# THE COMPLETE UNABRIDGED

# SUPER TRIVIA

## ENCYCLOPEDIA VOLUME III

### Fred L. Worth

(formerly titled:
Incredible Super Trivia)

WARNER BOOKS

A Warner Communications Company

Dedicated to my good friend David Strauss
who has always been there to lend a helping hand.

Warner Books, Inc.
666 Fifth Avenue
New York, N.Y. 10103

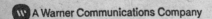 A Warner Communications Company

Printed in the United States of America

First Warner Books Printing: July, 1985

10  9  8  7  6  5  4  3  2  1

To know all things is not permitted.

Horace

# Note

As I have mentioned in my other books, mistakes will surface. I've had, I feel, some of the best trivia buffs in the country edit this edition for me, but that probably won't prevent an occasional mistake from appearing.

Compilers of dictionaries, encyclopedias, and other large works have an advantage in that they can correct previous errors in their latest editions.

Even when a book goes from hardcover to mass-market paperback, writers usually clear up their work. If you, the reader, spot an error, or, better yet, if you feel you can add to an entry, please drop me a line. Those nice people mentioned in the acknowledgments section of this book did just that, for which I am grateful.

# Acknowledgments

Missi Missildine, Steve Tamerius, Dave Strauss, Karin Fowler, James Worth, Venus Worth, Angela Worth, Kathryn Goldin, Marc L. Sperling, W. James Bastian, Michael E. Uslan, Kim Anne Moyer, Dave Glagovsky, Jeff Missinne, David Richard Baer, Brooks Darlington, Bob Eagelston, Mike Greenfield, David Rothel, David Bickel, Doug Ingeles, Douglas Brown, Tony Kalinski, Carol Capobianco, William F. Grant, L. M. Boyd, Charles Wirstrom, L. Edward Lucaire, J. N. Lockley, Helen Andrews, Barry Rutman, Kelly H. Blau, David C. Crockett, John Salerker, Don Curry, Herbert C. Tieseng, Susan M. Smith, Bruce R. Carr, Gordon Shriver, David L. G. Noakes, Rev. David Burd, David McCain, Laurence A. Yager, David H. Simon, Edward A. Koplowitz, Bruce A. Beebe, Bo Bokgren, Dianne Jessop, John A. Leipheimer, Glen A. Mitchell, Roger C. Dutton, Les Kangas, Jeffrey M. Loudon, Sherry Pritchard, Allen Shiloh, Warren Gondron, Dolores Harms, Linda C. Averille, Ben Woodhead, Dr. Rouneau, Barbara Stark, Jerry's Perchesky Radiola, Thomas Amodeo, Bruce R. Gilson, Forrest H. Ward, G. T. Zaucha, Donald James Tleugan, Tracy Gasfrey, Jon B. Jolly, Nina G. Fiore, Dan Koopmans, Don Bigger, Jim Wooten, David Mould, Tom Balint, Jonathan H. Mann, T. D. Grace, Bernie Rolnicki, Roy Nussbaum, John J. Zimkus, Michele Tover, Ahti Pursiainen, Jenifer Partridge, Beth Miles, Mary S. McCabe, Darrell L. Gamble, John Kaczenski, Jr., Diane Bechtol, Sheldon Dinerman, Christine B. McDevitt, Michael Steel, John L. Faundeen, Dan M. Brook, Char Knaus, Steven Btros, Joseph Smole, Susan Lentz, Rev. Brad Reynolds, Bill Bottomle, Donna Y. Onavin, Gregory Miller, William F. Walker, Joe M. Duncan, Richard W. Leche, Carlton F. Washburn, Bill Dictone, Jeffrey M. Smith, David Burd, Ray Kardas, Carolyn B. Johnes, Michael Arnold, John F. Hartter, Dave Miller, Laura Nickel, Chris Reynolds, Tom Hudson, Eileen Emerson, William J. Hudson, Jr., Andrew S. Klein, John G. Sisak, Bruce David Neiss, Charles Mitchell, Fred Carmichael, Sharon Kornbluth, Tom Battersby, E. I. Leach, Robert D. Trent, Leo Munro, David Nash, Carol Sickles, and Donna L. Nevin. If I have forgotten anyone, I apologize.

# Introduction

Just as there has been a *Superman III*, a *Friday the 13th Part 3 (3-D)*, and a *Rocky III*, here is the third part in the Super Trivia series.

After ten years of compiling books on facts and information (trivia), people finally know what trivia is. I no longer have to explain what trivia means, as the word has received much exposure over the last few years.

It fascinates me to see the information explosion going on around us. I can remember walking into a bookstore fifteen years ago and not being able to find a single book on either movies or rock 'n' roll music. For the young people of today, who are exposed to such a variety of books, this may sound hard to believe. It wasn't too long ago that encyclopedias on such subjects as television, country music, films, actors and actresses, radio, music, records, Elvis Presley, the Beatles, or monsters existed only in the minds of those who were putting them together.

Today we are just on the fringe of that information explosion that will one day enable us all to search out any oddball or hard-to-find facts by just typing requests into our home computers, which will be linked to data banks all over the world.

Those who love facts and information as much as I do will one day look back upon these times as the era when it all began, and will tell their children, "You may not believe this, but things weren't always as they are now."

# *Worth*while Trivia

Robert L. Ripley's Florida estate was situated on Lake *Worth*.

The winner of the 1912 Kentucky Derby was a horse named *Worth*.

Gary Cooper made his feature-movie debut in the 1926 film *The Winning of Barbara Worth*.

Frank *Worth* was the orchestra leader of the radio series *Richard Diamond, Private Eye*.

Herbert *Worth* played in just one game in his major-league career, in 1872.

Country singer Marion *Worth*'s biggest hit came in 1963 with "Shake Me I Rattle (Squeeze Me I Cry)."

Brian *Worth*, a leading man, born in Britain, has appeared in films since 1939.

Irene *Worth*, an American leading actress, has appeared in films since 1958.

The city of Fort Worth, Texas, was named for William Jenkins *Worth*.

Venus and Angela *Worth* are my two favorite little girls.

# A

**A4**

Paris theater stage trapdoor through which Carson Dyle (Walter Matthau) fell in the 1963 movie *Charade*.

**A-45200**

San Quentin Penitentiary number of inmate (future country singer) Merle Ronald Haggard, who was imprisoned from 1958 until 1963.

**AAA Diploma Company**

Delavan, Indiana, correspondence school from which Walter "Radar" O'Reilly (Gary Burghoff) graduated in the TV series "M*A*S*H." Lt. Col. Henry Blake (McLean Stevenson) gave him his final exam.

**AAU**

Amateur Athletic Union, founded in 1888.

**ABA**

American Bar Association, established in 1878.

**ABC, CBS, NBC, DuMont**

Four television networks:

American Broadcasting Company

Columbia Broadcasting System

National Broadcasting Company

There have been only four television series that have appeared on all four networks:

"The Arthur Murray Party"; "Down You Go"; "The Original Amateur Hour"; and "Pantomime Quiz."

**ABS**

American Bible Society

**A&F**

Initials on the back of the coveralls worn by Claude Fitzwilliam (Dick Van Dyke) and his henchmen when they stole camping supplies from a sports exhibit in the 1967 movie *Fitzwilly*.

**A.C.E.**

Initials given after the name of various film editors in movie credits. A.C.E. (American Cinema Editors) is an honorary society founded in 1950. The membership is very limited and only a few more than two hundred editors belong. The Eddie is A.C.E.'s annual award.

**AFL/CIO**

Two trade unions that merged in 1955. The initials stand for American Federation of Labor/Congress of Industrial Organizations.

**AFS 72485**

Serial number of the CIA's propaganda bomb that landed at the 4077th on the TV series "M*A*S*H." When the bomb exploded, it covered the camp with propaganda leaflets.

**AFTRA**

American Federation of Television and Radio Artists.

**AKC**

American Kennel Club.

**AM11**

British license plate number of Arthur Kipps's (Tommy Steele) white automobile in the 1969 movie *Half a Sixpence*.

**AMA**

American Medical Association, established in 1847.

**AN6530**

Numbers on the front of Wild Bill Kelso's (John Belushi) goggles in the 1979 movie *1941*.

**AP**

Associated Press news agency, first organized in 1848.

**ASE**

American Stock Exchange. It was given that name in 1953.

**ATlantic 6-3389**

Pittsburgh phone number that Glenn Griffin (Humphrey Bogart) has Mrs. Eleanor Hilliard (Martha Scott) call a Mrs. James, from a Mr. James in the 1955 movie *The Desperate Hours*.

**ATwater 9-3597**

New York City telephone number of the Fresh Air Taxi Cab Company on the TV series "Amos 'n' Andy."

**AWACS**
Airborne Warning and Control Systems. These highly sophisticated aircraft are radar-domed C-135 (Boeing 707) aircraft.

**AZ 1414**
Frank Morris's (Clint Eastwood) prison number at Alcatraz in the 1979 movie *Escape from Alcatraz*.

**Abbotsford**
Name of author Sir Walter Scott's estate in Scotland.

**Abraham Lincoln**
Philadelphia high school band that played at the dedication of the statue of Rocky Balboa (Sylvester Stallone) in the 1982 movie *Rocky III*.

**Abrahams, Harold M.**
Winner of the one-hundred-meter race in the 1924 Olympic Games. He is the only Englishman to have won an Olympic sprint title. Abrahams was portrayed by Ben Cross in the 1981 movie *Chariots of Fire*.

**Abrahamson, Tillie**
One-hundred-three-year-old woman who, on January 14, 1982, became the oldest person to have appeared on Johnny Carson's "The Tonight Show."

**Academy First Award To**
First four words engraved on the Oscar statuettes presented at the Academy Awards.

**Ace**
Maxine's (Tala Birel) German shepherd in the 1944 movie *The Monster Maker*.

**Ackerm, Jean**
Actress who married silent screen star Rudolph Valentino in November of 1919, only to leave him for good on their wedding night.

**Acme Collection Agency**
Agency that attempted to recover $370 for a ring that Marion Kirby (Anne Jeffreys) failed to pay off before she died in an avalanche on the TV series "Topper."

**Acme Plumbing**
Van that crashed into a fireworks store and exploded in the 1976 movie *The Gumball Rally*.

**Acme Saloon**
Carson City, Nevada, bar in which John Bernard Books (John Wayne) was shot to death on January 29, 1901, in the 1976 movie

*The Shootist.*

**Actor's Studio**

Actors' workshop in New York City, founded in 1947 by Cheryl Crawford, Elia Kazan, and Robert Lewis, which taught the Stanislavsky method of dramatic training. Lee Strasberg became the school's director in 1948. Some of its students have been Paul Newman, James Dean, Marlon Brando, Marilyn Monroe, Jane Fonda, Dustin Hoffman, and Al Pacino.

**Adams, William**

(1564–1620) Englishman who in 1600 traveled to Japan where he became the first non-Oriental samurai. Adams was portrayed by Richard Chamberlain (as John Blackthorne), in the 1980 TV miniseries *Shōgun*.

**A date that will live in infamy . . .**

Exact words of President Franklin Delano Roosevelt when he addressed the American people after the Japanese attack on Pearl Harbor, December 7, 1941. The quote is sometimes wrongly repeated as "A day that will live in infamy."

**Addie Rose**

Narrator of the 1948 movie *A Letter to Three Wives*. Provided by the uncredited voice of Celeste Holm.

**Admiral**

Colossal Film Company's star penguin, owned by Mr. Mack in the 1937 Humphrey Bogart movie *Stand-In*.

**Admiral Harold Harmon Hargrade**

Chief of CONTROL prior to Thaddeus (Edward Platt). He was played by William Schallert on the TV series "Get Smart."

**"Adventure of the Blanched Soldier, The" and "The Adventure of the Lion's Mane"**

Two Sherlock Holmes stories that are credited to Holmes, within the stories written by Sir Arthur Conan Doyle.

**Aeschylus**

(525–456 B.C.) "The father of Greek tragedy." Only seven of his ninety plays have survived:

1. *The Suppliants*
2. *The Persians*
3. *Seven Against Thebes*
4. *The Prometheus Bound*

The Orestean Trilogy

5. *Agamemnon*
6. *Choephoroi (The Libation Bearers)*

7. *The Eumenides (The Furies)*

Aeschylus was killed (according to legend) when an eagle dropped a tortoise on his bald head, mistaking it for a rock.

**Aethelnoth**

Lady Godiva's horse, upon which she rode naked through the town of Coventry. The mare was named after the Archbishop of Canterbury.

**Affluent Society, The**

Phrase coined by economist John Galbraith in 1958, as the title of his popular book.

**"After the Ball"**

Song written in 1892 by Charles K. Harris. It was the first song to sell five million copies of sheet music.

**"Again"**

Song composed in 1948 by Dorcas Cochran and Lionel Newman. It was introduced in the 1949 movie *Roadhouse* by Ida Lupino. Other film inclusions of the song were: *Island in the Sun* (1957) and *Best of Everything* (1959); it was the recurring theme song of the 3-D movie *Gorilla at Large* (1954).

**Agca, Mehmet Ali**

Turkish man who attempted to assassinate Pope John Paul II on May 13, 1981, when he fired several bullets at the pontiff in St. Peter's Square. Two American women, Ann Odre and Rose Hall, were wounded by stray bullets.

**Agent 13**

CONTROL agent played by David Ketchum on the TV series "Get Smart."

**Agent 22**

CONTROL agent played by Andrea Howard in the 1980 movie *The Return of Maxwell Smart* (AKA *The Nude Bomb*). In 1972, Agent 22 (age twenty-one) married Agent 78, who was forty-six years old and who died in 1975.

**Agent 34**

CONTROL agent played by Sylvia Kristel in *The Return of Maxwell Smart*.

**Agent 36**

CONTROL agent played by Pamela Hensley in *The Return of Maxwell Smart*.

**Agent 44**

CONTROL agent played by Victor French on the TV series "Get Smart."

**Agent 86**

CONTROL agent Maxwell Smart, played by Don Adams on the TV series "Get Smart" and in the movie *The Return of Maxwell Smart*.

**Ahoy!**

First greeting used in answering the newly introduced invention, the telephone, in 1876. "Ahoy" was quickly replaced by "hello," at Thomas Edison's suggestion.

**Aintree Course**

Liverpool, England, location of the Grand National Steeplechase since 1839.

**Air Force 191**

Call sign of the United States Air Force C-47 piloted by Captain Patrick Hendry (Kenneth Tobey) in the 1951 movie *The Thing (From Another World)*.

**Air Force Gold 10**

Call sign of the C-130 rescue aircraft piloted by Major Stoddard (Martin Milner) that flew into the eye of Hurricane Hilda in the 1974 TV movie *Hurricane*.

**"Air Force Takes Command, The"**

Theme song, performed by Victor Young, of the 1955 movie *Strategic Air Command*.

**Air France Flight 139**

Airline flight hijacked by the PLO (Palestine Liberation Army) on June 22, 1976, and taken by the hijackers to the Entebbe Airport at Uganda until the hostages were rescued by the Israeli commandos on July 4. The hijackers renamed the aircraft *Haifa*.

**Air-O-Doodle**

Howdy Doody's special vehicle that was a combination of automobile, ship, train, and airplane.

**Airport '80**

Title to which the title of the 1978 movie *Airport '79* was changed when the film was shown in Britain during 1980.

**Air raid . . . Pearl Harbor . . . This is no drill . . .**

Message sent out by Captain Logan C. Ramsey concerning the Japanese attack at Pearl Harbor, December 7, 1941. Previously, Ramsey had written an article in 1937, titled "Aerial Attacks on Fleets at Anchor."

**Ajax**

Montana mountain from which singer Hank Williams, Jr., fell on August 8, 1975, causing serious damage to his face, which had to be rebuilt. After the incident he wrote an autobiography, published during 1979, titled *Living Proof*, which became the basis of a 1983 TV movie.

**Ajax Express Company**
Trucking company from which ex-con Eddie Taylor (Henry Fonda) was fired in the 1937 movie *You Only Live Once*.

**Ajax Warehouse**
San Francisco warehouse, built in 1924, that Franklin M. Hart, Jr. (Dabney Coleman), used as a cover for his embezzlement in the 1980 movie *9 to 5*.

**Akihito**
(1933–      ) Son of Japanese Emperor Hirohito. In 1959 he became the first member of the Japanese royal family to marry a commoner.

**Ak-Sar-Ben**
Racetrack and convention facilities in Omaha, Nebraska. Ak-Sar-Ben is "Nebraska" spelled backwards.

**Alan**
Manager of the rock band Josie and the Pussycats, in the animated TV cartoon series "Josie and the Pussycats," voiced by Jerry Dexter.

**Alaska**
State that has the longest coastline in the United States (6,640 miles). Florida is second, at 1,350 miles. Alaska is the only one of the fifty states that does not have a motto.

**Alba, Maria**
Female singer on Archie Bleyer's 1954 hit recording "Hernando's Hideaway."

**Albert**
Alligator that bit off the right arm of Tee Hee (Julius Harris) in the 1973 James Bond movie *Live and Let Die*.

**Albert**
Chipmunk puppet on the 1951–1953 TV series "In the Park."

**Alderaan**
Home planet of Princess Leia Organa (Carrie Fisher) in the 1977 movie *Star Wars*.

**Alexander, Grover Cleveland**
(1887–1950) Major-league pitcher and member of the Baseball Hall of Fame, Alexander holds the National League record for most complete games (439) and total shutouts (90). He is tied with Christy Mathewson for the National League record of 373 games

won. In the 1926 World Series, he set a record by becoming the only pitcher to win two World Series games in a row (sixth and seventh). Ronald Reagan portrayed Grover Cleveland Alexander in the 1952 movie *The Winning Team*.

**Alexander Kieland**
Ten-thousand-ton floating hotel rig that overturned in the North Sea on March 27, 1980, killing 137 men.

**Alexander's**
New York City department store where Paula McFadden (Marsha Mason) shopped in the opening scene of the 1977 movie *The Goodbye Girl*.

**"Alfie"**
Hit song by Dionne Warwick, but sung by Cher in the 1966 movie *Alfie*. An instrumental version of the song is played at a high school reunion in the 1976 movie *Lifeguard*. In 1968, Stevie Wonder charted an instrumental version of the song under the pseudonym of Eivets Rednow (Stevie Wonder spelled backwards).

**Alfred**
Dog belonging to Mr. Johnson, the watchman at Grant Avenue Grammar School, in the TV series "Leave It to Beaver."

**Alfred Hitchcock**
Magazine read by Nicole Bonnet (Audrey Hepburn) while in bed in the 1966 movie *How to Steal a Million*.

**Ali, Rahamon**
Name that Muhammed Ali's brother, Rudolph Valentino Clay, chose as a Muslim when they both adopted the faith. Rahamon had a brief ring career.

**Alice**
Lisa Douglas's (Eva Gabor) favorite chicken on the TV series "Green Acres."

**Alice the Goon**
Large, heavy creature who was originally a slave to the Sea Hag in E. C. Segar's comic strips *Thimble Theatre* and *Popeye the Sailor*. Alice's language can only be understood by Wimpy. She made her comic strip debut in 1934.

**"All Aboard"**
Company song of the Lionel Train Company.

**"All American Smile, The"**
Short story written by Hubbell Gardner (Robert Redford) and read by his professor in the 1973 movie *The Way We Were*.

### Allan-A-Dale

Minstrel who was a member of Robin Hood's band of Merry Men in Sherwood Forest. He also appeared in Sir Walter Scott's *Ivanhoe*.

Movie characterizations:

| | |
|---|---|
| *The Bandits of Sherwood Forest* (1946) | Leslie Denison |
| *The Story of Robin Hood* (1952) | Elton Hayes |
| *Sword of Sherwood Forest* (1961) | Dennis Lotis |
| *A Challenge for Robin Hood* (1968) | Eric Flynn |
| *Robin Hood* (1973 animated movie) | voice of Roger Miller |

He was played by Bernie Kopell in the 1975 TV series "When Things Were Rotten," and by Bing Crosby in the 1964 "gangster parody" *Robin and the Seven Hoods*.

### "All Coons Look Alike to Me"

Song written in 1896 by black songwriter Ernest Hogan. Until then, "coon" was a slang word used when referring to white people. After that, it referred to blacks.

### Allentown

Pennsylvania hometown of Detective Arthur Dietrich (Steve Landesberg) on the TV series "Barney Miller." He attended St. Mary's School there. In 1983, "Allentown" became the title of a hit record by Billy Joel.

### Alley, Major Ronald E.

Only U.S. Army officer imprisoned for collaborating with the enemy during the Korean War. He was convicted in 1955 and sentenced to ten years' imprisonment.

### "All I Do Is Dream of You"

Arthur Freed/Nacio Herb Brown song sung by Debbie Reynolds in two movies; *Singin' in the Rain* (1952) and *The Affairs of Dobie Gillis\** (1953).

### Alligator

Logo of IZOD Lacoste shirts, a Swiss-based company.

### All My Best

Album of the biggest hits of country singer Slim Whitman that was sold on TV during 1979–1980. The album sold more than a million and a half copies.

### "All of Me"

Song written in 1931 by Seymour Simons and Gerald Marks and

---

\*Sung as a duet with Bobby Van.

performed in the following movies: *Careless Lady* (1932); *Meet Danny Wilson* (1952), sung by Frank Sinatra; and *Down Among the Sheltering Palms* (1953), sung by Gloria De Haven.

**All of Them Witches**
Book by J. R. Hanslet, read by Rosemary Woodhouse (Mia Farrow) in the 1968 movie *Rosemary's Baby*. The book was given to her by Hutch (Maurice Evans).

**All Souls Church**
Mayberry church attended by Andy and Opie Taylor, Aunt Bee, and Barney Fife on the TV series "The Andy Griffith Show." Rev. Hobart Tucker was the minister.

**All-Star Game (1949)**
First major-league baseball All-Star Game in which black players appeared.
They were
Jackie Robinson of the Brooklyn Dodgers
Roy Campanella of the Brooklyn Dodgers
Don Newcombe of the Brooklyn Dodgers
Larry Doby of the Cleveland Indians

**All the Fine Young Cannibals**
Movie (1960) directed by Michael Anderson, which was the only motion picture in which Natalie Wood and Robert Wagner appeared together. The pair, however, did appear together in two made-for-TV movies, *The Affair* (1973) and *Cat on a Hot Tin Roof* (1976).

**All the News That Fits**
Motto of *Rolling Stone* magazine.

**All the News That's Fit to Print**
Motto of the *New York Times*, coined by publisher Adolph S. Ochs (1896–1935).

**"All the Things You Are"**
Song written in 1939 by Oscar Hammerstein II and Jerome Kern. It was performed in the following MGM movies: *Broadway Rhythm* (1944); *Till the Clouds Roll By* (1946); and *Because You're Mine* (1952).

**"All the Way"**
Song written by Sammy Cahn and Jimmy Van Heusen and recorded by Frank Sinatra in 1957, played on a nightclub jukebox by Tim Culley (William Holden) in the 1981 movie *S.O.B.*

**All Through the Night**
Movie poster of the 1942 Humphrey Bogart film which hangs on

the wall of Assistant Purser Burl "Gopher" Smith's (Fred Grandy) stateroom (C123), on board the *Pacific Princess* in the TV series "The Love Boat."

**All work and no play makes Jack a dull boy . . .**
The sentence typed over and over again by Jack Torrance (Jack Nicholson) in the 1980 movie *The Shining*.

**Almond Joy**
Candy bar introduced by the Peter Paul Candy Company in 1947. Rock musicians Duane and Gregg Allman made their first record in 1966, "Spoonful" (Dial Records 406), as The Allman Joys.

**"Alone"**
Song written in 1935 by Arthur Freed and Nacio Herb Brown and performed in the MGM motion picture *A Night at the Opera* (1935) (sung by Kitty Carlisle and Allan Jones) and *Andy Hardy Meets a Debutante* (1940) (sung by Judy Garland).

**"Alphabet Song, The"**
Alternate title of the 1948 Buddy Kaye/Fred Wise/Sidney Lippman composition "A, You're Adorable."

**Alpha Delta Pi**
First sorority, formed at Wesleyan College on May 15, 1851, by sixteen women (until 1904, they were called the Adelphians).

**Al's Motel**
Seedy motel in Asbury Park where Mr. Beasley (John Astin) took Cathy Timberlake (Doris Day) in the 1962 movie *That Touch of Mink*.

**Alston, Walter Emmond**
(1911–    ) First manager of the Los Angeles Dodgers. Alston played in only one game in the majors, when, on September 27, 1936, he replaced Johnny Mize at first base. He made one error in two chances and was struck out by Lon Warneke in his only time at bat.

**Altamont**
Town in the fictitious state of Catawba in Thomas Wolfe's 1929 novel *Look Homeward Angel*. Supposedly the setting is based on the town of Asheville, North Carolina.

**Altman, Mike**
Son of director Robert Altman, he composed the lyrics of "Suicide Is Painless," the theme song of the 1970 movie *M*A*S*H* (which was directed by his father) and subsequently for the TV series.

**Altrock, Nick and Minnie Minoso**
Only two major-league baseball players to have played in five

different decades (1893–1933) and (1949–80) respectively.

## "Always True to You in My Fashion"

Song written by Cole Porter, in between the ground floor and the forty-first floor in the elevator of the Waldorf-Astoria, one day in 1948. Ann Miller and Tommy Rall sang the song in the 1953 movie *Kiss Me, Kate*.

## Alydar

Only horse ever to finish in the runner-up position in all three races for the Triple Crown, when, in 1978, Alydar finished second to Affirmed. In the Kentucky Derby, the Preakness, and the Belmont Stakes, Alydar was ridden by Jorge Velasquez. Alydar was the only horse ever to beat the 1978 Triple Crown winner Affirmed, which he beat twice, both times at Belmont Park.

## Amahl and the Night Visitors

First opera ever written for TV. Gian-Carlo Menotti, the opera's composer, first presented it on Christmas Eve, 1951, on NBC.

## Amalgamated Pictures, Inc.

Hollywood motion-picture studio headed by Dane Wharton (William Gargan) in the 1940 movie *Star Dust*.

## Ambassador

In-flight magazine given to the customers of TWA.

## Ambassador Auditorium

Pasadena, California, location where, on March 3, 1977, while taping a CBS TV special, singer Bing Crosby fell twenty feet into the orchestra pit as he was being given a standing ovation. He ruptured a disc in the fall.

## Ambassador of Love

Nickname conferred upon songstress Pearl Bailey by President Richard Nixon.

## Ambidextrously

Fourteen-letter word that has no repeating letters, using all five vowels.

## Amelito

Disfigured woman, played in the 1970 John Wayne movie *Rio Lobo* by model-turned-actress Sherry Lansing. In 1980, Lansing became the president of production of 20th Century-Fox.

## America—Love it or leave it . . .

Phrase coined by columnist Walter Winchell in 1940.

## "America"

Title of four different songs that appeared in the following movies:

*West Side Story* (1961); *Twilight's Last Gleaming* (1976); *The Muppet Movie* (1979); and *The Jazz Singer* (1980).

**American Airlines Flight 812**
Airliner that first sighted the UFO in the 1959 movie *Plan 9 from Outer Space*.

**"American Eagle"**
Western TV program that Ricky Nelson and his friends watched on TV in the 1952 movie *Here Come the Nelsons*.

**American flags**
Material used by the patients at Mineral Springs Asylum to make Bronco Billy McCoy's (Clint Eastwood) large rodeo tent in the 1980 movie *Bronco Billy*.

**American Graffiti**
1973 movie produced by Francis Ford Coppola and directed by George Lucas, which produced a large number of successful actors and actresses:

*TV Series*
Mackenzie Phillips
Cindy Williams
Ron Howard
Suzanne Somers
Susan Richardson

"One Day at a Time"
"Laverne and Shirley"
"Happy Days"
"Three's Company"
"Eight is Enough"

*Movies*
Richard Dreyfuss
Paul LeMat
Charles Martin Smith
Harrison Ford

*The Goodbye Girl* (1977)
*Melvin and Howard* (1981)
*The Buddy Holly Story* (1978)
*Star Wars* (1977)

**American hostages**
Employees of the American Embassy in Tehran, who were held against their will from November 4, 1979, until January 20, 1981, 444 days:

| | | |
|---|---|---|
| Thomas Ahern, Jr. | Robert Englemann | Joseph Hall |
| Clair Barnes | William Gallegos | Kevin Hermening[1] |
| William Belk | Bruce German | Donald Hohman |
| Robert Blucker | Duane Gillette | Leland Holland |
| Donald Cooke | Allan Golacinski | Michael Howland |
| William Daugherty | John Graves | Charles Jones[2] |

---

[1]Youngest—age nineteen.
[2]Only black hostage.

| Malcolm Kalp | James Lopez | Regis Ragan |
| Moorehead Kennedy, Jr. | John McKeel, Jr. | David Roeder |
| William Keough, Jr. | Michael Metrinko | Barry Rosen |
| Steven Kirtley | Jerry Miele[3] | William Royer, Jr. |
| Kathryn Koob | Michael Moeller | Thomas Schaefer |
| Frederick Kupke | Bert Moore | Charles Scott |
| L. Bruce Laingen | Richard Morefield | Don Sharer |
| Steve Lauterbach | Paul Needham | Rodney Sickman |
| Gary Lee | Robert Ode[4] | Joseph Subic, Jr. |
| Paul Lewis | Gregory Persinger | Elizabeth Ann Swift |
| John Limbert | Jerry Plotkin | Victor Tomseth |
| | | Phillip Ward |

## American Olympic decathlon winners:

| | *Points* |
| --- | --- |
| Harold Osborn (1924) | 7710.77[1] |
| James Bausch (1932) | 8462.23[1] |
| Glenn Morris (1936) | 7900.00[1] |
| Bob Mathias (1948) | 7139.00[2] |
| Bob Mathias (1952) | 7887.00[2] |
| Milton Campbell (1956) | 7937.00[2] |
| Rafer Johnson (1960) | 8392.00[2] |
| Bill Toomey (1968) | 8193.00[3] |
| Bruce Jenner (1976) | 8618.00[3] |

## American Overseas School

School in Rome, Italy, where Michael Endicott (John Forsythe) taught in the TV series "To Rome with Love."

## American Report, The

TV magazine for which Becky Tomkins (Priscilla Barnes) and Amy Waddell (Debra Clinger) worked as writers in the TV series "The American Girls."

## America's Boy

Nickname conferred upon child actor Jackie Cooper.

## American Vision, The

Book written by Secretary of State William Russell (Henry Fonda) in the 1964 movie *The Best Man*.

---

[3]Blindfolded on the first day, he was led around by his captors. His photo appeared on the front pages of newspapers all over the world.
[4]Oldest—age sixty-four.

---

[1]Original scoring system
[2]Revised scoring system
[3]New scoring system

**Amherst**
Massachusetts college (founded in 1821) attended by Sandy (Art Garfunkel) and Jonathan (Jack Nicholson) in the 1971 movie *Carnal Knowledge*. Amherst and Williams met in the first college baseball game at Pittsfield, Massachusetts, on July 1, 1859. Amherst won 73–32.

**"Am I Blue?"**
Song written in 1929 by Grant Clarke and Harry Akst and performed in the following motion pictures: *On With the Show* (1929), sung by Ethel Waters; *So Long, Letty* (1929); *The Hard Way* (1942), sung by Jack Carson and Dennis Morgan and *Is Everybody Happy?* (1943), sung by Nan Wynn.

**Amos B. Coogan**
New Prospect, Oklahoma, town barber/doctor played by Harry Morgan in the TV series "Hec Ramsey." Morgan also narrated the series.

**Amos 'n' Andy**
Santa Fe Railroad's nicknames for its *Super Chief*'s two diesel engines.

**Amphibious Fighters**
One-reel short subject (1942) for which sports writer Grantland Rice won an Academy Award.

**Amsterdam Construction Company**
Los Angeles firm located on 1281 George Street, which was run by Jack Amsterdam (Charles Durning) in the 1981 movie *True Confessions*.

**Anarene**
Small Texas town that provided the setting for the 1971 movie *The Last Picture Show*. In Larry McMurtry's novel, the town was Thalia. The actual town that was used for the film was Archer City, Texas, McMurtry's hometown.

**Anderson, Mary**
Inventor, in 1903, of the automobile windshield wiper.

**And that's the way it is . . .**
Tag line of CBS news anchorman Walter Cronkite, from April 16, 1962 to March 6, 1981.

**"And Then There's Maude"**
Theme song of the TV series "Maude," sung by Donny Hathaway.

**Andy Richards**
Bartender played by former United States President Gerald Ford's son, Steven Ford, on the TV soap opera "The Young and the

Restless.''

**Angel**

Secret Service code name for Air Force One.

**Angel Glow**

Brand of cosmetics that Stella Johnson (Barbara Eden) sold on the TV series ''Harper Valley PTA.''

**Angel Eyes**

Sadistic gunman played by Lee Van Cleef in the 1966 movie *The Good, the Bad and the Ugly* (he was ''the Bad'').

**Angel of the Battlefield**

Nickname of Civil War nurse Clara Barton, who, in 1881, founded the American Red Cross.

**Angels With Dirty Faces**

1938 Warner Bros. movie starring James Cagney, Pat O'Brien, Humphrey Bogart, Ann Sheridan, and the Dead End Kids. The movie was advertised on a sandwich sign carried by a man in the 1945 Jack Benny movie *The Horn Blows at Midnight*.

**Angel Unaware**

Book written by Dale Evans in 1953, about the life and death of her and Roy Rogers' young daughter Robin, who died of a heart condition at the age of two.

She wrote another book in 1964, titled *Dearest Debbie*, after her twelve-year-old daughter, Debbie, was killed in a bus crash.

Her book *Salute to Sandy* was written in honor of her son John, who had died at age eighteen.

**Angelus Temple**

Evangelist Aimee Semple McPherson's Los Angeles church, where she preached her International Institute of Four-Square Evangelism. Actor Anthony Quinn, in his youth, played saxophone there.

**Angus**

Role played by Art Carney on the radio series ''Lorenzo Jones.''

**Anibal, Benjamin H.**

Designer of the first Pontiac automobile (in 1926) for the Oakland Motor Company.

**A nickel ain't worth a dime anymore . . .**

One of many famous statements made by baseball star Yogi Berra.

**Animal Crackers**

The Marx Brothers' 1930 movie shown being advertised in the 1950 movie *Three Little Words*.

Ossie Schreckengost, the roommate of Rube Waddell, had a

clause written into Waddell's major-league baseball contract forbidding him to eat animal crackers in bed.

**Anna Owens**
British teacher who traveled to Siam in the 1860s to teach the children of royalty. Anna was played by Irene Dunne in the 1946 movie *Anna and the King of Siam*, by Deborah Kerr in the 1956 movie *The King and I*, and by Samantha Eggar in the 1972 TV series "Anna and the King," all based on Margaret Landon's novel *Anna and the King of Siam*.

**Annie**
Nine-year-old seller of artificial flowers in Bobby Darin's 1960 hit song "Artificial Flowers."

**Ann Reynolds**
Role played by Lee Merriweather on the TV soap "The Young Marrieds."

**"Another Rainy Day in New York City"**
Hit song recorded in 1976 by Chicago.

**Anson**
Middle name of science fiction writer Robert A. Heinlein.

**Ansonia Hotel**
Atlantic City, New Jersey, setting of the short-lived 1979 TV series "Big Shamus, Little Shamus."

**Antagonists, The**
Novel by Ernest Gann, published in 1970, upon which the 1981 TV miniseries "Masada" was based.

**Ant Hill Mob**
Penelope Pitstop's protectors in the animated TV series "The Perils of Penelope Pitstop." The members are Clyde, Dum Dum, Pockets, Snoozy, Softy, and Zippy.

**Anthony, Earl**
(1938– ) First man to win three Professional Bowlers Association Championships (in 1973, 1974, and 1975). On February 27, 1982, he became the first million-dollar winner in the history of the Professional Bowlers Association. On that date he took first prize of $38,000 at the Toledo Trust-PBA National Championship by defeating Charlie Tapp 233–192 at the Imperial Lanes in Toledo, Ohio. Anthony once pitched in the Baltimore Oriole chain; however, he gave it up after he experienced arm trouble.

**Anthony Wayne**
Submarine commanded by Commander Philip Kettehring (Leonard

Nimoy) in the 1970 TV movie *Assault on the Wayne*.

**Anti-Monopoly Party**
Party that nominated General Benjamin Franklin Butler for the Presidency of the United States in 1884.

**Anyone got a match?**
First line said by Lauren Bacall in her film debut in the 1944 movie *To Have and Have Not*.

**Anyone seeing a psychiatrist should have his head examined . . .**
Saying credited to movie producer Samuel Goldwyn, known as a Goldwynism. The line was said by Sam Carlson (Arthur Franz) in the 1951 movie *Submarine Command*.

**"Anywhere the Bluebird Goes"**
Original title of the 1939 song "Don't Sit Under the Apple Tree (with Anyone Else But Me)."

**Apartment, The**
Movie (1960) starring Jack Lemmon and Shirley MacLaine, upon which the 1968 musical play *Promises, Promises* was based.

**Apes in Myth and History**
Book that the chimp in the 1981 TV movie *The Return of the Beverly Hillbillies* was reading in Elly May Clampett's (Donna Douglas) office at Elly's Zoo.

**Ape Woman**
CB handle of Elly May Clampett (Donna Douglas) in the 1981 TV movie *The Return of the Beverly Hillbillies*.

**Applejack**
Word that triggered the memory bank of the Medfield College computers into revealing A. J. Arno's (Cesar Romero) illegal gambling information in the 1970 movie *The Computer Wore Tennis Shoes*.

**Appling, Luke**
(1908–    ) Chicago White Sox shortstop (1930–1950) and member of the Baseball Hall of Fame, who was portrayed by Dean White in the 1949 movie *The Stratton Story*. In the first Old Timers' Game, played in 1982, Luke hit a home run off pitcher Warren Spahn.

**April**
Month mentioned in the lyrics of the 1976 Barbra Streisand hit song "Evergreen" (theme song from *A Star Is Born*).

**April 6, 1956**
Day upon which the opening scenes of the 1956 movie *Written on the Wind* took place. The rest of the movie was told in flashback.

**April 7, 1847**
Birthdate of Bret Maverick (James Garner) on the TV series "Maverick."

**April 15**
Wedding anniversary of the Hartleys on the TV series "The Bob Newhart Show."

**April 22**
Day upon which Corporal Maxwell Q. Klinger (Jamie Farr) first began wearing female clothing at the 4077th on the TV series "M*A*S*H."

**April 23, 1616**
Date upon which William Shakespeare and Miguel de Cervantes both died.

**"April Showers"**
Song composed in 1921 by Buddy De Sylva and Louis Silvers and performed in the following movies: *Margie* (1946), sung by Jeanne Crain; *The Jolson Story* (1946), sung by Al Jolson (dubbing for Larry Parks); *Jolson Sings Again* (1949), sung by Al Jolson (dubbing for Larry Parks); *April Showers* (1948), sung by Jack Carson, Ann Sothern, and Bobbie Ellis.

**Archbury**
British town near which the United States Army Air Force 918th Bomber Group was based in the 1949 movie *Twelve O'Clock High.*

**Archery target**

| Area | Points |
| --- | --- |
| White | 1 |
| Black | 3 |
| Blue | 5 |
| Red | 7 |
| Gold (bullseye) | 9 |

**Archibald, Nate "Tiny"**
Shortest player (6' 1") ever to win an NBA scoring title (1972–1973 with the Kansas City Kings). He is the first guard in NBA history to score one thousand field goals.

**Arena**
Popular cafe on the TV soap "Another World."

**Arfie**
Name of the doggie in the window, according to the title of Patti Page's record "Arfie, the Doggie in the Window," a follow-up to her hit "Doggie in the Window," both of which were recorded in 1953.

**Argea, Angelo**
   Golfer Jack Nicklaus's caddy since 1964.
**Argentine Annie**
   Nickname given to the Argentine female broadcaster who called
   herself Liberty. In April of 1982, during the Falkland Island
   crisis, she began broadcasting in a pleasant voice to the British
   fleet, giving the men soccer scores in addition to psychological
   propaganda.
**Argonia, Kansas**
   First municipality in the United States to elect a female mayor,
   when, on April 4, 1887, it elected Susanna Medora Satler. She
   served for one year.
**Ariadne, HMS**
   British cruiser on which Lord Randolph Churchill first met his
   American wife, Jeanette Jerome, in August 1873. In 1874, their
   son Winston Churchill was born.
**Ariel**
   English poet Percy Bysshe Shelley's boat, from which he fell and
   drowned during a storm on July 8, 1822, in the Bay of Lerici.
**Arizona Pie**
   Racehorse ridden by Sarah (Tatum O'Neal) in the 1978 movie
   *International Velvet*.
**Arkansas**
   State in which the only diamond mine in North America is located.
**"Arkansas toothpick"**
   Nickname for the bowie knife.
**Arkham**
   Village haunted by Joseph Curwen (Vincent Price) in the 1964
   movie *The Haunted Palace* (based on the novel *The Case of
   Charles Dexter Ward* by H. P. Lovecraft). The town's tavern was
   called The Burning Man.
**Arlin, Harold**
   Announcer of the first baseball game to be broadcast over the radio.
   It was aired over Pittsburgh's KDKA radio on August 5, 1921,
   when the Pittsburgh Pirates defeated the Philadelphia Phillies with
   a score of 8 to 5.
**Army Officer's Guide, 1894**
   Excerpt: "Enlisted men are stupid, but they are sly and cunning and
   bear considerable watching."
**Arnie**
   Florida swamp alligator in the 1979 movie *The Muppet Movie*.

**Arno**
Actor Errol Flynn's pet schnauzer which he kept on his yacht *Sirocco*.

**Arnold Dingfilder Horshack**
Member of the Sweathogs at James Buchanan High in Brooklyn, who has a rather unusual laugh. Horshack was played by Ron Palillo in the TV series "Welcome Back Kotter."

**Arnold, Lt. H. H.**
First movie stuntman. He was hired on September 30, 1911, as a stand-in for the movie *The Military Air Scout*.

**Arrowhead Stadium**
Home of the Kansas City Chiefs' pro football team.

**Arrowhead Studios**
Hollywood motion picture studio that filmed the novel *Here Is Tomorrow* starring John Wayne as Rusty Thomas in the 1946 movie *Without Reservation*, with Lana Turner.

**Artanis**
Frank Sinatra's movie production company (Sinatra spelled backwards).

**Artesia Papageorge**
Jake Blues's mother, who delivered Jake at the Dwight, Illinois, Women's Correctional Institute. (The information was revealed in the book *Blues Brothers—Private*, by Judith Jacklin [wife of John Belushi] and Tino Insana.)

**ARTHUR**
New York State automobile license plate number of Arthur Bach's (Dudley Moore) Rolls-Royce in the 1981 movie *Arthur*.

**ARTHUR 2**
New York State automobile license plate number of Arthur Bach's (Dudley Moore) red convertible coupe in the 1981 movie *Arthur*.

**ARTHUR 3**
Name of Arthur Bach's (Dudley Moore) Porsche racing car in the 1981 movie *Arthur*.

**Arthur Lordly**
TV celebrity ("Hello-Hello-Hello") played by Ray Goulding in the 1965 movie *Cold Turkey*.

**Article 184**
United States Navy regulation invoked by Lt. Steve Maryk (Van Johnson) to relieve Captain Phillip Francis Queeg (Humphrey Bogart) as commander of the USS *Caine* in the 1954 movie *The Caine Mutiny*.

**Arvak**
Prince Valiant's horse, which died of old age.

**Ashdod**
Ship, weighing 4,500 tons, which, on April 30, 1979, became the first Israeli vessel ever to sail through the Suez Canal.

**Ashford, Emmett Littleton**
First black umpire in organized baseball, who started in 1951 in Class C Southwest International League and finished up in the American League, becoming the first black umpire in the major leagues. He played an umpire in the 1976 movie *The Bingo Long Traveling All-Stars and Motor Kings*.

**Ashley, Dr. Franklin**
Doctor who gave comedienne Phyllis Diller her two facelifts.

**Ash Wednesday**
First day of Lent. Also the title of a 1973 movie starring Elizabeth Taylor and Henry Fonda.

**Asian saga of James Clavell's novels**

| | |
|---|---|
| *Shōgun* | A.D. 1600 |
| *Tai-Pan* | A.D. 1841 |
| *King Rat* | A.D. 1945 |
| *Noble House* | A.D. 1963 |

**"Ask Me No Questions (I'll Tell You No Lies)"**
Theme song of the 1981 movie *Back Roads*, starring Sally Field and Tommy Lee Jones, which was sung by Sue Raney.

**As old as my tongue and a little bit older than my teeth . . .**
Kris Kringle's (Edmund Gwenn) age, as listed on his employment file card at Macy's department store in the 1947 movie *Miracle on Thirty-Fourth Street*.

**Asphalt State Park**
State park where Farly works as a ranger in the comic strip *Travels with Farly* by Phil Frank.

**Assignment: Munich**
1972 TV movie that served as the pilot film for the TV series "Assignment: Vienna."

**Astaire, Fred and Bob Dylan**
Only two people depicted on the cover of the Beatles' *Sgt. Pepper's Lonely Hearts Club Band* album who also later signed John Lennon's United States immigration petition.

**"As the Earth Turns"**
Maxwell Smart's (Don Adams) favorite TV soap opera in the 1980 movie *The Return of Maxwell Smart*.

**"As the World Turns"**
Television soap opera that First Lady Mamie Eisenhower watched five days a week when she lived in the White House.

**Astro**
Flying space whale in the 1965 animated movie *Pinocchio in Outer Space*.

**Atlanta National Bank**
Name of banking firm on the check for $300 written by Frank Kennedy (Carroll Nye) to Scarlett O'Hara (Vivien Leigh) in the 1939 movie *Gone With the Wind*. The bank's president, as indicated on the check, was A. Austell.

**Atlanta University**
Winner of the first black collegiate football game. It defeated Tuskegee Institute at Atlanta on January 1, 1897.

**"Atlantic City, My Old Friend"**
Song composed by Paul Anka and sung by Robert Goulet in the 1981 movie *Atlantic City*.

**Atlantic Picture Studios**
Hollywood motion picture studio for which Leo Harrigan (Ryan O'Neal), Tom "Buck" Greenway (Burt Reynolds), and Franklin Frank (John Ritter) worked at a salary of $150 per week until they were fired in the 1976 movie *Nickelodeon*.

**Atlas Savings and Loan of San Francisco**
First gay savings and loan company, opened in 1978. It is staffed by gay employees.

**Atlas Van Lines**
Moving company that transported the Freeling family's furniture in the 1982 movie *Poltergeist*. As mentioned in the credits, Gran Tree Furniture provided the furniture for the film.

**"At Sundown"**
Song composed in 1927 by Walter Donaldson and performed in the following movies: *The Bells of Capistrano* (1942); *Music for the Millions* (1944); *The Fabulous Dorseys* (1946); *Love Me or Leave Me* (1955).

**Attention Police, Call Evans—Treasury Radio Signal Fallon**
Message that Hank Fallon (Edmond O'Brien) left on a mirror of E. G. McClure's gas station in the 1949 movie *White Heat*.

**Attica**
New York State prison in which the inmates rioted and took some guards as hostages from August 22 to September 13, 1971, for twenty-three days. The riot caused more casualties than any other

single engagement between Americans since the Civil War. Within six minutes there were thirty-nine dead, twenty-nine of whom were prisoners, ten of whom were hostages. The name of the prison is mentioned in the movies *Dog Day Afternoon* (1975), *Saturday Night Fever* (1977), and *Cheech & Chong's Next Movie* (1980). The event became the subject of a 1980 TV movie titled *Attica*.

**Atticus**
Pet dog of 1972 Democratic Presidential candidate George McGovern.

**Audrey Rose**
Best-selling novel by Frank De Felitta. Model Brooke Shields posed for the paperback cover, even though she did not appear in the 1977 movie.

**"Auf Weidersehen, Sweetheart"**
Record by Vera Lynn that, on July 4, 1952, became the first song by a British artist to top the American *Billboard* chart.

**Augusta National Golf Club**
Golf facility in Augusta, Georgia, that is the site of the Annual Masters Tournament. Gene Sarazen was the winner of the first Masters in 1935.

**August 17**
Birthday of Tira (Mae West) in the 1933 movie *I'm No Angel*.

**August 8, 1944**
Birthdate of detective Thomas Magnum (Tom Selleck) on the TV series "Magnum P.I."

**August 14, 1961**
Opening date of the 1961 James Cagney movie *One, Two, Three*. That day, Roger Maris hit home runs number 44 and 45 while playing against the Washington Senators.

**August 18, 1973**
Date on which the 1974 cult movie *The Texas Chain Saw Massacre* took place.

**Austerlitz**
New York City play in which cowboy William S. Hart made his acting debut on January 21, 1889.

**Austin, Stephen Fuller**
(1793–1836) Texas colonizer who encouraged other Americans to move to Texas in order to help the republic become a state. He was portrayed by Ralph Morgan in the 1939 movie *Man of Conquest*.

**Austin, Thomas**
Man who introduced rabbits to Australia in 1859.

**Austin, Tracy**
Fourteen-year-old who, on June 22, 1977, became the youngest player ever to win a Wimbledon tennis match, defeating Elly Vessies-Appel of the Netherlands.

**Australia**
Country that Lex Luthor (Gene Hackman) wanted to rule in the 1981 movie *Superman II*. It was also the last surviving populated continent in the 1959 movie *On the Beach*.

**Author of *A Tale of Two Cities*—Charles Dickens**
Credit line in the production credits for the 1980 movie *Airplane!*

**Automobile Manufacturers (1980)**
*Largest in the United States* (according to size)
1. General Motors
2. Ford
3. Chrysler
4. American Motors
5. Volkswagen of America
6. Checker Motors Corporation

**Avalon, Frankie**
(1940–     ) Clean-cut, Philadelphia-born singer of hit songs in the late 1950s and early 1960s. Avalon made his first hit record "Dede Dinah" while holding his nose. He and Annette Funicello appeared together in a number of beach movies during the 1960s. In the 1978 movie *Grease*, Avalon played the role of Teen Angel. He was portrayed loosely by Paul Land in the 1981 movie *The Idolmaker* as Tommy Dee. Avalon made his acting debut in the 1960 Alan Ladd movie *Guns of the Timberland*.*

**Avco World Trophy**
Trophy presented to the winner of the World Hockey Association Championship.

**Avengers, The**
Signers of the ransom note for the return of Evangelist Aimee Semple McPherson, when she was supposedly kidnapped on May 18, 1926. After 37 days, she returned safely under a cloud of mystery.

**"Avenues and Alleyways"**
Theme song of the TV series "The Protectors," sung by Tony Christie.

---

*He had previously appeared in the 1957 rock 'n' roll movie *Jamboree*, in which he sang "Teacher's Pet."

**A verbal contract isn't worth the paper it's written on . . ..**
Saying credited to movie producer Samuel Goldwyn, known as a Goldwynism.

**Azra**
Winner of the eighteenth Kentucky Derby (May 11, 1892), in which only three horses ran. The other two horses, Huron and Phil Dwyer, were both owned by Ed Corrigan.

# B

**B12**
Puppet Johnny Jupiter's sidekick on the 1953 TV series *Johnny Jupiter*.

**BA52L3**
Pennsylvania license plate number of the broken-down Claremont Center school bus driven to the state of Washington by Joe Baxter (Richard Pryor) in the 1981 movie *Bustin' Loose*.

**BBJ128**
California automobile license plate number of Colonel Jim Caldwell's (Rock Hudson) white Valiant in the 1963 movie *A Gathering of Eagles*.

**B**
Blood type of both Captain John F. Xavier "Trapper John" McIntyre (Wayne Rogers) and Corporal Walter "Radar" O'Reilly (Gary Burghoff) in the TV series "M*A*S*H."

**B&O**
Railroad bridge from which Punjab (Geoffrey Holder) rescued Annie (Aileen Quinn) in the 1982 movie *Annie*.

**BAN-ONE**
License plate number of Bandit's (Burt Reynolds) Chevy Camaro "Trigger" in the 1977 movie *Smokey and the Bandit*. His CB handle was Bandit One.

**BMI**
Broadcast Music Incorporated

**BOQ**
Bachelor officers' quarters

**BTU**
British Thermal Unit

**Baba Wa Wa**

Popular nickname for newswoman Barbara Walters, because of her lisp. She was played by Gilda Radner on TV's NBC "Saturday Night Live."

**Babe Ruth**

Six-man British group who are the only rock 'n' roll band to be named after a major-league baseball player.

**Babe Ruth Story, The**

Movie premiere in New York City, which Babe Ruth attended on July 26, 1948. It was his last public appearance. The film featured William Bendix as the Babe.

**Baby**

Doug Quintain's (Humphrey Bogart) pet black Scottie dog, which he took with him everywhere in the 1937 movie *Stand-in*.

**"Baby"**

Song by Caesare (Peter Gallagher) that was at the number-one spot on the record charts for 25 weeks in the 1981 movie *The Idolmaker*. In actuality, no song has ever stayed at the top of the charts for that length of time.

**Baby Ruth**

Candy bar first produced by Curtiss Candy Company in 1921. The candy was named for President Cleveland's daughter, not for Babe Ruth. It is Howard Cunningham's (Tom Bosley) favorite candy on the TV series "Happy Days."* The Dionne quintuplets were featured in the advertisements for the candy bar.

**Bach**

Last name of Arthur, played by Dudley Moore in the 1981 movie *Arthur*.

**Bach, Johann Sebastian**

(1685–1750) German organist and composer who wrote a great number of vocal and instrumental compositions. His four sons also became musicians. Bach died, blind, in 1750. Bach was portrayed by Gustav Leonhardt in the 1969 movie *Chronicles of Anna Magdalena*.

**"Back Home"**

Number-one hit single in Britain, charted during August 1970 by

---

*In one 1980 episode, Mr. Cunningham told his daughter, in error, that the candy was named for Babe Ruth and on a 1982 episode of the TV series "Hart to Hart," Jonathan Hart (Robert Wagner) erroneously said to a small boy that a candy bar was named after Babe Ruth.

the English World Cup Squad. Previously, in 1976, the Manchester United Football Club charted "Manchester United," a song that only went to fiftieth place.

**"Back in Baby's Arms"**
Song which Loretta Lynn (Sissy Spacek) and Patsy Cline (Beverly D'Angelo) sang in duet in the 1980 movie *Coal Miner's Daughter*.

**Back-to-back no-hitters**
The first back-to-back no-hitters in major-league baseball were played on September 17, 1968, when Gaylord Perry of the San Francisco Giants pitched against the St. Louis Cardinals, and on the next day, September 18, 1968, when Ray Washburn of the Cardinals tossed a no-hitter against the San Francisco Giants.

**Back to Mono**
Two buttons worn by Phil Spector, dressed in a Santa Claus suit, on the cover of *Phil Spector's Christmas LP*. Spector hates stereo music.

**Backtrack**
TV movie (1969) made from episodes of two TV series, "Laredo" and "The Virginian."

**Badejo, Bolaji**
Stuntman who played the alien in the 1979 movie *Alien*.

**Badge 2**
Badge number of agent Ilya Kuryakin (David McCallum) on the TV series "The Man From U.N.C.L.E."

**Badge 14**
Badge number of detective Mark Saber (Tom Conway/Donald Gray) on the TV series "Mark Saber."

**Badge 79**
Badge number of Fearless Flanagan, hero of a story written by Wesley Winfield (Billy Gray), in the 1954 movie *By the Light of the Silvery Moon*.

**Badge 163**
Badge number of Sergeant Philip Esterhaus (Michael Conrad) on the TV series "Hill Street Blues."

**Badge 415**
Badge number of police officer Carl Levitt (Ron Carey) on the TV series "Barney Miller."

**Badge 437**
Badge number of the London bobbie (Peter Ellis), whom David Kessler (David Naughton) unsuccessfully tried to get to arrest him in the 1981 movie *An American Werewolf in London*.

**Badge 730**
Badge number of New York City policewoman Mary Beth Lacey (Tyne Daly) on the TV series "Cagney and Lacey."

**Badge 778**
Badge number on the police cap worn by Micky Dolenz on the cover of the Monkees' record album *Instant Replay*.

**Badge 1032**
Badge number of fireman Spike Ryerson (Vince Edwards) at Engine Company 23 in the 1973 pilot movie *Firehouse.* In the TV series, James Drury played Captain Spike Ryerson.

**Badge 2178**
Badge number of fireman Shelley Forsythe (Richard Roundtree) at Engine Company 23 in the 1973 pilot movie *Firehouse.*

**Badge 3146**
San Francisco Police Department (SFPD) badge number of Kate Moore (Tyne Daly) partner of "Dirty Harry" Callahan (Clint Eastwood) in the 1976 movie *The Enforcer*.

**Badge 5702**
Los Angeles Police Department badge number of Officer Brooks (Ronny Cox) in the 1979 movie *The Onion Field*.

**Badge 7332**
Badge number of Los Angeles undercover police officer Christie Love (Teresa Graves) on the TV series "Get Christie Love!"

**Badge 7691**
New York City police badge number of rookie cop Gabe Marino (Gabe Dell) in the 1948 Bowery Boys movie *Trouble Makers*.

**Badge 9735**
Badge number of New York police officer Beauregard "Bo" Lockley (Michael Moriarty) in the 1975 movie *Report to the Commissioner*.

**Badge 10532**
Badge number of Fozzie Bear on the TV series "The Muppet Show."

**Badge 13029**
New York City badge number of Officer John Joseph Vincent Murphy (Paul Newman) of the 41st Precinct in the 1981 movie *Fort Apache, the Bronx*.

**Badge 233451**
Badge number of Captain Barney Miller (Hal Linden) on the TV series "Barney Miller."

**Badge 549321**

Badge number of police detective Sergeant Stanley Taduce Wojehowicz (Max Gail) on the TV series "Barney Miller."

**Badges, we ain't got no badges. We don't need no badges. I don't have to show you no stinkin' badges!**

Line said by Alfonso Bedoya (as the bandit Gold Hat) in the 1948 movie *The Treasure of the Sierra Madre*.*

**Bailey, Pearl**

Only person ever to have danced with Egyptian President Anwar Sadat at a White House reception.

**Baird, John Logie**

Scotsman who, in 1944, received a United States patent for 3-D TV.

**Bakelite**

President Franklin D. Roosevelt's cigarette holder.

**Baker Bowl**

Philadelphia Phillies' baseball stadium (1887–1938) prior to the team's move to Shibe Park on July 4, 1938; Baker Bowl, which was previously known as Huntington Avenue Park, cost $80,000 to build.

**Baker, Kathlyn**

Actress who led a group of running nurses in the opening credits sequence of the TV series "M*A*S*H." She was paid $77.50 for appearing in the single scene (her only appearance on the show).

**Baker, Rick**

First winner of the Academy Award for Best Makeup. He won it *for the 1981 movie An American Werewolf in London*. He also appeared in Michael Jackson's video, *Thriller*, which was directed by John Landis.

**Baker, Frank "Home Run"**

(1886–1963) Major-league baseball player who led the American League in home runs in 1911, 1912, 1913, and 1914. For those four years, his combined totals were 29, an average of less than 10 a year. He played 13 years in the majors with the Philadelphia Athletics and New York Yankees and hit a lifetime total of 93 home runs. His highest total in one year was 12 (1913). Baker hit his only grand slam on April 24, 1909, off Frank Arellanes. Although not a great home-run hitter, he is the only player to have the nickname of

*A variation of the line was said in the 1974 movie *Blazing Saddles*: "Badges! We don't need no stinking badges!"

"Home Run." He starred in the 1912 movie *The Shortstop's Double*.

## Balfour, Arthur James

(1848–1930) English philosopher and statesman. He served as Prime Minister (1902–05) and was First Lord of the Admiralty, succeeding Winston Churchill (1915). His Balfour Declaration (November 1917) stated that the British government favored Palestine as the national home of the Jewish people. Balfour was portrayed by William Dexter in the 1972 movie *Young Winston*.

## "Ballad of John Chisum"

Theme song of the 1970 John Wayne movie *Chisum*, sung by Merle Haggard.

## "Ballad of Mashed Flagg, The"

Theme song of the 1969 Robert Mitchum movie *The Good Guys and the Bad Guys*, sung by Glenn Yarbrough.

## "Ballad of the Republic, Sung in the Year 1888, A"

Original title of Ernest L. Thayer's poem "Casey at the Bat," when it originally appeared in the *San Francisco Examiner* on June 3, 1888.

## "Ballbusters on Parade"

Title of the home movie shown by Jonathan (Jack Nicholson) in the 1971 movie *Carnal Knowledge*.

## Ball diameters

| | |
|---|---|
| 1½" | Table tennis ball |
| 1⅔" | Golf ball (American) |
| 1⅞" | Handball |
| 2⅛" | Snooker ball |
| 2¼" | Billiard ball (American pocket) |
| 2⅜" | Rounders ball |
| 2½" | Box lacrosse ball |
| 2½" | Tennis ball |
| 2½" | Lacrosse ball |
| 2⅞" | Cricket ball |
| 3" | Hockey |
| 3" | Baseball |
| 3⅛" | Hurling ball |
| 3¼" | Croquet ball (regulation) |
| 3⅜" | Croquet ball (American lawn) |
| 3⅝" | Croquet ball (association) |
| 3⅞" | Softball (regular) |

| | |
|---|---|
| 5″ | Duckpin ball |
| 5⅛″ | Softball (16 ounce) |
| 8½″ | Bowling ball |
| 8½″ | Volley ball |
| 8⅞″ | Soccer ball |
| 8⅞″ | Water polo ball |
| 9½″ | Basketball |

## Ball Four
1970 autobiographical book by major league pitcher Jim Bouton, which, in 1976, was made into a short-lived TV series, starring Bouton as Jim Barton. *Ball Four* is the best-selling sports book of all time. In 1983 Jim Bouton published *Ball Four Plus Ball Five*, an expanded edition of his book that covered the years 1970–1980.

## Ball, Larry
Football player who, in 1972, played for the Miami Dolphins (the team won every game that season) and, in 1977, played for the Tampa Bay Buccaneers (the team lost every game that season).

## Ball, Neal
(1881–1957) Cleveland shortstop who, on July 19, 1909, made the first unassisted triple play in major-league baseball (Boston's Amby McConnell hit into the play).

## Baltimore
Maryland city in which the 1979 movie . . . *And Justice for All* and the 1982 movie *Diner*, are set. The city is also mentioned in the lyrics of Bruce Springsteen's 1980 hit song "Hungry Heart."

## Baltimore Colts (1979)
NFL team with the most penalties in a single season (137).

## Baltimore Oriole
Official state bird of Maryland, since 1947.

## Bamm Bamm
The Rubbles' son on the TV cartoon series "The Flintstones," voiced by Don Messick. On the TV cartoon series "Pebbles And Bamm Bamm," voiced by Jay North.

## Banacek
Thomas Banacek, a Polish-American detective who worked as a free-lance investigator/bounty hunter for various insurance companies. He was played by George Peppard in a series of TV movies broadcast under the collective title *Banacek* on "The NBC Wednesday Mystery Movie" between 1972 and 1974. The following were the titles of the individual segments:

*Banacek:* (1972—pilot movie)
*Banacek: To Steal a King* (1972)
*Banacek: No Sign of the Cross* (1972)
*Banacek: Project Phoenix* (1972)
*Banacek: No Stone Unturned* (1973)
*Banacek: The Greatest Collection of Them All* (1973)
*Banacek: The Two Million Clams of Cap'n Jack* (1973)
*Banacek: Horse of a Slightly Different Color* (1974)
*Banacek: Now You See Me—Now You Don't* (1974)
*Banacek: The Vanishing Chalice* (1974)

## Banana Man
Character who appeared on the "Captain Kangaroo" TV series, played by Al Robbins.

## Bandit Sings Cole Porter, The
Unsuccessful record album recorded by the Bandit (Burt Reynolds) in the 1980 movie *Smokey and the Bandit Part II*.

## "Bandstand Boogie"
Instrumental by Les Elgart, played over a cassette tape in the yellow taxicab driven by Ernest Borgnine in the 1981 movie *Escape from New York*. "Bandstand Boogie," sung by Barry Manilow, is the closing theme song of Dick Clark's "American Bandstand" TV show.

## Bankhead, Dan
(1921–1976) Became the first modern-day black pitcher in the major leagues when he pitched for the Brooklyn Dodgers on August 8, 1947. In his first time at bat, on August 26, he hit his first and only home run. Bankhead pitched in a total of 52 games.

## Bank of the Pacific
Carmel, California, bank that Nicholas J. Gardenia (Chevy Chase) was forced to rob in the 1980 movie *Seems Like Old Times*.

## Banneker, Benjamin
(1731–1806) Black surveyor who assisted in mapping out Washington, D.C., beginning in 1789.

## Banthas
Animals ridden by the Sand People of Tatooine in the 1977 movie *Star Wars*.

## Bantu Wind
Tramp steamer captained by Katanga (George Harris) that transported the Ark of the Covenant until intercepted by a German submarine (U-26) in the 1981 movie *Raiders of the Lost Ark*.

**Bardwell's**
Department store in Hollywood where Laverne De Fazio (Penny Marshall) and Shirley Feeney (Cindy Williams) worked after moving from Milwaukee on the TV series "Laverne & Shirley."

**Barg, Sara**
Woman who has been married to country entertainers Mac Davis and Glen Campbell.

**Barnett, Marilyn**
Lesbian ex-lover of tennis star Billie Jean King. In May 1981, Barnett unsuccessfully sued King for lifetime support.

**Barney**
Corporal Randolph Agarn's (Larry Storch) horse on the TV series "F Troop."

**Baronet Theater**
New York City movie theater where the 1976 movie *Rocky* was previewed. Six years before, Sylvester Stallone was fired as an usher at the same theater when he tried to scalp a ticket to, of all people, Walter Reade, the owner of the theater (as revealed by Stallone in his book *Rocky*).

**Barragan, Cuno**
(1932–　　) Chicago Cubs catcher who, on September 1, 1961, hit a home run in his first time at bat in the major leagues. He never hit another home run in the rest of his three-season career (which consisted of just 163 times at bat).

**Barrett, Stan**
First man to travel faster than the speed of sound on land when, in 1979, he traveled 739.666 miles per hour in the Budweiser Rocket. Barrett had previously doubled for Paul Newman in the 1971 movie *Sometimes a Great Notion* and for Burt Reynolds in the 1978 movie *Hooper*.

**Barry, Joan**
Young actress who brought a paternity suit against Charles Chaplin in 1942. Chaplin, who had employed Jerry Giesler as his attorney, was found not guilty, but was still ordered to pay child support.

**Bartholdi, Charlotte Beysser**
Woman who modeled for the Statue of Liberty, which was sculpted by her son Frederic Auguste Bartholdi.

**Bartle, Joyce**
Twenty-two-year-old model who posed for the advertisement for the 1981 James Bond movie *For Your Eyes Only*. She is seen with

her legs spread apart, with James Bond (Roger Moore) off at a distance.

**Baseball—children**

| Little League | Ages 8 to 12 |
| Babe Ruth League | Ages 13 to 15 |
| American Legion Baseball | Ages 15 to 17 |

**Baseball Diamond**

Large jewel owned by Lady Holiday (Diana Rigg) which was stolen from her in the 1981 movie *The Great Muppet Caper*.

**Baseball scoring position numbers**

1 Pitcher
2 Catcher
3 First baseman
4 Second baseman
5 Third baseman
6 Shortstop
7 Left field
8 Center field
9 Right field

**Bases Loaded**

Joe Gillis's (William Holden) unproduced screenplay in the 1950 movie *Sunset Boulevard*.

**Basil the Defender**

Designer of the chalice used by Jesus at the Last Supper. He was portrayed by Paul Newman in the 1955 movie *The Silver Chalice* (his movie debut). Peter Reynolds played him as a boy.

**Bass and Marshall**

Manhattan law firm setting of the TV series "The Associates."

**Bates, Katharine Lee**

Composer of the song "America The Beautiful," after she had climbed Pikes Peak in 1893, from which she received her inspiration.

**Batjac**

Dutch trading company in the 1948 movie *Wake of the Red Witch*. John Wayne borrowed the name for his movie production company.

**Battle of the Century**

Laurel and Hardy comedy film in 1927, in which Lou Costello made his screen debut, playing a spectator at ringside during a boxing match.

**Baumholtz, Frankie**
(1919– ) Chicago Cubs member who, in the final game of the 1952 baseball season, became the only player ever to bat against pitcher Stan Musial in a major-league game. Baumholtz, who was ironically second to Musial for the batting title, got on base because of an error.

**Baxter College**
Connecticut school where the members of the Brewster House Sorority lived on the TV series "Co-ed Fever" (of which only one episode was shown, on February 4, 1979).

**Baylor, Don**
(1949– ) Only major-league baseball player caught stealing twice in the same inning. He set the unusual record in the ninth inning while playing for the Baltimore Orioles on June 15, 1974.

**Bayside High School**
New York school from which Edith Baines Bunker (Jean Stapleton) graduated on the TV series "All in the Family."

**Beans**
Boston terrier that appeared in the advertisements for Campbell's Baked Beans.

**Bear Flag Restaurant**
House of prostitution in Monterey in the 1945 John Steinbeck novel and 1982 movie *Cannery Row*.

**Bears**
Rollerskating team for which Johnny Caesar (Mickey Rooney) skated in the 1950 movie *Fireball*.

**Bea's Knees**
Short instrumental tune written by John Barry and later retitled by him "The James Bond Theme."

**Beasley, Robert**
Inventor of the approximately 34,000 heat-resistant tiles comprising the skin of the U.S. space shuttle *Columbia*.

**Beast Aftershave**
Men's lotion company for which Rocky Balboa (Sylvester Stallone) spent four hours in an attempt to film a TV commercial in the 1979 movie *Rocky II*.

**Beau**
Dave Barrett's (Ken Howard) pet dog on the 1974–75 TV series

"The Manhunter."

**Beauregard**

Weird British driver of a yellow London cab in the 1981 movie *The Great Muppet Caper*.

**Beauregard Chaulmoogra Frontenac de Montmingle Bugleboy**

Bloodhound in Walt Kelly's "Pogo" comic strip.

**Beautia**

Captain Marvel's girlfriend and the daughter of Dr. Sivana, the World's Wickedest Scientist. Her brother was Magnificus.

**"Beaver Gets Spelled"**

First telecast episode (of 234) of the TV series "Leave It to Beaver," which aired on October 4, 1957.

**Bechel, George**

On July 1, 1892, he became the first sports writer to be slugged by a major-league baseball player, when Chicago Cubs outfielder Jimmy Ryan punched the *Chicago Evening News* reporter in the face.

**Beecher's Corners**

Farming community where Luke (Tony Geary) and Laura (Genie Francis) spent their 1982 honeymoon on the TV series "General Hospital."

**Beechwood**

Town setting of the radio soap "When a Girl Marries."

**Beery, Wallace and Marie Dressler**

Their only two movie appearances together were *Min and Bill* (1933) and *Tugboat Annie* (1933). The two did appear, however, in a 1933 all-star-cast film titled *Dinner at Eight*.

**Beethoven, Ludwig van**

(1770–1827) German composer prolific in writing classical pieces, including nine symphonies (1800–23), sonatas, concertos, etc. He was portrayed by Carl Boehm in the 1960 movie *The Magnificent Rebel*.

**Before This Anger**

Working title of Alex Haley's best-selling novel *Roots*.

**Be fruitful and multiply . . .**

First commandment mentioned in the Bible (Genesis 1:27).

**"Begin the Beguine"**

Song composed by Cole Porter in 1935, which first appeared in the musical *Jubilee* (1935). The song also was heard in the following movies: *Broadway Melody* (1940); *Night and Day* (1946); *Aloha, Bobby and Rose* (1975). The recording by Artie Shaw was being played on a record player in the studio of photographer Tom Kelley the evening that he took the famous nude calendar photograph of Marilyn Monroe, on May 27, 1949.

**Behind the Green Door**
X-rated movie starring porno queen Marilyn Chambers, watched by the driver (Jackie Chan) in the black computerized Subaru 4WD in the 1981 movie *Cannonball Run*.

**Belasco, David**
(1854–1931) American playwright and producer. He wrote *The Girl of the Golden West* in 1905. Belasco was portrayed by Claude Rains in the 1940 movie *The Lady with Red Hair*.

**Beldon Cup**
Trophy presented to stationmaster Ballard (Henry Travers) for growing the Miniver rose in the 1942 movie *Mrs. Miniver*.

**Belham**
Small English village in which the Miniver family lives in the 1942 movie *Mrs. Miniver*.

**"Believe It or Not"**
Theme song subtitle for the TV series "The Greatest American Hero." It became a hit record by Joey Scarbury in July 1981.

**"Believe Me, If All Those Endearing Young Charms"**
Theme song of the radio series "Aunt Jenny's True-Life Stories."

**Belinda**
Joan Hill's (Farrah Fawcett) horse in the 1981 movie *Murder in Texas*. (Based on the book *Prescription: Murder* by Anne Kurth).

**Belinsky, Robert "Bo"**
(1936–    ) Los Angeles Angel who pitched a no-hitter game (May 5, 1962), beating Baltimore 2–0. He was also the losing pitcher to Don Wilson's no-hitter game on June 26, 1962. On April 20, 1966, he gave up Hank Aaron's four hundredth career home run. Belinsky played Bo Bo in the 1967 rock 'n' roll movie *C'mon, Let's Live a Little*. "Bo," who was once engaged to actress Mamie Van Doren, was married to Jo Collins, Playboy Playmate of the Year.

**Belle**
Dog in the 1962 movie *The Miracle Worker*.

**Bellini, Vincenzo**
(1801–1835) Italian opera composer who was portrayed by Phillips Holmes in the 1935 movie *The Divine Spark*.

**Belly Dancer**
Racing boat that J. J. McClure (Burt Reynolds) crashed into a

39

houseboat in the 1981 movie *Cannonball Run*.

**Belzer, Elizabeth**

First woman to graduate from the United States Naval Academy at Annapolis (1980).

**"Be My Little Baby Bumblebee"**

Song written in 1912 by Stanley Murphy and Henry Marshall, which was performed in the following movies: *When Irish Eyes Are Smiling* (1944); *By the Light of the Silvery Moon* (1953) performed by Doris Day and Russell Arms, and *The Eddie Cantor Story* (1954) performed by Eddie Cantor.

**Benedict, Clint**

Goalie for the Montreal Maroons, who, in 1929, became the first hockey goalie to wear a face mask.

**Benedict High School**

School in Arnold, California, attended by the students in the 1976 movie *Satan's Cheerleaders*.

**Ben-gals**

Cheerleaders for the Cincinnati Bengals football team.

**Ben Harper**

Role played by Christopher Reeve in the TV soap "Love of Life."

**Benjamin Harrison High**

School where thirty-one-year-old Sarah McDavid (Patty Duke Astin) taught English in the 1981 TV movie *The Violation of Sarah McDavid*.

**Bennett, Eddie**

Hunchback who, in the 1920s, became one of the most popular batboys in major-league history. Prior to going to bat, players would rub his hump for good luck. Eddie worked for the Brooklyn Dodgers, the New York Yankees, and the Chicago White Sox. He was the highest-paid batboy in major-league history.

**Bensfield**

Tennessee town in which Tom Holvak (Glenn Ford) was a minister in the TV series "The Family Holvak."

**Bergdorf Goodman**

Expensive New York City store where Linda Morrola (Liza Minnelli) shoplifted a tie in the men's department in the 1981 movie *Arthur*.

**Berg, Mrs. Hart**

First woman passenger in an airplane. In Auvers, France, in 1908, she took a two-minute ride with Wilbur Wright.

**Berg, Patty**

(1918–     ) Founder and first president of The Ladies Professional Golf Association (1951).

**Berkeley, William "Busby"**

(1895–1976) Broadway and Hollywood choreographer/director. He became famous for his spectacular movie musicals, such as *42nd Street* (1933), *Gold Diggers of 1935*, etc. Busby Berkeley was loosely portrayed by Douglas Fowley as Roscoe Dexter in the 1952 movie *Singin' in the Rain*.

**Berlin Ballet**

Ballet company performing at the Metropolitan Opera on July 23, 1980, on the evening when violinist Helen Hagnes was killed backstage, during an intermission.

**Berman, Stanley**

Brooklyn cabdriver who claimed to have been the World's Greatest Gate Crasher. In 1957 he posed as a waiter to get Queen Elizabeth II's autograph; he crashed John F. Kennedy's Inaugural Ball in 1961. That same year he jumped onstage in order to present host Bob Hope with a homemade Oscar at the Academy Award presentations. Berman died in 1968.

**Bernadine**

Movie (1957) in which Pat Boone made his motion-picture debut and in which Janet Gaynor made her last movie appearance.

**Bespin**

Cloud City, of which Lando Calrissian (Billy Dee Williams) is governor in the 1980 movie *The Empire Strikes Back*.

**Best Athlete (1944)**

Colegio Belen school title held by Fidel Castro in his youth.

**Best of Sam and Dave**

Eight-track tape being played inside the 1974 Dodge Monaco Bluesmobile in the 1980 movie *The Blues Brothers*.

**"Better than Ever"**

Song that Jessica Potter (Candice Bergen) wrote and sang to her ex-husband, Philip (Burt Reynolds), in the 1979 movie *Starting Over*. In actuality, Carole Bayer Sager composed the song.

**"Best That You Can Do (Arthur's Theme)"**

Theme song of the 1981 movie *Arthur*, sung by Christopher Cross. The song, which was composed by Burt Bacharach, Carole Bayer Sager, Peter Allen, and Christopher Cross, won the Academy Award for Best Song of 1981.

**Betty**

Name of the mummy mentioned in the lyrics of the 1958 novelty record "Dinner with Drac," by disc jockey John Zacherle.

**Betty and Vernon**

Two arguing public-service announcers at Los Angeles Airport in the 1980 movie *Airplane!*

**Betty Boop**

Sexy cartoon girl created by actress Helen Kane (the Boop-Boop-a-Doop Girl), and voiced by Mae Questel, Ann Rothschild, Margie Heinz, Kate Wright, and Bonnie Poe. Betty Boop debuted in the cartoon "Dizzy Dishes" (August 9, 1930).

**Beulah**

Land of sunshine and all delight in John Bunyan's 1678 work *Pilgrim's Progress*.

**Beulah**

Witch on the TV series "Kukla, Fran and Ollie." She was named for the show's producer, Beulah Zachary.

**Beverly Hills Fountain of Youth Health Spa**

Health clinic where Susan Hughes (Stockard Channing) worked on the TV series "Stockard Channing in Just Friends."

**Beverly Hills Unlisted Jazz Band**

Musical group for which actor George Segal plays banjo and sometimes sings.

**"Beyond the Blue Horizon"**

Song composed by Leo Robin, Richard A. Whiting, and W. Franke Harling in 1930, and sung by Jeanette MacDonald in two movies, *Monte Carlo* (1930) and *Follow the Boys* (1944).

**Bib-Label Litehearted Lemon-Lime Soda**

Original name of 7-Up when it was first invented by C. L. Grigg in 1929.

**Bible and Plutarch's Lives**

Two books that Milly (Jane Powell) had with her when kidnapped in the 1954 movie *Seven Brides for Seven Brothers*.

**Big Blue Wrecking Crew**

Vocal group who recorded the 45 RPM record "We Are Champions"/"New York, New York" in 1981. The group members were Los Angeles Dodgers Rick Monday, Jay Johnstone, Steve Yeager, and Jerry Reuss.

**Big Brother**

Ultimate ruler in George Orwell's novel *1984*, and in the 1956 movie version.

**Big Bundle, The**

Television game show hosted by Allen Ludden, which was shown in the opening sequence of the 1973 movie *Westworld*.

**Big Daddy's**
Nightclub where the kids hung out in the 1963 movie *Beach Party*. The house band was Dick Dale and the Deltones. Vincent Price played Big Daddy.

**Big Drag's Pit Stop**
Place where the surfers hung out in the 1964 movie *Bikini Beach*. Big Drag was played by Don Rickles.

**Big E**
Nickname of NBA star basketball player Elvin Hayes.

**Big Ethel**
Girlfriend of Jughead in the TV cartoon series *Archie*.

**Big Foot**
Four-wheel-drive blue Ford truck (Iowa license NCI 482) that Frank Macklin (Robert Hays) drove to victory (while wearing football jersey #12) at the brewery's annual picnic in the 1981 movie *Take This Job and Shove It*. Some of the trucks that Big Foot defeated were Silver Bullet, Palladin, and Thunder 'n' Lightnin'.

**Big Jack's**
Mobile, Alabama, nightclub which features a five-piece band in the lyrics of the 1968 Elvis Presley hit song "Guitar Man" on which Jerry Reed plays lead guitar.

**Big Muddy**
Nickname of the Missouri River.

**Big Red**
Irish setter befriended by fourteen-year-old orphan Rene Dumont (Gilles Payant) in the 1962 movie *Big Red*. Champion Red Aye "Scraps" played Big Red.

**Big Red**
Nickname of a Geronimo motorcycle owned by Rob Petrie on an episode of the TV series "The Dick Van Dyke Show." In the episode, Petrie was arrested as a result of being mistaken for a member of the Ramrods motorcycle gang, whom he had met at a diner called Hal's Eats.

**Big Red Line**
Cheerleaders for the St. Louis Cardinals football team.

**Big Rip-Off, The**
Pilot movie (1975) for the TV series "McCoy," starring Tony Curtis.

**Big Rip-Off, The**
Consumer-protection TV series shown on West Hollywood KXLA-TV, for which Susan Goodenow (Stockard Channing) was a researcher, in the TV series "The Stockard Channing Show."

**Big Sam Hollis**
Father of Charlotte Hollis (Bette Davis) in the 1964 movie *Hush, Hush, Sweet Charlotte*. Big Sam was played by Victor Buono, who, at the age of 26, played the father of 56-year-old Bette Davis. (They had previously appeared together in the 1962 movie *Whatever Happened to Baby Jane?*, his film debut.)

**Billy Comstock and the Counts**
Rock 'n' roll band that played at Richie Cunningham's (Ron Howard) Teen Angel Prom at Jefferson High School in the TV series "Happy Days."

**Billy Shears**
Singer with Sgt. Pepper's Lonely Hearts Club Band. Ringo Starr is Billy on the *Sgt. Pepper* album and refers to himself as Billy on his recording of "I'm the Greatest." Billy Shears was played by Peter Frampton in the 1978 movie *Sgt. Pepper's Lonely Hearts Club Band*. The real Billy Shears was supposedly a young man who won a Paul McCartney lookalike contest. In the 1951 movie *Along the Great Divide*, John Agar played a character named Billy Shear.

**Binaisa, Godfrey**
President of the African country of Uganda, who played bit parts in the 1950 movie *King Solomon's Mines* and the 1951 movie *The African Queen*.

**Biocarbon Amalgamated**
Canadian chemical plant founded by Dr. Paul Ruth (Patrick McGoohan) in 1942. The plant manufactured the chemical Emphemerol in the 1981 movie *Scanners*.

**Bip**
Princess Dawn's pet dog on the TV cartoon series "Here Comes the Grump."

**Blabber Mouse**
Sidekick of Super Snooper on the TV cartoon series.

**Black**
Color in which both Jack Haley, Jr., and Liza Minnelli were married in 1974.

**Black and Yellow**
Racing colors of the racehorse Man o' War.

**Black Angels**
Motorcycle gang led by a character named High Test (William P. Kelley) in the 1968 "B" movie *Big Enough 'n' Old Enough*.

**Black Babe Ruth, The**
Nickname of the Negro League's superstar, Josh Gibson, who hit

over 800 home runs in his baseball career.

**Black Bart**
Black sheriff hired to police the all-white western town of Rock Ridge in the 1974 movie *Blazing Saddles*. Lou Gossett played Sheriff Black Bart in an unsuccessful 1975 TV series called "Black Bart."

**Black Beauty**
Novel written by Anna Sewell, first published in 1877. It has been filmed in 1946, 1971, and in 1978 for TV. Dean Martin once stated that the only book he had ever read was *Black Beauty*.

**Black Dahlia**
Name given by the press to the dead woman whose nude body was found in a vacant lot in Los Angeles on January 15, 1947. Her body was cut in half. She was later identified as 21-year-old Elizabeth Short; however, her murder was never solved. Short was portrayed by Lucie Arnaz in the 1975 TV movie *Who Is the Black Dahlia?* The murder was used as the basis for a scene in the 1981 movie *True Confessions*. Miss Short was called the Black Dahlia because of her black hair and her fondness for black clothing. The name "Black Dahlia" was inspired by the title of a 1946 Alan Ladd–Veronica Lake film written by Raymond Chandler, titled *The Blue Dahlia*.

**Black Eagle**
Chester's (John Hall) fighting cock that he brought to Tahiti from San Francisco in the 1942 movie *The Tuttles of Tahiti*.

**Blackford**
Small California town setting of the 1980 movie *The Hearse*.

**Black Horse Vigilante Committee**
Organization of which Jason Maple (Porter Hall) was a member in the 1936 movie *The Petrified Forest*.

**Blackjack**
Charlie Malloy's (George Segal) horse, which is branded with a ㉑, in the 1976 movie *The Duchess and the Dirtwater Fox*.

**Black Jack**
Great Dane that appeared on the TV series "Blansky's Beauties."

**Black Legion**
Title of Norman Main's (James Mason) last movie, as given in the 1954 motion picture *A Star is Born*. It was made by the Oliver Niles Studios. As a billboard goes up for Vicki Lester's latest film, *Happiness Ahead*, Norman's billboard for *Black Legion* is being taken down.

**Black Maria**

Name on the cab of the eighteen-wheeler truck and trailer that ran over one of the cannibals in the 1974 movie *The Texas Chainsaw Massacre*.

**Black Pearl**

Nickname of soccer superstar Pelé.

**Black Pearl**

Three-masted barkentine ship half sunk in Sweethaven's harbor in the 1980 movie *Popeye*.

**Black Widows**

Pomona motorcycle club, led by Dallas (Bill McKinney), that pursues Philo Beddloe (Clint Eastwood) throughout the movies *Every Which Way But Loose* (1978) and *Any Which Way You Can* (1981).

**Blades**

Private British gambling club where agent James Bond (Sean Connery) gambled in an early scene of the 1963 movie *Dr. No*.

**Blaine, James Gillespie**

(1830–1893) United States congressman, senator, and Secretary of State. The Republican Presidential candidate against Grover Cleveland in 1884, Blaine was portrayed by Don Haggerty in the 1965 movie *The Great Sioux Massacre*.

**Blaisdell, George G.**

Inventor, in 1932, of the Zippo cigarette lighter. During World War II, American GIs used black Zippos, to eliminate reflections.

**Blaiz General Hospital**

Hospital where Nick Smith (Cecil Kellaway) spent two weeks recovering from an automobile accident injury, in the 1946 movie *The Postman Always Rings Twice*. His bill was $322. In James Cain's novel, the hospital was the Glendale.

**Blasphemer! Get him, he is a blasphemer!**

John Travolta's only line in his movie debut in *The Devil's Rain* (1975).

**Blast**

Radical magazine for which Dr. Hunter S. Thompson (Bill Murray) wrote in the 1980 movie *Where the Buffalo Roam*.

**Blazer**

Jock Ewing's (Jim Davis) horse at South Fork on the TV series "Dallas."

**Blazing Saddles**
   Mel Brooks movie being shown at Graumann's Chinese Theater in the 1974 movie *Blazing Saddles*.

**Bleier, Rocky**
   Pittsburgh Steelers football player who went back to playing football after receiving severe leg injuries in Vietnam. He was portrayed by Robert Urich in the 1980 TV movie *Fighting Back*.

**Blip**
   Space Ghost's chimp in TV cartoons.

**Blood and Swash**
   Book credited to Captain X but written by Lucy Muir (Gene Tierney), with the aid of Captain Daniel Gregg (Rex Harrison), in the 1947 movie *The Ghost and Mrs. Muir*. The book was published by Tacket and Sprogins.

**Blood Money**
   British release title of the 1962 American movie *Requiem for a Heavyweight*.

**Blood on the Badge**
   Book written by detective Ron Harris (Ron Glass), published by Wainwright Publishers, in the TV series *Barney Miller*. The book, which was originally titled *Precinct Diary*, had a Dewey Decimal number of 364.12.

**Bloods, Sherlocks, Diablos**
   Three different ethnic gangs in the TV series "Hill Street Blues": the Diablos were Hispanics, the Sherlocks were Irish, the Bloods were blacks.

**Blount, Barbara**
   First woman college student in the United States. Blount attended the University of Tennessee in 1794. She was the governor's daughter.

**Blozis, Al**
   Tackle for Georgetown University and college shot-put champion, who was named an All-League Tackle. During World War II, Lieutenant Blozis was killed in action at the Vosges Mountains in France.

**Blue**
   Color of Smurfs (their clothing is white).

**Blue**
   Color of paper on which Alexandre Dumas wrote his novels. He

used white paper for his magazine articles and yellow paper for his poetry.

**Blue**

Color of the devil's eyes in Terri Gibbs's 1981 hit song "Somebody's Knockin'."

**Blue**

Favorite color of Eunice Harper Higgins (Carol Burnett) on the TV series "The Carol Burnett Show."

**Blue Alexandria**

United States' 1847 five-cent stamp that sold for one million dollars in May 1981. The stamp was on a letter addressed to Jannett Brown of Richmond, Virginia, on November 25, 1847.

**Blue and white**

Colors of the caps worn by the two teams in a water polo game. Goalkeepers wear red caps trimmed in either blue or white.

**Blue Bonnet**

Former Alabama governor Cornelia Wallace's CB handle.

**Blue Bonnet**

Margarine for which baseball greats Mickey Mantle and Willie Mays made a 1980 TV commercial together, singing and wearing blue bonnets.

**Blue Dahlia, The**

Alan Ladd and Veronica Lake movie made in 1946, being shown on TV as Trisha (Lily Tomlin) watched in the 1978 movie *Moment by Moment*. She also watched the 1936 movie *My Man Godfrey*, starring William Powell and Carole Lombard. The movie's title, *The Blue Dahlia*, referred to the name of a restaurant.

**Blue Devil Cafe**

Bar in Sumatra where Bijou (Marlene Dietrich) was the cause of a barroom brawl in the 1940 movie *Seven Sinners*.

**Blue Eyes**

Movie debut of Dawn Bennett Youngblood (Melanie Griffith), which was directed by Danny Youngblood (Rock Hudson) within the 1981 TV movie *The Star Maker*. Melanie Griffith is the daughter of actress Tippi Hedren.

**Bluefin, USS**

Submarine that rescued the crew of the sunken submarine USS *Greyfish* in the 1958 movie *Torpedo Run*.

**Blue House**

South Korean presidential mansion.

**"Blue Moon"**

This song, written in 1934 by Richard Rodgers and Lorenz Hart, originally titled "Prayer," was to be sung by Jean Harlow in the movie *Hollywood Revue of 1933*, but the film was never completed. Hart then changed the lyrics and retitled the song "The Bad in Every Man." Shirley Ross sang it in the 1934 Clark Gable movie *Manhattan Melodrama*. Sha Na Na sang "Blue Moon" in the 1978 movie *Grease*, and Dudley Moore played part of "Blue Moon" in the 1981 movie *Arthur*.

**"Blue Moon"**

Opening theme, sung by Bobby Vinton, of the 1981 movie *An American Werewolf in London*.

Song sung by Sam Cooke as David Kessler (David Naughton) first turned into a werewolf in the 1981 movie *An American Werewolf in London*.

Closing theme, sung by the Marcels, of the 1981 movie *An American Werewolf in London*. The group had previously sung the song in the 1961 movie *Twist Around the Clock*.

**Blue 19**

Football play used by Frank Macklin (Robert Hayes) in Mooney's Tavern in the 1981 movie *Take This Job and Shove It*.

**Blue Note Cafe**

Favorite hangout of Casey (Staats Cotsworth) on the radio series "Casey, Crime Photographer."

**Bluerock**

Montana town from which the stranger came in Willie Nelson's hit song "Red Headed Stranger."

**"Blues in the Night"**

Song composed in 1941 by Johnny Mercer and Harold Arlen, which was sung by John Garfield in the 1943 movie *Thank Your Lucky Stars*.

**Blue, Vida**

(1949–     ) Only pitcher to start an All Star game in both leagues: National League (1971) and American League (1978).

In 1971, at the age of twenty-two, he became the youngest player to win the American League's Most Valuable Player and Cy Young awards.

**Blunderhead**

Horse of the puppet Buffalo Billy on the 1950 TV series "The Buffalo Billy Show."

**Boar's Nest**
Restaurant and bar owned by Mayor Jefferson Davis Hogg (Sorrell Brooke) on the TV series "The Dukes of Hazzard."

**Bob**
Ventriloquist Chuck Campbell's (Jay Johnson) dummy on the TV series "Soap."

**"Bobby's Girl"**
Hit song (1962) by Marcie Blaine. A band played an instrumental version of "Bobby's Girl" in the 1980 movie *It's My Turn*.

**Bob's Country Bunker**
Country-western club where Jake and Elwood Blues and their rhythm-and-blues band played one evening, singing such country songs as "Rawhide" and "Stand by Your Man" in the 1980 movie *The Blues Brothers*.

**Bocephus**
Nickname of country singer Hank Williams's son. On radio, Hank would say to him, "Don't worry, Bocephus, I'm coming home." Today, Bocephus is better known as Hank Williams, Jr.

**Bodar, Gus**
Toronto Maple Leafs rookie who, on October 30, 1943, set a NHL record by scoring his first goal only fifteen seconds into his first NHL game.

**"Body and Soul"**
Song composed in 1930 by Edward Heyman, Robert Sour, Frank Eyton, and John Green, performed in the following movies: *The Man I Love* (1946), *Body and Soul* (1947), and *The Eddy Duchin Story* (1956).

**Bogan County**
Fictitious southern setting of the Burt Reynolds movies *White Lightning* (1973) and *Gator* (1976).

**Bogart Slept Here**
Original title of Neil Simon's play that eventually became *The Goodbye Girl*. Simon originally wanted Robert DeNiro to play the lead role.

**Bohunk**
Ted's (Larry Nunn) pet dog in the 1941 movie *Men of Boy's Town*. Bohunk was killed by a car in the film.

**Boland, Bill**
Youngest jockey to ever win the Kentucky Derby. He won riding Middleground in 1950 at the age of sixteen.

**Bolivia and Paraguay**
Only two completely landlocked South American countries.

**Bombastic Bushkin**
Johnny Carson's financial advisor, Henry Bushkin, often referred to in Carson's monologues.

**Bondurant, Robert**
Racing car driver who trained actors James Garner and Yves Montand (for the 1966 movie *Grand Prix*) and Paul Newman and Robert Wagner (for the 1969 movie *Winning*) to competently drive racing cars.

**Bonner Hill**
Adam and Amanda Bonner's (Spencer Tracy and Katharine Hepburn) farm in the 1949 movie *Adam's Rib*.

**Bonnicut**
Bridge mentioned in the lyrics of the 1975 Frankie Valli hit song "My Eyes Adored You."

**Bonzo Runs for President**
Movie shown at the 4077th, as selected by Lieutenant Colonel Henry Blake (McLean Stevenson), on the TV series "M*A*S*H." (The title is fictitious.)

**Boo**
Pet cat of Jonathan "Musty" Muddlemore on the TV cartoon series "The Funky Phantom."

**Boogie Woogie**
Amanda Child's (Kristy McNichol) pet dog in the 1981 movie *The Night the Lights Went Out in Georgia*. Boogie was played by Kristy's own dog, LuLu McNichol.

**Book of Evil**
Ancient book sought by the monsters in the 1982 movie *Saturday the 14th*.

**Boom!**
Elizabeth Taylor/Richard Burton movie, made in 1968, which saw the rare film appearance of Miss Taylor's brother, Howard Taylor, playing a journalist.

**Booth Number Two**
Table at the Brown Derby restaurant, at 3377 Wilshire Boulevard, in Hollywood, where columnist Louella O. Parsons always sat.

**Booth Number Five**
Table at the Brown Derby restaurant where columnist Hedda Hopper always sat.

**Booth Number Seven**

Table at the Brown Derby restaurant where Clark Gable proposed to Carole Lombard in 1939.

**Bormann, Martin**

(1900–   ) German Nazi leader who, from 1933 until 1941, was Rudolf Hess's chief of staff.

Bormann was portrayed by Michael Lonsdale in the 1981 TV movie *The Bunker,* and by Derek Newark in the 1982 TV movie *Inside the Third Reich.*

**Born Again**

Ironic title of actor George Brent's last movie (1978). He died in 1979.

**Boss**

Tattoo on the right upper arm of Dr. Frank N. Furter (Tim Curry) in the 1975 movie *The Rocky Horror Picture Show.*

**Boston Braves**

NFL football team of 1932.

**Boston Braves**

Major-league baseball team whose previous names have been:

Red Caps (1876–1882)
Beaneaters (1883–1906)
Doves (1907–1908)
Pilgrims (1909–1911)
Braves (1912–1935)
Bees (1936–1940)
Braves (1941–1952)

In 1953 the franchise moved to Milwaukee.

**Boston Bruins**

First American hockey team in the NHL, joining the league in 1924.

**Boston Globe**

Newspaper subscribed to by Major Charles Emerson Winchester III (David Ogden Stiers) on the TV series "M*A*S*H."

**Boston Red Sox**

First major-league team to travel by air, when they flew from St. Louis to Chicago on July 30, 1936. Five players, however, did not fly with the team.

**Both Ends of the Candle**

British release title of the 1957 American movie *The Helen Morgan Story.*

**Both Mother and Father**
Fictional TV series of 1998, starring Monte Rushmore (Harvey Korman) in the 1979 movie *Americathon*.

**Bottleneck**
Wild West town tamed by Deputy Sheriff Thomas Jefferson Smith (James Stewart) in the 1939 movie *Destry Rides Again*.

**Boudreau Shift**
Defensive maneuver created by Cleveland Indians manager Lou Boudreau to enable his club to defend against Boston Red Sox hitter Ted Williams. He introduced the Shift in the second game of a double-header on July 14, 1946. It consisted of shifting almost the entire defense to the right, with the third baseman playing directly behind second, the left fielder covering left and center field, and everyone else to the right of them.

**BOwery 2-1000**
Phone number of the New York City morgue in the 1948 movie *Sorry, Wrong Number*.

**Bowl-A-Rama**
Bowling alley where the students of Rydell High go to bowl (and sing) in the 1982 movie *Grease 2*.

**Box A7**
Clark Kent's (George Reeves) box number at the Daily Planet in the TV series "The Adventures of Superman."

**Box 710**
Hollywood post office box where viewers are to write in order to submit a request to the TV series "You Asked for It." The show was revived in 1981 with host Rich Little, and in 1982, hosted by Jack Smith. If the program uses the request, the viewer receives fifty dollars. In 1982, Box 1980 was used.

**Box 25989**
Los Angeles post office box number where viewers are asked to write to the TV series "That's Incredible."

**Boxcar Willie**
Nickname of country singer Cecil "Marty" Martin.

**Boy Rangers**
Boys' club headed by Jefferson Smith (James Stewart) in the 1939 movie *Mr. Smith Goes to Washington*.

**Boy's Life, A**
Working title of the 1982 Steven Spielberg movie *E.T. the Extra-Terrestrial*.

**Bozo**

Carnival clown that is dunked by thrown baseballs. He was played by Frankie (Gary Busey) in the 1980 movie *Carny*.

**Brackman, Robert**

Artist who, in reality, painted the portrait of Jennie (Jennifer Jones) for the 1948 movie *A Portrait of Jennie*.

**Braddock University**

College of which Louis Harper (Bill Macy) was the president on the short-lived 1979 TV series "Hanging In."

**Brad Majors and Janet Weiss**

Young couple who are the subjects of the two films *The Rocky Horror Picture Show* (1975) and *Shock Treatment* (1981). Played by Barry Bostwick and Susan Sarandon in the first and by Cliff DeYoung and Jessica Harper in the sequel.

**Brady and Company**

Manhattan pocketbook firm for which Richard Sherman (Tom Ewell) worked as an editor in the 1955 movie *The Seven Year Itch*.

**Brady, William A.**

Producer of the 1929 Pulitzer Prize–winning play *Street Scene*. He is the only man ever to have managed two heavyweight boxing champions: James J. Corbett and James J. Jeffries.

**Brahms, Johannes**

(1833–1897) German composer and pianist who lived in Vienna from 1862. Brahms was portrayed by Robert Walker in the 1947 movie *Song of Love*.

**Brain, The**

Nickname given by writer Damon Runyon to gangster Arnold Rothstein.

**Brainstorm**

Motion picture that Natalie Wood was filming at the time of her death on November 29, 1981. In the movie, her son had a fear of drowning. The film was released in September 1983.

**Braithwaite, Edward Ricardo**

British Guiana schoolteacher who taught a tough class at a secondary school in London's East End during the 1950s. He was portrayed by Sidney Poitier (as Mark Thackeray) in the 1967 movie *To Sir With Love*.

**Brambell, Wilfred**

British actor who played Paul McCartney's grandfather in the 1965 movie *A Hard Day's Night*.

**Brandy Alexander**
Alcoholic drink that John Lennon was drinking the night he was thrown out of the Troubadour nightclub in Los Angeles in March of 1969.

**Braun, Eva**
(1912–1945) Mistress of Adolf Hitler. The two were married on the eve of their suicide, April 30, 1945.
Portrayals:
*The Magic Face* (1951), Patricia Knight
*Hitler* (1962), Marian Emo
*Hitler: The Last Ten Days* (1973), Doris Kunstman
*The Bunker* (1981 TV), Susan Blakely
*Inside the Third Reich* (1982 TV mini-series), Renee Southendijk

**Brave Stallion**
Title of the syndicated reruns of the TV series *Fury*.

**Brazzaville**
Title of the planned sequel film to the 1942 classic *Casablanca*. It was to star Humphrey Bogart, Geraldine Fitzgerald, and Sidney Greenstreet. However, it was never filmed.

**Breakers, The**
Closed and abandoned tavern that attorney Ned Rocine (William Hurt) burned down, with Mary Ann Simpson's (Kathleen Turner) husband's body inside, in the 1981 movie *Body Heat*.

**Breakfast at Tiffany's**
Phrase said in two movies that starred Audrey Hepburn: *Breakfast at Tiffany's* (1961) and *Paris When It Sizzles* (1964).

**Breakfast Food City**
Nickname of Battle Creek, Michigan, the birthplace of actress Betty Hutton on February 26, 1921.

**Breakfast of Champions**
Slogan on boxes of Wheaties breakfast cereal, created by Ivy Lee, the same man who created Betty Crocker.

**Break of Dawn Club**
New York City nightclub where Roberts (Tom Neal) played piano in the 1946 movie *Detour*.

**Bremen**
German ocean liner on which Captain Victor "Pug" Henry (Robert Mitchum) and his wife, Rhoda (Polly Bergen), traveled to Germany in 1939, in the TV mini-series *Winds of War*. *The Queen*

*Mary* was used during the filming of the series.

**"Bride and Groom"**

Radio series on which struggling actor Dick Van Dyke married his wife, Marjorie, on a program in 1948.

**Bridger Military Prison**

Government prison to which Amos (Tim Conway) and Theodore (Don Knotts) were sent to serve a thirty-year term for burning down Fort Concho in the 1979 movie *The Apple Dumpling Gang Rides Again*. Amos's prison number was 6321, and Theodore's was 3151.

**Brigadier Gordon**

Role played by Larry "Buster" Crabbe on the episode "Planet of the Slave Girls" (September 27, 1979) of the TV series "Buck Rogers in the 25th Century."

**BRighton 634**

Telephone number of Professor Peter Boyd (Ronald Reagan) in the 1951 movie *Bedtime for Bonzo*.

**Brill Building**

New York City building located at 1819 Broadway, which was the center of the rock 'n' roll music scene in the 1950s. Atlantic Records, Atco Records, and Wand Records were among the many record labels that had offices there. The building was also the location of many publishing firms for which Neil Sedaka, Carole King, Paul Simon, and others wrote songs.

**Bring on the Empty Horses**

Title of actor David Niven's 1975 autobiography. The line was originated by director Michael Curtiz, while he was filming the 1936 movie *The Charge of the Light Brigade*. He meant to say, "Bring on the riderless horses."

**Britannia**

Royal yacht on which Prince Charles and Lady Diana sailed on their Mediterranean honeymoon cruise in June 1981. (The ship's crew consisted of 276 men.)

**British Enterprise Four**

British oceanic vessel that was used in the attempts to rescue the sunken vessel *Goliath* on the 1981 TV mini-series *Goliath Awaits*.

**Broadwick, Georgia "Tiny"**

On June 21, 1913, at Los Angeles, she became the first woman to parachute from an airplane. The pilot was Glenn Martin.

**Bronko**

Dr. Hunter S. Thompson's (Bill Murray) pet Doberman pinscher in the 1980 movie *Where the Buffalo Roam*.

**Bronson, Charles and Jill Ireland**

Appeared together in:

*Villa Rides* (1968)
*Rider In The Rain* (1969)
*The Family* (1970)
*Cold Sweat* (1970)
*Someone Behind the Door* (1971)
*The Valachi Papers* (1972)
*The Mechanic* (1972)
*Chino* (1973)
*Breakout* (1973)
*Breakout* (1975)
*Hard Times* (1975)
*Breakheart Pass* (1976)
*From Noon Till Three* (1976)
*Love and Bullets* (1978)
*Death Wish II* (1982)

The pair have been married since 1968. Prior to that, Jill Ireland had been married from 1957 to 1967 to actor David McCallum.

**Brooklyn Dodgers**

1930–43 NFL football team
1946–48 AAFC football team
1911–1953 NL baseball team

**Brooklyn Dodgers**

Last major-league team to employ Babe Ruth. He coached for them in 1938.

**Brooklyn 21, New York 7**

Final score of the December 7, 1941, football game that Walt Dreiser (Dana Andrews) and Eloise Winters (Susan Hayward) attended in the 1949 movie *My Foolish Heart*.

**Brooks, Herb**

Coach of the American hockey team that won the Gold Medal at the 1980 Winter Olympics. He was portrayed by Karl Malden in the 1981 TV movie *Miracle on Ice*.

**Brothers Four**

Folk group who sang the title song for the 1966 movie *Alvarez Kelly*.

**Brown**

Color of Mary Lou's eyes in Rick Nelson's 1961 hit song "Hello Mary Lou" (on which his father, Ozzie Nelson, played a four-string guitar).

**Brown and black**

Mixed pair of shoes worn by Gerald Ford when he married Betty Bloomer on October 15, 1948.

**Brown Jack**

Horse upon which Steve Donaghue won the Ascot Gold Cup in six consecutive years, 1929–1934.

**Brown, Molly**

Affluent young lady who survived the sinking of the ocean liner *Titanic*. Molly was portrayed by Debbie Reynolds in the 1964 movie *The Unsinkable Molly Brown* and by Cloris Leachman in the 1979 TV movie *S.O.S. Titanic*.

**Brown, Sam**

Fourteen-year-old boy from Liberty, South Carolina, who traveled with three ex-Presidents (Richard Nixon, Gerald Ford, and Jimmy Carter) and the rest of the American delegation to Cairo for the funeral of Egyptian president Anwar Sadat. Sam and Sadat had previously corresponded with one another.

**Brown, Tom**

(1940–    ) Only player to have played in both a major-league baseball game and in the Super Bowl. In 1963 he played with the Washington Senators as a first baseman and outfielder (61 games) and then played with the Green Bay Packers in Super Bowls I and II.

**Bruce Carson**

Role played by Robby Benson on the TV soap "Search for Tomorrow."

**Brundland, Gro Harlem**

(1939–    ) First female prime minister of Norway (1981).

**Bruno**

Major Charles Emerson Winchester III's (David Ogden Stiers) dog back home in Boston on the TV series "M*A*S*H."

**BRyant 9-4099**

Peggy Brown (Debbie Reynolds) and Peter Harmond's (Tony Curtis) telephone number in apartment number 31 in the 1960 movie *The Rat Race*.

**Bryant High School**
Archie Bunker's (Carroll O'Connor) New York City alma mater*
on the TV series *All in the Family*.

**Buchanan, Jack**
(1891–1959) Song-and-dance man who appeared on Broadway as
well as in movies in both Britain and the United States. He made
his Broadway debut with Beatrice Lillie and Gertrude Lawrence in
*Charlot's Revue* in 1924. He was portrayed by Garrett Lewis in the
1968 movie *Star!*

**Buck**
Deputy sheriff played by James Arness on an episode of the TV
series "The Lone Ranger." On the episode, Arness talked like
John Wayne, and Tonto got hit over the head and knocked out
twice (as usual).

**Buck**
Slim Mosley's (Dean Martin) horse in the 1956 movie *Pardners*.

**Buckeroos**
Term used by Gabby Hayes to describe his young fans.

**Buck, Frank**
African big-game hunter of the 1930s and author of the book *Bring
'Em Back Alive*. He and Clyde Beatty appeared together in the 1950
Abbott and Costello film *Africa Screams*. Buck was portrayed by
Bruce Boxleitner on the TV series "Bring 'Em Back Alive."

**Buck Gannon**
Grizzly, one-eyed outlaw played by the Lone Ranger (Clayton
Moore) in one of his disguises on the TV series "The Lone
Ranger."

**Buckingham Palace**
London residence of British royalty since 1837. It was built by the
Duke of Buckingham in 1703.

**Buddy**
Ted Dodd's (Travis Lemmond) dog in the 1960 movie *My Dog,
Buddy*, played by London.

**Budge, J. Donald**
(1915–      ) First winner of tennis's Grand Slam, which he won in

---

*He was also known to have attended Flushing High School, and in one episode Edith
revealed that Archie had never graduated from high school. Continuity problems of this
sort occur often on television.

1937–38. His autobiography is titled *A Tennis Memoir*.

**Buffalo Vic**

Buffalo Bob's brother, played on the TV show "Howdy Doody" by Bob Smith's real brother, Vic.

**Buffy**

Cartoon elephant's head that readers were asked to draw for Art Instruction School's magazine ads.

**Buhl, Bob**

(1928–    ) Major-league pitcher who holds the record for appearing the most times at bat in a single season without a hit. He set the record in 1962 when he failed to get a single hit in seventy times at bat.

**Buick 88**

Automobile mentioned in the lyrics of the 1956 Little Richard hit song "Rip It Up."

**Bulova Watch Company**

Firm for which General Omar N. Bradley served as chairman from 1958 to 1973.

**Bulkeley, Lieutenant John D.**

U.S. Navy officer who evacuated General Douglas MacArthur and his family from Corregidor to Mindanao in 1942. He was portrayed by Robert Montgomery (as Lieutenant John Brickley) in the 1945 movie *They Were Expendable* and by William Wellman, Jr., in the 1977 film *MacArthur*.

**Bullet Records**

Nashville's first record label, which was established there in 1945.

**Bull Tales**

Comic strip that Gary Trudeau drew for the Yale *Daily News*. Mike Doonesbury was the featured character.

**Bunker Hill**

Military academy featured in the 1981 movie *Taps*.

**Bunny Wigglesworth**

Don Diego Vega's (Zorro) gay twin brother. Both were played by George Hamilton in the 1981 movie *Zorro, the Gay Blade*.

**Burch, Yvonne**

Thirteen-year-old who became the first girl to play in the Babe Ruth Baseball League.

**Burger Buddy**

Catsup used in Rough House's Cafe in the 1980 movie *Popeye*.

**"Burning Bridges"**
Song sung by the Mike Curb Congregation in the 1970 movie *Kelly's Heroes*.

**Burns, Elizabeth**
Hollywood actress who became an alcoholic, then was saved by religion. She was portrayed by Anne Baxter in the 1971 movie *The Late Liz*.

**Burstyn, Ellen**
(1932–    ) Academy Award–winning actress who, in 1982, became the first female president of Actor's Equity since its founding in 1913.

**Burt**
Animated turtle who instructs schoolchildren on how to react in the event of an atomic bomb attack, shown in a film within the 1982 movie *The Atomic Cafe*.

**Burton, Richard**
(1925–    ) Actor born in Pontrhydfen, South Wales. He appeared on Broadway, and in 1949 made his movie debut in *The Last Days of Dolwyn*. Twice he has been married to actress Elizabeth Taylor. Burton was nominated for an Oscar six times without ever winning one. Frank Gorshin's voice was used for that of Burton reciting "Camelot" in the closing scenes of the 1981 TV movie *Jacqueline Bouvier Kennedy*.

**Burton, Sir Richard**
(1821–1890) English explorer and scholar who translated *The Arabian Nights* into English.

**Bus**
Word in the title of both a Marilyn Monroe (*Bus Stop*—1956) and a Jayne Mansfield (*The Wayward Bus*—1957) movie.

**Buster**
Bronco Billy McCoy's (Clint Eastwood) trick horse in the 1980 movie *Bronco Billy*.

**Busy Bee**
Los Angeles car wash into which Ellen Wagstaff Arden (Doris Day) drove her blue Imperial convertible, lowering the top as she went through in the 1963 movie *Move Over Darling*.

**Butch Cassidy and the Sundance Kid**
Nickname of the Miami Dolphins' running backs Larry Csonka and Jim Kiick.

**Butcher, The**

Boxer whom Bags (Tim Conway) knocked out to become the heavyweight boxing champion of the world in the 1979 movie *The Prize Fighter*. Michael LaGuardia played the Butcher.

**Butler, Jean Marie**

First woman graduate from the United States Coast Guard Academy, on May 21, 1980. She was also the first woman to graduate from a U.S. service academy.

**BUtterfield 8-1098**

New York City home phone number of Alice Hammond (Donna Reed) in the 1956 movie *The Benny Goodman Story*.

**Butterfield, Tom**

Young man who established a home for unwanted boys and girls. At the age of twenty-one, he became the first single male to become a foster parent in the state of Missouri. Tom was portrayed by Fred Lehne in the 1981 TV movie *The Children Nobody Wanted*.

**Butterfingers**

Candy bar introduced by the Curtiss Candy Company in 1923.

**Button Nose**

Nickname that Ronald Reagan used for his actress wife, Jane Wyman.

**"Buttons and Bows"**

Academy Award–winning song introduced by Bob Hope in the 1948 movie *The Paleface*. The song was composed by Jay Livingston and Ray Evans. It was again sung in *Son of Paleface* (1952).* The song was also sung by a group in a bar in the 1950 movie *Sunset Boulevard*.

**Butts, Alfred Mosher**

Inventor, in 1932, of the game Scrabble, which he first called Lexico.

**Bye-Bye Blackbird**

Song that Howard Hughes (Jason Robards) sang with Melvin Dummar (Paul LeMat) in Dunmar's pickup truck in the 1980 movie *Melvin and Howard*. The song was composed in 1926 by Mort Dixon and Ray Henderson, and was heard in the following films: *Rainbow Round My Shoulder* (1952), sung by Frankie Laine; *River of No Return* (1954), sung by Marilyn Monroe; *The Eddie Cantor Story* (1954), sung by Eddie Cantor.

---

*Robert L. Welch, who produced both films, *Paleface* and *Son of Paleface*, is the father of Bob Welch, ex-member of the rock band Fleetwood Mac.

# C

**C125**

*Pacific Princess* cruise director Julie McCoy's (Lauren Tewes) cabin number on the TV series "The Love Boat."

**CF**

First two letters of boat registration numbers in California.

**CORE**

Congress of Racial Equality.

**COYOTE**

Acronym for Call Off Your Old Tired Ethics, the name of the first prostitutes' union. It was introduced in San Francisco in 1972 by Margo St. James.

**C-T-R**

Computer-Tabulating-Recording, the original name of IBM.

**Cactus**

Secret Service code name for Camp David, the Presidential retreat.

**Cadillac**

Name of the lion at the city zoo where Veldini (Donald Sutherland) worked cleaning out animal cages, in the 1973 movie *Steelyard Blues*.

**Cadillac**

Automobile mentioned in the lyrics of the songs "Maybellene" by Chuck Berry (1955), "Beep Beep" by the Playmates (1958), "Mary Lou" by Ronnie Hawkins (1959), "A Worried Man" by the Kingston Trio (1959), "Do-Wacka-Do" by Roger Miller (1964), "Nadine" by Chuck Berry (1964), "Long Black Limousine" by Elvis Presley (1969), and "You Don't Mess Around with Jim" by Jim Croce (1972).

**Cadillac, Lincoln, Mercury, Subaru**
Four automobiles mentioned in the lyrics of "Rapture," a number-one hit record by Blondie in 1981.

**Caesar**
Mr. Magoo's pet hamster in his TV cartoon series.

**Caesar**
Name of Kimba's father on the TV cartoon series "Kimba."

**Caesar**
White workhorse of Pa Baxter (Gregory Peck) in the 1946 movie *The Yearling*.

**Cahn, Sammy**
(1913–     ) Highly prolific lyricist who has been composing successful songs since 1935. Some of his better-known compositions are "I'll Walk Alone," "I Believe," "It's Magic," and "It's Been a Long Long Time." Sammy Cahn made a cameo appearance in the 1979 movie *Boardwalk*.

**Calder Memorial Trophy**
Trophy awarded to the NHL's Rookie of The Year. Established in 1936, it was named for Frank Calder, the NHL's first president.

**Caledonia II**
Yacht owned by Osgood Fielding III (Joe E. Brown) in the 1959 movie *Some Like It Hot*. Osgood referred to the vessel as "the *New Caledonia*."

**Calhoun**
Tanker commanded by Captain Bart Manson (Edward G. Robinson) in the 1944 movie *Tampico*.

**Calhoun, Haystacks**
Six-hundred-pound professional wrestler whom 196-pound Mountain Rivera (Anthony Quinn) is about to wrestle in the closing scene of the 1962 movie *Requiem for a Heavyweight*.

**California Dolls**
Harry's (Peter Falk) female wrestling team that he takes to the championship in the 1981 movie *All the Marbles*. The Dolls were Iris (Vicki Frederick) and Molly (Laurene Landon), and their specialty was the "Sunset Flip."

**California Stars**
Major-league baseball team for which Ralph Hinkley (William Katt) signed a $3-million-a-year contract as a pitcher. He pitched (uniform number 1) against the Oakland Mets, beating them by throwing three straight strikes and hitting a home run the next day

to win the pennant for the Stars on the TV series "The Greatest American Hero."

**Call me Ishmael . . .**
Opening line of the narrative in Herman Melville's 1851 novel *Moby Dick*.

**Calugcug, Lou**
Nineteen-year-old student at the University of the Phillippines, who rushed toward Pope John Paul II at the Santo Tomas University in Manila, on February 17, 1981, only to be stopped by police. Calugcug, who had "I Love You" printed on his T-shirt, later got a chance to embrace the pope. For some reason, that story made the front page of newspapers throughout the world.

**Calvin**
Cigarette-smoking crow puppet on the 1951–1953 TV series *In the Park*.

**Calvin Klein**
Brand of jeans modeled suggestively in advertisements and commercials by fifteen-year-old Brooke Shields. Brooke Shields's body can be seen advertising the jeans on a TV inside an automobile in the 1982 movie *Private Lessons*.

**Camel**
Animal mentioned in the lyrics of the two hit records, "Ahab the Arab" by Ray Stevens (1962) and "Midnight at the Oasis" by Maria Muldaur (1974).

**Camelot**
Palace of King Arthur, leader of the Knights of the Round Table.

**Camille**
Movie (1936), based on the Dumas novel, starring Greta Garbo and Robert Taylor, which Gwen Terasaki (Carroll Baker) and Hidenari Terasaki (James Shigeta) watch in the 1961 movie *Bridge to the Sun*. The movie was also seen by Richard Rodgers (Tom Drake) in the 1948 movie *Words and Music*. In the 1982 movie *Annie*, the picture is shown at the Radio City Music Hall, attended by Annie, Daddy Warbucks, Grace, and Sandy. Julie Marsten (Bette Davis), in the 1938 movie *Jezebel*, mentions having seen the play. Actress Ruth Gordon made her acting movie debut in the 1915 movie *Camille*, and Joan Leslie made her film debut in the 1936 version.

**Campaign Special**
President Richard M. Nixon's campaign DC-9 aircraft (N933F), loaned to him by Evergreen International (owned by the CIA), in

the 1980 movie *Where the Buffalo Roam*.

**Campbell, Glen and Tanya Tucker**
Couple who sang the National Anthem to open the Republican National Convention in Detroit, in July 1980.

**Campbell's Mushroom Soup**
Soup that Lieutenant Colonel Wilbur P. "Bull" Meechum (Robert Duvall) hid in his coat and spilled on the house band in a Spanish restaurant as he pretended to throw up in the 1980 movie *The Great Santini*. The band had been playing the song "Fascination."

**Camp Colfax**
Desert U.S. Army base setting of the 1963 movie *Captain Newman, M.D.*

**Camp Crystal Lake**
Summer camp established in 1935 that is the setting of the 1980 movie *Friday the 13th* (as well as its sequels).

**Camp Divine**
Girls' summer camp headed by Mahalia May Gruenecker (Alice Nunn) on the TV series "Camp Runamuck."

**Camp Little Wolf**
Girls' camp attended by Angel (Kristy McNichol) and Ferris (Tatum O'Neal) in the 1980 movie *Little Darlings*. The boys' camp across the lake was Camp Tomahawk.

**Camp Mohawk**
Children's summer camp for three hundred rich children ($1,000 per week) and rivals of Camp North Star, in the 1979 movie *Meatballs*.

**Camp North Star**
Summer camp headed by Tripper (Bill Murray) in the 1979 movie *Meatballs*. The camp opened on June 25. Their rival was Camp Mohawk, whose camp color was orange.

**"Camptown Races"**
Song that the cartoon rooster, Foghorn Leghorn, often sings. The character's voice is that of Mel Blanc.

**Canaan, Peter**
San Francisco motorcycle police officer who arrested Attorney F. Lee Bailey on the morning of February 28, 1982, for drunk driving. In a trial that cost $100,000, Bailey was acquitted.

**Canada, Lena**
Author of the touching book *To Elvis With Love*, about a crippled young girl named Karen who was a fan of Elvis Presley, with whom she corresponded. Lena Canada was portrayed by Deborah

Raffin and Karen was portrayed by Diane Lane in the 1980 movie *Touched by Love* which was based on the book.

**Canada's First Lady of Song**
Title held in the 1950s by singer Giselle MacKenzie.

**CAnal 6-109**
Telephone number on a yellow taxicab in the 1953 movie *Houdini*.

**Canby, General Edward Richard Sprigg**
(1817–1873) U.S. Army general who was shot and killed by Indian leader Captain Jack while the two were negotiating an Indian surrender on April 11, 1873. He was the only general killed while fighting Indians (Custer was a lieutenant colonel when he was killed).

**Canfield, Porter**
Vice-President featured in Spiro T. Agnew's novel *The Canfield Decision*. The name of the president in the novel was Hurly.

**Can Hieronymus Merkin Ever Forget Mercy Humppe and Find True Happiness?**
Movie (1969) made in Great Britain, directed by Anthony Newley and starring Newley, Milton Berle, and George Jessel.

**C.A.P.**
Initials of musical composer Cole Albert Porter (1893–1964).

**Cape Flattery**
Small town in Washington State where the Kettles lived in the *Ma and Pa Kettle* movie series.

**Cappeletti, John**
Heisman trophy winner and receiver who caught the last pass that Joe Namath completed throwing as a pro football player (1977).

**Capitol Studios**
Motion picture studio featured in the 1981 movie *S.O.B.*

**Capra (Frank) heroes**
Good, honest men who are the subject of films produced and directed by Frank Capra:

| | |
|---|---|
| Longfellow Deeds (Gary Cooper) | *Mr. Deeds Goes to Town* (1936) |
| Jefferson Smith (James Stewart) | *Mr. Smith Goes to Washington* (1939) |
| John Doe (Gary Cooper) | *Meet John Doe* (1941) |
| George Bailey (James Stewart) | *It's a Wonderful Life* (1946) |

**Captain, The**
Chubby, mustached German character featured in the comic strip series "The Katzenjammer Kids" and "The Captain and the Kids." The captain has appeared in the MGM cartoon series "The Captain and the Kids" (voice of Billy Bletcher). Debut: "Clean-

ing House'' (February 19, 1938)

**Captain Chaos**

Secret identity of do-gooder Victor (Dom De Luise) in the 1981 movie *Cannonball Run*. At the movie's end, he became Captain U.S.A.

**Captain Collins**

Commander of the U.S. gunboat *San Pablo*. He was played by Richard Crenna in the 1966 movie *The Sand Pebbles*.

**Captain Crackie**

Southern gentleman puppet on the TV series "Kukla, Fran and Ollie."

**Captain Dana E. Holmes**

United States Army officer who commanded G Company at Schoefield Barracks in Hawaii, in the novel *From Here to Eternity*, by James Jones. He was played by Philip Ober in the 1953 movie and by Roy Thinnes in the 1979 TV mini-series and weekly series.

**Captain Doreen Lewis**

United States Army WAC officer played by Eileen Brennan in the 1980 movie *Private Benjamin* and in the spinoff TV series.

**Captain Frank Furillo**

Officer in charge of the Hill Street police station, played by Daniel J. Travanti on the TV series *Hill Street Blues*.

**Captain Frank Kennelly**

New York City police officer played by Everett Sloane in the 1953–56 radio series *The 21st Precinct*.

**Captain John Blackthorne**

First Englishman to set foot on Japanese soil, in 1600. He was portrayed by Richard Chamberlain in the 1980 TV mini-series *Shōgun*. *(see Adams, William)*.

**Captain Jonathan Tuttle**

Fictitious, six-foot-four-inch, 195-pound, hazel-eyed, auburn-haired U.S. Army surgeon (serial number 39729966), born to Harry and Freeda Tuttle in Battlecreek, Michigan in 1924. He attended medical school at Berlin Polytechnic and died when he bailed out of a helicopter without his parachute. All of this was a creation of the imagination of Captain Benjamin Franklin Pierce (Alan Alda) on the TV series "M*A*S*H." In the episode's credits, Captain Tuttle was billed as playing himself.

**Captain Lee Quince**

Captain of the U.S. Cavalry post Fort Laramie in Wyoming, played by Raymond Burr in the radio series "Fort Laramie."

## Captain Louis Renaud

Head of the Vichy French police in Casablanca. Captain Renaud was played in the 1942 movie *Casablanca* by Claude Rains and on the 1955–1956 TV series *Casablanca* by Marcel Dalio (who played Emile, the croupier at Rick's Cafe Américain, in the movie).

## Captain McCavish

Black Scottie dog that Philo Vance (William Powell) entered (#292) in the Long Island Kennel Club dog show in the 1933 movie *The Kennel Murder Case*.

## Captain Wilson

Pilot of the airliner who passed out due to food poisoning in the 1957 movie *Zero Hour!* (basis for the 1980 movie *Airplane!*), played by football star Elroy "Crazylegs" Hirsch. The movie was based on Arthur Hailey and John Castle's novel *Runway Zero-Eight*. (*Runway Zero-Eight* also provided the basis for the 1971 TV movie *Terror in the Sky*).

## Caputo, Philip

United States Marine lieutenant who wrote about his tours in Vietnam. He was portrayed by Brad Davis in the 1980 TV movie *A Rumor of War*.

## Cardinal

Official state bird of Indiana (1933) and Kentucky (Kentucky cardinal).

## Carew, Rod

(1945–      ) Rodney Cline Carew, first American League batting champion (1972) not to have hit a home run that season (.318). He set the American League record with hits in 131 games. Rod was born on a train en route to Colón in the Panama Canal Zone on October 1, 1945.

## Carey Hotel

Wichita, Kansas, hotel that, on December 27, 1900, became the first bar "raided" by hatchet-swinging prohibitionist Carrie Nation.

## Carey, Mary

Fifteen-year-old Indian wife of an Englishman. She was the only woman among the 145 men who spent the night of June 21, 1756, in an 18-by-14-foot, 10-inch cell in Calcutta, historically called the "Black Hole of Calcutta." Mary Carey was among the twenty-three survivors.

**Carfield Place**

Four-hundred-acre English estate where Barbara Cartland writes her romantic novels (one every two weeks). Beatrix Potter wrote her *Peter Rabbit* stories there many years before.

**Cargo Hold Number Nine**

Location of the fuel Byzantium on board the sunken oceanliner *Titanic*, in the 1980 movie *Raise the Titanic!*

**Caribbean Star**

Freighter registered in Panama that is featured in the 1977 movie *Golden Rendezvous*, based on Alistair MacLean's novel of the same name.

**Carl**

Good Seasons vegetable man, played in TV commercials by Squire Fridell.

**Carl Harper**

Father of Eunice Harper Higgins (Carol Burnett), who was heard but never seen. He was always in the bathroom, where he eventually died. Carl Harper was voiced by Dick Clair on "The Carol Burnett Show."

**Carlson, Chester**

Inventor of the Xerox photocopying machine.

**Carl Yastrzemski**

Boston Red Sox player whose autograph was on the Louisville Slugger baseball bat used by Wendy Torrance (Shelley Duvall) to hit her deranged husband, Jack (Jack Nicholson), in the 1980 movie *The Shining*.

**Carmen**

Opera being performed at the Metropolitian Theater in the 1944 movie *Going My Way*.

**Carnera, Primo**

(1906–1967) Six-foot-five-and-¾-inch, 260-pound Italian-born boxer who became the heavyweight boxing champion when he defeated Jack Sharkey on June 29, 1933. He lost the title to Max Baer on June 14, 1934, by a KO in the eleventh round (Baer had floored him eleven times). After giving up boxing, he became a wrestler, then a referee. Carnera died on June 29, 1967, exactly thirty-four years after he won the heavyweight crown. He appeared in the 1949 movie *Mighty Joe Young* and in other films. Primo Carnera was portrayed loosely by Mike Lane, as Toro Moreno, in the 1956 movie *The Harder They Fall*.

**Carnes, Clarence**

Youngest inmate at Alcatraz (number 714AZ), at age eighteen. He was involved in a robbery in which his accomplice shot and killed a grocery clerk. While in prison, Carnes educated himself by reading almost every book in the prison library. Carnes was portrayed by Michael Beck in the 1980 TV movie *Alcatraz: The Whole Shocking Story*.

**Carney, Bill**

Young man who, after being injured in a jeep during a weekend of Army reserve duty in 1976, became a paraplegic. Carney fought to retain custody of his small sons, Willie and Eddie; however, his wife won the case even though she had originally deserted them. After the California Supreme Court overturned the lower court's decision on April 2, 1981, Bill Carney was returned custody of his young sons. Carney was portrayed by Ray Sharkey in the 1981 TV movie *The Ordeal of Bill Carney*.

**Carpetbaggers, The**

Novel written by Harold Robbins, which was based loosely on the life of Howard Hughes. It was made into a movie in 1964, starring Carroll Baker and George Peppard. *The Carpetbaggers* was the only book ever read (up to page 19) by Sandy Hinkle (Judi West), wife of Harry Hinkle (Jack Lemmon), in the 1966 movie *The Fortune Cookie*.

**Carr, Elizabeth Jordon**

First test tube baby to be born in the United States (December 28, 1981).

**Carroll, Lewis**

(1832–1898) Pseudonym of Charles Lutwidge Dodgson, author of children's books, his most famous being *Alice's Adventures in Wonderland* (1865) and *Through the Looking Glass* (1872). Lewis Carroll was also a respected mathematician. He was portrayed by Stephen Murray in the 1951 movie *Alice in Wonderland*.

**Carroll, Leo G.**

(1892–1972) British-born actor who appeared in the following Alfred Hitchcock movies: *Rebecca* (1940), *Suspicion* (1941), *Spellbound* (1945), *Strangers on a Train* (1951), and *North By Northwest* (1959).

**Carter**

Clementine's (Cathy Downs) last name in the 1946 movie *My*

*Darling Clementine*.

**Carter family**

A black family who passed for white over a twenty-five-year period. Their story is told in the 1949 movie *Lost Boundaries*.

**Casablanca**

Warner Bros. 1942 movie starring Humphrey Bogart, Ingrid Bergman, Paul Heinried, and Claude Rains. Originally considered for the two leads were Ronald Reagan and Ann Sheridan. Alan Ladd, Hedy Lamarr, and John Loder all performed in the presentation of *Casablanca* on the "Lux Radio Theatre," broadcast on January 24, 1944. Charles McGraw played Rick Jason in the 1955–1956 TV series "Casablanca." In 1955, *"The Lux Video Theatre"* telecast a production of "Casablanca" starring Paul Douglas, Arlene Dahl, and Hoagy Carmichael, and in 1983, David Soul played Rick on a four-episode TV series titled "Casablanca," with Scatman Crothers playing Sam. *Casablanca* is the most shown movie on TV and was President John F. Kennedy's favorite motion picture. Scenes from *Casablanca* are seen on a TV in the 1969 movie *The Happy Ending* and in the 1972 movie *Play It Again, Sam*.

**Casa Del Whackos**

Los Angeles mental institute where Dr. Timothy Leary was employed in the 1981 movie *Nice Dreams*.

**Casanova**

Baxter family pet cat in the 1952 movie *It Grows on Trees*.

**Casebook of Simon Brimmer, The**

Radio program of criminologist Simon Brimmer (John Hillerman) on the TV series "Ellery Queen."

**Caspian Sea**

Largest lake in the world (152,239 square miles) located in the USSR and Iran. It is over five times the size of the second largest lake, Lake Superior.

**Cassim Baba**

Brother of Ali Baba in *The Arabian Nights*.

**Cat**

McCoy's (Burt Reynolds) pet cat in the 1973 movie *Shamus*. Played by Lucky, who would later play Morris the Cat in the 9-Lives TV commercials.

**Cat and Mouse**

West German film made in 1969, which starred Lars and Peter Brandt, the sons of ex-Chancellor Willy Brandt.

## Cat Ballou

Movie (1965) starring Lee Marvin as Kid Shelleen and Tim Strawn, and Jane Fonda as Cat Ballou. Marvin won an Oscar as Best Actor for playing the dual role, an Academy first.* Two TV series pilots, both titled "Cat Ballou," were made in 1971, one with Lesley Ann Warren and the other with Jo Ann Harris.

## Catcher in the Rye, The

Novel by J. D. Salinger** being read by Wendy Torrence (Shelley Duvall) in the beginning of the 1980 movie *The Shining*. Freddie Clegg (Terence Stamp) bought a copy of the book for his prisoner Miranda Grey (Samantha Eggar) and then read it himself in the 1965 movie *The Collector*. It was also the book that the assassin of John Lennon, Mark David Chapman, had on him when he shot and killed Lennon on the evening of December 8, 1980.

## Catch-22

"There was only one catch and that was Catch-22, which specified that a concern for one's own safety in the face of dangers that were real and immediate was the process of a rational mind. [A pilot] was crazy and could be grounded. All he had to do was ask; and as soon as he did he would no longer be crazy and would have to fly more missions. [He] would be crazy to fly more missions and sane if he didn't, but if he was sane he had to fly them. If he flew them, he was crazy and didn't have to; but if he didn't want to he was sane and had to. . . ."

—from Joseph Heller's novel *Catch-22*

## Catfish

Nickname of major-league pitcher James Augustus Hunter. He received the nickname as a young boy, when he brought home two catfish after he was supposed to have run away.

## Catnip Gang, The

Foes of Mighty Mouse. The gang members were Shorty the Runt (leader), No-Chin Charlie, and Pinhead Schlabotka.

## Cato, Roberto

Driver of the van that, on the night of September 6, 1982, ran into

---

*Fredric March won an Oscar for *Dr. Jekyll and Mr. Hyde* (1932); however, he played one person with two distinct personalities, whereas Lee Marvin played two different persons.

---

**Author Jerome David Salinger was born on January 1, 1919, the same day as actress/authoress Carole Landis.

the taxicab in San Francisco, at California and Franklin Streets, in which actresses Mary Martin and Janet Gaynor were injured. Ben Washer, Martin's press agent, was killed. The cab was driven by Ronald Drury. Cato, who was arrested for running a red light that evening, was convicted of manslaughter and drunken driving in February 1983, and sentenced to three years in jail. The custom license of Cato's van was CREAM.

## Caudill, Bill
Chicago Cubs pitcher who is the only major-league player ever to strike out one hundred or more players (104) and have only one victory for the entire season; 1-7 (1979).

## Cavalier
Secret Service code name for President Jimmy Carter's Vice-President, Walter "Fritz" Mondale.

## Cavalry Trilogy
Three movies directed by John Ford and starring John Wayne. All were based on *Saturday Evening Post* stories by James Warner Bellah:

| Motion picture title | Story title | John Wayne's role |
|---|---|---|
| Fort Apache (1948) | "Massacre" | Captain Kirby York |
| She Wore a Yellow Ribbon (1949) | "War Party" | Captain Nathan Brittle |
| Rio Grande (1950) | "Mission with No Record" | Lieutenant Colonel Kirby York |

## Cedar, Cedar, Cedar and Boddington
Law firm representing the Semple fortune in the 1936 movie *Mr. Deeds Goes to Town*.

## Cell 13
Singer Merle Haggard's cell number in South Block, Tier 4, B Section, of San Quentin Prison.

## Cell 33
Prison cell of Joe Gallo (Peter Boyle) in the 1974 movie *Crazy Joe*.

## Cell 109
Frank Lee Morris's (Clint Eastwood) D Block cell number at Alcatraz Prison in the 1979 movie *Escape from Alcatraz*.

## Cell 363
Larry Poole's (Bing Crosby) cell number in prison in the 1936 movie *Pennies from Heaven*.

**Centralia**
   Pennsylvania town that has had a coal fire burning underneath it
   since 1965. The town of Carbondale, 50 miles away, had a 33-
   year-long fire finally put out in 1965.
**Century Turns, The**
   TV pilot movie (1972) for the TV series "Hec Ramsey" starring
   Richard Boone.
**Cervantes, Miguel de**
   (1547–1616) Spanish author who, between 1605 and 1615, wrote
   the classic novel *Don Quixote*. He was portrayed by Peter O'Toole
   in the 1972 movie *Man of La Mancha*.
**Challenger**
   One of the sister craft of the space shuttle *Columbia;* another is the
   *Enterprise*.
**Challenger**
   Judith Traherne's (Bette Davis) thoroughbred racehorse in the 1939
   movie *Dark Victory*.
**Chamberlain, Neville**
   (1869–1940) British statesman who, in 1937, succeeded Stanley
   Baldwin as Prime Minister. He declared war on Germany on
   September 3, 1939. Chamberlain resigned as Prime Minister in
   May of 1940. He was portrayed by Lester Matthews in the 1968
   movie *Star!*, by Jeremy Child in the 1972 movie *Young Winston*,
   and by Robin Bailey in *The Gathering Storm*, a 1974 "Hallmark
   Hall of Fame" TV presentation. His father, Joseph Chamberlain,
   was portrayed by Basil Dignam in the 1972 movie *Young Winston*.
**Chamberlin, Christopher**
   In November 1979, he became Canada's first blind policeman.
   Chamberlin, who was blind when the Ontario Police hired him,
   deciphers tapes and monitors wiretaps.
**Chandler, Don**
   Green Bay Packers kicker who kicked the first extra point in the
   first Super Bowl game (1967).
**Channel 2**
   TV channel mentioned in the lyrics of the Coasters' 1959 hit song
   "Along Came Jones."
**Channel 3**
   TV channel through which the Freeling family can talk to their five-
   year-old daughter Carole Anne (Heather O'Rourke) in the 1982
   movie *Poltergeist*.

**Chapman, Ben**

(1906–    ) Major-league outfielder who, as a New York Yankee, was replaced in 1936 by Joe DiMaggio, and as a Boston Red Sox player was replaced in 1939 by Ted Williams.

**Chapman, Eddie**

British safecracker-turned-counterspy for the British against the Germans during World War II. He was portrayed by Christopher Plummer in the 1967 movie *Triple Cross*.

**Chapman, Mark David**

Twenty-five-year-old slayer of singer John Lennon, outside the Dakota Apartments, in New York City, on December 8, 1980.

**Charge at Feather River, The**

In the 1954 movie *A Star Is Born*, this was the name of the 3-D movie that was being screened for studio brass when Vicki Lester (Judy Garland) walked in front of the screen.

**Charioteers**

Black gospel group with whom Frank Sinatra recorded a number of songs in 1945, such as "Jesus is a Rock in the Weary Land" and "I've Got a Home in the Rock."

**Charity Hope Valentine**

Dance-hall hostess played by Shirley MacLaine in the 1969 movie *Sweet Charity*.

**Charlemane**

Lion puppet on the 1951–1952 TV program "The Whistling Wizard."

**Charlene**

Cocktail waitress at the Silver Slipper Club, with whom Ed Higgins (Harvey Korman) ran off in August 1977, leaving Eunice (Carol Burnett) behind, in "The Carol Burnett Show."

**Charles and Edward**

Two of Queen Elizabeth II's sons (eldest and youngest, respectively).

**Charles, Ezzard**

(1921–    ) Heavyweight boxing champion (1949–1951) who has fought in more bouts (122) than any other heavyweight champion. He won 96 of those matches.

**Charley**

Bartender at Duffy's Tavern, played by Jimmy Conlin in the TV series "Duffy's Tavern."

**Charlie**
Soldier who is shot with an arrow in a hit novelty song of 1960 titled "Mr. Custer," sung by Larry Verne.

**Charlie**
Dog rescued from the yacht *Gatsby* in the 1980 movie *The Final Countdown*.

**Charlie's Bar**
San Francisco pub where Dora Lee Rhodes (Dolly Parton), Violet Newstead (Lily Tomlin), and Judy Bernley (Jane Fonda) went to drink in the 1980 movie *9 to 5*.

**Charlotte**
Pregnant elephant being transported from Miami to Texas in the 1980 movie *Smokey and the Bandit II*. Cledus (Jerry Reed) named the elephant after his aunt.

**Charlotte's Web**
Title of a 1973 animated movie based on E. B. White's book, and the title of a song sung by the Statler Brothers in the 1980 movie *Smokey and the Bandit II*.

**Charly Gordon**
Retarded thirty-year-old man who possesses the mind of a child until he is operated on in an experiment that increases his intelligence. He was played by Cliff Robertson in both the 1961 "U.S. Steel Hour" TV presentation of "The Two Worlds of Charly Gordon" and in the 1968 movie *Charly*, for which Robertson won an Academy Award as Best Actor. Both versions were based on the novel *Flowers for Algernon* by Daniel Keyes, which also inspired the short-lived Broadway musical *Charly and Algernon*.

**Charter Arms**
Maker of the .38-caliber revolver used by Arthur Herman Bremer when he shot Alabama Governor George C. Wallace on May 15, 1972, and of the pistol used by Mark David Chapman to shoot and kill John Lennon on December 8, 1980.

**Chateau Marmont Hotel**
Los Angeles hotel where actor John Belushi died on March 5, 1982.

**Chaz**
After-shave that Tom Selleck advertised in TV commercials.

**Cheerios**
Cereal that young Clark Kent (Jeff East) ate for breakfast in the

1978 movie *Superman*.

**Cheerios by General Mills**
Credit line in the 1978 movie *Superman*.

**Cherokee**
Indians who lived on the reservation, in the 1971 Paul Revere and the Raiders hit "Indian Reservation."

**Cherry Street Gang**
Rival gang of the Clancy Street Boys (Leo Gorcey, Huntz Hall, Billy Halop) in the 1943 East Side Kids film *Clancy Street Boys*.

**Chesapeake**
United States frigate upon which Captain James Lawrence gave his famous order "Don't give up the ship," on June 1, 1813.

**CHestnut 7878**
Telephone number of Johnny Webb's (Pat O'Brien) office in the 1940 movie *Slightly Honorable*.

**Chevrolet**
Make of automobile mentioned in the lyrics of Don McLean's 1971 hit song, "American Pie." The Chevy was driven to the levee.

**Chevrolet, Gaston**
Winner of the 1920 Indianapolis 500 race. He drove a Monroe car.

**Chic**
Magazine read by Mary Marshall (Ginger Rogers) on board a train to Pinehill in the 1944 movie *I'll Be Seeing You.*

**Chic**
Nickname that Archie Andrews asked Betty Cooper to call him in his debut comic strip in December 1941. The nickname, however, was never used afterwards.

**Chicago and Los Angeles**
Two cities mentioned in the lyrics of The Rolling Stones' version of "Route 66" and Martha Reeves and the Vandellas' "Dancing in the Streets."

**Chicago Sun-Times**
Newspaper for which Ernie Souchak (John Belushi) was an investigative columnist in the 1981 movie *Continental Divide*.

**Chiefettes**
Cheerleaders for the Kansas City Chiefs football team.

**Chief Hawkeye**
Owner of the New Mexico trading post on the TV series "Guestward Ho," played by J. Carroll Naish.

**Chief Thunder Chicken**
Character who appeared on the TV show "Howdy Doody," played

**by** Alan Swift.

## Chipmunks
Baseball team of which Jonathan Winters is a member on a Chee-tos TV commercial.

## Chippewa Falls
Wisconsin hometown of Annie Hall (Diane Keaton) in the 1977 movie *Annie Hall*.

## Chockie, Michael B.
First U.S. serviceman to fire a shot at the enemy during World War I. He fired the first of three shots across the bow of a German launch at Guam on April 6, 1917. Chockie died in 1980, at the age of 91.

## Chop, Chop, sweet Charlotte . . .
Cruel little chant sung by a group of boys to Charlotte Hollis (Bette Davis) in the 1965 movie *Hush, Hush Sweet Charlotte*.

## "Chopsticks"
Quick piano exercise written in 1877 by a sixteen-year-old girl named Euphemia Allen, using the pseudonym of Arthur de Lulli.

## Chris
Gunfighter played by Yul Brynner in the 1960 movie *The Magnificent Seven* and in the 1966 sequel *Return of the Seven*. George Kennedy played Chris in the sequel film *Guns of the Magnificent Seven* (1969), and Lee Van Cleef in *The Magnificent Seven Ride* (1972).

## Chris
Helen Belson's (Lori Nelson) German shepherd in the 1955 movie *Revenge of the Creature*. She often called him Boy.

## Christian
Both actor Buddy Ebsen and football quarterback Sonny Jurgen-son's Christian names.

## Christiania
Previous name of Oslo, Norway.

## Christie
Barbie doll's black friend, who was introduced in 1968.

## "Christmas Don't Be Late"
Subtitle of "The Chipmunk Song" which was sung by the Chip-munks (David Seville).

## "Christmas Song, The"
Subtitle of the song "Chestnuts Roasting on an Open Fire" com-posed in July 1946 by Robert Wells and Mel Tormé, and recorded by both Mel Tormé and Nat "King" Cole.

**Christopher**

Secret Service code name for President Nixon's friend, Bebe Rebozo.

**Christopher Casanova**

Adventurer played by Errol Flynn in his 1952 radio series "The Adventures of Casanova."

**Chrysanthemum**

Yellow flower that the prison warden (Patrick McGoohan) crunched up, only to find another one on the rocks after Frank Lee Morris (Clint Eastwood) and two other men escaped Alcatraz, in the 1979 movie *Escape from Alcatraz*.

**Chubbuck, Chris**

Sarasota, Florida, morning talk-show hostess ("Suncoast Digest") who, during her July 15, 1974, show, stopped her reading to say: "In keeping with Channel 40's policy of bringing you the latest in blood and guts in living color, you are going to see another first—attempted suicide," after which the thirty-year-old woman took a .38 pistol from her purse and fatally shot herself in the head.

**Chubby Checkers**

Weight-loss organization that Dominick (Dom De Luise) joined in the 1980 movie *Fatso*.

**Chu Chu**

Chan family's pet dog (voice of Don Messick) on the animated TV cartoon series "The Amazing Chan and the Chan Clan."

**Chuck E. Cheese**

Mechanical rat that is the mascot of Chuck E. Cheese's Pizza Time Theaters. Nolan Bushnell, who founded the pizza parlors, had previously founded the video game company, Atari.

**Chuckles the Clown**

On "The Mary Tyler Moore Show," Chuckles was the host of a kiddie show on Minneapolis's TV station WYM, playing the characters of Peter Peanut, Billy Banana, Aunt Yoohoo, and Mr. Fee-Fi-Fo. His real name was George Bowderchuck, and his wife was named Louise. His daughter, Betty (played by Arlene Golontca), was once infatuated with anchorman Ted Baxter. At the end of each show, Chuckles recited the Credo of a Clown: "A little song, a little dance, a little seltzer down your pants." Chuckles was killed by a rogue elephant named Jocko in a circus parade, while he was dressed as Peter Peanut. He was played by Mark Gordon and

Richard Schaal.*

**Chuck Rodent**

Name listed in the credits for the puppet gopher in the 1980 movie *Caddyshack*.

**Chuckwan, USS**

U.S. Navy vessel upon which rock 'n' roll singer Eugene Vincent Caddock (Gene Vincent) was stationed in 1955.

**Chukker**

Time period of play in a polo game.

**Chunky**

Brand of candy of which retired Yankee outfielder Mickey Mantle was given a year's supply on Mickey Mantle Day, September 18, 1965. He was also given a Mercury 95-horsepower outboard motor, a set of Wilson golf clubs, and other gifts.

**Churchill**

Bulldog in the 1981 movie *Take This Job and Shove It*.

**Cinderella Club**

Black New York City club where Jess Robin (Neil Diamond) attempted to pass himself off as black, with a musical group called the Four Brothers, in the 1980 movie *The Jazz Singer*. He sang "You Baby" on stage before a fight broke out.

**Cindy**

FBI chief J. Edgar Hoover's pet cairn terrier dog.

**Cinerama's Russian Adventure**

Travelogue filmed in the Soviet Union (1966) and narrated by Bing Crosby.

**Circle**

Taxicab company for which Wardell Franklin (Bill Cosby) drove in the 1974 movie *Uptown Saturday Night*.

**City College of New York**

Only college ever to win both the NCAA and NIT tournaments in the same year (1950).

**City Dump 32, East River, Sutton Place**

Imaginary address given by Godfrey Parke (William Powell) as where he lived in New York in the 1936 movie *My Man Godfrey*.

**City Hospital**

New York City medical facility that is the setting of the 1982 movie *Young Doctors in Love*.

---

*Then real-life husband of Valerie Harper (who played Rhoda).

**City of New York**
Official name of New York City.

**City Sheet Metal Works**
Firm from which the robot was obtained in the 1952 movie serial *Zombies of the Stratosphere*.

**C.J. (Clyde Jr.)**
Actual name of the 135-pound orangutan that showed an interest in Jane (Bo Derek) in the 1981 movie *Tarzan the Ape Man*. C.J. and his father, Clyde, previously appeared in the 1980 movie *Any Which Way You Can*.

**Clansman, The**
D. W. Griffith silent film (1915) being premiered in the 1976 movie *Nickelodeon*. The movie was later retitled *The Birth of a Nation*. (Future director John Ford played the bit role of a Ku Klux Klan member in the film.)

**Clarion Records**
Record label that signed the Blues Brothers to a recording contract, giving them an advance of $10,000, in the 1980 movie *The Blues Brothers*. In reality, Clarion was a budget label of Atlantic Records, the company that released the film's soundtrack album.

**Clark, J. M.**
Transsexual who, as a male (Michael), spent nineteen years (beginning in 1959) in the U.S. Navy, after which he was discharged. Previously, in 1955, as a woman (Joan Michelle), she had joined the U.S. Army Reserves.

**Clawhammer**
Secret Service code name for General Alexander Haig (circa 1978).

**Clayton, Zack**
First black to referee a heavyweight title fight. He refereed the June 6, 1952, fight between champion Jersey Joe Walcott and challenger Ezzard Charles.

**Clear and Present Danger, A**
TV pilot movie (1970) for the TV series "The Senator." The title refers to air pollution.

**Clearwater**
Sloop built by singers Pete Seeger and Don McLean in between concert performances.

**Clearwater, Texas**
Setting of the 1965 John Wayne movie *The Sons of Katie Elder*.

**Cleary, Idaho**
Hometown of Dave Barrett (Ken Howard) on the TV series

*Manhunter.*

**Clementine**

Name given to the giant forked fingers that were used to raise part of a sunken Russian submarine by the *Glomar Explorer* in August of 1974.

**"Clementine"**

Dick Allen's (Robert Preston) favorite tune, which he sang to himself in the 1939 movie *Union Pacific*. Also the favorite song of Huckleberry Hound on his TV cartoon show.

**Cleopatra**

Cat in the 1964 Vincent Price horror film *The Comedy of Terrors*, played by Rhubarb.

**Cleopatra**

Name of the woman who is made into the freak called "the feathered hen," played by Olga Baclanova, in the 1932 movie *Freaks*.

**Cleopatra**

Movie made in 1963, starring Elizabeth Taylor, Richard Burton, and Rex Harrison. For making the film, Taylor became the first person to receive $1 million. The movie was a financial failure, and at the time the most expensive ever made. Cleopatra was banned for more than fifteen years in Egypt because Elizabeth Taylor had converted to Judaism.

**Cleopatra**

Old prospector's pack horse in the 1976 movie *The Duchess and the Dirtwater Fox*.

**Cleveland, Dr. David**

First man to register at the Barbizon Hotel in New York City, in 1980.

**Cleveland Indians**

NFL football team of 1921 and 1923.

**Climax Studios**

Hollywood movie studio that first signed Vince Everette (Elvis Presley) as an actor in the 1957 movie *Jailhouse Rock*.

**Clock stopped**

Situations in the NFL in which the time clock is stopped:

1. After a team scores
2. When a ball carrier goes out of bounds
3. After an incomplete pass
4. After a player is injured
5. After completion of a first down

6. At a two-minute warning
7. During a time out by either team
8. While a penalty is marked off

**Clorese**
Amos (Tim Conway) and Theodore's (Don Knotts) mule that followed them everywhere in the 1979 movie *The Apple Dumpling Gang Rides Again*.

**Closed on Account of the TV**
Sign left on the door of the Chicken Ranch, after it was closed for good in the 1982 movie *The Best Little Whorehouse in Texas*.

**Close Encounters of the Third Kind (Special Edition)**
Videocassette movie sold by Columbia's Home Entertainment Club that became the first videotape to sell gold (20,000 units, equaling one million dollars in retail sales).

**"Clouds"**
Subtitle of Judy Collins's 1968 hit song "Both Sides Now," which was composed by Joni Mitchell.

**Clown**
Name used by Larry (Peter Fonda) when conversing over the two-way radio with police sheriff Franklin (Vic Morrow) in the 1974 movie *Dirty Mary and Crazy Larry*.

**Clown Prince of Baseball**
Nickname of major-league player Al Schacht.

**Clubber Lang**
Chicago boxer weighing 235 pounds, who defeated 202-pound Rocky Balboa (Sylvester Stallone) for the heavyweight boxing championship, by a knockout in the second round on August 15, 1981. Thirty-four-year-old, 191-pound Rocky defeated 237-pound Lang played by Mr. T. (Lawrence Tero) in the third round of the rematch in the 1982 movie *Rocky III*.

**Club Palisades**
Nightclub where Tommy Dee (Paul Land) sang with the band the Kingbees prior to his being discovered in the 1981 movie *The Idol Maker*.

**Club Paradise**
Los Angeles bar where Cheech and Chong were hired as male strippers in the 1981 movie *Nice Dreams*.

**Club Xanadu**
Chicago club where Mickey One (Warren Beatty) is a stand-up comedian in the 1965 movie *Mickey One*.

**Clyde**
Bugs Bunny's nephew in TV cartoons.
**Clyde**
Chimpanzee in the 1964 movie *Bikini Beach*.
**Coco**
Chimpanzee that appeared in the 1940 Dorothy Lamour movie *Typhoon*.
**Codex Leicester**
Thirty-six-page manuscript written by Leonardo da Vinci. It is the only work signed by him. In December 1980, American oil magnate Armand Hammer bought the manuscript for $5.1 million. The manuscript is titled *On the Nature, Weight, and Movement of Water*.
**Cody, Wyoming**
Birthplace of the fictional Roy Rogers (on TV). The real Roy Rogers (Leonard Slye) was actually born in Cincinnati, Ohio.
**Coed Frenzy**
Cheap horror film being made by Independent Pictures of Philadelphia, for which Jack Terry (John Travolta) is the sound man in the 1981 movie *Blow Out*. During a scene in which a girl is stabbed in the shower, Jack used the actual screams of his dying girlfriend, Sally (Nancy Allen).
**Cohn, Harry**
(1891–1958) Hollywood movie producer and founder of Columbia Pictures in 1924. Cohn, nicknamed ''White Fang'' by Ben Hecht, was one of the most hated men in Hollywood. He was portrayed by Vic Tayback in the 1980 TV movie *Moviola*.
**Cole, Nat "King"**
(1917–1965) Popular singer of the 1940s and 1950s (born Nathaniel Adams Coles). In 1939 he formed the Nat Cole Trio, but later went solo. Some of his biggest hits songs were ''Mona Lisa,'' ''Too Young,'' and ''Pretend.'' He was the father of popular singer Natalie Cole. Nat Cole sang the theme song of the 1958 movie *Raintree County* and appeared in a number of movies, including *Cat Ballou* (1965).
**Collier, Robert**
(1876–1918) Son of Peter Collier, the founder of *Collier's Weekly* magazine in 1896. From 1909 until his death, Robert served as the president of the magazine. Collier was portrayed by Philip Reed in the 1955 movie *The Girl in the Red Velvet Swing*.

**Collins, Floyd**

Explorer who, in March of 1925, became trapped in a cave near Cave City, Kentucky. He lived for eighteen days in a hole five feet in diameter. Twenty-one-year-old reporter William Miller of the *Louisville Courier-Journal* descended into the tunnel five times to talk to Collins. Miller won a Pulitzer Prize for the reports. During the time that Collins was trapped, the area around the cave took on a carnival-like atmosphere. Kirk Douglas mentioned Floyd Collins by name in the 1951 movie *The Big Carnival* (AKA *Ace in the Hole*).

**Collins, Gary**

Scorer of the first touchdown on "Monday Night Football" in a game played on September 21, 1970, at Cleveland. The Browns defeated the New York Jets 31 to 21.

**Collins, Marva**

Black Chicago schoolteacher who, after fourteen years teaching in public schools, quit to open her own school, named the Westside Preparatory School. Marva was portrayed by Cicely Tyson in the 1981 TV movie *The Marva Collins Story*.

**Collins, Michael**

U.S. astronaut born in Rome, Italy.

**Collins, Nancy**

Reporter who asked author Truman Capote if he was gay, to which Capote replied "yes." Collins was the first person ever to have asked Capote that question, according to Capote himself.

**Colonel Sam Flagg**

Strange-acting CIA agent who sometimes visited the 4077th on the TV series "M*A*S*H." Played by Edward Winter, some of his other identities are those of officers named Klein, Brookes, Carter, Troy, and WAC Captain Louise.

**Colonel Edward Gray**

Commanding officer of Camp Henderson, played by Forrest Compton on the TV series "Gomer Pyle, USMC."

**Colonel Jeff Bartin**

First human to travel to the planet Venus (the spacecraft's call sign was "Venus One"), played by William Shatner on an episode of the TV series "The Outer Limits." Project Vulcan was to be the colonization of the planet Mars.

**Colonel Steve West**

The title role, played by Alex Rebar, in the 1977 movie *The Incredible Melting Man*.

**Colorado University Trivia Bowl**
   Annual trivia contest held, since 1968, at the University of Colorado at Boulder.* The contest was first organized by Dr. David Bowen. The first winning team was the Beagle Boys.

**Colossal Studios**
   Hollywood movie studio for which Douglas Quintain (Humphrey Bogart) was a producer in the 1937 movie *Stand-In*. Colossal's two competitors were Excelsior and National Pictures.

**Colt .45**
   The only film (1950) in which both Randolph Scott and Zachary Scott appeared together.

**Colt 45s**
   Previous name of the Houston Astros baseball team (1962–1964) when they first received their National League franchise.

**Columbia**
   U.S. space shuttle first flown on April 12, 1981, by astronauts Robert Crippen and John Young. The shuttle completed thirty-six orbits of the earth during its 54½-hour flight, after which it landed at Edwards Air Force Base in California.

**Coming Around the Mountain**
   Song whistled by a nervous man as a group of anxious people await the arrival of a fleet of UFOs in the 1977 movie *Close Encounters of the Third Kind*.

**Commandant**
   Warden of Devil's Island Penal Colony, played by Dalton Trumbo (who wrote the screenplay), in the 1973 movie *Papillon* (based on Henri Charriere's book of the same title).

**Commander John Koenig**
   Commander of Moonbase Alpha on the surface of the moon. He became head of the base in September 1999 in the TV series "Space: 1999."

**Commissioner Anthony X. Russell**
   New York City police commissioner played by Henry Fonda in the 1968 movie *Madigan*.

**Commissioner Howard Knight**
   New York City police commissioner played by Raymond Burr in the 1979 TV series "Eischied."

---

*The author has had the opportunity to play in this bowl, which is professionally organized, entertaining, and just great fun!

**Common Clay**

Movie (fictitious) starring Molly Adair (Alice Faye) that premiered at Graumann's Egyptian Theater in the 1939 movie *Hollywood Cavalcade*. The advertisement for the film read "Molly Adair Talks in Common Clay."

**Communion**

Horror movie of 1976, which was the debut of Brooke Shields. She played a small girl who got killed in a church in the opening scenes. The film was later re-released under the titles *Holy Terror* and *Alice, Sweet Alice*.

**Communist Dream, The**

Book by P. Tolskin that was banned from the Kentport Free Library from which Alicia Hull (Bette Davis)* was fired as the librarian in the 1956 movie *Storm Center*.

**Company's Coming Cookbook**

Book written by singer Kate Smith in 1958.

**Complete and Uncut**

The only book ever billed on the cover this way was *The White House Transcripts*, published by Bantam Books in 1974.

**Compton, Betty**

Chorus girlfriend of New York City Mayor Jimmy Walker. She was portrayed by Vera Miles in the 1957 movie *Beau James*.

**Comstock**

Western town where Frame Johnson (Ronald Reagan) became marshal after leaving Tombstone in the 1953 movie *Law and Order*.

**Comstock Bank and Trust**

San Francisco bank for which Jim Corbett (Errol Flynn) worked in the 1942 movie *Gentleman Jim*.

**Concur**

Six-letter word that a woman caller is trying to find out for the *Los Angeles Examiner's* daily crossword puzzle (51 Down). Thirty-six Across was the word *par*. William Conrad finally gave her the answer in the 1959 movie *-30-*.

**Confederate Air Force**

Society located in Harlington, Texas, created to restore and fly World War II aircraft.

**Confederate Gallery 1897**

Gallery at the old Ryman Theater in Nashville, Tennessee.

---

*Bette Davis replaced Mary Pickford in the role.

**Congo**

Gorilla that starred in the movie *Sex and Satan*, which Colossal Film Company was filming during the 1937 Humphrey Bogart movie *Stand-In*.

**Conley, Kathleen**

First woman to graduate from the U.S. Air Force Academy (1980).

**Connecticut Yankee in King Arthur's Court, A**

Novel written by Samuel Clemens (Mark Twain) in 1899 that is being read by nurse Alex Price (Jenny Agutter) in the 1981 movie *An American Werewolf in London*.

**Connors, Eugene "Bull"**

Birmingham police chief during the civil rights protests in the South during the 1950s, who took a hard stand against the peaceful demonstrators in his city. He once had blind singer Al Hibbler arrested. Connors was portrayed by Kenneth McMillan in the 1978 mini-series *King*. Bull Connors himself played a character named Bull in the 1963 movie *Common-Law Wife*.

**Conroy, Pat**

Writer and teacher who traveled to an island off the South Carolina coast to teach black children. There the youngsters called him Conrack. Conroy was the author of the book *The Water Is Wide*, about his experiences on the island. In 1974, Jon Voight portrayed him in the movie *Conrack*. Pat Conroy also authored the book *The Great Santini*, whose protagonist is based upon his Marine Corps pilot father. In 1979 *The Great Santini* was filmed, starring Robert Duvall as Bull Meecham. It was originally released as *The Ace*. Another of his books, *The Lords of Discipline*, was made into a movie in 1983.

**Con Sec**

Canadian firm for which Dr. Paul Ruth (Patrick McGoohan) worked in the 1981 movie *Scanners*.

**Consolidated Airlines Flight 22**

Los Angeles-to-Seattle jetliner that crashed in the 1964 movie *Fate Is the Hunter*.

**Consolidated Companies**

San Francisco firm for which Violet Newstead (Lily Tomlin), Judy Bernley (Jane Fonda), and Dora Lee Rhodes (Dolly Parton) worked in the 1980 movie *9 to 5*.

**Consolidated Insurance**

Cleveland insurance company that represented a million-dollar suit against CBS, the Cleveland Browns, and the Municipal Stadium, which was brought by Harry Hinkle (Jack Lemmon), who was represented by his lawyer (and brother-in-law) Willie Gingrich (Walter Matthau) in the 1966 movie *The Fortune Cookie*.

**Constellation**
U.S. frigate that is the oldest American fighting ship still in existence. It was launched in 1797, and is now berthed at Newport, Rhode Island.

**Constitution**
Mother ship in the TV series "Buck Rogers in the 25th Century." Its commander was Admiral Asimov (Jay Gardner).

**Contasino, Mario**
Man who, while driving down Fifth Avenue in New York City on December 13, 1931, accidently struck Winston Churchill, who had been walking toward the home of Bernard Baruch. Churchill was then taken to Lenox Hill Hospital.

**Contessa**
Magazine on whose cover Mandy Summers's (Maude Adams) picture appeared in the 1981 movie *Tattoo*. Mandy also made TV commercials for Aphrodite Perfume.

**Contestoga 1**
Privately owned rocket that was launched on September 9, 1982, and flew 192 miles into space (321 miles downrange from the Matagorda, Texas, launching pad).

**Cook County, Oregon**
County that has supported every winning Presidential candidate since 1892. (Emmetsburg, Iowa, has done the same since 1896).

**Cooke, Janet**
Reporter for the *Washington Post* who won the 1981 Pulitzer Prize for journalism, until it was revealed that she had fabricated her story on "Little Jimmy."

**Cooney, Jim and Johnny Neun**
Major-league infielders who made unassisted triple plays on successive days. Chicago Cubs shortstop Jim Cooney made his on May 30, 1927, and Detroit Tigers first baseman, Johnny Neun, made his on May 31, 1927.

**Coos Bay**
Oregon hometown of boxer Johnny Captor (Marc Singer) in the short-lived TV series "The Contender."

**Cooter Smith**
Eugene Smith's singing uncle on the TV series "Mr. Smith Goes To Washington," played by country artist Red Foley.

**Copacabana School of Dramatic Art**
   School of which Addison DeWitt (George Sanders) said, sarcastic-
   ally, that Miss Caswell (Marilyn Monroe) was a graduate, as he
   was introducing her to Margo Channing (Bette Davis), in the 1950
   movie *All About Eve*.

**Coppertone Girl**
   Small girl in Coppertone suntan lotion advertisements, whose bare
   rear end is exposed when her dog pulls on her bathing suit. Jacquie
   Callaway claims to have posed for the original photo for the ad,
   which was taken by her father, Clark Wills, in April 1941. Jodie
   Foster posed her bottom for one of the advertisements when she
   was three years old.

**Corbett, Sergeant Boston**
   Soldier who, on April 26, 1865, allegedly shot and killed President
   Abraham Lincoln's assassin, John Wilkes Booth, in a barn.

**Corncracker**
   Black colt owned by Dick Handley (Sterling Hayden) as a small
   boy in the 1950 movie *The Asphalt Jungle*.

**Cornstalk Hotel**
   New Orleans hotel that detective Lew Archer (Paul Newman) broke
   into in the 1976 movie *The Drowning Pool*.

**Corporal/Sergeant Maxwell Q. Klinger**
   U.S. Army enlisted man (serial number 19571782, Social Security
   number 556-78-2613), assigned to the 4077th M*A*S*H unit during the Korean War. He replaced Walter "Radar" O'Reilly as the
   company clerk. In hopes of receiving a Section Eight discharge
   from the Army, Klinger wore female clothing, but to no avail. Born
   at 1215 Michigan Street in Toledo, Ohio, Klinger was briefly
   married to Laverne Esposito. Klinger was played by Jamie Farr on
   the TV series "M*A*S*H."
      In the last episode of "M*A*S*H," Klinger married a Korean
   girl named Soon Lee (Rosalind Chao). The pair appeared as husband and wife on the TV series "AfterMash."

**Corporal Walter Eugene O'Reilly**
   U.S. Army company clerk (serial number 3911810, blood type B),
   at the 4077th M*A*S*H unit, nicknamed "Radar" because he can
   anticipate what will happen next. Radar's home is a small farm in
   Ottumwa, Iowa. Played by Gary Burghoff in the 1970 movie and
   on the TV series. Burghoff was one of the only two actors to appear
   in both the movie and the TV productions, in the same roles. G.
   Wood (as General Hammond) was the other actor.

**Corridon, Fiddler**
(1880–1941) Chicago Cubs pitcher who is credited with inventing the spitball, in 1904.

**Cory, Joel**
Voice of the following TV commercial products: Cricket (Cricket cigarette lighters), Helpin Hand (Hamburger Helper), and the Sun (Raisin Bran).

**Cosby, Bill**
(1937–    ) Comedian whose photograph hangs on the wall of *Daily Planet* editor-in-chief Perry White's (Jackie Cooper) office in the 1981 movie *Superman II*.

**Cosmic Breath**
Term that Mork (Robin Williams) called the Orkan Leader, Orson, resulting in his being sent to Earth as a punishment on the TV series "Mork and Mindy."

**Cosmic Cow**
Comic book for which Henry Rush (Ted Knight) is an artist on the TV series "Too Close for Comfort."

**Cosmic Venus**
Pinball machine on which Harold "the Whale" (Charles Durning) beat fourteen-year-old Brenda "Tilt" Davenport (Brooke Shields) in the 1979 movie *Tilt*. The machine was manufactured by Koala.

**Cotopaxi**
Ship found in the middle of the Gobi Desert in Mongolia in the 1980 re-release of the movie *Close Encounters of the Third Kind*.

**Cottonmouth**
CB handle of the assembly-line manufacturer who is putting together a Cadillac car from parts he has been sneaking out of the factory since 1949 in Johnny Cash's 1976 hit record "One Piece at a Time."

**Cottonwood, owl, and dove**
Tree and two birds mentioned in the lyrics of the 1957 song "Tammy" by Debbie Reynolds.

**Councilman, James "Doc"**
Oldest man ever to swim the English Channel, which he did on September 14, 1979, at the age of fifty-eight.

**Count of Monte Cristo**
Edmond Dantes, hero of the 1844 novel *The Count of Monte Cristo* by Alexandre Dumas. Played in the movies by Robert Donat (1934), by Jean Marais (1954), by Louis Jourdan (1961), and by

Richard Chamberlain (1975).

**Coupon Queen**

Nickname of Mary Anne Hayes who, in 1979, wrote the book *Ask the Coupon Queen*.

**Counter Attack**

Movie (1945) starring Paul Muni and Larry Parks that was advertised on a New York City movie marquee in the 1973 movie *The Way We Were*. Also advertised was the 1940 Marx Brothers movie *Go West* (along with a Donald Duck cartoon).

**Covent Garden**

Section of London where Professor Henry Higgins met Eliza Doolittle for the first time in the musical *My Fair Lady*.

**Cowboy**

Downtown Dallas nightclub where Bud Davis (John Travolta) went in the 1980 movie *Urban Cowboy*. The other nightclub in the film was Gilley's in Pasadena, Texas.

**Cowen, Joshua Lionel**

Creator of Lionel electric trains, in 1902.

**Cowhide**

Material from which footballs are made, though the covering is usually referred to as "pigskin."

**Cox, Archibald**

(1912– ) Special Prosecutor for the Watergate investigation. On October 20, 1973, President Richard Nixon ordered Attorney General Eliot Richardson to fire Cox. He refused and resigned. Deputy Attorney General William Ruckelshaus also refused and was fired. U.S. Solicitor Robert Bork, who was named Acting Attorney General, fired Cox. Cox was portrayed by Byron Morrow in the 1978 movie *Born Again*.

**C. P. Huntington**

Name of Southern Pacific's first locomotive. It had originally been built for the Central Pacific Railroad in 1864.

**Cracker Jack**

Candy created in 1872, named in 1896, with prizes added in 1912. It is Susan Reedquist who picks out the prizes to be placed in Cracker Jack boxes (two million boxes a day).

**Craig, Roger**

(1931– ) New York Mets pitcher who, in the very first major-league season game ever played by the Mets, on April 11, 1962, committed a balk in the first inning, allowing Bill White of the St.

Louis Cardinals to score the very first run against the new team.

**Crazy Quilt (Billy Rose's Crazy Quilt)**
Broadway follies produced by Billy Rose (James Caan) and starring Fanny Brice (Barbra Streisand) with Bert Robbins (Ben Vereen), in the 1975 movie *Funny Lady*.

**Crakor**
Robot on board the spaceship PXL 1236, played by Stan Jenson on the TV series "Far Out Space Nuts."

**Crate 1444**
Packing crate that contained the pregnant elephant Charlotte in a Miami warehouse in the 1980 movie *Smokey and the Bandit II*.

**Crater Lake**
Oregon lake, situated on top of an extinct volcano, which is the deepest lake in the United States (1,932 feet).

**Crawford High**
School setting of the 1981 movie *Happy Birthday to Me*.

**Crawford, Jerry**
Umpire into whose face Pittsburgh Pirates third baseman Bill Madlock shoved a glove in a game at Montreal on May 1, 1980. Because of the incident, Madlock was given a then-record fifteen-day suspension and was fined $5,000.

**Crawfordville**
Small-town setting of the 1981 TV movie *Coward of the County*, starring Kenny Rogers.

**Crest Ridge High School**
Crest Ridge, California, school attended by Matthew Star (Peter Barton) in the TV series "The Powers of Matthew Star."

**CRestview 5-4699**
Home phone number of Ellen Arden (Doris Day). After her five-year absence, it was changed to 213-275-4699, in the 1963 movie *Move Over Darling*. Later in the film, the number 235-5405 was mentioned.

**Crichton**
Superior-type robot on the TV series "Buck Rogers in the 25th Century."

**Cripple Creek**
Arizona town where Johnny Concho (Frank Sinatra) lived in the 1956 movie *Johnny Concho*.

**Crock Dip, Arkansas**
Birthplace of Lieutenant Sonny Fuzz in the "Beetle Bailey" comic strip.

**Crocker, Charles**
 (1822–1888) American financier and member of the California Big Four, who built the Central Pacific Railroad (1863–69). He became the president of the Southern Pacific Railroad in 1871. Crocker was portrayed by Harry Crocker in the 1942 movie *Gentleman Jim*.

**Crosley Field**
 Cincinnati baseball stadium where the first night game in major-league baseball was played. That evening (May 24, 1935) the Cincinnati Reds defeated the Philadelphia Phillies by a score of 2 to 1.

**Crossfire**
 Movie (1947) starring three Roberts: Robert Ryan, Robert Mitchum, and Robert Young.

**Croves, Hal**
 Pseudonym used by the mysterious author of the novel *The Treasure of the Sierra Madre*, known as B. Traven, when he visited the set of the 1948 film.

**Crown**
 Secret Service code name for the White House.

**Crown Point Prison**
 Maximum security prison in Indiana from which John Dillinger escaped in a sheriff's car on March 3, 1934.

**Crumb, Robert**
 Underground cartoonist who designed the album cover for Janis Joplin and Big Brother and the Holding Company's 1968 album *Cheap Thrills*.

**Crystal Palace**
 Delia's nightclub in the TV soap "Ryan's Hope."

**Cubby**
 Cartoon bear's head that the reader is asked to draw for Art Instruction School's ads in magazines.

**Cuddles**
 Bull purchased by Wade Kingsley (Jerry Lewis) for $7500 from Slim Mosley (Dean Martin) in the 1956 movie *Pardners*.

**Cuddle Up a Little Closer**
 Song composed in 1908 by Otto Haverbach and Karl Hoschna, which is heard in the following movies: *The Story of Vernon and Irene Castle* (1939), *The Birth of the Blues* (1941), *Is Everybody Happy?* (1943), *Coney Island* (1943), *On Moonlight Bay* (1951), and *Tall Story* (1960).

**Cuesta Verde**
 Southern California housing community built over a cemetery in

the 1982 movie *Poltergeist*.

**Culver Hotel**

Culver City hotel whose name was changed to Hotel Rainbow by the owner's son in the 1981 movie *Under the Rainbow*. Otis (Freeman King) was the elevator operator. The hotel served Hills Bros. Coffee.

**Cunningham, Randall**

First American air ace in the Vietnam War. He shot down his first MIG in his Navy F4 on January 19, 1972. His third, fourth, and fifth were shot down on May 10, 1972.

**Cupid**

Roman god of love—winged, blindfolded little boy who carries a bow and arrow. When he hits someone with his arrow, he or she falls in love shortly afterwards. Cupid has been the subject of two Top Twenty hit songs, "Stupid Cupid" by Connie Francis, in 1958, and "Cupid"* by Sam Cooke, in 1961.

**Cupid's Hot Dogs**

Van Nuys diner where Donna DiVito (Didi Conn) worked in the 1978 movie *Almost Summer*.

**Curious Dream, A**

Movie (1907) in which author Mark Twain (Samuel Clemens) portrayed himself.

**Curl Up and Dye**

Beauty salon where the mystery woman (Carrie Fisher) worked in the 1980 movie *The Blues Brothers*.

**Curmudgeon, HMS**

British gunboat commanded by Lieutenant Commander Finch-haven (David Niven) in the 1969 movie *The Extraordinary Seaman*.

**Curragh**

Edward Kennedy's $200,000 yacht, which he sold when he divorced his wife Joan in 1982.

**Cushman, Mary Ellen**

Last surviving member of the *Mayflower* voyage; she died in 1699.

**Custer College**

School for which Ray Blant (Anthony Perkins) was the star player (number 44) in the 1960 movie *Tall Story*. Custer College defeated the Russian basketball team, the Sputniks, by a score of 81 to 80.

---

*In 1980, the Spinners sang "Cupid" in medley with "I've Loved You for a Long Time." It peaked at Number Four.

The school radio station is KLUS.

**Custer, Tom**
Brother of Lieutenant Colonel George Armstrong Custer, who, along with a third brother, Boston, was killed at the Battle of the Little Bighorn on June 25, 1876. Tom had twice won the Congressional Medal of Honor. He was portrayed by John Napier in the 1965 film *The Great Sioux Massacre*.

**Cutters**
Local Bloomington bicycle racing team that won the Little 500 Race (200-lap event) in the 1979 movie *Breaking Away*. Dave Stoller (Dennis Christopher) led the team.

**Cutter's Goose**
Jake Cutter's (Stephen Collins) Grumman sea plane in the TV series "Tales of the Gold Monkey."

**Cycle Sluts**
X-rated movie in which Doris Waverly (Barbra Streisand) starred in the 1970 movie *The Owl and the Pussycat*.

**Cyclone**
Horse ridden by Tom "Buck" Greenway (Burt Reynolds) in a play at the New Amsterdam Theater while the song "'Dixie'" was being played in the 1976 movie *Nickelodeon*.

**CYpress 2-6725**
First telephone number of singer Bobby Darin's family in the Bronx in the 1950s. On his deathbed at Cedars of Lebanon Hospital, on December 18, 1973, the telephone number was the very last thing that Bobby Darin said before he died. The reason will never be known.

# D

**D**

Brand of the Dunston Ranch, owned by Tom Dunston (John Wayne) in the 1948 movie *Red River*. Director Howard Hawks gave Wayne a belt buckle with the brand on it, which the Duke wore in *Red River* (1948), *Rio Bravo* (1959), *True Grit* (1969), *McLintock* (1963), *The Sons of Katie Elder* (1965), and *The Shootist* (1976).

**DBC**

Divinity Broadcasting Corporation. Network in Springfield which broadcast the religious program "The Freddy Stone Hour" in the 1982 TV movie *Pray TV*.

**DC-269**

North Carolina automobile license plate number of Andy Taylor's (Andy Griffith) automobile in the TV series *The Andy Griffith Show*.

**D-Day**

Time setting (June 6, 1944) of the last televised episode of the TV series "The Waltons."

**D-Day**

Nickname of motorcycle-riding Delta Tau Chi fraternity member Daniel Simpson Day (Bruce McGill) in the 1978 movie *National Lampoon's Animal House* and in the TV series "Delta House."

**DE 745**

Identification letters of the World War I biplane upon which Cameron (Steven Railsback) performed his stunts in the 1980 movie *The Stunt Man*.

**D6**

Yeoman-Purser Burl "Gopher" Smith's (Fred Grandy) cabin on

board the *Pacific Princess* in the TV series "The Love Boat."

**"Da Doo Run Run"**
Hit song by the Crystals in 1966 and by Shaun Cassidy in 1977. Russell (Harold Ramis) had his English speaking class sing the chorus while he sang the lead in the 1981 movie *Stripes*.

**Dagwood**
Black cat that was seen playing Ping-Pong in a sequence on a Movietone News film during the 1950s. It was shown on an episode of the TV series "M*A*S*H."

**Dahlgren, Babe**
(1912– ) New York Yankee who, during a game on May 2, 1939, replaced first baseman Lou Gehrig after he had appeared in a record 2,130 consecutive games. He was portrayed by Chicago Cub first baseman Glenn "Rip" Russell in the 1942 movie *Pride of the Yankees*.

**Dahl, Roald**
Author who is the ex-husband of actress Patricia Neal. He wrote many children's stories, including the novel *Charlie and the Chocolate Factory*, from which the 1971 movie *Willie Wonka and the Chocolate Factory* was made. In 1979 he hosted the TV series "Roald Dahl's Tales of the Unexpected." He also coined the word *gremlin* (as a euphemism for the "unexplainable" in aviation) during World War II. Dahl was portrayed by Dirk Bogarde in the 1981 movie *The Patricia Neal Story*.

**Daily Chronicle**
Newspaper for which Kermit the Frog and Fozzie Bear are reporters and Gonzo is a photographer in the 1981 movie *The Great Muppet Caper*. Their competitors are the *Express*, the *Times*, and the *Herald*.

**Daisy**
Walter Eugene "Radar" O'Reilly's pet white mouse that ran against the U.S. Marines' black mouse, Sluggo, in an episode of the TV series "M*A*S*H."

**Daisy Mae**
Two-headed cow in the Freak Animal Show in the 1981 movie *Fun House*.

**"Daktari"**
First American TV series to air in the Soviet Union.

**Dallas**
Barbie's (the doll) white horse that winks. She also signs souvenir photographs with a stamp on her hoof.

**Damn . . .**

Last word on the flight recorder from American Airlines DC-10 Flight 191, which crashed on May 25, 1979, in Chicago.

**Damn Yankees**

Horton High School play in which Polly Hines (Kristy McNichol) sang in the 1981 movie *Only When I Laugh*.

**Dan**

Cowboy mentioned in the lyrics of the classic Western song "Cool Water," made popular by the Sons of the Pioneers.

**Dan**

Pony that dies in the snow with his master just one hundred yards from the house of Mary Ann's, in Jim Reeves's song "The Blizzard."

**"Dance of the Cuckoos"**

Laurel and Hardy's theme song (also known as "The Ku-Ku Song") composed by T. Marvin Hatley. The Dead End Kids whistled the tune in the 1938 movie *Crime School*.

**Dancing Bear**

Indian mentioned in the lyrics of the country song "Cherokee Boogie."

**"Dancing in the Streets"**

Hit record (1964) by the Motown vocal group Martha Reeves and the Vandellas. The cities mentioned in the song's lyrics are Chicago, New Orleans, New York City, Philadelphia, Baltimore, Washington, D.C., Detroit (Motor City), and Los Angeles.

**Dandi**

Actual name of the lion that appeared in the 1981 Bo Derek movie *Tarzan the Ape Man*.

**Dandilo**

White cat that was dematerialized into oblivion in the 1958 movie *The Fly*.

**Daniel**

Hebrew prophet who is mentioned in the Old Testament and who lent his name to the Book of Daniel. He interpreted dreams of Nebuchadnezzar and the handwriting on the wall for Belshazzar. He was thrown into the lions' den but survived. Daniel was portrayed by David Birney on the TV series "Greatest Heroes of the Bible."

**Daphne Harridge**

Role played by Kate Jackson on the TV soap "Dark Shadows."

**Dartmouth**

Hanover, New Hampshire College once attended by Captain "Trapper" John McIntyre (Elliott Gould) in the 1970 movie *M\*A\*S\*H*.

**Darwin, Charles**

(1809–1882) Naturalist who sailed on the ship *Beagle* in order to study animal life on land at numerous ports (1831–1836). He was the author of several important works, such as *On the Origin of Species by Means of Natural Selection* (1859). He was portrayed by Malcolm Stoddard in the 1980 TV mini-series *Voyage of Charles Darwin*.

**Dating Game, The**

TV game show (1966–1970) hosted by Jim Lange. Lenny and Squiggy made an appearance on the show in an episode of the TV series "Laverne and Shirley." The show also appeared in the 1979 movie *The Onion Field* and can be heard on a TV at a strip joint in the 1975 movie *Hustle*. Actor Tom Selleck appeared on the TV program twice, as Bachelor Number Two. Both times he lost.

**Dave's Discount Records**

Record store that supplied the grand prize of one hundred record albums for the winner of the Rydell High School Talent Contest in the 1982 movie *Grease 2*.

**David Chetley**

Anchorman played by Bob Elliott in the 1965 movie *Cold Turkey*.

**David Copperfield**

Novel by Charles Dickens that Melanie (Olivia de Havilland) read to the other women as they awaited the return of their husbands in the 1939 movie *Gone With the Wind*. In the novel upon which the film was based, she was reading Victor Hugo's *Les Miserables*.

**Davidoff, Constantino**

Argentine scrap-metal dealer whose action of raising the Argentine flag on a Falkland Island whaling station at South Georgia Island in 1982 caused the international incident that led to the Argentine-British war over the Falkland Islands.

**Davidson, Sergeant R. A.**

California Highway Patrolman who arrested entertainer Dean Martin for drunk driving in West Hollywood on May 9, 1982.

**David Susskind Show, The**

TV talk show first broadcast in 1958. It was the TV series on which Mary Hartman (Louise Lasser) had a nervous breakdown on the TV series "Mary Hartman, Mary Hartman."

**Davis, Nancy**

(1921–     ) Wife of President Ronald Reagan and First Lady of the United States. Her film roles have been:

| | |
|---|---|
| *The Doctor and the Girl* (1949) | Marlette |
| *East Side, West Side* (1949) | Helen Lee |
| *Shadow on the Wall* (1950)* | Dr. Caroline Canford |
| *The Next Voice You Hear* (1950) | Mrs. Joe Smith |
| *Night Into Morning* (1951) | Katherine Mead |
| *It's a Big Country* (1952) | Miss Coleman |
| *Shadow in the Sky* (1952) | Betty |
| *Talk About a Stranger* (1952) | Marge Fontaine |
| *Donovan's Brain* (1953) | Janice Corey |
| *Hellcats of the Navy* (1957) | Helen Blair |
| *Crash Landing* (1958) | Helen Williams |

**Davis, Zachary Taylor**

Architect who built both Comiskey Park, in 1910, and Wrigley Field, in 1914 (both located in Chicago).

**Dayan, Moshe**

(1915–1981) Former Israeli defense minister. He was Israel's Minister of Defense during the Six-Day War. Dayan lost his left eye in 1941, when he led a Jewish company against the Vichy French in Syria. Dayan portrayed himself in the 1977 Israeli movie *Operation Thunderbolt*, and was portrayed by Yossi Graber in the 1982 TV movie *A Woman Called Golda*. (Yul Brynner portrayed a character named Commander Asher Gonen, who was loosely based on Dayan, in a 1966 movie, *Cast a Giant Shadow*).

**Day in the Life of a Number One DJ, A**

Documentary film about Cleveland disc jockey Bill Randle, which was made on October 20, 1955. The film, which is also known by the title *The Pied Piper of Cleveland*, contained the film debuts of Elvis Presley, Bill Haley, and Pat Boone. To date, it has never been released.

**Dazzle-Dent Toothpaste**

Product for which "the girl" (Marilyn Monroe) does a TV commercial in the 1955 movie *The Seven Year Itch*.

**Dead and Buried**

Title of actor Jack Albertson's last movie appearance, released in 1981, after his death.

---

*Though released third, this film was actually made first.

**Dead Giveaway**
   Original title of Ringo Starr's 1981 album, until the death of John Lennon, at which time it was changed to *Can't Fight Lightnin'*.
**Deadly Game, The**
   Pilot film (1976) for the TV series "Serpico," starring David Birney.
**Dean, Maureen**
   Wife of John Dean, the White House counsel to President Nixon. She was portrayed by Theresa Russell in the 1977 TV mini-series *Blind Ambition*, based in part on her autobiography, *Mo*.
**DEarborne 5-2750**
   Telephone number of the Chicago restaurant called Adam's Ribs in the TV series "M*A*S*H."
**DEarborne 5-7500**
   Phone number of the Dearborne Station in Chicago, Illinois, where Colonel Henry Blake (McLean Stevenson) met his wife, Lorraine, in the TV series "M*A*S*H."
**"Dear Mom and Dad"**
   Theme song of the single-episode (February 4, 1979) TV series "Coed Fever," performed by Henry Mancini.
**Death in the Library**
   Mystery novel by Philip Ketchum, which, in 1943, became the first paperback book published by Dell Books.
**Death in the Night and A Study in Homicide**
   Two books on the nightstand of Carlye Hardwicke (Kim Novak) in the 1962 movie *The Notorious Landlady*.
**Death Trap**
   Movie (1982) being watched by the passengers of United Airlines Flight 95 (Boston to San Francisco), which, on July 16, 1982 experienced severe turbulence. Ex-major-league baseball player Dom DiMaggio was injured in the mishap.
**Death Valley**
– Nickname given to the deepest part of left center field in Yankee Stadium.
**De Busschere, Dave**
   (1940–     ) New York Knicks basketball player who pitched two seasons (1962–63) for the Chicago White Sox (ERA 2.90) with a 3–4 record. In 1962 he played for the White Sox and was a player-coach for the Detroit Pistons basketball team.
**December 2, 1941**
   Date of the first scene in the 1942 movie *Casablanca*.

**December 2, 1969**

Date upon which Major Tony Nelson (Larry Hagman) married Jeannie (Barbara Eden) on the TV series "I Dream of Jeannie."

**December 25, 1893**

Date on which Robert L. Ripley ("Ripley's Believe It or Not") claimed to be born. He was actually born the next day.

**December 31, 1899**

Date of the first scene in the 1960 movie *The Time Machine* (based on the H. G. Wells novel of the same title).

**December 31, 1970**

Date that the last cigarette commercial was broadcast on U.S. TV.

**Dee, John**

Mathematician who, in 1580, invented the first crystal ball used by fortune-tellers.

**Dee-Lux**

Name of the Los Angeles car wash featured in the 1976 movie *Car Wash*.

**"Deep in the Heart of Texas"**

Song written in 1941 by June Hershey and Don Swandler, which was heard in the movies *Heart Of The Rio Grande* (1942), *Hi Neighbor* (1942), *Thirty Seconds Over Tokyo* (1944), *I'll Get By* (1950), *Rich, Young and Pretty* (1951), *With a Song in My Heart* (1953), *How to Marry a Millionaire* (1953), and *Teahouse of the August Moon* (1957).

**"Deep Purple"**

Song that Lou Peckinpaugh (Peter Falk) and Betty De Boop (Eileen Brennan) sang in an attempt to drown out the singing of "Watch on the Rhine" by a group of Germans in the 1978 movie *The Cheap Detective*.

**Deep Quest**

Deep-sea research vessel that located the sunken liner *Titanic* on the floor of the Atlantic Ocean (12,700 feet down) in the 1980 movie *Raise the Titanic!*

**Deep Walls**

Ranger station where Rango (Tim Conway) was posted in the TV series "Rango."

**Defense of Fort McHenry, The**

Original title of Francis Scott Key's poem, later to be known as "The Star-Spangled Banner."

**Defiance Castle**
Crusader Rabbit's home in Galahad Glen in the TV cartoon series "Crusader Rabbit" (the first cartoon series made specifically for television).

**Del Mar High School**
California high school from which Rick Carlson (Sam Elliott) graduated in 1960 in the 1976 movie *Lifeguard*. In 1975, he attended his fifteen-year reunion.

**De Lorean**
Irish-built automobile that entertainer Johnny Carson was driving on the evening of February 27, 1982, on La Cienaga Boulevard in Beverly Hills when he was arrested for drunken driving. The arresting officer was M. Angel.

**Del Rio**
Texas town near Bryant's Gap in the 1981 movie *The Legend of the Lone Ranger*. The town paper is the *Dispatch*.

**Delta Gamma**
Richie Cunningham's (Ron Howard) college fraternity on the TV series "Happy Days."

**Democratic Party**
Political party to which Captain Hawkeye Pierce (Alan Alda) belongs on the TV series "M*A*S*H."

**Denmark Speaks**
Porno film being shown in a Los Angeles theater in the 1973 movie *Save the Tiger*.

**Denton High School**
High school attended by Janet Weiss (Susan Sarandon) and Brad Majors (Barry Bostwick) in the 1975 movie *The Rocky Horror Picture Show*.

**Denton, Ohio**
Home of Brad Majors (Barry Bostwick) and Janet Weiss (Susan Sarandon) in the 1975 movie *The Rocky Horror Picture Show*.

**DePalma, Ralph**
Racing car driver who, in the 1915 Indianapolis 500 race, got out and pushed his Mercedes for the last mile and a half across the finish line to win the race.

**Depression**
Subject of Bob Hartley's doctoral thesis in the TV series "The Bob Newhart Show."

**Deputy Inspector Frank Hovannes**
New York City cop played by Frank Sinatra in his TV movie debut *Contract on Cherry Street* (1977).

**Deriabar**
Birthplace of Sinbad the Sailor, which is located "where a star is over a mountain."

**Derringer**
Small pistol invented by Philadelphia gunsmith Henry Derringer in 1835.

**Desert Flower Hotel**
Las Vegas Strip hotel built in 1946 by gangster Benjamin "Bugsy" Siegel in the 1974 TV movie *The Virginia Hill Story*. In reality, the hotel that Siegel built was the Flamingo.

**Detective Arthur Dietrich**
Extremely intelligent police officer played by Steve Landesberg in the TV series "Barney Miller."

**Detective Buck Rogers**
Police officer played by Robby Weaver (Dennis Weaver's son) in the TV series "Stone."

**Detective Spoofs**

*Murder by Death* (1976 movie):

| Spoof of | Character's name | Actor |
|---|---|---|
| Sam Spade | Sam Diamond | Peter Falk |
| Hercule Poirot | Milo Perrier | James Coco |
| Charlie Chan | Sidney Wang | Peter Sellers |
| Nick and Nora Charles | Dick and Dora Charleston | David Niven and Maggie Smith |
| Miss Marple | Jessica Marbles | Elsa Lanchester |

*Murder Can Hurt You* (1980 TV movie):

| | | |
|---|---|---|
| Baretta | Lambretta | Tony Danza |
| Columbo | Palumbo | Burt Young |
| Starsky and Hutch | Studsky and Hatch | Jamie Farr and John Byner |
| Kojak | Nojack | Gavin MacLeod |
| Ironside | Iron Bottom | Victor Buono |
| McCloud | MacSkye | Buck Owens |
| Police Woman | Salty | Connie Stevens |
| Mrs. Columbo | Mrs. Palumbo | Liz Torres |

**DeToth, André**
One-eyed director of the 3-D movie *House of Wax*, made in 1953.

**Detroit**

Pet dog of the Fitzpatrick family on the TV series "The Fitzpatricks."

**Detroit Lions (1937)**

NFL team with the fewest penalties in a single season (nineteen for 139 yards).

**Detroit Redwings**

NHL team that was previously called the Cougars (1926–1930), then the Falcons (1932–1933), before becoming the Redwings in 1933.

**Devil and Max Devlin, The**

Movie (1981) starring Bill Cosby and Elliott Gould. It was the first "R"-rated movie produced by Walt Disney Studios (changed on appeal to the MPAA to PG).

**DeVries, Ned**

Midwestern dairy farmer whose herd was killed by the toxic chemical PPB, which was mistakenly packaged in his cattle feed. DeVries was portrayed in the 1981 TV movie *Bitter Harvest* by Ron Howard (his friend, Walter, was played by Art Carney).

**Dewey, Thomas Edmund**

(1902–    ) Lawyer, U.S. Attorney, and Special Prosecution Investigator of organized crime (1935–1937) and governor of New York from 1942 to 1954. He was the unsuccessful Republican candidate for President against Harry S Truman in 1948. Dewey was the inspiration and model for the radio series "Mr. District Attorney." Dewey was portrayed in the movies *Lepke* (1975) by Richard C. Adams and *FDR: The Last Year* (1980 TV play) by Kenneth Welsh. He was portrayed loosely by Humphrey Bogart (as David Graham) in the 1937 movie *Marked Woman*, and by Jim Conway in the 1938 movie *Smashing the Rackets*.

**DeWitt's Jewelry**

Firm in the town of Sheridan, from which Bonzo stole a necklace in the 1951 movie *Bedtime for Bonzo*.

**Dickens, Charles**

(1812–70) British novelist who wrote such classic works as:

*The Pickwick Papers* (1836–37)
*Oliver Twist* (1837–39)
*A Christmas Carol* (1843)
*Dombey and Son* (1846–48)
*David Copperfield* (1849–50)

*A Tale of Two Cities* (1859)
*Great Expectations* (1860–61)

He sometimes wrote under the pseudonym Boz. Charles Dickens was portrayed in the 1946 movie *Devotion* by Reginald Sheffield, and in the 1969 movie *The Best House in London* by Arnold Diamond. Ron Moody played his "ghost" in Bing Crosby's last Christmas TV special (1977).

**Dick Grosvenor**

Son-in-law of Stella Dallas on the radio soap "Stella Dallas," who was played at various times by Richard Widmark, Frank Lovejoy, MacDonald Carey, Barry Sullivan, and Jim Backus, among others.

**Di Dia**

Hand-built aluminum custom car once owned by singer Bobby Darin. The $150,000 automobile took 6½ years to build.

**Die jacet Arturus, Rex quondam, Rexque futurus**

Inscription on the tomb of King Arthur.

**Diemer, Walter**

Inventor of bubble gum in 1928.

**Dietrich, Marlene**

(1901–     ) Berlin-born actress who made her movie debut in 1923 in *Der Kleine Napoleon*. In 1930 she played the classic role of Lola Lola in *The Blue Angel*. In 1939 Miss Dietrich became an American citizen, and she entertained U.S. troops during World War II. It was Marlene Dietrich who nicknamed Ernest Hemingway "Papa." She was portrayed by Torill in the 1982 TV movie *The Day the Bubble Burst*.

**Dig You Later**

Words on the screen in lieu of "The End" in the 1957 movie *Don't Knock the Rock*.

**DiHigo, Martin**

Only member of the Baseball Hall of Fame who was born in Cuba. DiHigo, who played in the Negro, Latin American, and Mexican leagues, was elected to the Hall of Fame in 1977.

**Diners Club**

Organization founded in 1950 by Ralph Schneider. Diners Club introduced the use of credit cards.

**Dingleberry**

Name that Larry (Peter Fonda) called Mary Coons (Susan George) in the 1974 movie *Dirty Mary and Crazy Larry*.

**Dinky**

Pet white poodle of singer Jerry Lee Lewis and his young bride

Myra Gale Brown in the late 1950s.

**Dirango Records**
Nashville Record company that wanted to record Travis Child (Dennis Quaid) before he was killed in the 1981 movie *The Night the Lights Went Out in Georgia*.

**Diaster '76**
Movie takeoff on every conceivable disaster film. It was shown at the Alamo Drive-In in the 1976 movie *Drive-In*.

**Discourse on the Aborigines of the Valley of Ohio**
Only book ever written by President William Henry Harrison. It was published in 1839.

**Diskay, Joseph**
First person to ghost-sing in motion pictures. He dubbed in the singing voice of Warner Oland in the 1927 movie *The Jazz Singer*.

**Dixie Shopping Center**
Calumet City, Illinois, shopping center wrecked by Jake and Elwood Blues in an automobile chase in the 1980 movie *The Blues Brothers*.

**Dixon, Jeane**
Noted psychic and author of numerous books on parapsychology. Her brother, Ernest Pinckert, was an All-American football player at USC and later played pro ball for the Washington Redskins from 1932 to 1940.

**Doberman Gang**
Five Doberman pinschers that were the subject of the movies *The Doberman Gang* (1972), *The Daring Dobermans* (1973), *The Amazing Dobermans* (1976), and *Alex and the Doberman Gang* (1980\*). In the movies the dogs are named Sheba, Adam, Seth, Eve, and Micah.

**Dobkin, Mary**
Baltimore woman who, although handicapped (she had spent thirty-three years in hospitals, undergoing 130 leg operations), managed boys' baseball teams over a thirty-five-year period. She was portrayed by Jean Stapleton in the 1979 TV movie *Aunt Mary*.

**Dr. Alan Stewart**
Physician played by Gil Gerard on the TV soap "The Doctors."

**Doctor Bob and Bill W.**
Founders of AA (Alcoholics Anonymous) on June 11, 1935. Last names are never mentioned at AA meetings.

---

\*In this TV movie, the dogs are named Duke, Gable, Harlow, Little Bogie, and Rocky.

**Dr. Bruce Banning**
Physician played by Barnard Hughes on the TV soap "The Guiding Light."

**Dr. Caroline Canford**
Physician played by Nancy Davis in the 1949 movie *Shadow on the Wall,* her third movie.

**Dr. Chapstick**
Basketball player Julius Irving on TV advertisements. (In the ad, a clock in the background shows 4:30).

**Dr. Chernak**
Physician played by Paul Michael Glaser on the TV soap "Love Is a Many Splendored Thing."

**Dr. Claire**
Physician played by Mariette Hartley on the TV soap "Peyton Place."

**Dr. Everett Scott**
Science teacher at Denton High School in Denton, Ohio, played by Jonathan Adams in the 1975 movie *The Rocky Horror Picture Show.*

**Dr. Frank N. Furter**
Mad doctor who brings Rocky Horror to life; played by Tim Curry in the 1975 movie *The Rocky Horror Picture Show.*

**Dr. Helena Russell**
Chief medical officer at Moonbase Alpha, played by Barbara Bain on the TV series "Space: 1999."

**Dr. Irving Finegarden**
Hollywood doctor who carried with him many drugs for his clients. He was played by Robert Preston in the 1981 movie *S.O.B.*

**Dr. J**
Nickname of basketball player Julius Irving.

**Dr. James Frazier**
Physician played by James Earl Jones on the TV soap "The Guiding Light."

**Dr. Jeffrey Latimer**
Head doctor of City Hospital in the 1979 TV series "Doctors' Private Lives," played by John Gavin.

**Dr. Jerome "Jerry" Merle Robinson**
Associate and friend of Dr. Bob Hartley (Bob Newhart), played by Peter Bonerz on the TV series "The Bob Newhart Show."

**Dr. Jerry Turner**
Physician played by James Earl Jones on the TV soap "As the

World Turns.''

**Dr. Joan Dale**
Girlfriend of Spaceman Tom Corbett, played by Margaret Garland on the TV series "Tom Corbett, Space Cadet."

**Dr. Joe Corelli**
Physician played by both Paul Michael Glaser and Tony LoBianco on the TV soap "Love of Life."

**Dr. Johnny Fever**
Disc jockey (Johnny Caravella) at radio station WKRP, played by Howard Hesseman on the TV series "WKRP in Cincinnati."

**Dr. John Wayne**
Glens Falls physician played by Martin Gabel, Paul McGrath, and Staats Cotsworth on the radio soap "Big Sister."

**Dr. Joseph Harris**
Lucy Ricardo's (Lucille Ball) obstetrician while she was pregnant with her son, Ricky, on the TV series "I Love Lucy."

**Dr. MacArthur St. Clair**
Physician at Webster Memorial Hospital played by Louis Gossett, Jr., on the 1979 TV series "The Lazarus Syndrome."

**Dr. Mark Chadwick**
Physician played by Peter Fonda in the 1963 movie *Tammy and the Doctor*, in his movie debut.

**Dr. Noah Drake**
Physician played by singer Rick Springfield on the TV soap "General Hospital." Dr. Noah Drake is paged over an intercom in the 1981 hit song "General Hospi-Tale," by the Afternoon Delights.

**Dr. Paul Hunter**
Physician played by David Hartman on the TV series "The Bold Ones."

**Dr. Stevens**
Assumed name used by God (George Burns) during the meeting of psychiatrists in the 1980 movie *Oh God! Book Two*.

**Dr. Vinnie Boombotz**
Physician referred to by Rodney Dangerfield in comedy monologues.

**Dr. Wheeler**
Role played by Roy Scheider on the TV soap "Search for Tomorrow."

**Dr. Woo Woo**
Supposedly Richard Dawson's doctor, often referred to by Dawson on the TV game show "Family Feud."

**"Does Your Heart Beat for Me?"**
   Theme song of singer Russ Morgan, which he composed.

**Doghouse Riley**
   Name that detective Philip Marlowe (Humphrey Bogart) gave as his name to Vivian Sternwood Rutledge (Lauren Bacall) in the 1946 movie *The Big Sleep*.

**Dogpatch Red**
   Call sign of Colonel James Shannon's (John Wayne) jet aircraft in the 1957 movie *Jet Pilot*.

**Dolly**
   Old white horse bought by Private Gomer Pyle (Jim Nabors) on the TV series "Gomer Pyle, USMC." He gave it to a retired man.

**Dolly Dimples**
   Computerized twelve-foot-tall hippopotamus at Chuck E. Cheese's Pizza Time Theaters. When she sings, she sounds like Pearl Bailey.

**Dolores Dragon**
   Cousin of Oliver J. Dragon (Ollie) on the TV program "Kukla, Fran and Ollie."

**Dolphin**
   Parick Fairlie's (Ray Milland) yacht in the 1953 movie *Jamaica Run*.

**Dome City**
   Central location of the people in the novel, movie, and TV series *Logan's Run*.

**Donaldson, William H.**
   (1864–1925) Founder of *Billboard* magazine in 1894.

**Donnelly, Dorothy**
   (1880—1928) Lyricist-librettist of Broadway musicals. She wrote the lyrics for the songs "Deep in My Heart," "Song of Love," and "Silver Moon," among others. Miss Donnelly also appeared in several silent films. She was portrayed by Merle Oberon in the 1954 movie *Deep in My Heart*.

**Donovan, Art Jr.**
   Member of the Professional Football Hall of Fame who has both a father (Mike Donovan) and a grandfather (Arthur Donovan, Sr.) in the Boxing Hall of Fame.

**Don's Diner**
   Diner where Clark Kent was beat up by a truckdriver named Rocky (Pepper Martin). Clark Kent, having regained his super powers, later returned to the diner to become the victor in the 1981 movie *Superman II*. JVC is the brand of TV in the diner.

**Don't sell that cow . . .**
Punchline to the joke that Buck Barrow (Gene Hackman) told in the 1967 movie *Bonnie and Clyde*.

**Don't Spit on the Floor**
Red sign on the wall of the holding cell at the 12th Precinct on the TV series "Barney Miller."

**Don't Worry, We'll Think of a Title**
A 1966 movie starring Morey Amsterdam and Rose Marie.

**Doolie**
Word used by Olympic hockey team member Mike Eruzione to describe his team after their Olympic gold medal victories in the 1980 Olympics. He said that the word meant big wheel, or big shot.

**Doomsday Plane**
Name given to the $117-million Boeing 747 Presidential aircraft intended to serve as an airborne command post in the event of a nuclear war.

**"Doo Wah Diddy Diddy"**
A 1964 hit song by Manfred Mann. Privates John (Bill Murray) and Russell (Harold Ramis) sang the song as they marched with their platoon (Third Platoon, B Company, 41st Armored Division) in the 1981 movie *Stripes* (see "Da Doo Run Run").

**Dopey**
One of Radar O'Reilly's (Gary Burghoff) pet hamsters at the 4077th in the TV series "M*A*S*H."

**Dora Lee Rhodes**
Sexy secretary played in the 1980 movie *9 to 5* by Dolly Parton and in the 1983 TV series by Rachel Dennison, Dolly Parton's youngest sister.

**Doris**
Computer with a female voice at the Institute for Advanced Concepts in the 1980 movie *Simon*.

**Dorrington, Arthur**
First black player to play in professional hockey. On November 15, 1950, he signed a contract with Atlantic City.

**Dorsset, Sybil**
Young girl who, under psychiatric help, was revealed to have had sixteen distinct personalities. She was portrayed by Sally Field (Natasha Ryan as a child) in the 1976 TV movie *Sybil*, based on Flora Rheta Schreiber's book of the same title. The movie won four Emmy awards. Sybil's psychiatrist, Dr. Cornelia Wilbur, was portrayed by Joanne Woodward.

**Doss, Corporal Desmond T.**
First conscientious objector to receive the Congressional Medal of Honor. A Seventh-Day Adventist, he served as an Army medical corpsman during World War II.

**Doubleday**
New York City bookstore where Fred "Felix" Sherman (George Segal) worked in the 1970 movie *The Owl and the Pussycat.*

**Double Doody**
Howdy Doody's twin brother (voice of Bob Smith) on the TV series "Howdy Doody Time."

**Double Indemnity**
The 1944 Paramount movie starring Fred MacMurray, Barbara Stanwyck, and Edward G. Robinson which was being shown over KBAC-TV on Vince Newman's (George Peppard) apartment TV in the 1974 movie *Newman's Law.* Some scenes from *Double Indemnity* were used in the 1982 movie *Dead Men Don't Wear Plaid.*

**Double 00**
Name of the mechanical bull at Glenboro State Prison Farm in the 1980 movie *Stir Crazy.*

**Dougherty, Jim**
First husband of actress Marilyn Monroe (1944–46). He was portrayed by Kevin Geer in the 1980 TV movie *Marilyn: The Untold Story.*

**Douglas, David**
(1798–1834) Scotsman who lent his name to that of the Douglas fir tree.

**"Down in the Valley"**
Song that 6-foot, 6-inch, 380-pound prisoner, Grossman (Erland Van Lidth DeJeude*), sang in his cell in the 1980 movie *Stir Crazy.*

**"Down in the Valley"/"Michael"/"Tom Dooley"**
Three songs that a group of camp counselors sang in front of the fireplace in the 1980 movie *Friday the 13th.*

**"Do You Ever Think of Me?"**
Popular song composed in 1920 by Earl Burnett, Harry D. Kerr, and John Cooper (the father of actor Jackie Cooper).

**Dozier, Brigadier General James**
U.S. Army general who, in February 1982, was rescued by Italian

---

*DeJeude has been both an alternate for the 1976 Olympic wrestling team and an up-and-coming opera singer.

police after he was abducted and held captive by terrorists for forty-two days.

**Dragonfish, USS**

Submarine that came to the rescue of the team raising the liner *Titanic*, to stave off the Russian vessel *Mikhail Kurkov* in Clive Cussler's 1976 novel *Raise the Titanic!*

**Dragonfly Ripple**

Ice cream cone that Kermit ate in the 1979 movie *The Muppet Movie*. The ice cream man was played by Bob Hope.

**Drake**

Ship that caught fire and sank in the 1979 movie *The Black Stallion*.

**Drake McHugh**

Role played by Ronald Reagan in the 1941 movie *King's Row*, and by Robert Horton on the 1955–56 TV series of the same title.

**Drasin, Ric**

Actor who played the Hulk in transition between Dr. David Banner (Bill Bixby) and the Hulk (Lou Ferrigno) on the TV series *The Incredible Hulk*. (He appeared in the second season only.)

**"Dream"**

Recording by Frank Sinatra being played as Jonathan (Jack Nicholson) and Bobbie (Ann-Margret) are making love in the 1971 movie *Carnal Knowledge*.

**Dreams Don't Lie**

Novel written by blind author Harold Meredith (Jack Warden), as mentioned in the 1979 movie *Beyond the Poseidon Adventure* (based on Paul Gallico's novel of the same name).

**Dream Without End**

Movie for which Esther Hoffman (Janet Gaynor) won the Academy Award for Best Actress for her role of Anna, in the 1937 movie *A Star is Born*.

**Dress for Success**

Paperback book written by John T. Malloy, which was read by Officer Andy Corelli (Ken Wahl) in a police car in the 1981 movie *Fort Apache—The Bronx*.

**Dribbles**

The Harlem Globetrotters' dog on their cartoon TV series.

**Drink to me . . .**

Last words of artist Pablo Picasso. They became the title of a song by Paul McCartney and Wings (upon a dare by actor Dustin

Hoffman to McCartney to write a song about Picasso's death).

**Driscoll, Paddy**
Member of both the Chicago Cubs baseball team (1917) and of the Chicago Bears football team (1920s).

**Dropo, Walt "Moose"**
(1924–     ) Detroit Tigers baseball player who, on July 14–15, 1952, made twelve consecutive hits.

**Drunkard**
Reply by Rick Blaine (Humphrey Bogart) when asked his nationality in the 1942 movie *Casablanca*.

**DuBois, W. E. B. (William Edward Burghardt)**
(1868–1963) American educator who was the first black to earn a Ph.D. from Harvard.

**Duck Dodgers**
Space character played by Daffy Duck in Warner Bros. cartoons. The voice was that of Mel Blanc. Duck Dodgers debuted in a cartoon titled *Duck Dodgers in the 24th-and-a-Half Century* (July 25, 1953).

**Duck Kee Market**
Berkeley, California, corner grocery store shown on the cover of the 1968 Creedence Clearwater Revival album *Willy and the Poor Boys*.

**Ducky Boys**
Large gang of youths that rumble with the Wanderers, the Wons, and the Mau-Maus in the 1980 movie *The Wanderers*.

**Dubin, Al**
(1891–1945) Lyricist who collaborated with composer Harry Warren. Some of his better known songs were "42nd Street," "I Only Have Eyes For You," and "Lullaby of Broadway." He and Harry Warren played songwriters in the 1933 movie *42nd Street*.

**Duke**
German shepherd that attacked Army Sergeant Zachary Morgan (Joseph Cotten) in the 1944 movie *I'll Be Seeing You*.

**Duke of Paducah**
Nickname of country singer Francis "Whitey" Ford.

**Dull Men's Hall of Fame**
First three inductees: Ozzie Nelson, Nigel Bruce, and Robert Young. It was established by the Carroll, Iowa, Chamber of Commerce.

**Dumbo the Elephant**
The one ride that Harry S Truman refused to have anything to do

with at Disneyland when he and his wife, Bess, visited there in 1957. Truman explained that the elephant was a Republican symbol.

**Dump, The**
Nightclub built by "Duke" Godfrey Parke (William Powell) to replace the home of the derelicts in the 1936 movie *My Man Godfrey*.

**Dunbar, Reggie**
Pseudonym used by Murray Wilson, the father of Dennis, Carl, and Brian Wilson of the Beach Boys, when he composed songs.

**Duncan, Christopher**
Fourteen-year-old boy who, in March, 1978, became the first person to skateboard on the Great Wall of China.

**Duncan, Dave and Joe Torre**
On June 30, 1975, Dave Duncan became the last player to hit four doubles in a single game; on July 21, 1975, Joe Torre became the last player to hit into four double plays in a single game.

**Dunns River**
Connecticut town setting of the TV series "Soap."

**Durant, William**
(1861–1947) American industrialist and chairman of the board of the Buick Motorcar Company in 1905 and founder of the General Motors plant in 1908. After losing control of GM in 1920, he founded the Durant Motor Company. Durant later went into the manufacture of rayon. He was portrayed by David Ogden Stiers in the TV movie *The Day the Bubble Burst*.

**Durante, Sal**
Nineteen-year-old truck driver who caught Roger Maris's sixty-first home run of the season, which was hit on October 2, 1961, at Yankee Stadium.

**Durso, Joseph**
Co-author, with Eleanor Gehrig, of the book *My Luke and I*. He was portrayed by Robert Burn in the 1978 TV movie *A Love Affair: The Eleanor and Lou Gehrig Story*.

**Duse, Eleanora**
(1858—1924) The first woman to have her portrait on the cover of *Time* magazine, July 30, 1923. She was an Italian stage actress and Sara Bernhardt's rival.

**Dusty**
Name of the horse that was shot out from under Ranger John Reid (the Lone Ranger) when he was ambushed by Butch Cavendish's

gang. The next horse that the Lone Ranger rode was named Silver which he captured in Wild Horse Canyon. (Dusty is only mentioned in a few sources).

# E

**8**

Engine number of the passenger train bound for Grease City, on which Flower Belle Lee (Mae West) met Cuthbert J. Twillie (W. C. Fields), in the 1940 movie *My Little Chickadee*.

**8**

Round in which welterweight champion Roberto Duran threw up his hands and quit in the championship fight with Sugar Ray Leonard, in the Superdome, on November 26, 1980. Duran claimed to be suffering from stomach cramps.

**8**

Cleveland Indians uniform number of outfielder Benjamin Lewin, Jr. (Michael Douglas), in the 1980 movie *It's My Turn*. At the Old Timers Game at Yankee Stadium, he caught a ball that had been hit by Mickey Mantle.

**8**

Major-league record for the most home runs hit in four consecutive games. It was set between September 10 and 12, 1947, by Ralph Kiner. R. Dale Long, of the Pittsburgh Pirates, once hit eight home runs in eight straight games, from May 19 to May 28, 1956.

**8 minutes**

Length of time that Anthony Quinn appeared on the screen as artist Paul Gauguin, in winning the Academy Award for Best Supporting Actor for the 1956 movie *Lust for Life*. Quinn's time on the screen was the briefest ever for an Oscar winner.

**8A8769**

New York State license plate number of the Larabee family Rolls-Royce in the 1954 movie *Sabrina*.

**8B0237**

California license plate number of Tom Spellacy's (Robert Duvall) blue 1948 Ford in the 1981 movie *True Confessions*.

**8 Pounds**

Weight of Corporal Maxwell Q. Klinger (Jamie Farr) of the TV series "M*A*S*H," at the time of his birth.

**8 pounds, 10 ounces**

Weight of Jesse Robins (Neil Diamond) and Molly Bell's (Lucie Arnaz) baby boy, Charles Parker Rabinovitch, in the 1980 movie *The Jazz Singer*.

**8 seconds**

Length of time that Julie Andrews went topless in the 1981 movie *S.O.B.*

**8 years old**

Age of Dorothy Gale in L. Frank Baum's 1900 novel *The Wizard of Oz*.

**8:00**

Time for dinner in the Lorenz Hart–Richard Rodgers song "The Lady Is a Tramp."

**8:00, 9:00, 9:45**

Three times mentioned in the lyrics of the 1951 Pee Wee King country hit song "Slow Polk." The last time was given as "a quarter to ten."

**8:26 A.M.**

Time that Robert Anthony Hartley leaves for work each day on the TV series "The Bob Newhart Show."

**8:30**

Time on Ben Davidson's watch that he gave to an inquirer as he is arm-wrestling in a 1982 Miller Lite Beer TV commercial.

**8:40**

Time at which the steeple clock stopped on top of the house of Miss Havisham in Charles Dickens's novel *Great Expectations*. It was the time at which her wedding was called off.

**8:40**

Time shown on the clock tower of St. Anthony's College when in actuality it was nine o'clock (in the 1953 John Wayne movie *Trouble Along the Way*).

**11**

Number of times that Max Baer knocked boxing champ Primo Carnera down in the heavyweight title fight on June 14, 1934. The fight was stopped after eleven rounds.

**"Eleven Months and Twenty-nine Days"**

Title of a hit country song by Johnny Paycheck. It is the length of time that the singer once spent in prison.

**11 years old**

Perpetual age of Little Orphan Annie.

**11 years, 10 months, and 1 week**

Length of time that Caryl Chessman spent on Death Row at San Quentin Prison before being executed on May 2, 1960.

**11:10 P.M.**

Time that Robert Anthony Hartley (Bob Newhart) goes to sleep each night after ten minutes of reading his newspaper, on the TV series "The Bob Newhart Show."

**11:15**

Time that Professor Charles W. Kingsfield, Jr.'s law class began on the TV series "The Paper Chase."

**80 Steps to Jonah**

Movie released in 1969 that starred singer Wayne Newton.

**83**

Customer service number taken by Dominick (Dom DeLuise) at a bakery in the 1980 movie *Fatso*.

**83**

Number of times that comedian Alan King appeared on the TV series "The Ed Sullivan Show," a record for any one guest.

**84**

Milwaukee fire station that answered the call when Rhoda's apartment caught fire in the TV series "The Mary Tyler Moore Show."

**85**

Home runs hit in a single season by Josh Gibson of the Homestead Grays of the old Negro League.

**86**

Number of games canceled during the 1972 baseball strike (712 games were canceled in the 1981 baseball strike).

**86**

Number of days left until Christmas vacation, as mentioned by Sandy Olsen (Olivia Newton-John) on the first day of school at Rydell High School in the 1978 movie *Grease*.

**87**

Buford Davis's (John Travolta) contestant number in the mechanical bull-bucking contest at Gilley's in the 1980 movie *Urban Cowboy*.

**87th Precinct**

New York police station where Henrietta Robbins (Barbra Streisand) was incarcerated in the 1974 movie *For Pete's Sake*.

**89**

Entry number of skier Jill Kinmont (Marilyn Hassett) in the event in which she became involved in a tragic fall that totally paralyzed her, in the 1975 movie *The Other Side of the Mountain*.

**803**

NHL record of consecutive hockey games in which a player has appeared. The record is held by Garry Unger of Toronto, Detroit, and St. Louis (1967–1979).

**804**

Number on the taxicab seen during the closing credits of the TV series "Taxi."

**804 Schrum Road**

Calumet City, Illinois, address of Ray's Music Exchange and Pawn Shop in the 1980 movie *The Blues Brothers*. Ray was played by singer Ray Charles.

**818**

Major-league record number of games started by one pitcher. Cy Young accumulated the record over twenty-two years (1890–1911). He also completed a record 753 games and pitched a record 7,356 innings. Young had 511 career wins.

**840**

NBA record number of free throws made in a single season. It was set in 1966 by Los Angeles Laker Jerry West.

**850TLX**

California state license plate number of Brewster Baker's (Kenny Rogers) motor home in the 1982 movie *Six Pack*.

**881 Seventh Avenue**

New York City address of Carnegie Hall.

**885DJC**

California automobile license plate of Blanche Tyler's (Barbara Harris) Ford Mustang in the 1976 movie *Family Plot*.

**1801**

Date on a bottle of Chivas Regal Blended Scotch Whiskey. It is the date that the company was founded.

**1803**

Time setting of the 1937 movie *Old Louisiana*.

**1830**

Time setting of the 1952 Kirk Douglas movie *The Big Sky*.

**1844**

Time setting of the 1980 TV series *The Chisholms* and the 1946 movie *Dragonwyck*.

**1854**

Year in which the 1981 movie *The Legend of the Lone Ranger* begins and in which the 1979 TV movie *Orphan Train* is set.

**1855**

Time setting of the 1979 Sean Connery movie *The Great Train Robbery*.

**1861**

Time setting of the 1961 TV series "The Americans."

**1862**

Time setting of the 1946 movie and the TV series based on the book *Anna and the King of Siam*.

**1863**

Time setting of the 1959 John Wayne movie *The Horse Soldiers*.

**1866**

Year in which the 1939 Errol Flynn movie *Dodge City* begins.

**1867**

Time setting of the 1965 Burt Lancaster movie *The Hallelujah Trail*.

**1869**

Time setting of the 1943 movie *Frontier Badmen*.

**1870**

Time setting of the 1944 movie *Gaslight*.

**1873**

Time setting of the 1956 Richard Widmark movie *The Last Wagon*.

**1874**

Time setting of the 1953 John Wayne movie *Hondo*.

**1875**

Year in which the 1954 movie *River of No Return*, starring Robert Mitchum and Marilyn Monroe, is set. Also the setting of the 1956 Frank Sinatra movie *Johnny Concho*.

**1878**

Time setting of the 1972 John Wayne movie *The Cowboys*.

**1882**

Time setting of the 1976 movie *The Dutchess and the Dirtwater Fox*.

**1889**

Time setting of the 1964 movie *Law of the Lawless*.

**1897**

Time setting of the 1953 movie *City of Bad Men* and the 1956 movie *The First Traveling Saleslady*.

**1899**

Year in which actors Humphrey Bogart (January 23), James Cagney (July 14), and Pat O'Brien (November 11) were born. It was the same year that composer Johann Strauss died. Others born in 1899 were Charles Boyer (August 28), Alfred Hitchcock (August 13), and George Cukor (July 7).

**8,063**

Number of points that Rafer Johnson scored in the decathlon in the 1960 Olympics. (Bruce Jenner scored 8,618 in the 1976 Olympics).

**8130.3**

Star date in the opening scene of the 1982 movie *Star Trek II: The Wrath Of Khan*.

**8,147**

Times at bat for Harmon Killebrew over his 22-year major-league career, without once laying down a sacrifice bunt.

**8410 North Turtle Dove Drive**

Los Angeles home address of Richie Brockelman (Dennis Dugan) on the TV series "Richie Brockelman, Private Eye."

**8757**

Combination for opening the cargo hold door of the Concorde in the 1979 movie *The Concorde—Airport '79*.

**80 676**

License plate number of the yellow taxicab driven by Beauregard through London in the 1981 movie *The Great Muppet Caper*.

**83750**

Rusty Morgan's (Red Skelton) prison number in the 1957 movie *Public Pigeon Number One*.

**86,400**

Number of seconds in a single 24-hour day.

**860 OCO**

California license number of the runaway Volkswagen (with a little girl inside) that Maximillian, the bionic dog, stopped in an episode on the TV series "The Bionic Woman."

**896586**

Prison number of the escaped convict who tunnels to a Fotomat store in a 1981 Fotomat TV commercial.

**(800) 555-6864**

Springfield telephone number that viewers call to pledge financial support for a religious program, "The Freddy Stone Hour," in the 1982 TV movie *Pray TV*. On the evening that the movie was aired, 15,000 viewers actually attempted to call the number, only to receive a recorded voice stating that their call could not be completed as dialed.

**E**

Letter at the top of optometrists' eye-test charts.

**ELL 485C**

British license number of Harry Morgan's (Telly Savalas) white Jaguar in the 1975 movie *Hitler's Gold* (originally titled *Inside Out*). The car was repossessed.

**EM50**

Top-secret project using a converted GMC motor home as a military vehicle (license number M94201), at Fort Milano, Italy, in the 1981 movie *Stripes*.

**EST**

Erhard Seminars Training

**E6837**

Registration number of the biplane on the cover of Joe Walsh's album *The Smoke You Drink, the Player You Get*.

**E.T.**

Three-foot-six-inch-tall extraterrestrial hero of the 1982 Steven Spielberg movie *E.T. the Extra-Terrestial*. The model for E.T. was created by Carlo Rambaldi, his voice was provided by Pat Walsh (sixty-five years old) and actress Debra Winger (who played a cameo role in costume in the film), and the character was "played" by two dwarves—forty-pound, 2½-foot-tall Tamara De Treaux and thirty-four-year-old Pat Bilon (walking up the ramp into the spacecraft)—and a legless seventh-grader, Matthew Merritt, who walked on his hands. E.T.'s hands were those of Caprice Rothe, and Howie Hammerman did the character's belching. The eyes were a composite of Albert Einstein's, Ernest Hemingway's, and Carl Sandburg's. An E.T. Halloween costume can be seen in the 1983 movie *Mr. Mom*. E.T. is thanked in the liner notes of Michael Jackson's album *Thriller* (Jackson narrated an album telling the story of E.T.).

**EUC 812**

British license plate number of the blue London cab in which

German spy Henry Faber (Donald Sutherland) is followed in the 1981 movie *Eye of the Needle*.

**EWING I**

California automobile license plate number of actor Jim Davis's Cadillac from the TV Series *Dallas*.

**Eagle Saloon**

Pittsburgh, Pennsylvania, pub where Stephen Foster's song "Oh Susanna" was first sung professionally, on September 11, 1847.

**Earn Your Vacation**

Radio series that was hosted by both Jay C. Flippen and Steve Allen.

**East Houston**

Idaho town terrorized by General Zod (Terence Stamp) and his two companions in the 1981 movie *Superman II*. (These sequences were actually filmed at Pinewood Studios in England.)

**East Pittsburgh Steel**

Steel mill where Peter "Skag" Skagska (Karl Malden) worked as a foreman in the 1980 TV series "Skag."

**Eastwood, Clint/Sondra Locke films**

Movies in which the couple has appeared together:

*The Outlaw Josey Wales* (1976)
*The Gauntlet* (1977)
*Every Which Way But Loose* (1978)
*Bronco Billy* (1980)
*Any Which Way You Can* (1980)
*Sudden Impact* (1983)

**Egan, Eddie**

New York City police officer who was the inspiration for Jimmy "Popeye" Doyle, played by Gene Hackman in the 1971 movie *The French Connection* (in which Egan played a bit role) and in the 1975 sequel, *The French Connection II*. Egan was also the subject of a 1973 movie, *Badge 373*, which starred Robert Duvall as Eddy Ryan (Eddie Egan played the role of Scanlon in the film). An unsuccessful TV pilot titled *Egan* was filmed in 1973, with Eugene Roche portraying Eddie Egan. In the 1978 TV movie *To Kill a Cop*, Eddie Egan appeared as Chief Ed Palmer. Egan was a regular on the TV series "Joe Forrester" and "Eischield."

**Eggleton, Robert**

Driver of the flatbed tractor-trailer truck that, on July 17, 1981, collided with the automobile driven by singer Harry Chapin on the

Long Island Expressway in Jericho. Chapin was killed in the accident.

**Ehmke, Howard**
(1894-1959) Major-league pitcher off whom Babe Ruth hit the greatest number of his 714 home runs (12 home runs).

**Eiffel, Alexandre-Gustave**
(1832–1932) French engineer who designed the Eiffel Tower and the frame for the Statue of Liberty.

**Eighth Wonder of the World**
Billing of Bonzo, the world's most educated chimpanzee, in the 1952 movie *Bonzo Goes to College*. The title had previously been conferred upon King Kong in the 1933 movie.

**Easy Street**
Television game show, hosted by Wally "Mr. Love" Williams (Robert Ridgely), on which Lynda Dummar (Mary Steenbergen) won the grand prize, the Golden Gate (Curtain Number Two), in the 1980 movie *Melvin and Howard*.

**Eat at Elis' Joint**
Advertisement on a balloon blown up on the finger of a hand sticking out of the sand on a beach during the filming of a World War I film in the 1980 movie *The Stunt Man* (you must see it to understand it). Elis Cross (Peter O'Toole) is the director of the film-within-a-film.

**Ebbets, Charles**
President of the Brooklyn Dodgers, who, at the very first official game played at Ebbets Field, on April 9, 1913, sang the National Anthem.

**E. Buzz**
The Freeling family's pet dog in the 1982 movie *Poltergeist*, played by Rip, who was owned and trained by Richard L. Calkins.

**E-coupon rides**
Disneyland rides for which so-called E-coupons are required:
Matterhorn
Bobsled
Pirates of the Carribbean
Space Mountain
Jungle Cruise
Submarine Voyage
Big Thunder Railroad
Tiki Room

Monorail
Country Bear Jamboree
It's a Small World

**Eddie**

Johnny Carson's ventriloquist dummy used by him early in his career.

**Edens, Roger**

(1905–1970) Composer, producer, and arranger. He composed music for Judy Garland in films and won an Academy Award for several of his musical collaborations. Edens was portrayed by Michael Parks in the 1978 TV movie *Rainbow*.

**Ed Forbes**

Boyfriend of Roberta Stevens (Marilyn Monroe) in the 1951 movie *Love Nest*, played by Jack Paar.

**Ed Gibson**

Lawyer played by Larry Hagman on the TV soap "The Edge of Night."

**Edna**

Radar O'Reilly's (Gary Burghoff) family cow back home in Ottumwa, Iowa, on the TV series "M*A*S*H."

**Edward "Eddie" Clark Haskell III**

Mischievous, sneaky, cunning, underhanded friend of Wally Cleaver (Tony Dow), played by Ken Osmond on the TV series "Leave It to Beaver." Eddie's dog was named Wolf.

**Edward L. Grant**

Liberty ship launched in June 1943. It was the only one to be named for a major-league baseball player, who served in World War I.

**Edwin**

Kipps's (Tommy Steele) pet cat in the 1969 musical *Half a Sixpence*.

**Efficiency-System-Economy**

Golden rule of Shalfords Emporium in London, where Kipps (Tommy Steele) works in the 1969 musical *Half a Sixpence*.

**Effie**

UNIT's computer on the 1979 TV series "A Man Called Sloane," whose voice was that of Michele Carey.

**Einstein, Albert**

Real name of comedian Albert Brooks. Brooks's father, Harry Einstein, was radio's Parkyakarkas on "The Eddie Cantor Show." His brother, Robert, was a comedy writer for "The Smothers

Brothers Show.''

**El Cid**
(1040–1099) Rodrigo Diáz de Bivar. Spanish soldier and ruler who has become a romantic hero in Spanish literature. In 1094 he captured Valencia, where he ruled until he was killed by Almoravides. He was portrayed by Charlton Heston in the 1961 movie *El Cid*.

**Elderberry wine**
Beverage used by the Brewster sisters (Josephine Hull and Jean Adair) to poison the lonely old men in the 1944 movie *Arsenic and Old Lace* (based on the play of the same title by Joseph Kesselring).

**Eldridge Street**
New York street upon which Jess Robin (Neil Diamond) lived in the 1980 movie *The Jazz Singer*.

**Eleanor**
Elephant puppet on the 1952 TV program "Willie Wonderful."

**Electric Ladyland**
Recording studio built by Jimi Hendrix shortly before his death in 1971.

**Electric Mayhem**
Muppet rock band in the 1979 movie *The Muppet Movie*. The band's leader is Doctor Teeth.

**Elia Kazan**
Magic words said by the villainous puppet Spider Lady in order to perform her black magic on the 1951–1952 TV program "The Whistling Wizard."

**Elinore**
Lisa Douglas's (Eva Gabor) favorite cow in the TV series "Green Acres."

**Elite**
Magazine seen with Cinnamon Carter's (Barbara Bain) photo on the cover in the early episodes of the TV series "Mission: Impossible."

**Elizabeth Parker**
Jane Parker's (Bo Derek) mother, as mentioned in the 1981 movie *Tarzan the Ape Man*.

**Ellie**
Annual award for a performance in a movie musical, given by the National Film Society, named for Eleanor Powell.

**Elmer**
Ethel Thayer's (Katharine Hepburn) toy wooden sailor doll in the

1981 movie *On Golden Pond*.

**Elmer Gantry**

Academy Award–winning Burt Lancaster film being shown at an Indianapolis movie theater to which Jim Jones (Powers Boothe) bought 350 tickets in order to desegregate the theater, in the 1980 TV movie *Guyana Tragedy: The Story of Jim Jones*. The novel *Elmer Gantry*, by Sinclair Lewis, was the first paperback book ever published by Avon Books (1941).

**Elm Farm Ollie**

First American cow to fly in an airplane. The event took place on February 18, 1939.

**El Presidente Country Club**

Golf course where pro golfer Mike Banning (Robert Wagner) worked in the 1967 movie *Banning*.

**Elsie**

Nicky Arnstein's (Omar Sharif) racehorse in the 1968 movie *Funny Girl*.

**Elting Theater**

San Francisco's Chinatown theater showing a Charlie Chan film in the 1981 movie *Charlie Chan and the Curse of the Dragon Queen*.

**Emerald City, The**

Working title of L. (Lyman) Frank Baum's classic novel *The Wizard of Oz* (1900).

**Emily**

Dancing housewife played by Ann Miller in "The Great American Soup Commercial" on TV, in which she is featured dancing and singing with a chorus line.

**Emma**

The Kettles' family horse in the Ma and Pa Kettle movie series.

**Emmetsburg**

Small Iowa town that has voted for the winner of every Presidential election since 1896.

**Emotion**

Word that the criminologist (Charles Gray) looked up in a dictionary in the 1975 movie *The Rocky Horror Picture Show*.

**Empire Theater**

Theater where Anthony John (Ronald Coleman) performed *Othello* in the 1947 movie *A Double Life*.

**Empress of Britain**

Hotel that Field Marshal Rommel (Erich von Stroheim) used as his headquarters in the 1943 movie *Five Graves to Cairo*.

**Enchanted Hour, The**
Vicki Lester's (Janet Gaynor) movie debut in the 1937 movie *A Star is Born*.

**Endeavor**
Windjammer captained by Chet King (Joe James) on the TV series "Barrier Reef."

**End of the World**
Name of the sailboat owned by Pete (Cliff Robertson) and Kit (Lana Turner) Jordan in the 1965 movie *Love Has Many Faces*.

**Enemies of the People**
British release title of the 1931 American movie *Public Enemy*.

**Enforcer, The**
Title of two different movies in which Humphrey Bogart (1951) and Clint Eastwood (1976) have each appeared.

**Engine Number 2440**
Engine of the Southern Pacific train robbed of $300,000 in Treasury notes by Cody Jarrett (James Cagney) and his gang in the 1949 movie *White Heat*.

**England**
Fifty-seventh state of the United States in the 1979 movie *Americathon*.

**English Triple Crown of Horseracing**
The Epsom Derby, the St. Leger Stakes, and the Two Thousand Guineas.

**"Enjoy the Ride"**
Theme song of the TV series "House Calls."

**Erasmus**
Major John Blackthorne's (Richard Chamberlain) Dutch vessel in the 1980 TV mini-series *Shōgun* (based on James Clavell's novel of the same title). In making the film, the vessel used was the *Golden Hind*.

**Ergenstrasse**
German tramp steamer skippered by Karl Ehrlich (John Wayne) in the 1955 movie *The Sea Chase*.

**Erin**
Captain B.J. Hunnicut's (Mike Farrell) daughter back home in Mill Valley, California, on the TV series "M*A*S*H." The first person Erin ever called "daddy" was Walter "Radar" O'Reilly (Gary Burghoff) who visited with her and her mother, Peg, as he

passed through San Francisco on his way home.

**Ernest P. Duckweather**

Janitor (Vaughn Taylor) character who appeared on the 1953 TV program "Johnny Jupiter."

**"Ernie (The Fastest Milkman in the West)"**

Number-one hit song in Britain, charted in 1971 by comedian Benny Hill.

**Eros**

Alien played by Dudley Manlove (previously the voice of Ivory Soap commercials) in the 1959 movie *Plan 9 From Outer Space*.

**Errand Boy, The**

Movie (1961) starring Jerry Lewis. Posters advertising the movie can be seen in the 1962 Jerry Lewis movie *It's Only Money*.

**Eruzione, Mike**

Captain of the American hockey team that won the Gold Medal at the 1980 Winter Olympics. He was portrayed by Andrew Stevens in the 1981 TV movie *Miracle on Ice*.

**Escudero**

Race horse purchased and trained by Joel Tarrant (Ty Hardin) in the 1963 movie *Wall of Noise*.

**Esmeralda**

Lucy Ricardo's (Lucille Ball) middle name on the TV series "I Love Lucy."

**Essex**

Name on the gasoline truck almost blown up by General Zod (Terence Stamp) in the 1981 movie *Superman II*.

**Essex Hotel**

New York City hotel from which singer Donny Hathaway fell to his death from the fifteenth floor on January 13, 1979.

**Esteemed Brain Tonic and Intellectual Beverage**

How chemist John S. Pemberton described his new beverage, called Coca-Cola, which he created on March 29, 1886.

**Ester**

Maid who was cleaning room 1912 on the cover of REO Speedwagon's 1982 album *Good Trouble*.

**Esther Smith**

Young lady who lived with her middle-class family around the turn of the century, played in the 1944 movie *Meet Me in St. Louis* by Judy Garland and on the 1950 radio series of the same title by Peggy Ann Garner.

**Ethel**
Name of the interviewed person's wife in the 1974 novelty record "The Streak," recorded live by Ray Stevens.

**Eucalyptus leaves**
Only food eaten by koala bears.

**Euphoria II**
Singer Jimmy Buffett's forty-eight-foot ketch.

**Eureka**
California town that was Jack Dunne's (Henry Winkler) destination in the 1977 movie *Heroes*.

**Eureka Cafe**
Restaurant in Mineral City, of which Dale Evans is the proprietor, on TV's "The Roy Rogers Show."

**"Ever Onward"**
Title of IBM's corporate anthem.

**Everybody Goes to Rick's**
Unpublished and unperformed play by Murray Burnett and Joan Alison, on which the 1942 movie *Casablanca* was based.

**Everybody's Cheering**
British release title of the 1949 Busby Berkeley movie *Take Me Out to the Ball Game*, starring Frank Sinatra, Esther Williams, and Gene Kelly.

**Every Frenchman Has One**
Autobiography (1961) of actress Olivia de Havilland. What she is referring to is the French liver. Due to the amount of drinking that occurs in the country, Frenchmen spend a great deal of time discussing their livers.

**Every Little Movement Has a Meaning of Its Own**
Song composed in 1910 by Otto Haverbach and Karl Hoschna. The song is heard in the following motion pictures: *Shine on Harvest Moon* (1944), *Presenting Lily Mars* (1945), *April Showers* (1948), and *On Moonlight Bay* (1951).

**Every Secret Thing**
Revealing autobiography written by Patricia Campbell Hearst, published in 1981.

**"Everything's Coming Up Roses"**
Song written in 1959 by Stephen Sondheim and Jule Styne, introduced by Ethel Merman in the musical *Gypsy* and sung by Lisa Kirk, for Rosalind Russell, in the 1962 movie of the same title. Part of it was sung by Ethel Merman in the 1980 movie *Airplane!*

**"Ev'ry Man a King"**

Presidential campaign song of Huey P. Long.

**Excedrin Headache Number 48**

Excedrin pain reliever TV commercial filmed by the rock group Alice Cooper in December 1969, but never shown.

**Expletive deleted**

Phrase used to indicate deletion of any profanity used by President Nixon or his advisors on the Watergate tapes.

**Exshaw, Sir Eyre Massey**

British man who won a gold medal in the 1900 Olympics in the yachting event (eight-meter-class yacht race, on board *Ollie*). At the age of seventy, he became the oldest winner of an Olympic gold medal.

**"Eye of the Tiger"**

Number-one hit song by Survivor, theme song of the 1982 movie *Rocky III*.

**"Eyewitless News"**

Evening news program on TV's "The Steve Allen Show" (1980–81).

# F

**4**

Michael Andropolis's (Michael Douglas) entry number in the marathon race in the 1976 Olympics at Montreal in the 1979 movie *Running*. He wore Number 46 in the Olympic trials in Boston.

**4 for 4**

Only three major-league players have hit four *consecutive* home runs in a single game: Robert L. Love, playing for the Boston Braves, on May 30, 1894; Lou Gehrig, playing for the New York Yankees, on June 3, 1932; and Rocky Colavito, playing for the Cleveland Indians, on June 10, 1959.

**4 hours and 18 minutes**

Longest *nine-inning* major-league baseball game in modern-day records. It was played on October 2, 1962, when the Los Angeles Dodgers defeated the San Francisco Giants (8 to 7).

**4 steps to manhood**

Author Ernest Hemingway once wrote that a man must do four things in his life to demonstrate his manhood:

1. Plant a tree
2. Fight a bull
3. Write a book
4. Have a son

**4:10**

Time on the Independence Hall clock, as depicted on the reverse side of a one-hundred-dollar bill.

**4:30**

Time mentioned in the lyrics of the Monkees' 1966 hit "Last Train to Clarksville," indicating the time one must leave by.

**4:45**

Time that Rick Blaine (Humphrey Bogart) was to meet Ilsa Lund Laszlo (Ingrid Bergman) at the Paris railroad station in the 1942 movie *Casablanca*. However, she didn't show up.

**4:59**

Time shown on a digital street clock in New York City in the opening scene of the 1949 movie *Adam's Rib*.

**5**

Major-league record number of grand-slam home runs hit in a single season. The record is held by both Ernie Banks of the National League (1955) and by Jim Gentile of the American League (1961).

**5**

Roulette wheel number on which Harpo repeatedly won so much money that he broke the bank in the 1946 Marx Brothers movie *A Night in Casablanca*.

**5**

Roulette wheel number that Vivian Sternwood Rutledge (Lauren Bacall) bet on, winning $28,000 in the 1946 movie *The Big Sleep*.

**5 cents and 25 cents**

Amount of money that Doc (Nick Nolte) paid for frogs and turtles respectively, in the 1982 movie *Cannery Row*.

**5 pounds**

Weight of singers Hank Williams (1923) and Elvis Presley (1935) at the time of their births.

**5 years**

Age at which a filly becomes a mare, and a colt becomes a horse.

**5 years and 3 days**

Length of time that Ellen Wagstaff Arden (Doris Day) and Steve Burkett (Chuck Connors) were marooned together on a South Pacific island in the 1963 movie *Move Over, Darling*.

**5 feet 9 inches**

Height of Lady Diana Spencer, as compared to 5-foot-10-inch-tall Prince Charles. When both were honored on an official British postage stamp, Charles stood on a box so as to appear several inches taller than his lady.

**14**

Age to which the right to vote was lowered in the 1968 movie *Wild in the Streets*.

**14**

Days in a fortnight.

**14**

Number of times that Marion Crane (Janet Leigh) was stabbed in the shower at the Bates Motel in the 1960 movie *Psycho*.

**14 ounces**

Size of the coffee cups served at Mel's Diner on the TV series "Alice."

**14 to 13**

Final score of the Chicago–North Dallas playoff football game in the 1979 movie *North Dallas Forty*, in which Dallas won.

**14th Precinct**

New York City precinct for which Chris Cagney (Meg Foster\*) and Mary Beth Lacey (Tyne Daly\*\*) work as female detectives on the TV series "Cagney and Lacey." Meg Foster was replaced by Sharon Gless after a few episodes.

**15**

Record number of appearances of a female actress on "The Lux Radio Theater" held by Barbara Stanwyck. Loretta Young and Claudette Colbert are tied for second place, with fourteen appearances each.

**40**

Most points scored by one player in a pro football game. Ernie Nevers scored six touchdowns and four after-touchdown points while playing for the Chicago Cardinals against the Chicago Bears, on November 28, 1929.

**41**

Football jersey number worn by Stephen Stills, on horseback, on the back cover of his 1970 album *Stephen Stills*.

**41**

Major-league record for the most batters hit by a pitcher in a single season. Brooklyn Dodgers pitcher Joe McGinnity set the record in 1900.

**41**

Major-league record for the most games won by a pitcher in a single season. It was set in 1904 by New York Yankees pitcher Jack Chesbro, who also lost thirteen games that season.

**42**

Mobey Tech football jersey worn by Boze Hertzlinger (Dick Foran)

---

\*Played by Loretta Swit in the 1982 TV pilot movie.

\*\*Wife of actor Georg Stanford Brown and daughter of actor James Daly and character actress Hope Newell.

in the 1936 movie *The Petrified Forest*.

**42**

NFL record for the most passes intercepted in a single season. George Blanda set the dubious record in 1962, when he was a quarterback for the Houston Oilers.

**42**

Number of gallons in a barrel of oil.

**44**

Ben Meechum's (Michael O'Keefe) jersey number as a basketball player for the Beaufort High Eagles in the 1980 movie *The Great Santini*. The Eagles were beaten by the Dolphins.

**44**

Jersey number of the Cleveland Browns' 220-pound halfback, Luther "Boom Boom" Jackson (Ron Rich), who accidently knocked down Harry Hinkle (Jack Lemmon), a CBS TV cameraman, on the thirty-yard line during a football game against the Minnesota Vikings in the 1966 movie *The Fortune Cookie*. The Vikings won.

**49**

Brewster Baker's (Kenny Rogers) auto racing number in the 1982 movie *Six Pack*.

**49-0**

Score of the first Tournament of Roses football game at Pasadena, California, when the University of Michigan defeated Stanford on January 1, 1902.

**"50 Ways to Leave Your Lover"**

Number-one hit song by Paul Simon in 1975. The five guys that he mentions in the lyrics are Jack, Stan, Roy, Gus, and Lee.

**51**

Number that the Miami Dolphins had affixed to the right rear of their helmets during the 1981 season, in memory of team member Rusty Chambers who had died in July of 1981.

**52**

Jersey number in the photo of Ed Asner, when he played tackle at Wyandotte High in Kansas City, Kansas. The photo hung on the wall of Lou Grant's (Ed Asner) office on the TV series "The Mary Tyler Moore Show."

**52 Bedford Place**

London house address of Daphne Caldwell (Ann Field) in the 1962 movie *The War Lover*.

## $53

Amount of money that Curly (Gordon MacRae) bid for Laurey's (Shirley Jones) picnic basket in the 1955 movie *Oklahoma!* In order to raise the money, he had to sell his saddle for ten dollars, his horse Blue for twenty-five dollars, and his gun for eighteen dollars. Curly's rival Jud (Rod Steiger) had bid all the money he had, stopping at $42.31.

## 58

NFL record number of fumbles by one team in a season. The record was set by the Minnesota Vikings in 1963.

## .408

Joe DiMaggio's batting average during his fifty-six-game hitting streak, from May 15 through July 16, 1941.

## 411 Elm Street

Mayberry home address of deputy Barney Fife (Don Knotts) on the TV series "The Andy Griffith Show."

## $413.50

Monthly pay of Captain Hawkeye Pierce (Alan Alda) on the TV series "M*A*S*H."

## 431

Home phone number of Barney Fife (Don Knotts) in Mayberry on the TV series "The Andy Griffith Show."

## 441 Olive Street

New York City house address of Ruby Carter (Mae West) in the 1934 movie *Belle of the Nineties*. Her phone number was DAvenport 7000.

## 444

Number of days that the fifty-two American hostages were held in Tehran, Iran, from November 4, 1979, until January 20, 1981 (the day that Ronald Reagan was inaugurated as President).

## 456 and 457

Numbers of the two atomic bombs hijacked from NATO flight 759 (Vulcan bomber) by SPECTRE in the 1965 movie *Thunderball*.

## 457

Individual credits listed for the 1978 movie *Superman*. It is the longest list in motion picture history.

## 457

Major-league record for total bases in a single season, set in 1921 by Babe Ruth.

## 463 East 76th Street
New York City address of Katie Robbins's (Shirley MacLaine) apartment in the 1961 movie *All in a Night's Work*.

## 472 minutes
NHL record for time spent in the penalty box. Dave Schultz of the Philadelphia Players set the record during the 1974–1975 season. During the next season the Players broke the record for the most time in penalties assessed against them as a team with 1,980 minutes.

## .477
Willie Mays's batting average for the New York Giants farm club in Minneapolis, at the time he was called up to the majors on May 25, 1951.

## 483 feet
Distance from home plate to the center-field stands in New York City's Polo Grounds, the longest such distance in baseball. Only three players ever hit home runs into the center-field bleachers: Henry Aaron, Joe Adcock, and Lou Brock.

## 502
Police Penal Code punishable by a term from fifty to three hundred years, for "devouring maidens out of season," in the 1953 novelty song "St. George and the Dragonet" by Stan Freberg.

## 502
Number of official plate appearances a batter must have in the major leagues to qualify him for a batting title in a 162-game schedule.

## 528
NBA record for the most foul shots missed in a single season. It is held by Wilt Chamberlain.

## 579 feet
Estimated distance of a home run that Boston Red Sox outfielder Babe Ruth hit at Tampa, Florida, in an exhibition game played on April 4, 1919. George Smith of the New York Giants pitched the ball. Many baseball buffs consider this the longest home run ever hit.

## 593 feet
Distance from home plate to the center-field stands in Boston's Fenway Park before it was rebuilt in 1934. After the rebuilding, center field was brought in to 390 feet.

**4,007 yards**

NFL record set by New York Jets quarterback Joe Namath in 1967, for the most yards passed in a single season.

**4,029**

NBA record number of points scored by one player in a single season, set in 1962 by Wilt Chamberlain of the Philadelphia '76ers.

**4070**

Number on the locomotive of the eight-car passenger train whose name is also the title of the 1976 movie *Silver Streak*.

**4,191**

Major-league record for the most lifetime hits, held by Ty Cobb, who hit 3,902 for Detroit (1905–1926) and 289 for Philadelphia (1927–1928).

**4221 Vermont Street**

Philadelphia home address of Angie Falco Benson (Donna Pescow) on the TV series "Angie."

**4227 Shady Lane**

Home address of Dagwood and Blondie Bumstead, as mentioned in several movies of the *Blondie* movie series.

**4267**

House number of the Freeling family's home in Cuesta Verde (built in 1976) in the 1982 movie *Poltergeist*.

**4873**

Georgia automobile license plate number of Sergeant Whittaker's (Robert Vibaro) 1958 Oldsmobile 98 police car in the 1975 movie *Return to Macon County.*

**4960 Terrace Drive**

Address of the Venus DiMillo Arms Apartments in Rome, the setting of the cartoon TV series "Roman Holidays."

**5412 Grove Avenue**

Del Mar Vista, California, home address of Chester A. Riley and family, after moving from 1313 Blueview Terrace in 1956, on the TV series "Life of Riley." Riley's best friend, Jim Gillis, lived upstairs at 5420 Grove Avenue (also referred to in the series as Grove Street and Grove Place).

**5523**

Prison number of the inmate who borrowed Lex Luthor's (Gene Hackman) Liberace records in the 1981 movie *Superman II*.

**4-1250**

Telephone number of the pay phone at the Twin Oaks Tavern in the

1981 movie *The Postman Always Rings Twice*.

**43648E**

California license number of Fred Sanford's (Redd Foxx) red Ford pickup truck on the TV series "Sanford and Son."

**43-758**

New York state license number of the steamroller that ran over Hiram Jaffe (Elliott Gould) in the 1970 movie *Move*.

**$50,000**

Amount of money that comedian W. C. Fields kept in a German bank during World War II. The reason, as he once stated, was "in case the little bastard wins."

**$50,000**

Amount of money that Buddy Evans (Burt Reynolds) paid Maggie (Beverly D'Angelo) to have his baby in the 1981 movie *Paternity*. He later married her instead.

**50574**

New Jersey prison number of Vincent Canelli (Edward G. Robinson) in the 1954 movie *Black Tuesday*.

**53834**

Prison number of convict Joe "Red" Kennedy (Humphrey Bogart) in the 1937 movie *San Quentin*.

**40-2344**

Serial number of the B-25 that Col. James Doolittle flew from the aircraft carrier USS *Hornet* on his raid over Tokyo on April 18, 1942.

**40-36-10/104-44-30**

Numbers sent out by the aliens in response to the Earth message of musical notes. The numbers are the latitude and longitude of Devil's Tower in Wyoming in the 1977 movie *Close Encounters of the Third Kind*.

**407610**

Pennsylvania license nmber of Jack Terry's (John Travolta) Jeep Renegade in the 1981 movie *Blow Out*.

**4-82850**

License number of the yellow 1957 Chevrolet driven by Bo Hollinger (Nick Nolte) and Harley McKay (Don Johnson) in the 1975 movie *Return to Macon County*. They claimed that the car could do a quarter-mile in 8.7 seconds. In the opening scenes, the odometer read 31192 miles.

**485963**

Joliet prison number of Professor Peter Boyd's (Ronald Reagan) father in the 1951 movie *Bedtime for Bonzo*. His father, who was also named Peter Boyd, went by the nickname Silky.

**566497**

Boxcar that was supposedly transporting Warsaw Ghetto Jews to the Ukraine (a journey of several days). However, it was discovered that the same car returned seven hours after the trip began in the 1982 TV movie *The Wall* (based on John Hersey's novel).

**5C8230**

California license number of Michael Carrington's (Maxwell Caulfield) motorcycle in the 1982 movie *Grease 2*.

**466-2495**

Dr. Quincy's (Jack Klugman) work phone number on the TV series "Quincy."

**555-0267 (prefix 213)**

Telephone number of the Townsend Agency on the TV series "Charlie's Angels."

**555-1212**

Telephone number shown in *Century 21* real estate commercials on TV. It is the number used for directory information.

**555-2131**

Home telephone number of private detective Thomas Magnum (Tom Selleck) on the TV series "Magnum, P.I."

**555-2368**

Home telephone number of the Jarretts in Forest Hill, Illinois, in the 1980 movie *Ordinary People*.

**555-2834**

Home telephone number of Vera Louise Gorman (Beth Howland) on the TV series "Alice."

**555-3233**

Telephone number of Hart Industries, owned by Jonathan Hart (Robert Wagner) on the TV series "Hart to Hart." It has also been given as 555-6903.

**555-3310**

Kate Palmer's (Lee Remick) New York City apartment telephone number in the 1968 movie *No Way to Treat a Lady*.

**555-3567**

Telephone number of Portland, Oregon, radio station KLOW, where Larry Adler (McLean Stevenson) worked on the 1979 TV series "Hello Larry."

**555-4012**

Telephone number on the side of the Checker Special Cab shown on the cover of the Temptations' *Reunion* album (1982).

**555-4124**

Telephone number of Ann Romano (Bonnie Franklin) on the TV series "One Day at a Time."

**555-4242**

Home telephone number of Jennie Picolo (Cathy Silvers) on the TV series "Happy Days."

**555-4521**

Portland, Oregon, home telephone number of Larry Adler (McLean Stevenson) on the 1979 TV series "Hello Larry."

**555-5261**

Telephone number of the phone booth across the street from the apartment leased by Paula McFadden (Marsha Mason) in the 1977 movie *The Goodbye Girl*.

**555-6634**

Home telephone number of Ed and Eunice Higgins on the TV series "The Carol Burnett Show."

**555-7382**

San Francisco telephone number of the law firm of Carl Palmer and Associates on the TV series "Hagen."

**555-8675 (Area Code 415)**

Twenty-four-hour hotline at the San Francisco Memorial Hospital. The phone is a pay telephone in the hallway on the TV series "Trapper John, M.D." ("Hotline, you've got a friend.")

**555-8760**

San Francisco telephone number written on a brick thrown through a window in the 1981 movie *Charlie Chan and the Curse of the Dragon Queen*. The number was that of Al's Window and Brick Repair.

**555-9970**

Telephone number of New York City's Chelsea Hotel, where twenty-two-year-old *Rolling Stone* magazine writer Christopher Adams (Hart Bochner) was staying in the 1981 movie *Rich and Famous*.

**555-WKRP**

Telephone number of radio station WKRP on the TV series "WKRP in Cincinnati."

**584-2121**

Telephone number on the top sign of John Winger's (Bill Murray) yellow taxicab in the 1981 movie *Stripes*. Strangely, there was a different number on the door: 636-5511. There was no license plate on either the front or the rear of the vehicle.

**657-2036**

Dr. Smith's answering service in the 1967 movie *The Graduate*.

**480-07-7456**

Social Security number of President Ronald Reagan.

**556-78-2613**

Corporal Max Klinger's (Jamie Farr) Social Security number on the TV series "M*A*S*H."

**516-472-3402**

Home telephone number of David Kessler (David Naughton) in the 1981 movie *An American Werewolf in London*.

**43,252,003,274,489,856,000**

Exact number of positions that a Rubik's Cube (created by Dr. Erno Rubik) can be twisted into.

**F**

Key in which the majority of American automobile horns sound.

**F (c) 3**

Bound-delegate rule. The Democratic rule that binds delegates to vote on the first convention ballot for the Presidential candidate that they supported in the year's primaries and caucuses. This was the subject of controversy in the 1980 Presidential election.

**F7**

Berth on Battleship Row at Pearl Harbor where the battleship USS *Arizona* was tied on December 7, 1941, before being sunk by Japanese aircraft.

**FELIX**

California license number of Felix Farmer's (Richard Mulligan) white Cadillac in which he tried to asphyxiate himself, in the 1981 movie *S.O.B.*

**FMLY OF 8**

One-millionth personalized license plate to be issued in the state of California. It was issued in March 1982.

**FOX 6612**

British license number of the automobile in which rock singer Marc Bolan was killed, on September 16, 1977, when the car hit a tree. His girlfriend, Gloria Jones, was the driver.

**FT 268**

U.S. Air Force jet piloted by Clint Eastwood as the flight leader in the 1955 movie *Tarantula*.

**FVB**

Future Villain Band—evil rock group played by Aerosmith in the

1978 movie *Sgt. Pepper's Lonely Hearts Club Band*.

**Fabian**

(1943–    ) Popular teenage singer and idol of the late 1950s and early 1960s, born Fabino Forte. Although he couldn't sing very well, his good looks made him popular with the girls. Fabian Forte also appeared in a number of films in the late 1950s and early 1960s: *Hound Dog Man* (1959); *North to Alaska* (1960); *The Longest Day* (1962); and *Ten Little Indians* (1965). Fabian was loosely portrayed by Peter Gallagher, as Caesare, in the 1981 movie *The Idolmaker*.

**Facts**

Original title considered for *Time* magazine.

**Fagan, Michael**

Thirty-year-old man who sneaked into Buckingham Palace on July 12, 1982. Fagan entered Queen Elizabeth's room, sat on her bed, and talked to her for approximately ten minutes.

**Fagin**

Sinister man who employed a gang of thieves made up of young boys in Charles Dickens's 1838 novel *Oliver Twist*. He taught them how to pick pockets and commit other forms of robbery. Played in films by Alec Guinness (1948) and George C. Scott (1982—TV). Ron Moody played Fagin in the musical version, called *Oliver!*

**Faggot**

Miles Mellough's (Jack Cassidy) dog in the 1975 movie *The Eiger Sanction*.

**Fairchild**

Pet bear of Elly May Clampett (Donna Douglas) in the TV series "The Beverly Hillbillies."

**Faithful, Starr**

Prostitute who was found murdered in Long Beach, California, in 1931. She was the subject of John O'Hara's novel *Butterfield 8*, and was played by Elizabeth Taylor, as Gloria Wandrous, in the 1960 movie, for which she won an Oscar as Best Actress.

**FALL GUY**

California truck license plate number as well as the CB handle of Colt Sievers (Lee Majors) in the TV series "The Fall Guy." The license plate actually belongs to Hollywood stuntman Jack Gill (husband of actress Morgan Brittany), and is the license number of his Datsun 280ZX.

**Fall Guy**

Title of the 1980 autobiography of stuntman Chuck Robertson, who, for thirty years, doubled for John Wayne in many films.

**Family of Fine Cars**
Inscription on sets of keys of Ford Company automobiles.

**Famous Amos' Chocolate Chip Cookies**
Successful brand of cookies created by black actor Wally Amos.

**Famous Driving School**
Driving school run by Jim Douglas (Dean Jones) on the TV series "Herbie the Love Bug." The telephone number is 555-7636.

**Famous feuds**
Bob Hope and Bing Crosby
Jack Benny and Fred Allen
Charlie McCarthy and W. C. Fields
Tommy Smothers and Dick Smothers
Hatfields and McCoys
Dean Martin and Jerry Lewis
Don Rickles and everybody
Walter Winchell and Ben Bernie

**Fandango Ballroom**
Cheap New York City dancehall where Charity Hope Valentine (Shirley MacLaine) was a hostess in the 1969 movie *Sweet Charity*.

**Fanfare**
Movie being filmed by Bellamy Pictures in the TV movie *Valley of the Dolls 1981* (loosely based on Jacqueline Susann's novel). In the film-within-a-film, Neely O'Hara (Lisa Hartman) won the Best Supporting Actress Award from the National Film Awards.

**Fanny Hill**
Innocent country girl who used her charms to amass a fortune, in John Cleland's 1749 novel *Fanny Hill, or the Memoirs of a Woman of Pleasure*. The following is a list of titles of movies based upon the novel or the character of its heroine, with the names of the actresses who have played Fanny Hill:

*Fanny Hill: Memoirs of a Woman of Pleasure* (1965), with Letitia Roman; *Fanny Hill Meets Dr. Erotico* (1967), *Fanny Hill Meets Lady Chatterly* (1967), *Fanny Hill Meets the Red Baron* (1968), all with Sue Evans; and *Fanny Hill* (Sweden, 1969) with Diana Kjaer.

Fanny Hill is mentioned by Henry Fonda in the 1968 movie *Yours, Mine, and Ours*. The book was read surreptitiously by Abbey (Darleen Carr) in the 1968 movie *The Impossible Years*.

**Fant, Lou**
Ace Hardware Store man in Ace Hardware TV ads, with both

Connie Stevens and Suzanne Somers. The son of deaf parents, Lou Fant is well known for his work with the deaf.

**"Farewell Amanda"**
Cole Porter song that is sung briefly by Frank Sinatra on a record player in the 1949 movie *Adam's Rib*. He had recorded the song especially for the film.

**Farewell to the Master**
Novella by Harry Bates, on which the 1951 movie *The Day the Earth Stood Still* was based. Ironically, in the original story it was the robot who was the master, not the character of Klaatu (Michael Rennie).

**Farmer Alfalfa**
Farmer who is forever trying to use the latest improvements on his farm. He debuted in the 1916 cartoon "Farmer Alfalfa's Catastrophe."

**Farnham, Joseph**
Only person to receive an Academy Award for writing titles for silent films. In 1928 he received three Oscars.

**Farrell, Carolyn**
First Catholic nun to serve as mayor of an American city, when she was elected mayor of Dubuque, Iowa, in 1980.

**"Fascination"**
Song that Lucas Lorenzo Spencer (Tony Geary) and his bride, Laura Baldwin (Genie Francis), danced to on their wedding day on November 17, 1981, on the TV series "General Hospital." The song, which was adapted from "Valse Tziganne" by F. D. Marchetti, can be heard in the 1957 movie *Love in the Afternoon*. Several versions of the song made the record charts in 1957.

**Father Guido Sarducci**
Hip Catholic priest played by Don Novello, who, while on a visit to the Vatican in 1981, was arrested and stripped of his priestly garments.

**Father MacKenzie**
Clergyman mentioned in the lyrics of the Beatles' hit song "Eleanor Rigby."

**Father of Comedy**
Appellation of Athenian playwright Aristophanes (448–380 B.C.).

**Father of History**
Appellation of Greek historian Herodotus (fifth century B.C.).

**Father of the Bride**

Movie (1950) starring Spencer Tracy* and Elizabeth Taylor. Scenes from the film were shown in the 1971 movie *The Last Picture Show* as well as in the 1969 film *The Happy Ending*. Vickie LaMotta (Cathy Moriarty) told her husband, Jake (Robert DeNiro), that she went to see the film, in the 1980 movie *Raging Bull*.

**Father of the Year 1975**

Title conferred upon actor Ted Knight.

**Father Paul**

Catholic priest who headed St. Michael's Church, in Carlton, Pennsylvania. He was played by Frank Sinatra in the 1948 movie *The Miracle of the Bells*.

**"Fat Man, The"**

Song sung by six-hundred-pound Harold, the carnival fat man, nicknamed Henry (Ken McMillan), in the 1980 movie *Carny*. The song was originally recorded by Fats Domino in 1949 and is considered by some rock historians to be the first rock 'n' roll song.

**Faul, Bill**

(1940–     ) Chicago Cubs pitcher who was on the mound each of the three times that the Cubs executed a triple play in 1965.

**February 1895**

Month and year in which George Herman "Babe" Ruth, George Halas, and George Gipp were all born.

**February 29, 1904**

Birthdate of orchestra leader Jimmy Dorsey and major-league baseball player Johnny "Pepper" Martin.

**February 14, 1913**

Birthdate of sportscaster Mel Allen, coach Woody Hayes, and union leader Jimmy Hoffa.

**February 12, 1980**

Date of the opening scenes of the 1981 movie *My Bloody Valentine*.

**Federal General Studios**

Hollywood movie studio where Laverne DeFazio (Penny Marshall) and Shirley Feeney (Cindy Williams) did stunt work in a Troy Donahue movie titled *Before Time Began* in the TV series "Laverne and Shirley."

---

*Jack Benny turned down the role.

**Federated Broadcasting System**

Radio network that broadcast "The Paradise Coffee Program" in the 1945 Jack Benny movie *The Horn Blows At Midnight*.

**Feldman, Jacob**

Holder of Peace Corps card number 0001.

**"Felicidad"**

Song that actress Sally Field recorded in 1967. It made *Billboard*'s Hot 100, peaking at Number 94. She sang it on her TV series "The Flying Nun."

**Feller, Bob**

(1918–  ) Only major-league pitcher ever to pitch a no-hitter on an opening day. He set the record in 1940 while pitching for the Cleveland Indians in a game against the Chicago White Sox. During a Mother's Day game at Comiskey Park in 1939, Bob Feller's mother was hit on the head and knocked unconscious by a foul ball.

**Female Instinct**

Pilot movie (1972) for the TV series "The Snoop Sisters." It appeared as a segment of the NBC Mystery Movie, and became a regular part of its rotating series the following season.

**Fencing**

Sports scholarship through which singer Neil Diamond was accepted to NYU, where he majored in biology in hopes of becoming a doctor.

**Fenelon, Fania**

Parisian cabaret singer of Jewish descent, who was interned at Auschwitz in 1944. There she performed in a prisoner's orchestra that played for the SS. She was portrayed by Vanessa Redgrave* in the 1980 TV movie *Playing For Time*.

**Fenwick Diversified Industries, Incorporated**

Cara Wilton's (Cara Williams) place of employment as a file clerk on the TV series "The Cara Williams Show."

**Ferguson, Joe**

Buffalo Bills quarterback, who holds the NFL record for the fewest passes being intercepted in a single season. In 1976 he had only one pass intercepted out of 151 throws.

---

*The casting of Vanessa Redgrave caused some controversy because of her anti-Zionist politics.

**Ferguson, Miriam**
First woman governor of Texas, elected in 1924.

**Fidelio**
Beethoven's only opera, which he wrote in 1805. He originally titled it *Leonore*.

**Fiesta**
Original title of Ernest Hemingway's 1926 novel *The Sun Also Rises*.

**Fi Fi**
Last fully operational B-29 in the world. It is presently flown by the Confederate Air Force.

**Figueroa, Ed and Jose**
Only two major-league baseball players whose same last names contain all five English vowels.

**Fillmore**
North Dakota hometown of Ester Blodgett (Janet Gaynor) in the 1937 movie *A Star Is Born*.

**Final score 2–0**
St. Louis Cardinals defeated the hometown Chicago Cubs. Dave Kingman made the last out by hitting into a double play in the play *Bleacher Bums*.

**Finch, Pat**
First guest on the premiere showing of the TV show "What's My Line?" on February 2, 1952. Her occupation was that of a hatcheck girl. The occupation of the second guest was that of an executive of a diaper service. The third and last was the "mystery guest," baseball player Phil Rizzuto.

**Fingers, Rollie**
(1946–      ) First relief pitcher to be named Most Valuable Player (American League, 1981).

**Fireman Save My Child**
Movie (1954) in which Bud Abbott and Lou Costello were to appear. However, they walked off the set after already having filmed some stunt work. Actors Hugh O'Brian and Buddy Hackett, who resembled the pair from a distance, took over the two roles.

**First four radio sponsors of Jack Benny:**
1. Canada Dry
2. General Motors
3. General Tires
4. General Foods

**First Impressions**
Working title of Jane Austen's 1813 novel *Pride and Prejudice*.

**First Lady**
Senior-class (1939) high-school play in which First Lady Nancy Davis Reagan appeared. Her only line was "They ought to elect the First Lady and then let her husband be President."

**First Monday in October**
Opening day of each term of the United States Supreme Court, established in the Judiciary Act of 1789. Also the title of a 1981 Walter Matthau–Jill Clayburgh movie, and the original Broadway play starring Henry Fonda and Jane Alexander (this was Fonda's last appearance on the New York stage).

**Fisch, Adolf**
Young man who saved Albert Einstein's life when both were in their youth. As they climbed an 8,000-foot mountain, Einstein slipped. Fisch grabbed him by the hand, stopping him from falling. *Both* men thus changed the course of history.

**Fisher, Jack**
(1939–      ) Baltimore pitcher off whom Ted Williams hit the last home run of his career (521) on September 28, 1960. It was also Williams's last time up at bat.

**Five basic swimming strokes**
American Crawl (freestyle)
Backstroke
Breaststroke
Butterfly
Sidestroke

**Flack, Max and Cliff Heathcote**
Right-fielder for the Chicago Cubs and St. Louis Cardinals respectively, who, between games of a double-header played on May 30, 1922, were traded to each other's teams, for which they played right field during the second game.

**Flagship National Bank**
Miami bank from which forty-seven-year-old Michael Collin Gallagher (Paul Newman) drew two checks—one for $3,000 and one for $9,000—to be given to the Committee for the Betterment of Miami, in the 1981 movie *Absence of Malice*.

**Flaming Arrow**
Scout patrol to which Lionel "Whitney" Brown (Jeff Goldblum) belonged as a young boy, in the TV series "Tenspeed and

Brownshoe.''

**Flaming Arrow**

Indian, 147 years old, played by Phil Harris on the TV series "F Troop.''

**Flanders, Ralph**

Vermont Republican senator who introduced on the Senate floor the resolution to censure Joseph McCarthy on July 30, 1954.

**Flapjack**

Bull ridden by inmate Skip Donahue (Gene Wilder) in the 1980 movie *Stir Crazy*.

**Flash**

Sheriff Roscoe P. Coltrane's (James Best) pet dog on the TV series "The Dukes of Hazzard.''

**Fleeson, Plunket**

Inventor of wallpaper, in Philadelphia, in 1793.

**Fleetwood Coupe de Ville**

Name of the cowardly lion played by Ted Ross in the 1979 movie *The Wiz* (a role he originated in the original Broadway musical).

**Fleming, Sir Sandford**

(1827–1915) Canadian railway engineer who, in 1878, established the twenty-four time zones of the world.

**Fleming, Walter Millard**

Doctor (M.D.) who in 1870 established the fraternal organization called the Ancient Arabic Order of Nobles of the Mystic Shriners of North America.

**Fletcher Rabbit**

Postman puppet on the TV show "Kukla, Fran and Ollie.''

**Flimm Building**

Downtown Cincinnati high-rise where radio station WKRP has its offices on the 14th floor, on the TV series "WKRP in Cincinnati.''

**Flippy**

Trained porpoise at Ocean Harbor Amusement Park in the 1955 movie *Revenge of the Creature*.

**"Flo"**

TV series starring Polly Holliday as waitress Florence Jean Castleberry. It was a spinoff of the TV series "Alice,'' which was based in turn on the 1974 movie *Alice Doesn't Live Here Anymore*.

**Floating Island**

Dessert served by Bunny Watson (Katharine Hepburn) to Richard Sumner (Spencer Tracy) in her New York City apartment in the

1957 movie *Desk Set*.

**Florida**

State that has the most lakes (30,000).

**"Flo's Golden Rose"**

Theme song of the TV series "Flo," sung by Hoyt Axton.

**Flournoy, T. J.**

(1902–1982) Fayette County sheriff nicknamed "Sheriff Jim," who served in that capacity for thirty-four years until he retired in 1980. He defended the Chicken Ranch brothel until it was closed in 1973, and was loosely portrayed by Burt Reynolds in the 1982 movie *The Best Little Whorehouse in Texas* (as Sheriff Ed Earl Dodd).

**Floyd R. Turbo**

Redneck hunter who editorializes. He is played by Johnny Carson on "The Tonight Show." The *R* stands for *Arthur*.

**Flushing**

Part of the New York City borough of Queens where the first *Charmin* TV commercial was filmed, with Mr. George Whipple (Dick Wilson) begging the women not to squeeze the toilet paper.

**Flying Phoenix**

Spacecraft commanded by Commander Mark on the TV cartoon series "Battle of the Planets."

**Flynn, Fireman Jim**

Only boxer to ever knock out Jack Dempsey. Flynn floored Dempsey in the first round in a fight on February 13, 1917. On February 14, 1918, Dempsey knocked Flynn out in the return bout.

**Folkestone Station**

Destination of the London train in the 1979 movie *The Great Train Robbery*.

**Football stadiums—NFL**

*AFC*

West

| | | |
|---|---|---|
| 1. Denver Broncos | Mile High Stadium | Denver, Colo. |
| 2. Kansas City Chiefs | Arrowhead Stadium | Kansas City, Mo. |
| 3. Los Angeles Raiders | Coliseum | Los Angeles, Cal. |
| 4. San Diego Chargers | Jack Murphy Stadium | San Diego, Cal. |
| 5. Seattle Seahawks | Kingdome | Seattle, Wash. |

Central

| | | |
|---|---|---|
| 1. Cincinnati Bengals | Riverfront Stadium | Cincinnati, Ohio |
| 2. Cleveland Browns | Municipal Stadium | Cleveland, Ohio |
| 3. Houston Oilers | Astrodome | Houston, Texas |
| 4. Pittsburgh Steelers | Three Rivers Stadium | Pittsburgh, Pa. |

East

| | | |
|---|---|---|
| 1. Baltimore Colts | Memorial Stadium | Baltimore, Md. |
| 2. Buffalo Bills | Rich Stadium | Orchard Park, N.Y. |
| 3. Miami Dolphins | Orange Bowl | Miami, Fla. |
| 4. New England Patriots | Schaefer Stadium | Foxboro, Mass. |
| 5. New York Jets | Giants' Stadium | East Rutherford, N.J. |

*NFC*

West

| | | |
|---|---|---|
| 1. Atlanta Falcons | Atlanta Stadium | Atlanta, Ga. |
| 2. Los Angeles | Anaheim Stadium | Anaheim, Cal. |
| 3. New Orleans Saints | Louisiana Superdome | New Orleans, La. |
| 4. San Francisco 49ers | Candlestick Park | San Francisco, Cal. |

Central

| | | |
|---|---|---|
| 1. Chicago Bears | Soldier Field | Chicago, Ill. |
| 2. Detroit Lions | Pontiac Metropolitian Stadium | Pontiac, Mich. |
| 3. Green Bay Packers | Lambeau Field | Green Bay, Wis. |
| 4. Tampa Bay Buccaneers | Tampa Bay Stadium | Tampa Bay, Fla. |
| 5. Minnesota Vikings | Metropolitan Stadium* | Burlingham, Minn. |

East

| | | |
|---|---|---|
| 1. Dallas Cowboys | Texas Stadium | Dallas, Texas |
| 2. New York Giants | Giants' Stadium | East Rutherford, N.J. |
| 3. Philadelphia Eagles | Veterans Stadium | Philadelphia, Pa. |
| 4. St. Louis Cardinals | Busch Memorial Stadium | St. Louis, Mo. |
| 5. Washington | R. F. Kennedy Stadium | Washington, D.C. |

## Ford, John

(1895–1973) Successful Hollywood director famous for his colorful Westerns, many of them starring John Wayne, such as: *Fort Apache* (1948), *She Wore a Yellow Ribbon,* (1949), and *Rio Grande* (1950). His brother is actor Francis Ford, who appeared in several of his films. During World War II, Ford served with the OSS. He portrayed himself in the 1929 movie *Big Time,* and was loosely portrayed by Ward Bond as John Dodge in the 1957 movie *The Wings of Eagles,* and by James Chandler in the 1983 TV movie *Grace Kelly*.

## Ford Model S

First production-line model Ford (1908).

## Ford, Rev. Arthur

Believer in the supernatural and author of a number of books on the subject, such as *The Book of the Damned*. He was portrayed by Bill Bixby in the 1976 TV movie *The Great Houdinis*.

---

*Seats only 48,446, the smallest of all the stadiums.

**Foreman, George**
(1948– ) Heavyweight boxing champ (1973–1974), and 1968 Olympic heavyweight champion. On January 22, 1973, when he defeated Joe Frazier in a championship bout, it was his twenty-fifth birthday. He holds the Heavyweight record for the most consecutive knockouts, with eighteen.

**Forever in My Heart**
Diana Barrymore's (Dorothy Malone) movie debut within the 1958 movie *Too Much, Too Soon.* Produced by Imperial films, the film-within-a-film bombed. (In actuality, Diana Barrymore's debut was in *Eagle Squadron* [1942]. *Forever in My Heart* is a fictitious movie.)

**For Every Young Heart**
Book written by singer Connie Francis and published in 1962.

**Forget-Me-Not**
Billy Bright's (Dick Van Dyke) first full-length comedy, made in 1926, in the 1969 movie *The Comic*.

**"For He's a Jolly Good Fellow"**
Theme song of "The Henry Morgan Show" on radio.

**For Pete's Sake!**
Movie (1966) that starred evangelist Billy Graham, as himself.

**Forsch, Ken and Bob**
(1946– ) (1950– ) First brothers to each throw a no-hit game in the major leagues. Ken's occurred on April 7, 1979, against the Atlanta Braves, and Bob's on March 30, 1978, against the Philadelphia Phillies.

**Forsyte Saga, The**
NET TV series (based on the novels of John Galsworthy) that ran from 1969 to 1970. It was the last major TV series to be filmed in black and white.

**Fort Arnold**
U.S. Army camp where John Winger (Bill Murray) underwent his basic training in the 1981 movie *Stripes*. The movie was actually filmed at Fort Knox, Kentucky.

**Fortas, Abe**
(1910–1982) U.S. Supreme Court Associate Justice from 1965 until he resigned in 1969 at the age of fifty-eight. His nephew, Alan Fortas, was a member of Elvis Presley's inner circle of friends known as the Memphis Mafia. Abe Fortas was portrayed by Jose

Ferrer in the 1980 TV movie *Gideon's Trumpet*.

**Fort Concho**
U.S. Cavalry fort, commanded by Major T. P. Gaskill (Harry Morgan), that Amos (Tim Conway) and Theodore (Don Knotts) accidentally burned down in the 1979 movie *The Apple Dumpling Gang Rides Again*.

**Fort Donelson**
Confederate fort in Tennessee which Simon Buckner surrendered to General Ulysses S. Grant on February 16, 1862. Grant demanded and received "no terms except an unconditional and immediate surrender," after which he was nicknamed by some "Unconditional Surrender" Grant. Buckner, who turned over to Grant fourteen thousand men and their supplies, had previously been a classmate of Grant's at West Point, and in 1885 served as one of the pallbearers at Grant's funeral.

**Forten, Dr. Robert**
Medical technical advisor for the TV series "Marcus Welby, M.D."

**Fort Hays**
U.S. Cavalry fort commanded by Brigadier General Alfred Terry (Robert F. Simon) in the TV series "Custer."

**"For the Last Time"**
Last recording of Bob Wills and His Texas Playboys before Wills's death on May 13, 1975.

**Fort Invisible**
U.S. Cavalry fort attacked by Apache Indians in the 1951 movie *Only the Valiant*.

**Fort McClelland**
U.S. Army post where Laverne DeFazio (Penny Marshall) and Shirley Feeney (Cindy Williams) underwent their basic training on the TV series "Laverne & Shirley."

**Fort McCleod**
U.S. Army fort where Dagwood Bumstead (Arthur Lake) underwent his basic training when he joined the Army reserves in the 1949 movie *Blondie's Hero*.

**Fort Peck Dam**
Montana Dam on the Missouri River that was photographed by Margaret Bourke-White for the very first cover of *Life* magazine on November 23, 1936 (the issue's cover price was ten cents). It is the

largest dam in the United States.

**Fort Point**

U.S. Cavalry fort near San Gil, founded in 1858, where Colonel Jeb Britten (Bruce Bennett) was the commander in the 1951 movie *The Last Outpost*.

**Fort Russell**

U.S. Cavalry outpost south of Cheyenne, Wyoming, commanded by Colonel Thaddeus Gearhardt (Burt Lancaster), in the 1965 movie *The Hallelujah Trail*.

**Fort Sam Houston**

Medical school attended by Colonel Sherman Potter (Harry Morgan) on the TV series "M*A*S*H."

**Fort Shafter**

U.S. Army post from which Private Robert E. Lee Prewitt (Montgomery Clift) transferred to Schofield Barracks in the 1953 movie *From Here to Eternity*.

**Fort Stark**

Cavalry fort where Captain Nathan Brittle (John Wayne) and his men were posted in the 1949 movie *She Wore a Yellow Ribbon* and where Lieutenant Colonel Kirby York (John Wayne) and his men were posted in the 1950 movie *Rio Grande*.

**Fort Travis**

Biloxi, Mississippi, U.S. Army camp where Private Judy Benjamin (Lorna Patterson) underwent basic training on the TV series "Private Benjamin."

**Fortunia**

Foreign country setting of the 1961 movie *Snow White and the Three Stooges*.

**Fort Val Verde**

U.S. Cavalry fort where an experiment of having soldiers ride camels was undertaken in the 1976 movie *Hawmps*.

**Fort Wayne, Indiana**

Hometown of Major Frank Burns (Larry Linville) on the TV series "M*A*S*H."

**Fort Wood**

U.S. Army fort that once stood on the site of the Statue of Liberty.

**Fosse, Bob**

(1927–      ) Director, choreographer, and dancer. In 1973 he won a Tony for *Pippin*, an Emmy for "Liza With a Z," and an Oscar for *Cabaret*. He was loosely portrayed by Roy Scheider as Joe Gideon in the 1979 movie *All That Jazz* (directed by Bob Fosse).

**Foster Grants**
   Sunglasses worn by Jake Blues (John Belushi) in the 1980 movie *The Blues Brothers*.

**Foster, Robert**
   Designer of the first rooster used as a logo for Bantam Books (1945). The rooster has changed design a number of times through the years.

**Fouke**
   Town that is terrorized by a hairy monster in the 1972 movie *Legend of Boggy Creek*.

**Fountain, Deborah Ann**
   Miss New York, who was disqualified from the 1981 Miss U.S.A. Contest because she padded her swimsuit.

**Fountainebleau Hotel**
   Miami hotel where Cha Cha O'Brien (Margarita Sierra) sang in the Boom Boom Room in the TV series "Surfside Six."

**Fountainhead, The**
   Novel by Ayn Rand that is Susan's (Candice Bergen) favorite book in the 1971 movie *Carnal Knowledge*. *The Fountainhead* was made into a film in 1949 starring Gary Cooper and Patricia Neal.

**Four Corners**
   Location in the United States where four states touch: Utah, Colorado, Arizona, and New Mexico.

**Four countries**
   Only four countries have competed in *all* of the modern summer Olympic Games: Australia, Greece, Great Britain, and Switzerland.

**Four for Texas**
   Only movie (1963) in which Frank Sinatra and the Three Stooges appeared together.

**Four Hundred, The**
   Term representing the upper crust of society, coined by Ward McAllister in referring to the number of guests that Mrs. Astor's ballroom could hold.

**Four Jacks and a Six of Hearts**
   Winning poker hand that Henry Gondorff (Paul Newman) used to beat banker Doyle Lonnegan's (Robert Shaw) four nines and a ten of spades, in a game on board the Twentieth Century Limited, in the 1973 movie *The Sting*.

**Fox, Terry**
   Twenty-two-year-old youth who ran halfway across Canada (3,317 miles) in 4½ months on one artificial leg, in 1980, helping in the

raising of over $20 million for cancer research. In 1977, Fox had lost his leg due to cancer, and in July 1981 he died of lung cancer. In late 1981, Rod Stewart and Bernie Taupin wrote the song "Never Give Up on a Dream" in tribute to Terry Fox. Fox was portrayed by one-legged Eric Fryer in the 1983 HBO movie *The Terry Fox Story*.

## Foxx, Redd

(1922–     ) Black comedian (born John Elroy Sanford) who, for years, specialized in "party" records (he recorded a total of fifty-four LPs). In 1964, Foxx* made his TV debut on "The Today Show." His own TV series, "Sanford and Son," premiered in 1972. He was the only entertainer to attend Elvis Presley's wedding to Priscilla Beaulieu, on May 1, 1967.

## Francie

Barbie's cousin, introduced in 1966. In 1967 she was reintroduced as a black doll; however, she did not sell. Christie, another black doll, marketed later, did sell.

## Francis Kane

Hero of Harold Robbins's first novel, *Never Love a Stranger* (1948). Francis Kane is Robbins's real name. In the 1958 movie *Never Love a Stranger*, John Drew Barrymore played Francis Kane, and Dolores Vitina played Frances Kane.

## Frank Black

Name to which Gene Kelly's first agent, Johnny Darrow, tried unsuccessfully to have him change his own actual name.

## "Frankie and Igor at a Rock and Roll Party"

One of several rock 'n' roll single records recorded by poet Rod McKuen under the pseudonym of Bob McFadden in 1962.

## Franklin High School

St. Louis school setting of the TV series "Making the Grade."

## Frankie Jay and the Red Peppers

Name of the jazz band that a group of men claimed they were members of, in order to steal five of Pete Harmond's (Tony Curtis) musical instruments in the 1960 movie *The Rat Race*.

## Frazier, "Smokin'" Joe

(1944–     ) Olympic heavyweight champion (1964), and ex-heavyweight champion (1970–1973). He was introduced in the ring at the Bicentennial bout in the 1976 movie *Rocky*.

---

*In 1939 he won second place on radio's "Major Bowes and His Original Amateur Hour." He played in a bass tub band.

**Fred**

Pet dog of the porter, Mr. Starr (John Carter), on the TV series "The Duchess of Duke Street."

**Fred C. Dobbs**

Name of the prospector played by Humphrey Bogart in the 1948 movie *The Treasure of the Sierra Madre*. It was the assumed name used by Peter J. Ingers (Jerry Lewis) as an Australian sheepherder in the 1969 movie *Hook, Line and Sinker*. In the 1965 movie *The Great Sioux Massacre*, the film's screenwriter is listed as Fred C. Dobbs.

**Frederick, Johnny**

(1901–      ) Brooklyn Dodgers player who, in 1932, set the record for the most pinch-hit home runs in one season, with six.

**Fred Flintstone**

Heavyset, lovable citizen of Bedrock on Hanna-Barbera TV cartoons. His voice was provided by Alan Reed (and later by Henry Corden in "The New Fred and Barney Show").

**Freed, Arthur**

(1891–1973) Hollywood producer and lyricist. He produced musicals for MGM for a number of years. Freed was portrayed by Philip Sterling in the 1978 TV movie *Rainbow* and loosely portrayed by Millard Mitchell, as R. F. Simpson, in the 1952 movie *Singin' in the Rain*.

**Freed, Barry**

Name under which the fugitive 1960s Yippie antiwar leader Abbie Hoffman surfaced on September 3, 1980, at the age of forty-three.

**Freedom One**

Name of the U.S. Air Force DC-9 that brought the fifty-two American hostages to Washington, D.C., from Germany in January 1981.

**Freedom Road**

TV movie (1979) in which Muhammad Ali played the lead role (based on the novel by Howard Fast).

**Freezer, The**

Play that was among the Best Short Plays of 1968. It was written by actress Candice Bergen.

**Fremont**

Missouri town where Fred Sanford (Redd Foxx) married his wife, Elizabeth, in the TV series "Sanford and Son."

**Frémont, John C.**

(1813–1890) American explorer and Army officer nicknamed "the

Pathfinder." While in the U.S. Army, he was court-martialed for mutiny, and convicted, but later his penalty was remitted. He ran for U.S. President on the Republican ticket in 1856. Frémont was portrayed by Dana Andrews in the 1940 movie *Kit Carson*.

## Friday
Day that the singer was fired, as mentioned in the lyrics of Frank Sinatra's 1968 hit record "Cycles." The day is also mentioned in the 1964 hit "Popsicles and Icicles" by the Murmaids.

## Frieda
Little girl introduced in Charles Schulz's comic strip *Peanuts* in 1961. Her pet cat is named Faron (Schulz named him for country singer Faron Young).

   *A Boy Named Charlie Brown* (1969)  Voice of Linda Mendelson
   *Snoopy Come Home* (1972)      Voice of Linda Mendelson
On TV specials voiced by Ann Altieri (1965–67) and Linda Mendelson (1971).

## Friendships, Secrets and Lies
Movie (1979) made for TV that holds the distinction of being the first TV movie with an all-female cast.

## Friends of the Italian Opera
Convention (tenth annual) attended by Spats Columbo (George Raft) at the Seminole-Ritz Hotel in Florida in the 1959 movie *Some Like It Hot*. He and his gang are machine-gunned there.

## Frisky
Little girl's white cat rescued from a tree by Superman (Christopher Reeve) in the 1978 movie *Superman*.

## Frou-Frou
Beatrice Reiner's pet Pekinese dog in the 1935 movie *A Night at the Opera*.

## Fruit, Garden and Home
Original title of the magazine *Better Homes and Gardens*, when it came into existence in 1922 (the same year as *Readers Digest*).

## Frye, Marquette
Black man who was arrested by CHP officer Lee Minikus on August 11, 1965. It was over this incident that the Watts Riots began.

## Fugi
Pet dog of the Osmond Brothers on the TV cartoon series "The Osmonds"; its voice was provided by Paul Frees.

## Fujimoto, Shun
Japanese gymnast who won a gold medal in the rings competition in

the 1976 Olympic games with his leg in a cast (he had just broken it).

**Full House**

J. Geils Band's 1972 record album that shows the poker hand of three jacks, a queen of hearts, and a king of spades on the cover, obviously *not* a full house.

**Funk, Casimir**

Polish-American chemist who, in 1912, discovered vitamins.

**Fuzz**

Ziggy's pet dog in the newspaper cartoon "Ziggy" by Tom Wilson.

# G

**G-BAKS**

Registration letters of Universal Imports' red and white helicopter, which James Bond (Roger Moore) flew, dropping Ernst Stavro Blofeld into a huge chimney, in the prologue of the 1981 movie *For Your Eyes Only*.

**Gabriel**

Archangel who told Mary that she would become the mother of Jesus Christ.

**Gadsby**

Novel containing fifty thousand words, written in 1939 by Ernest Vincent. In the entire text there is not one letter *e*, the most commonly used letter in the English alphabet.

**"Galactica"**

Theme song of the TV series "Battlestar Galactica," composed by Stu Phillips and the show's creator, Glen A. Larson (ex-member of the vocal group The Four Preps).

**Galan, Augie**

Chicago Cubs baseball player who sportscaster Ronald Reagan told his WHO radio audience was fouling off pitch after pitch, during a six-minute-forty-five-second broadcast blackout in which the reprints of the game over the telegraph went dead. (In actuality, Galan popped out on his first pitch).

**Galaxy Pictures**

Hollywood motion picture studio headed by Kenneth Regan (Joseph Cotten) in the 1966 movie *The Oscar*.

**Gallant Lad and Avalanche**

Two racehorses that were switched for each other on board ship in the 1936 movie *Charlie Chan at the Racetrack*.

**"Gallant Men"**
Recording made by Senator Everett McKinley Dirksen for Capitol Records. The record made the *Billboard* Hot 100 chart in 1967, peaking at Number 29. The speech was written by CBS newsman Charles Osgood.

**Garden of Allah**
Hollywood hotel on Sunset Boulevard, where author F. Scott Fitzgerald first met columnist Sheilah Graham in 1937. The hotel, which was originally the home of actress Alla Nazimova, was torn down in 1959. The hotel was the subject of a book written by Sheilah Graham.

**Garrett's Barn**
Site located fifty miles south of Washington, D.C., where President Abraham Lincoln's assassin, John Wilkes Booth, was trapped and shot to death (possibly by Sergeant Boston Corbett), on April 26, 1865.

**Garvey, Steven Patrick**
(1948–    ) Only living baseball player who has a public school named after him: Steve Garvey Junior High School, in Lindsay, California. Steve played an extra in the 1974 movie *The Godfather Part II*.

**Gashouse Gang**
Nickname conferred upon the 1931–1932 Toronto Maple Leafs hockey team.

**Gates, David**
Singer of the theme song of the 1977 movie *The Goodbye Girl*. He performed with the rock group "Bread."

**Gates, Walter**
Piano player on Danny and the Juniors' number-one hit song, in 1957, "At the Hop."

**Gatlin Brothers**
Country-Western singing group; the brothers' first names are Larry, Rudy, and Steve.

**Gator Motel**
Texas motel home of Beau "Bandit" Darber (Burt Reynolds) in the 1980 movie *Smokey and the Bandit II*.

**Gatsby**
Yacht that two Japanese Zero aircraft strafed in the 1980 movie *The*

*Final Countdown.*

**Gauric, Gabbo**

Only person to have kicked goals in both the National Football League and the North American Soccer League.

**Gay Deceivers**

Euphemism used by Amanda for the word "falsies" in Tennessee Williams' play *The Glass Menagerie*.

**Gay Lady**

Dodge City saloon run by Jeff Surrett (Bruce Cabot) in the 1939 movie *Dodge City*.

**GAXZN**

Registration number of the police aircraft flown by Sergeant Howie (Edward Woodward) in the 1973 movie *The Wicker Man*.

**Gee and haw**

Words said in order to instruct a horse to turn right or left, respectively.

**Gehrig, Adeline**

National Women's Foil Champion, 1920–1923. She was the sister of baseball great Lou Gehrig.

**Gehrig, Eleanor**

Wife of New York Yankee first baseman Lou Gehrig, for eight years. She wrote the memoir *My Luke and I*. Eleanor was portrayed by Teresa Wright in the 1942 movie *The Pride of the Yankees*, and by Blythe Danner in the 1978 TV movie *A Love Affair: The Eleanor and Lou Gehrig Story*.

**Gehrke, Fred**

Los Angeles Rams player who, in 1948, designed the first logo for a football helmet. Gehrke later became general manager of the Denver Broncos.

**General Belgrano**

Argentine cruiser that was sunk by the British submarine *Conqueror* on May 2, 1982. The vessel had previously been named the USS *Phoenix*, and had been present at Pearl Harbor on December 7, 1941. It was the first known ship ever to be sunk by a nuclear submarine.

**General Benjamin "Mustard Ben" Kaye**

U.S. Army officer with whom Francis the Talking Mule once served at the Burma Bridge. When Francis learned to talk, he decided to imitate the general's voice. Played by Chill Wills in the 1954 movie *Francis Joins the WACS*. (Chill Wills also provided

Francis's voice).

**General Della Rovere**
Italian motion picture (1960), directed by Roberto Rossellini, that was the first movie shown in the White House after John F. Kennedy became President of the United States.

**General Hospital**
TV soap opera watched by Jimmy Smith (Franklyn Seales) in the 1979 movie *The Onion Field*.

**General Indemnity Insurance**
Insurance company for which Bill Gruen (Robert Duvall) worked in the 1981 movie *The Pursuit of D. B. Cooper*.

**General "Iron Guts" McGinty**
U.S. Army officer who visited Fort Baxter, Kansas. McGinty, who closely resembled Private Duane Doberman, was played by Jim Williams on the TV series "You'll Never Get Rich" (later titled "The Phil Silvers Show").

**General Zod**
Superman's arch-nemesis, played by Terance Stamp, in the 1978 movie *Superman* and in its 1981 sequel, *Superman II*.

**Genesis**
Scientific project that creates new life on desolate planets in the 1982 movie *Star Trek II: The Wrath of Khan*.

**Genesis 6:12, 13**
Bible verses used as an epigraph in George Pal's 1951 movie *When Worlds Collide*.

**Genevieve**
Kathy Anderson's (Lauren Chapin) doll on the TV series "Father Knows Best." It was also the name of Jill Young's (Terry Moore) doll in the 1949 movie *Mighty Joe Young*.

**Genova**
One of the lifeboats belonging to the ocean liner *Andrea Doria*, which sank on July 26, 1956. The boat was discovered in some reeds on a secluded beach near New York City in August 1981, by a power station worker named Fred Lennox.

**George**
Alfred's pet mouse, put into the beer stein of the Kandi Grand Master (Walter Massey) at the Silent Woman Inn in the 1980 movie *Happy Birthday to Me*.

**George**
Name of the goldfish in the Larabee Estate fountain in the 1954

movie *Sabrina*.

**George**
Milkman played by Herb Vigran on Kellogg's Graham Crackers TV advertisements.

**George and Mildred**
British TV series upon which the U.S. series "The Ropers" was based. (It was a spinoff of "Man About the House," upon which the U.S. series "Three's Company" was based).

**George Chapstick**
Name that George Willig, who climbed the World Trade Center, used in the Chapstick TV commercials.

**George, Robert**
Official Presidential Santa Claus since President Dwight D. Eisenhower named him to that post.

**George Spedlap**
Rita Marlowe's (Jayne Mansfield) long-lost love, played by Groucho Marx in the 1957 movie *Will Success Spoil Rock Hunter?*

**Gertrude**
Norman Thayer's (Henry Fonda) canoe in the 1981 movie *On Golden Pond*.

**"Get Along, Little Dogie"**
Song that Public Enemy Number One, John Dillinger, sang during his escape from prison on March 3, 1934.

**"Get Back"**
Song performed by the Beatles (with Billy Preston) in the 1970 movie *Let It Be*, by Rod Stewart in the 1976 movie *All This and World War II*, and by Billy Preston in the 1978 movie *Sgt. Pepper's Lonely Hearts Club Band*.

**Get Outta My Hair**
Phoenix, Arizona, Cortez High School newspaper column written by musician Alice Cooper (Vincent Furnier) as a student.

**Gets Ya There and Gets Ya Back**
Advertising slogan for the Model T Ford.

**Giacobbo, Placido**
Al Capone's chauffeur.

**Gibb, Russ**
Disc jockey at Detroit radio station WKNR-FM who, on October 12, 1969, along with his listening audience, began compiling the many little "clues" in the Beatles songs and on their album jackets to prove that Paul McCartney was dead. He deduced that Paul had been killed in an automobile accident on November 9, 1966.

**Gibbs, Lois**

Niagara Falls, New York, housewife who began a campaign to draw government attention to a chemical hazard at the Love Canal. Her persistence finally led to the U.S. government's buying the houses of eight hundred families. She was portrayed by Marsha Mason in the 1982 TV movie *Lois Gibbs and the Love Canal*. The movie was based on Lois Gibbs's autobiography, *Love Canal, My Story*.

**Gibbson, Tommy and Mike**

Only brothers in the Boxing Hall of Fame.

**Gibson, Charles Dana**

(1867–1944) American illustrator and creator, in 1912, of the Gibson Girl. He modeled the first Gibson Girl after his wife, Irene Langhorne. Dana was portrayed by Richard Travis in the 1955 movie *The Girl in the Red Velvet Swing*.

**Gibraltar of the Pacific**

Nickname given to Diamond Head in the Hawaiian Islands.

**Giddyap Gourmet**

Television chef Randy Robinson (Charles Nelson Reilly) on the TV series "Arnie."

**Gif me a viskey, ginger ale on the side, an' don't be stingy, baby!**

Greta Garbo's first words ever uttered in a movie, *Anna Christie* (1930), which was advertised with the phrase "Garbo Talks!"

**Gigot**

Movie (1962) directed by Gene Kelly, starring Jackie Gleason as a deaf mute. The film was taken from an original story written by Gleason.

**Gig Young**

Role played by actor Byron Barr in the 1945 movie *The Gay Sisters*. It was this name that Barr chose as his stage name after making the film.

**Gilbert**

Lanville County town one mile from the Chicken Ranch, in the 1982 movie *The Best Little Whorehouse in Texas*. The weekly town newspaper was the *Gazette*.

**Gilberto, Astrud**

Female singer on Stan Getz's 1964 hit recording "The Girl from Ipanema."

**Gilda**

Movie (1946) starring Rita Hayworth and Glenn Ford that was being shown on TV in the room of Diane Barrie (Maggie Smith) in the 1978 movie *California Suite* and on the TV in Georgia Hines's (Marsha Mason) apartment in the 1981 movie *Only When I Laugh*. A section of it is performed by Lynda Carter as Rita Hayworth in the 1983 TV movie *Rita Hayworth: The Love Goddess*.

**Gilda Badney**

Mysterious woman, played by Madeline Kahn, in the 1978 movie *The Cheap Detective*. Her aliases in the film were Denise Manderley, Natasha Oublenskaya, Sophia DeVega, Wanda Coleman, Chloe LaMarr, Alma Chatmers, Vivien Purcell, Lady Edwina Morgan St. Paul, and Diane Glucksman.

**Girad**

Puppet giraffe on the 1952 TV show "Willie Wonderful."

**"Girl from Ipanema, The"**

Song being played in the elevator of the Richard J. Daley Building in Chicago, as Jake and Elwood Blues rode inside (up to the eleventh floor) in the 1980 movie *The Blues Brothers*.

**Girls Want to Go to a Nightclub, The**

Title of the first episode of the TV series "I Love Lucy," first broadcast at 9:00 P.M., Monday, October 15, 1951.

**Girl Who Stole the Eiffel Tower, The**

Movie screenplay being written by Richard Bensen (William Holden) and typed by Miss Gabrielle Simpson (Audrey Hepburn), in the 1964 movie *Paris When It Sizzles*. Frank Sinatra sang the movie's theme song, "The Girl Who Stole the Eiffel Tower Also Stole My Heart."

**G.I.'s General**

Nickname of U.S. Army general Omar Nelson Bradley.

**"Give a Little Bit"**

Song by Supertramp heard on Lois Lane's (Margot Kidder) car radio, just before the earthquake began, in the 1978 movie *Superman*.

**Gladiators**

San Francisco street gang headed by Orenthal James "O.J." Simpson, when he was thirteen years old.

**Gladney, Edna**

Founder of an adoption agency foundation in Fort Worth, Texas. She was portrayed by Greer Garson in the 1941 movie *Blossoms in the Dust*.

**Glendora**

Tiny Mediterranean kingdom that was the setting of the TV series "The Quest."

**Glen Hamilton**
Role played by Bert Convy on the TV soap "Love of Life."

**Glenn, Howard**
Last professional football player to die in a football game. As a player for the New York Titans, he received a broken neck in a game at Houston on October 9, 1960.

**Global 505**
Arriving Boeing 747 flight to Las Vegas that almost collided with Ralph Hinckley (William Katt) on an episode of the TV series "The Greatest American Hero."

**Globatron Corporation**
Company that was the setting of the short-lived 1977 TV series "All That Glitters."

**Globe**
Culver City taxicab company featured in the 1981 movie *Under the Rainbow*. Their cabs were painted yellow.

**Globe Cinema**
Scottish movie theater in which the German spy Henry Faber (Donald Sutherland) watched a newsreel in the 1981 movie *Eye of the Needle*, based on the novel by Ken Follet.

**Globe Pictures**
Hollywood motion picture studio headed by Mike Kirsch (Rod Steiger) in the 1967 TV movie *The Movie Maker*.

**Gloomy Gus**
Pappy Poopdeck's boat, on which Popeye was born during a typhoon off the coast of Santa Monica, California. (Popeye is perpetually thirty-four years old).

**Gloria**
Role played by Marilyn Chambers in the X-rated movie *Behind the Green Door*.

**Gloria Schaeffer**
Maiden name of Felix Unger's wife, who threw him out of their apartment on November 13. She was played by Janis Hansen on the TV series "The Odd Couple."

**Glory for Me**
Novel by MacKinlay Kantor that became the basis for the 1946 movie *The Best Years of Our Lives*.

**"Glory of Love, The"**
Song composed in 1936 by Billy Hill. It was sung by a chorus over the opening credits of the 1967 Spencer Tracy/Katharine Hepburn movie *Guess Who's Coming to Dinner?* The song was also played

by a dance band at a college dance in the 1973 movie *The Way We Were*.

**Glory Prison**

Prison where Mattis Appleyard (James Stewart) spent forty years for the theft of $25,452.32, before being released in 1935, in the 1971 movie *Fool's Parade*.

**"Glowworm"**

Tune played by Laura Petrie's (Mary Tyler Moore) jewelry box on the TV series "The Dick Van Dyke Show."

**Gluck, Alma**

(1884–1938) Singer of the 1915 hit "Carry Me Back to Old Virginny," the first single recording to sell more than a million copies. Alma Gluck is the mother of actor Efrem Zimbalist, Jr.

**Goat Gap Texas Chili**

Chili bean dish created by President Ronald Reagan's press secretary, Jim Brady.

**"Gob Is a Slob, A"**

Original title of the 1952 Doris Day hit song "A Guy Is a Guy."

**Godfather, The**

Best-selling novel by Mario Puzo that Theresa Dunn (Diane Keaton\*) was reading in the 1977 movie *Looking for Mr. Goodbar*. A copy of the paperback can be seen on a shelf in the home of Roy Fehler (Stacy Keach) in the 1972 movie *The New Centurions*.

**Godfather Part II, The**

Movie (1974) that won the Academy Award for Best Picture. It became the first sequel film to win such an award.

**Godolphin College**

Setting of the 1968 Walt Disney movie *Blackbeard's Ghost*.

**"Go for It"**

Theme song of the 1979 movie *Fast Break*, sung by Billy Preston and Syreeta. (Syreeta Wright was once married to Stevie Wonder.)

**Gogo**

Chimpanzee that appeared in the 1936 Dorothy Lamour movie *The Jungle Princess*. During the filming, he scratched one man's back so badly that the man died.

**Gold**

Color of the helmets of the football players of both Annapolis and West Point.

---

\*Diane Keaton appeared in the movies *The Godfather* (1972) and *The Godfather Part II* (1974).

**Golden Cherry Motel**
Henleyville motel where union organizer Rubin Washopsky (Ron Leiberman) stayed, in room 31, in the 1979 movie *Norma Rae*.

**Golden, Colorado**
Site of the Coors brewery.

**Golden Gate**
First horse that Willie Shoemaker rode to victory (April 20, 1949) in his career. It was a nine-to-one shot.

**Golden Horseshoe**
Western saloon in Disneyland's Frontierland where Steve Martin has appeared as a comedian.

**Golden, Howard, and Sebastian Leone**
Two borough presidents of Brooklyn whose names have been shown on signs in the credits of the TV series "Welcome Back Kotter."

**Golden Muscle**
Brand of mustard used in Rough House's Cafe in the 1980 movie *Popeye*.

**Golden Poppy Cafe**
Small Monterey restaurant where Suzy (Debra Winger) worked in the 1982 movie *Cannery Row*.

**Golden Turkey Awards**
Award created in 1980 by humorous writers Harry and Michael Medved for the worst movies, actors, and actresses that Hollywood has ever produced.

**Goldie**
Smokey the Bear's mate, who mothered their son, Smokey II.

**Goldman, Sylvan**
Inventor of the shopping cart, introduced in 1937.

**Gold Rush**
California town that was the landing place of the alien family in the 1981 movie *Earthbound*.

**Goliath**
Sideshow gorilla in the 1954 3-D movie *Gorilla at Large*.

**Gomez, Lefty**
(1908–     ) New York Yankees player who was the winning pitcher in the very first All-Star Game, played at Comiskey Park on July 6, 1933, when the American League won 4–2.

**"Goodbye Blues"**
Theme song of the Mills Brothers, which was first recorded by them in 1931.

**Goodbye from Joe Young**
Closing words on screen of the 1949 movie *Mighty Joe Young*, used in place of "The End."

**Good Company**
Interview TV series (1967) hosted by attorney F. Lee Bailey.

**Good for Nothing**
Charlie Chaplin film during which W. C. Fields (Rod Steiger) got sick while watching it being shown in the 1976 movie *W. C. Fields and Me*. Fields envied Chaplin's talents.

**Goodman Trio, Benny**
Benny Goodman, clarinet; Teddy Wilson, piano; Gene Krupa, drums. The Benny Goodman quartet used the additional services of Lionel Hampton on vibes.

**"Goodness Gracious Me"**
Duet by Peter Sellers and Sophia Loren that went to number four on the British charts in 1960.

**Goodness had nothing to do with it . . .**
Line said by Mae West in the 1932 movie *Night After Night*, and also said by Steve McQueen in the 1962 movie *The War Lover*.

**Good night and May God Bless, thank you . . .**
Comedian Richard "Red" Skelton's sign-off on radio and TV.

**"Good Night My Someone"**
Ballad sung in *The Music Man* which has the same tune as the faster-tempo song "76 Trombones," both of which were composed by Meredith Willson.

**"Goodnight, Sweetheart, Goodnight"**
Closing song of the rock 'n' roll group Sha Na Na on their TV series.

**Good Prospect**
Horse from which Prince Charles fell twice within four days in March 1981, during steeplechases.

**Goose Lodge 17**
Fraternity lodge where Joe Baxton (Richard Pryor) ripped off a money-making trapezoid scheme for $15,000 in the 1981 movie *Bustin' Loose*.

**Go Quietly . . . Or Else**
Memoirs (1980) of ex-U.S. Vice-president Spiro T. Agnew.

**Gordon Sims**
Real name of WKRP disc jockey Venus Flytrap, played by Tim Reid in the TV series "WKRP in Cincinnati."

**Goresh, Paul**

Photographer who, earlier in the day of December 8, 1980, photographed John Lennon autographing his *Double Fantasy* album for Mark David Chapman outside the Dakota Apartments in New York City. Later that day, Chapman shot and killed Lennon.

**Gorman, Miki**

Japanese long-distance runner who began running seriously at the age of thirty-three. She was AAU Best Runner of the Year for 1976. In 1977 she won both the New York and the Boston marathons and is the only woman to have won both races twice. She was portrayed by Yoko Shimada in the 1981 movie *My Champion*.

**Gort Baringa . . .**

Words spoken by Klaatu to command his robot, Gort, to stand guard outside their spacecraft in the 1951 movie *The Day the Earth Stood Still*.

**Gortner, Marjoe**

Child evangelist who eventually rejected the ministry to become an actor. He portrayed himself in the 1972 movie *Marjoe*. His first name is derived from a combination of the names Mary and Joseph.

**Governor Garfield Burns**

Governor of Oklahoma played by ex-Georgia governor Lester Maddox in the 1975 TV movie *The Kansas City Massacre*.

**Governor Stanford**

Central Pacific Railroad's first locomotive, built in Pennsylvania in 1862. It was transported around Cape Horn in 1863 on board the sailing ship *Herald of the Morning* and was named for California Governor Leland Stanford.

**Governing Texas**

Title of the book that J.R. Ewing (Larry Hagman) was reading when Sue Ellen Ewing (Linda Gray) came back to Southfork on the TV series "Dallas."

**Go West**

Marx Brothers movie (1940) that is advertised on a poster on the cover of Elton John's 1973 album *Don't Shoot Me, I'm Only the Piano Player*. The movie was advertised on a theater marque in the 1973 movie *The Way We Were* (also advertised was the 1945 Paul Muni movie *Counter Attack*, in addition to a Donald Duck cartoon).

**G-Players**

Men who played for the 1934 Detroit Tigers and are now members of the Baseball Hall of Fame: Hank Greenberg (first base); Charlie Gehriager (second base); and Goose Goslin (left field).

**Grace Bolton**
Role played by Jill Clayburgh in the TV soap "Search for Tomorrow."

**Graceland Cemetery**
Chicago graveyard where two heavyweight boxing champions are buried within two hundred feet of one another: Bob Fitzsimmons (1862–1917)* and Jack Johnson (1878–1946).

**Grace, Martin, and Wendy Leach**
Stunt doubles for Harrison Ford and Karen Allen in the 1981 movie *Raiders of the Lost Ark*. Martin Grace also doubled for Roger Moore in *Moonraker* (1979) and *The Spy Who Loved Me* (1977).

**Graham, June**
Betty Furness's stand-in, who couldn't open the door of the Westinghouse refrigerator during a live commercial on early TV in the 1950s. The door would only open when the appliance was plugged in. At the time that June attempted to open it, the plug had fallen out of the wall socket.

**Gramaldi, Joseph**
(1778–1821) Theater clown who was the first man to wear a clown suit and to paint his face. He played a character named Joey, a name that is synonymous with the word *clown*, even today.

**Granby's Green Acres**
Radio series (1950s) starring Gale Gordon, which was the basis of the TV series "Green Acres."

**Grand Hotel**
Old hotel located in Chicago, where Richard Collier (Christopher Reeve) goes back in time, from 1980 to 1912. The transformation took place in room 313 of the hotel, where it was achieved through the power of suggestion (by use of a Dynarange Recorder and 1912 replicas). Collier meets and falls in love with Elise McKenna (Jane Seymour), who was in room 117. McKenna checked into the hotel on June 27, 1912, while Collier checked in at 9:18 A.M. in room 416, the next day, in the 1980 movie *Somewhere in Time*. Collier died in Room 313.

**Grand National**
Annual steeplechase held at Aintree, England, since 1839. The

---

*In 1973 it was discovered that the name on the tombstone was erroneously spelled Fitzimmons, after which it was changed.

horses make thirty jumps over the four-mile, 856-yard course.

## Grand Slam of Bowling

All-Star World's Invitational, PBA National, and ABC Masters Tournament.

## Grand slams

Only three baseball players have hit grand slams in two consecutive innings: Jim Gentile (Baltimore) May 9, 1961; Jim Northrup (Detroit) June 24, 1968; and Frank Robinson (Baltimore) June 26, 1970.

## Grand slams in a single game

Of the seven major-league players who have hit two grand slams in a single game, three are named Jim: Jim Tabor (Boston) July 4, 1939; Jim Gentile (Baltimore) May 9, 1961; and Jim Northrup (Detroit) June 24, 1968.

Of the nine major-league players who have hit grand slams in consecutive games, four are named Jim: Jimmy Bannon (Boston) August 6–7, 1897; Jimmy Sheckard (Brooklyn) September 23–24, 1901; Jimmy Foxx (Boston) May 20–21, 1940; and Jim Busby (Cleveland) July 5–6, 1956.

## Granite Life Insurance and Casualty Company

Insurance company for which Peter J. Ingers (Jerry Lewis) worked in the 1969 movie *Hook, Line and Sinker.*

## Granny

Owner of Tweety Bird in Warner Bros. Merrie Melodies cartoons, whose voice was that of June Foray. Debuted in *A Tale of Two Kitties* (November 21, 1942).

## Grant, Cary

(1904–      ) Hollywood actor born Archibald Leach in Bristol, England. After moving to the United States in 1920, he spent time as a lifeguard at Coney Island, then sang in twelve operettas, finally making his first movie, *This Is the Night,* in 1932. He made his last movie, *Walk, Don't Run,* in 1966. His wives have been Virginia Cherrill (1933–35); Barbara Hutton (1942–45)*; Betsy Drake (1949–59); Dyan Cannon (1965–68); and Barbara Harris, whom he married in 1978. He was been portrayed in the movies by Bert Convy in *Act One* (1963) and by John Gavin in the 1980 TV movie *Sophia Loren: Her Own Story.*

---

*Barbara Hutton, heiress to the Woolworth fortune, has been called the world's wealthiest woman.

**Grant, Len**
Onetime intercollegiate heavyweight boxing champion and football player at NYU, who, while playing golf, was struck by a bolt of lightning and killed.

**Grant Memorial Hospital**
New York city setting of the TV series "Nurse."

**Grave Digger Jones and Coffin Ed Johnson**
Two black detectives played by Godfrey Cambridge and Raymond St. Jacques in the 1970 movie *Cotton Comes to Harlem* and in the 1972 sequel *Come Back Charleston Blue*.

**Gray, Dolly**
(1897–1953) Washington pitcher who walked a record number of men in a single inning, on August 28, 1909. In the second inning of a double-header, Gray walked eight men.

**Gray, Hugh**
First person to photograph the Loch Ness Monster, near Inverness, Scotland, on November 12, 1933.

**Gray, Janice**
Policewoman who, on June 13, 1977, became the first woman law enforcement officer in the United States to shoot and kill a person in the line of duty.

**Grayson, Admiral Cary**
President Woodrow Wilson's personal physician. He was portrayed by Stanley Ridges in the 1944 movie *Wilson*.

**Graziano, Rocky**
(1922–    ) Middleweight boxing champion, born Rocco Barbella, in New York City. He won the title from Tony Zale in 1946, only to lose it to him in 1948. After defending the title twenty-one times, he finally lost to Sugar Ray Robinson, by a KO in the third round, on April 16, 1952. Rocky was portrayed by Paul Newman in the 1956 movie *Somebody Up There Likes Me*.

**Greaser's Hall**
Hangout of the rock group Sha Na Na, on their TV series.

**Greaseweed City**
Destination of Flower Belle Lee (Mae West) and Cuthbert J. Twillie (W. C. Fields) in the 1940 movie *My Little Chickadee*.

**Great American Carnival**
Traveling carnival for which Frankie (Gary Busey) worked as a clown in the 1980 movie *Carny*.

**Great Compromiser, The**
Appellation of Henry Clay.

**Great Neck, Long Island**
New York setting of the 1972 TV series "The Don Rickles Show."

**Greeley, Horace**
(1811–1872) American journalist and political leader. In 1841 he founded the *New York Tribune*. It was Greeley who signed Confederate President Jefferson Davis's bail bond after the Civil War. Greeley was nominated for U.S. President in 1872, but lost. He is known for his saying "Go west, young man, go west," which was actually coined by newsman John B. Soule, in 1851. Greeley was portrayed by Davison Clark in the 1934 movie *The Mighty Barnum*.

**Green Book**
Washington, D.C.'s, social register.

**Greenbrier**
Miss Hannah Hunter's (Constance Towers) Southern plantation, from where she was taken prisoner by Colonel John Marlowe (John Wayne) in the 1959 movie *The Horse Soldiers*.

**Green, Ernest**
First black to graduate from Central High School in Little Rock, Arkansas, in 1958. He was portrayed by Calvin Levels in the 1981 TV movie *Crisis at Central High*.

**"Green Grow the Lilacs"**
Popular song sung by the cowboys in the early West. The Mexicans began calling cowboys "gringos" from the first two words of the song.

**"Green Leaves of Summer"**
Theme song of the 1960 movie *The Alamo*.

**Green Manors**
Mental institution where Dr. Constance Peterson (Ingrid Bergman) worked as a psychologist in the 1945 movie *Spellbound*.

**Green Mill Cocktail Lounge**
Chicago bar owned by Frank (James Caan) in the 1981 movie *Thief*. He later blew it up.

**Greenwood, Chester**
Inventor of earmuffs, in 1873.

**Greenwood, John**
Dentist who fashioned President George Washington's false teeth.

**Gregory**
Wesley Winfield's (Billy Gray) pet turkey in the 1954 movie *By the Light of the Silvery Moon*.

**Gregory, Jim**
First white athlete to play football (third-string quarterback) at the

Louisiana college, Grambling, beginning in 1968. He was portrayed by Bruce Jenner in the 1981 TV movie *Grambling's White Tiger*.

**Gregory Moxley**

Corpse played by Errol Flynn in the 1935 movie *The Case of the Curious Bride*.

**Gregory, Texas—1944**

Setting of the 1981 movie *Raggedy Man*. The first scene, however, took place in Edna, Texas, in 1940.

**Gregson, Richard**

Man to whom actress Natalie Wood was married (1969) in between her two marriages to actor Robert Wagner, the first from 1957 to 1962, and the second from 1970 until her death in 1981.

**Greyfish, USS**

World War II submarine commanded by Lieutenant Commander Barney Doyle (Glenn Ford) in the 1958 movie *Torpedo Run*.

**Grey Ghost**

Name of Charlie Callahan's (Robert Blake) gray GMC General diesel truck in the 1980 movie *Coast to Coast*. The printing on the door read SUPER C TRUCKING, MASSILLON, OHIO 555-8603.

**Grey, Sir Edward**

(1862–1933) Grandson of Sir George Grey. He consolidated the Triple Entente that united Great Britain, France, and Russia. He also helped to negotiate the 1919 peace settlement. Grey was portrayed by Sir Ralph Richardson in the 1969 movie *Oh! What a Lovely War*.

**Griffin, Archie**

Ohio State running back who became the only two-time winner of the Heisman Trophy (1974 and 1975).

**Griffin, Merv**

(1925– ) Onetime singer with the Freddy Martin band and later TV talk-show host from 1962. In 1948 he recorded his theme song, "I've Got a Lovely Bunch of Coconuts" (for which he received only fifty dollars). He has appeared in several movies. In the 1953 movie *I Confess*, Merv Griffin's voice can be heard over a telephone. He appeared in the 3-D movie *Phantom of the Rue Morgue* (1954).

**Grigg, Charles L.**

Man who introduced the soft drink 7-Up, in October 1929. It was originally called Bib-Label Lithiated Lemon-Lime Soda.

**Grille**

Adolf Hitler's personal yacht.

**Grodd**

Super-gorilla that appears in Flash comic book stories.

**Gross, Gary**

Photographer who took nude photographs of Brooke Shields when she was only ten years old. In November 1981, Miss Shields's mother took him to court to halt publication of the photos, but lost the case.

**Grossmobile**

Ross Whitman's (Marc McClure) customized automobile in the short-lived TV series "California Fever."

**GRosvenor 7060**

Frances Andros's (Elizabeth Taylor) London home phone number in the 1963 movie *The VIPs*. In actuality, it was the phone number of MGM's London office.

**Grove Falls**

Town setting of the 1953 TV series "My Son Jeep."

**"Guantanamera"**

Hit recording (1966) by the Sandpipers. Two other versions of the song can be heard in the 1974 movie *The Godfather Part II*, first by a roving band and next by an orchestra at a New Year's Eve party in Havana.

**Guardian**

Russian computer in the 1970 movie *Colossus: The Forbin Project*.

**Guardian Angel, The**

Canadian movie (1978) that starred Margaret Trudeau, estranged wife of Canadian Prime Minister Pierre Trudeau.

**Guiding Light, The**

Soap opera that has had the longest continuous network (radio and TV) run. It debuted on radio in 1935 and transferred to TV in 1952, where it is still on the air today.

**Guido Panzini**

Italian golf pro played by comedian Pat Harrington on "The Steve Allen Show."

**Gullfire**

Glider on which Snake Plissken (Kurt Russell) flew into Manhattan Island in order to rescue the President of the United States (Donald

Pleasence) in the 1981 movie *Escape From New York*.

**Gun Fury (1953) and Gorilla at Large (1954)**

Two movies filmed in 3-D in which Lee Marvin appeared.

**Gunga Din**

Indian waterboy who was loyal to the British soldiers in India. The subject of the Rudyard Kipling poem "Gunga Din" and his 1887 story "Soldiers Three." He died blowing his trumpet, which warned the British of an ambush. Gunga Din was played by Sam Jaffe in the 1939 movie *Gunga Din* and by Sammy Davis, Jr., as Jonah Williams, in the 1962 movie *Sergeants 3*. Jim Backus provided his voice as Mr. Magoo in a cartoon version of the classic tale.

**Gunn, Richard**

British featherweight boxer who, in the 1908 Olympic Games in London, won a gold medal, thus becoming, at age thirty-eight, the oldest man to win an Olympic boxing title.

**Guthrie, Arlo**

(1947–     ) Folksinger son of Woody Guthrie. He introduced his classic song "Alice's Rock 'n' Roll Restaurant" at the 1967 Newport Folk Festival, and recorded the 1972 hit song "City of New Orleans." He portrayed himself in the 1969 movie *Alice's Restaurant* and was portrayed by Calvin Butler in the 1970 movie *Chicago 70*.

**Guy Named Joe, A**

Movie (1943) starring Spencer Tracy and written by Dalton Trumbo, which was playing on the Freeling's TV set in the 1982 movie *Poltergeist*.

**Gwinnett, Button**

(1735–1777) One of the fifty-six signers of the Declaration of Independence. Because he was killed in a duel one year after signing the document, his signature is considered one of the most valuable in the world. William Shakespeare's signature is the most valuable.

**Gygax, Gary**

Ex–shoe repairman who invented the game Dungeons & Dragons.

# H

**H&R Block**
Henry and Richard Block, tax experts who founded their multimillion-dollar company in 1956.

**Hadaway, William S.**
American inventor of the electric stove, in 1896.

**Haddix, Harvey**
(1925– ) Pittsburgh Pirates pitcher who, on May 26, 1959, threw a perfect game for twelve innings. He lost the game in the thirteenth inning when Joe Adcock of the Braves hit a home run. Adcock passed Hank Aaron, who was on base, and was declared out and his home run was downgraded to a double. Felix Mantilla, also on base, scored the winning run.

**Haddonfield**
Illinois town setting of the 1978 movie *Halloween* and the 1981 sequel, *Halloween II*.

**Haggard, Merle Ronald**
(1937– ) Country artist who, as a youth in 1957, was charged with attempted burglary and sentenced to six months to fifteen years at San Quentin. He was released in 1963. Haggard was in the audience when Johnny Cash went there to perform. He was finally given a complete pardon in 1972, by California governor Ronald Reagan. After becoming a successful artist, Haggard has reached superstar status. In 1970 he recorded the controversial record "Okie From Muskogee." In 1981, Merle Haggard published his autobiography, titled *Sing Me Back Home*. Merle Haggard was the first country artist to be featured on the cover of *Downbeat* magazine.

**Haggerville**
Wyoming town in which boxer James J. Corbett (Steve Oliver) beat up Tom Horn (Steve McQueen) in the 1980 movie *Tom Horn*.

**Haines, Byron**
University of Washington halfback who, during a game against Southern California, on December 7, 1935, scored all the game's points. He scored a touchdown for Washington and, in addition, a safety for Southern California.

**Haircut, The**
Nickname of TV comedian Garry Moore, who for years wore a crewcut.

**Halaby, Elizabeth**
American woman who married King Hussein of Jordan in 1978, thus becoming Queen Nur.

**Haley Green**
First Los Angeles woman firefighter, played by Martina Deignan in the TV series "Code Red."

**Half a Sixpence**
Musical based on the 1905 book *Kipps,* written by H. G. Wells.

**Halijian, Peter Paul**
Founder of the Peter Paul Candy Company, manufacturer of Mounds (1921) and Almond Joy (1947).

**Hall, Charles B.**
First black American pilot in World War II who was officially credited with shooting down a German plane.

**Hall of Fame for Famous Legs**
Society created in 1980. Its first inductee was dancer Cyd Charisse.

**Halpin, Maria Croft**
Widow with whom it is believed by some that then bachelor Grover Cleveland fathered a son before he became President of the United States.

**Ham Hock**
Miss Piggy's CB handle in the 1981 movie *The Great Muppet Caper*.

**Hamlet**
Mr. Quincy Magoo's pet hamster in the Mr. Magoo TV cartoons. The name has also been given to his pet dog.

**Hamlet**
Glenda Barnes's (Goldie Hawn) pet St. Bernard in the 1980 movie *Seems Like Old Times*.

**Hamlin, William James**

Creator of Orange Julius orange drink. He named it after one of his employees, Julius Freed, at their first stand, which was located at 820 South Broadway in Los Angeles.

**Hammer, Armand**

(1898– ) President of Occidental Petroleum Corporation, the nation's eleventh largest oil company. He also founded the Arm & Hammer Baking Soda company. Hammer was loosely portrayed by Marlon Brando in the 1980 movie *The Formula*.

**Hammerin' Hank**

Nickname of two members of the Baseball Hall of Fame: Hank Greenberg and Hank Aaron.

**Hammond**

Portable typewriter used by Rob Petrie (Dick Van Dyke) at his office on the twenty-eighth floor of the office building where "The Alan Brady Show" was produced on the TV series "The Dick Van Dyke Show." Neither the *E* nor the *C* keys worked properly.

**Hampton, Lionel**

(1913– ) First black musician to play at a Presidential inauguration, that of Harry S Truman in 1949.

**Hangout, The**

Nightclub hangout of Theresa Dunn (Diane Keaton) in the 1977 movie *Looking for Mr. Goodbar*.

**Hank Patterson**

Stableman played by Hank Patterson on the TV series "Gunsmoke."

**Hanks, Sam**

Oldest man to win the Indianapolis 500, when he won the race in 1957, just a few weeks short of his forty-third birthday. Twenty-two-year-old Troy Ruttman was the youngest to win the race (1952).

**Hannah Huntley School**

Connecticut girls' school where Dorothy Banks (Dorothy Loudon) taught, in the short-lived 1979 TV series "Dorothy."

**Hannon, Judge James**

Judge who tried folksinger Arlo Guthrie for littering. He portrayed himself in the 1969 movie *Alice's Restaurant*.

**Hans Delbruck**

Dead man whose brain Igor (Marty Feldman) was to have stolen in the 1974 movie *Young Frankenstein*. Igor dropped Delbruck's brain and substituted an abnormal one instead.

**Hans Kleinberg**

Role played by author Erich Segal in the 1972 movie *Without Apparent Motive*.

**Happiness Hotel**

Rundown London hotel where Kermit the Frog, Fozzie, and Gonzo stayed in the 1981 movie *The Great Muppet Caper*.

**Happy Birthday, Uncle Otis . . .**

Angie Dickinson's sole line in her movie debut in *Lucky Me* (1954).

**Happy Christmas to all and to all a good night . . .**

Last line of Clement Clarke Moore's poem "A Visit From Saint Nicholas." Most people erroneously call the poem "The Night Before Christmas" and give the last line as "Merry Christmas to all and to all a good night."

**Happy Hour Bar**

Pub near WJM's television studio, frequented by Lou Grant (Ed Asner) and the WJM employees on the TV series "The Mary Tyler Moore Show."

**Happy Milk**

Company for which Breezy Albright (Jimmy Durante) delivered milk in the 1951 movie *The Milkman*.

**Happy Soap**

Sponsor of the TV series "Happy Playhouse." Beverly Boyer (Doris Day) signed a fifty-two-week contract at $1,500 a week to advertise the soap in the 1963 movie *The Thrill of It All*.

**Hard Hat**

Jamie Bonham's (Joey Floyd) pet turtle in the 1980 movie *Honeysuckle Rose*.

**Hard Hat Days and Honky Tonk Nights**

Wording on posters for the 1980 movie *Urban Cowboy*.

**Harding, You're the Man for Us**

Republican campaign song of Warren G. Harding in his campaign for President. The song was written by singer Al Jolson.

**Hargitay, Mickey**

Mr. Universe of 1955. In 1958 he married actress Jayne Mansfield, only to divorce her in 1964. He was portrayed in the 1980 TV movie *The Jayne Mansfield Story* by Arnold Schwarzenegger (one Mr. Universe portraying another).

**Harlequin Enterprises, Ltd.**

Largest publishing company in Canada.

**Harley-Davidson**

Make of motorcycle shown on the cover of Paul McCartney and Wings' 1973 album *Red Rose Speedway*.

**Harley-Davidson Service Manual**

Book used by Bruce Dern in his attempt to marry a young couple in the 1970 movie *The Rebel Rousers*.

**Haroldson Lafayette**

First and middle name of billionaire H. L. Hunt, who came by his first oil well in a poker game in El Dorado, Arkansas, at the age of thirty-two.

**Harrah's**

Las Vegas casino where Matilda the kangaroo fought Lee Dockerby (Larry Pennell) for the heavyweight championship of the world in the 1978 movie *Matilda*.

**Harrah, Toby**

(1948–     ) Shortstop for the Texas Rangers who played in a double-header on June 26, 1976, without once being involved in a fielding play.

**Harris, Jean**

Woman convicted of the murder of the Scarsdale diet doctor Herman Tarnower, author of *The Scarsdale Diet*. She was portrayed by Ellen Burstyn in the 1981 TV movie *The People vs. Jean Harris*.

**Harris, Julie**

Winner of the most Tony Awards, with five.

**Harry and Grace**

Two rare tropical fish mentioned by Richard Sumner (Spencer Tracy) in a detective deduction quiz, asked of Bunny Watson (Katharine Hepburn) in the 1957 movie *Desk Set*.

**Harry and Joe's**

Manhattan nightclub where Don Birnam (Ray Milland) got drunk and tried to steal a purse in order to get ten dollars in the 1945 movie *The Lost Weekend*. As Don was being thrown out, the crowd sang "Somebody Stole My Purse."

**Harry (Dirty Harry)**

Eleventh atomic bomb to be exploded in the Nevada desert, May 1953. Just downwind from the bombsite, the Howard Hughes movie *The Conqueror* was being filmed in St. George, Utah. The fallout has been blamed for the deaths of the following people connected with the film, all of whom died of cancer: Pedro Armendariz (1963), Dick Powell (1963), Agnes Moorhead (1974), Ted de Corsia (1973), John Wayne (1979), and Susan Hayward (1975).

Lee Van Cleef is the only surviving principal player. An estimated ninety-one of the 220 cast and crew members have developed cancer, and forty other associates have died of it.

**Harry Hare**

Magician Gilbert Wooley's (Jerry Lewis) white rabbit that he pulled out of a hat in the 1958 movie *The Geisha Boy*.

**Harry "Rabbit" Angstrom**

Hero of John Updike's three novels: *Rabbit Run* (1960), *Rabbit Redux* (1971), and *Rabbit Is Rich* (1981). *Rabbit Is Rich* won the 1982 Pulitzer Prize for fiction.

**Hart to Hart**

TV series starring Robert Wagner and Stefanie Powers. Before he died, on October 16, 1981, the last person to talk to William Holden was his girlfriend, Stefanie Powers. Before she died, on November 29, 1981, the last person to talk to Natalie Wood was her husband, Robert Wagner.

**Harvard, Yale, Cornell, and Princeton**

Universities attended by Charles Foster Kane (Orson Welles) in the 1941 movie *Citizen Kane*. He failed to graduate from any of them.

**Harvey**

Elliot, Mike, and Gerti's pet dog in the 1982 movie *E.T. the Extra-Terrestrial*.

**Has Anybody Here Seen Kelly?**

Silent movie being shown at the Strand Theater in the 1952 movie *Has Anyone Seen My Gal?*

**Haunted Forest—Witches Castle—1 Mile**

One of two signs in the forest in the 1939 movie *The Wizard of Oz*. (The other sign read "I'd Turn Back If I Were You!")

**"Have Yourself a Merry Little Christmas"**

Song sung by Frank Sinatra on the film soundtrack, as a U.S. soldier is executed, in the 1963 movie *The Victors*. (The scene was based on the execution of Private Eddie Slovik, the only U.S. soldier executed for desertion during World War II.) Judy Garland sang the song to Margaret O'Brien in the 1944 movie *Meet Me in St. Louis*. The song was sung by Al Martino on the soundtrack of the 1972 movie *The Godfather*.

**Havoc, June**

(1916–     ) Actress, born June Hovick, in Vancouver, B.C., in 1916. She is the sister of stripper/actress Gypsy Rose Lee. In 1948 she married producer William Spier, who died in 1973. June made her movie debut in the 1941 film *Four Jacks and a Jill*. Her 1959 autobiography is titled *Early Havoc,* and a later autobiography is titled *More Havoc.* She was portrayed by Ann Jillian as "Baby" June and by Suzanne Cupito (Morgan Brittany) as "Dainty" June in the 1962 movie *Gypsy.*

**"Hawaiian War Chant"**
Song popularized by the Tommy Dorsey Orchestra, which was played at the second marriage ceremony of Linda (Mary Steenbergen) and Melvin Dumar (Paul LeMat) in the 1980 movie *Melvin and Howard.*

**Hawksworth, Henry**
Man who possessed multiple personalities. He was portrayed by David Birney in the 1981 TV movie *The Five of Me,* as Dana, Johnny, Pete, Phil, and finally Henry.

**Hawthorne, Nathaniel**
Author to whom Herman Melville dedicated his 1851 novel *Moby Dick.*

**Hayden, Carl Trumball (1877–1972)**
Late Arizona senator who held the record for tenure in Congress (fifty-six years, 1912–1969).

**Hayes, Rutherford Birchard**
(1822–1893) Nineteenth President of the United States. He served as a brigadier general during the Civil War and was the governor of Ohio (1868–1872 and 1876–1877). Hayes was portrayed by John Dilson in the 1944 movie *Buffalo Bill.*

**Haymes, Dick**
(1918–1982) Popular crooner of the 1930s and 1940s, born in Buenos Aires, Argentina. He replaced Frank Sinatra twice—when Sinatra left the Harry James band and again when he left the Tommy Dorsey Orchestra. He was married to Edith Harper (1938), JoAnne Dru (1941–1949), Nora Eddington (1950), Rita Hayworth (1953–55), Fran Makais (1956), Fran Jefferies (1957), and Wendy Smith (1958).

**Hayward, Leland**
(1902–1971) Broadway and movie producer. Hayward produced the films *Mister Roberts* (1955), *The Spirit of St. Louis* (1957), and *The Old Man and the Sea* (1958). He was married to actress Margaret Sullavan from 1937 until 1947 and is the father of actress Brooke Hayward. Hayward was portrayed by Jason Robards in the 1980 TV movie *Haywire.*

**Hazzard County Gazette**
Local newspaper in Hazzard County on the TV series *The Dukes of*

*Hazzard.*

**Haze**

Last name of Lolita, as played by Sue Lyon in the 1962 movie *Lolita*.

**Head, Edith**

(1907–1981) Hollywood fashion designer who won a record eight Academy Awards (out of thirty-five nominations) for her designs: *The Heiress* (1949), *Samson and Delilah* (1950), *All About Eve* (1950), *A Place in the Sun* (1951), *Roman Holiday* (1953), *Sabrina* (1954), *The Facts of Life* (1960), and *The Sting* (1973). Her 1959 autobiography is titled *The Dress Doctor*. Ironically, the 1966 movie in which she made a personal appearance was titled *The Oscar*. Head was portrayed by Edith Fellows in the 1983 TV movie *Grace Kelly*.

**"Heartaches"**

Recording (1932) by Ted Weems that can be heard over a radio in the 1980 movie *Raging Bull*. Elmo Tanner did the whistling on the song, which became a hit in 1932 and again in 1947.

**"Heartaches by the Number"**

Hit song (1959) by Ray Price, on which Willie Nelson played bass guitar.

**Heart of Darkness**

Novel (1902) by Joseph Conrad that was used as the basis for the 1979 movie *Apocalypse Now*.

**Heather Grant**

Role played by Georganne LaPiere, the sister of singer Cher, on the TV series "General Hospital."

**Heathway, Granville**

Orgy sequence advisor (as credited) for the 1959 movie *Solomon and Sheba*.

**Heavenly Blues**

Leader of a motorcycle gang, played by Peter Fonda in the 1966 movie *The Wild Angels*.

**Heaven's Gate**

Three-hour-and-forty-five-minute, $40-million movie flop, starring Kris Kristofferson, that was withdrawn by United Artists after its debut in December 1980. It was released again in April 1981. The movie was mentioned in the 1980 movie *Modern Romance*. In 1983 the film was re-released in a much shorter version. It was the first movie that Michael Cimino had directed after winning the

Academy Award as Best Director for *The Deer Hunter*.

**He best serves himself who serves others . . .**

Motto of the Screen Actors' Guild.

**Hedley Lamarr**

Role played by Harvey Korman in the 1974 movie *Blazing Saddles*.

**Hefner, Hugh**

(1926– ) Founder of *Playboy* magazine, which he introduced in December 1953. The magazine's success eventually made possible the creation of the Playboy Clubs throughout the world. Hefner played a cameo role in the 1981 movie *History of the World, Part I* and was portrayed by Mitchell Ryan in the 1981 TV movie *Death of a Centerfold: The Dorothy Stratten Story*, and by Cliff Robertson in the 1983 movie *Star 80*.

**Heinz**

The Flanagans' family dog on the TV series "A New Kind of Family."

**Hekawi**

Indian tribe headed by Chief Wild Eagle (Frank deKova) on the TV series "F Troop." According to legend, they received their name from their first chief, who said, "I think we're lost. We're the Hekawi." ("Where the heck are we?")

**Helen**

Name of the deceased wives of all the following: Tom Corbett (Bill Bixby) on the TV series "The Courtship of Eddie's Father"; Barnaby Jones (Buddy Ebsen) on "Barnaby Jones"; Quincy (Jack Klugman) on "Quincy, M.E."; and Dr. Richard Kimble (David Jannsen) on "The Fugitive."

**Helena Cassadine**

Role played by Elizabeth Taylor when she appeared in five episodes (November 10, 12, 16, 17, and 19, 1982) of the TV soap "General Hospital." She donated her salary for these appearances to two Virginia hospitals.

**He-Man Woman Haters Club**

Club that Spanky, Alfalfa, and Darla are talking about at the beginning of REO Speedway's "Tough Guy" track on their 1981 Grammy Award–winning *Hi-Infidelity* album.

**Hemingway, Leicester**

(1915–1982) Sixty-seven-year-old brother of author Ernest Hemingway, who committed suicide by shooting himself with a pistol on September 12, 1982. Both his Nobel Prize–winning brother and their father had also committed suicide.

**Hendrich, Tommy**

(1913–    ) New York Yankees player whose thirty-six-ounce bat Joe DiMaggio borrowed for ten days, during his fifty-six-game hitting streak in 1941. DiMaggio's regular bat had been stolen between the games of a double-header and was finally returned ten days later.

**Henry**

King family dog in the 1948 movie *Sitting Pretty*.

**Henry Henshaw**

Melody Jones's (Gary Cooper) horse in the 1945 movie *Along Came Jones*.

**Henry Street**

Lower East Side New York City street on which Fanny Brice (Barbra Streisand) lived in the 1968 movie *Funny Girl*.

**Henson, Les**

Virginia Tech basketball player who, on January 21, 1980, made the longest successful basket shot in collegiate play. The ball traveled 89 feet and 3 inches.

**Henson, Lisa**

Daughter of muppet creator Jim Henson. In 1980 she was elected as the first woman president of the *Harvard Lampoon* organization in its 105-year history.

**He played too much football with his helmet off . . .**

Statement attributed to Lyndon B. Johnson about Gerald Ford.

**Hera**

In Greek mythology, the queen of the Olympian Gods and the protectress of women. She is both the sister and wife of Zeus and the mother of Ares and Hephaestus. Hera was played in the 1963 movie *Jason and the Argonauts* by Honor Blackman, and in *Clash of the Titans* (1981) by Claire Bloom.

**Herald**

Newspaper of which Blake Washburn (Jeffrey Lynn) is the editor in the 1951 movie *Hometown Story*. The office girl, Miss Martin, was played by Marilyn Monroe.

**Herbert Hoover High School**

School attended by Sally Rogers (Rose Marie) in the TV series "The Dick Van Dyke Show."

**Herbie**

Robot of the Fantastic Four on the TV cartoon series "The Fantastic Four." His voice is that of Frank Welker.

192

**Hercules**

Brand name of the vacuum cleaner sold by Benny Miller (Lou Costello) in the 1946 movie *Little Giant*.

**Hercules**

Hero of both Greek and Roman mythology. He was the son of Zeus and Alcmene. After his death, he ascended to Mt. Olympus, where he married Hebe.

*Movie portrayals:*

*Hercules* (1959), Steve Reeves

*Hercules Against the Barbarians* (1960), Mark Forrest

*Hercules Against Rome* (1960), Alan Steel

*Hercules and the Black Pirates* (1960), Alan Steel

*Hercules and the Masked Rider* (1960), Alan Steel

*Hercules and the Treasure of the Incas* (1960), Alan Steel

*Hercules Unchained* (1960), Steve Reeves

*Venus Meets the Son of Hercules* (1960), Massimo Serato (a.k.a. Mars, God of War)

*Hercules in the Haunted World* (1961), Reg Park

*Ulysses Against Hercules* (1961), Michael Lane

*Hercules vs. Ulysses* (1962), George Marchal

*The Three Stooges Meet Hercules* (1962), Samson Burke

*Son of Hercules in the Land of Fire* (1962), Ed Fury

*Hercules Against the Sons of the Sun* (1963), Mark Forrest

*Hercules and the Captive Women* (1963), Reg Park

*Jason and the Argonauts* (1963), Nigel Green

*Son of Hercules in the Land of Darkness* (1963), Dan Vadis

*Terror of Rome Against the Son of Hercules* (1963), Mark Forrest

*Triumph of the Son of Hercules* (1963), Kirk Morris

*Tyrant of Lydia Against the Son of Hercules* (1963), Gordon Scott

*Ulysses Against the Son of Hercules* (1963), George Marchal

*Hercules Against the Moon Men* (1964), Alan Steel

*Hercules and the Ten Avengers* (1964), Dan Vadis

*Hercules and the Tyrants of Babylon* (1964), Rock Stevens

*Hercules in the Vale of Woe* (1964), Kirk Morris

*Hercules of the Desert* (1964), Kirk Morris

*Hercules, Prisoner of Evil* (1964), Reg Park

*The Triumph of Hercules* (1964), Dan Vadis

*Hercules, Samson and Ulysses* (1965), Kirk Morris

*Hercules* (1983), Lou Ferrigno

**"Here Comes the Night"**
Theme song of the 1979 movie *The Bell Jar*.

**"Here I Come to Save the Day"**
Mighty Mouse's theme song actually voiced by Tom Morrison. Comedian Andy Kauffman used this song in a comedy routine in which he lip-synch's Mighty Mouse's singing.

**"Here Is My Love"/"Sweet Little Lover"**
Tommy Dee's (Paul Land) first record, which became a hit in the 1981 movie *The Idolmaker*.

**Here Is Tomorrow**
Novel written by Christopher Madden (Claudette Colbert), in the 1946 movie *Without Reservations*, which spent sixteen consecutive weeks as number one on the best-seller list. When the book was to be filmed, Miss Madden chose a U.S. Marine captain named Rusty Thomas (John Wayne) to play the lead of Mark Winston (Cary Grant, who made a cameo in the film, was originally selected), opposite Lana Turner.

**Herman**
The dog that chased Roger (Gig Young) into a taxi in the 1962 movie *That Touch of Mink*.

**Herman Gutman Mail Order Catalogue**
Company for which Stuart Hibbard (Oliver Clark) worked as a copywriter in the TV series "We've Got Each Other."

**Herman P. Willis**
Favorite pseudonym of country singer Hank Williams, when he wished not to be recognized.

**Herman Smith**
Name of the Wiz, from Atlantic City, New Jersey, played by Richard Pryor in the 1979 movie *The Wiz*.

**Herman, Victor**
American-born Russian who, in 1934, set the world parachute-jump record but refused to allow the Soviets credit, claiming he was an American. For refusing the Stalin Medal, he was sentenced to ten years hard labor in Siberia. In 1976 he finally returned to Detroit. Herman was portrayed by John Savage in the 1982 TV movie *Coming Out of the Ice*.

**Hermes**
Olympian god in Greek mythology, the son of Zeus and Maia. He is the god of commerce, and of thieves. Hermes was played by Michael Gwynn in the 1963 movie *Jason and the Argonauts*.

**Hermes**

British Royal Navy aircraft carrier that sailed to the Falkland Islands in order to take back the Islands from the invading Argentines in April 1982. A second carrier, *Invincible,* led the task force.

**Herrmann, Bernard**

(1911–1975) Composer to whom the 1976 movie *Taxi Driver* was dedicated. Herrmann died one day after completing the movie's score.

**Hershey Horowitz and Mary Elizabeth Doyle**

Comic characters played by Jerry Stiller and Anne Meara. The pair played the characters on Ed Sullivan's TV show on thirty-four occasions.

**Hershey, Milton S.**

Candy manufacturer who, in 1894, introduced the Hershey bar.

**"He's Only a Man"**

Theme song of the 1970–1971 TV series "Headmaster," sung by Linda Ronstadt.

**Hess, Rudolph**

(1896–      ) Member of Adolf Hitler's Third Reich. He was second in succession to Hermann Goering for dictatorship of Germany. In 1941 he flew to Scotland, after which he was held in the Tower of London as a prisoner of war. Hess was portrayed by Victor Varconi in the 1944 movie *The Hitler Gang,* and by Maurice Reeves in the 1982 TV mini-series *Inside the Third Reich.*

**He Stooped to Kill**

Pulp magazine read by Robert Tracey (Jack Lemmon) in the opening scene of the 1954 movie *Phffft!*

**He treated her rough—and she loved it!**

Publicity line for the 1932 Clark Gable/Jean Harlow film *Red Dust.*

**"Hey, Little Goldfish"**

Song that Richard Dreyfuss sang to a porpoise in the 1969 movie *Hello Down There.*

**H. G. Wells**

Patrick Glover's (Patrick Cargill) pet dog on the 1977 TV series "Father Dear Father."

**Hickock, Richard E., and Perry E. Smith**

Murderers of the four-member Clutter family of Holcomb, Kansas, on November 15, 1959; the pair robbed the family of just forty-three dollars. Author Truman Capote befriended the two men in prison and wrote the best-selling book *In Cold Blood* about the pair's crime. The two were executed on April 14, 1965. They were portrayed by Scott Wilson and Robert Blake, respectively, in the 1967 movie *In Cold Blood*. Woody Allen mentioned Hickock and Smith in the 1977 movie *Annie Hall*.

**Hicks, Sue K.**
(1896–1980) Man named for his mother, who had died while giving birth to him. This was the inspiration for cartoonist and songwriter Shel Silverstein to write the 1969 Johnny Cash hit song "A Boy Named Sue." Hicks was the assistant prosecutor in the July 1925 Scopes "monkey trial."

**Hiding Plalce, The**
Novel upon which the 1965 Robert Redford movie, *Situation Hopeless, But Not Serious*, is based. The book was written by actor Robert Shaw.

**High and the Mighty, The**
Movie theme whistled by Nicholas J. Gardenia (Chevy Chase) after kissing Glenda (Goldie Hawn) goodbye, in the 1980 movie *Seems Like Old Times*.

**High-Bouncing Lover, The**
Original title considered for the F. Scott Fitzgerald novel *The Great Gatsby*.

**Highway 41**
Highway mentioned in the lyrics of the Allman Brothers' 1973 hit song "Ramblin' Man."

**Hildegarde and Buffy**
Female names used by Henry Desmond (Peter Scolari) and Kip Wilson (Tom Hanks) when in drag, in the TV series "Bosom Buddies."

**Hilldale**
Hometown of the Stone family on the TV series "The Donna Reed Show."

**Hillsboro**
Town setting of the 1960 movie *Inherit the Wind*.

**Hillsdale High School**
Alma mater of Jennifer Edwards Hart (Stephanie Powers) on the TV series "Hart to Hart."

**Hill Street Blues**
Television series that holds the record for winning the most Emmys in a single season, when, in 1981, it received eight out of twenty-one nominations. The season before, the series had placed eighty-

ninth out of the top ninety-nine programs on TV. It was almost canceled at that point.

**Hilton, Daisy and Violet**
Siamese twins who appeared in the 1932 movie *Freaks*.

**Hinckley, Jr., John Warnock**
Twenty-five-year-old man who shot President Ronald Reagan in the chest with a Roehm RG-14 .22-caliber pistol outside of the Washington Hilton, on March 30, 1981. Press Secretary James Brady was shot in the head and placed on the critical list, but survived the ordeal. Policeman Thomas K. Delahanty and Secret Service agent Timothy J. McCarthy were also wounded. Hinckley claimed his motive was to win the attention of eighteen-year-old actress Jodie Foster. Ironically, John Hinckley's brother, Scott, was to have had dinner with Vice-President George Bush's son Neil the very next night.

**Hinckley, Ohio**
Town where the turkey buzzards return each year on approximately March 19 (the same date that the swallows return to Capistrano), a tradition that goes back 160 years.

**His and Hers**
Nicknames of the pistols that President Franklin D. Roosevelt and his First Lady, Eleanor, kept under their respective pillows at night.

**H Is for Harlot**
Title of the paperback book being read in the bathtub by a member of the Go Go's on the back cover of their debut album *Beauty and the Beat*.

**History of Tom Jones, a Foundling, The**
Complete title of Henry Fielding's 1749 novel *Tom Jones*.

**Hitchcock, Constance**
First woman to pilot a sailboat from San Francisco to Hawaii (1946).

**Hi-yo, Silver, Awa-a-a-aaayy!**
Cry of the Lone Ranger to his horse, Silver. In the 1981 movie *The Legend of the Lone Ranger*, starring Klinton Spilsbury, it was actor James Keach who dubbed in the famous cry as well as his entire dialogue. The expression "Hi-yo, Silver" appears in the hit records "Honey Hush" by Big Joe Turner (1953) and "Elvira" by the Oak Ridge Boys (1981).

**Ho Chi Minh City**
New name given to Saigon, the capital of South Vietnam, after the

Communists gained complete control of the country, in 1973.

**Hoff-Federated Pictures**

Hollywood motion picture studio headed by Stanley Hoff (Rod Steiger) in the 1955 movie *The Big Knife*.

**Hogan**

Role played by Jack Lemmon in two movies: *Operation Mad Ball* (1957) and *Under the Yum Yum Tree* (1963).

**Hogg, Ima**

Only daughter of Texas governor Jim Hogg (1891–1895).

**Hogs**

Nickname that Major Bull Meechum (Robert Duvall) calls his children in the 1980 movie *The Great Santini*.

**Hog's Breath Inn**

Pub in Carmel, California, owned by actor Clint Eastwood, where Dirty Harry Burgers and Fistfuls of T-Bones are served.

**Hoisington, Elizabeth P.**

First woman general in the U.S. armed forces. In June of 1970, she was promoted to the post of director of the Women's Army Corps.

**Holden, Thomas James**

First person to be put on the FBI's Ten Most Wanted Fugitives list, when he was selected on March 14, 1950. Holden had killed his wife and her two brothers. He died in prison in 1953.

**"Hold Me"**

Theme song of the 1967 Dean Martin movie *Rough Night in Jericho*, sung by the Kids Next Door.

**Holiday, Billie**

(1915–1959) Black torch singer, born Eleanor Gough and nicknamed Lady Day. The illegitimate daughter of guitarist Clarence Holiday, she sang with Benny Goodman, Count Basie, and Artie Shaw. Billie, who always wore a white gardenia in her hair when she performed, became involved with drugs, and spent time in jail. Three of her most well-known songs are "God Bless the Child," "Strange Fruit," and "Lover Man." Billie was portrayed by Diana Ross in the 1972 movie *Lady Sings the Blues*.

**Hollen, Andrea**

First woman to graduate from the United States Military Academy at West Point (1980).

**Hollis House**

Louisiana plantation inherited by Charlotte Hollis (Bette Davis) in the 1965 movie *Hush, Hush, Sweet Charlotte*.

**Hollywood Studio Club**
   Women's boardinghouse where Herbert H. Hebert (Jerry Lewis) worked as a handyman in the 1961 movie *The Ladies' Man*.
**"Home"**
   Theme song of the short-lived 1980 TV series "The Six O'Clock Follies," sung by Joe Cocker.
**Home Cookin'**
   Novel by Merry Noel Blake (Candice Bergen), that won a literary award in the 1981 movie *Rich and Famous*.
**Home-run leaders (major leagues)**

| Hank Aaron | 755 | (6' tall) |
|---|---|---|
| Babe Ruth | 714 | (6' 2" tall) |
| Willie Mays | 660 | (5' 10½" tall) |
| Frank Robinson | 586 | (6' 1" tall) |
| Harmon Killebrew | 573 | (6' tall) |
| Mickey Mantle | 536 | (5' 11½" tall) |
| Jimmie Foxx | 534 | (6' tall) |
| Ted Williams | 521 | (6' 3" tall) |
| Willie McCovey | 520 | (6' 4" tall) |
| Ernie Banks | 512 | (6' 1" tall) |
| Eddie Matthews | 512 | (6' 1" tall) |
| Mel Ott | 511 | (5' 9" tall) |

   Out of the twelve, only Mel Ott, Willie Mays, and Mickey Mantle were under six feet tall.
**Honda 350**
   Motorcycle on which Gilda Texter rode nude in the 1971 movie *Vanishing Point*.
**Honey Badger, The**
   Novel (1964) by Robert Ruark that reporter Dorothy Kilgallen was reading when she died in bed on November 8, 1965.
**Honeymoon Haven Hotel**
   Niagara Falls resort where Clark Kent (Christopher Reeve) and Lois Lane (Margot Kidder) got a honeymoon suite under the name of Mr. and Mrs. Smith (room number 6) in order to cover a story in the 1981 movie *Superman II*.
**Honeymoon Hotel**
   First Merry Melodies cartoon made in color (February 17, 1934).
**Honk**
   Pet space creature on board the PXL 1236 spacecraft on the TV series "Far Out Space Nuts," played by Patty Maloney.

**"Hooray for Spinach"**

Song sung by Zelda Manion (Ann Sheridan) in the 1939 movie *Naughty But Nice*.

**Hooterville World-Guardian**

Hooterville town newspaper, with 138 subscribers. During the week of September 10–16, 1924, it did not publish anything, because nothing happened, on the TV series "Petticoat Junction."

**Hopkins Realty Company**

Real estate firm from which the Stevenses bought their first home on the TV series "Bewitched." The company's phone number was 474-6925.

**Hopkins, Samuel**

First person granted a patent by the United States, on July 31, 1790, for a process of making potash and pearl ash.

**Horatio**

Caterpillar puppet on the 1951 TV show "Ozmoe."

**"Hooray for Santa Claus"**

Theme song sung by a group of children in the 1964 movie *Santa Claus Conquers the Martians* (actually sung by Milton DeLugg and the Little Eskimos).

**Horn, Tom**

Bounty hunter of the Wild West, portrayed by John Ireland in the 1967 movie *Fort Utah*, by David Carradine in the 1977 TV movie *Mr. Horn*, and by Steve McQueen in the 1980 movie *Tom Horn*.

**Horrible Hill, Transylvania**

Setting of the 1965–1967 TV cartoon series "Milton the Monster."

**Horticulture**

Word that writer and wit Dorothy Parker was once challenged to create a saying about. Her reply was "You can lead a horticulture, but you can't make her think."

**Hot Blood**

Original title under which the 1954 movie *The Wild One* was released, only to be withdrawn and retitled. The movie was banned in Britain for twelve years.

**Hotel Continental**

Washington, D.C., hotel in which Tom Tinston (Cary Grant) unsuccessfully tried to house his three children in the 1958 movie *Houseboat*.

**Hotel Electra**

Hotel where Red Stone (a.k.a. Quintet) stayed in room 243 in the

1979 movie *Quintet*. Red Stone was played by Paul Newman.

**Hotel Ivanhoe**

Philadelphia hotel where Cash McCall (James Garner) lived, paying $1,000-a-month rent for the entire tenth floor, in the 1959 movie *Cash McCall*.

**Hotel Louis XIV**

Paris hotel where Pa Kettle (Percy Kilbride) stayed in room 419 in the 1953 movie *Ma and Pa Kettle on Vacation*.

**Hotel Washington**

Washington, D.C., hotel where Michael Corleone (Al Pacino) and his wife, Kay (Diane Keaton), stayed while he testified before Congress in the 1974 movie *The Godfather, Part II*.

**Hot enough for June?**

Agent Nicholas Whister's (Dirk Bogarde) password to his contact in Prague in the 1965 British movie *Agent 8¾*. His countersign was "Ah, but you should have been here last November."

**"Hot Voodoo"**

Song sung by Marlene Dietrich while dressed in an ape suit in the 1932 movie *Blonde Venus*.

**Hough, David**

Confederate soldier who became the first person officially killed during the Civil War, when he died after his cannon exploded. The incident occurred during the fifty-gun salute that the Confederates were shooting off to celebrate the surrender of Fort Sumter on April 12, 1861, which was taken without a single fatality.

**Hound Dog**

Sergeant Jim Rockford's (James Garner) nickname while with the Fifth Regimental Combat Team in Korea, on the TV series "The Rockford Files." Actor Jim Garner actually served in Korea, and was wounded there. (He was the first man drafted from his home state of Oklahoma).

**House, Edward Mandell**

(1858–1938) American diplomat known as Colonel House. He was a close personal friend and advisor to President Woodrow Wilson. House was portrayed by Charles Halton in the 1944 movie *Wilson*.

**Houston, USS**

Cruiser from which the American named Shears (William Holden) is a survivor in the 1957 movie *The Bridge on the River Kwai*.

**Howard**

Professor Chandler's (Elliot Gould) pet basset hound in the 1981 movie *Dirty Tricks*.

**Howard, Elston**

(1929–　　) New York Yankees catcher who, in 1969, introduced the use of the donut weight put on the baseball bat in the on-deck circle.

**Howard Phillips**

First and middle name of horror-fiction writer H. P. Lovecraft.

**Howard, Tom**

Photographer for the *Chicago Tribune* who was hired by the New York *Daily News* to secretly take photos of the January 1928 electric-chair execution of Ruth Snyder at Sing Sing prison. Snyder had murdered her husband with the help of Henry Judd Gray.

**"How Deep Is the Ocean?"**

Song composed in 1932 by Irving Berlin and performed in the following films: *Alexander's Ragtime Band* (1938); *Blue Skies* (1946); and *Meet Danny Wilson* (1952).

**How'd you like to tussle with Russell?**

Publicity line for Howard Hughes's 1943 movie *The Outlaw*, starring Jane Russell.

**Howe, Gordie**

Winner in 1974 of the Gordie Howe Trophy for the Most Valuable Player in the WHA.

**Howell, Trevor**

Twenty-four-year-old man who threw musician Frank Zappa from the stage of the London Rainbow Theater on December 10, 1971. In the fall, Zappa broke a leg and an ankle and fractured his skull.

**Howe, Marty and Mark**

Gordie Howe's two sons, with whom he played on the Houston Aeros team beginning in June 1973.

**Howe, William**

(1729–1814) Lieutenant general who commanded the British at the battle of Bunker Hill (1775). He defeated the Americans on Long Island and captured New York City (1776). Howe, who was the brother of British naval officer Admiral Richard Howe (1726–1799), was portrayed by Wilfrid Hyde-White in the 1979 TV mini-series *The Rebels*, and by Laurence Olivier in the 1959 movie *The Devil's Disciple*.

**How I Did It**

Title of the book written by his grandfather, discovered by Frederick Frankenstein (Gene Wilder) in the 1974 movie *Young Frankenstein*.

## How I Lost 400 Pounds
Autobiography of circus fat lady Dolly Dimples (real name Celesta Geyer) who, in 1967, reduced her weight from 550 pounds to 110 pounds.

## How It Happened
Television talk show on which Eddie "Kid Natural" Scanlon (Ryan O'Neal) and his opponent, Hector Mantea (Richard Lawson), appeared in the 1979 movie *The Main Event*.

## How to Make Your Husband Happy
Book written by Dr. Blossom Franklin that Martha Strabel (Gene Tierney) went to a bookstore to buy, only to be talked out of the purchase by Henry Van Cleve (Don Ameche), in the 1943 movie *Heaven Can Wait*.

## Hoyt, Ed
Only man killed by Wyatt Earp (July 26, 1879) as marshal of Dodge City.

## "H" Presidents who were never reelected
William H. Harrison, Benjamin Harrison, Rutherford B. Hayes, Warren G. Harding, and Herbert Hoover.

## H. R. Pufnstuf
Puppet character, created by Sid and Marty Krofft, who has a head that resembles a hamburger. When McDonald's brought out their character, Mayor McCheese, the Kroffts successfully sued the company for $50,000 in damages.

## Hubbs, Ken
(1941–1964) Chicago Cubs player whose picture appeared erroneously on a Topps bubble gum card in 1966 under the name of pitcher Dick Ellsworth. Hubbs had been killed in an airplane crash two years earlier.

## Hudson, Jeffrey
Dwarf in the court of King Charles II of England. Author Michael Crichton once wrote under the pseudonym of Jeffrey Hudson.

## Hudson, Robert
Last person to leave the *Andrea Doria* on the morning of July 26, 1956. As a passenger, he slept through the collision and rescue operations. When he woke up, he found no one else on board. Hudson was finally rescued after the captain and crew had already departed.

## Hull brothers
NHL players Bobby and Dennis.

**Human Beings**

TV talk show for which Isaac Davis (Woody Allen) worked in New York City as a writer in the 1979 movie *Manhattan*.

**Humans and pigs**

Only two animals that sunburn.

**Humbert Humbert**

Role played by James Mason in the 1962 movie *Lolita* (based on the Vladimir Nabokov novel of the same title).

**Hummingbird Hill**

Book written by Lynn Belevedere (Clifton Webb) in the 1948 movie *Sitting Pretty*.

**Hungry**

Baby elephant in the 1963 movie *Tarzan's Three Challenges*.

**Hungry House Cafe**

Restaurant mentioned in the lyrics of the Oak Ridge Boys' 1981 hit record "Elvira."

**Hunt, E. Howard**

White House consultant under President Richard Nixon. He served two years and eight months in prison for his involvement in the Watergate scandal. He was portrayed by William Zukert in the 1978 movie *Born Again*, and by James Greene in the 1979 TV mini-series *Blind Ambition*.

**Hunt, Ron**

(1941–    ) Baseball player who holds the major-league record for being hit with pitched balls in a single season. In 1971, Hunt was hit on fifty occasions. He also holds the career record for being hit the most: 243 times over his twelve-year career.

**Hunter College**

Marjorie Morningstar's (Natalie Wood) alma mater in the 1958 movie *Marjorie Morningstar*.

**Huntington, Collis Potter**

(1821–1900) American railroad builder who, in conjunction with Mark Hopkins, Charles Crocker, and Leland Stanford (the California Big Four), built the Central Pacific Railroad (1861–1869), which connected with the Union Pacific at Promontory Point, Utah. Huntington was portrayed by Henry O'Hara in the 1942 movie *Gentleman Jim*.

**"Hunting We Will Go,"**

Song usually sung by Elmer Fudd whenever he went hunting for rabbits in Warner Bros. cartoons.

**Hurlbutt, Gertrude**
Winner of $100 when she named the game of trapshooting "Skeet" in a national contest held by *National Sportsman Magazine*, thus coining the term "skeet shooting."

**Hurly**
Original name of the game of hockey.

**Hurst, Fannie**
(1889–1968) Novelist who wrote such classics as *Humoresque* (1919), *Back Street* (1931), and *Imitation of Life* (1933). Hurst was the first recipient of *Photoplay* magazine's Gold Medal Award.

**Hustler**
Porno magazine published by Larry Flynt. Theresa Dunn (Diane Keaton) carried a copy of the magazine on board a streetcar in the 1977 movie *Looking for Mr. Goodbar*.

**"Hut Sut Song"**
Novelty song (1939) written by Leo V. Killian, Ted McMichael, and Jack Owens. The song can be heard in the 1941 movie *San Antonio Rose*, and in the 1953 film *From Here to Eternity*. The song features the line "Hut-sut rawlson on the Rillerahead and a brawla, brawla soo-it."

**Hutton, Maude**
Oldest woman to record a hole-in-one in golf, which she made in 1980, at the age of eighty-six.

**Huxton Dairy**
Dairy that employed the Nash family milkman, Mr. Hastings, on the TV series "Please Don't Eat the Daisies."

**Hyatt Wilshire**
Los Angeles hotel where New York Yankees owner George Steinbrenner had an altercation in the elevator with two Dodgers fans on October 26, 1981. Steinbrenner broke his right hand in the melee. The Dodgers beat the Yankees in the series, four games to two.

**Hyde, Johnny**
William Morris Agency executive. He was the agent for Marilyn Monroe, Bob Hope, Betty Hutton, Rita Hayworth, Lana Turner, and Esther Williams. Hyde was portrayed by Richard Basehart in the 1980 TV movie *Marilyn: The Untold Story*, and by Lloyd Bridges in the 1980 TV mini-series *Moviola* (a.k.a. *The Secret Love of Marilyn Monroe* and *This Year's Blonde*.

**Hyman Roth**
Mobster played by Lee Strasberg in his film debut, *The Godfather,*

*Part II* (1974), for which he was nominated for an Oscar as Best Supporting Actor.

**Hype, The**

Working title of Christina Crawford's revealing autobiography, *Mommie Dearest*.

# I

**I**

Theodore Roosevelt was the only President who did not use the word "I" during his inaugural address (March 4, 1905).

**ICC**

Interstate Commerce Commission.

**IM 863**

Code used to interface with Biocarbon Amalgamated's computer in the 1981 movie *Scanners*.

**IM 69268**

California automobile license plate number of the white Chevy van "borrowed" by Cheech (Richard Marin) and Chong (Thomas Chong) in the 1980 movie *Cheech and Chong's Next Movie*.

**I Am Curious (Blue)**

X-rated Swedish movie (1970) sequel to the 1969 X-rated film *I Am Curious (Yellow)*. Lena Nyman starred in both films.

**I Am Legend**

Novel (1954) written by Richard Matheson. The book was the basis of two movies: *The Last Man on Earth* (1964), starring Vincent Price, and *The Omega Man* (1971), starring Charlton Heston.

**I am not an animal, I am a man!**

Line said by Lord John Morgan (Richard Harris) in the 1970 movie *A Man Called Horse*, and by John Merrick (John Hurt) in the 1980 movie *The Elephant Man*.

**"I Am the Very Model of a Modern Major-General"**

Song composed by William S. Gilbert and Arthur Sullivan, which was used as background music in the 1962 movie *The Notorious*

*Landlady*.

**Iberia**
National airline of Spain.

**"I Can Dream, Can't I?"**
Record by the Andrews Sisters that, on January 6, 1950, became the first number-one hit song on the *Billboard* charts for the 1950s.

**"I Can't Begin to Tell You"**
Song recorded by Ruth Haag with the Harry James Orchestra. Ruth Haag was a pseudonym used by James's wife, Betty Grable, because her studio, 20th Century-Fox, would not permit her to make any recordings.

**"I Can't Believe That You're in Love With Me"**
Theme song of the 1954 movie *The Caine Mutiny*. It is also sung by Sue Harvey (Claudia Drake) in the 1946 movie *Detour*.

**"I Can't Get Started with You"**
Song composed in 1936 by Ira Gershwin and Vernon Duke, which was introduced in the musical *Ziegfeld Follies of 1936* by Bob Hope and Eve Arden. Bunny Berigan's version is played over the closing credits of the 1973 movie *Save the Tiger*. The song is also heard in the 1974 movie *Chinatown*.

**"I Can't Give You Anything But Love, Baby"**
Song composed in 1936 by Ira Gershwin and Vernon Duke. The song can be heard in the following motion pictures:
> *Bringing Up Baby* (1938), sung by Katharine Hepburn
> *I Can't Give You Anything But Love, Baby* (1940)
> *Seven Sinners* (1940)
> *True to the Army* (1952), sung by Allan Jones
> *Stormy Weather* (1943), sung by Lena Horne
> *Jam Session* (1944)
> *So This Is Paris* (1955), sung by Gloria DeHaven
> *The Eddy Duchin Story* (1956)
> *The Helen Morgan Story* (1957), sung by Gogi Grant (dubbed for Ann Blyth)

**"I Can't Stand the Rain"**
Song that John Lennon and Harry Nilsson sang from the audience during a comedy routine of the Smothers Brothers at the Troubador Club in Los Angeles on the evening of March 12, 1974. John Lennon was evicted from the club.

**"I Could Love a Million Girls"**
Song that was being played when Harry K. Thaw shot architect

Stanford White on June 25, 1906. In the 1981 movie *Ragtime*, Donald O'Connor sang the song during the famous scene.

**I Couldn't Wait for Success, So I Went on Ahead Without It**
Title of the autobiography of comedian Jonathan Winters.

**I'd like to help you, but it's not my picture . . .**
Sole line said by John Wayne to Bob Hope in a cameo appearance in the 1972 movie *Cancel My Reservation*.

**I'd like to kiss you, but I just washed my hair . . .**
Famous line said by Bette Davis in the 1932 movie *Cabin in the Cotton*.

**"I Don't Like Mondays"**
Recording (1980) by the Boomtown Rats, based on the incident in which high school student Brenda Spenee shot eleven people in San Diego on Monday, January 29, 1979.

**"I Enjoy Being a Girl"**
Christine Jorgensen's theme song in her nightclub act.

**"If I Could Tell You"**
Opening theme song of the radio series "The Voice of Firestone."

**If music be the food of love, play on . . .**
First line of William Shakespeare's play *Twelfth Night*. It is said by the character of Orsino, the Duke of Illyria.

**If the people don't want to come out to the park, nobody's going to stop 'em . . .**
One of many famous statements made by Yogi Berra.

**"If You Believe in Me"**
Original title of the song "It's Only a Paper Moon" when it first appeared in the 1932 play *The Great Magoo*.

**"I Get a Kick Out of You"**
Song to which Velma Goodhue (Joan Leslie) danced after the operation that cured her clubfoot in the 1941 movie *High Sierra*. Ethel Merman and Bing Crosby sang the Cole Porter song in the 1936 movie *Anything Goes*. It is also heard in the movies *Night and Day* (1946), *On the Sunny Side of the Street* (1951), *Anything Goes* (1956), and a variation of it in *Blazing Saddles* (1974).

**Iggy**
Female cat that D.C. courts in the 1965 movie *That Darn Cat*.

**"I Got Rhythm"**
Song composed in 1930 by George and Ira Gershwin. Ethel Merman introduced the song in the 1930 Broadway musical *Girl Crazy*. The song can also be heard in the films *Girl Crazy* (1932),

*When the Boys Meet the Girls* (1943), *Rhapsody in Blue* (1945), and *Girl Crazy* (1965).

**I had a monumental idea this morning, but I didn't like it . . .**
Saying credited to movie producer Samuel Goldwyn, known as a Goldwynism.

**"I Have a Dream"**
Only recording made by a Nobel Prize winner to make *Billboard*'s Hot 100. It was a selection from Rev. Martin Luther King's speech. The record, released in March 1968 on Gordy Records, peaked at number 88.

**I have gathered a posie of other men's flowers and nothing but the thread that binds them is my own . . .**
John Bartlett's own quotation at the beginning of his world-famous work *Bartlett's Familiar Quotations*.

**"I Have No Words"**
Original title of the Howard Dietz/Arthur Schwartz 1930 composition "Something to Remember You By."

**I like nothing better than a big bowl of Wheaties!**
Line once said by New York Yankees first baseman Lou Gehrig, while doing a live commercial on the radio program "Believe It Or Not!" The only problem with Gehrig's line was that the show was sponsored by Huskies, a competitor of Wheaties.

**"Illegal Smile"**
Theme song of the TV series "The Texas Wheelers," composed by John Prine.

**"I'll live to see you, all of you, hanging from the highest yardarm in the British fleet . . .**
Famous line said by Captain Bligh (Charles Laughton) to the mutineers in the 1935 movie *Mutiny on the Bounty* (based on the book of the same title by Charles Nordhoff and James Hall).

**"I'll String Along With You"**
Song composed in 1934 by Al Dubin and Harry Warren and introduced by Dick Powell and Ginger Rogers in the 1934 movie *Twenty Million Sweethearts*. The song can also be heard in the films *The Hard Way* (1942), *My Dream Is Yours* (1949), *The Jazz Singer* (1953), and *Battle Cry* (1954). The song was played over a car radio in the 1955 movie *Rebel Without a Cause*.

**I'll take lemonade—in a dirty glass . . .**
Line said by Bob Hope in a rough Alaskan bar in the 1945 movie *The Road to Utopia*.

**I'll tell you right out, I'm a man who likes talking to a man who likes to talk . . .**

Line said by Sidney Greenstreet to Humphrey Bogart in the 1941 movie *The Maltese Falcon*.

**"I Love the Night Life"**

Song sung by Alicia Bridges, to which Count Dracula (George Hamilton) and Miss Newman (Susan Saint James) disco together, in the 1979 movie *Love at First Bite*.

**"I'm Always Chasing Rainbows"**

Song composed by Joseph McCarthy and Harry Carroll in 1918. The song can be heard in the following movies:

*Rose of Washington Square* (1939)
*Ziegfeld Girl* (1941)
*The Merry Monahans* (1944)
*The Dolly Sisters* (1945), sung by John Payne
*Rainbow* (1978—TV), sung by Andrea McArdle

The song's melody was taken from the *Fantaisie Impromptu* in C-Sharp Minor by Frédéric Chopin.

**IM COOL**

Personalized New York State automobile license plate number on Bill Blazerjowski's (Michael Keaton) custom Cadillac in the 1982 movie *Night Shift*.

**I'm Mad As Hell**

Autobiography of income-tax fighter Howard Jarvis, who made a cameo appearance in the 1980 movie *Airplane!*

**I Me Mine**

Last song recorded by the Beatles (January 3, 1970).

**I Me Mine**

Autobiography of musician George Harrison. One thousand copies of the original book were printed, at a cost of $250 each, prior to its becoming a popular hardcover book.

**I'm in Pittsburgh and it's raining . . .**

Mountain Rivera's (Anthony Quinn) answer to the question "Where are you?" after a bout in which Cassius Clay knocked him out in the seventh round. Actually, he was in St. Christopher's Arena in Pittsburgh in the 1962 movie *Requiem for a Heavyweight*.

**Imogene**

Dorothy Gale's pet cow in the 1902 musical play *The Wizard of Oz*.

**Imperial Films**

Movie studio headed by Charles Snow (Murray Hamilton), with

which Diana Barrymore (Dorothy Malone) signed a contract in the 1958 movie *Too Much, Too Soon* (the studio was fictitious). Her first picture was *Forever in My Heart*.

**Imperial Theatre**

New York City theater where, on May 24, 1936, Joe Helbock presented the first swing music concert.

**"I'm So Lonesome I Could Cry"**

Hank Williams song of which pro quarterback Terry Bradshaw made a recording in May of 1976. It peaked at number 91 on *Billboard*'s Hot 100 chart.

**I'm Superman . . .**

Line said by Pat Talbot (John Wayne) in the 1942 movie *Reunion in France*.

**"I'm the Man Who Broke the Bank at Monte Carlo"**

Song that Thomas Edward Lawrence (Peter O'Toole) sang aloud in a valley that gave off an echo in the 1962 movie *Lawrence of Arabia*.

**Include me out . . .**

Saying credited to movie producer, Samuel Goldwyn, known as a Goldwynism.

**In Cold Blood**

In-flight movie being shown on TWA flight 602 to London in the 1979 movie *Love at First Bite*. *In Cold Blood* (1967) was based on Truman Capote's book of the same title.

**Independence, Missouri**

Birthplace of President Harry S Truman (1884) and actress Ginger Rogers (1911).

**Independent Pictures, Incorporated**

Philadelphia motion picture company for which Jack Terry (John Travolta) was employed as a sound man, in the 1981 movie *Blow Out*. The company's five pictures were: *Bad Day at Bloodheart*, *Bloodbath*, *Bloodbath II*, *Bloodbath Beach*, and *Coed Frenzy*.

**Indiana Jones, Dr.**

Archeologist and adventurer hero of the 1981 movie *Raiders of the Lost Ark*. Harrison Ford, who played the lead role, was not the first choice. The role was originally offered to Tom Selleck, but he was unavailable. He was originally to have been named Indiana Smith (Indiana is the name of George and Marcia Lucas's first child).

**Indianapolis, Indiana**

Setting of the 1955 Humphrey Bogart movie *The Desperate Hours*.

**Infant Care**
   Title of the U.S. government's best-selling publication in print
   since 1914.
**Ingersoll, Robert**
   According to Thomas Jefferson, he was the first man to write the
   title "The United States of America."
**Ingram, Rex**
   (1892–1950) Hollywood director of such films as *The Four Horse-
   men of the Apocalypse* (1921), *The Prisoner of Zenda* (1922), and
   *Scaramouche* (1923). Ingram was portrayed by Michael Thoma in
   the 1975 TV movie *The Legend of Valentino*.
**In His Own Write**
   Book by John Lennon, seen in a dressing room in the 1964 movie *A
   Hard Day's Night*.
**Initials**

| William F. Buckley | Frank |
| George C. Scott | Campbell |
| J. D. Souther | John David |
| B. J. Thomas | Billy Joe |
| T. S. Eliot | Thomas Stearns |
| Y. A. Tittle | Yelberton Abraham |
| A. J. Foyt | Anthony Joseph |
| O. J. Simpson | Orenthal James |

**"In My Garden"**
   Closing theme song of the radio series "The Voice of Firestone."
**In 1600 an Englishman named Will Adams went to Japan and
become a samurai . . .**
   Single sentence in his nine-year-old daughter's history textbook
   that inspired author James Clavell to write his 802-page novel
   *Shōgun*.
**Inquiry Within**
   Dictionary for people who can't spell, being written by Miss Vicki
   Woodsworth (Edith Evans) in the 1967 movie *Fitzwilly*. Opal
   Pictures paid her $500,000 for the book, letters *A* to *K*.
**Inspector Frank B. Luger**
   Police inspector played by James Gregory on the TV series "Bar-
   ney Miller."
**"In Spite of All the Danger"**
   First recording ever made by the Quarrymen (the Beatles). They cut
   the record in a Liverpool studio in 1958. Backed with John Lennon

singing lead on "That'll Be the Day," there exists only one copy of the record, which fell into the hands of the Quarrymen's piano player, Duff Lowe.

**In Tandem**

Pilot TV movie (1974) for the TV series "Movin' On."

**International Projects**

New York City–based conglomerate, founded by Edward L. McKeever (Paul Douglas), in the 1956 movie *The Solid Gold Cadillac*.

**In the beginning God created the heaven and the earth . .**

First ten words of the first verse of the Bible (Genesis 1:1).

**In the Clouds**

Actress Sarah Bernhardt's only novel, which she wrote in 1878.

**In the Kitchen With Love**

Cookbook written by actress Sophia Loren in 1972.

**Iodent**

Toothpaste with Miracle K-69, which sponsored Bert Healy's (Peter Marshall) radio program in the 1982 movie *Annie*.

**I once was so poor I didn't know where my next husband was coming from . . .**

Line said by Lady Lou (Mae West) to her maid, Pearl (Louise Beavers), in the 1933 movie *She Done Him Wrong*.

**Ipana**

Toothpaste that a young Grace Kelly advertised on TV in the 1950s.

**IQ's in fiction**

185   Howie Dickerson (John Calvin), in the TV series "The Paul Lynde Show."

162   Dr. Richard Burrows (Elliott Gould), in the 1970 movie *I Love My Wife*.

161   Lt. "Doc" Ostrow (Warren Stevens), in the 1956 movie *Forbidden Planet*.

152   Doc (Nick Nolte), in the 1982 movie *Cannery Row*.

147   Elliott Garfield (Richard Dreyfuss), in the 1977 movie *The Goodbye Girl*.

120   President Chet Roosevelt (John Ritter), in the 1979 movie *Americathon*.

**Ira**

The Interagency Defense Command computer on the TV series "The New Adventures of Wonder Woman." Ira's voice was supplied by Tom Kratochzil.

**Iraq**
Country in which the prologue to the 1973 movie *The Exorcist*, and the William Peter Blatty novel of the same name, is set.

**Irene**
Ship commanded by Captain Svevo Stefan (Telly Savalas) in the 1979 movie *Beyond the Poseidon Adventure*.

**Irma**
Young lady to whom Dagwood Bumstead was engaged, prior to his meeting Blondie. He actually "married" Irma, but the ceremony wasn't legal because he didn't sign the proxy, in the Chic Young comic strip *Blondie*.

**Iron Cross**
Highest military decoration awarded by the German government.

**Iron Fist**
Brand of spinach eaten by Popeye in the 1980 movie *Popeye*.

**Iron Man**
Secret identity of Tony Stark. Iron man was created by Stan Lee, and debuted in *Tales of Suspense* comics number 39, in March of 1963.

**Isabel Street**
Street in a Lux liquid detergent ad on TV, in which the women on the west side were given a maid for a week, while those on the east side did their own dishes in Lux. No difference was found in the smoothness of their hands.

**"Is It Because of Love?"**
Theme song of the 1980 TV series "Me And Maxx," sung by Lenore O'Malley.

**I Steal . . .**
Last words spoken by Paul Muni in the 1932 movie *I Am a Fugitive From a Chain Gang*.

**Is This the End?**
How the 1965 movie *The Curse of the Fly* ends.

**It**
First word that teacher Annie Sullivan taught her pupil, Helen Keller, to articulate.

**I take this step in the journey of peace for all mankind . . .**
Words said by Colonel Charles Brubaker (James Brolin) when their landing craft *Capricorn One* landed on Mars (fictitiously filmed in a studio) in the 1978 movie *Capricorn One*.

**It Boy**
Nickname conferred on actor Gary Cooper for a short time after he

co-starred in the 1927 movie *It*, with Clara Bow, the "It" Girl.

**"It Can't Be Wrong"**
Song by Kim Gannon and Max Steiner introduced in the 1942 movie *Now, Voyager*. It was the love song of Charlotte Vale (Bette Davis) and Jerry Durrence (Paul Henreid).

**It Could Happen to You**
Morty S. Tashman's (Jerry Lewis) first motion picture for Paramutual Pictures in the 1961 movie *The Errand Boy*.

**"It Had to Be You"**
Song written in 1924 by Gus Kahn and Isham Jones. It can be heard in the following motion pictures:
  *Casablanca* (1942), sung by Dooley Wilson
  *Is Everybody Happy?* (1943)
  *Show Business* (1944)
  *The Incendiary Blonde* (1945)
  *It Had to Be You* (1947)
  *South Sea Sinner* (1950)
  *I'll See You in My Dreams* (1951)
  *Hell on Frisco Bay* (1955)

**I think Little League is wonderful. It keeps the kids out of the house . . .**
One of many famous statements made by Yogi Berra.

**It is a far, far better thing that I do, than I have ever done; it is a far, far better rest that I go to, than I have ever known . . .**
Last line of Charles Dickens's 1859 novel *A Tale of Two Cities*.

**It is well . . .**
Dying words of George Washington (December 14, 1799).

**It Must Be Good**
Musical presented at the Knickerbocker Theatre in New York City in the 1952 movie *April in Paris*.

**"I Told Ev'ry Little Star"**
Song introduced by actor Walter Slezak in the 1932 musical play *Music in the Air*.

**It rolls off my back like a duck . . .**
Saying credited to movie producer Samuel Goldwyn, known as a Goldwynism.

**It's a Bikini World**
Movie (1965) starring Tommy Kirk and Deborah Walley and scored by Mike Curb.

**"It's All Right, Ma (I'm Only Bleeding)"**
Bob Dylan song that Jimmy Carter quoted as part of his acceptance speech at the 1976 Democratic National Convention. The line he used was "He who is not busy being born is busy dying."

**It's a New World**
Movie in which Vicki Lester (Judy Garland) has her first starring role, in the 1954 movie *A Star Is Born*.

**It's been a long time since I was a pony . . .**
First words that Mr. Ed said to Wilbur Post (Alan Young) on the debut episode (October 1, 1961) of the TV series "Mr. Ed."

**Its Called Tomorrow**
Movie in which Sally Ross (Lauren Bacall) appeared, prior to making the musical play *Never Say Never* in the 1981 movie *The Fan*.

**"It's De-Lovely"**
Cole Porter song (1936) that was the very first song Dinah Shore sang on her first TV show, "The Dinah Shore Show," on November 27, 1951. The song was introduced in the 1936 musical *Red, Hot and Blue* by Ethel Merman and Bob Hope, and sung in the 1956 movie *Anything Goes* by Donald O'Connor and Mitzi Gaynor.

**It seems every Tom, Dick, and Harry is named Sam . . .**
Saying credited to movie producer Samuel Goldwyn, known as a Goldwynism.

**It's never too late . . .**
Mulligan's law, as quoted by Leo Harrigan (Ryan O'Neal) in the 1976 movie *Nickelodeon*.

**"It's Not Easy Being Green"**
Theme song of Kermit the Frog (written by Rod McKuen).

**It's Not Just a Job, It's an Adventure**
Recruiting slogan for the U.S. Navy in the 1980s.

**IT'S VE DAY**
Headline of the *Los Angeles Tribune* the day that the war with Germany ended, May 8, 1945, as seen on a wall in the TV series "Lou Grant."

**"Itsy Bitsy Teenie Weenie Yellow Polka Dot Bikini"**
Rock 'n' roll song played by the East German soldiers in order to torture Otto Ludwig Piffl (Horst Buchholz) in the 1961 movie *One, Two, Three*. Sixteen-year-old Brian Hyland's version of the song

went to number one in 1960.

**"It was love at first sight . . ."**
First line of Joseph Heller's novel *Catch-22*.

**"I've Been Working on the Railroad"**
Theme song of the radio show, "The Railroad Hour." The song was sung by Lewt McCanles (Gregory Peck) after he derailed a train, in the 1946 movie *Duel in the Sun*.

**I've Got a Secret**
Television game show created by comedian Allan Sherman.

**"I Want It All"**
Theme song of the TV series "Blansky's Beauties," sung by Cyndi Grecco.

**"I Wish I Were Eighteen Again"**
Hit country song of 1980, recorded by eighty-three-year-old comedian George Burns. (It peaked at number 49 on the *Billboard* Pop Singles Chart).

**Ixcatlan**
Mexican village that hired seven gunfighters to protect them in the 1960 movie *The Magnificent Seven*.

# J

**J**

The names of all three wives of TV's "Tonight Show" host Johnny Carson begin with the letter "J": Jody Wolcott (1949–63), Joanne Copeland (1963–72), Joanna Ulrich (1972–83).

**J**

Letter that no street name in Washington, D.C., begins with, because the letter *J* too closely resembles the letter *I*.

**JAPS**

Japanese Amateur Photographic Society. Group of twenty Japanese men who stayed at Hollywood's Hotel Rainbow in the 1981 movie *Under the Rainbow*.

**J. Fred Muggs Award**

Annual list of awards to those who excelled at making monkeys of themselves within the preceding year. First awarded by *TV Guide* in 1982 (for 1981).

**J.G.**

Initials of three catchers who have played for the New York Mets: Joe Ginsberg, Jesse Gonder, and Jerry Grote.

**J. J. Ewing**

Cattle baron played by Jason Robards, Jr., in the 1978 movie *Comes a Horseman,* in which actor Jim Davis (who played John "Jock" Ewing on the TV series "Dallas") also appeared.

**JL Cattle Ranch**

Jim Ed Love's (Chill Wills) cattle ranch, setting of the TV series "The Rounders." The nearby town was Hi Lo.

**JKR269**

California automobile license plate number of Tom Spellacy's

(Robert Duvall) Plymouth Fury in the 1981 movie *True Confessions*.

**JOBS**

Job Opportunities in the Business Sector.

**J. R. Ewing (John Ross Ewing II)**

Unscrupulous head of Ewing Oil, played by Larry Hagman on the TV series "Dallas."

**Jack**

Jake Cutter's (Stephen Collins) one-eyed (left) dog on the TV series "Tales of the Gold Monkey." If the dog barked twice it meant yes; if he barked once it meant no.

**Jack and Jill**

Boy and girl who are the subject of a nursery rhyme: "Jack and Jill went up the hill . . ." Played by James Martin and Ilana Dowding in the 1961 movie *Babes in Toyland*. "Jack and Jill" was the title of a 1978 hit record by Raydio.

**Jack-Be-Nimble**

Nursery-rhyme character who jumped over a candlestick. Played by John Perri in the 1961 movie *Babes in Toyland*.

**Jack Davis**

Character played by Martin Sheen on the TV soap "As the World Turns."

**Jack Flash**

Character in children's literature. He is mentioned in the lyrics of the Rolling Stones' 1968 hit "Jumpin' Jack Flash" and in Don McLean's 1971 hit song "American Pie."

**Jacobsen, Christine**

Twenty-seven-year-old woman who doubled for Brooke Shields in the lovemaking scenes of the 1981 movie *Endless Love*. Miss Jacobsen is the daughter of the film's soundman.

**Jaguar**

Actor Alan Ladd's movie production company.

**Jai**

Elephant boy who appeared in two Tarzan movies. Played by Jai in the 1962 movie *Tarzan Goes to India*, starring Jock Mahoney, and by Manuel Padilla, Jr., in the 1970 movie *Tarzan's Jungle Rebellion*, starring Ron Ely.

**Jaklin Klugman**

Actor Jack Klugman's racehorse, which ran in the 1980 Kentucky Derby.

**James, Joni**
Singer of the title song of the 1956 Barbara Stanwyck movie *The Maverick Queen,* which was taken from the Zane Grey novel of the same title.

**James Mead**
Character who is identified as hijacker D. B. Cooper in the 1981 movie *The Pursuit of D. B. Cooper,* played by Treat Williams.

**Janney, Eli H.**
Inventor who patented (No. 138,405) the first American railroad coupler on April 29, 1873.

**Jansen, Raymond William**
(1890– ) St. Louis Browns' player who, in a game on September 30, 1910, had four hits out of five times at bat. It was his first, last, and only major-league game.

**January 10, 1778**
Date of the letter supposedly written by George Washington, discovered in the 1981 movie *Dirty Tricks.*

**January 29, 1901**
Day on which John Bernard Books (John Wayne) is killed in the Acme Saloon in Carson City, Nevada, in the 1976 movie *The Shootist.* It was also his birthday.

**January 1999**
Opening month and year of Ray Bradbury's 1946 SF novel/collection of science fiction stories, *The Martian Chronicles.*

**Japan**
Country that was scheduled to host the 1940 Summer Olympics, in Tokyo, until they were canceled by the outbreak of World War II.

**Jarvis, Al**
First disc jockey, originating his "Make-Believe Ballroom" on KFWB, in Los Angeles, in the 1930s.

**Jason**
Killer of the young men and women in the movies *Friday the 13th* (1980),* *Friday the 13th, Part II* (1981), and *Friday the 13th, Part III* (1982). Jason was played by Ari Lehman, Warrington Gillette, and Richard Brooker.

**Jeannie**
Beautiful genie, played by Barbara Eden, whose master was Captain (later Major) Anthony Nelson (Larry Hagman) on the 1965–70

---

*In the first movie it was Jason's mother who committed the murders.

TV series "I Dream of Jeannie." In the spinoff TV cartoon series "Jeannie," her voice was that of Julie McWhirther.

**Jed Andrews**

Role played by Tom Selleck in the TV soap "The Young and the Restless."

**Jeepers Creepers**

Racehorse in the 1939 movie *Going Places*. The horse's groom was played by Louis Armstrong, who sang the popular novelty song "Jeepers Creepers."

**Jefferson High**

High school setting of the 1960 movie *Because They're Young*, starring Dick Clark. The movie, based upon John Farris's novel *Harrison High*, was filmed in Glendale, California.

**"Jeff's Collie"**

Syndication title of the original "Lassie" TV series.

**Jelly Belly**

Brand of jelly beans served in the White House during President Ronald Reagan's administration.

**Jenkins, Ferguson**

(1943–  ) Last American League pitcher to get a hit before the introduction of the designated hitter, when, on October 2, 1974, he singled off pitcher Jim Hughes.

**Jenner, Bruce**

(1949–  ) Olympic champion who won the decathlon in the 1976 Olympics (with a record 8,618 points). He is a descendant of Edward Jenner, the British physician who developed the vaccine for smallpox. Like previous Olympic decathlon winner Bob Mathias, Jenner's picture appeared on packages of Wheaties cereal. He was given a screen test for the lead role in the 1978 movie *Superman*. Jenner made his movie debut in the 1980 musical movie *Can't Stop the Music*. He drove for twenty-four hours in the 1980 Daytona race, driving a March Engineering BMW M-1, teamed with Jim Busby and Rick Knoop. He is presently married to Elvis Presley's ex-girlfriend Linda Thompson.

**Jennifer Place**

Housewife played by Morgan Fairchild on the TV soap "Search for Tomorrow."

**Jennings, Waylon**

(1937–  ) Popular country-western "outlaw" singer who once played with Buddy Holly's Crickets on the road. In fact, it was Buddy Holly who bought Jennings his first bass guitar. He is married to guitarist Duane Eddy's ex-wife, Jessi Colter. He and his band, the Waylors, sang the theme song for the TV series "The Dukes of Hazzard." Waylon also narrates the series. Jennings was loosely portrayed by Rip Torn as Maury Dann in the 1972 movie *Payday*.

## Jenny
Mike Turner's (Michael Caine) tugboat in the 1979 movie *Beyond the Poseidon Adventure*, which was named after his mother, who died at his birth.

## Jeremiah
Bullfrog in Three Dog Night's 1971 hit song "Joy to the World."

## Jeremiah Peabody's Poly-Unsaturated, Quick-Dissolving, Fast-Acting, Pleasant-Tasting Green and Purple Pills
Title of the 1961 hit recording, by Ray Stevens, on Mercury Records. It is the longest title of any song to make *Billboard*'s Top 40.

## Jernberg, Sixten
Swedish skier who has won more medals in the Winter Olympics than any other competitor. As an individual participant in cross-country races and in team relays, he won four gold, three silver, and two bronze medals in the 1956, 1960, and 1964 Olympic Games.

## Jerry Helper
Dentist who lived next door* to Rob Petrie (Dick Van Dyke) in New Rochelle in the TV series "The Dick Van Dyke Show." He was played by Jerry Paris, who went on to be the director of the TV series "Happy Days."

## Jerry Mahoney
Precocious little boy dummy of ventriloquist and inventor Paul Winchell. Frank Marshall, a professional carver of dummies, designed the twenty-five-pound Jerry.

## Jesse
Louise MacFay's (Virginia Grey) pet dog who was killed in the 1939 movie *Another Thin Man*.

## Jetexas Company
Jet Rink's (James Dean) oil company in the 1956 movie *Giant*.

## Jewels of the Crown
Fraternal organization to which Sam 'n' Henry (Freeman Gosden and Charles J. Correll) belonged on their radio series (This predated

---

*On the first episode, the Petries had different neighbors.

Amos 'n' Andy's Mystic Knights of the Sea.)

**Jill**
Woman who works at Murphy's Union 76 Gasoline Station on TV commercials.

**Jills**
Cheerleaders for the Buffalo Bills football team.

**Jim and Della**
Husband and wife who exchanged gifts in O. Henry's short story "The Gift of the Magi." Della had her hair cut and sold in order to buy Jim a chain for his watch, while he sold his watch to buy her tortoiseshell combs for her long hair.

**"Jim Bowie"**
Theme song of the 1955 movie *The Last Command*, sung by Gordon MacRae.

**Jim Gavin**
Role played by Efrem Zimbalist, Jr., on the TV soap "Concerning Miss Marlow."

**Jimmie Dykes Day**
Special day in Chicago, celebrated on May 15, 1941. During the game in which White Sox pitcher Edgar Smith defeated the New York Yankees 13 to 1, Joe DiMaggio made his first hit in his 56-game hitting streak (Jimmie Dykes was a Chicago veteran player).

**Jimmu**
First Emperor of Japan. He ascended the throne in 660 B.C.

**Jim Smith**
Frontiersman played by John Wayne in the 1939 movie *Allegheny Uprising*. Richard Arlen played a Jim Smith in the 1943 movie *Minesweeper*.

**"Jingle Bells"**
Christmas song sung by Patti Page in the 1961 movie *Dondi*.

**Jobete**
Music publishing company of Motown Records. The name was derived from daughters of Robert Gordy, the brother of the label's president, Berry Gordy (*Jo*ann, *Be*tty, and *Te*rry).

**Jockey Hall of Fame**
Located at Pimlico, Maryland. The first three inductees (November 17, 1955) were Eddie Arcaro, Earle Sande, and George Woolf.

**Jocko**
Monkey puppet that appeared with Miss Frances (Dr. Frances Horwich) on the TV program "Ding Dong School."

**Joe Rossi**
Name of characters played by Humphrey Bogart in the 1943 movie *Action in the North Atlantic* and by Robert Walden in the TV series "Lou Grant."

**Joey**
Prison bloodhound in the 1971 movie *Fools' Parade*.

**John Barnes**
Role played by Barry Newman on the TV soap "The Edge of Night."

**John Boy**
John Curtis Walton, eldest of the Walton children, played in the TV series "The Waltons" by Richard Thomas (1972–1977) and Robert Wightman (1979–1982). In the Earl Hamner novels on which the series is based, the character was known as Clay Boy.

**John Davidson High School**
School where Curtis Lewis (Bill Russell) was the basketball coach of an all-white basketball team on the skit titled "The Black Shadow" on the TV series "Saturday Night Live."

**John Davidson Show, The**
TV talk show on which singer Andy Gibb and actress Victoria Principal first met in 1981.

**Johnny**
Rival about whom the Everly Brothers sang in their 1958 million-selling song "Bird Dog." It is also the name of the prospective bridegroom in Lloyd Price's 1959 hit, "I'm Gonna Get Married," and the name of the youth who beat the Devil in a fiddling contest in the Charlie Daniels Band's 1979 hit song "The Devil Went Down to Georgia."

**Johnny Doughboy**
Only movie (1943) in which both George "Spanky" McFarland and Carl "Alfalfa" Switzer appeared together, other than in Our Gang/Little Rascals episodes.

**John Q. Public**
Alias used by Virgil Starkwell (Woody Allen) when he went for a job interview in the 1969 movie *Take the Money and Run*.

**Johnson, Gus**
Baltimore Bullets basketball player who demolished a backboard in Oakland in 1963, in St. Louis in 1965, and in Milwaukee in 1971.

**Johnson, Jerome**
Twenty-four-year-old man who was shot to death after he had

gunned down Mafia chief Joseph Columbo, who died several months later, in 1971.

**Johnson, Ray**
Armed robber who made the only successful escape from California's Folsom Prison.* After his recapture, he became involved in prison reform. Johnson was portrayed by Beau Bridges in the 1982 TV movie *Dangerous Company*. The real Ray Johnson played the bit role of Gallagher in the TV movie based on his autobiography *Too Dangerous to Be at Large*.

**Johnson, Victoria Lynn**
*Penthouse* magazine pinup who stood in for actress Angie Dickinson in the nude shower scenes in the 1980 movie *Dressed to Kill*.

**John Wayne**
The Americans' password into the Alamo in the 1969 movie *Viva Max*. The Mexicans' password was "Richard Widmark."

**John Wayne**
Motion-picture actor of whom Sheriff Riley (Keenan Wynn) had a photograph in his locker in the 1972 movie *Cancel My Reservation*.

**John Wayne Airport**
Name of the airport at Santa Ana, Orange County, California.

**Jo Jo's Dance Factory**
New York City dance school where Sally Ross (Lauren Bacall) and her company rehearsed for the play *Never Say Never* in the 1981 movie *The Fan*.

**Joliet**
Illinois prison where Frank (James Caan) spent eleven years (1959–70), for stealing forty dollars. He killed a man while in prison, in the 1981 movie *Thief*.

**Jones, Charlie "Bumpus"**
(1870–1938) Only pitcher to throw a no-hitter in his first major-league game (October 15, 1892). It was the only game he pitched that year. He set the unusual record pitching for the Cincinnati Reds against the Pittsburgh Pirates. For the remainder of his career, Jones won only one other game and left baseball with a career record of 2–4.

**Jones, Gloria**
Girlfriend of rock singer Marc Bolan, who was driving the car in which Bolan was killed on September 16, 1977, when the auto-

---

*Missi Missildine, who typed the manuscript of the book you are now reading, is currently employed by Folsom State Prison.

mobile hit the Barnes Bridge in London. She recorded the original version of the song "Tainted Love."

## Jordan, Ohio
Setting of the 1947 Ronald Reagan/Shirley Temple movie *That Hagen Girl*.

## Joseph
Husband of the Blessed Virgin Mary, who cared for her and helped raise Jesus to manhood. Portrayals: Laurence Payne in *Ben-Hur* (1959); Gerard Tichy in *King of Kings* (1961); and Robert Loggia in *The Greatest Story Ever Told* (1965). Joseph was portrayed by Sam Bottoms on the TV series *Greatest Heroes of the Bible*, and by Jeff East in the 1979 TV movie *Mary and Joseph: A Story of Faith*.

## Joseph P. Kennedy, Jr., USS
U.S. destroyer on which Robert Kennedy served for a few months at the close of World War II. The ship had been christened by Jean Kennedy and was named for their brother, who had been killed on a secret mission on August 12, 1944. Ironically, the vessel was used to help turn back Soviet missiles during the Cuban missile crisis in 1963.

## Joshua
Successor of Moses as leader of the Hebrews. He blew the trumpet that knocked down the walls of Jericho and, during the battle in the Ajalon Valley, he made the sun stand still. Joshua was portrayed by Robert Culp on the TV series "Greatest Heroes of the Bible," and by John Derek in the 1956 movie *The Ten Commandments*.

## Joshua Cabe
Western hero who was played in TV movies by Buddy Ebsen in *The Daughters of Joshua Cabe* (1972); Dan Dailey in *The Daughters of Joshua Cabe Return* (1975); John McIntire in *The New Daughters of Joshua Cabe* (1976).

## Joshua Tree Motel
Motel in Joshua Tree National Monument, where rock musician Graham Parsons died on September 19, 1973, from a drug overdose (his body was later stolen). He was cremated, which had been his request.

## Journeymen Printers Union
First union in the United States to go on strike officially (in New York in 1776).

## Judge Henry T. Fleming
Baltimore judge, played by John Forsythe, accused of rape in the 1979 movie . . . *And Justice for All*.

227

**Judith Cole**

Role played by Marsha Mason on the TV soap "Love of Life."

**Julesburg**

Town where the forty-unit Wallingham wagon train of Whiskey (driven by Irish teamsters) originated on its westward trek to Denver in the 1965 movie *The Hallelujah Trail*.

**Julie Andrews**

Magic words said by George Spiggot (Peter Cook) in order to grant Stanley Moon's (Dudley Moore) wishes in the 1967 movie *Bedazzled*.

**Julie Murano**

Role played by Jessica Walter on the TV soap "Love of Life."

**Julio McCaw**

Horse that Jesse Owens beat in a 100-yard dash. The event took place in Havana on December 27, 1936. Owens, who began the race forty yards ahead of the horse, beat the gelding by twenty yards.

**Julius**

Goat on Ma and Pa Kettle's Farm.

**July 4, 1921**

Date of an Independence Day ball at the Overlook Hotel. In the photograph of the participants can be seen Jack Torrance (Jack Nicholson), in the 1980 movie *The Shining*,

**July 13, 1945**

Day on which Italy declared war on Japan.

**July 21, 1899**

Birthdate of authors Ernest Hemingway and Hart Crane, both of whom committed suicide.

**July 26**

Date on which George Webber's (Dudley Moore) driver's license expired in the 1979 movie *10*.

**July 31, 1944**

Date on which Lieutenant Commander Philip Francis Queeg (Humphrey Bogart) was relieved of duty by his officers in the 1954 movie *The Caine Mutiny*.

**July 1979**

Date stamped on the box of rations left on a Hawaiian island with Commander Richard Owens (James Farentino) and Laurel Scott (Katharine Ross) in the 1980 movie *The Final Countdown*.

**June 3 and June 4**

Two dates mentioned in Neil Diamond's 1978 hit song "Desiree."

**June 8, 1960**
Date of the beginning of James Clavell's 1982 novel *Noble House*.

**June 13**
Time setting of the 1980 movie *Friday the 13th*. There was a full moon that night.

**June 25**
Date of the opening scenes of the 1979 movie *Meatballs*.

**June 25, 1950**
Day on which the North Koreans crossed the thirty-eighth parallel to invade South Korea. It is the date the 1982 movie *Inchon* begins.

**June 29**
Date on which Primo Carnera beat Jack Sharkey for the heavy-weight title in 1933. Carnera died thirty-four years later, to the day, in 1967.

**Junior Miss (1963)**
Title won by CBS TV "Morning Show" hostess Diane Sawyer.

**Junior Orange Bowl Queen**
Beauty-contest title once held by TV soap actress Deidre Hall.

**Junior Proplinski**
Character played by eleven-year-old Robert Blake in the 1945 Jack Benny movie *The Horn Blows at Midnight*.

**Jupiter Effect**
March 10, 1982, a date on which all of the planets of our Solar System lined up on the south side of the sun.

**Jupiter 16**
U.S. manned space capsule hijacked by another space vehicle in the 1967 movie *You Only Live Twice*.

**"Just Around the Corner, There's a Rainbow in the Sky"**
Theme song of the radio series "Father Knows Best."

**Justice Magazine**
Magazine for which Jessica Drew (voice of Joan Van Ark) was the editor in the 1979–1980 animated cartoon series "Spider-Woman."

**Just Me**
Autobiography of silent star Pearl White, published in 1916. It was the first autobiography of a movie star.

**Just Plain Jane**
Radio soap opera sponsored by Beautee Soap in the 1947 movie *The Hucksters*. Beautee Soap was the firm for which Victor Albee Norman (Clark Gable) worked in advertising.

# K

**KAB**

Antonio Bay, California, radio station (1340 on the dial, FCC license number 66W9) owned by Stevie Wayne (Adrienne Barbeau) in the 1980 movie *The Fog*. The station's telephone number was 555-2131.

**KB**

Radio call letters of the aircraft carrier *USS Nimitz* in the 1980 movie *The Final Countdown*.

**KCAA**

Southern California radio station heard in the 1956 movie *Invasion of the Body Snatchers*.

**KHJP**

Melrose Springs radio station that broadcast the program "The Homemaker" hosted by Honest Harold Hemp (Hal Peary), on the radio program "The Hal Peary Show—Honest Harold."

**KHOW**

Denver radio station listened to by Dick Halloran (Scatman Crothers) in a rented car in the 1980 movie *The Shining*.

**KID-TV**

Television station that interviewed Santa Claus (John Call) in his workshop in the 1964 movie *Santa Claus Conquers the Martians*.

**KLA**

Los Angeles (Channel 6) television station on which Jessica Novak (Helen Shaver) was a reporter for "Closeup News" on the TV series "Jessica Novak."

**KL 93**

Plastic that was stronger than steel, in which the U.S. Army encased the robot Gort in the 1951 movie *The Day the Earth Stood Still*.

**KLOW**

Portland, Oregon, radio station for which Larry Adler (McLean Stevenson) worked as a talk-show host on the 1979 TV series "Hello, Larry."

**KLVW**

San Francisco radio station sign seen outside of detective Sam Spade's (Humphrey Bogart) office window in the 1941 movie *The Maltese Falcon*.

**K9**

Dr. Who's robot dog, which debuted in the 1977 episode "The Invisible Enemy," on the TV series "Dr. Who."

**K Ranch**

Ranch near Carsonville, in Carson Valley, for which Slim Mosley (Dean Martin) was the foreman in the 1956 movie *Pardners*.

**KRKR-TV**

Television station in the 1958 movie *Attack of the Fifty-Foot Woman*.

**KTNS**

Boulder, Colorado, TV station (Channel 31) where Mindy McConnell (Pam Dawber) worked as a newscaster on the TV series "Mork and Mindy."

**KVQ326**

Texas license number of Bobby Lee's (Bruce Dern) $40,000 1980 white Porshe 928 in the 1980 movie *Middle-Age Crazy*.

**KWK**

Radio station for which Chet Huntley played a sportscaster in the 1952 movie *The Pride of St. Louis*.

**KXLA-TV**

West Hollywood television station that televised the consumer show "The Big Rip-Off" on the TV series "The Stockard Channing Show."

**Kailua Club**

San Diego club advertised on a matchbook used by Commander Christopher Draper (Paul Mantee) in the 1964 movie *Robinson Crusoe on Mars*.

**Kaiser, Henry J. (John)**

(1882–1967) American industrialist whose companies constructed many large projects in the United States, such as the Bonneville Dam (1934) and the Grand Coulee Dam (1939) and built many ships during World War II. He also helped Howard Hughes construct the huge aircraft called the Spruce Goose. Kaiser has had two automobiles named after him, the Henry-J and the Kaiser, and was portrayed by Garry Walberg in the 1977 TV movie *The Amazing Howard Hughes*.

**Kalamazoo**

Michigan city in which the Checker Motors Corporation, manufacturer of the Checker Cab, was located. Checker cabs used Chevrolet engines.

**Kane, James**

*New York Journal* photographer who, in 1912, coined the term "cheesecake" when referring to a sexy photograph.

**"Kan-gu-wa"**

Song once recorded on Imperial Records by an obscure group called the Scholars in 1957. The band, which included a young singer named Kenny Rogers, cut the song because it was composed by gossip columnist Louella Parsons; they hoped she would mention the recording in her column. She didn't.

**Kanoga Falls**

Setting of the soap opera "When the Stomach Turns" on the TV series "The Carol Burnett Show."

**"Kansas City"**

Title of two different songs, one in the 1955 musical movie *Oklahoma!* and one in the 1970 musical movie *Let It Be*.

**Kansas City, Missouri**

Setting, in 1933, of the short-lived 1978 TV series "Apple Pie."

**Kansas Star**

Passenger train with which young Clark Kent (Jeff East) ran a foot race and beat to a crossing in the 1978 movie *Superman*.

**Kappa Alpha Theta**

First sorority established in the United States. It was founded at DePauw University in 1870.

**Karate for Lovers and Other Strangers**

Title of the book written by Mr. Yamamoto (Pat Morita) in the 1972 Bob Hope movie *Cancel My Reservation* (based on the Louis L'Amour novel *Broken Gun*).

**Karl, Harry**

Millionaire shoe magnate who was married to actresses Marie McDonald (twice), Joan Cohn (widow of Harry Cohn)* and Debbie Reynolds (1960–1973).

---

*Their marriage lasted only three weeks.

**Karman, Steve**
Clio-winning composer of the commercial jingles "I Love New York," "Aren't You Glad You Used Dial," "When You Say BUD-WEISER," "Doublemint," "Michelob (Weekends were made . . .)," "General Tire," and "Juicy Fruit."

**Karnak**
Steamer that sails on the Nile in the 1978 movie *Death on the Nile*.

**Karr, Andy**
Eleven-year-old whose dead body can be seen in the bed of a pickup truck in one of the most shown photographs of the May 18, 1980, Mount St. Helen's eruption damage. Andy's father and brother, who were in the cab of the Chevy truck, were also killed. Upon seeing this photograph, Andy's mother, Barbara Karr, learned of the death of her family.

**Karras brothers**
NFL players Ted, Lou, and Alex. Alex played for Iowa and the Detroit Lions. Ted played for Indiana, the Pittsburgh Steelers, and the Chicago Bears. Lou played for Purdue and the Washington Redskins. All were tackles.

**KARTEL**
Evil organization that opposed the government agency UNIT on the TV series "A Man Called Sloane."

**Kasanof's**
Boston rye bread bakery for which Charley Gordon (Cliff Robertson) worked as a janitor in the 1968 movie *Charly*.

**Katie**
Cleaning lady on TV's Pine Sol commercials.

**Katy "Scarlett" O'Hara Hamilton Kennedy Butler**
Scarlett O'Hara's (Vivien Leigh) name after her three marriages in the 1939 classic movie *Gone With the Wind*.

**Kazoo**
Musical instrument that Paul McCartney played on Ringo Starr's 1974 hit "You're Sixteen." It is the only number-one song ever to feature a kazoo.

**Keeler, Wee Willie**
(1872–1923) Member of the Baseball Hall of Fame who, in 1897, set the major-league record for the most singles in a season, with 199. Keeler used the shortest bat in baseball history; it was only 21½ inches long.

**"Keeps Rainin' All the Time"**
Subtitle of the 1933 Ted Koehler–Harold Arlen song "Stormy

Weather."

## Kellogg, W. K. (William Keith)

Founder of the Kellogg Company of Battle Creek, Michigan, in 1906.

## Kelly, Emmet

(1898–1979) Sad-faced circus clown since 1921, when he developed his clown named Willie the Tramp. He joined the Ringling Bros. Barnum & Bailey Circus in 1942. Emmet Kelly played himself in the 1951 movie *The Fat Man* and in the 1952 James Stewart movie *The Greatest Show on Earth*. He starred as the Piper in the 1968 movie *The Clown and the Kid*. In 1957, the Brooklyn Dodgers hired Emmet Kelly to entertain their fans.

## Kelly, Grace

(1928–1982) Actress born in Philadelphia in 1928. After making eleven films in Hollywood, she married Prince Rainier III of Monaco. She and Bing Crosby recorded the million-selling duet "True Love" (making her the only princess to record a million-selling record and win an Academy Award). Her eleven movie appearances were:

| | |
|---|---|
| *Fourteen Hours* (1951) | Bit part as a lady in a lawyer's office |
| *High Noon* (1952) | Amy Kane |
| *Mogambo* (1953) | Linda Nordley |
| *Dial M for Murder* (1954) | Margot Winders (Directed by Alfred Hitchcock) |
| *Rear Window* (1954) | Lisa Fremont (Directed by Alfred Hitchcock) |
| *The Country Girl* (1954) | Georgie Elgin (Academy Award for Best Actress) |
| *Green Fire* (1954) | Catherine Knowland |
| *The Bridges at Toko-Ri* (1955) | Nancy Brubaker |
| *To Catch a Thief* (1955)* | Frances Stevens (Directed by Alfred Hitchcock) |
| *The Swan* (1956)* | Princess Alexandra |
| *High Society* (1956) | Tracy Lord |

Grace Kelly was portrayed by Cheryl Ladd in the 1983 TV movie *Grace Kelly* (with Christina Applegate portraying her as a girl).

## Kelly, John B. (Jack)

Winner of three Olympic gold medals for the United States, for rowing in the 1920 and 1924 Olympic Games. He was the husband of swimming star Mary Freeman and the father of Princess Grace Kelly. John Kelly was portrayed by Lloyd Bridges in the 1983 TV movie *Grace Kelly*. John Kelly's brother, George Kelly, won the

---

*In both films, Jessie Royce Landis played her mother.

Pulitzer Prize for the 1926 play *Craig's Wife* (only brothers who have won an Olympic Medal and a Pulitzer Prize).

**Kelly, Paula**
Original female member of the vocal group the Modernaires. She was the wife of member Hal Dickinson.

**Kennelly, Thomas**
Man who looked for his family for eight years after they were hidden from him by the U.S. Department of Justice. He was portrayed by James Caan in the 1980 movie *Hide in Plain Sight*.

**Ken Norton**
Role played by Tyrone Power in the 1939 movie *Daytime Wife*.

**Ketchel, Stanley**
(1887–1910) Middleweight boxing champion and member of the Boxing Hall of Fame, born Stanislaus Kiecal and nicknamed the Michigan Assassin. On October 15, 1910, he was shot and killed by Walter Display in Conway, Missouri. Ketchel was portrayed by Maxie Rosenbloom in the 1944 movie *When Irish Eyes are Smiling*.

**Kid Andrew Cody and Julie Sparrow**
First novel (1977) written by actor Tony Curtis under his real name, Bernard Schwartz.

**"Kid" boxing champions**

| | |
|---|---|
| Charles "Kid" McCoy | Middleweight |
| Kid Graves | Welterweight |
| Ted "Kid" Lewis | Welterweight |
| Kid Gavilan | Welterweight |
| Benny "Kid" Paret | Welterweight |
| Dixie Kid | Welterweight |
| Jack "Kid" Berg | Junior welterweight |
| George "Kid" Lavigne | Lightweight |
| Steve "Kid" Sullivan | Junior lightweight |
| Kid Chocolate | Featherweight |
| Louis "Kid" Kaplan | Featherweight |
| Hogan "Kid" Bassey | Featherweight |
| Jack "Kid" Wolfe | Junior featherweight |
| Kid Murphy | Bantamweight |
| Kid Williams | Bantamweight |

**Kid Chocolate**
Name under which rock 'n' roll singer Lee Dorsey fought professionally as a light heavyweight contender.

**Kid Doctor**
Name under which 175-pound Captain Trapper John McIntyre (Wayne Roger) fought and defeated the 3099th MASH's boxer, Sergeant John "Killer" Blocker. Kid Doctor defeated him in the second round with the aid of chloroform in the "M*A*S*H" episode "Requiem for a Lightweight".

**Kid McCoy**
(1873–1940) Ring name of middleweight boxing champion (1897–1898) Norman Selby. He is the only boxing champion to have been married nine times. His lifetime record was eighty-one wins, six losses, nine draws, and nine no-decisions. He appeared in a number of films, several of them directed by Cecil B. DeMille.

**Kid Natural**
Ring name of 177-pound boxer Eddie Scanlon (Ryan O'Neal) in the 1979 movie *The Main Event*.

**Kill Devil Hill**
Actual location of the Wright Brothers' historical December 17, 1903, flight. It is located four miles south of Kitty Hawk, North Carolina.

**Killer**
Nickname of baseball great Harmon Killebrew and of rock 'n' roll great Jerry Lee Lewis.

**Killer Kane**
Heavyweight boxing champ whom John "Cash" Evans (Randolph Scott) beat by staying in the ring with him for three minutes in the 1942 movie *Pittsburgh*.

**Kimberly Jim**
South African movie (1965) that starred country singer Jim Reeves (his only acting role).

**Kincsem**
Horse that holds the record for winning the most races without a defeat. In his career, Kincsem won fifty-four races.

**Kind, Roslyn**
Recording artist, half-sister of Barbra Streisand. She recorded several albums in the 1960s.

**King**
David Chandler's (David Ladd) pet dog, played by Lance, in the 1958 movie *The Proud Rebel*.

**King**
Computerized lion at Chuck E. Cheese Pizza Time Theaters.

**King Achaemenides**
Persian king of the seventh century B.C., the ancestor of Cyrus the Great. He was loosely portrayed by Sean Connery in the 1981 movie *Time Bandits* (the character was really a composite of Achaemenides and Agamemnon).

**King, Alan**
(1927–    ) Comedian who appeared on TV's "The Ed Sullivan Show" more often than any other act. He appeared eighty-three times on the show.

**King, Clyde W.**
U.S. Navy admiral who, in 1919, as a midshipman, scored all the points as a tackle in the Army-Navy game at Annapolis. He kicked two field goals. A year later he was a member of the American Olympic team that won a gold medal in the 1920 games.

**King Cole Trio, The**
First number-one LP when *Billboard*'s Album Chart began on March 15, 1945. The trio was lead by singer/piano player Nat "King" Cole.

**Kingdome**
Fully enclosed playing field in Seattle, Washington.

**King Edward**
(1002–1066) Last king of the Anglo-Saxon line, portrayed by Eduard Franz in the 1955 movie *Lady Godiva*.

**King Find-All**
Ruler in the children's radio series "Land of the Lost."

**King Friday XIII**
Royal puppet that appears on the "Mister Rogers' Neighborhood" TV series; his voice is that of Fred Rogers.

**King George V**
(1865–1936) George Frederick Ernest Albert, King of Great Britain and Northern Ireland, and Emperor of India (1910–1936). He was portrayed by Marius Goring in the 1980 TV mini-series "Edward and Mrs. Simpson" and by Rene Krande in the 1980 movie *The Fiendish Plot of Dr. Fu Manchu*.

**King Louis VII**
(1121–1180) King of France (1137–1180), called the young son of Louis VI. He was portrayed by John Gielgud in the 1964 movie *Becket*.

**Kings in the deck of playing cards**
Alexander, Caesar, Charles, and David.

**Kingsley College**

School attended by Phineas and Vicky Whipsnade, the son and daughter of Larson E. Whipsnade (W. C. Fields) in the 1939 movie *You Can't Cheat an Honest Man*.

**Kingsport**

Setting of the short-lived (1953) TV soap opera "The Bennetts" (also known as "The Bennett Story").

**King, Stephen**

The King of the horror novel:

*Carrie* (1975; movie 1976)
*Salem's Lot** (1975; mini-series 1979)
*The Shining* (1977; movie 1980)
*The Stand* (1978)
*The Dead Zone* (1979; movie 1983)
*Firestarter* (1980; movie 1984)
*Cujo* (1981; movie 1983)
*Christine* (1983; movie 1983)
*Pet Semetary* (1983)

He is the only male American writer ever to have three "real"** books on the *New York Times* best-seller lists at the same time (1980): *Firestarter*, *The Dead Zone*, and *The Shining*. (The only female American writer to do the same is Danielle Steel). His short story "The Children of the Corn" (from his anthology *Night Shift*) provided the basis for 1984 film of the same title. He wrote the story for the 1982 movie *Creepshow*.

**Kingston, Cohen, and Vanderpool, Inc.**

Firm for which Don Robinson (Don Rickles) worked on the TV series "The Don Rickles Show."

**King, William**

(1786–1853) Vice-President to President Franklin Pierce. He took his oath of office in Cuba, where he was hospitalized with tuberculosis. He died in 1853, before he ever officially took office.

**Kinma**

Trophy award (Golden Horse) given in Taiwan, Nationalist Chinese equivalent of the Oscar.

**Kirkland, Willie**

(1934–      ) First San Francisco Giant to hit a home run in Candle-

---

*Originally titled *The Second Coming*.
**In 1982, Jim Davis had a record seven Garfield "non-books" on the *New York Times* best-seller list.

stick Park in San Francisco, on April 13, 1960. In answer to the question "Who was the first Willie to hit a home run in Candlestick Park?" chances are the answer will be given erroneously as either Willie Mays or Willie McCovey.

**Kirk, Lisa**
Singer who sang for Rosalind Russell in the 1962 movie *Gypsy*. She sang "Everything's Coming Up Roses" and other songs.

**Kirk Ohanian**
Role played by Mike Connors in the 1976 TV movie *The Killer Who Wouldn't die*. Connors real last name is Ohanian.

**"Kisses and Tears"**
Song recorded in duet by Frank Sinatra and Jane Russell in 1950.

**Kissinger, Henry**
(1923–    ) Secretary of State in President Richard Nixon's administration. He was awarded the Nobel Peace Prize in 1973. Kissinger was portrayed by Peter Jurasik in the 1978 movie *Born Again*.

**Kissinger Rule**
Harvard University rule that limits senior theses to 40,000 words. It was passed as a result of Henry Kissinger's 377-page thesis *The Meaning of History*, which he wrote in his senior year, 1950.

**Kiss my grits . . .**
Favorite expression of Florence "Flo" Jean Castleberry (Polly Holliday) on the TV series "Alice" and "Flo."

**Kiss of Love**
Perfume ($25 an ounce) worn by Dagmar (Virginia Grey) in the 1948 Abbott and Costello movie *Mexican Hayride*.

**Kiss Them for Me**
Movie (fictitious) in which Rita Marlowe (Jayne Mansfield) appeared with Cary Grant, as mentioned in the 1957 movie *Will Success Spoil Rock Hunter?* The 1957 movie was actually made with Mansfield and Grant in the leads.

**KISSY**
Miss Piggy's custom-made automobile license plate on *Miss Piggy's 1982 Calendar*.

**KITT**
Michael Knight's (David Hasselhoff) special black Pontiac Trans-Am in the TV series "Knight Rider." KITT, which stands for Knight Institute Two Thousand, is voiced by William Danielson.

**Kitts, Swan**
Tennessee highway patrolman who gave chauffeur Charles Carr a $25 ticket for speeding on January 30, 1953, remarking that Carr's

boss, in the back seat, looked dead. A while later, Carr pulled over to a stop in Oak Hill, West Virginia, and discovered that his boss, singer Hank Williams, was indeed dead.

**Kitty**

Kimba's girlfriend on the TV cartoon series "Kimba the White Lion."

**Kitty Hawk**

First balloon to cross the American continent (May 8–12, 1980). The trip took 99 hours and 54 minutes and covered 3,400 miles. The balloon was piloted by Maxie Anderson and his son Kris.

**Klement, Ricardo**

Name under which German Nazi official Adolph Eichmann was living in Argentina, until his discovery and capture by the Isarelis in 1960.

**KLondike 5-2463**

Phone number of Jake LaMotta's brother Joey (Joe Pesci), in the 1980 movie *Raging Bull.*

**KLondike 5-4648**

Phone number of Reverend Billy (Wolfman Jack) in the 1980 movie *Motel Hell.*

**KLondike 5-8372**

Telephone number of George and Dorothy Baxter (Don DeFore and Whitney Blake) on the TV series "Hazel."

**Klondike Kat Always Gets His Mouse**

Motto of Klondike Kat on the TV cartoon series.

**Klute**

Movie (1971) mentioned by Chuck Lumley (Henry Winkler) in the 1982 movie *Night Shift.*

**Knapp, Bridget**

Original Ivory Soap baby. She was seen on TV in 1954 and is today a member of the comedy team called the Loose Connection.

**Knickerbacker Savings and Loan Company**

Company that held the mortgage on St. Dominic's church in the 1944 movie *Going My Way.*

**Knockout Driving Academy**

Long Beach school owned by Eddie "Kid Natural" Scanlon (Ryan O'Neal) in the 1979 movie *The Main Event.*

**Knockout Hope**

Boxing-glove-wearing character played by Bob Hope on Texaco TV commercials (1980–1982). His gloves were red.

**Knott, Walter**

Founder of the Southern California amusement park called Knott's Berry Farm, the third largest amusement park in the United States. He developed the boysenberry in 1932, coining the name himself.

**Knowles, Darold**

(1941– ) Only pitcher to appear in all the games of a seven-game World Series, when he pitched in the 1973 series with the Oakland A's. He pitched a total of 6⅓ innings.

**Knox, Henry**

(1750–1806) Brigadier general during the American Revolution. He established the U.S. Military Academy at West Point in 1779, and served as the United States's first Secretary of War, from 1785 to 1794. Knox was portrayed by John Chappell in the 1979 TV mini-series "The Rebels."

**Kobayashi Maru**

Space vessel in distress, located in a restricted zone in a simulation test at the Federation Academy, in the 1982 movie *Star Trek II: The Wrath of Khan*.

**Koshay, Bobbie**

Judy Garland's double as Dorothy Gale in the 1939 movie *The Wizard of Oz*.

**Krakow**

Polish hometown of Mike Stivic's (Rob Reiner) parents on the TV series "All in the Family."

**Kramer Candy Kitchen**

Candy factory where Lucy Ricardo (Lucille Ball) and Ethel Mertz (Vivian Vance) got a job working in the wrapping department on the TV series "I Love Lucy" episode "Job Switching," first aired on September 15, 1952. Their job of candy-wrapping turns into a catastrophe when the conveyor belt speeds up.

**Krockmeyer's Department Store**

Los Angeles store where Walter Burnley (John McGiver) worked as the manager of the complaint department on the TV series "Many Happy Returns."

**Kruml, Stan**

Thirty-six-year-old man who nearly lost his fingers when he attempted to run through a 150-foot-long burning tunnel, only to emerge partway through with his fire-retardant suit aflame. The incident was shown on the TV series "That's Incredible" in March 1980.

## Ku Klux Klan Organization

Secret society founded in Pulaski, Tennessee, in December 1865.

| | |
|---|---|
| Imperial Wizard | (Invisible Empire) |
| Grand Goblin | (Eight Domains) |
| Grand Dragon | (50 Realms) |
| Great Titan | (Provinces) |
| Exalted Cyclops | (Local Chapter) |

## Kuscik, Nina

First female to finish in the Boston Marathon. In 1972 she finished first among the women, at 3 hours, 10 minutes, and 58 seconds.

# L

**L75249382G**
Serial number of the dollar bill that Tom Petty is seen tearing up on the July 23, 1980, edition of *Rolling Stone* magazine.

**LSP93**
British license plate number of the motorcycle stolen by German spy Henry Faber (Donald Sutherland) in the 1981 movie *Eye of the Needle*. He dumped the bike when it ran out of gas.

**LT34X**
Model of the sunlamp that turned Jeff Gerber (Godfrey Cambridge) into a negro in the 1970 movie *Watermelon Man*. The lamp's serial number was 3677231.

**L.O.O.M.**
Loyal Order of the Moose.

**Ladies Tea Society**
Woman's club to which Blondie Bumstead belongs in the comic strip "Blondie."

**Lady Astor**
(1879–1954) First woman to serve in the House of Commons. Her full title was Viscountess Nancy Astor.

**Lady Chatterley's Lover**
Classic work by D. H. Lawrence being memorized by a Tibetan apostle, played by David Niven in a cameo appearance, in the 1962 movie *The Road to Hong Kong*.

**Lady Dilke**
(1840–1904) Second wife of Sir Charles Wentworth. She was an author and a historian of French art, and worked for the betterment of working conditions for women. She was portrayed by Jan Holden in the 1969 movie *The Best House in London*.

**Lady Hamilton**
Movie (1941) filmed in Great Britain, starring Vivien Leigh and Laurence Olivier, about the romance between Lady Emma Hamilton and Lord Admiral Nelson. The movie was the favorite film of world leaders Sir Winston Churchill and Joseph Stalin.

**"Lady Is a Tramp, The"**
Song composed by Lorenz Hart and Richard Rodgers, in 1937. Sung in three films: *Babes in Arms* (1939), by Judy Garland; *Words and Music* (1948), by Lena Horne; and *Pal Joey* (1957), by Frank Sinatra. It was to this song that President Gerald Ford asked Queen Elizabeth II to dance, at the Bicentennial Ball in the White House.

**Laisure, Donald Lee**
Texas millionaire who, in 1981, married Susan Atkins (who is serving a life sentence for her part in the Charles Manson clan murders). Laisure claims to have been married and divorced at least thirty times.

**Lake Itasca**
Minnesota lake that is the origin of the Mississippi River.

**Lakeside Orphanage**
Orphanage where Elizabeth Blair (Shirley Temple) spent some time in the 1935 movie *Curly Top*.

**Lala**
Lost cat found by Charlie Chan (Peter Ustinov) in the 1981 movie *Charlie Chan and the Curse of the Dragon Queen*.

**LaMotta, Vicki**
Beautiful ex-wife of middleweight boxing champ Jake LaMotta. In November 1980, as a grandmother, at the age of fifty-one, she posed nude for *Playboy* magazine. Vicki was portrayed by Cathy Moriarty in the 1980 movie *Raging Bull*.

**Lamplighter**
London restaurant where William Gridley (Jack Lemmon) took Carlye Hardwicke (Kim Novak) to dinner in the 1962 movie *The Notorious Landlady*.

**Lancia**
Custom sports car in which Aly Khan was killed in a head-on collision in Paris, near the Bois de Boulogne on May 12, 1960.

**Land, Edwin H.**
(1909–  ) Inventor of the self-developing Polaroid camera, in 1947, and of polarized sunglasses.

**Land of Dreams**
Striptease house where Gypsy Rose (whose real name is Mary Jo)

dances in Tony Orlando and Dawn's 1973 hit "Say, Has Anybody Seen My Sweet Gypsy Rose?"

**Landseer, Sir Edwin**
(1802–1873) British artist who first began showing St. Bernard dogs carrying little brandy casks around their necks, even though the real rescue dogs never carried them.

**Lang, Donald**
Seventeen-year-old deaf and illiterate black youth who was accused of murder in Chicago in 1962. His lawyer was Lowell Myers, then the only deaf trial lawyer in America. In the 1979 TV movie *Dummy*, Donald Lang was portrayed by LeVar Burton, and Myers was portrayed by Paul Sorvino.

**Lark**
Bird mentioned in the lyrics of the songs "On the Street Where You Live" and "You'll Never Walk Alone."

**Larry Carter**
Role played by Hal Linden on the TV soap "Search for To-morrow."

**Larry Krandall College**
School setting of the 1979 TV series "Brothers and Sisters." The two featured societies were the Pi Nu fraternity and the Gamma Delta Iota sorority.

**Last Month's Newsletter**
Official publication of the Procrastinators' Club of America, Inc.

**"Last night I dreamt I went to Manderley again . . ."**
Opening line in the 1940 movie *Rebecca*, said by the second Mrs. de Winter (Joan Fontaine). The film was based on Daphne du Maurier's novel.

**Last of the Apaches**
New Western movie that producer George Bissinger (Patrick O'Neal) was showing in his home when it was discovered that his house was bugged, in the 1973 movie *The Way We Were*.

**Last One**
Tuna boat which "Sperm Whale" Whalen (Charles Durning) bought after retiring from the Los Angeles police department, in the 1977 movie *The Choirboys*.

**Last Picture Show, The**
First picture show for model-turned-actress Cybill Shepherd, who debuted in this 1971 movie.

**"Last Time I Saw Paris, The"**
Song Written in 1940 by Oscar Hammerstein II and Jerome Kern.

Hammerstein was inspired to write this song after the German occupation of the French city in June 1940. The song was used in the films *Lady, Be Good* (1941), sung by Ann Sothern; *Till the Clouds Roll By* (1946), sung by Dinah Shore; and in *The Last Time I Saw Paris* (1954), as the main musical theme.

**Latynina, Larissa**

Russian woman-gymanst who won a record eighteen Olympic medals: Six gold medals, three team gold medals, five silver medals, and four bronze medals.

**"Laura"**

Recurring theme song of the 1944 movie *Laura*, starring Gene Tierney and Dana Andrews. Composed by Johnny Mercer and David Raskin, the song can also be heard playing in a homosexual bar in the 1968 Frank Sinatra film *The Detective*.

**Laura Petrie**

Rob Petrie's (Dick Van Dyke) beautiful wife, played by Mary Tyler Moore, on the TV series "The Dick Van Dyke Show." Laura was played by Barbara Britton on the pilot show, called "Head of the Family."

**Lavender**

Scrawny gray horse that Mary Pickford befriended in the 1920 silent film *Suds*.

**Laver, Rod**

(1938– ) Australian-born tennis player who is the only person to have won the Grand Slam of tennis twice (1962 and 1969).

**Lawes, Lewis, E.**

Warden of Sing Sing Prison, who hosted the TV series "Twenty Thousand Years in Sing Sing." He also wrote several books that were made into films, such as: *20,000 Years in Sing Sing* (1933), *Invisible Stripes* (1940), and *Castle on the Hudson* (1940).

**Lawler, Jerry**

Professional wrestler, weighing 234 pounds, who hospitalized comedian Andy Kaufman in an exhibition bout on April 5, 1982, by slamming Kaufman's head onto the mat.

**Lawrence of Arabia**

Movie (1962) directed by David Lean, starring Peter O'Toole, Alec Guinness, Anthony Quinn, Jack Hawkins, Claude Rains, Anthony Quayle, Arthur Kennedy, Omar Sharif, and Jose Ferrer, about the life of T. E. Lawrence. The movie, which had no women in the cast, was made in Great Britain and became the second foreign film to win the Academy Award for Best Picture. (*The Bridge on the River Kwai* (1957), also directed by Lean, was the first.)

**Lawson, Lieutenant Ted**
Pilot of the B-25 *The Ruptured Duck*, one of sixteen aircraft that took part in Lieutenant Colonel Doolittle's raid on Tokyo on April 18, 1942. Lawson was portrayed by Van Johnson in the 1944 movie *Thirty Seconds Over Tokyo*.

**Lazy Ace**
One-hundred-acre ranch outside of Sweetwater, bought by Bret Maverick (James Garner) for $50,000 in the 1981 TV series "Bret Maverick." The spread had previously been called Miller's Place.

**Lazy Acres Bar M**
Country bar through which Carol Bell (Sally Field) drove a red Camaro in order to rescue Jack Dunne (Henry Winkler) in the 1977 movie *Heroes*.

**Lazzeri, Tony**
(1903–1948) New York Yankees second baseman whom St. Louis Cardinals pitcher Grover Cleveland Alexander struck out with bases loaded in the seventh inning of the decisive seventh game of the 1926 World Series. Lazzeri was portrayed by James Luisi in the 1978 TV movie *A Love Affair: The Eleanor and Lou Gehrig Story*.

**Leadership 80**
Ronald Reagan's leased Boeing 727 campaign jet.

**Leather Face**
Butcher of human beings, played by Gunner Hansen in the 1974 movie *The Texas Chainsaw Massacre*.

**Leaves of Grass**
Book of poetry by Walt Whitman, into which Louise Bryant (Diane Keaton) put a love letter from Eugene O'Neill (Jack Nicholson), in the 1981 movie *Reds*.

**Lederer, Jules**
Ex-husband of columnist Ann Landers, who borrowed $5,000 and turned it into the Budget Rent-a-Car Company, which he sold in 1970 for $10 million.

**Lee Curtis and the All Stars**
Liverpool band that drummer Pete Best joined after being fired from the Beatles in 1963, in order to make room for Ringo Starr.

**Leeds, Crystal**
Woman union labor organizer in the garment industry, loosely portrayed by Sally Field in the 1979 movie *Norma Rae*, as Norma

Rae Webster.

**Leeland**

Blind jazz pianist George Shearing's guide dog, who died in 1975 after guiding his master for twelve years. Shearing never replaced Leeland.

**Lee, Richard Henry**

(1732–1794) American revolutionary statesman who was a delegate to the Continental Congress and a signer of both the Declaration of Independence and the Articles of Confederation. Lee was portrayed by Ronald Holgate in the 1972 movie *1776*.

**Lee Tripper**

Sophisticated, well-educated brother of Jack Tripper on the TV series "Three's Company." Played by John Krutz. Whenever the two get together, Jack becomes a klutz.

**Lee, W. Howard**

Houston oilman who has been married to actresses Hedy Lamar (1953–1960) and Gene Tierney (1960–    ).

**Lefty**

Nickname of Baseball Hall of Fame member Robert Moses Grove.

**"Legend of Mackie Messer, The"**

Kurt Weill song performed in the 1933 musical *The Threepenny Opera*. The song was later retitled "Mack the Knife."

**Legion of Decency**

Official U.S. Catholic organization that passed judgment on the latest movie releases, condemning many and forbidding Catholics to see them. It was established in 1935 by Joseph Breen and was finally disbanded in 1980.

**Legion of Honor**

Highest military decoration awarded by the French government.

**Leif Erickson High School**

Roseburg, Minnesota, high school, 125 miles from Minneapolis, attended by Mary Richards (Mary Tyler Moore), who graduated in 1959, on the TV series "The Mary Tyler Moore Show." Another school, Roseburg High, was also mentioned in several episodes.

**Lenya, Lotte**

Tony Award–winning actress whose name Louis Armstrong inserted in his version of the song "Mack the Knife," from *The Threepenny Opera*. Lotte is the widow of German composer Kurt Weill, who wrote the music for *The Three Penny Opera*.

**Leo**

Pet dog of the 4077th, for a short time, on the TV series

"M*A*S*H," as shown in only one episode.

**Leo**
Black-and-white pet dog of Alice Forsyte (Tatum O'Neal) in the 1976 movie *Nickelodeon*.

**Leona**
First name of both the first and third wives of country singer Merle Haggard.

**Le Roi des Champs Elysees**
Only film (1935) in which comic Buster Keaton smiled.

**Leroy**
U.S. Army chimpanzee that was scheduled to travel into space in a rocket in the 1958 movie *Rally 'Round the Flag, Boys*.

**"Let Me Call You Sweetheart"**
Song composed in 1910 by Beth Slater Whitson and Leo Friedman. The young lady who posed for the cover of the sheet music was Virginia Rappe, whom comic Fatty Arbuckle was tried and acquitted for raping and killing on September 5, 1921.

**"Let's Dance"**
Song written in 1935 by Joseph Bonime and Gregory Stone, with words by Fanny Baldridge. The song can be heard in the films *The Powers Girl* (1942), *The Gang's All Here* (1943), *Sweet and Low Down* (1944), and *The Benny Goodman Story* (1956).

**"Let's Do Something Cheap and Superficial"**
Song recorded in 1980 by actor Burt Reynolds, which peaked at number 88 on the *Billboard* Pop Singles Chart.

**"Let's Fall in Love"**
Song written in 1933 by Ted Koehler and Harold Arlen. The song was heard in the films *Let's Fall in Love* (1934); *Slightly French* 1949), sung by Don Ameche and Dorothy Lamour; *Tell It to the Judge* (1949), sung by Robert Cummings; *On the Sunny Side of the Street* (1951); *It Should Happen to You* (1954), sung by Judy Holliday and Jack Lemmon; and *The Eddy Duchin Story* (1956), played by Carmen Cavallaro.

**Let's Get Small**
Comedy album by Steve Martin. It became the first comedy album record to earn a platinum record (one million unit sales).

**Let's Make a Deal**
TV game show hosted by Monty Hall. The game show can be seen on a TV in the hotel room of a dead man in the 1975 movie *The Black Bird*, in Folsom Prison in the 1979 TV movie *The Jericho Mile*, on a TV in the 1980 movie *Middle Aged Crazy*, and in the

1982 movie *The Thing*.

**Letters of transit**
Official documents that allowed the bearer to travel without interference or questions. The term is totally fictitious, but was utilized in the 1943 movie *Casablanca*.

**"Let the Good Times In"**
Partridge family's demo song, which they played for Reuben Kinkaid (Dave Madden), who then became their agent on the TV series "The Partridge Family."

**"Let the Good Times Roll"**
Song by Louis Jordan on the 78 RPM Decca record played by Elroy Blues (Dan Ackroyd) in his room, in the 1980 movie *The Blues Brothers*.

**Levy, Benn**
Writer who is credited with "additional dialogue" for the 1936 movie *Romeo and Juliet*, starring Leslie Howard and Norma Shearer.

**Lewis, Joe E.**
(1902–1971) Nightclub comedian of the 1930s and 1940s who became involved with the Syndicate when they "borrowed" him to work in their Chicago club, the New Rendezvous Cafe. He was coerced by the mob to work at the club, which he did, after which he was beaten by the owners of his previous club, the Green Mill. He was portrayed by Frank Sinatra in the 1957 movie *The Joker Is Wild*. He later played himself in the 1968 Sinatra film *Lady in Cement*.

**Lewis, Steve**
Twenty-five-year-old man who broke his foot in an attempt to jump over two oncoming automobiles traveling at 100 miles per hour. Misjudging, Lewis hit his foot against the windshield of the first car. The incident was shown on the TV series "That's Incredible" in July 1980.

**LExington 0-5549**
Los Angeles home phone number of Judy (Natalie Wood) in the 1955 movie *Rebel Without a Cause*.

**Ley, Willy**
(1906–1969) German-born physicist and writer, he was the technical advisor for the early 1950s TV series "Tom Corbett, Space Cadet."

**Libby**
Waitress on the cover of the Supertramp album "Breakfast in

America'' (the name is on her name tag).

**Liberace's movie appearances**
*South Sea Sinner* (1950)
*Footlight Varieties* (1951)
*Sincerely Yours* (1955)
*The Loved One* (1965)
*When the Boys Meet the Girls* (1965)

**Liberty Bell Motel**
Philadelphia motel in which Judy Benjamin Goodman (Goldie Hawn) hid from the world for eight days and from which, at night, she poured her heart out on the ''Night Owl'' radio show, using the name of Jessica, in the 1980 movie *Private Benjamin*.

**Liddell, Eric**
Winner of the 400-meter race in the 1924 Olympic Games, nicknamed the Flying Scotsman. Liddell was born in China to Scottish parents, and later became a missionary. He was portrayed by Ian Charleson in the 1981 movie *Chariots of Fire*.

**Lieutenant Brass Bancroft**
Secret Service agent played by Ronald Reagan in four movies: *Secret Service of the Air* (1939), *Code of the Secret Service* (1939), *Smashing the Money Ring* (1939), and *Murder in the Air* (1940).

**Lieutenant Colonel Alvin F. Houlihan**
Major Margaret Houlihan's (Loretta Swit) father,* nicknamed ''Howitzer Al'' on the TV series ''M*A*S*H.'' He was played by Andrew Duggan, in the 1980–81 episode ''Father's Day.''

**Lieutenant Commander Barney Doyle**
Commander of the submarine USS *Greyfish* in the 1958 movie *Torpedo Run;* played by Glenn Ford.

**Lieutenant Francis Xavier Pope**
New York City policeman played by Norman Mailer in the 1968 movie *Beyond the Law*. Mailer wrote, produced, edited, and directed the movie.

**Lieutenant Maggie Dish**
Army nurse, played by Jo Ann Pflug in the 1970 movie *M*A*S*H*, her film debut. Lieutenant Dish was played by Karen Philipp in the pilot episode of the TV series.

**Life Achievement Awards**
Honor given by the American Film Institute awarded to:

---

*One of the series' few continuity errors was that in different episodes Margaret gave conflicting stories as to whether her father was alive or dead.

| John Ford | 1973 |
| James Cagney | 1974 |
| Orson Wells | 1975 |
| William Wyler | 1976 |
| Bette Davis | 1977 |
| Henry Fonda | 1978 |
| Alfred Hitchcock | 1979 |
| James Stewart | 1980 |
| Fred Astaire | 1981 |
| Frank Capra | 1982 |
| John Huston | 1983 |

**Lifeboat 7**

First lifeboat launched from the ocean liner *Stockholm* on the night that she rammed and sank the *Andrea Doria,* July 25, 1956.

**Lifeboat 13**

First lifeboat launched from the sinking *Andrea Doria* on the night of July 25, 1956.

**Life in the Woods**

Subtitle of Henry David Thoreau's classic 1854 American book, *Walden.*

**Life magazine**

July 22, 1946, issue that had an advertisement for the drug Emphemerol, in the 1981 movie *Scanners.*

**Liger**

Cross between a lion and a tiger.

**Lightning**

Racehorse that can't stand the smell of sardines, played by Marauder in the 1969 movie *The Reivers* (based on the novel of the same title by William Faulkner).

**Limelight**

Only movie in which Charles Chaplin and Buster Keaton appeared together. Chaplin won an Oscar for the musical score for this 1952 film.

**Lincoln and 46th**

Location of the drugstore in Ricky Nelson's 1958 hit recording of "Waitin' in School."

**Lionel Twain**

Millionaire played by author Truman Capote in the 1976 movie *Murder by Death.*

**Lions View State Asylum**

Mental institution where Dr. Cukrowicz (Montgomery Clift) was the head physician in the 1959 movie *Suddenly Last Summer*.

**Lisa Crowder**

Role played by Dyan Cannon on the TV soap "Full Circle."

**"Lisbon Antigua"**

Instrumental hit record (1956) by Nelson Riddle, being played on the car radio while Buddy Holly and the Crickets are en route to Nashville for a recording session in the 1978 movie *The Buddy Holly Story*.

**Little Al**

Name that Ellie Morgan Decker (Farrah Fawcett) gave to the giant teddy bear that Jake Decker bought her in the 1979 movie *Sunburn*. Little Al got shot in an attempted murder of Jake and Ellie.

**Lindstrom, Freddie**

(1905– ) Youngest person to play in a World Series game. As a New York Giants outfielder (at eighteen years and ten months of age), he appeared in all seven games of the 1924 World Series.

**Little Bend**

Western town that Flower Belle Lee (Mae West) was run out of in the 1940 movie *My Little Chickadee*.

**Little Bend**

Small Arizona town setting of the 1972 movie *Cancel My Reservation*.

**Little Boy Blue**

Little boy of the nursery rhyme, who is thought to have been Cardinal Wolsey as a lad. He was played by Johnny Downs in the 1934 movie *Babes in Toyland*, and by Kevin Corcoran in the 1961 movie *Babes in Toyland*.

**Little Buzzard 2-9824**

Phone number in Little Buzzard, Arizona, of Sally Hobson (Barbara Eden) in the 1961 movie *All Hands on Deck*. Sally was a reporter for the *Phoenix Independent* newspaper.

**Little Caesar**

Movie (1930) heard on a TV set in Chance's (Peter Sellers) bedroom, while Eve (Shirley MacLaine) stripped, in the 1979 movie *Being There*.

**Little Facts About Well-Known People**

Radio series (1943) hosted by Dale Carnegie. It was also the title of a best-selling book written by Carnegie.

**"Little Ole Wine Drinker, Me"**

Song that made the *Billboard* Hot 100 chart in 1967 for actors Dean Martin (peaked at number 38) and Robert Mitchum (peaked at number 96).

**Little Orphan Annie Secret Service Club**
    Club to which listeners could become members by sending in a silver inner seal from a jar of Ovaltine. Included was a code so that listeners could decipher the secret messages given out at the end of each program (which, in many cases, were commercials for Ovaltine).

**Little Orphan Otto**
    Original title of Harold Gray's cartoon "Little Orphan Annie" until *Chicago Tribune* publisher Joseph Patterson told him one day in 1924, "Put a skirt on the kid and call her Little Orphan Annie."

**Little pig droppings**
    Name that Miss Hanagan (Carol Burnett) called the little girls in her Hudson Street Home orphanage in the 1982 movie musical *Annie*.

**Little Richard Simmons**
    Musical exercise fanatic played by comedian Eddie Murphy on "Saturday Night Live." He was a parody of rock singer Little Richard and diet expert Richard Simmons.

**Little Sprout**
    Friend of the Jolly Green Giant on TV commercials; voice of Paul Frees.

**Little Sure Shot**
    Nickname of marksman Annie Oakley (Phoebe Anne Oakley Mozee). The nickname was given to her by Bill Cody but attributed to Sitting Bull.

**Little White House**
    President Franklin D. Roosevelt's retreat in Warm Springs, Georgia.

**Little Yola**
    Female dummy that Jack Dunne (Henry Winkler) used to entertain Carol Bell (Sally Field) in the 1977 movie *Heroes*.

**Livermore, Jesse**
    New York financier who made millions from the stock market crash. He made $30 million by selling short the day before the crash of November 29, 1929. Livermore, who committed suicide (his last words being "My life is a failure") was portrayed by Richard Crenna in the 1980 TV movie *The Day the Bubble Burst*.

**Liverpool, England, streets names for the Beatles in December of 1981**
    John Lennon Drive
    Paul McCartney Way

George Harrison Close
Ringo Starr Drive

**Living Dead**
Motorcycle gang featured in the 1972 British movie *Psychomania*.

**Lizzie**
Movie (1957) in which Johnny Mathis introduced his hit song "It's Not For Me to Say."

**LoBall**
Bret Maverick's (James Garner) horse, which he won in a poker game in the 1981 TV series "Bret Maverick."

**Local Hoedown**
Album of country songs recorded by horse race jockey Steve Cauthen.

**Local 343**
Cedar Rapids, Iowa, chapter of the Amalgamated Shirt and Pajama Workers of America, of which Katie "Babe" Williams (Doris Day) was head of the grievance committee in the 1957 movie *The Pajama Game*.

**Lockwood, Belva Ann**
(1830–1917) Feminist and lawyer who was the first woman to plead a case before the United States Supreme Court. She initiated Congress to pass a bill giving women government workers equal pay with men. Mrs. Lockwood ran for President of the United States twice (in 1884 and in 1888) on the National Equal Rights Party ticket. She later served on the Nobel Peace Prize nominating committee.

**Loes, Billy**
(1929–     ) Only major-league baseball player who was present on all of the occasions when the following players hit four home runs in a single game:

Gil Hodges (August 31, 1950)
Joe Adcock (July 31, 1954)
Rocky Colavito (June 10, 1959)
Willie Mays (April 30, 1961)

**Loftin, Cary**
Stunt driver of the mysterious tanker truck in the 1971 TV movie *Duel*.

**Logan, Harvey**
Western outlaw who was a member of Butch Cassidy and the Sundance Kid's Hole in the Wall gang. He was portrayed by Ted Cassidy in the 1969 movie *Butch Cassidy and the Sundance Kid,*

255

and by John Schuck in the 1979 movie *Butch and Sundance: The Early Days*.

**Lois**

Name of the ex-wife of airline pilot Howard Borden (Bill Daily), on the TV series "The Bob Newhart Show."

**Lola Lola**

Sexy Berlin nightclub singer, played by Marlene Dietrich in the 1930 German-made film *The Blue Angel*, and by May Britt in the 1959 remake. The Blue Angel was the name of a cabaret.

**Lolita**

U.S.-British-made film (1962) based on the Nabokov novel and directed by Stanley Kubrick and starring James Mason, Peter Sellers, Shelley Winters, and Sue Lyon. The movie was advertised on a Los Angeles movie theater marquee in the 1979 movic *The Onion Field*.

**Lollipop**

Streamliner Jones's (John H. Allen) pet monkey in the 1936 movie *Charlie Chan at the Racetrack*.

**London, Tom**

Real-life locomotive engineer in the 1903 movie *The Great Train Robbery*. London went on to appear in over two thousand movies, setting a record.

**"Lonely Girl"**

Theme song of the 1965 Paramount-Embassy film *Harlow*, sung by Bobby Vinton.

**Lone Wolf of Wall Street**

Appellative conferred upon Joseph P. Kennedy, Sr., the father of John F. Kennedy.

**Longacre, Sarah**

Daughter of the U.S. Mint's chief engraver, James Longacre. It was Sarah who posed for the Indian-head penny issued between 1859 and 1909.

**LOngbeach 4-5620**

The Corleone estate's phone number in Long Beach, Long Island, in the 1972 movie *The Godfather*.

**Long, Herman C.**

(1866–1909) Major-league baseball player who holds the lifetime record for the most errors. In his fifteen-year career (1889–1904) he made 1,037 errors.

**Long Island Bucks**

Great Neck softball team for which Monte Miller (Rob Reiner) played third base in the 1982 TV movie *Million Dollar Infield*.

**Long Live Flash Gordon**
Red graffiti on the walls of the torture chamber where Flash Gordon (Sam J. Jones) and Dr. Zarkov (Topol) were held prisoner in the 1980 movie *Flash Gordon*.

**"Look How Far We've Come"**
Theme song of the TV series "The Family Holvak," sung by Denny Brooks.

**"Looking for Love"**
Hit record by Johnnie Lee that was Buford "Bud" Davis's (John Travolta) favorite song. The song is heard, in part, three times in the 1980 movie *Urban Cowboy*.

**Look: We've Come Through**
Burt Reynolds's first Broadway play; it closed after only five performances in October 1961.

**Lopes, Davey**
(1946– ) Los Angeles Dodgers second baseman who made a record six errors during the 1981 World Series.

**Lopez, Vincent**
(1898– ) Popular bandleader since 1918. In 1921 he became the first bandleader to broadcast on radio, over WJ2 from Newark. His band's theme song was "Nola."

**Lord Baltimore**
Full-blooded Oklahoma Indian who, with a posse, tracked Butch Cassidy (Paul Newman) and the Sundance Kid (Robert Redford) into the mountains in the 1969 movie *Butch Cassidy and the Sundance Kid*.

**Lord Byron**
(1788–1824) George Gordon Byron, English poet, who was portrayed in the 1954 movie *Beau Brummel* by Noel William, in the 1972 movie *Lady Caroline Lamb* by Richard Chamberlain, and in the 1973 TV movie *Frankenstein: The True Story* by David McCallum. Despite a clubfoot, he led the life of dashing adventurer, with scandal following him wherever he went (his longest-lasting liaison being with his own half-sister). He is perhaps best known for his masterpiece *Don Juan* (1819). He died while training troops for the Greeks in their fight for independence from Turkey.

**Lord Cardigan (James Thomas Brudenell)**
(1797–1868) British army officer who became a lieutenant colonel after serving as an M.P. He purchased his commission in 1830, after which he became unpopular with his men. In 1840 he fought a

duel with a fellow officer, and in 1854 he commanded the cavalry that led the famous Charge of the Light Brigade at the battle of Balaklava in the Union War. Lord Cardigan became the first man to reach the Russian lines. In 1861 he was promoted to lieutenant general. Cardigan was portrayed by Trevor Howard in the 1968 movie *The Charge of the Light Brigade*.

**Lords**

Gang made up of Chico (Perry King), Stanley Rosiello (Sylvester Stallone), Butchey (Henry Winkler), and Wimpy (Paul Mace), in the 1974 movie *The Lords of Flatbush*.

**Loren, Sophia**

(1934– ) Italian actress, born Sofia Scicolone. After growing up in poverty, she made her first film, along with her mother, in the 1949 movie *Quo Vadis* (they appeared in bit roles). In 1957 she married producer Carlo Ponti by proxy, and then again in 1966. She won the Academy Award as Best Actress for the 1961 movie *Two Women*. Romano Mussolini, the son of Benito Mussolini, was Sophia's brother-in-law. Sophia was portrayed by herself in the 1980 TV movie *Sophia Loren: Her Own Story* (she also portrayed her own mother) and by Ritza Brown (at age 16) and Chiara Ferraro (at age 47).

**Loretta**

Actress Colleen Moore's favorite doll. It was after this doll that actress Gretchen Young named herself, becoming Loretta Young.

**Lorraine**

Colonel Henry Blake's (McLean Stevenson) wife back home in Bloomington, Illinois. Her measurements were 36-24-34, and she was played in a home movie by Kathleen Hughes. Their two daughters are Molly and Janey, in the TV series "M*A*S*H."

**Los Angeles Rams**

In exhibition games on August 4, 1951, the pro football team defeated three teams, playing each for 20 minutes:

| | |
|---|---|
| The Marine Recruiting Depot | 13 to 0 |
| Camp Pendleton Marines | 21 to 2 |
| San Diego Training Center | 21 to 0 |

**Los Angeles Standard**

Newspaper for which Maggie Day (Cloris Leachman) was a columnist on the TV series "Advice to the Lovelorn."

**Los Angeles Sun**

Newspaper for which Vince Perrino (David Janssen) worked as a columnist in the 1980 TV movie *City in Fear.*

**Los Angeles Times**
Newspaper that Benjamin ''Bugsy'' Siegel was reading when he was shot to death in the home of girlfriend Virginia Hill, on June 20, 1947.

**LOS GUYS**
California license number of Cheech and Chong's low-riding white Chevy ice cream truck (number 333) in the 1981 movie *Cheech & Chong's Nice Dreams.*

**Lot**
Nephew of Abraham whom God allowed to leave the doomed city of Sodom with his family. Unfortunately, his wife looked back at the destruction and was turned into a pillar of salt. He was portrayed by Stewart Granger in the 1961 movie *Sodom and Gomorrah,* and by Ed Ames on the TV series ''Greatest Heroes of the Bible.''

**Louis-Conn fight**
Heavyweight championship fight between Joe Louis and Billy Conn, which Louis won by a KO in the eighth round. In the 1980 movie *The Final Countdown,* the crew heard this fight over the radio on December 6, 1941, although the fight had actually been fought on June 18, 1941.

**Louise**
Captain ''Trapper''˙ John McIntyre's (Wayne Rogers) wife on the TV series ''M*A*S*H.'' Their two daughters are named Kathy and Becky.

**Louise**
Major Frank Burns's (Larry Linville) wife back home in the States, played by Jeannie Shulherr in a home movie on the TV series ''M*A*S*H.'' In the home movie, the bride and bridegroom drove away on their honeymoon in a 1940 Ford convertible, with Louise doing the driving.

**''Louise''**
Song written in 1929 by Leo Robin and Richard A. Whiting, heard in the movies *Innocents of Paris* (1929) and *A New Kind of Love* (1963), sung in both films by Maurice Chevalier; also heard in *Halfway to Heaven* (1929), *You Can't Ration Love* (1944), and in *The Stooge* (1952), sung by Jerry Lewis.

**Lou King**
Ring name under which actor Lou Costello boxed in his youth. His

amateur record was eleven wins and one draw.

**Love Among the Stars**
Theme of the Bates High School Senior Ball attended by Carrie White (Cissy Spacek) in the 1976 movie *Carrie* (based on the Stephen King novel of the same title).

**Love and Kisses**
Motion picture (1965) produced, written, and directed by Ozzie Nelson. It starred Rick Nelson and his real-life wife Kristin (daughter of football great Tom Harmon and actress Elyse Knox), as husband and wife.

**"Love and Let Love"**
Song for which Neely O'Hara (Patti Duke) won a Grammy Award in the 1967 movie *Valley of the Dolls*.

**"Love and the Happy Day"**
Segment on the TV series "Love, American Style," first aired in February 1972, from which the TV series "Happy Days" was a spinoff. Ron Howard and Anson Williams appeared in the segment.

**Love-Hate**
Letters on the knuckles of Eddie (Meat Loaf) in the 1975 movie *The Rocky Horror Picture Show* (Robert Mitchum had had a similar tattoo in the 1955 movie *The Night of the Hunter*).

**Love Is on the Air**
Movie (1937) debut of Ronald Reagan.

**"Love Me Tender"**
Popular ballad written by Ken Darby (although credited to his wife, Vera Matson). It was first recorded by Elvis Presley in 1956, reaching number one on the pop charts. The song was based on the 1861 ballad "Aura Lee." Elvis Presley sang "Love Me Tender" in the 1956 movie *Love Me Tender*, and Linda Ronstadt sang the song in the 1978 movie *FM*. Actress Frances Farmer sang "Aura Lee" in the 1936 movie *Come and Get It*. In late 1983, "Love Me Tender" was used to advertise Tender Chunks dog food.

**"Lovesick Blues"**
Song that Hank Williams sang on his debut on "The Grand Ole Opry" on June 11, 1949. The crowd loved the performance so much that he sang it a second time. His son, Hank Williams, Jr., also sang "Lovesick Blues" in his first professional appearance, in Swain Shore, Georgia, when he was eight years old. Hank Wil-

liams's recording of "Lovesick Blues" can be heard in the 1971 movie *The Last Picture Show*.

**"Love Song of the Waterfall"**

Country song being sung by Slim Whitman over the radio as Indiana police cars go through a toll booth into Ohio, in the 1977 movie *Close Encounters of the Third Kind*.

**Love Ya Blues**

Slogan of the Houston Oilers football team, coined by medical secretary Donna Agner.

**L. Q. Jones**

Soldier played by actor L. Q. Jones in the 1955 movie *Battle Cry*, billed under his real name, Justus E. McQueen. After making this film, McQueen changed his name to L. Q. Jones.

**Lucas Lorenzo Spencer**

Luke's (Tony Geary) full name on the TV soap opera "General Hospital."

**Lucas, Sam**

First black actor to play a leading role in an American film, when he starred in the 1914 movie *Uncle Tom's Cabin*.

**Lucky**

Rabbit puppet that appeared with Miss Frances on the TV program "Ding Dong School."

**Lucky Dan**

For the "big sting," horse that Doyle Lonnegan (Robert Shaw) is told to "place" his $500,000 bet on, at the third race at Riverside Park, at odds of four to one. The horse came in second (place), but Lonnegan lost because he "placed" the bet to win, in the 1973 movie *The Sting*.

**Lucky Jackpot Program, The**

Radio program on which Irma Peterson (Marie Wilson) won the $50,000 first prize by guessing the correct answer to the mystery song "Buttons and Bows" sung by Bing Crosby, in the 1949 movie *My Friend Irma*.

**Lucy**

Guitar that Eric Clapton gave to his close friend, George Harrison, in 1968.

**Lucy Van Pelt**

Militant little girl who is in love with Schroeder in Charles Schulz's comic strip "Peanuts." She was introduced into the strip in 1952.

Her voice was provided in the movie *A Boy Named Charlie Brown* (1969) by Pamelyn Ferdin,* and in *Snoopy Come Home* (1972) by Robin Kohn. On "Peanuts" TV specials, her voice has been provided by Tracy Stratford (1965), Sally Dryer (1966–1968), Pamelyn Ferdin (1969–1971), Robin Kohn (1972–1973), Melanie Kohn (1974–1975), Lynn Mortensen (1976), Sarah Beach (1976), Michelle Muller (1977–1979), and Cindi Reilly (1981).

## LUDES

California automobile license plate of the pickup truck belonging to the Pud Pullers in the 1981 movie *Cheech & Chong's Nice Dreams*.

## Luke

Roscoe "Fatty' Arbuckle's pet dog, which appeared with him in films.

## Luke Skywalker

Hero of George Lucas's 1978 movie *Star Wars*, the 1980 sequel *The Empire Strikes Back*, and the 1983 sequel *Return of the Jedi*. He is the son of Darth Vader and brother of Princess Leia (Carrie Fisher). Luke was played by Mark Hamill.

## "Lullaby of Broadway"

Song composed in 1935 by Al Dubin and Harry Warren. It was given the Academy Award for Best Song when it was used in the 1935 movie *Gold Diggers of Broadway*. The song was played in the 1940 movie *City of Fear*, and Doris Day sang it in the 1951 movie *Lullaby of Broadway*.

## Luther

Merlin's (Barnard Hughes) pet owl on the TV series "Mr. Merlin."

## Lycanthropy

Study of werewolves (also sometimes used as the name for the disease of werewolfism).

## Lyons, Ted

(1900–   ) Only member of the Baseball Hall of Fame to have walked more batters (1,121) than he struck out (1,073) in his career.

---

*Pamelyn Ferdin and Doney Oatman both played Felix Unger's daughter, Edna, on the TV series "The Odd Couple."

# M

**M.B.S.C.S.D.D.**
Master of Back Stabbin', Corkscrewin' and Dirty Dealin'—self-conferred title of Mordecai Jones (George C. Scott) in the 1967 movie *The Flim-Flam Man*.

**MDCCCLXXXVIII**
Roman numeral for the year 1888.

**M.S.**
Initials of actresses who won the Oscar for Best Supporting Actress from 1978 to 1981.

| 1978 | Maggie Smith | *California Suite* |
| 1979 | Meryl Streep | *Kramer vs. Kramer* |
| 1980 | Mary Steenburgen | *Melvin and Howard* |
| 1981 | Maureen Stapleton | *Reds* |

**M-1026-A**
Greek license plate number of the yellow Citröen 2CV automobile driven by both Melina (Carol Bouquet) and James Bond (Roger Moore) in the 1981 movie *For Your Eyes Only*.

**M29750**
License plate number of the police car on the picture sleeve of the 45 RPM record of the "Hill Street Blues Theme," a 1981 hit recording by Mike Post.

**M52519**
U.S. Army serial number of Francis the Mule, assigned to the 123rd Mule Detachment in the *Francis the Talking Mule* movie series.

**Ma and Pa Kettle Have a Baby**
One of the fictitious movies shown at the 4077th in the TV series "M*A*S*H."

**MacCracken, Mary**
   Volunteer teacher who dedicated her life to helping emotionally
   disturbed children. She was portrayed by Jane Alexander in two TV
   movies: *A Circle of Children* (1977) and *Lovey: A Circle of Children, Part Two* (1981).

**MacDonald, Ryan**
   Actor who appeared on the TV soap opera "Days of Our Lives."
   He was the first centerfold for *Playgirl* magazine.

**"Mad About the Boy"**
   Noel Coward song sung by Yul Brynner, dressed as a lady singer,
   to Roman Polanski in the 1970 movie *The Magic Christian*.

**Madame Tinkertoy's House of Blue Lights**
   Whorehouse in New Orleans visited by Wyatt (Peter Fonda) and
   Billy (Dennis Hopper) during Mardi Gras in the 1969 movie *Easy
   Rider*.

**MAdison 4307**
   Telephone number of private detective Jake J. Gittes (Jack Nicholson) in the 1974 movie *Chinatown*.

**MAdison 5-0100**
   Home phone number of Dr. Myles Binnell (Kevin McCarthy) in the
   1956 movie *Invasion of the Body Snatchers*.

**Maggie the Cat**
   Nickname of Margaret Pollitt, played by Elizabeth Taylor in the
   1958 movie *Cat on a Hot Tin Roof* and by Natalie Wood in the
   1976 TV movie of the same title (based on the Pulitzer Prize–
   winning play by Tennessee Williams).

**Magnolia Drive-In**
   Drive-in restaurant where Georgette Thomas (Lee Remick) worked
   in the 1965 movie *Baby, the Rain Must Fall*.

**Maid of the Mist IV**
   Sightseeing boat at Niagara Falls in the 1981 movie *Superman II*.
   (*Maid of the Mist II* could be seen in the 1953 movie *Niagara*.)

**MAine 4-9970**
   Telephone number of Mrs. Connie Bailey (Thelma Todd) in the
   1932 movie *Horse Feathers*.

**Major Amos Charles Dundee**
   U.S. Army officer, played by Charlton Heston in the 1965 movie
   *Major Dundee*.

**Major Domo**
   Johnny Jupiter's robot on the 1953 TV puppet show "Johnny
   Jupiter."

**Major Erik Dorf**
German SS officer, played by Michael Moriarty in the 1978 TV mini-series "Holocaust."

**Major General Walter Kroll**
Union officer under whom James T. West (Robert Conrad) served during the Civil War. He was played by Kevin McCarthy in an episode of the TV series "The Wild Wild West."

**Major T.J. "King" Kong**
U.S. B-52 pilot whose aircraft penetrated Soviet airspace, after which he rode to earth on an H-bomb, in the 1964 movie *Dr. Strangelove*. He was played by Slim Pickens, although Peter Sellers was originally cast in the role, until he broke his ankle. (As it was, Sellers played three other major roles in the film.)

**Major Weldon Penderton**
U.S. Army officer played by Marlon Brando in the 1967 movie *Reflections in a Golden Eye*.

**Make Way for Glory**
Movie that Zachary Morgan (Joseph Cotten) took Mary Marshall (Ginger Rogers) to see at a Pinehill theater in the 1944 movie *I'll Be Seeing You*. *Romantic Rhapsody* was to be the next movie they would see.

**Making My First Million**
Book written by B. P. Morrow and read by Sermon Jones (Gordon MacRae) in the 1953 movie *Three Sailors and a Girl*.

**Makin' It**
Television series (1979) in which David Naughton both starred and sang the theme song, "Makin' It," with background disco music by the Bee Gees. The song, which made it to number five in 1979, can also be heard in the 1979 movie *Meatballs*.

**Malacca, SS**
Tramp steamer upon which Bijou (Marlene Dietrich) sailed after she was deported from Sumatra in the 1940 movie *Seven Sinners*.

**Malinou, Sherri**
Mickey Spillane's second wife (twenty-four years his junior) who posed nude for the cover of his novel *The Erection Set*.

**Mallory Gallery**
London museum where Lady Holiday's (Diana Rigg) jewel "the Baseball Diamond" was kept in the 1981 movie *The Great Muppet Caper*.

**Mallory, George Leigh**
British mountain climber who led an expedition to climb Mount

Everest in 1924. All of the members perished on June 28, 1924. Some people believe that they died after successfully making it to the top, which would mean that they were the first, beating Sir Edmund Hillary by twenty-nine years.

**Malpractice and Its Defense and Profit in Healing**
Two books written by Dr. Lloyd Axton (Jeff Morrow) on the TV series "The New Temperature's Rising."

**Malvinas**
Argentine name for the Falkland Islands.

**Mama and the Hospital**
Short story that Katrin Hanson (Barbara Bel Geddes) sold to a publisher for five dollars in the 1948 movie *I Remember Mama*.

**Mammoth Studios**
Hollywood motion picture studio that is the setting of the 1945 movie *Abbott and Costello in Hollywood*.

**Man About the House**
British TV series upon which the U.S. series "Three's Company" is based. The British series "George and Mildred" was a spinoff of "Man About the House," while the American series "The Ropers," which was based upon the British series "George and Mildred," became a spinoff of "Three's Company." (Confused??)

**Managers traded for baseball players**
Rogers Hornsby for Frankie Frisch and Jimmy Ring (1926)
Chuck Tanner for Manny Sanguillan (1953)
Gil Hodges for Bill Denehy (1967)

**"Man and a Train, A"**
Theme song of the 1973 movie *Emperor of the North Pole*, sung by Marty Robbins.

**Mandrell, Barbara**
(1948–    ) Extremely talented and beautiful country singer who sings and plays the guitar, steel guitar, banjo, and saxophone. She heads a cowboy band called the Do-Rites. Born on December 25, 1948, she was portrayed as a little girl by Georgi Irene, on her TV series, "Barbara Mandrell and the Mandrell Sisters."

**Mandrell Sisters**
Family of talented country performers: Barbara, Louise, and Irlene.

**Manhattan Garage**
Garage where the members of the musical *U.S.S. Texas* rehearsed in the 1953 movie *Three Sailors and a Girl*. The phone number

there was CIrcle 2-4300.

**"Man in the Mask, The"**
Theme song of the 1981 movie *The Legend of the Lone Ranger*, sung by Merle Haggard, who also narrated the film.

**Man on the Outside, The**
TV pilot movie (1973) for the TV series "Griff."

**Mansfield, Arabella**
First woman to be admitted to the law bar in the United States (1869).

**"Man Trap, The"**
First episode of the TV series "Star Trek," aired originally on September 8, 1966.

**Mapes, Cliff**
(1922–   ) New York Yankee who wore uniform number 3 after Babe Ruth retired, and number 7 prior to Mickey Mantle. When Mantle wanted number 7, Mapes then chose number 13.

**Maranville, Walter "Rabbit"**
(1891–1954) Major-league player who holds the record for the most at-bats (672) in a single season (1922) without hitting a single home run.

**Marberry**
Exclusive New York City hotel where Apple Annie (Bette Davis) received mail, using the name of Mrs. E. Worthington Manville, from her daughter, Louise (Ann-Margret), in Barcelona, Spain, in the 1961 movie *Pocketful of Miracles*.

**Marcelle, Lou**
Uncredited narrator of the 1943 movie *Casablanca* and of the 1943 movie *Destination Tokyo*.

**March 5, 1944**
Date on which Lieutenant Steve Maryk (Van Johnson) started his medical log about Captain Philip Francis Queeg (Humphrey Bogart) in the 1954 movie *The Caine Mutiny*.

**Margaret**
Danny Williams's (Danny Thomas) first wife on the 1953–1964 TV series "Make Room for Daddy," played from 1953 to 1957 by Jean Hagen. The following season the program title was changed to "The Danny Thomas Show" and Danny Williams had a new wife named Kathy, played by Marjorie Lord. It was explained that Margaret had died.

**Maria**
Title of a song sung in two different musical plays: *West Side Story* and *The Sound of Music*.

**Mariah**
Speedboat driven by mailman Charlie Martin (William Lanteau) in the 1981 movie *On Golden Pond*.

**Marigold**
Girlfriend of Tom Slick on TV cartoon series.

**Marine Lagoon**
Western White House of President Chet Roosevelt (John Ritter) in the 1979 movie *Americathon*.

**Mario**
Workman who attempts to rescue the blond woman in the video game *Donkey Kong*.

**Marion Hargrove**
Newspaper reporter who was drafted into the U.S. Army in September 1943. He was played by Robert Walker in two films: *See Here, Private Hargrove* (1944) and *What Next, Corporal Hargrove?* (1945). Marion Hargrove is the actual name of the author of the novel on which the films are based.

**Mark Spitz**
Singer Dolly Parton's pet Spitz dog.

**Marlowe**
Rick Simon's (Gerald McRaney) pet dog on the TV series "Simon and Simon."

**Marquee Club**
Soho, London, club where, on Thursday night, July 12, 1962, the Rolling Stones made their debut as a band.

**Marr, Eddie**
Actor who asked Jack Benny the famous question, "Your money or your life?" to which Jack answered (after a *long* pause), "I'm thinking!" on "The Jack Benny Program" on radio.

**Marriage—A Fraud and a Failure**
Book written by Mortimer Brewster (Cary Grant) in the 1944 movie *Arsenic and Old Lace*.

**"Married Man"**
Recording with which actor Richard Burton made the *Billboard* Hot 100 chart in 1965, peaking at number 64 (MGM 13307).

**Marsha**
Name that Rhoda's mother, Ida (Nancy Walker), originally wanted

to give her on the TV series "Rhoda."

**Marshall, Mike**
(1943–   ) Baseball player who, in 1974, set the major-league record for the most games pitched in a season, when he pitched in 106 games for the Los Angeles Dodgers. His record that season was 15–12, with 21 saves. That year he became baseball's first relief pitcher to win the Cy Young Award.

**Marsoupial**
Name given to the possum in the closing credits for the 1981 movie *The Pursuit of D. B. Cooper*.

**Martha Frazier**
Character on the TV soap opera "The Guiding Light," played at different times by Ruby Dee and Cicely Tyson.

**Martino, Al**
Singer of the theme song of the 1965 movie *Hush, Hush, Sweet Charlotte*. It was Patti Page, however, who had the hit record of the song.

**Martin, Sir James**
Inventor of the aircraft ejection seat, first successfully tested on July 24, 1946.

**Marty White**
Character played by Dickie Moore in the 1942 Shirley Temple movie *Miss Annie Rooney*. In the movie, Dickie Moore gave Shirley Temple her first romantic screen kiss.

**Marucci, Bob**
Manager of rock artists Frankie Avalon and Fabian Forte in the 1950s and 1960s. He was loosely portrayed by Ray Sharkey, as Vinnie Vacarri, in the 1980 movie *The Idolmaker*, on which Bob Marucci served as technical advisor.

**Mary**
Spokesperson for the Iranian students who held the fifty American hostages at the American Embassy in Tehran from November 4, 1979, until January 19, 1981.

**Mary**
Real name of the rhinoceros that Johnny Weissmuller rode in the 1934 movie *Tarzan and His Mate*.

**Mary and Sue**
Two girls mentioned in the lyrics of three hit songs: "Honey Babe," by Art Mooney (1955); "Finger-Poppin' Time," by Hank Ballard and the Midnighters (1960); and "What's Your Name," by

Don and Juan (1962).

**Mary Christmas**

Hollywood gossip columnist played by Mary Astor on the radio series "The Merry Life of Mary Christmas."

**Mary D.**

Dr. Marcus Welby's (Robert Young) fishing boat on the TV series "Marcus Welby, M.D."

**Mary Goodnight**

Secretary of Agent 007, James Bond (Roger Moore), in the 1974 movie *The Man with the Golden Gun* (loosely based on the novel of the same title by Ian Fleming). Miss Goodnight was played by Britt Ekland.

**Mary Hill**

Naughty young woman who was the subject of Billy Joe Royal's 1969 hit song "Cherry Hill Park."

**Mary Lou**

Girl mentioned in the lyrics of the following songs: the Cheers' 1955 hit, "Black Denim Trousers and Motorcycle Boots"; Claudine Clark's 1962 hit, "Party Lights"; and Jim Stafford's 1973 hit, "Spiders and Snakes."

**Mary Lou**

Name of the python in the 1965 movie *Clarence, the Cross-Eyed Lion*.

**Mary Westmascott**

Pseudonym used by British novelist Agatha Christie when she wrote romantic novels.

**Master Sergeant Milton Warden**

U.S. Army sergeant who fell in love with Captain Dana Holmes's wife, Karen. He was played by Burt Lancaster in the 1953 movie *From Here to Eternity*, and by William Devane in the TV series of the same title (both based on the novel by James Jones).

**Masterson, Bill**

First NHL player to die as the result of injuries that occurred in a game. Masterson, of the Minnesota North Stars, died two days later of a brain injury incurred in a game on January 13, 1968, against the Oakland Seals.

**Mathewson, Christy**

(1880–1925) Major-league baseball player who shut out the Philadelphia Athletics three times in the 1905 World Series. In 1936 he became the third man (of the first five) to be elected to the Baseball

Hall of Fame. On July 15, 1901, he became the youngest pitcher to throw a no-hitter, at age twenty years, eleven months, and three days. Mathewson was portrayed by Fay Thomas in the 1942 movie *The Pride of the Yankees*.

**Mathewson, Christy and Henry**

Major-league pitching brothers. Christy holds the National League record for the most consecutive innings (sixty-eight innings, in 1913) without allowing a base on balls, and Henry holds the National League record for the most bases on balls in one game (with fourteen in a game) in 1906. Together, the brothers are the second winningest pitching brothers, after the Perry brothers. Christy won 373 games, but Henry won none in three appearances.

**Matrix Club**

San Francisco nightclub where the rock band the Jefferson Airplane made their first professional appearance on August 13, 1965.

**Maureen Mooney**

Role played by Gloria De Haven in the TV soap opera "As the World Turns."

**Mauser, Lillie**

Grandmother of Senate Majority Leader Howard Baker. In 1927 she became the first woman sheriff in Tennessee (she died in 1981, at the age of 101).

**"Maverick Didn't Come Here to Lose"**

Theme song of the 1981 TV series *Bret Maverick*, sung by James Garner.

**Maverick, Maury**

Texas congressman who, in 1944, coined the term "gobbledygook."

**Max**

Havelock's (Jack Hedley) pet parrot in the 1981 movie *For Your Eyes Only*. His favorite expression was "Give me a kiss."

**Max**

Wesley Winfield's (Billy Gray) pet dog in the 1951 movie *On Moonlight Bay* and in the 1954 sequel, *By the Light of the Silvery Moon*.

**Maximillian**

Robot on board the space vessel *Cygnus* in the 1979 movie *The Black Hole*.

**Maxply McEnroes**

Dunlop tennis rackets for which Wimbledon champ John McEnroe appeared in TV commercials.

**May**

Month mentioned in the lyrics of the Temptations' 1965 hit, "My Girl."

**May 26, 1900**

Birthdate of German spy Henry Faber (Donald Sutherland) in the 1981 movie *Eye of the Needle* (based on the novel of the same title by Ken Follett).

**May 28, 1908**

Birthdate of James Bond's archenemy, Ernst Stavro Blofeld. (In actuality, it was the birthdate of author Ian Fleming.)

**May 9, 1940**

Date of the opening scenes of the 1942 Joan Crawford/John Wayne movie *Reunion in France*.

**May 1972**

Date of the opening scenes of the 1980 movie *Somewhere in Time*, starring Christopher Reeve and Jane Seymour.

**Mayberry**

Town (population 1,200) in the northern part of North Carolina, founded by James Meriweather and Chief Noogatuck, on the TV series "The Andy Griffith Show." It is the hometown of Sheriff Andy Taylor, Barney Fife, Aunt Bee, Goober Pyle, Gomer Pyle, and others.

**Mayberry After Midnight**

Gossip column in the *Mayberry Gazette* newspaper on the TV series "The Andy Griffith Show." It was also known as "The Mayberry Merry-Go-Round."

**Mayberry Gazette**

Small-town newspaper of Mayberry, North Carolina, on the TV series "The Andy Griffith Show."

**Mayberry Union High**

High school in Mayberry, North Carolina, from which Andy Taylor and Barney Fife graduated on the TV series "The Andy Griffith Show."

**May, Carlos**

(1948–     ) Only major-league baseball player to wear both the month and day of his birth on his uniform. May, whose uniform number was 17, was born on May 17 (1948).

**Mayo Clinic/City Hospital/Mt. Sinai**

Three wall clocks on the operating-room wall, representing the times at the various medical facilities in the 1982 movie *Young Doctors in Love*.

**Mayor Carmine De Pasto**
Mayor of the college town near Faber College; played by Cesare Danova in the 1978 movie *National Lampoon's Animal House*.

**Mayor Frank Skeffington**
Boston city mayor, played by Spencer Tracy, who ran for, but lost, reelection in the 1958 movie *The Last Hurrah*. Also played by Carroll O'Connor, in the 1977 film of the same title. (Both movies were based on the novel *The Last Hurrah* by Edwin O'Connor.)

**Mayor Hiram J. Slade**
Mayor of the town of Bottleneck, played by Samuel S. Hinds in the 1939 movie *Destry Rides Again*.

**Mayor Jefferson Davis "Boss" Hogg**
Mayor of Hazzard County, played by Sorrell Brooke on the TV series "The Dukes of Hazzard." His twin brother (also played by Sorrell Brooke) is Abraham Lincoln Hogg. Boss Hogg's wife is named Lulu.

**Mayor Merle Jeeter**
Mayor of the town of Fernwood, Ohio, played by Dabney Coleman on the TV series "Mary Hartman, Mary Hartman."

**Mayor of Harlem**
Nickname of dancer Bill "Bojangles" Robinson.

**Mayor Otis Harper**
Mayor of Harper Valley, played by George Gobel on the TV series "Harper Valley PTA."

**Mayor Stonefeller**
Mayor of Sweethaven, the hometown of Popeye; played by Paul Zegler in the 1980 movie *Popeye*.

**"May the Good Lord Bless and Keep You"**
Closing theme song sung each week by Tallulah Bankhead on the radio series "The Big Show."

**McBarker**
Mr. Magoo's pet bulldog on the cartoon TV series "What's New, Mr. Magoo?" Voiced by Robert Ogle.

**McCarthy, Joe**
(1887–1978) Manager of the New York Yankees for fifteen seasons, winning eight pennants and seven World Series, and a member of the Baseball Hall of Fame (1957). McCarthy was portrayed by Harry Harvey in the 1942 movie *The Pride of the Yankees*.

**McCay, Windsor**
Cartoonist who created the comic strip "Little Nemo" in 1905. He

played himself in the 1924 silent movie *The Great White Way*.

**McCormick, Pat**

Texas woman who, in 1952, became the first woman bullfighter. She performed in Mexico, killing eighty bulls in her first two years.

**McCosky, Barney**

(1918–      ) Philadelphia A's and Detroit Tigers player who was the only regular American League player not struck out by Bob Feller during the 1946 season. (He did not face Feller that season.) Of course, this excludes Feller's own teammates.

**McCovey, Willie**

(1938–      ) In his very first major-league game (on July 30, 1959), he got four hits, including two triples and two doubles, against Robin Roberts. McCovey is the only player to have hit two home runs in one inning, on two separate occasions: April 12, 1973 (fourth inning), and June 27, 1977 (sixth inning).

**McDermott, Terry**

Only American athlete to win a gold medal in the 1964 Winter Olympics at Innsbruck, Austria. He won it for the 500-meter speed-skating race.

**McDowell, Ephraim**

(1771–1830) Frontier doctor who, in 1809, performed the first removal of an ovarian tumor. He was portrayed by Paul Guilfoyle in the PBS TV movie *Ephraim McDowell's Kentucky Ride*.

**McDowell, Ronnie**

Elvis Presley sound-alike singer who provided the singing for the 1979 Dick Clark-produced TV movie *Elvis!* in which Kurt Russell portrayed Elvis.

**McGraw, Cari**

Tug McGraw's daughter, who appeared with her father in several TV commercials for 7-Up. Her sole line in one commercial was, "Lucky for you that pitch was low and outside" (circa 1981–1982).

**McLean, Ray "Scooter"**

Chicago Bears player who made the very last dropkick in an NFL game. He made the dropkick in the 1941 championship game (played on December 21) in which the Chicago Bears defeated the New York Giants 37 to 9.

**McLeod, Don**

Actor who appears in American Tourister (1980–1981) TV commercials as an ape.

**McManus, George**
Cartoonist who created the comic strip "Bringing Up Father" in 1913. He played himself in the 1924 silent movie *The Great White Way*.

**McMillian, Kirkland**
Scottish blacksmith who, in 1840, invented the first bicycle with pedals.

**McNally, Dave**
(1942–     ) Baltimore Orioles pitcher who, on October 13, 1970, became the only pitcher ever to hit a grand slam in a World Series game.

**McNamara, James C.**
Newscaster for KLAC radio, who interviewed Howard Hughes at the controls of his experimental aircraft, the Spruce Goose, which he flew for the first and only time on November 9, 1947.

**McNeill, Anna**
Artist James Whistler's mother, whom he painted in 1871.

**McPherson, Aimee Semple**
(1890–1944) Woman evangelist who founded the Angelus Temple in Los Angeles, teaching her "Foursquare Gospel." She had a very large following and was mysteriously "kidnapped" in May of 1926, but returned safely some thirty-seven days later. Aimee baptized a young girl in 1926 named Norma Jeane Mortenson, who later became known as Marilyn Monroe. McPherson was portrayed by Faye Dunaway in the 1976 TV movie *The Disappearance of Aimee* (a role originally meant for Ann-Margret). Bette Davis played her mother, Minnie Kennedy, in the film. Aimee McPherson was loosely portrayed by Geraldine Page in the 1975 movie *The Day of the Locust*.

**McWilliam, Willie B.**
Delta Airlines pilot who landed his aircraft at MacDill Air Force Base in Florida, on June 20, 1980, thinking it was his destination of Tampa.

**"Me and My Shadow"**
Song composed in 1927 by Billy Rose, Dave Dreyer, and Al Jolson, which was sung by the six "time bandits" on stage, to Napoleon, in the 1981 movie *Time Bandits*.

**Meat Cutters**
Butcher Sam Franklin's (Allan Melvin) bowling team on the TV series "The Brady Bunch."

**Medea**

Princess of Colchis in Greek mythology. She aided Jason in his quest for the Golden Fleece. Medea was played by Nancy Kovack in the 1963 movie *Jason and the Argonauts*.

**Medicine Bow Saloon**

Town tavern where Trampas and the Virginian played poker. When Trampas said to the Virginian, "Your bet, you son of a b____," the Virginian replied, "When you call me that, smile!" in Owen Wister's 1902 novel *The Virginian*.

**Meet me in the lounge—God**

Message found by Tracy (Louanne) in her fortune cookie at the Red Dragon restaurant in the 1980 movie *Oh God! Book II*. A second cookie said, "I mean you, Tracy—God."

**Meet Whiplash Willie**

British release title of the 1966 American movie *The Fortune Cookie*.

**Megapolitan**

Hollywood motion picture studio where Sir Francis Hinley (Sir John Gielgud) worked as an art director in the 1965 movie *The Loved One*.

**Melanie**

Trapper John's (Pernell Roberts) ex-wife, played by Jessica Walter on the TV series "Trapper John, M.D."

**Mellonville**

Canadian town from which Channel 109 is transmitted in the TV series "SCTV" (Second City Television).

**Memory of Eva Ryker, The**

TV movie (1980) starring Natalie Wood and Ralph Bellamy, in which Natalie Wood's character drowned. The film was shown on TV two months prior to her actual drowning death, which occurred on November 29, 1981.

**Mene, Mene, Tekel, Upharsin**

Four Aramaic words written on the wall at Belshazzar's feast, mentioned in the Bible (Daniel 5:25). It was Daniel who interpreted the words as "numbered, numbered, weighed, divided," meaning that Belshazzar's kingdom was about to come to an end.

**Mensa**

Organization comprised of people with IQs of 140 and above. (Its name is from the Latin word "mind.")

**Mercury (1971)**

Automobile in which blues guitarist Mike Bloomfield was found dead from a drug overdose on February 15, 1981.

**Meriden-Cleghorn High**

Des Moines, Iowa, school that bought the uniforms designed for former President Nixon's White House guards. The school bought the uniforms for ten dollars each, to be used for their school's marching band.

**Merle Johnson**

Character played by Troy Donahue in the 1974 movie *The Godfather, Part II*. Merle Johnson is Troy Donahue's real name.

**Merlin, Joseph**

Belgian man who, in 1760, invented the first roller skates.

**Merrill**

Three-year-old bull that walks around in a china shop without knocking anything down, on TV commercials for Merrill-Lynch. The standby bull was named Lynch.

**Mickey Goldmill**

(April 7, 1905–August 15, 1981) Rocky Balboa's (Sylvester Stallone) manager in the movies *Rocky* (1976), *Rocky II* (1979), and *Rocky III* (1982), played by Burgess Meredith.

**Middleweight**

Private Robert E. Lee Prewitt's (Montgomery Clift) pugilistic weight classification in the 1953 movie *From Here to Eternity*.

**Mid-Morning Manhattan**

Morning TV show that Nan Gallagher (Mimi Kennedy) co-hosts on the TV series "The Two of Us." It is televised from Studio 12.

**Midnight**

Old Rivers's plow mule in the 1962 hit record "Old Rivers," sung by actor Walter Brennan.

**Midnight**

Only bucking bronco to appear at the Calgary Stampede—Calgary, Alberta, Canada, on twelve occasions without a single rider being able to stay on his back for the mandatory eight seconds.

**"Midnight Plane to Houston"**

Original title of the 1973 Gladys Knight and the Pips hit, "Midnight Train to Georgia."

**"Midsummer's Day"**

Song used in the 1942 movie *Mrs. Miniver*, composed by actor

Gene Lockhart.

**Mijbil**

Otter hero of the 1969 movie *Ring of Bright Water*.

**Mikan, George**

First pro basketball player to score 10,000 points in his career (1945–1954).

**Mike**

Boomer Bate's (Todd Ferrell) pet dog on the 1957–1964 version of the "Lassie" TV series.

**Milburn**

Small-town setting of the Doris Day/Gordon MacRae movies *On Moonlight Bay* (1951) and *By the Light of the Silvery Moon* (1953).

**Milky Way**

Candy bar introduced by Mars Candy Company in 1923.

**Millard Fillmore High**

School setting where Diana Swanson (Lynn Redgrave) taught in the TV series "Teachers Only."

**Miller, Gerry**

Woman who came out of a cake nude (except for pasties on her breasts), at Mick Jagger's twenty-ninth birthday party in New York, on July 26, 1972.

**Miller, Hugh Barr**

Surprised guest on the January 30, 1957, TV episode of "This Is Your Life." This was the only time that Ralph Edwards did not host the show. Ronald Reagan was the guest host.

**Miller, Johnny**

New York Yankees player who hit a home run in his very first time at bat in the majors (September 11, 1966). He hit only one other home run in his major-league career.

**Miller, Kathy**

Thirteen-year-old girl who made a miraculous recovery after being hit by an automobile in an accident that left her brain-damaged and crippled. Within six months after the accident, she overcame her injuries to run in a marathon race. She was portrayed by Helen Hunt in the 1981 TV movie *The Miracle of Kathy Miller*. Kathy's father, Larry Miller (portrayed by Frank Converse), had played pro baseball with the New York Mets.

**Miller, Ralph Darwin**

(1873–1973) First former major-league baseball player to live to the age of one hundred. Born on March 15, 1873, he died on May

8, 1973, at the age of one hundred years and fifty-four days.

**Miller, Robert**

Name of two pitchers on the original Mets baseball team (1962). Robert G. Miller was nicknamed Righty, and Robert L. Miller was nicknamed Lefty.

**Miller's Music Store**

Metcalf record store where Miriam Joyce Haines (Laura Elliott) worked in the 1951 movie *Strangers on a Train*.

**Millfield College**

College in Chicago attended by both Elsie McKenna (Jane Seymour) prior to 1912, and Richard Collier (Christopher Reeve), in 1972, in the 1980 movie *Somewhere in Time*.

**Mills, Jack**

Engineer of the Royal Mail train, robbed of $7 million on August 8, 1963, at Buckinghamshire, England.

**"Mill Valley"**

Record that reached number 90 on the *Billboard* Hot 100 chart in August 1970. The song was sung by Miss Abrams and the Strawberry Point School third-grade class.

**Milwaukee Braves and Milwaukee Brewers**

Only three players have played for both baseball teams: Hank Aaron, Phil Roof, and Felipe Alou.

**Milwaukee Journal**

Newspaper for which Richie Cunningham (Ron Howard) worked part-time while in college on the TV series "Happy Days."

**Mind Your Own Business**

Motto first inscribed on U.S. coins, beginning in 1789.

**Mine**

Pet dog of six-foot-five-inch-tall, 255-pound Father John Michael Landon (Merlin Olsen) in the TV series "Father Murphy."

**Mineral City**

Town in Paradise Valley, near the Double R Bar Ranch, on the TV series "The Roy Rogers Show."

**Ming the Merciless**

Emperor of the planet Mongo, and Flash Gordon's foe. He was played in the Buster Crabbe movies by Charles Middleton, and in the 1980 movie *Flash Gordon* by Max von Sydow. Ming was played on the "Flash Gordon" radio series by Bruno Wick.

**Minneapolis–St. Paul International**

Airport where the location scenes for Lincoln International Airport in the 1970 movie *Airport* were filmed.

**Minnonette**

Name that William G. Morgan originally gave to the game of volleyball, which he created at the Holyoke, Massachusetts, YMCA, in 1895.

**Miracle**

Fast white horse seen in the 1981 movie *The History of the World, Part I*.

**Miracle Pictures**

"If it's a good picture, it's a Miracle." Motion picture studio (fictitious) in the 1938 movie *Hollywood Hotel*, and in the 1976 movie *Hollywood Boulevard*. The corporate name was also used by "Face" (Dick Benedict) in an episode of the TV series "The A-Team."

**Mirth**

Mork and Mindy's baby, who was hatched in 1981 on the TV series "Mork and Mindy." He was played by Jonathan Winters.

**Miss Alabama**

Title once held by author Truman Capote's mother, Nina.

**Miss Alabama**

Beauty contest title once held by actress Pam Long of the TV soap "Texas."

**Miss America 1942**

Title held by Jo-Carroll Dennison, actress and onetime wife of comedian Phil Silvers (1946–1950).

**Miss America 1958**

Title held by Marilyn Van Durber, who was named Woman of the Year in 1976.

**Miss America 1973**

Title held by actress Lindsay Bloom, who plays Cousin Mabel on the TV series "The Dukes of Hazzard."

**Miss America 1976**

Title held by Los Angeles newscaster Tawny Godin.

**Miss America 1983**

Title held by Debra Sue Maffett, who underwent cosmetic surgery to fix her nose in 1980, after losing the Miss Texas Pageant.

**Miss Barbara Stanwyck**

How actress Barbara Stanwyck was billed on the TV series "The Big Valley."

**Miss California 1982**

Title held by Suzanne Duwames. She wore the same dress that her mother had worn when she won the title of Miss Texas, twenty-five years earlier.

**Miss Cha Cha Cha of 1957**
Title held by Peggy Brown (Debbie Reynolds) in the 1960 movie *The Rat Race*.

**Miss Giovanna Goodthighs**
Role played by Jacqueline Bisset in the 1967 movie *Casino Royale*.

**Miss Indiana 1972**
Title held by Kellee Patterson, who made the *Billboard* Hot 100 chart with the song "If It Don't Fit, Don't Force It" in January 1978. It only reached number 75.

**Miss Iowa**
Contestant played by Barbi Benton in the 1973 TV movie *The Great American Beauty Contest*.

**Miss Miami**
Title held by actress Victoria Principal at the age of seventeen.

**Miss Morrow**
Proponent of Cross Your Heart bras, played by Eve Arden in TV commercials.

**Miss Nevada 1971**
Title held by Saundra "Sony" Campbell Revere, wife of musician Paul Revere. They were married on July 4, 1976, the United States Bicentennial. The minister was dressed as Uncle Sam.

**Miss New Jersey**
Title once held by Victoria King, the sister of actor Michael Landon.

**Miss Oceanside**
Beauty contest title once held by country singer Barbara Mandrell.

**Missouri**
State that borders eight other states: Iowa, Nebraska, Kansas, Oklahoma, Arkansas, Illinois, Kentucky, and Tennessee.

**Misspelled**
One of the most commonly misspelled words in the English language.

**Miss Poker Face**
Nickname of tennis star Helen Wills.

**Miss Prissy**
Girlfriend of cartoon rooster Foghorn Leghorn in Warner Bros. cartoons.

**Miss Sweden**
Title held by Miss Universe runner-up Sür Auberg, hostess on the

TV series "The Gong Show."

**Miss Sweden 1956**
Title held by Ingrid Goude, who, in 1957 and 1958, appeared as herself on the TV series "The Bob Cummings Show."

**Miss Teenage America**
Title once held by Barbi Benton.

**Miss Texas**
Contestant played by Farrah Fawcett in the 1973 TV movie *The Great American Beauty Contest*. She went uncredited in the film.

**Miss Togar**
Principal of Vince Lombardi High School, played by Mary Woronou in the 1979 movie *Rock 'n' Roll High School*.

**Miss Universe 1953**
Title held by Mexican actress Christiane Martel.

**Miss Universe 1954**
Title held by actress Myrna Hansen.

**Miss USA 1968**
Title held by Didi Anstett, who, in 1978, wed basketball star Bill Russell.

**Mr. and Mrs. Thomas Hardy**
Name that Prince Charles and Princess Diana used when they traveled to the Bahamas in March 1982.

**Mr. Babbitt**
The Monkees' landlord; played by Henry Corden on the TV series "The Monkees."

**Mr. Bill**
Comic clay character created by Walter Williams for "Saturday Night Live." Mr. Bill is always getting killed ("Ooh Nooo!") by his nemeses, Mr. Hands and Sluggo. His dog's name is Spot. In November 1981, a U.S. District Court decided that Williams had to share his ownership of Mr. Bill with Vance de Generes and David Derickson.

**Mr. Blair**
Theodore "Beaver" Cleaver's (Jerry Mathers) first male teacher at Grant Avenue Elementary School; played by Wendell Holmes on the TV series "Leave It to Beaver."

**Mr. Clean**
Nickname of major-league baseball player Steve Garvey, coined by comic Don Rickles.

**Mr. Clutch**
Autobiography of basketball star Jerry West.

**Mr. Cool**
Fonzie's pet dog, whose voice is that of Frank Welker, on the 1980 animated cartoon series "Fonz and the Happy Days Gang."

**Mr. Featherstein**
Fred and Wilma Flintstone's mailman on the TV cartoon series "The Flintstones."

**Mr. Kennedy, you can't say that Dallas doesn't love you . . .**
What Texas governor John Connally's wife said to President Kennedy just a few seconds before Kennedy was shot and killed in Dallas on November 22, 1963. The Connallys and the Kennedys were riding in the same automobile.

**Mr. Potts**
Man who appears in TV advertisements for Soup Starter, played by Jack Mullaney.

**Mr. Pro Football**
Appellative conferred upon Chicago Bears player/owner/coach George Halas.

**Mr. Rogers**
Fred Rogers, host of the children's TV show "Mr. Rogers' Neighborhood." He was seen on a TV set in the 1981 movie *Paternity*, and in the 1982 movie *Poltergeist*.

**Mr. Shirley Temple**
How actor John Agar was referred to by some after his marriage in 1945 to actress Shirley Temple.

**Mr. Spock**
Dolphin that Golden State Warriors center Clifford Ray helped to operate on at Marine World, Redwood City, California, on February 28, 1978, when he used his long arm to retrieve a large steel screw that Mr. Spock had swallowed.

**Mr. Thompson**
Man who helps sell Fit 'n' Trim Dog Food on TV, played by Frank Cady.

**Mrs. C**
How the Fonz (Henry Winkler) refers to Mrs. Cunningham (Marion Ross), on the TV series "Happy Days."

**Mrs. Johnson**
Hospital patient played by Carol Burnett on the March 16, 1976, episode of the TV soap opera "All My Children."

**Mrs. Miniver**
Kay Miniver, British housewife and mother during World War II, played by Greer Garson in the 1942 movie *Mrs. Miniver* and its

1950 sequel, *The Miniver Story*. She was also played by Judith
Evelyn and Gertrude Warner on the radio series "Mrs. Miniver."

**Mrs. Mississippi**
Title held by Annabel Noris (Marilyn Monroe) in the Mrs. America
Contest in the 1952 movie *We're Not Married*. After finding out
that she wasn't legally married, she then entered and won the *Miss
Mississippi* contest.

**Mrs. Peterson**
Role played by Margaret Hamilton on the TV soap opera "As the
World Turns."

**Misty Waters**
Mermaid puppet on the 1951 TV show "Ozmoe."

**Mitchell, Billy**
(1879–1936) U.S. Army officer born in Nice, France. He joined
the Army in 1898 as a private, and was promoted to brigadier
general in 1920. He was court-martialed for insubordination because he criticized both the War and Navy departments. Billy
Mitchell was portrayed in the 1955 movie *The Court-Martial of
Billy Mitchell*\* by Gary Cooper.

**Mitchell, Leslie**
Britain's first TV announcer, beginning in 1936, who portrayed
himself in the 1953 movie *Genevieve*.

**Mitsouko**
Actress Jean Harlow's favorite perfume.

**Mitsubishi, Subaru, Volkswagen, and Toyota**
Four foreign automobiles that were advertised on TV during the
showing of Super Bowl XVI in 1982. No American cars were
advertised.

**Modern Sperm**
Magazine that Captain Oveur (Peter Graves) glanced at in the
airport terminal in the 1980 movie *Airplane!*

**Moe**
First name of three players for the Chicago Cubs: Moe Drabowsky
(1956–1960), Moe Thacker (1958–1962), and Moe Morhardt
(1961–1962).

**Moen, Kevin**
University of California defensive back who scored the winning
touchdown in the November 20, 1982, Big Game between Stanford

---

\*This film was also the movie debut of Elizabeth Montgomery.

and California. The touchdown, which came on the last play of the game, with four seconds left, occurred in the following sequence: Mark Harmon of Stanford kicked off the ball with Stanford leading 20–19. Kevin Moen got the ball and started to run until he was trapped. He then lateraled it to Richard Rodgers, who in turn lateraled it to Dwight Garner, who gave it back to Rodgers, who this time lateraled it back to Kevin Moen, who ran it to the end zone, where he knocked down Stanford band trombone player Gary Tyrell.

## Moe the Gimp
Nickname of the mobster Martin Snyder, husband of Ruth Etting, portrayed by James Cagney in the 1955 movie *Love Me or Leave Me*.

## Moffett, Ken
Federal mediator of the baseball strike of 1981.

## Moffett, W. A. (Rear Admiral USN)
Head of the Navy Bureau of Aeronautics from 1921 to 1933, who was killed in the crash of the dirigible *Akron* in 1933. He was portrayed by Edmund Lowe in the 1957 movie *The Wings of Eagles*.

## Moll Flanders
Heroine of the 1721 novel by Daniel Defoe titled *Moll Flanders*. She was played by Kim Novak (and by Claire Ufland as a girl) in the 1965 movie *The Amorous Adventures of Moll Flanders*, and by Julia Foster on the PBS TV mini-series "Moll Flanders."

## Molly
Henchwoman to the villain, Riddler. Molly, played by Jill St. John, was the first person to be killed on the TV series "Batman" (remember, Catwoman had nine lives).

## Molly
Name of the singer's wife in the song "My Blue Heaven."

## "Mona Lisa"
Hit record by Nat "King" Cole, recorded in 1951. When Cole recorded the tune, some of the musicians laughed at the song because they thought it was a joke. The song can be heard on the soundtrack of two movies: *Captain Carey, U.S.A.* (1950), where it won an Academy Award for Best Song, and on a radio in *Raging Bull* (1980).

## Monkey Bar
Jake Cutter's (Stephen Collins) hangout on the South Sea Island of Bora Gora on the TV series "Tales of the Gold Monkey."

**Monkey Puzzle Tree**
Tree at Gull Cottage, planted by Captain Daniel Gregg (Rex Harrison), only to be chopped down by Lucy Muir (Gene Tierney), in the 1947 movie *The Ghost and Mrs. Muir*.

**Mon-Lei**
Robert L. Ripley's fifty-foot-long Chinese junk, built in 1939, which he bought in 1946. He sailed the vessel often.

**Monroe, James**
(1758–1831) Fifth President of the United States. He was the first President to have served as a senator. His daughter, Maria, was married in the White House in 1820. James Monroe was portrayed by Emmett King in the 1925 silent movie *The Man Without a Country*.

**Montana, Joe**
Quarterback of the San Francisco 49ers who helped to win the 1982 Super Bowl. During the week of the game, Montana had his photo on the cover of *Time, Newsweek,* and *Sports Illustrated* magazines.

**Montana Overland Stage**
Stage line seen in the opening credits of the TV series "Best of the West."

**Montanez, Juan**
Twenty-six-year-old Puerto Rican who killed sax player "King" Curtis Ousley in a fight in New York City on August 13, 1971 (Friday the thirteenth).

**Monte Jarrad**
Outlaw whom the townsfolk at Painful think cowpoke Melody Jones (Gary Cooper) is because of the MJ brand on his horse, in the 1945 movie *Along Came Jones*.

**Monte Sano Hospital**
San Francisco medical facility, set in 1968, in which the 1980 movie *Where the Buffalo Roam* opens.

**Montgomery (Monty)**
Charly's landlady Miss Apple's (Ruth White) pet bulldog in the 1968 movie *Charly*.

**Montgomery, Alastair**
Second known test-tube baby. He was born in January 1979.

**Monty**
Miss Piggy's agent in the 1979 film *The Muppet Movie*.

**"Moonbeam"**
Original title of the 1955 song "Young at Heart."

**Mooney's**
   Dubuque, Iowa, tavern hangout of the workers at Pickett's Brewery in the 1981 movie *Take This Job and Shove It*.

**"Moonlight and Shadows"**
   Song composed in 1936 by Leo Robin and Frederick Hollander. Dorothy Lamour introduced it in the 1936 movie *Jungle Princess*.

**"Moonlight on the Granges"/"A Blues Serenade"**
   First record that Glenn Miller recorded under his own name, on April 25, 1935. Ironically, the first word of the "A" side and the last word of the "B" side combined to read "Moonlight Serenade," which became one of Miller's biggest hits when he recorded it four years later, in 1939.

**Moonrunners**
   Movie (1974) starring James Mitchum and Kiel Martin, in which Waylon Jennings and Spanky McFarland appeared. The film was the basis for the TV series "The Dukes of Hazzard."

**"Moon Over Naples"**
   Original title of the song "Spanish Eyes."

**Moon Spinners**
   Rock 'n' roll band for which six-foot-three-inch-tall author Stephen King played rhythm guitar during his high school years.

**Moore, Archie**
   (1916–    ) Light heavyweight boxing champion (1952–1960). He was the only man to have met both Rocky Marciano (1955) and Muhammad Ali (1962) in the ring. He lost both bouts.

**Moorehouse, Homer**
   First recorded fatality in a dance marathon. He died during a contest at North Tonawanda, New York, in 1923.

**Moore, Hugh**
   Inventor of the Dixie Cup (the first paper cup) in 1912. He made his invention after dropping out of Harvard University.

**Moore, Mona Claywood**
   Twenty-seven-year-old woman who underwent plastic surgery in 1978, in order to look like the late blues artist Janis Joplin.

**Moreno, Rita**
   Only person to have *won* a Tony, an Oscar, an Emmy, a Grammy, and a Golden Globe Award. (Barbra Streisand was "given" a special Tony.)

|  |  |
|---|---|
| Tony | *The Ritz* (1975) |
| Oscar | *West Side Story* (1961) |

| Golden Globe | *West Side Story* (1962) |
| Emmy | "The Muppet Show" (1976–1977) and |
| | "The Rockford Files" (1977–1978) |
| Grammy | "The Electric Company" (1972) |

## "More Than You Know"

Song written in 1929 by Billy Rose, Edward Eliscu, and Vincent Youmans. Humphrey Bogart's future wife, Mayo Methot, introduced the song in the musical *Great Day*. The song appeared in the 1975 movie *Funny Lady*.

## Morgan, Gary

Stuntman who played the boxing kangaroo in the 1978 movie *Matilda*.

## Morgan, Julia

First woman to graduate from the University of California's College of Civil Engineering, and the first woman architectural graduate of the Ecole des Beaux Arts in Paris. Miss Morgan was the designer of Hearst Castle at San Simeon.

## Morning Post

London newspaper for which Winston Churchill was once a news correspondent.

## Morris, Jan

Only person to have scaled Mount Everest and to have undergone a sex change. Jan was previously named James.

## Morris, Jim

Mr. America 1974, who is the personal bodyguard of singer Elton John.

## Morrison, Herb

News reporter for Chicago radio station WLS, who broke down in tears as he described the *Hindenburg*'s exploding in flames as it attempted to moor at Lakehurst, New Jersey, on May 6, 1937. Herb Morrison was portrayed by Greg Mullavey in the 1975 movie *The Hindenburg*.

## Mortimer, Elias

President Warren G. Harding's personal bootlegger during Prohibition.

## Moschitta, John

Fast-talking businessman on TV's Federal Express ads (circa 1981–1983). He can speak at a rate of 530 words a minute. Moschitta says in the Federal Express ads:

"Okay, Eunice, travel plans. I need to be in New York on Monday, L.A. on Tuesday, New York on Wednesday, L.A. on

Thursday, New York on Friday. Got it? Good." (Three seconds.)

"Pete, you did a bang-up job, I'm putting you in charge of Pittsburgh. I know it's perfect, Peter, that's why I picked Pittsburgh. Pittsburgh's perfect, Peter. May I call you Pete?" (Three seconds.)

"Wonderful, wonderful, wonderful, and in conclusion, Jim, Bill, Bob, Carl, Fred, Load, Dork, Adolf, and Ted, business is business. And as we all know, in order to get something done, you've got to do something. In order to do something, you've got to work, so let's get to work. Thanks for taking this meeting." (Five seconds.)

He recited the Academy Award rules at the fifty-fifth annual Oscar Awards in 1983. He can be heard in a Federal Express ad on two different channels on a TV in the 1983 movie *Flashdance*.

**Moses**

Name of different characters played by Benjamin Sherman "Scatman" Crothers in two films, *Bloody Mama* (1970) and *The Shootist* (1976). Ex–Little Rascal Stymie Beard played a man named Moses in the 1940 film *The Return of Frank James*.

**Moses and Oliver**

Pet Irish wolfhound dogs of James Parker (Richard Harris) in the 1981 movie *Tarzan the Ape Man*. It was Moses who knocked Jane Parker (Bo Derek) into the river.

**Moses supposes his toeses are roses but Moses supposes erroneously . . .**

Tongue-twister used by a dialogue coach in helping Don Lockwood (Gene Kelly) to enunciate his words for the making of talking pictures. Don and his friend Cosmo Brown (Donald O'Connor) sing and dance a parody of the saying in the 1952 movie *Singin' in the Rain*.

**Mosienko, Bill**

Chicago Black Hawks hockey player who, in a game against the New York Rangers at Madison Square Garden on March 23, 1952, scored three goals in just twenty-one seconds.

**Mosrite**

Brand of guitars used exclusively by the rock 'n' roll instrumental group the Ventures, as mentioned in the liner notes of their 1960s albums.

**Mossmoor Prison**
Indiana state prison from which Roy Earle (Humphrey Bogart) was released after serving an eight-year sentence for bank robbery in the 1941 movie *High Sierra*.

**"Most Beautiful Girl in the World, The"**
Song sung by Stephen Boyd in the 1962 MGM movie *Jumbo*. His voice was dubbed by singer James Joyce.

**Most Colossal Flop**
Annual award given by the Harvard Lampoon to the 1939 movie *The Wizard of Oz*.

**Most exclusive club in the world**
Phrase relating to the U.S. Senate.

**Most Popular Film Performer of the Year—1926**
Title held by canine star Rin Tin Tin.

**"Mother I Still Have You"**
Song composed by Louis Silvers, which was the first song ever written for a motion picture. It was sung by Al Jolson in the 1927 movie *The Jazz Singer*.

**Mother of God!**
Last words said by a crew member before the Air Force C-130 "Gold 10" blew up in the 1974 TV movie *Hurricane!*

**Mother of Mercy, is this the end of Little Rico?**
Line said by C. R. MacNamara (James Cagney) in the 1961 movie *One, Two, Three*. This was a parody of Edward G. Robinson's line, "Mother of Mercy, is this the end of Rico?" in the 1930 movie *Little Caesar*.

**"Mother o' Mine"**
Song sung by Al Jolson in the 1927 movie *The Jazz Singer*. It was the first soundtrack recording ever released.

**Mother Hubbard**
Character of folklore. Accompanied by her dog, she became a character in nursery rhymes, "Old Mother Hubbard went to her cupboard to get her poor dog a bone . . ." She was played by Alice Cooke in the 1934 movie *Babes in Toyland*.

**Motion picture ratings**
G     General Audience
PG   Parental Guidance Suggested
R      Restricted—under seventeen not admitted without a parent or guardian
X      Adults Only—under seventeen not admitted
(Prior to 1968, "M" was used instead of "PG," standing for

"Mature Audience.")

**Motion pictures in color? I won't believe it until I see it in black and white . . .**

Saying credited to movie producer Samuel Goldwyn, known as a Goldwynism.

**Mott Hotel**

Sleazy San Francisco hotel where Virgil Stockwell (Woody Allen) lived after getting out of prison (the first time) in the 1969 movie *Take the Money and Run*.

**Mounds**

Candy bar introduced by the Peter Paul Candy Company in 1921.

**Mount Evans**

Highest mountain in the United States that one can drive a car to the top. Situated in Colorado, Mr. Evans is 14,260 feet high.

**Mount Katahdin**

Location in the state of Maine from where the sun is first seen in the United States each morning.

**Mount Kenya Game Ranch**

Actor William Holden's 1,256-acre estate near Nairobi, Kenya, Africa.

**Mount Walaleale, Hawaii**

Wettest place in the world, due to its record amount of rainfall.

**Mountain McClintock**

Heavyweight boxer who later became a wrestler. He is a loose portrayal of heavyweight boxing champ Primo Carnera. Mountain was played by Jack Palance in the 1956 TV play *Requiem for a Heavyweight* (screenplay by Rod Serling), by Anthony Quinn (as Mountain Rivera) in the 1962 movie *Requiem for a Heavyweight*, and by Sean Connery in the BBC TV play *Requiem for a Heavyweight*.

**Mountain Top Picnic Grounds**

Location of the Ebenezer Church annual picnic in the 1974 movie *Uptown Saturday Night*.

**Mouschi**

Anne Frank's pet cat, who lived with her and her family in Amsterdam, before they hid from the Germans in 1942–1944. (It is to this cat, whom she called Kitty, that Anne's diary is "written.")

**Mozart, Wolfgang Amadeus**

(1756–1791) Musical child prodigy who composed more than six hundred works, including several operas. Portrayed by Stephen Haggard (and by Pat Fitzpatrick as a boy) in the 1940 movie

*Mozart*, and by Pavlos Bekiaris in the 1980 movie *Mozart, a Childhood Chronicle*. He was also played by Tim Curry in the original Broadway production of Peter Schaffer's play *Amadeus*, and by Thomas Hulce in the 1984 film version.

**MS MOM**
California automobile license plate of Pat Kramer's (Lily Tomlin) yellow station wagon in the 1981 movie *The Incredible Shrinking Woman*.

**Mucki**
German Field Marshal Hermann Göring's pet lion.

**Muffin**
Stanley and Helen Roper's pet dog on the TV series "The Ropers."

**Muffin**
Aspiring actress Dorothy Stratten's (Jamie Lee Curtis) pet white kitten in the 1981 TV movie *Death of a Centerfold: The Dorothy Stratten Story*.

**Muffy**
Pet dog of Laura Manion (Lee Remick) in the 1959 movie *Anatomy of a Murder*.

**Muhammad**
Most common name in the world.

**Mulander 165**
Computer onboard the Earth Ship *Ark* in the 1973 TV series "The Starlost."

**Muldowney, Shirley "Cha Cha"**
First woman licensed in the United States to drive top-fuel dragsters. She was portrayed by Bonnie Bedelia in the 1983 movie *Heart Like a Wheel*.

**Mulligan or Shapiro**
Name for a free golf shot.

**Mullins, Priscilla**
Female mentioned in Henry Wadsworth Longfellow's poem "The Courtship of Miles Standish," in which John Alden asks Captain Miles Standish to propose to her for him. She was played by Dawn Addams in the 1952 movie *Plymouth Adventure*, and by Jenny Agutter in the 1979 TV movie *Mayflower: The Pilgrims' Adventure*.

**Murder in Thornton Square, The**
British release title of the 1944 American movie *Gaslight*.

**Murf and Surf**
Emily Hartley's (Suzanne Pleshette) two hamsters in her school classroom on the TV series "The Bob Newhart Show."

**MUrray Hill 1-098**
New York City home phone of Mrs. Matildo Kingsley (Agnes Moorehead) in the 1956 movie *Pardners*.

**MUrray Hill 8529**
New York City phone number of the J. P. Morgan Library, where Colehouse Walker, Jr. (Howard E. Rollins) held out with five other men in the 1981 movie *Ragtime*.

**MUrray Hill 3-6599**
New York City phone number of Nanny Ordway (Peggy Ann Garner) in the 1954 movie *Black Widow*.

**MUrray Hill 5-9975**
The Ricardos' apartment phone number on the TV series "I Love Lucy." Two other phone numbers mentioned in the series were MUrray Hill 5-9099 and CIrcle 7-2099.

**MUrray Hill 7-7430**
Dr. Frederick Steele's (George Brent) night answering service in the 1939 movie *Dark Victory*.

**Murray, James, A. H.**
Author of the first edition of *The Oxford English Dictionary*, in 1884.

**Musical Contributors**
For the "Happy Days" TV series, as listed in the credits, were: Ike Cole, Fats Domino, Connie Francis, Johnnie Ray, Kay Starr, and Anson Williams.

**Music Box, The**
Only Laurel and Hardy feature or short to win an Oscar (for "Best Live-Action Comedy Short Subject of the Year 1931–1932").

**Musty**
Skunk on the 1973–1975 cartoon TV series "Lassie's Rescue Rangers."

**Mutual Films**
New York film company that signed a contract with Mexican guerrilla warrior Pancho Villa on January 3, 1914. The agreement gave Villa $25,000 in exchange for allowing the film company to film Villa's revolution.

**"My Canary Has Circles Under His Eyes"**
Singing debut of Dinah Shore. She sang the song in a school

assembly while in the eighth grade, accompanying herself on the ukulele. She was booed.

**My Capitol Secrets**
Revealing book written by Congressman John Jenrette's estranged wife, Rita Jenrette.

**My Darling Clementine**
Movie (1946) directed by John Ford, starring Henry Fonda and Linda Darnell. The film is Colonel Sherman Potter's (Harry Morgan) all-time favorite on the TV series "M*A*S*H."

**"My Life"**
Theme song of the TV series "Bosom Buddies," composed by Billy Joel.

**"My Lucky Star"**
Song written by Arthur Freed and Nacio Herb Brown in 1935, introduced in the 1935 movie *The Broadway Melody of 1936* by Eleanor Powell, and heard in the films *Babes in Arms* (1939), *Born to Sing* (1942), *The Stratton Story* (1949), and *Singin' in the Rain* (1952). It is the song that Warren Attinger (Tom Ewell) was whistling as he walked down a New York street in the 1949 movie *Adam's Rib*.

**My name is Bond, James Bond . . .**
How agent James Bond introduces himself in movies.

**My Official Wife**
Silent movie made in the United States in 1916, in which future Russian Communist leader Leon Trotsky appeared under the name of Mr. Brown.

**Myrtle**
Dodie Harper Douglas's (Dawn Lynn*) doll on the TV series "My Three Sons."

**Mysterious Planet Debbie, The**
Movie being shown on TV while Oscar Madison (Jack Klugman) was running for city council. He made a speech during the commercial break, on the TV series "The Odd Couple."

**"My Two Front Teeth"**
Only number-one hit song ever recorded by Spike Jones and the City Slickers (1949).

---

*Sister of singer Leif Garrett.

# N

**NASA**
National Aeronautics and Space Administration.

**NHL (National Hockey League)**
Formed in 1917. The four original teams were:
Toronto Arenas
Ottawa Senators
Montreal Canadiens
Montreal Wanderers

**NHRA**
National Hot Rod Association.

**NYC-1**
New York state license number of Oliver "Daddy" Warbucks's (Albert Finney) black Rolls-Royce in the 1982 movie *Annie*.

**NYC-2**
New York state license number of Oliver "Daddy" Warbucks's (Albert Finney) blue Deusenberg convertible in the 1982 movie *Annie*.

**N1AP**
Call sign of golf champion Arnold Palmer's Cessna Citation (C-500) jet aircraft.

**N1JN**
Call sign of golf champion Jack Nicklaus's Cessna Citation (C-500) jet aircraft.

**N25GM**
Registration number of the white Green Mountain Airways airplane (call sign: Green Mountain Airways 123) that Flash Gordon (Sam J. Jones) crashed into Dr. Hans Zarkov's (Topol) laboratory in the 1980 movie *Flash Gordon*.

**N70JF**

Registration number of the Ewing family jet on the TV series "Dallas."

**N464CL**

Learjet flown by Vince Ricardo (Peter Falk) in the 1979 movie *The In-Laws*.

**N564CL**

Learjet weighing 7 tons and costing $2 million that magician David Copperfield made "disappear" on the TV special "The Magic of David Copperfield," telecast on October 26, 1981. The aircraft, which is owned by Clay Lacey, has appeared in TV movies such as *Knight Rider* (1982).

**NC678**

Experimental aircraft piloted by Morgan Wale (John Carroll) that made an emergency landing in the 1945 movie *Her Favorite Patient*.

**N5886**

Call letters of the red aircraft that crashed in Alaska, in which two people survived for forty-nine days. The two survivors, Ralph and Helen, were portrayed by Ed Asner and Sally Struthers in the 1975 TV movie *Hey, I'm Alive*.

**N9014F**

Registration number of the blue and white helicopter shown on the introduction of the TV series "Hawaii Five-O."

**N1239R**

Balloon in which Sgt. Pepper's Lonely Hearts Club Band (the Bee Gees) and Billy Shears (Peter Frampton) left Heartland for Hollywood in the 1978 movie *Sgt. Pepper's Lonely Hearts Club Band*.

**N3254S**

White Cessna flown to a Nevada brothel by Tom Hagen (Robert Duvall) in the 1974 movie *The Godfather, Part II*.

**N56949**

Registration number of the yellow biplane that Jim Mead (Treat Williams) crashed in the 1981 movie *The Pursuit of D. B. Cooper*.

**N59395**

Registration number of the Ewing family helicopter on the TV series "Dallas."

**N91329**

Call letters of the B-29 that crashed onto a South Pacific island in the 1980 movie *The Last Flight of Noah's Ark*.

**9**

Number of laps in the Roman chariot race won by Judah Ben-Hur (Charlton Heston), in the 1959 movie *Ben Hur*.

**9**

Major-league record number of hits in a single game, set by Cleveland Indians shortstop John Burnett in an eighteen-inning game on July 10, 1932.

**9**

Number of at-bats that Yogi Berra accumulated in his short time with the New York Mets, in 1965.

**9G 893**

License number of Maxwell Smart's (Don Adams) sports car on the TV series "Get Smart."

**9 to 1**

Final score of the last game played by the New York Giants when, on September 29, 1957, they were defeated by the Pittsburgh Pirates. The next season, the team was called the San Francisco Giants.

**9 A.M. to 4 A.M.**

Hours of operation of Archie Bunker's Place on the TV series "Archie Bunker's Place."

**9 Madryrn Street**

Address of the house in Liverpool, England, where Richard "Ringo Starr" Starkey was born on July 7, 1940.

**19**

Major-league record number of consecutive games won by New York Giants pitcher Rube Marquard up to July 3, 1912.

**19 to 18**

Lowest winning score in an NBA game, when Detroit defeated Minneapolis on November 22, 1950.

**19th Precinct**

New York City police precinct for which Detective Bruce (George Raft) worked. His office was in room 222 in the 1954 movie *Black Widow*.

**90 Church Street**

New York City address of the U.S. Navy office, where Lieutenant Robert Tracey (Jack Lemmon) worked, in the 1954 movie *Phffft!*

**94**

Major-league record number of batters struck out in World Series play. The record is held by New York Yankees pitcher Whitey

Ford.

**94 MPH**

Speed of the eight-inning fast ball thrown by Goose Gossage during the fifth game of the 1981 World Series, on October 25, 1981, between the Dodgers and the Yankees. It hit batter Ron Cey's helmet, knocking him down and out of the game. Ken Landreaux replaced Cey as a pinch-runner.

**98.5 degrees Fahrenheit**

Proper temperature at which sake should be served.

**921 Fifth Avenue**

New York City bar address of Henry Van Cleve (Don Ameche) in the 1943 movie *Heaven Can Wait*.

**935 Fifth Avenue**

New York City home address of Frieda Winter (Genevieve Page) in the 1964 movie *Youngblood Hawke*.

**956 years**

Prison sentence given to Digby Geste (Marty Feldman) in the 1977 movie *The Last Remake of Beau Geste*.

**938**

Major-league record number of stolen bases, set by Lou Brock between 1961 and 1979 (yet he only stole home once).

**987 Fifth Avenue**

New York City home address of Oliver "Daddy" Warbucks's (Albert Finney) mansion in the 1982 movie *Annie*.

**1900**

Year in which the 1941 movie *The Sea Wolf* and the 1958 movie *Gigi* are set.

**1901**

Year when Vito Corleone immigrated to the United States as shown in the 1974 movie *The Godfather, Part II*.

**1901**

Year in which the 1954 movie *The Naked Jungle* is set.

**1902**

Time setting for the 3-D movie *House of Wax* (1953).

**1905**

Year in which the French lighthouse was built in Korea in the 1982 movie *Inchon*.

**1906**

Time setting of the 1935 Mickey Rooney movie *Ah, Wilderness* (based on the Eugene O'Neill play of the same title) and of the 1975 movie *Bite the Bullet*.

**1907**

Opening date of the 1981 TV series "The Gangster Chronicles," and the time setting of the 1953 movie *White Witch Doctor*.

**1908**

Time setting of the 1965 movie *The Great Race*, as well as the time setting of the 1976 movie *The Great Scout and Cathouse Thursday*.

**1910**

Year in which the 1981 John and Bo Derek–produced movie *Tarzan, the Ape Man* is set; also the year in which the Chicken Ranch was established in the 1982 movie *The Best Little Whorehouse in Texas*.

**1915**

Time setting of the 1951 Humphrey Bogart movie *The African Queen*.

**1923**

Date on the large prop silver dollar used in a dance sequence in the 1981 Steve Martin movie *Pennies from Heaven*.

**1926**

Time setting of the 1966 Steve McQueen movie *The Sand Pebbles*.

**1928**

Year in which the 1961 Natalie Wood/Warren Beatty movie *Splendor in the Grass* is set.

**1929**

Time setting of the 1959 Marilyn Monroe movie *Some Like It Hot*.

**1931**

Time setting of the 1972 Liza Minnelli movie *Cabaret*.

**1933**

Time settings of the TV series "The Family Holvak" and the 1978 TV series "Apple Pie."

**1934**

Time settings of the 1981 movie *Pennies from Heaven* and the 1982 movie *Victor/Victoria*.

**1935**

Time setting of the TV series "Palmerstown, U.S.A."

**1936**

Year in which the 1981 movie *Raiders of the Lost Ark* is set.

**1937**

Only year in which there was a Triple Crown winner in both baseball (Joe Medwick) and horse racing (War Admiral, ridden by

Charlie Kurtsinger).

**1938**

Year in which the 1981 movie *Under the Rainbow* is set.

**1940**

Date of the opening scenes in London of the 1981 movie *Eye of the Needle*.

**1942**

Time setting of the 1980 TV series "Goodtime Girls."

**1944**

Year in which the 1982 movie *The World According to Garp* begins.

**1946**

Time setting of the 1978 Sylvester Stallone movie *Paradise Alley*.

**1954**

Time setting of the 1982 movie *My Favorite Year*, the 1982 movie *Porky's*, and the 1983 movie *Porky's II*.

**1959**

Time setting of the 1982 movie *Diner*.

**1961**

Time setting of the 1982 movie *Grease II*.

**1961**

Year in which the American League changed from a 154-game to a 162-game schedule.

**1962**

Year in which the National League changed from a 154-game to a 162-game schedule.

**1962**

Time settings of the 1973 movie *American Graffiti*, the 1978 movie *National Lampoon's Animal House*, and the 1979 movie *The Great Santini*.

**1962 Linden Boulevard**

Brooklyn address of the Kotter family, apartment number 409, after they moved from 711 East Ocean Parkway, on the 1975–1979 TV series "Welcome Back Kotter."

**1963**

Time setting of the opening scenes of the 1978 movie *Halloween*. During the film, the setting is moved up to October 30, 1978.

**1964**

Time setting, in Chicago, of the 1975 movie *Cooley High*.

**1979**

Only year in which the New Orleans Mardi Gras has been canceled since 1875; the cancellation was caused by a police strike.

**1979**

Year on the penny that triggered Richard Collier's (Christopher Reeve) return to the present time, ultimately causing his death, in the 1980 movie *Somewhere in Time*.

**1997**

Time setting of the 1981 movie *Escape from New York*.

**1997**

Year in which the city of Singapore returns to China's rule. China's lease with Britain expires in 1997.

**1998**

Time setting of the 1979 movie *Americathon*.

**9114 South Central**

Los Angeles home address of Fred Sanford's (Redd Foxx) junkyard in the TV series "Sanford and Son." Later, it became the address of the Sanford Arms on the TV series "Sanford Arms."

**9595**

Latest year mentioned in the Zager and Evans 1969 number-one hit song "In the Year 2525."

**9,887**

NBA record number of lifetime assists, set by Oscar Robertson (1961–1974).

**979345**

State penitentiary number of prisoner Leo Bloom (Gene Wilder) in the 1967 movie *The Producers*.

**9906753**

Serial number stenciled on the Top Secret, U.S. Army Intelligence crate in which the Ark of the Covenant was stored and hidden away in a U.S. government warehouse in the 1981 movie *Raiders of the Lost Ark*.

**900-410-6272**

Dial an astronaut—special telephone number set up so the public could listen to the crew of the space shuttle *Columbia* in July 1982.

**Nagra III**

Hand-carried tape recorder used by Jack Terry (John Travolta) when he taped a rifle shot before Governor McRyan's automobile tire blew out, causing the car to crash, in the 1981 movie *Blow Out*.

**Naked Lust**

Original title of William Burroughs's novel until author Jack Kerouac mispronounced it *Naked Lunch*, which Burroughs liked better.

**Naked Nymphomaniac, The**
Porno film produced by Herbert G. Maloney and starring Lois LaRue, that the Supreme Court viewed in order to make a decision in the 1981 movie *First Monday in October*.

**Narab**
Martian played by Leonard Nimoy in the 1952 Republic serial *Zombies of the Stratosphere*.

**Narcissus**
Shuttlecraft of the spacecraft *Nostromo* in the 1979 movie *Alien*.

**Nardico, Danny**
Only fighter ever to knock middleweight Jake LaMotta off his feet during a bout. Nardico knocked LaMotta down in the seventh round in a fight on December 31, 1952, winning with an eighth-round TKO, after the referee stopped the fight.

**Nassau County Cafe**
Luckenbach, Texas, cafe owned and run by Stewart Lewis (Gabe Kaplan) in the TV series "Lewis and Clark."

**Nathaniel Ulysses Turtle**
Mascot of the Turtle Organization, who turned 9,950 years old on June 1, 1982.

**Neal**
Laboratory chimpanzee in the 1955 movie *Revenge of the Creature*.

**Neal, Patricia**
(1926– ) Hollywood actress born in Packard, Kentucky, in 1926. She made her debut in the 1949 Ronald Reagan movie *John Loves Mary*. In 1953 she married British writer Roald Dahl. Ten years later she won the Academy Award as Best Actress for the 1963 movie *Hud*. In 1965, Neal suffered a severe stroke that left her semiparalyzed and with impaired speech. With the help of her husband, she fought back and made a remarkable recovery. In 1968 she made her comeback when she appeared in the film *The Subject Was Roses*. Neal played a U.S. Navy nurse in two John Wayne movies: *Operation Pacific* (1961) and *In Harm's Way* (1965). She was portrayed by Glenda Jackson in the 1982 TV movie *The Patricia Neal Story*.

**"Neapolitan Nights"**
Theme song of the radio series "Mr. First Nighter."

**Nell**
Shadd's (Richard Thomas) shipboard computer in the 1980 movie *Battle Beyond the Stars*.

**Nelson, David**
(1936–     ) Actor son of Ozzie Nelson and Harriet Hilliard, and brother of singer Rick Nelson. In a baseball game between Hollywood High and Van Nuys, in which a young high school pitcher named Don Drysdale pitched a one-hitter, David Nelson was the player who got the one hit, in the ninth inning.

**Nelson's Blood**
British Navy's daily supply of rum (grog).

**Neptune**
Two-person submarine piloted by James Bond (Roger Moore) and Melina (Carol Bouquet) in order to locate the sunken British spy ship *St. Georges* in the 1981 movie *For Your Eyes Only*.

**Nesbit, Evelyn**
(1884–1967) Estranged wife of Harry K. Thaw, who had had an affair with architect Stanford White. Thaw shot and killed White at Madison Square Garden on July 25, 1906. Nesbit was portrayed by Joan Collins in the 1955 movie *The Girl in the Red Velvet Swing* and by Elizabeth McGovern in the 1981 film *Ragtime*, and she portrayed herself in the 1907 movie *The Great Thaw Trial*, as well as in the 1917 movie *Redemption*.

**Neumann, John Nepomucene**
First American male saint. He died on January 5, 1860, and was canonized by Pope Paul VI.

**Neurofibromatosis**
Physical ailment from which John Merrick, the Elephant Man (1863–1890) suffered.

**Nevele Pride**
Horse that holds the mile record for a trotter. He set the record in 1969, at one minute and fifty-four seconds.

**"Never Say Goodbye"**
Theme song from the 1981 movie *Continental Divide* sung by Helen Reddy.

**Nevers, Ernie**
(1903–     ) Chicago Cardinals player who set an unusual football record in November 1929. In a game against Dayton on November 21, he scored all of his team's 19 points; the following week, in a game against the Chicago Bears, he scored all of his team's 40 points. Thus he scored 59 consecutive points, setting a record. In 1927, while pitching for St. Louis, he gave up two (number 8 and number 41) of Babe Ruth's 60 home runs that season. This makes him the only member of the Pro Football Hall of Fame to give up

two of Babe Ruth's 60 home runs in 1927.

**New City**
Texas oil boomtown (originally named White Sage Junction) in which Lucy Gallant (Jane Wyman) created a multimillion-dollar department store in the 1955 movie *Lucy Gallant*. The Red Derrick was the town's saloon.

**Newell, Pete**
Only basketball coach to have won an NIT title (San Francisco), an NCAA championship (University of California at Berkeley), and an Olympic gold medal (1960).

**New Hampshire**
State that has held the Presidential primaries first since 1920. The town of Dixville Notch votes at one minute past midnight, thus registering the state's earliest returns.

**New Orleans Saints and Los Angeles Rams**
A 1981 season football game being played on TV at the Freelings' home in the 1982 movie *Poltergeist*. Player Jim Youngblood was shown catching a pass. The neighbor's TV kept interrupting the game with "Mister Rogers' Neighborhood."

**Newsday**
Magazine that published photographs taken of Governor McRyan's automobile accident in the 1981 movie *Blow Out*.

**"New Step Every Day, A"**
Original title of the Gershwin song "I'll Build a Stairway to Paradise."

**Newsworld**
Magazine on which John Winger (Bill Murray) is shown on the cover ("The New Army, Can America Survive?") in the 1981 movie *Stripes*.

**New York Bulls**
Football team featured in the 1980 TV series "Semi-Tough."

**New York Daily Mail**
Newspaper for which Louise "Babe" Bennett (Jean Arthur) worked as a reporter in the 1936 movie *Mr. Deeds Goes to Town*.

**New York Dispatch**
Newspaper for which Susan Williams (Susan Anton) was employed as a photographer on "Stop Susan Williams" (part of the "Cliffhangers" TV series).

**New York Eagle**
Newspaper for which David Farrell (played at different times by Richard Widmark, Carleton Young, and Staats Cotsworth) worked

as a reporter on the radio series "Front Page Farrell."

**New Yorker**
Magazine that can be seen floating in the water in the opening scene of the 1944 movie *Lifeboat*.

**New York Forum**
Newspaper for which Mike Andros (James Sutorius) was a reporter on the TV series "The Andros Targets."

**New York Mail**
Newspaper featured in the 1934 movie *It Happened One Night*.

**New York Mets' first game**
Played on April 11, 1962; the final score was St. Louis 11, New York 4.

**"New York, New York"**
Song that Jimmy (James Coco) sang to himself in the 1981 movie *Only When I Laugh*.

**New York teams**
In 1956 the New York Yankees won the pennant, the Brooklyn Dodgers won the pennant, and the New York Giants won the NFL championship.

**New York Titans**
Previous name of the AFL football team the New York Jets, until it was changed on March 28, 1963.

**New York Tribune**
Newspaper for which Karl Marx was once a correspondent.

**New York Yankees (1932)**
Only major-league baseball team to play an entire season without being shut out (155-game season).

**New York Yankees**
1926 AFL football team
1927–1928 NFL football team
1946–1948 AAFC football team
1913–     AL baseball team

**Nicholson, Jack**
Actor in whose house director Roman Polanski was accused of raping a thirteen-year-old girl on March 10, 1977. Nicholson was away on vacation at the time.

**Nichols, Red**
(1905–1965) Popular American jazz bandleader, born Ernest Loring. He was billed as Red Nichols and His Five Pennies. Some of the members of his band were Benny Goodman, Tommy and Jimmy Dorsey, Glenn Miller, Gene Krupa, and Jack Teagarden.

Nichols was portrayed by Danny Kaye in the 1959 movie *The Five Pennies*.

**Nick**

Grocer proponent of Fantastik Spray Cleaner, played in TV commercials by Cliff Norton.

**Nieman, Bob**

(1927–     ) St. Louis Browns outfielder who hit a home run on each of his first two times at bat in the major leagues, on September 14, 1951, off Red Sox pitcher Mickey McDermott, in Fenway Park. In his twelve years in the majors, he hit only 125 home runs.

**"Night and Day"**

Song written in 1932 by Cole Porter and introduced in the 1934 movie *The Gay Divorcee* by Fred Astaire. The song was sung by Deanna Durbin in the 1945 movie *Lady on a Train* and in 1946 became the title for the screen biography of Cole Porter. "Night and Day" was sung by Katharine Hepburn in the 1957 movie *Desk Set*.

**Night on Bald Mountain, A**

Classical piece by Modest Petrovich Moussorgsky (1835–1881) that appeared in Walt Disney's 1940 animated movie *Fantasia*. It was also used as the theme song of the radio series "Escape." (A disco version of it can be heard in the 1977 movie *Saturday Night Fever*, under the title "A Night on Disco Mountain.")

**"Night the Animals Talk, The"**

Annual Christmas episode on the TV series "I Remember Mama."

**Night Wind**

Movie produced by Felix Farmer (Richard Mulligan) at Capitol Studios in the 1981 movie *S.O.B*. He turned it from a $30-million flop into a risqué hit film by having his wife, Sally Miles (Julie Andrews), show her breasts.

**Nimitz, USS**

U.S. aircraft carrier from which eight rescue helicopters were launched in the unsuccessful attempt to rescue the fifty-two American hostages in Tehran on April 14, 1982. It was also the nuclear carrier that was caught in a time warp and reappeared at Pearl Harbor on December 6, 1941, in the 1980 movie *The Final Countdown*.

**Nimrod**

Agents James T. West's (Robert Conrad) and Artemus Gordon's (Ross Martin) private railroad car on the TV series "The Wild Wild West."

306

**Nine Sisters**

Album produced by Air Flow Records on which Kira (Olivia Newton-John) mysteriously appeared on the cover in the 1980 movie *Xanadu*.

**Nissho Maru**

Last Japanese freighter sunk by an American submarine (April 8, 1981), when the U.S. submarine *George Washington* collided with the vessel in the East China Sea.

**Nixon, Agnes**

Creator of soap operas such as "All My Children," "One Life to Live," and "Loving."

**Noah**

Man whom God selected to build a huge ark in order that he, his family, and pairs of every kind of animal might escape the Great Flood. Noah was portrayed by John Huston in the 1966 movie *The Bible*, and by Lew Ayres in the 1978 TV mini-series "Greatest Heroes of the Bible." Comedian Bill Cosby has also played Noah in one of his classic standup routines.

**Nobody**

Answer written on a chalkboard by Bonzo the chimp at a carnival, in response to the question from the audience, "Who played the fiddle while Rome burned?" in the 1952 movie *Bonzo Goes to College*. When Bonzo was challenged on his answer, he then wrote, "Nero played the lute."

**Nobody's Perfect**

Slogan for the "Nobody for President" campaign launched for the 1980 elections.

**"Nobody's Sweetheart"**

Song written in 1924 by Gus Kahn, Ernie Erdman, Billy Meyers, and Elmer Schoebel. It can be heard in the film's *Red Headed Woman* (1932), *I'm Nobody's Sweetheart Now* (1940), *Atlantic City* (1944), and *I'll See You in My Dreams* (1951).

**No Chance Saloon**

Carsonville town saloon in the 1956 Dean Martin/Jerry Lewis movie *Pardners*.

**Noel-Baker, Lord Philip John**

(1890–1982) Member of the House of Commons who won a silver medal in the 1,500-meter run in the 1920 Olympics, as well as the Nobel Peace Prize in 1959, for his relief work to aid victims of Russian famine in the 1920s, as well as for post–World War II disarmanent efforts, including the drafting of the UN charter.

## Noguchi, Thomas

Japanese-born Los Angeles County coroner who personally performed the autopsies on the following celebrities: Marilyn Monroe (1962), Robert Kennedy (1968), Janis Joplin (1970), William Holden (1981), Natalie Wood (1981), and John Belushi (1982).

Noguchi was supposedly the model for Dr. Quincy (played by Jack Klugman) on TV. In all but Kennedy's autopsy, Dr. Noguchi once stated that he found either drugs or alcohol in each of the above victims' bodies. In 1983 his autobiography, *Coroner*, was released.

## No-hitter

Oakland A's pitchers Vida Blue, Glenn Abbott, Paul Linblad, and Rollie Fingers combined to pitch a no-hit game against the California Angels on September 28, 1975 (5–0). Vida Blue, who pitched the first five innings, was credited as the winning pitcher. Only four men have pitched three or more no-hitters in their careers:

Cy Young (1897, 1904, 1908), total three
Bob Feller (1940, 1946, 1951), total three
Sandy Koufax (1962, 1963, 1964, 1965), total four
Nolan Ryan (1973 [2], 1974, 1975, 1981), total five

## Noise from the Deep, A

Silent film (1913) in which, for the first time, a pie (tossed by Mabel Normand) was thrown in a film.

## Nola

U.S. Marshal Rooster J. Cogburn's (John Wayne) ex-wife in the 1969 movie *True Grit*.

## Non-rhyming color words

Orange, silver, purple.

## North Dakota

First all-gay state of the 1998 Union in the 1979 movie *Americathon*.

## North Dallas Bulls

Football team for which Maxwell (number 16, Mac Davis) and Phillip Elliott (number 28, Nick Nolte) played in the 1979 movie *North Dallas Forty*.

## Northern Pacific

Airliner Flight 305 that D. B. Cooper (Treat Williams) hijacked on November 24, 1971, escaping with $200,000. (The airliner that the real D. B. Cooper hijacked belonged to Northwest Airlines.) The registration of the aircraft was N690WA; it was owned by World

Airways, but repainted for the movie.

**North Star**
Summer camp attended by Tripper (Bill Murray) in the 1979 movie *Meatballs*. The rival camp is Mohawk.

**Northumberland**
Sailing vessel that caught fire and exploded in the 1980 movie *The Blue Lagoon*, shipwrecking Emmeline (Brooke Shields) and Richard (Christopher Atkins).

**Northwestern and Brown**
First winning and losing teams (respectively) on the TV series "G. E. College Bowl," hosted by Allen Ludden, on January 4, 1959.

**Northwest Louisiana State University**
Last concert appearance of singer Jim Croce, who was killed in a plane crash shortly afterward (September 20, 1973) while en route to Sherman, Texas.

**Norton, Jerry**
St. Louis Cardinals player who, on two occasions, intercepted four passes in a single game (November 20, 1960, and November 26, 1961).

**Norton, Ken**
(1945–     ) Only heavyweight champion who has never won a heavyweight championship fight. Prior to being acclaimed the champ by the WBC, he lost to both George Foreman and Muhammad Ali and afterwards, as champ, lost his first defense when Larry Holmes beat him. Therefore, he lost his only three title bouts, yet served as the champion. John L. Sullivan and Ken Norton were the only two heavyweight champions to have attended college. Norton appeared in the movies *Mandingo* (1975) and *Drum* (1976).

**"Notre Dame Victory March"**
Song played over the closing credits in the 1980 movie *Airplane!*

**Nova**
Original name of *Omni* magazine. The name was changed prior to the publication of the first issue.

**November 1**
Date on which a UFO crashed near the North Pole in the 1951 movie *The Thing*. The monster (played by Bob Steel, Billy Curtis, and James Arness) died on November 3.

**November 3, 1979**
Date on which Mr. Roarke (Ricardo Montalban) married Helena Marsh (Samantha Eggar) on the TV series "Fantasy Island." Mrs.

Roarke died soon afterward, from a brain tumor.

**November 9, 1977**

Date on which Tom Bradford (Dick Van Patten) married Abby Abbott (Betty Buckley) on the TV series "Eight Is Enough."

**November 10, 1947–October 11, 1963**

Dates on Judith Myers's gravestone, which was put at the head of a bed by the "shape," Michael (Tony Moran), in the 1978 movie *Halloween*.

**November 11, 1984**

Date on which World War III began, in Sir John Hackett's novel *The Third World War*.

**November 13**

Date on which Gloria Unger (Janis Hansen) threw Felix (Tony Randall) out of their house on the TV series "The Odd Couple."

**November 17, 1981**

Date on which Luke Spencer (Tony Geary) married Laura Webber Baldwin (Genie Francis) on the TV series "General Hospital."

**November 20, 1903**

Date on which Tom Horn (Steve McQueen) was hanged in the 1980 movie *Tom Horn*.

**November 25, 1960 (Friday)**

Last broadcast of soap operas on radio. That day saw the last episodes of "Ma Perkins," "Young Doctor Malone," "The Second Mrs. Burton," and "Right to Happiness."

**November 30, 1936**

Second edition of *Life* magazine ever issued. It showed a military plebe at attention while eating at a table. It was this issue of *Life* (cost ten cents) that a Nazi officer was reading on board the Pan American clipper in the 1981 movie *Raiders of the Lost Ark*.

**No War This Year**

Headline of the *Daily Express* newspaper floating in the water in the 1942 movie *In Which We Serve*.

**No Way to Treat a Lady and W. C. Fields and Me**

Movies (1968 and 1976, respectively) in which Rod Steiger impersonated W. C.Fields. In the first, he only did it for a few seconds; but in the second he portrayed the great comedian.

**Nowhere**

California town where the Kallikak family lived in the TV series "The Kallikaks."

**Nurse Linda Cooper**

Nurse played by actress Linda Cooper in the TV soap "General Hospital."

**Nurse Withers**

Role played by ninety-three-year-old actress Estelle Winwood in the 1976 movie *Murder by Death*.

# O

**OGRE**
Organization of Generally Rotten Enterprises, evil organization on the animated TV cartoon series "The Dark Pack."

**0-1**
U.S. Army service number of General John J. Pershing, who was issued the first service identification number in 1918.

**0-1305301**
U.S. Army serial number of Captain Benjamin L. Willard (Martin Sheen) in the 1979 movie *Apocalypse Now*.

**1**
Lowest paid attendance for a college football game, when, on November 12, 1955, Washington State and San Jose State played a game in Pullman, Washington.

**1Lt 2Rt 3Lt 4Rt**
Combination of the safe at the 12th Precinct on the TV series "Barney Miller."

**$1.00**
Annual salary paid to singer Frank Sinatra for advertising Chrysler automobile products in 1980. Chrysler also gave Sinatra the first 1981 Chrysler Imperial that came off the assembly line.

**$1.50**
Amount per mile that B. J. McCabe (Greg Evigan) charges for hauling cargo on the TV series "B.J. and the Bear."

**1 mile, 427 yards**
Length of the Olympic rowing course.

**One Hundred American Poems**
Collection of poems, edited by Selden Rodman, that became the

first paperback book published by Signet Books (1948).

**100 plus**

Only twice have two players on the same team combined to hit over one hundred home runs:

    1927   Babe Ruth (60) and Lou Gehrig (47), total 107

    1961   Roger Maris (61) and Mickey Mantle (54), total 115

All were members of the New York Yankees.

**100 West James Street**

Apartment 23, address of Franz Liebkind (Kenneth Mars), the author of the play *Springtime for Hitler*, in the 1968 movie *The Producers*.

**100.9 MPH**

Fastest pitch clocked in the major leagues by a pitcher. It was thrown at Anaheim Stadium by the California Angels' Nolan Ryan, on August 20, 1974.

**101**

Highway terrorized by the motorcyclist in the 1955 hit song "Black Denim Trousers and Motorcycle Boots" sung by the Cheers (actor Bert Convy was a member).

**103**

NHL record number of shut-outs, held by goalie Terry Sawchuck over his twenty-season career.

**103 Brown Street**

Address of Gus's Gas, owned by Gus Gardician (Paul Michael) in the 1976–1977 TV series "Muggsy."

**105**

Age mentioned by Frank Sinatra in the lyrics of the 1954 hit song "Young at Heart."

**105**

NFL career record for the most fumbles by a quarterback. Six-foot-four-inch former Los Angeles Rams quarterback Roman Gabriel holds the record.

**105 degrees**

Temperature in Martinique, in the Marilyn Monroe version of the song "Tropical Heat Wave" from the 1954 movie *There's No Business Like Show Business*.

**106**

Major-league record of games in which a pitcher appeared within a single season. The record was set by Los Angeles Dodgers pitcher Mike Marshall in 1974.

**107 Marietta Street**

Address of the drugstore in Atlanta, Georgia, where, on May 8, 1886, Dr. John Styth Pemberton created the soft drink Coca-Cola.

**109 degrees**

Temperature mentioned in the 1972 Elvis Presley hit song "Burning Love."

**110–44**

The New York Yankees' win-loss record for the 1927 season.

**111**

Career bouts of boxer Mountain Rivera (Anthony Quinn) in the 1962 movie *Requiem for a Heavyweight*. He lost his last bout to Cassius Clay in the seventh round.

**111**

Number of the yellow school bus (T&T Bus Service) that Beaver Cleaver (Jerry Mathers) rode to school in the TV series "Leave It to Beaver."

**111 to 94**

Final score of the first All-Star basketball game, played in 1951, in which the East beat the West.

**112 North Las Palmas**

Los Angeles street address of Hart Industries on the TV series "Hart to Hart."

**113**

Combined points scored in an NFL game to set a record, when, on November 27, 1966, the Washington Redskins beat the New York Giants 72 to 41.

**115 yards**

Run credited to Wyllys Terry of Yale in a game against Wesleyan on November 4, 1884. Rules today state that players cannot be credited with more than one hundred yards in a full-field run; so his record will never be tied or broken.

**120 MPH**

Top speed of the Cadillac in the 1958 Playmates' hit song "Beep Beep."

**122 15th Street**

Address of Father Dan Cleary's (McLean Stevenson) mission to help the poor in the 1978 TV series "In the Beginning."

**123**

Major-league career number of bases stolen by Babe Ruth.

**125 years**
Prison sentence given to Skip Donahue (Gene Wilder) and Harry Monroe (Richard Pryor) for armed bank robbery in the 1980 movie *Stir Crazy*.

**125–134**
Beats per minutes in a disco song.

**126 pounds**
Weight that all horses in the Triple Crown must carry.

**127**
NBA record number of lifetime games in which a player was fouled out. It was set by Vern Mikkelsen of the Minneapolis Lakers (1949–1950/58/59 seasons).

**127**
NFL record number of consecutive games in which Harold Carmichael of the Philadelphia Eagles caught a pass.

**127**
World seasonal record for number of goals scored. Soccer star Pelé set the record in 1959 with the Brazilian national team.

**127 feet, 3⅜ inches**
Distance between home plate and second base on a regulation baseball diamond.

**128 West 48th Street**
Home address in New York City of Miss Ethel S. Jackson (Doris Day) in the 1952 movie *April in Paris.*

**132**
Islands that make up Hawaii. They are spread out over 1,500 square miles.

**132**
NHL record number of points scored by a team in a single season. It was set by the Montreal Canadiens in 1976–1977, in an eighty-game schedule.

**132 YEB**
California license number of Mary Taylor's (Dee Wallace) silver Audi 5000S in the 1982 movie *E.T. the Extra-Terrestrial.*

**137**
Number of the Soviet submarine, commanded by Captain Pyotr Gushin, that ran around in Swedish waters in October of 1981.

**140 MPH**
Speed "without bein' floored" of the Ford in the 1963 Beach Boys

hit song "Little Deuce Coupe."

## 143BLA
New York state license number of Dectective Phillip Fish's (Abe Vigoda) car, as mentioned in an episode of the TV series "Barney Miller."

## 154 MPH
Fastest recorded tennis serve. It was served by Michael Sangster of Great Britain in 1963.

## 156 West Patrick Street
Address of the house of Union patriot Barbara Fritchie, who, in September 1862, waved the Union flag from her second-story window as Stonewall Jackson and his men passed through Frederick, Maryland.

## 160 acres
Size of the Green Acres farm on the TV series "Green Acres."

## 163 pounds
Weight of Dagwood Bumstead (Arthur Lake) in the Blondie movie series.

## 166
Issue number of *Mad* magazine (April 1977) that showed a hand "giving the bird" to the reader. The publishers of *Mad* sent a letter to its subscribers apologizing for the bad taste displayed by the cover.

## 168 Riverside Drive
Manhattan home address of Miss Vicki Woodsworth (Edith Evans) in the 1967 movie *Fitzwilly*.

## 170
Major-league record number of bases on balls, set by the New York Yankees' Babe Ruth, over 152 games in 1923.

## 176
NFL record number of points scored during a single season. It was established by Paul Hornung of the Green Bay Packers in the 1960 season, when he scored 15 touchdowns, 41 points-after-touchdowns, and 15 field goals.

## 177 East 104th Street
New York City address of the 23rd Precinct police station in the 1968 movie *Coogan's Bluff*.

## 181
Total number of bases stolen by three Oakland A's players: Bill North (75), Bert Camparnaris (54), and Don Baylor (52), in 1976. They set a record of having three players on a single team steal

more than 50 bases each in a single season.

**190**

Major-league record number of RBIs accumulated in one season. Hack Wilson established the record in the 1930 season, the year that he hit 56 home runs.

**191**

Amount of kisses given by Don Juan (John Barrymore) in the 1926 silent film *Don Juan*.

**1,000 miles**

Length of the Great Wall of China, in the lyrics of Paul Simon's hit song "Something So Right."

**1011 Fifth Avenue**

New York City home address of Irene Bullock (Carole Lombard) in the 1936 movie *My Man Godfrey*.

**$1,040**

Amount of money for which one of actress Marilyn Monroe's bras was sold, on June 10, 1981. An American, who kept his identity secret, purchased the clothing article.

**1064**

Patrol car unit used by Officers Murphy (Paul Newman) and Corelli (Ken Wahl) in the 1981 movie *Fort Apache—The Bronx*.

**1066th General Hospital**

U.S. Army setting of the 1957 movie *Operation Mad Ball*.

**1069**

Name to which Minnesota resident Michael Herbert Dengler changed his given name in 1977. It is now the name on his Social Security card and checkbooks.

**1,070**

Major-league record number of games in which a single pitcher has made an appearance. The record is held by Hoyt Wilhelm, who played for nine teams over his twenty-one-year career (1952–1972).

**1,099**

NBA record number of assists made in a single season, set by Kevin Porter of the Detroit Pistons in 1979.

**1,117**

National League record for the most consecutive games played by one player, Billy Williams of the Chicago Cubs. (Lou Gehrig holds the American League record, with 2,130 games.)

**1150**

Engine number of the train that took reporter John Reed (Warren

Beatty) and his wife, Louise Bryant Reed (Diane Keaton), to Petrograd, Russia, in the 1981 movie *Reds*.

**1202 Circle Drive**

Birchfield California, home address of the Mulligan family in the 1977 TV series "Mulligan's Stew."

**1215 Michigan Street**

Address of the house in Toledo, Ohio, where Maxwell Klinger (Jamie Farr) was born, on the TV series "M*A*S*H."

**1230 Holland Street**

Pasadena, California, home address of the Lawrence family in the TV series "Family."

**1246**

Prison number that Lex Luthor (Gene Hackman) wore while serving a sentence of life plus twenty-five years in the 1981 movie *Superman II*. He resided in Cell 383.

**1260 Avenue of the Americas**

New York City address of Radio City Music Hall.

**1,270**

NBA record number of lifetime games, set by John Havlicek from 1963 to 1978.

**1,274 yards**

NFL record for the most yards on penalties in a single season, set by the Oakland Raiders in 1969.

**1,281**

Career number of goals scored by Edson Arantes do Nascimento (Pelé) in the 1,363 games in which he played.

**1313 Pleasant Avenue**

Flatbush, Brooklyn, home address of Henry Limpet (Don Knotts) in the 1964 movie *The Incredible Mr. Limpet*.

**1335 Cliff Drive**

Street address of scientist Dr. Egor Markof (J. Carrol Naish) in the 1944 movie *The Monster Maker*. Actually, the real doctor was murdered by the "fake" Dr. Markof, who took over his life.

**1344 Hartford**

Indianapolis, Indiana, home address of Ann Romano (Bonnie Franklin) and her daughters (in apartment 402) on the TV series "One Day at a Time."

**1400 Tower Road**

Beverly Hills home address of John Barrymore's (Errol Flynn) mansion in the 1958 movie *Too Much, Too Soon*.

**1407 East Figueroa**
Los Angeles street address of the Hannigan Detective School and Agency in the short-lived 1979 TV series "Detective School."

**1451 Blue View Terrace**
Los Angeles home address of Babs Riley Marshall (Lugene Sanders) and her husband Don Marshall (Martin Milner), on the TV series "The Life of Riley."

**1,687**
NHL record of the most career games played, held by Gordy Howe, who played from 1946 to 1971.

**1,700**
Families that make up the Nielsen ratings. In 1982 the number increased from 1,200.

**1,752**
Number of spectators who witnessed the last baseball game played at the Polo Grounds, when the New York Mets were defeated by the Philadelphia Phillies, 5 to 1. The winning pitcher was Chris Short. Craig Anderson was the loser.

**1808 Walnut Street**
Philadelphia address of the St. Dismas Thrift Shop, a fence for stolen goods, in the 1967 movie *Fitzwilly*.

**1836 Loma Linda Drive**
Los Angeles home address of the two families, the Stones and the Flanagans, in the 1979 TV series "A New Kind of Family."

**1873 Bodega Lane**
Address in Bodega, California, of the schoolhouse next to which the birds gathered in the 1963 movie *The Birds*. Today the schoolhouse houses the Galley Restaurant.

**1881**
Number of the locomotive in the 1981 movie *Terror Train*. Carne (Ben Johnson) was the train's conductor.

**1972 Canyon Drive**
Los Angeles address of the house where Evelyn Mulwray (Faye Dunaway) was keeping her daughter (and sister) Hollis (Darrell Zwerling), in the 1975 movie *Chinatown*.

**12,093**
Major-league record number of at-bats in a lifetime for one player, set by Hank Aaron.

**14863**
Larry Poole's (Bing Crosby) prison number in the 1936 movie

*Pennies From Heaven.*

**102395**

New York state license number of Colehouse Walker, Jr.'s (Howard E. Rollins) black Model T Ford automobile in the 1981 movie *Ragtime.*

**105353**

Lieutenant James Schyler Dunbar's (Don Taylor) army serial number in the 1953 movie *Stalag 17.*

**137047**

Police identification number of singer Billie Holiday (Diana Ross) in the opening scene of the 1972 movie *Lady Sings the Blues.*

**137,132**

Largest free crowd to view a boxing match, when Tony Zale knocked out Billy Pryor in Milwaukee, Wisconsin, in 1941.

**141077**

B-25 aircraft that crashed on takeoff, in which Walt Dreiser (Dana Andrews) and all crew members died, in the 1949 movie *My Foolish Heart.*

**$1 million**

Amount of money offered to, but turned down by, Babe Ruth in 1946 to become the president of the newly founded Mexican Baseball League.

**$1.6 million**

Initial settlement won by actress Carol Burnett when she sued the *National Enquirer* in march 1981 over an article that stated that Burnett was drunk in the company of Henry Kissinger in a Washington, D.C., restaurant. In October 1983, an appeals court reduced the amount.

**19571782**

U.S. Army serial number of Corporal (later Sergeant) Maxwell Q. Klinger (Jamie Farr) on the TV series "M*A*S*H."

**19905607**

U.S. Army serial number of Captain Hawkeye Pierce (Alan Alda) on the TV series "M*A*S*H."

**106 43 2185**

Social Security number of Alex Wood (Slim Pickens) in the 1979 movie *1941.*

**O**

Blood type of the Dionne Quintuplets.

**Oakie Doakie**

Andy the alien's dog on the TV cartoon series "My Favorite

Martian.''

**Obber, Horst**

Waiter who worked at the Star Club in Hamburg, Germany, who sang on two songs played by the Beatles on their 1977 album *The Beatles Live at the Star Club*. The two songs, which were tape-recorded in 1962, were titled ''Be-Bop-a-Lulu'' and ''Hallelujah, I Love You So.''

**OB-CPO**

Call letters of the seaplane by which Indiana Jones (Harrison Ford) escaped a South American tribe in the 1981 movie *Raiders of the Lost Ark*. Josh (Fred Sorenson) was the pilot.

**O'Connor, Sandra Day**

(1930–      ) Fifty-one-year-old Arizona State Court of Appeals judge, whom President Reagan selected in 1981 as the first woman to serve on the U.S. Supreme Court, replacing retiring Justice Potter Stewart. She was confirmed on September 25, 1981. Sandra O'Connor had attended Stanford University, graduating in the same 102-student class as William H. Rehnquist. (He ranked first in the class and she ranked third.)

**October 9, One Zillion B.C.**

Opening date of the 1981 Ringo Starr movie *Caveman*.

**October 17, 1947**

Date on which Beech Bonanza Model 35, N3794N, was manufactured. The aircraft was destroyed in a crash on February 3, 1959, killing pilot Roger Peterson and passengers Buddy Holly, J. P. Richardson (The Big Bopper), and Ritchie Valens.

**October 26**

Birthdate of two heavyweight boxing champions, Jack Sharkey (1902) and Primo Carnera (1906). Carnera beat Sharkey for the title on June 29, 1933.

**Odd Couple, The**

Jack Lemmon and Walter Matthau movie (1968) being shown at the Pix Theater in the 1969 movie *Goodbye Columbus*. Jack Klugman, who appeared in *Goodbye Columbus,* played the Matthau role of Oscar Madison on TV.

**''Ode on the Intimations of Immortality from Recollections of Early Childhood''**

Poem by English poet William Wordsworth (1770–1850) from which came the phrase ''Splendor in the Grass,'' which was used as the title of the 1961 Warren Beatty/Natalie Wood movie *Splendor in the Grass*.

**O'Donnell, Jake**

Only man to have refereed in both major-league baseball and major-league basketball (1968–1972).

**O'Donnell, James**

Author of the 1978 book *The Bunker*, about the last days of Adolf Hitler. He was portrayed by James Naughton in the 1981 TV movie *The Bunker*.

**Oenology**

Science of wine and winemaking.

**Officer Frank Murphy**

Los Angeles police officer; played by Charles Durning in the TV series "The Cop and the Kid."

**Officer Mike Breen**

Los Angeles police officer (played by Mark Harmon) who owned the Labrador retriever, Sam (played by Sam), on the 1978 TV series "Sam."

**Officer William "Obie" Obanhein**

Policeman who arrested singer Arlo Guthrie for littering after he found a letter addressed to Guthrie in the trash. He portrayed himself in the 1969 movie *Alice's Restaurant*.

**OFP857**

California license number of the 1963 Volkswagen named Herbie, in the TV series "Herbie the Love Bug."

**O'Hair, Madelyn Murray**

Athiest who took her case to the Supreme Court and won, thus ending student prayer in public schools. She was the first guest on the TV show "Donahue," on November 6, 1967, in Dayton, Ohio.

**O'Hara, Jill**

Singer who introduced the songs "Good Morning Starshine," in the 1967 musical play *Hair*, and "I'll Never Fall in Love Again," in the 1968 musical *Promises, Promises*.

**O'Hare**

Chicago airport that is the busiest in the world. It was named after U.S. Navy aviator Edward Henry O'Hare, who died on November 27, 1943, after he shot down five Japanese planes. He was credited with saving the U.S. aircraft carrier *Lexington*.

**OH5630**

Illinois license number of the Jarrett family's Buick in the 1980 movie *Ordinary People*.

**Ohio State**

Alma mater of Henry Desmond (Peter Scolari) and Kip Wilson

(Tom Hanks) in the TV series "Bosom Buddies."

**"Oh, Susanna"**
Tune that Ozzie Bates (Patrick O'Moore) played on the harmonica in order to show the Germans that they (the trapped Allies) had plenty of water in the 1943 movie *Sahara*. Also the tune that Molly (Shirley Temple) played on the piano in the 1935 movie *Our Little Girl*.

**"Oh, You Beautiful Doll"**
Song composed in 1911 by A. Seymour Brown and Nat D. Ayer. It can be heard in the films *Wharf Angel* (1934), *The Story of Vernon and Irene Castle* (1939), *For Me and My Gal* (1942), *Oh, You Beautiful Doll* (1949), *The Eddie Cantor Story* (1954), and *All the Marbles* (1981).

**Oil**
Original proposed title of the 1981 TV series "Dynasty."

**Oilcan Harry**
Nemesis of Mighty Mouse in cartoons, voiced by Alan Oppenheimer on the TV series "The New Adventures of Mighty Mouse and Heckle and Jeckle."

**Oklahoma Kid**
Book written by Holly Martins (Joseph Cotten), carried by Baron Kurtz so that Martins would recognize him, in the 1949 movie *The Third Man*. Two other books by Martins were *The Lone Rider of Santa Fe* and *The Death of the Double X Ranch*.

**Oklahoma—original cast album**
First album to sell a million copies in the United States. This album was first released in 1949.

**Okron, Tommy**
Ten-year-old boy who offered Mean Joe Greene his Coca-Cola, for which Joe gave him his jersey, on TV commercials. In order to get an acceptable take, Joe downed eighteen bottles of Coca-Cola (sixteen ounces each). On November 8, 1981, a one-hour special, titled "The Steelers and the Pittsburgh Kid," featured Joe Greene and a boy named Henry Thomas (Tommy Okron had grown too much since the commercial). Henry Thomas went on to play the role of Elliott in the 1982 film *E.T. the Extra-Terrestrial*.

**Oland, Warner**
First actor to have his singing dubbed into a movie: *The Jazz Singer* (1927). His voice was dubbed by Joseph Diskay.

**Old Crow**
Whiskey that General/President Ulysses S. Grant drank.

**Old Dunlap Ranch**

Homestead purchased by Lucas McCain (Chuck Connors) on the very first episode (September 30, 1958) on the TV series "The Rifleman."

**Older, Charles**

Judge at the trial of mass-murderer Charles Manson. He was portrayed by Skip Homeier in the 1976 TV movie *Helter Skelter*.

**Old Harper**

Brand of whiskey asked for by the Toad (Charles Martin Smith) at the drive-in liquor store in the 1973 movie *American Graffiti*.

**Old King Cole**

Nursery rhyme character: "merry old soul who called for his bowl and he called for his pipe and he called for his fiddlers three." He was played in the 1934 movie *Babes in Toyland* by Kewpie Morgan, and by Hugh Herbert in the 1936 movie *Mother Goose Goes Hollywood*.

**"Old Man Moon"**

Song sung by George and Marion Kirby (Cary Grant and Constance Bennett) accompanied by a piano player named Bill (Hoagy Carmichael) until they were thrown out of a bar just prior to their fatal accident in the 1937 movie *Topper*.

**Old Paint**

Nickname of Pete Cochrane's (Michael Cole) Mercury "Woody" station wagon on the 1968–1973 TV series "The Mod Squad."

**Old Shep**

Robert Hartley's (Bob Newhart) dog that ran away from home when he was a boy, on the TV series "The Bob Newhart Show."

**Old silk hat**

Object that brought Frosty the Snowman to life when it was placed on his head.

**"Old Turkey Buzzard"**

Song sung by José Feliciano for the 1969 movie *McKenna's Gold*.

**Oliver Niles Studio**

Hollywood movie studio for which both Norman Maine (James Mason) and his wife, Vicki Lester (Judy Garland), made motion pictures in the 1954 movie *A Star Is Born*.

**Oliver Twist**

Orphaned nine-year-old boy who lived in nineteenth-century London. He was the subject of Charles Dickens's 1838 novel of the same title. In movies, he has been played by Dickie Moore (1933), John Howard Davies (1948), and by Richard Charles in the 1982

TV movie. He was played by Mark Lester in the 1968 musical *Oliver!*

**Olivia Dragon**

Oliver J. Dragon's (Ollie) mother on the TV puppet show "Kukla, Fran and Ollie."

**Olivier, Laurence**

(1907– ) British actor whose name Tony Manero (John Travolta) didn't recognize after hearing it mentioned by Stephanie (Karen Lynn Gorney) in the 1977 movie *Saturday Night Fever*. (Stephanie knew him as the guy who made camera commercials.) Olivier won an Academy Award for his portrayal of Hamlet in 1947, and was knighted on July 8 of that year, becoming the youngest actor (age forty) ever knighted. He was married to actress Vivien Leigh from 1940 to 1960.

**O Lost**

Original title of Thomas Wolfe's 1929 novel *Look Homeward, Angel*, which is subtitled *A Story of the Buried Life*.

**Olympian**

School paper of Carvel High in the Andy Hardy movie series.

**Olympic Club**

Private San Francisco athletic club of which fighter James J. Corbett (Errol Flynn) was a member in the 1942 movie *Gentleman Jim*.

**Olympic gold medalists who became heavyweight boxing champions:**

| | | |
|---|---|---|
| Floyd Patterson | 1952 | Middleweight |
| Cassius Clay | 1960 | Light heavyweight |
| Joe Frazier | 1964 | Heavyweight |
| George Foreman | 1968 | Heavyweight |
| Leon Spinks | 1976 | Light heavyweight |

**Olympic gymnastic events for women**

Floor exercise
All-around
Balance beam
Vaulting
Uneven parallel bars
Team championship

**Olympics 1980**

First U.S. stamp (fifteen cents) to be pulled off the market since the Civil War.

**Omni**

Small time machine in the TV series "Voyagers!"

**Omnitech**
   Giant corporation that had a suit filed against it, which the Supreme
   Court was to hear in the 1981 movie *First Monday in October*.
**Once and Future King, The**
   Book (1958) by T. H. White upon which the 1967 movie *Camelot*
   was based.
**O'Neal, Steve**
   New York Jets kicker who holds the NFL record for the longest
   punt (98 yards), set in a game on September 21, 1969, against the
   Denver Broncos.
**One Born Every Minute**
   British release title of the 1967 American movie *The Flim-Flam
   Man*.
**"One Love"/"Give Her Love"**
   Forty-five RPM single recorded by major-league pitcher Don Drys-
   dale in 1963 on Reprise Records.
**One-Lung**
   Oliver "Daddy" Warbucks' dog in the "Little Orphan Annie"
   comic strip.
**"One More Hour"**
   Theme song of the 1981 movie *Ragtime*, sung by Jennifer Warnes.
**One-Night Stands of a Noisy Passenger**
   Play, starring Robert DeNiro, which was written by Shelley
   Winters.
**One Special Summer**
   Book written by sisters Jackie Bouvier and Lee Radzewill about
   their trip through Europe during the summer of 1951.
**One, Two, Buckle My Shoe (nursery rhyme)**
   One, two, buckle my shoe
   Three, four, shut the door
   Five, six, pick up sticks
   Seven, eight, lay them straight
   Nine, ten, a good fat hen
   Eleven, twelve, dig and delve
   Thirteen, fourteen, maids a-counting (or "a tambourine")
   Fifteen, sixteen, maids a-kissing (or "the sea is green")
   Seventeen, eighteen, maids a-waiting
   Nineteen, twenty, my platter's empty
**One Way Passage**
   Movie (1932) starring Kay Francis and William Powell, seen by
   Alva Starr (Natalie Wood) and Owen Legate (Robert Redford) in

the 1966 movie *This Property Is Condemned.*

**"On the Sunny Side of the Street"**

Song composed in 1930 by Dorothy Fields and Jimmy McHugh. It is heard in the following movies:

*Is Everybody Happy?* (1943)
*Two Blondes and a Red Head* (1947)
*This Earth Is Mine* (1949)
*On the Sunny Side of the Street* (1951), sung by Frankie Laine
*The Eddy Duchin Story* (1956)
*The Benny Goodman Story* (1956)
*The Helen Morgan Story* (1957), sung by Gogi Grant
*The Way We Were* (1973)

**"On Top of Old Smokey"**

Recurring theme song of the 1945 movie *Along Came Jones.*

**"On Wisconsin"**

School song for which the music was originally written for the University of Minnesota.

**Operation Undertow**

British Secret Service assignment to recover electronic gear from the British spy ship *St. Georges* in the 1981 movie *For Your Eyes Only.*

**OPW654W**

License number of James Bond's (Roger Moore) white Lotus Turbo Esprit that blew up when someone attempted to get in it, in the 1981 movie *For Your Eyes Only.*

**Orange**

Color of the golden Gate Bridge, also Frank Sinatra's favorite color.

**ORchard 9-9539**

Telephone number of Don Vito Corleone (Marlon Brando) in the 1972 movie *The Godfather.*

**Ordinary People**

Movie (1980) that was Robert Redford's first film as a director, for which he won an Oscar.

**O'Ree, Willie**

First black to play in the National Hockey League. He was a forward for the Boston Bruins, first playing on January 18, 1958.

**Oregano**

Miller family pet dog in the 1979–1980 TV series "Shirley."

**Oregon Pacific and Eastern**

Railroad for which Shack (Ernest Borgnine) was an engineer

(engine number 19) in the 1973 movie *Emperor of the North*.

**Organization of World Management**
Evil organization whose scheme is to shrink the world's population in the 1981 movie *The Incredible Shrinking Woman*.

**Original Radio Girl**
Appellative of singer Vaughn DeLeath, the first female to sing on radio.

**Orion**
Nebula that Simon (Alan Arkin) thought he came from in the 1980 Orion-produced movie *Simon*.

**Orly County**
Georgia setting of the TV series "Lobo," later retitled "The Misadventures of Sheriff Lobo."

**Or the Decline and Fall of the British Empire**
Subtitle of Ray Davies's rock opera *Arthur*.

**Ortiz, Antulio Ramirez**
First person to hijack an aircraft from the United States (Miami) to Cuba (1961).

**O'Ryan Funeral Home**
Place from which Felix Farmer's (Richard Mulligan) body was stolen in the 1981 movie *S.O.B.*

**Osborne Enterprises**
Factory for which Harry Grafton (Phil Silvers) was employed as a foreman on the TV series "The New Phil Silvers Show."

**Otello**
Opera written by Giuseppe Verdi in 1887, which Big Eddie (Richard Kiel) wrecks in the 1981 movie *So Fine*.

**Otto**
Name given to the inflatable autopilot in the credits of the 1980 movie *Airplane!*

**Our comedies are not to be laughed at . . .**
Saying credited to movie producer Samuel Goldwyn, known as a Goldwynism.

**"Our Day Will Come"**
Number-one hit song (1963) by Ruby and the Romantics. It is the only song that can be heard in both of the sequel movies *More American Graffiti* (1979) and *Grease 2* (1982).

**"Out of Nowhere"**
Theme song of the 1945 movie *You Came Along*, in which Lizabeth Scott made her film debut.

### "Out of Time"
Recording by the Rolling Stones that can be heard at both the beginning and closing of the 1978 movie *Coming Home*.

### Overland Flyer
Last U.S. train held up by Butch Cassidy (Paul Newman) and the Sundance Kid (Robert Redford) in the 1969 movie *Butch Cassidy and the Sundance Kid*. They blow the baggage car up.

### Overlook Hotel
Colorado hotel, built in 1907, which was the setting of the 1980 movie *The Shining* (based on the novel by Stephen King). The hotel's ballroom was called "the Gold Room," and their CB radio call letters were KDK-12.

### Owens Falcons
College football team that played against Pawlton University and featured the chimpanzee named Bonzo as quarterback (uniform number 5) in the 1952 movie *Bonzo Goes to College*.

# P

**PATCO**

Professional Air Traffic Controllers Organization, the union that was busted by the Federal Government in 1982. PATCO is one of the few unions that have been outlawed in the history of the United States.* A controller wearing a PATCO insignia on his pocket protector can be seen in the 1973 movie *Magnum Force*.

**P.C.**

Earl Eischied's (Joe Don Baker) pet cat on the TV series "Eischied."

**P.O.S.H.**

Portside Outbound, Starboard Homeward. Cabin reservations for ship travel.

**PRLFQ**

How Scotty spelled "Mom and Dad" in the 1971 Bobby Golds-boro song "Watching Scotty Grow." The song was based on an actual incident involving composer Mac Davis's four-year-old son Scotty.

**P.S. 46**

School attended by Jeff Williams (Ronald Reagan) in his youth, in the 1951 movie *Hong Kong*.

**PXJ 432**

California license plate hanging in one of the Thunderbirds' lockers at Rydell High School in the 1982 movie *Grease 2*.

---

*Ironically, at the same time that PATCO was outlawed, U.S. policy was to support the "illegal" union Solidarity in Communist Poland, an interesting contrast in policy. In 1983, the head of Solidarity, Lech Walesa, was awarded the Nobel Peace Prize, while that same year several U.S. air traffic controllers were sent to jail because of their strike.

**PXL1236**

NASA spaceship upon which Junior (Bob Denver) and Barney (Chuck McCann) were launched into space on the TV series "Far Out Space Nuts."

**PA2246**

Landing craft in which Major Huxley (Van Heflin) and his men landed on the beach in the 1955 movie *Battle Cry*.

**Pacific High**

Southern California high school featured in the 1978 movie *Almost Summer*. The school team was the Panthers. Darryl Fitzgerald (John Friedrich) won the election for student body president.

**Pacific Island divisions**

Micronesia: Caroline, Gilbert, Marshall, and Marianas Islands.

Indonesia: Malay Archipelago and New Guinea

Polynesia: Hawaiian Islands, New Zealand Islands of Oceania

**Pacino, Al**

(1940–     ) Actor who has appeared on the stage (Obie and Tony winner), as well as receiving Oscar nominations for film performances *The Godfather* (1972, Best Supporting Actor); *Serpico* (1973, Best Actor); *The Godfather, Part II* (1974, Best Actor); *Dog Day Afternoon* (1975, Best Actor); . . . *And Justice for All* (1979, Best Actor). He made his movie debut in the 1969 film *Me, Natalie*. He was at the bedside of Lee Strasberg when the actor/director died, on February 17, 1981. They had appeared together in the 1974 movie *The Godfather, Part II* (Strasberg's film acting debut). Pacino was Tony Manero's (John Travolta) idol in the 1977 movie *Saturday Night Fever;* there was a poster of Pacino on Tony's bedroom wall. At the 2001 Disco in the same film, a girl calls Tony "Al Pacino." Elliott Garfield (Richard Dreyfuss) mentions Pacino's name in the 1977 movie *The Goodbye Girl*. He is also mentioned in the 1980 movie *The Competition*, and by Inspector Clouseau (Peter Sellers) in the 1978 movie *Revenge of the Pink Panther*.

**Paciorek, John**

Seventeen-year-old who played in only one baseball game in the majors. In the last game of the 1963 season, he was called up from the minors by the Houston Colt 45s, and in his one game he got three hits for three at-bats, and two walks, scoring four runs and driving in three. He never played in the majors again.

**Packard**

Engines (three each) used in U.S. PT (or Mosquito) boats during

World War II.

## Pac-Man

Extremely popular video game that first came into use in 1980. The four opponents of Pac-Man and their nicknames are:

| Red | Shadow | "Blinky" |
| Pink | Speedy | "Pinky" |
| Blue | Bashful | "Inky" |
| Yellow | Pokey | "Clyde" (Replaced by "Sue" in the *Ms. Pac-Man* game) |

*Extra points:*

Cherries = 100
Strawberry = 200
Orange = 500
Pretzel = 700
Apple = 1,000
Pear = 2,000
Banana = 5,000

The game spun off several books, a board game, and a 1982 hit record "Pac-Man Fever" by Buckner and Garcia, as well as a breakfast cereal. Marty Ingels is the voice of Pac-Man on a Saturday morning TV cartoon series. Ted Trenton (Danny Pintauro) has a Pac-Man lunchbox in the 1983 movie *Cujo*.

## Pad 39A

Cape Canaveral launching pad from which the space shuttle *Columbia* made its maiden flight on April 12, 1981. Apollo 11 was launched from Pad 39A on July 16, 1969.

## Paddy

J. L. Kraft's first horse, which pulled his cheese wagon. He purchased both the horse and the wagon in 1903 for sixty-five dollars.

## Page 80

Page of the *Wizard of Oz* movie script in which the Japanese agent hid the invasion map in the 1981 movie *Under the Rainbow*.

## Paine's Pure Pickles

Paine family business on the TV series "Thicker Than Water," starring Julie Harris.

## Painful

Town that Melody Jones (Gary Cooper) rode into in the 1945 movie *Along Came Jones*.

## Palace Chop House

Newark, New Jersey, restaurant where Arthur "Dutch Schultz"

Flegenheimer was assassinated on the orders of Charles "Lucky" Luciano, on October 23, 1955.

**Palace Hotel**

Large hotel at Lake Wazapamoni, 106 miles from Chicago, where the Blues Brothers, Jake and Elwood, performed to a capacity crowd (including the Illinois state police and the Good Ole Boys western band) in the 1980 movie *The Blues Brothers*.

**Palace of the Governors**

Oldest public building in the United States, built in 1610 in Santa Fe, New Mexico.

**Palett, Pilar**

John Wayne's third wife (1954–1979) and the daughter of a Peruvian senator. A photo of Pilar was used as Dan Roman's (John Wayne) dead wife in the 1954 movie *The High and the Mighty*.

**Palinkas, Pat**

First woman to "play" professional football when, on August 15, 1970, she held the football for her husband, Orlando Panthers (Atlantic Coast football league) place kicker Steve Palinkas.

**Pallas, Peter Simon**

(1741–1811) German naturalist famous for his collection of natural history specimens.

**Palma, Emilio Marcos**

First baby ever born on the continent of Antarctica. He was born on an Argentine military base in January 1978.

**Palm Drive**

Los Angeles street on which Helen Trent lived on the radio soap opera "The Romance of Helen Trent."

**Palmer, Arnold**

First golfer to win more than $100,000 in one year (1973). He appeared as himself in the 1963 Bob Hope movie *Call Me Bwana*.

**Pamela**

Chimpanzee that two thieves substituted for Bonzo at Pawlton's football game in the 1952 movie *Bonzo Goes to College*.

**Pan American Flight 323**

Boeing 707 on which James Bond (Sean Connery) traveled from London to Kingston, Jamaica, in the 1962 movie *Dr. No*.

**Pan American Flight 603**

Airliner on which Cathy Timberlake (Doris Day) traveled from New York to Bermuda, at 31,000 feet, as the plane's only passenger. The pilot was Captain Miller in the 1962 movie *That Touch of Mink*.

**Pancho**
Johnson family thoroughbred horse that Arthur Bach (Dudley Moore) kisses in the 1981 movie *Arthur*.

**Pandora Sparks**
Credit line for the role of Serena on the TV series "Bewitched," although Elizabeth Montgomery (Samantha) played her.

**Papp, Laszlo**
Hungarian boxer who won the Olympic gold medal for the middleweight category in 1948, the gold medal for light middleweight in 1952, and the gold medal for the light middleweight category again in 1956.

**Pappy Yokum**
Father of Li'l Abner, played by Clarence Hartzell on the radio series "Li'l Abner."

**Parachute Jumper**
Movie (1933) starring Bette Davis which was shown on TV in the 1962 movie *Whatever Happened to Baby Jane* (the only film appearance of both Bette Davis and Joan Crawford together). It was shown as one of Jane Hudson's (Bette Davis) old movies.

**Paradise Burlesque**
Theater where Professor Kropotkin (Hans Conreid) played violin in the radio series "My Friend Irma."

**Paradise Cove Trailer Colony**
Malibu, California, location of Jim Rockford's (James Garner) mobile home on the TV series "The Rockford Files."

**Paradise Lost**
Epic poem by John Milton, written in 1667, that is being taught at Faber College by Professor Dave Jennings (Donald Sutherland) in the 1978 movie *National Lampoon's Animal House*.

**Paramount Apartments**
Hollywood apartment house that inspired William Wadsworth Hodkinson, in 1917, to name his movie studio Paramount Pictures.

**Paramutual Pictures, Inc.**
Hollywood motion picture company headed by Mr. T.P. (Brian Donlevy) in the 1961 movie *The Errand Boy*.

**Pardo, Don**
Announcer for the TV game show "Jeopardy," which was hosted by Art Fleming. His life was humorously reviewed on a skit on the TV series "Saturday Night Live," (for which Pardo was also the announcer). Don Pardo appeared on the cover of Frank Zappa's 1978 album *In New York*.

**Paris**
Ship upon which Errol Flynn first sailed to America, in November of 1934.

**Paris Club**
Nightclub in London where Ed Bolland (Robert Wagner) took Daphne Caldwell (Ann Field), only to meet Buzz Rickson (Steve McQueen), in the 1962 movie *The War Lover*.

**Park Bearcats**
Kids' basketball team that defeated the Third Street Lions with the help of an alien team member, in the 1981 movie *Earthbound*.

**Park Central Hotel**
New York City hotel where, on November 4, 1928, gambler Arnold Rothstein was shot to death in room 349.

**Parker's Roller Rink**
Lubbock, Texas, roller rink where Buddy Holly and the Crickets played on KDAV's "Holly Hayride" in the 1978 movie *The Buddy Holly Story*.

**Parkersville**
Hometown of Portia Blake Manning (Lucille Ball) on the radio soap "Portia Faces Life."

**Parkettes**
Cheerleaders for the Minnesota Vikings football team.

**Parkhouse, Albert J.**
Inventor, in 1903, of the wire coat hanger.

**Park Street**
Most popular street name in the United States.

**Parson Brown**
Minister mentioned in the lyrics of the song "Winter Wonderland."

**Partridge Club**
Chicago gambling casino owned and run by Charles "Lucky" Luciano (Michael Nouri), Ben "Bugsy" Siegel (Joe Penny), and Michael Lasker (Brian Benben) in the TV series "Gangster Chronicles."

**Paschal, Ben**
(1895–1974) Major-league player who hit two inside-the-park home runs in a single game in 1925.

**Passionate Plumber, The**
X-rated movie that the Sweathogs brought to Buchanan High and was mistakenly shown to the parents on the TV series "Welcome Back Kotter."

**Passion Play, The**
Religious play about the suffering and death of Jesus, performed in Latin; after the fifteenth century, it was performed in German, at Oberammergau, Bavaria, every ten years.

**Passkey**
Secret Service code name for U.S. President Gerald Ford.

**Pathe's Rooster**
Rooster mascot of Pathe's newsreels. Brad Barker provided the rooster's crow.

**"Patricia"**
Instrumental song being played in the opening scene of the 1969 movie *Goodbye Columbus*. "Patricia" had been a number-one song for Perez Prado in 1958.

**Patrick J. Duffy**
Full name of Duffy on the radio series "Duffy's Tavern." Duffy was never heard.

**Patrolman Joe Coffey**
Policeman who works for the Hill Street Precinct of the Metropolitan Police on the TV series "Hill Street Blues." He was played by ex-Chicago Bears running back Ed Marinaro, who rushed for 4,715 yards in three seasons. The part was originally intended as a "guest star"/semi-continuing character who would be terminated after the first season (the last episode of which has him getting his throat slashed by a hooker). However, due to his popularity, he was allowed "to survive" and became a "regular" the next season.

**Patterson, Floyd**
(1935–    ) Heavyweight boxing champion who, at the age of twenty-one, became the youngest fighter to win the heavyweight title. He is the only heavyweight to have been outweighed in all of his thirteen heavyweight championship bouts.

**Patterson, Roger, and Bob Gimlin**
Two hunters who took the famous moving pictures of Bigfoot in Northern California on October 20, 1967. Although the film only lasted a few seconds, it showed an animal that was estimated to have stood seven feet tall and weighed 350 pounds. It was also determined that it was female.

**Paul Hardly**
News commentator played by Bob Elliott in the 1965 movie *Cold Turkey*.

**Paul French**

Pseudonym for prolific writer Isaac Asimov, who wrote six books (the "Lucky Starr" series) using that name.

**Pawlton**

University attended by Bonzo the chimpanze, where he played on the football team as a quarterback in the 1952 movie *Bonzo Goes to College*. Tom Harmon gave the game's play-by-play account.

**"Pay as You Go"**

TV game show on which Laura Petrie (Mary Tyler Moore) once appeared. The show was hosted by Johnny Patrick on the TV series "The Dick Van Dyke Show."

**Peabody**

Employee who created the Firestone 721 Belted Radial, in 1980 TV commercials.

**Peace and Freedom Party**

Political party for which comedian Dick Gregory ran for President of the United States in 1968.

**Peace Bug**

Psychedelic 1960 BMW Isetta 300 car in the 1968 movie *I Love You, Alice B. Toklas*.

**Pearl is in the river, the**

Recognition phrase that a Japanese agent was to use when he met the Nazi, Otto (Billy Barty), in the 1981 movie *Under the Rainbow*.

**Pearl Pureheart**

Girlfriend of Mighty Mouse, whose voice was that of Diane Pershing on the TV series "The New Adventures of Mighty Mouse and Heckle and Jeckle."

**"Pearly Shells"**

Theme song of the 1963 movie *Donovan's Reef*.

**Pecan tree**

Tree in Natchitoches, Louisiana, into which the twin-engine airplane carrying singer Jim Croce and five other people crashed after takeoff on September 20, 1973.

**Pecos, New Mexico**

Setting of the 1964 movie *Invitation to a Gunfighter*.

**Peel, Sir Robert**

Founder, on February 5, 1788, of the Metropolitan Police in London. From his first name was derived the term "bobbie." He was portrayed by Michael Barrington in the TV series "Edward the King," and by Nicholas Hannen in the 1942 movie *The Prime Minister*.

**Peepo**

Small robot member of the Blue Team on the TV series "Space Academy."

**Peerless Radio and Television Company**

Firm for which Chuck (Farley Granger) worked in the 1950 movie *Our Very Own*.

**Peggy Hayden**

Maiden name of Captain B. J. Hunnicutt's (Mike Farrell) wife on the TV series "M*A*S*H." Their wedding anniversary was May 23. Peg was played in one episode by Catherine Bergstrom, via home movies.

**Peletier, Nicolas Jacques**

Frenchman who, on April 25, 1792, became the first person to die on the guillotine.

**Pelican**

Official state bird of Louisiana.

**Pelzer, Lorne Parke**

Twenty-three-year old U.S. Navy pilot whose Douglas Dauntless dive bomber was lost during a flight on March 13, 1943, in Shasta County, California. The aircraft was finally discovered in September 1981.

**Pen and Pencil**

Miami bar frequented by Michael Collin Gallagher (Paul Newman) and Megan Carter (Sally Field) in the 1981 movie *Absence of Malice*. They also dined at Caramba's Restaurant.

**Penny**

Male wirehaired terrier pet dog of the Blaisdell family in the 1952 movie *Has Anybody Seen My Gal?*

**People (fictitious covers)**

Magazine that had New York Jets quarterback Flash Gordon's (Sam J. Jones) picture on the cover in the 1980 movie *Flash Gordon*. Michael Dorsey (Dustin Hoffman), as Dorothy Michaels, appeared with Andy Warhol on the cover of *People* in the 1982 movie *Tootsie*. Male model Tyler Burnett (Jon-Erik Hexum) appeared on the cover in the 1983 TV movie *The Making of a Male Model*.

**"People Alone"**
Love theme from the 1980 movie *The Competition*, sung by Randy Crawford.

**People Crackers**
Dog treats by French's, containing figures of a policeman, a milkman, a dog catcher, a fireman, a burglar, and a mailman.

**People who were never seen or heard in radio and TV series**

| | | |
|---|---|---|
| Duffy | radio series | "Duffy's Tavern" |
| Mrs. Bloom | radio series | "The Goldbergs" |
| Madge | TV series | "The Dick Van Dyke Show" |
| Gladys | TV series | "December Bride" |
| Mr. Dunahy | TV series | "The Jackie Gleason Show" |

**Pepe Le Moko**
Crook, played by Charles Boyer, in the 1938 classic film *Algiers* (which was later made into the musical *Casbah*). The character is originally from the 1937 French film *Pepe Le Moko* with Jean Gabin in the title role.

**Peppermint Patty Reichardt**
Little girl in Charles Schulz's comic strip "Peanuts." Her father calls her "his rare gem." On the "Peanuts" TV specials, Peppermint Patty's voice was provided by Sally Dryer (1965), Lisa DeFaria (1966), Gail DeFaria (1967–1968), Kip DeFaria (1971–1973), Donna Forman (1974), Linda Ercoli (1974), Stuart Brotman (1975–1976), Laura Planting (1977), Patricia Patts (1979–1980), and Brent Hauer (1980–1981). In the 1969 movie *A Boy Named Charlie Brown*, her voice was that of Sally Dryer, and in the 1972 movie *Snoopy Come Home*, her voice was provided by Chris DeFaria.

**"Pepper Pot, The"**
Original title of Don McNeill's radio series "Breakfast Club."

**Pep, Willie**
(1922–     ) Only boxing champion (featherweight) to survive a plane crash that took place while he was the champ (January 8, 1947). The crash, which occurred at Newark, New Jersey, killed five people.

**Percy, Eileen**
Hollywood actress born in Belfast in 1899. After becoming a Ziegfeld girl, she made her movie debut in *Wild and Woolly*, in 1917. In 1936 she married composer Harry Ruby. Eileen Percy was

portrayed by Arlene Dahl in the 1950 movie *Three Little Words*.

**Peridromophilia**

Collecting of bus or trolley transfers.

**Perkins, Josephine**

First woman in the United States to be convicted of horse theft (1839).

**Perma 1**

Space station setting of the TV series "Quark."

**Perpetual Virgin**

Appellative conferred upon actress/singer Doris Day.

**Perrin, Vic**

"Control voice" for the introduction and closing of the TV series "Outer Limits." He also did the voice of the Metron Controller for the "Star Trek" episode entitled "Arena." The introduction and closing narrations of "The Outer Limits" were as follows:

*Introduction:*

"There is nothing wrong with your television set; do not attempt to adjust the picture. We are controlling transmission. If we wish to make it louder, we will bring up the volume. If we wish to make it softer, we will tune it to a whisper. We will control the horizontal; we will control the vertical. We can roll the image . . . make it flutter. We can change the focus to a soft blur or sharpen it to crystal clarity. For the next hour, sit quietly and we will control all that you see and hear. We repeat—there is nothing wrong with your television set. You are about to participate in a great adventure. You are about to experience the awe and mystery which reaches from the inner mind to . . . the Outer Limits."

   (The introduction varied slightly during the series' two-year run.)

*Closing:*

"We now return control of your television set to you until next week at this same time, when the Control Voice will take you to . . . the Outer Limits."

**Perth Amboy High**

School attended by Walter Mitty (Danny Kaye) in the 1947 movie *The Secret Life of Walter Mitty*.

**Petaluma**

California town that hosts the World's Wrist Wrestling Championship each year since 1953.

**Peter Brown**

Name mentioned in the lyrics of the 1969 song "The Ballad of John and Yoko" by the Beatles.

**Peter Emil Flick**

Pseudonym used by San Francisco reporter Pierre Salinger in a scheme to be arrested in both Stockton and Bakersfield, California, in 1953 so that he could expose the jail conditions. His newspaper stories led to a number of jail reforms.

**"Peter Gunn"**

TV series with a musical score by Henry Mancini, beginning in 1958. It became the first TV soundtrack album to sell a million copies. The theme song can be heard in the 1978 movie *The Blues Brothers*.

**Peter, Laurence Johnston**

(1919–     ) Father of the Peter Principle: "In a hierarchy, every employee tends to rise to his level of incompetence."

**Peter Pan Peanut Butter jingle**

"Picky people pick Peter Pan peanut Butter, it's the peanut butter picky people pick" (tongue-twister used in 1981 TV commercials).

**Peter Perfect**

Boyfriend of Penelope Pitstop on the TV cartoon series "The Wacky Races."

**Peters, Gary, and J. C. Martin**

Two chicago White Sox players who had their pictures switched on Topps bubble gum cards in 1960.

**Peters, Jean**

(1926–     ) Hollywood actress and former Miss Ohio State (1946). She made her film debut in the 1947 movie *Captain from Castile*. In 1957 she secretly married billionaire Howard Hughes and divorced him in 1971. Jean Peters was portrayed by Carol Bagdasarian in the 1977 TV movie *The Amazing Howard Hughes*.

**Peter Stirling**

Owner of Francis the Talking Mule, in films; played by Donald O'Connor in all except the last movie in the series, in which Mickey Rooney played the role. Peter Stirling graduated 647th in his class at West Point, the bottom man. In actuality, Peter Stirling was the real name of David Sterns, the man who created Francis.

**Pfennig, Ernst**

Chicago dentist who, in 1903, became the first person to purchase an automobile from the Ford Motor Company.

**Phantom Zone**
Dimension to which the planet Krypton sentenced its criminals. General Zod (Terence Stamp), Non (Jack O'Halloran), and Ursa (Sarah Douglas) were entrapped there in the 1978 movie *Superman*, and in the beginning of the 1981 movie *Superman II*. A hydrogen bomb hurled into space by Superman exploded the Phantom Zone in *Superman II*, setting the trio free.

**Phil**
Baby robot in the 1982 movie *Heartbeeps*.

**Philadelphia**
Rocky Balboa's (Sylvester Stallone) hometown in the *Rocky* movie series.

**Philadelphia Athletics**
Major-league baseball team for which Doc Eddie "the Blur" Daniels (Nick Nolte) pitched until he beaned Maxie Baker (Sunshine Parker), putting him out of baseball. Doc left the game with a record of 21 wins and 10 losses for his last season. He previously pitched seasons in which he won 25 and 26 games, in the 1982 movie *Cannery Row*.

**"Philadelphia Freedom"**
Song written and recorded by Elton John in 1975 as a dedication to tennis star Billie Jean King and her team, the Philadelphia Freedoms.

**Philharmonic**
Middle name of Throckmorton P. Gildersleeve, "The Great Gildersleeve," played on radio by Hal Peary, and on radio and TV by Willard Waterman.

**Phillie Phanatic**
Comical costumed mascot of the Philadelphia Phillies baseball team.

**Phillips Dance Studio**
Dance studio where nineteen-year-old Tony (John Travolta) practiced dancing in the 1977 movie *Saturday Night Fever*.

**Phineas Q. Throckmorton**
Young boy puppet hero of the 1952 TV series "Willie Wonderful."

**Phipps, James**
Eight-year-old boy who became the first person to receive a smallpox vaccination when Dr. Edward Jenner inoculated him on May 14, 1796.

**Phobus 4**
Evil warrior robot in the 1979 movie *The Shape of Things to Come*. Phobus 4 was captured and rebuilt and renamed Sparks.

**Phoebe and Franklin**
First names of Ma and Pa Kettle. In some films, Pa is also referred to as Elwin.

**Phyl and Mikhy**
TV sitcom on which several facts were read by Truck (Jack Dodson) from *The Complete Unabridged Super Trivia Encyclopedia,* in an episode telecast on June 9, 1980. Truck's favorite question was "What was the name of Adolf Hitler's dog?"*

**"Piano Man"**
Music sheet sitting on Sally Miles's (Julie Andrews) piano in the 1981 movie *S.O.B.* "Piano Man" was composed by Billy Joel, who had a hit with the autobiographical song in 1974.

**Picasso**
Name of the family cat owned by the Brents in the 1957 movie *Tammy and the Bachelor*.

**Pickett's**
Premium beer brewed in Dubuque, founded by Charles Pickett (Art Carney) in the 1981 movie *Take This Job and Shove It*. The company was previously known as Dubuque Star Beer.

**Piece Corps**
Bad San Diego motorcycle club headed by Scum (Meatloaf) in the 1980 movie *Scavenger Hunt*. They hung out at a pub called Chez Death.

**"Piece of the Action, A"**
Theme song of the very short-lived 1980 TV series "Roughnecks," sung by Juice Newton.

**Pigeon-Toed Orange Peel, The**
Psychedelic New York City dance hall where Watt Coogan (Clint Eastwood) went to trace his runaway prisoner in the 1968 movie *Coogan's Bluff*.

**Piggly Wiggly**
First self-service grocery store chain. It was begun by Clarence Saunders in 1916.

---

*Answer: Blondi.

**Piggott, Lester**

(1935–     ) Grandson of a two-time winner of the Grand National, Piggott won the Derby at Epsom on eight occasions. His mounts were:

Nevere Sy Die (1954)
Crepello (1957)
St. Paddy (1960)
Sir Ivor (1968)
Nijinksy (1970)
Roberto (1972)
Empery (1976)
The Minstrel (1977)

**Pike Bishop**

Role played by William Holden in the 1969 movie *The Wild Bunch*.

**Pilgrim Hotel**

Roxford hotel that Daniel (Cecil Kellaway) set on fire, where Jennifer (Veronica Lake) first met Wallace Wooley (Fredric March) in the 1942 movie *I Married a Witch*.

**Pinafore**

Secret service code name for Mrs. Betty Ford.

**Pine Bluff**

Arkansas town that erected a $10,000 life-size bronze bust of Martha Mitchell.

**Pinetree**

Code name for the Eighth Air Corps headquarters in the 1949 movie *Twelve O'Clock High*.

**Ping Bodie**

New York Yankee Babe Ruth's fictitious roommate when the Yankees were on the road. In order to room alone, he would sign the name of Ping Bodie next to his.

**Pingree, Hazen S.**

Man who once served as the mayor of Detroit and the governor of Michigan at the same time.

**Pink Cloud Motel**

Bakersfield, California, motel where Philo Beddoe (Clint Eastwood) and his orangutan, Clyde, stayed in separate rooms with their girlfriends in the 1980 movie *Any Which Way You Can*.

**Pink Pulky Doo**

Bright red, horrible-smelling, six-hundred-foot-tall tree that Randall (David Rappaport) created, which caused the Supreme Being to downgrade the six dwarves' jobs in the 1981 movie *Time Bandits*.

**Pinstripes**
Design of the New York Yankees' uniforms. They were first introduced in a game on April 22, 1925.

**Pioneer Stage Lines**
Stagecoach on which Thomas Jefferson Destry (James Stewart) rode into Bottleneck from Omaha, in the 1939 movie *Destry Rides Again*.

**Pippin**
Little dog of the Jarrett family in Forest Hills, Illinois, in the 1980 movie *Ordinary People*.

**Pirate Club**
Exclusive New York City nightclub shaped like a pirate ship, where Stan Laurel and Oliver Hardy were mistaken for their lookalikes in the 1936 movie *Our Relations*.

**Pirate Cove, The**
Author Roger Crane's (Fredric March) first children's novel in the 1935 movie *The Dark Angel*.

**Pirate's Cove**
Bar tended by Isaac Washington (Ted Lange) on board the liner *Pacific Princess* on the TV series "The Love Boat."

**Pistol Pete**
Nickname of NBA star Pete Maravich.

**Pitt-Phil Steagles**
Name of the football team that resulted from combining the NFL teams the Philadelphia Eagles and the Pittsburgh Steelers, in 1943, due to the war.

**Pittsburgh**
Super Chicken's hometown on the TV cartoon series. It is also the point of departure in Dave Dudley's 1963 hit song "Six Days on the Road." In 1952, Guy Mitchell had a hit with the song "Pittsburgh, Pennsylvania." On December 1, 1913, the first drive-in gasoline station opened there. Pittsburgh was the setting of the 1983 movie *Flashdance*.

**Pittsburgh**
Names of characters played by Randolph Scott in the 1942 movie *Pittsburgh* and by Charles Bronson in the 1954 movie *Vera Cruz*.

**Pittsburgh Pirates**
NFL football team from 1933 to 1939.
**Pittsburgh Pirates**
First major-league baseball team to field an all-black lineup (September 1, 1971).
**Pittsburgh Pisces**
Basketball team featured in the 1979 movie *The Fish That Saved Pittsburgh*. The team was previously called the Pythons
**Pixie**
Tagg Oakley's (Jimmy Hawkins) horse on the TV series "Annie Oakley."
**Pizaz**
Fashion magazine on the cover of which Cindy Sondheim (Susan Saint James) appeared in the 1978 movie *Love at First Bite*.
**Piz Gloria**
Mountain restaurant nestled 9,712 feet above sea level, which was a front for SPECTRE in the 1969 movie *On Her Majesty's Secret Service*.
**Place in the Sun, A**
Movie (1951) based on Theodore Dreiser's novel *An American Tragedy*, starring Montgomery Clift, Elizabeth Taylor, and Shelley Winters. It was Skip Donahue's (Gene Wilder) favorite movie in the 1980 film *Stir Crazy*.
**Place, Martha M.**
First woman to be executed in the electric chair. The execution took place at Sing Sing on March 20, 1899. She was convicted of murdering her stepdaughter, Ida.
**Plain Dealer, The**
Newspaper read by Janet Weiss (Susan Sarandon) in the 1975 movie *The Rocky Horror Picture Show*.
**Plains Monitor**
Plains, Georgia, newspaper purchased by *Hustler* magazine owner Larry Flynt.
**Plane 22**
Aircraft that took Joe Pendleton (Robert Montgomery) to heaven in the 1941 movie *Here Comes Mr. Jordan*.
**Plan 9 from Outer Space**
Movie (1959) directed by Edward Wood, Jr. This film, which was Bela Lugosi's last, is considered by many critics to have been the worst movie ever made.

**Plato**

Rutledge University's mascot goat on the TV series "The Wonderful World of Philip Malley."

**Playmate of the Year (1969)**

Title held by the late actress Claudia Jennings.

**Play to Win**

Motto of millionaire game inventor Milton Parker (Vincent Price) in the 1980 movie *Scavenger Hunt*.

**Plaza 2-3391/MUrray Hill 3-1099/PLaza 2-3931**

Three telephone numbers that Richard Sumner (Spencer Tracy) asked Bunny Watson (Katherine Hepburn) to repeat from memory in order to test her recall in the 1957 movie *Desk Set*.

**PLaza 5-1598**

Telephone number of the Manhattan Home for Unwed Mothers in the 1962 movie *That Touch of Mink*.

**PLaza 7-9970**

Phone number of the Miller residence in New York City in the 1967 movie *Fitzwilly*.

**"Please Don't Talk About Me When I'm Gone"**

Song sung by Patricia Neal in the 1950 movie *The Breaking Point*.

**"Please put $50,000 into this bag and act natural. I am pointing a gun at you . . ."**

Wording of the hold-up note used by Virgil Stockwell (Woody Allen) in his unsuccessful attempt to rob a bank, when the bank officials thought that the word "gun" was spelled "gub" in the 1969 movie *Take the Money and Run*. Some employees thought the word "act" was "abt," causing still more confusion. The attempt got Virgil ten years in prison.

**Plenty O'Toole**

James Bond's (Sean Connery) temporary love interest in the 1971 movie *Diamonds Are Forever*, played by Lana Wood (sister of Natalie Wood).

**Plummer Brothers**

Outlaw brothers who had killed the Ringo Kid's (John Wayne) father and brother, in the 1939 movie *Stagecoach*. The Plummer's names were Hank (Vester Pegg), Luke (Tom Tyler), and Ike (Joe Rickson).

**Pluto**

Name of the boat that Bruno Anthony (Robert Walker) rode through the Tunnel of Love in the 1951 Alfred Hitchcock movie

*Strangers on a Train*, at Magic Isle Amusement Park.

**Poe**

Crow puppet on the 1951 TV show "Ozmoe."

**Poetry Day**

Commemorated on October 15 each year.

**Point 33**

Position of the statue of Christ on a cross where the German soldiers attempted to ambush the 16th Infantry in the 1980 movie *The Big Red One*.

**Poker Night, The**

Original title considered for Tennessee Williams's play *A Streetcar Named Desire*.

**Pokey and Jack**

Lieutenant Hunter's (James Sikking) two basset hounds on the TV series "Hill Street Blues."

**Poland is not under Soviet domination . . .**

False statement made by President Gerald Ford during the 1976 Presidential debates.

**Polar Borer**

Intra-earth capsule launched by THRUST in the 1977 TV movie *The Last Dinosaur*.

**Polka Dottie**

Girlfriend of puppet Rootie Kazootie on the 1950 "Rootie Kazootie" TV program.

**Polo**

Only sport that officially bars left-handed players. As of January 1, 1977, the U.S. Polo Association ruled that all players in a polo match must use their right hands to swing their sticks. Players who had used their left hands prior to the rule were allowed to continue playing.

**Palomar Hotel**

Laredo hotel where the poker game took place in the 1966 movie *A Big Hand for the Little Lady*.

**Polony, Frank**

Photographer who took the enlarged picture of actress Gene Tierney for the portrait of Laura Hunt in the 1944 movie *Laura*. The photograph was brushed over to look like a painting.

**Polovchak, Walter**

Twelve-year-old boy who was allowed to stay in the United States after his parents decided to return to the Soviet Ukraine in August 1980.

**Ponsonby**

Reginald Perrin's (Leonard Rossiter) pet cat on the PBS TV series "The Fall and Rise of Reginald Perrin."

**Ponti, Carlo**

(1910–     ) Italian movie producer. In 1957 he married actress Sophia Loren in Mexico. In 1964 he became a French citizen. He was sentenced in absentia by an Italian court in 1970 to four years in jail and was fined $25 million for income tax evasion. Carlo Ponti was portrayed by Rip Torn in the 1980 TV movie *Sophia Loren: Her Own Story*.

**Pontipee**

Family name of the seven brothers, Adam, Benjamin, Caleb, Daniel, Ephraim, Frank, and Gideon, in the musical play, 1954 movie, and TV series *Seven Brides for Seven Brothers*.

**Ponzi, Charles A.**

Italian-American who, in 1920, created the first money pyramid. It took in $20 million before his scheme was exposed.

**Poodle cut**

Popular women's hairstyle introduced by actress Gina Lollobrigida in the 1956 movie *Trapeze*.

**Pooh Bah**

Lord High Everything Else, in the comic opera *The Mikado* by Gilbert and Sullivan.

**Pookie**

British release title of the 1969 American movie *The Sterile Cuckoo*.

**Poopsie**

Nickname that Zelda Gilroy (Sheila James) called Dobie Gillis (Dwayne Hickman) in the TV series "The Many Loves of Dobie Gillis."

**Pope Innocent III**

(1161–1216) Roman Catholic pope (1198–1216) portrayed by Finlay Currie in the 1961 movie *Francis of Assisi*.

**Pope Joan Anglicus**

Alleged pope of the Catholic Church (818–855) who masqueraded as a man until she gave birth to a baby. Joan was portrayed by Liv Ullmann in the 1972 movie *Pope Joan*.

**Population 152**

Population of the small town of Seattle on the TV series "Here Come the Brides."

**Porthos**

Pet English bulldog of John K. M. McCaffery, who, from 1953 until 1955, hosted the TV game show "What's the Story?" Porthos was the show's mascot.

**Potemkin**

Russian cruiser on which the ship's commanding officer, Captain Golikov, was killed in a mutiny by the crew on June 13, 1905. This incident was immortalized in the 1925 Sergei Eisenstein film *Battleship Potemkin*.

**Poultry Hall of Fame**

Located in Beltsville, Maryland.

**Pound of feathers**

Weighs more than a pound of gold. Feathers are weighed in avoirdupois (16 ounces per pound); gold is weighed in troy (twelve ounces per pound).

**Power of Love**

First 3-D movie, released on September 27, 1922.

**Powder Puff Special**

Racing car of Penelope Pitstop in TV cartoons. It is also known as the Compact Pussycat.

**Power Pellet Forest**

Forest in which Pac-Man (voice of Marty Ingels) is a security guard in the TV cartoon series "Pac-Man."

**Powers, Johnny**

New York Giant who, on Sepember 29, 1957, hit the last home run at the Polo Grounds.

**Prasada**

New York City apartment building where actress Sally Ross (Lauren Bacall) lived in the 1981 movie *The Fan*.

**Precious Pup**

Granny Sweet's "lovable" pet dog, who is actually sneaky and mischievous. Voiced by Don Messick on the Hanna-Barbera TV cartoon "Precious Pup."

**Prelude to Love**

Code name of the 1949 movie *Battleground*, prior to the story's being finished.

**Presidential Inauguration Day**

January 20 (each January after a Presidential election).

**Presidents of the International Olympic Committee:**
Demetrius Vikelas—Greece (1894–1896)
Baron de Coubertin (1896–1925)
Henri de Baillet-Latour—Belgium (1925–1946)
Sigfrid Edström—Sweden (1946–1952)
Avery Brundage—the United States (1952–1972)
Lord Killanin—Great Britain (1972–     )

**Presley, Vernon**
(1916–1979) Father of Elvis Presley. He was married to Gladys Smith from 1933 until her death in 1958. In 1960 he married Dee Stanley, whom he divorced in 1977. Portrayed in movies by Bing Russell in *Elvis* (1979—TV); John Crawford in *Elvis and the Beauty Queen* (1981—TV); and Lawrence Killer in *This Is Elvis* (1981).

**Prettiest Baby—1930**
Title held by six-month-old David Harold Meyer from Naponee, Nebraska, in a national contest sponsored by Sears, Roebuck. Little David became known as actor David Janssen.

**"Pretty Girl Is Like a Melody, A"**
Song composed in 1919 by Irving Berlin. Theme song of the Ziegfeld Follies. The song is heard in the movies *The Great Ziegfeld* (1936), *The Powers Girl* (1943), and *There's No Business Like Show Business* (1954).

**Pretty Lady**
Musical comedy feature within the 1933 movie *42nd Street*.

**"Price Is Right, The"**
TV game show watched by Vince Ricardo (Peter Falk) in a New York bar in the 1979 movie *The In-Laws*. Vince had never seen the program before. It is also the game show appearing on a TV in the 1977 movie *Looking for Mr. Goodbar*.

**Priesand, Sally Jane**
First woman rabbi (thirty-six years old), ordained in the Isaac M. Wise Temple in Cincinnati, Ohio, on June 3, 1972.

**Prince of Darkness**
Title belonging to Count Dracula.

**Prince Oxford**
Sire of the Barkley cattle herd. The Barkleys once turned down $10,000 for the bull on the TV series "The Big Valley."

**Prince Publishing Company**
New York City firm that published author Youngblood Hawke's (James Franciscus) novel *Arms of the Oblivion* in the 1964 movie

351

*Youngblood Hawke* (based on the novel of the same title by Herman Wouk).

**Princess Nia**
Mermaid that appeared on episodes of the TV series "Fantasy Island," played by Michelle Philips.

**Prince Yousopov**
Alleged killer of the "mad monk," Rasputin. He was portrayed by John Barrymore, as Prince Paul Chegodieff,* in the 1932 movie *Rasputin and the Empress*.

**Priscilla Hotel**
New York City setting of the 1967 movie *Thoroughly Modern Millie*. The hotel was run by Mrs. Meers (Beatrice Lillie).

**"Prisoner of Love"**
Song composed in 1931 by Leo Robin, Russ Columbo, and Clarence Gaskill. Both Russ Columbo's (1931) and Perry Como's (1946) versions of the song can be heard in the 1980 movie *Raging Bull*.

**Pritchard, Terry**
Art director of the 1981 movie *The French Lieutenant's Woman*, who appeared in the distance, looking out over the breakwater, in the opening scene of the movie, in which he is actually doubling for actress Meryl Streep.

**Private Life of Henry VIII, The**
Movie (1933) starring Charles Laughton as King Henry VIII, watched on TV by Dominick (Dom DeLuise) in the 1980 movie *Fatso*.

**Private Robert E. Lee Pruitt**
U.S. Army bugler stationed at Schofield Barracks in Hawaii in 1941. He was played by Montgomery Clift in the 1953 movie *From Here to Eternity*, by Steve Railsback in the 1979 TV mini-series of the same title, and by Gary Swanson in the 1980 spinoff TV series.

**Proctor, Louis**
Calgary, Alberta, man who, in 1981, became the first black man to join the Ku Klux Klan.

**Professor Peter Boyd**
Role played by Ronald Reagan in the 1951 movie *Bedtime for Bonzo*.

---

*The real Prince Yousopov successfully sued because his name was not used, while a real Prince Chegodieff also successfully sued because his name *was* used.

**Professor Thomas Boswell**
Role played by Dana Andrews on the TV soap "Bright Promise."

**Project Azorian**
CIA mission to raise a sunken Russian submarine that sank on April 11, 1968. The 36,000-ton mining ship *Glomar Explorer* was used in the attempt.

**Proud Flesh**
Original title of Robert Penn Warren's 1947 Pulitzer Prize-winning novel, *All the King's Men*.

**Prowler Fouler**
Ralph "Papa" Thorson's (Steve McQueen) special shock gun in the 1980 movie *The Hunter*.

**Pruitt, Kenneth**
Impressionist who provided the duck's voice on Rick Dee's 1976 hit record "Disco Duck."

**Psalter**
Volume of psalms and hymns of Henry Ainsworth, which was the only book that the Pilgrims brought over on the *Mayflower*.

**Psychology**
Subject that Professor Peter Boyd (Ronald Reagan) taught at Sheridan College in the 1951 movie *Bedtime for Bonzo*.

**"Puberty Love"**
Rock song played to destroy the invading tomatoes in the 1978 movie *Attack of the Killer Tomatoes*.

**Pugach, Burt**
New York lawyer who hired a man to throw lye in the face of his girlfriend, Linda Riss, blinding her for life. After spending fourteen years in prison (1959–1974) for the crime, he married Linda.

**Pulitzer, Joseph**
(1847–1911) Journalist born in Mako, Hungary. He became the owner of several newspapers: the *St. Louis Dispatch* (1878), the *New York World* (1883), etc. Later he became a member of the U.S. House of Representatives from New York (1885–1886). Pulitzer established the Pulitzer Prizes for the encouragement of public service, public morals, American literature, and the advancement of education. He was portrayed by John Randolph in the 1981 TV movie *The Adventures of Nellie Bly*.

**Purgatory, Colorado**
Western town setting of the movies *Support Your Local Sheriff* (1969) and *Support Your Local Gunfighter* (1971), both starring James Garner as Jason McCullough.

**Purgatory Cove**

New Hampshire lake cove, with numerous rocks in it, where Billy Ray Wayne (Doug McKeon) accidentally drove the Chris-Craft *Thayer IV* onto a rock, in the 1981 movie *On Golden Pond*.

**Purtell, Billy**

(1886–1962) White Sox third baseman who, during the sixth inning of a game on May 10, 1910, became the first major-league player to strike out twice in the same inning.

**Pussycat Theater**

Los Angeles porno theater where the X-rated film *Deep Throat* ran for ten years (1971–1981).

**Put all your eggs in one basket and watch that basket . . .**

Best advice, as given in a *Herman Joseph* TV commercial.

**Pye, Phillips, Columbia, HMV, and Decca**

British record labels that turned down the Beatles before Parlaphone Records signed the group in 1962.

# Q

**Q and Z**
   Highest valued letters in the Game Scrabble; both are worth ten points.
**Qantas**
   Queensland and Northern Territory Aerial Services, the national airline of Australia.
**QB**
   Brand of football used in the game between the inmates and the guards in the 1974 movie *The Longest Yard*.
**QSKY**
   Los Angeles FM radio station (711 FM) owned by the Billings Radio Division in the 1978 movie *FM*.
**QSKY-FM**
   California license plate of Los Angeles FM radio station manager Jeff Dugan's (Michael Brandon) yellow Porshe in the 1978 movie *FM*.
**Quaker State Audio and Video**
   Stereo store where Joe Baxter (Richard Pryor) was arrested after attempting to steal a truckload of electronic equipment in the 1981 movie *Bustin' Loose*.
**Queen**
   Rock band whose music was featured in the 1980 movie *Flash Gordon*.
**Queen of Brazil, SS**
   Rio line ship upon which Scat Sweeney (Bing Crosby) and Hot Lips Barton (Bob Hope) stowed away in the 1947 movie *The Road to Rio*.

**Queen of Folk Music**

Title conferred upon folksinger Joan Baez.

**"Queen of the Blues"**

Subtitle of Ray Stevens's 1970 hit record, "Bridget the Midget."

**Queen of the Creepies**

Appellative of actress Jamie Lee Curtis (daughter of actor Tony Curtis and actress Janet Leigh). She has appeared in such horror movies as *Halloween* (1978), *The Fog* (1980—Janet Leigh also appeared in this film), *Terror Train* (1980), *Prom Night* (1980), and *Halloween II* (1981).

**Queen of the Mist**

Name on Annie Edison Taylor's barrel that she rode over Niagara Falls on October 24, 1901, on her forty-third birthday. She became the first woman to survive the ordeal.

**Queen of the Screamers**

Appellative of actress Evelyn Ankers, because of her numerous horror film appearances.

**Queen, Richard**

American diplomat freed after 250 days of captivity in the U.S. Embassy in Tehran, Iran (released on July 10, 1980), due to an illness.

**Queen Sara Saturday**

Royal puppet that appears on the "Mister Rogers' Neighborhood" TV program. Her voice is that of Fred Rogers.

**Queens in a deck of playing cards**

Argine, Esther, Judith, and Pallas.

**Queens Memorial Hospital**

Medical facility where Edith Baines Bunker (Jean Stapleton) passed away in 1980 on the TV series "Archie Bunker's Place."

**Queen Tika**

Queen of the Muranians in the 1935 movie serial *Phantom Empire*, starring Gene Autry.

**"Quentin's Theme"**

Theme song of the 1966–1971 TV daytime serial "Dark Shadows." "Quentin's Theme," by Charles Randolph Grean Sounde, which has thirteen letters in the title, peaked at number thirteen in 1969.

**Quenton High School**

High school attended by Latitia "Buddy" Lawrence (Kristy McNichol) on the TV series "Family."

**Quiet Man, The**
Movie (1952) starring John Wayne and Maureen O'Hara, being shown on TV in the California suburban house in the 1982 movie *E.T. the Extra-Terrestrial*.

**Quinn, Jack**
(1884–1946) Oldest baseball player to play in a World Series game. Quinn (John Quinn Picus), who was forty-six years, two months, and twenty-nine days old, pitched two innings for Philadelphia in the third game (October 4) in the 1930 World Series between the Athletics and the St. Louis Cardinals. Quinn ended his career with the Cincinnati Reds in 1933, at the age of forty-nine.

**Quonset Point, Rhode Island**
Location for which quonset huts were named. They were manufactured there during World War II.

# R

**R**

First initial of Dr. Quincy (Jack Klugman) on the TV series "Quincy." A closeup of Quincy's business card once showed the name R. Quincy.

**RFD**

Rural Free Delivery.

**RHIP**

Rank Has Its Privileges.

**RSVP**

*Respondez s'il vous plait* (please reply).

**R1J775**

California license number of the 1966 Corvette Stingray driven by singer Jan Berry, which ran into the back of a parked truck near Dead Man's Curve on Whittier Boulevard in Hollywood in April 1966.

**R2D2**

Princess Leia's (Carrie Fisher) small android, played by three-foot, eight-inch Kenny Baker in the 1977 movie *Star Wars*. The robot's name was borrowed from "Reel 2, Dialogue 2," as cued in the sound mixing process of filmmaking.

**R17**

Jail cell number of Joe Collins (Burt Lancaster) in the 1947 movie *Brute Force*.

**R 6255987**

New York City police identification number of Chuck Lumley (Henry Winkler), when he was arrested on December 26, in the 1982 movie *Night Shift*.

**R 6255988**
New York City police identification number of Bill Blazerjowski (Michael Keaton), when he was arrested on December 26, in the 1982 movie *Night Shift*.

**Rachel, Kansas**
Setting of the 1966 Don Knotts film *The Ghost and Mr. Chicken*.

**Rachmaninoff Rhapsody**
Theme based on Paganini's Opus 43, Variation XXVI, which was Richard Collins's (Christopher Reeve) favorite melody in the 1980 movie *Somewhere in Time*.

**Radar**
Big Bird's teddy bear on the TV series "Sesame Street."

**Radcliffe**
Women's college affiliated with Harvard University, founded in Cambridge, Massachusetts, in 1879, one of the "seven sisters." It was the alma mater of Brenda Patimkin (Ali McGraw) in the 1969 movie *Goodbye, Columbus* (based on the Philip Roth novel of the same title).

**Rader, Dave**
(1948–    ) Chicago Cubs catcher who, aside from appearing as himself, was also misidentified as Larry Cox on two other Topps baseball cards in 1979.

**Radio City Music Hall**
Theater located in the original fourteen-building complex called Rockefeller Center. It was opened in 1933. Actors Larry Parks and Gregory Peck were once tour guides there.

**Radner, Gilda**
Her comic roles on "Saturday Night Live" were Roseanne Roseannadanna, Judy Miller, Emily Litella, Baba Wawa, Lisa Lupner, Rhonda Weiss, and Candy Slice.

**Raffles Hotel Bar**
Singapore bar run by Myles Delaney (Sean McClory) in the TV series "Bring 'em Back Alive."

**Rain**
Beatles sound-alike group that provided the music for the 1979 TV movie *Birth of the Beatles* (produced by Dick Clark).

**Rains, Claude**
(1889–1967) Actor who played the Invisible Man in the 1933 movie *The Invisible Man* (his film debut). In the 1951 film *Abbott and Costello Meet the Invisible Man*, a photograph of Claude Rains

can be seen hanging on a wall.

**Rajah**
Bengal tiger in the 1964 Walt Disney movie *A Tiger Walks*.

**Ralph and Norma**
Husband and wife spokespersons on radio/TV commercials for Winchell's Donuts. They are never seen.

**Ralph Hinkley**
Hero of the TV series "The Greatest American Hero," starring William Katt. After John W. Hinckley, Jr., shot President Ronald Reagan on March 30,1981, the show's producer decided to change the character's name to Hanley. In the very next episode (April 11), the name Hanley was dubbed in. After a few episodes the name was changed back to Hinkley.

**Ramblin' Rose**
Fifty-five-foot cruiser on which Robert Wagner remarried Natalie Wood, on July 15, 1972. The vessel was named after Nat "King" Cole's 1962 hit song.

**Rampo Medical Arts Building**
Chicago building where psychiatrist Robert Hartley's (Bob Newhart) office is located, on the seventh floor, on the TV series "The Bob Newhart Show."

**Randolf and Matilda**
Two ostriches appearing in the silent movie *Romeo's Balloon*, within the 1976 movie *Nickelodeon*.

**Ranger Jace Pearson**
Texas Ranger played by Joel McCrea in the radio series "Tales of the Texas Rangers," and by Willard Parker on the 1958–1959 TV series of the same name.

**Ranger Matt Harper**
Sierra National Park ranger in the short-lived TV series "Sierra." He was played by Ernest Thompson, who went on to write the play and subsequent screenplay for the 1981 movie *On Golden Pond*.

**Ranger 19**
SAC call sign of the B-52 piloted by Colonel Jim Caldwell (Rock Hudson), which declared an emergency because of a fuel leak during refueling with a KC-135, in the 1963 movie *A Gathering of Eagles*. He landed the aircraft safely.

**Rankin, Judy**
First professional woman golfer to earn more than $100,000 in a

single season (1976).

**Raschi, Vic**

(1919–      ) St. Louis Cardinals pitcher who, on April 23, 1954, served up Hank Aaron's first major-league home run.

**Rather, Dan**

(1931–      ) Television news anchorman who was beaten up on the floor of the 1968 Democratic National Convention. Rather was also only thirty yards from the grassy knoll in Dallas when President John F. Kennedy was assassinated on November 22, 1963.

**Rats**

Motorcycle gang led by Eric Von Zipper (Harvey Lembeck) in the movies *Beach Party* (1963), *Bikini Beach* (1964), *Beach Blanket Bingo* (1965), *How to Stuff a Wild Bikini* (1965), and *The Ghost in the Invisible Bikini* (1966). The female members of the gang are called Mice.

**Ratso Rizzo**

Seedy character in the novel *Midnight Cowboy* by James Leo Herlihy, from which the 1969 film of the same title was made. Dustin Hoffman played the role. The name of Ratso Rizzo was mentioned in the movie *Almost Summer* (1978).

**Ravagers, The**

Next Matt Helm movie to star Dean Martin, as announced at the end of the 1969 movie *The Wrecking Crew*. The film was never made.

**Raven Bar**

Himalayan bar owned by Marion Ravenwood (Karen Allen), before it was burned down in the 1981 movie *Raiders of the Lost Ark*.

**Ravenscroft, Raphael**

Musician who performs the sax solo on Gerry Rafferty's 1978 hit record ''Baker Street.''

**''Rawhide'' and ''Peter Gunn''**

Two TV series theme songs that can be heard in the 1980 movie *The Blues Brothers*.

**Ray and Charles**

Michael Jackson's pet mice on the TV cartoon series ''The Jackson 5.''

**Ray-Ban**

Brand of sunglasses (No. 5022-G15) worn by Elwood Blues (Dan

Aykroyd), in the film *The Blues Brothers*.

**RCB824**

Metropolis license plate number of the bus destroyed by General Zod (Terence Stamp) and his companions in the 1981 movie *Superman II*. On the side of the bus, the play *Evita* was advertised.

**Reagan, Ronald, and Ann Sheridan films**

> *Cowboy from Brooklyn* (1938)
> *Naughty but Nice* (1939)
> *Angels Wash Their Faces* (1939)
> *King's Row* (1941)
> *Juke Girl* (1942)

Ann Sheridan's name was mentioned in the 1942 Reagan movie *Desperate Journey*.

**Reagan, Ronald, and Jane Wyman films**

> *Brother Rat* (1938)
> *Brother Rat and a Baby* (1940)
> *An Angel from Texas* (1940)
> *Tugboat Annie Sails Again* (1940)
> *It's a Great Feeling* (1949)

The two were married from 1940 to 1948.

**Reagan the Man, the President**

Book written by five correspondents of the *New York Times* and published in 1980. Steve Freeling (Craig T. Nelson) was reading the book in bed in the 1982 movie *Poltergeist*.

**Reasoner, USS**

U.S. Navy frigate on which the Village People were videotaped on March 5, 1978, in San Diego, singing their hit song "In the Navy." For the publicity stunt (used by both the group and the Navy), the ship was cleaned up and repainted.

**Rebecca Randall**

Ten-year-old heroine of the children's novel *Rebecca of Sunnybrook Farm*, by Kate Douglas Wiggin.

**Rebel**

Ricky North's (Barry Curtis) pet dog on the TV series "The Adventures of Champion."

**Rebel Without a Cause**

Movie (1955) directed by Nicholas Ray and produced by David Weisbart. The film starred James Dean, Sal Mineo, Nick Adams, and Natalie Wood. All of these stars have met early tragic deaths, leading to what may be referred to as the "Rebel Without a Cause

Curse."

**Rebley**
Father Brown's (Barnard Hughes) pet dog in the 1979 TV movie *Sanctuary of Fear* (a.k.a. *Girl in the Park*).

**Red Boy One**
Call sign of Hawk's (Thom Christopher) space vehicle on the TV series "Buck Rogers in the 25th Century."

**"Red Channels"**
Booklet that first appeared in June of 1950, which listed liberals in the radio, television, and movie industries with reputed Socialist leanings. This was one of the contributing factors to the blacklistings.

**Red Dog Saloon**
Saloon mentioned in the lyrics of Johnny Horton's 1968 hit song, "When It's Springtime in Alaska."

**Red Dog 2**
Rescue seaplane that spotted Captain Casey Abbott (Ronald Reagan) and his crew after their submarine USS *Starfish* had been sunk by the Japanese in the 1957 movie *Hellcats of the Navy*.

**Red Dragon**
Bar where Ginny Tremaine (Gloria Grahame) worked in the 1947 movie *Crossfire*.

**Red Dragon**
Chinese restaurant where Don Richards (David Birney) took his daughter Tracy (Louanne) to eat whenever he visited with her in the 1980 movie *Oh God! Book II*.

**Redford, Robert**
(1937–      ) Popular Hollywood actor, born Charles Robert Redford, who won an Academy Award for Best Director for the 1980 movie *Ordinary People*. Redford became the first male to appear on the cover of *Ladies' Home Journal* magazine (he appeared with a woman on the cover).

**Red Gulch**
Western town setting of the 1945 movie *Frontier Gal*.

**Red Lantern**
Big fish that guided the children on an adventure each week on the radio series "Land of the Lost."

**Red Ox Saloon**
Sweetwater town bar won by Bret Maverick (James Garner), with four aces and an eight of diamonds, in a poker game on the 1981

TV series "Bret Maverick." Tom Guthrie (singer Ed Bruce), co-owner, ran the place for Bret.

**"Red River"**
Working title of the Henry Mancini/Johnny Mercer Academy Award-winning song "Moon River" from the 1961 movie *Breakfast at Tiffany's*.

**"Red River Valley"**
Song played by the Space Cowboy (George Peppard) on the harmonica in the 1980 movie *Battle Beyond the Stars*.

**REDRUM**
Word that Danny Torrence (Danny Lloyd) wrote with red lipstick on a door in the 1980 movie *The Shining*. The word, as later revealed through its mirrored reflection, is "murder" spelled backwards.

**Reese's Pieces**
Candy (introduced in 1978 by Hershey) that Elliot (Henry Thomas) gave to E.T. when he first met him in the 1982 movie *E.T. the Extra-Terrestrial*. In the tie-in novel by William Kotzwinkle, the candy was M&M's. The makers of M&M's were first offered the opportunity to promote the film in exchange for using their product, but they turned Steven Spielberg down. This turned out to be a very costly mistake.

**REgent 4-8499**
Telephone number of Elizabeth Martin (Shirley Jones) in the 1963 movie *The Courtship of Eddie's Father*.

**Reggie**
Pet snake of seaplane pilot Jock (Fred Sorenson) in the 1981 movie *Raiders of the Lost Ark*. Jock wore a New York Yankees baseball cap.

**Regis, Billy**
Trumpeter who soloed on the 1955 Perez Prado number one hit song "Cherry Pink and Apple Blossom White."

**Regular 1**
Scientific space station run by Dr. Carol Marcus (Bibi Besch) in the 1982 movie *Star Trek II: The Wrath of Khan*.

**Regulator**
Brand of pendulum clock seen in the 1952 movie *High Noon*.

**Reid, Tim**
Doorman at the Dakota Apartments, who was an eyewitness when Mark David Chapman shot singer John Lennon to death on December 9, 1980.

**Reilly, Catherine**

Model who appeared as the nun in the ads and commercials for Blue Nun wine. In July 1982, she killed her boyfriend and then committed suicide.

**Reiner, Carl**

(1922–     ) Comedian born in New York City. He appeared with Sid Caesar in the TV series "Your Show of Shows" and played the role of Alan Brady on the TV series "The Dick Van Dyke Show." He is the father of actor Rob Reiner. He was loosely portrayed by Reni Santoni (as David Kolowitz) in the 1967 movie *Enter Laughing* (based on his 1958 autobiographical play).

**Reliant, USS**

Federation starship (NCC 1864) taken over by Khan (Ricardo Montalban) in the 1982 movie *Star Trek II: The Wrath of Khan.*

**Remulack**

Home planet of the Coneheads, even though they tell everyone that they are from France, in a series of skits on the TV show "Saturday Night Live."

**Renaud, Louis**

French fashion designer who, in 1946, introduced the bikini; it was named after Bikini Island, site of nuclear tests in the Pacific Ocean.

**Replicant**

Cloned cyborgs of the twenty-first century that are sought out and destroyed by "blade runners" in the 1982 movie *Blade Runner.*

**Requiem**

Mozart's musical work that was performed at the funerals of Franz Joseph Haydn (1809), Ludwig van Beethoven (1827), and Frédéric Chopin (1849). Luigi Lablanche (1794–1858), who taught Queen Victoria to sing, sang at all three funerals.

**Resko, John**

Man who, in 1931, during the Great Depression, killed a shopkeeper, after which he was sentenced to be executed at Sing Sing, only to have his sentence changed to life imprisonment. After failing to escape from Dannemora prison in two attempts, he took up drawing and became successful at it. Resko was finally paroled in 1949. He was portrayed by Ben Gazzara in the 1962 movie *Convicts 4*. In the film, Carl Carmen, the art critic who helped Resko's works to be discovered, was portrayed by Vincent Price.

**"Respect"**

Song composed by Otis Redding that became a hit for Aretha Franklin in 1967. A few lines of the song can be heard from a prisoner and a nun in the 1980 movies *Brubaker* and *Airplane!* respectively.

**Reulbach, Ed**
(1882–1961) Chicago Cubs pitcher who died on July 17, 1961, the same day as Ty Cobb.

**Reverend Charles Brown**
The Petries' and Helpers' family minister on the TV series "The Dick Van Dyke Show."

**Reverend Clayton Brooks**
Pastor of the Eagle Rock Community Church in the 1965 movie *Cold Turkey*. He was played by Dick Van Dyke.

**Reverend Cleophus James**
Minister of Chicago's Baptist Triple Rock Church, played by singer James Brown in the 1980 movie *The Blues Brothers*.

**Reverend Matthew Fordwick**
Country preacher played by John Ritter (1972–1977), on the TV series "The Waltons."

**Rex**
Riley's family dog on the TV series "The Life of Riley." In 1957 the family acquired a dog named Baskerville, who had previously belonged to old man Dobson (Paul Bryar).

**Rex Olcott**
Role played by Neil Reagan (brother of Ronald Reagan) in the 1940 movie *Tugboat Annie Sails Again*. This was one of only two movie appearances by the President's brother.

**Rhinos**
Football team for which Ed Huddles and Bubba McCoy played in the cartoon TV series "Where's Huddles?"

**Rhodes, James A.**
Governor of the state of Ohio at the time of the Kent State shootings (May 4, 1970). He was portrayed by Jerome Dempsey in the 1981 TV movie *Kent State*.

**Rhodesia**
Former name of the African country of Zimbabwe.

**Rhyme**
How both Underdog and Yogi Bear usually spoke in their respective TV cartoon series.

**Rhyne, Erin**
Woman who underwent plastic surgery in 1978 to look like the late singer Elvis Presley.

**Ribbons awarded in a contest:**

| | |
|---|---|
| Blue | First place |
| Red | Second place |
| Yellow | Third place |
| White | Fourth Place |
| Pink | Fifth place |
| Green | Sixth place |
| Purple | Seventh place |
| Brown | Eighth place |

**Rice, Dan**

(1823–1900) Popular American clown born Daniel McLaren. He worked for P. T. Barnum for awhile before starting his own circus. In 1868 he ran for the Republican nomination for President of the United States. He had a pet pig named Lord Byron. It was Dan Rice who later became the model for the early paintings of Uncle Sam.

**Rice-Davies, Mandy**

Girlfriend of Christine Keeler who introduced her to osteopath Stephen Ward. She starred in the 1976 Israeli movie *Kuni Lemel in Tel Aviv,* and was portrayed by Alicia Brandet in the 1964 movie *The Christine Keeler Affair.*

**Richard Allen, Jr.**

Pet dog of the Harris family in the short-lived 1979 TV series "*Harris and Company.*"

**Richard, James Rodney**

(1950–  ) Houston Astros pitcher who, at six feet, eight and a half inches, is the tallest man ever to play in the major leagues.

**Richards, Ellen Swallow**

First female graduate of the Massachusetts Institute of Technology.

**Richelieu**

Miss Gabrielle Simpson's (Audrey Hepburn) pet canary in the 1964 movie *Paris When It Sizzles.*

**RIchmond 2-1818**

Special phone number of the Boston Police Department, for leads leading to the capture of the Boston Strangler, in the 1968 movie *The Boston Strangler.*

**Rick's Place**

Hangout in the short-lived 1980 TV series "*California Fever.*"

**Ride, Sally K.**

Thirty-one-year-old woman who, in 1983, became the first American woman in space.

**Ride the Man Down**
Zane Grey paperback book read in bed by Colonel Sherman Potter (Harry Morgan) in an episode of the TV series "M*A*S*H."

**Rid-O-Rat**
Rat poison "accidentally" used by Violet Newstead (Lily Tomlin) instead of Skinny and Sweet in her boss's, Franklin M. Hart, Jr.'s (Dabney Coleman), coffee in the 1980 movie *9 to 5*.

**Riff Raff**
Butler at Dr. Frank N. Furter's castle, played by Richard O'Brien in the 1975 movie *The Rocky Horror Picture Show*. O'Brien is the British actor who co-wrote the musical.

**Rift Raft**
Wolf nemesis of Underdog on the TV cartoon series.

**Riker, Marguerite Norris**
President of the Detroit Red Wings, and the only woman whose name is inscribed on the Stanley Cup; her team won it in 1952 and 1955.

**Ring**
Magazine read by George Raft while portraying himself in the 1961 Jerry Lewis movie *The Ladies' Man*.

**Ring of Fear**
Warner Bros. movie (1954) in which animal trainer Clyde Beatty and author Mickey Spillane played themselves.

**Ripe Program**
Plan to give pregnant mothers the chemical Ephemerol, to insure that their babies are born "scanners," in the 1981 movie *Scanners*.

**Ripley, Robert Leroy**
(1893–1949) Cartoonist who, in 1918, created a cartoon of unusual sports feats, titled "Champs or Chumps," featured in the *New York Globe*. On December 19, 1918, the cartoon made its debut under the name of "*Believe It or Not!*" and became world-famous over the years. Robert Ripley portrayed himself in the 1924 movie *The Great White Way*. Ripley was mentioned by Bob Hope in the 1941 movie *Louisiana Purchase*. In 1980, Robert Ripley became the first inductee in *Trivia Unlimited* magazine's Trivia Hall of Fame.

**Ripon, Wisconsin**
Town in which the Republican Party was founded in 1828. A liberal wing of the Republican Party is known as the Ripon Society in honor of the town.

**Rippling Rhythm Orchestra**
Shep Fields's musical band from 1931 to 1963.

**Rita**

Boat that traveled the Amazon River in the 3-D movie *The Creature from the Black Lagoon,* made in 1954.

**Rita II**

Boat that traveled the Amazon River in the 3-D movie *Revenge of the Creature,* made in 1955.

**Rita Marlowe and Rina Marlow**

Blond Hollywood beauty queen/actress played by Jayne Mansfield and Carroll Baker, respectively in the 1957 movie *Will Success Spoil Rock Hunter?* and in the 1964 movie *The Carpetbaggers.*

**Rive Gauche**

Washington, D.C., restaurant in which the *National Enquirer* claimed that comedienne Carol Burnett was boisterous and argumentative with Henry Kissinger. Carol Burnett successfully sued the magazine for $1.6 million. The settlement was later reduced.

**Rivera**

Last name of the boxer Filipe played by Richard Conte, in the 1952 movie *The Fighter,* and that of boxer Mountain, played by Anthony Quinn in the 1962 movie *Requiem for a Heavyweight.*

**Riverfront Stadium**

Home baseball stadium of the Cincinnati Reds. The first game played there was on June 30, 1970, in which Atlanta beat Cincinnati, 8 to 2. The stadium is built on the site of the house (412 Second Street) in which actor Roy Rogers was born on November 5, 1912 (approximately where second base is located).

**River Queen**

Mississippi riverboat on which Kenny Rogers hosted the 1971–1973 TV series "Rollin' on the River."

**Riverside**

Huge land development being built in 1946, in the 1967 movie *Hurry Sundown.*

**River Street**

Honolulu street on which the New Congress Club was located in the 1953 movie *From Here to Eternity.*

**Riverview**

Hotel for which Bill "Bonjangles" Robinson played the doorman in the 1938 movie *Just Around the Corner.*

**Roaring 20's Club**

San Francisco nightclub where Kelly Sherwood (Lee Remick) went to meet Red Lynch (Ross Martin), only to miss him, in the 1962 movie *Experiment in Terror*.

**Robbie**

Raccoon on the 1973–1975 cartoon TV series "Lassie's Rescue Rangers."

**Robert**

Pet rattlesnake of Alice Forsythe (Tatum O'Neal) in the 1976 movie *Nickelodeon*.

**Robert**

First name of the nine-year-old boy who, on February 25, 1981, robbed the New York Bank for Savings of $118 at gunpoint. The boy later surrendered to the FBI.

**Robert E. Lee**

Riverboat mentioned in the lyrics of the song "The Night They Drove Old Dixie Down" recorded by both the Band and Joan Baez. Actor Rex Ingram was born aboard the *Robert E. Lee* on October 20, 1895.

**Robert E. Peary**

Liberty ship built during World War II, in four days and fifteen hours, a record that, to this day, has never been broken.

**Robert Marmaduke Hightower**

Western bank robber played by John Wayne in the 1948 movie *The Three Godfathers*.

**Roberto Clemente High School**

Chicago high school named for the late Pittsburgh Pirates baseball player.

**Robert Rich**

Pseudonym used by blacklisted Hollywood writer Dalton Trumbo, when he wrote the Academy Award-winning screenplay for the 1956 movie *The Brave One*.

**Roberts, Robin**

(1926–  ) Major-league pitcher who gave up the most home runs in a single season (forty-six, in 1956), and in a career. He pitched for nineteen seasons (1948–1966), serving up 502 home runs. In 1952 and 1955, he was named Pitcher of the Year by *Sporting News*.

**Robin and Whippoorwill**

Birds mentioned in the lyrics of the Hank Williams's classic sad song "I'm So Lonesome I Could Cry."

**Robinson, Brooks**

(1937–  ) Holder of the major-league record for the most games played by a third baseman (2,349), and the record for hitting into more triple plays (four) than any other major-league player. His uniform (number 5) has been retired by the Orioles.

**Robinson, Sugar Ray**

(1920–  ) Fighter who became World Middleweight Champion in 1951, when he defeated Jake LaMotta by a KO. He won the middleweight title a record five times:

| February 14, 1951 | Jake LaMotta | KO in thirteen rounds |
| September 12, 1951 | Rawry Turpin | KO in ten rounds |
| December 9, 1955 | Bubo Olsen | KO in two rounds |
| May 1, 1957 | Gene Fullmer | KO in five rounds |
| March 25, 1958 | Carmen Basilio | |

Robinson was portrayed by Johnny Barnes in the 1980 movie *Raging Bull*. He portrayed himself in the 1968 movie *Paper Lion*.

**"Rock Around the Rock Pile"**

Hit record made by Jerri Jordan (Jayne Mansfield) in the 1956 movie *The Girl Can't Help It*. The song was composed by Bobby Troup.

**Rockdale High School**

School attended by Tony (Michael Landon) in the 1957 movie *I Was a Teenage Werewolf*.

**Rock Doc**

Nickname of Dr. William Abruzzi, who handled five thousand cases during the Woodstock Festival of 1969. He handled two deaths and two births, as well as several thousand drug-related illnesses.

**Rocket**

Real name of the white horse ridden by Dr. Indiana Jones (Harrison Ford) in the 1981 movie *Raiders of the Lost Ark*.

**Rocket Motor Sales**

Chicago used-car lot owned and later destroyed by Frank (James Caan) in the 1981 movie *Thief*.

**Rock-ola**

Brand of jukebox at the Delta House in the 1978 movie *National Lampoon's Animal House*.

**"Rock, Roll and Shake"**

Rock 'n' roll TV show hosted by Gary Nelson (Touch Connors)* in the 1956 movie *Shake, Rattle and Rock*.

**Rock Springs**

Western town setting of the 1956 Barbara Stanwyck movie *The*

---

*Touch Connors was the previous film name of Mike Connors.

*Maverick Queen.*

**Rockwell Community Church**
Church of which Reverend Grady Williams (Grady Nutt) was the minister in the 1981 pilot TV series "The Grady Nutt Show."

**Rockwood Dairy**
Bellflower, California, milk company for which Melvin Dummar (Paul LeMat) drove a delivery truck in the 1980 movie *Melvin and Howard.*

**Rocky Horror Picture Show, The**
Zany 1975 cult film watched by the students of Performing Arts High School in the 1980 movie *Fame.*

**Rocky Horror Show, The**
Musical upon which the 1975 movie *The Rocky Horror Picture Show* was based.

**Rodeo**
Magazine that featured Norman "Sonny" Steele (Robert Redford) on its cover in the 1979 movie *The Electric Horseman.*

**Rodriquez, Aurelio, and Aurelio Lopez**
Only two major-league baseball players whose first names contain all five English vowels.

**Roebuck, Ed**
(1931–   ) Only player to ever hit the *roof* of the Astrodome. He did it with a fungo bat, prior to a game between the Phillies and the Astros, on September 14, 1964.

**Roget, Peter Mark**
Doctor who, in 1852, authored *Roget's Thesaurus.*

**Rogue Song, The**
MGM movie (1930), which was the only color motion picture in which Stan Laurel and Oliver Hardy appeared.

**Rollin, Betty**
Television newswoman who underwent a modified radical mastectomy, which she wrote about in her 1975 book *First You Cry.* She was portrayed by Mary Tyler Moore in the 1981 TV movie of the same title.

**"Rolling Stone"**
Song sung by James Stewart and Henry Fonda in the 1970 movie *The Cheyenne Social Club.*

**Rolls-Royce (1981)**
Automobile that singer Teddy Pendergrass was driving when he became involved in an accident on March 18, 1982. He suffered serious spinal cord damage resulting in paralysis.

**Romanoff Diamonds**
Missing jewels that are being sought in the 1949 movie *Love Happy*.

**Romanos**
Dog act on "*The Ed Sullivan Show*" seen in the 1978 movie *I Wanna Hold Your Hand*.

**Romantic Egoists, The**
Original title of Ernest Hemmingway's 1926 novel *The Sun Also Rises*.

**Romeo and Juliet**
Tootie Ramsey's (Kim Fields) pet rabbits on the TV series "The Facts of Life."

**Romeo's Balloon**
Silent movie produced and directed by Leo Harrigin (Ryan O'Neal), starring Tom "Buck" Greenway (Burt Reynolds), in the 1976 movie *Nickelodeon*. The best shots in the film were created by accident.

**Ron**
Name of the dog on the cover of Rick Springfield's album *Working Class Dog*, released in 1981.

**Rookies**
British release title of the 1941 Abbott and Costello movie *Buck Privates*.

**Rookies Come Home**
British release title of the 1947 Abbott and Costello movie *Buck Privates Come Home*.

**Room 23**
Room at St. Joseph's Hospital in South Bend, where George Gipp (Ronald Reagan) died in the 1940 movie *Knute Rockne—All-American*.

**Room 136**
Simon Dermott's (Peter O'Toole) room at the Hotel Ritz in Paris in the 1966 movie *How to Steal a Million*.

**Room 209**
The Freeling family's room at the Holiday Inn on Interstate 74, in the closing scene of the 1982 movie *Poltergeist*.

**Room 216**
Room at the Hotel Bella Vista in England, where Mimi Glossop (Ginger Rogers) stayed in the 1934 movie *The Gay Divorcee*.

**Room 237**
Haunted room at the Overlook Hotel in the 1980 movie *The*

*Shining*.

**Room 304**

Room number at the Golden Hotel, where Walt Coogan (Clint Eastwood) stayed while in New York City, in the 1968 movie *Coogan's Bluff*.

**Room 304**

Dale Tremont's (Ginger Rogers) room number at the Lido Hotel, just below that of Room 404, which belonged to Jerry Travers (Fred Astaire) in the 1935 movie *Top Hat*.

**Room 416**

Suite at the Windsor Hotel in London, where Miles Kendig (Walter Matthau) stayed while he hid out from the CIA in the 1981 movie *Hopscotch*.

**Room 511**

Room at the Culver Hotel (renamed Hotel Rainbow), where Annie Clark (Carrie Fisher) stayed in the 1981 movie *Under the Rainbow*.

**Room 796**

Room number of the fictitious George Kaplin at the Plaza Hotel in New York City in the 1959 movie *North by Northwest*.

**Room 903**

Count Dracula's (George Hamilton) room number at the New York Plaza in the 1978 movie *Love at First Bite*.

**Room 2421**

New York City hotel room number from which Ace Stamper (Pat Hingle) jumped to his death in the 1961 movie *Splendor in the Grass*.

**Rooney, Art**

Owner of the Pittsburgh Steelers football team and a member of the Pro Football Hall of Fame. Rooney was portrayed by Art Carney in the 1980 TV movie *Fighting Back*.

**Roseanne Roseannadanna**

Obnoxious newswoman played by Gilda Radner on the TV series "Saturday Night Live."

**Rosebud**

Movie (1975) debut of ex–New York City Mayor John V. Lindsay.

**Rose Caleti**

Childhool girlfriend whom "Arnold" Matsuo Talahashi (Pat Morita) is always talking about on the TV series "Happy Days."

**Rose, Fred**

(1897–1954) Singer/songwriter who co-founded Acuff-Rose Music in 1942. He composed songs in collaboration with both Gene Autry and Hank Williams. Fred Rose was at one time a pianist with Paul Whiteman's Orchestra. He wrote or co-wrote "Deed I Do," "Kaw-liga," "Blue Eyes Crying in the Rain," and "Crazy Heart." Rose was portrayed by Arthur O'Connell in the 1964 movie *Your Cheatin' Heart*.

**Rosenbloom, Maxie**

(1904–1976) World Light Heavyweight Champion (1930–1934), nicknamed "Slapsie Maxie" by Damon Runyon. He made a number of radio, movie, and TV appearances. He fought 410 bouts in his fight career. Maxie portrayed himself on the comedy radio series "The Slapsie Maxie Show," in 1956. He played a washed-up fighter on the "Playhouse 90" presentation of "Requiem for a Heavyweight," and he portrayed himself in the 1942 movie *Harvard Here I Come*, appearing in the lead role.

**Rosenthal**

Name used by Kermit the Frog in order to visit Miss Piggy in prison, in the 1981 movie *The Great Muppet Caper*.

**Rose, Pete**

Only baseball player selected to play on a team for the annual All-Star Game at five different positions:

| | |
|---|---|
| 1965 | Second base |
| 1973 | Left field |
| 1974 | Left field |
| 1975 | Right field |
| 1976 | Third base |
| 1978 | Third base |
| 1981 | First base |

**Rose, Ralph**

Flagbearer of the U.S. flag in the 1908 Olympic games in London, who refused to dip the stars and stripes for King Edward VIII. This began a tradition that has never been changed.

**Rosey**

Name tattooed on the singer's chest in the lyrics of Dion's 1962 hit song "The Wanderer."

**Rosie**

Real name of the tarantula that crawled on James Bond's (Sean Connery) arm in the 1962 movie *Dr. No*. Stuntman Bob Simmons's arm was actually used.

**Rosie**

Irene Sperry's (Hope Lange) Irish setter in the 1961 Elvis Presley movie *Wild in the Country*.

**Ross Jeanelle**
Role played by Tony Dow on the TV soap "General Hospital."

**Round-Up**
Original code name considered for the Normandy Invasion of June 6, 1944, but never used, because Winston Churchill did not like it. Churchill chose "Overlord" instead.

**Route 66**
Nat "King" Cole hit song written by Bobby Troup. The following towns are mentioned in the lyrics: Chicago, Los Angeles, St. Louis, Joplin, Oklahoma City, Amarillo, Gallup, Flagstaff, Winslow, Kingman, Barstow, and San Bernardino.

**Rover**
Family's Pekinese dog in the 1982 movie *Saturday the 14th*.

**Rover 3500**
British automobile that Princess Grace was driving on a Monte Carlo road when she experienced a stroke, causing the car to crash, on September 14, 1982.

**Royal Dale Condominium Town House**
Chevia Hills, California, home, located at 46 Peacock Drive, of Stanley (Normal Fell) and Helen (Audra Lindley) Roper, on the TV series "The Ropers."

**Royal flush of hearts**
Winning hand held by Freddie Hunter (Bob Hope) in the 1949 movie *The Great Lover*.

**Royal Order of Leopards**
Lodge (number 196) to which Howard Cunningham (Tom Bosley) belonged, and of which he was later elected Grand Pooba, on the TV series "Happy Days."

**Royal Order of the Goose**
Lodge 117—hall where the pyramid scheme called "Dare to Be Rich" was being presented in the 1981 movie *Bustin' Loose*.

**"Rubber Duckie"**
Hit record (1970) made by Sesame Street muppet Ernie, on Columbia Records. It peaked at number 16.

**Rubin, Barbara Jo**
On February 22, 1969, at Charlestown Racetrack in West Virginia, she became the first female jockey to win a horserace, when she rode Cohesian to victory.

**Rubin, Glynn**
Actress Farrah Fawcett's stunt double on the TV series "Charlie's

Angels."

**Ruby**

Tony's (Jack Lemmon) fishing trawler in the 1957 movie *Fire Down Below*.

**Rueckheim, F. W.**

Chicago vendor who created Cracker Jack in 1893. He began putting prizes in the boxes in 1921.

**Ruick, Barbara**

(1933–1973) Actress to whom the 1974 movie *California Split* was dedicated, as she died during the making of the film. Barbara Ruick was the wife of composer John Williams.

**Ruiz, Rosie**

Woman who supposedly won the women's division of the 1980 Boston Marathon, with a time of 2:31.56. In her only other race (the New York Marathon) she finished 621st, with a time of 2:56 (about a 25-minute difference). A week after the Boston race, she was disqualified when officials could not find her in any of the thousands of feet of film taken. Jacqueline Garean was declared the winner.

**Rumble in the Jungle**

Name given to the heavyweight championship fight in which Muhammad Ali defeated George Foreman in Kinshasa, Zaire, on October 30, 1974.

**Rum Runner**

Michael Collin Gallagher's (Paul Newman) 1934 Chris-Craft in the 1981 movie *Absence of Malice*.

**Rupert**

Cute pet squirrel in the 1950 Jimmy Durante film *The Great Rupert*.

**Rupert of Hentzau**

Anthony Hope's 1893 sequel novel to *The Prisoner of Zenda*. It has been filmed twice.

**Rusty**

Barney Hefner's (Allan Melvin) pet dog on the TV series "Archie Bunker's Place."

**Rule Britannia**

Words on the bottom of Bullwinkle's left foot (TV cartoon).

**Ruth**

Real name of the dog that pulled on Burt Reynolds's shirt in the beginning of the 1978 movie *Starting Over*. Ruth also played Toto in the 1978 movie *The Wiz*.

**Ruth, Claire**

Wife of George Herman "Babe" Ruth. She wrote the autobiography *The Babe and I*. Ruth was portrayed by Claire Trevor in the 1948 movie *The Babe Ruth Story*, and by Georgia Engel in the 1978 TV movie *A Love Affair: The Eleanor and Lou Gehrig Story*.

**Rutledge University**

College at which Philip Malley (Stephen Nathan) is a science professor in the TV series "The Wonderful World of Philip Malley." The school teams are the Wasps.

**Rye**

Liquor consumed by Don Birnam (Ray Milland) in the 1945 movie *The Lost Weekend*.

# S

**6**

Record number of consecutive walks given to a single player in a major-league baseball game set by Jimmie Foxx on June 16, 1938.

**6**

Number of white horses mentioned in the folk song "She'll Be Comin' Around the Mountain."

**6**

Number of weeks that Judy Benjamin (Goldie Hawn) was married to her first husband and the number of hours that she was married to her second spouse before both men died, in the 1980 movie *Private Benjamin*.

**6½ minutes**

Duration of the longest swordfight to appear in a Hollywood film. The duel took place between Stewart Granger and Mel Ferrer in the 1953 movie *Scaramouche*.

**6⅞ pounds**

Weight of Bugs Bunny.

**6 feet 4 inches**

Height of Leroy Brown in the 1973 Jim Croce song "Bad Bad Leroy Brown." Leroy was "badder than a junkyard dog."

**6 feet 6 inches, 245 pounds**

Size of the coal miner named John, who died after saving twenty miners in Jimmy Dean's 1961 hit song "Big Bad John."

**−7**

NFL record for the lowest number of total yards for a team. It was set by the Seattle Seahawks while playing the Los Angeles Rams at the Kingdome on November 4, 1979.

**7**

NFL record for kicking the most field goals in one game. It was set on September 24, 1967, by Jim Bakken of the St. Louis Cardinals, playing against the Pittsburgh Steelers.

**7**

NFL record number of fumbles by a single player in a single game. It was set by Len Dawson of Kansas City on November 15, 1964.

**7**

Number of gold medals that the United States won in the 1904 Olympic boxing competition. They were won in all seven weight classifications. Oliver Kirk won the medal in both the Feather-weight and Lightweight classifications.

**7**

Record number of goals scored by Joe Malone of the Quebec Bulldogs, against the Toronto St. Patricks (10–6) in a hockey game played on January 31, 1920.

**7**

Number pinned to the coat of the young Vito Corleone (Oreste Baldini) at Ellis Island in the 1974 movie *The Godfather, Part II*. At the time, Vito Corleone was named Vito Andolini.

**7**

Record number of times that a player has stolen home in a single season. The record is shared by Pete Reiser (1946) and Rod Carew (1969).

**7**

Major-league record for the most consecutive hits by a single player during a World Series. The record was set by Thurman Munson during the 1976–1977 Series.

**7**

Modern major-league record number of hits in a nine-inning game since 1900. It was established by Rennie Stennett of the Pittsburgh Pirates on September 16, 1975, when he hit four singles, two doubles, and one triple.

**7**

Number of years in a single term of office for the President of France.

**7–0**

Score in a forfeited softball game.

**7:00 A.M.**

Time that the alarm clock went off in the opening scene of the 1981 movie *9 to 5*.

**7 feet 3 inches**
Height of Herman Munster (Fred Gwynne) on the TV series "The Munsters."

**7 and 7**
Seagram's 7 and 7-Up. Drink ordered by Tony (John Travolta) at the 2001 Odyssey Disco in the 1977 movie *Saturday Night Fever*. A "7 and 7" is sometimes referred to as a "14."

**7 hours and 23 minutes**
Length of the longest game played in the history of major-league baseball, September 11, 1974. The San Francisco Giants beat the New York Mets at Shea Stadium, with a final score of 8 to 6 after 23 innings of play.

**7-Up**
Soft drink introduced in 1929. The "7" stood for "seven-ounce bottle," and the "Up" stood for "bottoms up."

**7F2690**
Washington, D.C., automobile license number of Supreme Court Justice Ruth Loomis (Jill Clayburgh), in the 1981 movie *First Monday in October*.

**16**
Number of times that New York Yankees' Lou Gehrig and Babe Ruth hit back-to-back home runs.

**62 Sutton Place South**
Home address of G. D. Abercrombi, to whom butler Claude R. Fitzwilliam (Dick Van Dyke) billed the sterling silver he stole in the 1967 movie *Fitzwilly*.

**−62.8 degrees**
Body temperature of Herman Munster (Fred Gwynne) on the TV series "The Munsters."

**63**
Age of Walter "Radar" O'Reilly's (Gary Burghoff) father at the time that Radar was born, on the TV series "M*A*S*H."

**66**
Notre Dame jersey number of legendary football player George Gipp.

**66**
Number of days that jailed IRA member Bobby Sands was on a hunger strike before he died (on May 4, 1981).

**70/70**
Doctor Who's constant blood pressure, in the TV series "Doctor Who."

**72**

Numbers of times that Babe Ruth hit two home runs in a single game in the majors.

**72 degrees Fahrenheit**

Constant temperature at the Harris County Domed Stadium (the Astrodome).

**72 inches**

Height of the staff that holds the medallion of Ra, which shows the location of the Well of Souls when the sun shines through it, in the 1981 movie *Raiders of the Lost Ark*.

**73**

Aircraft shot down (seventy-one confirmed, two probable) by RAF Wing Commander Walter Mitty (Danny Kaye) in one of his dreams in the 1947 movie *The Secret Life of Walter Mitty*.

**75**

Record number of World Series games in which Yankee catcher Yogi Berra appeared.

**$75.63**

Monthly rent of Paul Bratter (Robert Redford) and his wife, Corey's (Jane Fonda) fifth-story flat in the 1967 movie *Barefoot in the Park*.

**78**

NBA record number of consecutive free throws made by Calvin Murphy of the Houston Rockets, between December 27, 1980, and February 28, 1981.

**79**

NFL record number of career interceptions, held by Emlen Tunnell, with the Giants (1948–1958) and the Packers (1959–1961).

**666**

Winning combination for the Pennsylvania Lottery, drawn Thursday, April 24, 1980. The sixes and fours were later found to have been weighed down.

**705**

Major-league record number of at-bats for a single season, set in 1980 by Willie Wilson of the Kansas City Royals.

**712**

Number of games canceled by the 1981 baseball strike (eighty-six games were canceled in the 1972 baseball strike).

**723**

National Hockey League record of consecutive games played by a single player, set by Garry Unger.

**724**

Daisy's number when she was taken to the dog pound in the 1949 movie *Blondie's Secret*.

**$750**

Amount of money that Henry Winkler made for an episode of the TV series "Happy Days," when the series began in 1974. By 1980 he was making $80,000 an episode, and by 1982 he was making $175,000 per show.

**751**

Major-league record number of lifetime completed baseball games, set by Cy Young (1890–1911).

**763 North Gilbert**

Chicago address of the Cabrini Housing Project, where the Evans family lives (apartment 17C), on the TV series "Good Times" (in some episodes the address is given as 963 North Gilbert).

**769 Oakwood**

Harper Valley, Ohio, home address of Stella Johnson (Barbara Eden) on the TV series "Harper Valley PTA."

**786**

NHL record of most career goals in regular season play, held by Gordie Howe, who played between 1946 and 1971.

**6123**

Chicago Transit Authority subway train on which Ralph "Papa" Thorson (Steve McQueen) rides on the roof in pursuit of a killer, in the 1980 movie *The Hunter*.

**6239**

Prison number of Vince Everett (Elvis Presley) in the 1957 movie *Jailhouse Rock*.

**6306**

Prison number of Sue Ellen Ewing (Linda Gray), when she was booked for suspicion of the attempted murder of J. R. Ewing in the TV series "Dallas."

**6,467**

NFL record number of lifetime passes attempted, set by Fran Tarkenton (1961–1971), who completed 3,686 throws.

**6633PP**

British license number of Seymour's (Roger Moore) battleship-gray Aston Martin. The plate also rotates to show P4C597E, in the 1981 movie *Cannonball Run*.

**6,845**

Points that Jim Thorpe accumulated to win the decathlon in the

1912 Olympics.

**6,856**

Major-league lifetime record for most total bases, held by Hank Aaron, who played from 1954 to 1976.

**7289**

Prison number of Hunk Houghton (Mickey Shaughnessy) in the 1957 movie *Jailhouse Rock*.

**7,377**

Major-league record number of innings pitched by a single pitcher, set by Cy Young.

**7,694**

NBA record number of lifetime free throws, set by Oscar Robertson (1961–1974).

**7777**

New agent number issued to James Bond, to replace his 007 number, when he became part of the Diplomatic Section of the Secret Service, in Ian Fleming's novel *You Only Live Twice*.

**64696**

Prison number of three-hundred-pound inmate Grossman (Erland Van Lidth de Jeude) in the 1980 movie *Stir Crazy*.

**65984**

Glenboro State Prison number of inmate Harry Monroe (Richard Pryor), who is serving a 125-year sentence for armed bank robbery in the 1980 movie *Stir Crazy*.

**65985**

Glenboro State Prison number of inmate Skip Donahue (Gene Wilder), who is serving a 125-year sentence for armed bank robbery of the Glenboro State Bank, in the 1980 movie *Stir Crazy*.

**$70,000**

Annual salary contract signed by New York Yankees player Babe Ruth on March 2, 1927.

**73004**

Prison number of Walter Upjohn Ballentine (George C. Scott) in the 1974 movie *Bank Shot*.

**78,672**

Major-league attendance record for a single game, set at the Los Angeles Coliseum on April 18, 1958. That day, the Dodgers played the San Francisco Giants.

**78-11-22**

Combination of the ship's safe on board the *Pacific Princess* on the

TV series "Love Boat."

**60-3847**

License number of Lieutenant Colonel Wilbur "Bull" Meechum's (Robert Duvall) 1955 Chevrolet station wagon in the 1980 movie *The Great Santini*.

**606491**

Los Angeles police arrest record of editor Lou Grant (Ed Asner) when he was arrested for drunk driving, in an episode of the TV series "Lou Grant."

**619028**

Number on Eddie's (Meat Loaf) motorcycle in the 1975 movie *The Rocky Horror Picture Show*.

**637867**

Czechoslovakian concentration-camp identification number of the small boy that the Sergeant (Lee Marvin) befriends, only to have him die, in the 1980 movie *The Big Red One*.

**688-5549**

Home telephone number of Linda Morrola (Liza Minnelli) in the 1981 movie *Arthur*.

**69-9-46-10 and 25-6-27-7**

Two combinations to the safe at the Atlantic and Pacific Bank in Berkeley Square, London, in the 1979 movie *A Nightingale Sings in Berkeley Square*.

**(202) 252-3271**

Phone number of Chief Justice Crawford (Barnard Hughes) in the 1981 movie *First Monday in October*.

**(714) 555-2895**

Telephone number of Simon and Simon Courtesy Service in the TV series "Simon and Simon."

**$750 million**

Amount of money that Arthur Bach (Dudley Moore) is due to inherit in the 1981 movie *Arthur*.

**66 West Twelfth Street**

New York City address of five-foot, eleven-inch, 180-pound Warren Francis Attinger (Tom Ewell), in the 1949 movie *Adam's Rib*.

**72 Blinker Street**

New York City home address of Dominick (Dom DeLuise) in the 1980 movie *Fatso*.

**77 Kantwell Drive**

Beverly Hills home address of Evelyn Lewis (Marguerite Ray) on the TV series "Sanford Arms."

**602 Kings Beach Road**
Lake Tahoe, Nevada, home address of Shirley Miller (Shirley Jones) in the 1979–1980 TV series "Shirley."

**617 North Elm Street**
Home address in Pinehill of Mary Marshall's (Ginger Rogers) uncle Henry, in the 1944 movie *I'll Be Seeing You*.

**623 Eucalyptus Avenue**
Detroit home address of the Wabash family on the TV series "Joe's World."

**660 South Marshall**
Chicago address of the drugstore where the off-track betting tip-offs of winning horses are telephoned in the 1973 movie *The Sting*.

**704 Prester Road**
Henleyville address where thirty-one-year-old Norma Rae Webster (Sally Field) lived in the 1979 movie *Norma Rae*.

**708 Gower Street**
San Francisco home address of Lucy Carmichael (Lucille Ball) on the TV series "The Lucy Show" (after 1965).

**710 West Street**
Home address of J. Pinkham Whinney (W. C. Fields) in the 1934 movie *Six of a Kind*.

**711 East Ocean Parkway**
Brooklyn home address of Gabe and Julie Kotter (Gabe Kaplan and Marcia Strassman) on the TV series "Welcome Back Kotter."

**6459 North Preston**
Indianapolis home address of the Hilliard family in the 1955 movie *The Desperate Hours*.

**7244 LaVerne Terrace**
Eddie Mars's (John Ridgely, Jr.) Los Angeles house address, off Laurel Canyon Drive, in the 1946 movie *The Big Sleep*.

**S**
Letter being researched by Professor Bertram Potts (Gary Cooper) while editing an encyclopedia in the 1941 movie *Ball of Fire*.

**"SAC Song, The"**
Theme song of the 1963 Rock Hudson movie *A Gathering of Eagles*. The song, sung by Rod Taylor, was composed by Tom Lehrer.

**SCCA**
Sports Car Club of America.

## Sacco and Vanzetti

Nicola Sacco (1891–1927) and Bartolomeo Vanzetti (1888–1927). Two Italians arrested and found guilty for the murder of a shoe-factory paymaster and a guard at South Braintree, Massachusetts, on April 15, 1920. Their trial was extremely controversial, with many people believing they were framed. They were electrocuted on August 23, 1927. The pair were portrayed by Martin Balsam and Steven Hill in a TV play, "The Sacco-Vanzetti Story," presented on "The Armstrong Circle Theatre," telecast on June 3, 1960, and by Gian Maria Volonte and Ficcardo Cucciola in the 1971 movie *Sacco and Vanzetti*.

## Sackter, Bill

Mentally retarded fifty-one-year-old man who had spent forty-four of those years in institutions. He was portrayed by Mickey Rooney (who won an Emmy) in the 1981 TV movie *Bill*, and again in the 1983 TV movie *Bill: On His Own*. Sackton was finally helped by a young filmmaker named Barry Morrow (Dennis Quaid), who helped him adjust to living outside an institution. Bill died in June 1983.

## Sacraments of the Catholic Church

1. Baptism
2. Penance
3. Holy Communion
4. Confirmation
5. Matrimony
6. Holy Orders (Priesthood)
7. Extreme Unction (Sacrament of the Sick)

## Sadat, Anwar

(1918–1981) President of Egypt from 1970 until his death on October 6, 1981, when he was the victim of an assassination. He was *Time* magazine's 1977 Man of the Year, and he and Israeli prime minister Menachem Begin were jointly awarded the 1978 Nobel Peace Prize. Sadat was portrayed by Robert Loggia in the 1982 TV movie *A Woman Called Golda* and by Lou Gossett, Jr., in the 1983 TV mini-series "Sadat."

## Sadi

White poodle that appears on Barbra Streisand's album *Songbird*. Barbra stated, on her 1978 album, "Sorry, I couldn't find a bird."

## Safari

Word that a Bogan County police officer was trying to figure out

for a crossword puzzle, from the clue "an African trip," in the
1973 movie *White Lightning*.

**Sagan, Linda**

Wife of astronomer/writer Carl Sagan. It was Linda who drew the
plaques depicting a nude male and female, which were attached to
the Pioneer 10 and 11 spacecraft.

**Sage of Baltimore**

Appellative of writer H. L. Mencken (Henry Louis Mencken,
1880–1956).

**St. Ambrose**

San Francisco hospital where Franklin M. Hart, Jr. (Dabney Coleman), was taken in a Newberry ambulance in the 1980 movie *9
to 5*.

**St. Ann's**

Mission run by Father Tim Mullin (Spencer Tracy) in the 1936
movie *San Francisco*.

**St. Anthony's College**

Catholic university, headed by Father Matthew William Burke
(Charles Coburn), for which Steven Aloysius Williams (John
Wayne) is head football coach, in the 1953 movie *Trouble Along
the Way*.

**St. Augustine, Florida**

Oldest city in the United States, founded by Menéndez de
Avilés, in September of 1565.

**St. Charles Hotel**

New York City hotel where Mary McKinley (Patricia Neal) lived
with her parents in the 1949 Ronald Reagan movie *John Loves
Mary*.

**St. Christopher**

Former patron saint of travelers, whom the Catholic Church de-
moted from sainthood in 1969.

**St. Eligius**

Boston hospital that is the setting of the TV series "St. Else-
where."

**St. Elizabeth's Hospital**

Washington, D.C., medical facility where poet Ezra Pound was
confined for twelve years, and where John W. Hinckley, Jr., was
incarcerated in 1982, after being found not guilty by reason of
insanity in the shooting of President Reagan.

**St. Georges**

British fishing "spy" vessel sunk off the Albanian coast by a mine in the 1981 movie *For Your Eyes Only*. It sank in 584 feet of water.

**St. Helen's of the Blessed Shroud**
Calumet City, Illinois, Catholic school at 2138 Patricia Street, founded in 1923 and headed by Sister Mary Stigmata (Kathleen Freeman), which was attended by Jake and Elwood Blues in their youth, in the 1980 movie *The Blues Brothers*. The phone number there was 862-3129.

**St. Louis**
City mentioned in the lyrics of "Route 66," composed by Bobby Troup, and "Sweet Little Sixteen," by Chuck Berry.

**St. Louis Zoo**
Zoo where Ranger Smith always threatened to send Yogi Bear if he didn't behave himself in Yogi Bear TV cartoons.

**St. Mark's Hospital**
Cleveland hospital where CBS cameraman Harry Hinkle was hospitalized (in room 403) for a back injury in the 1966 movie *The Fortune Cookie*.

**St. Martin's Hospital**
London medical facility where David Kessler (David Naughton) recovered (in room 21) from his werewolf attack in the 1981 movie *An American Werewolf in London*.

**St. Paul's Cathedral**
London church where Prince Charles (age thirty-two) married Lady Diana Spencer (age twenty) on July 29, 1981.

**St. Thomas Beach**
Beach mentioned in the lyrics of Kenny Nolan's 1977 hit song "I Like Dreaming."

**Sally**
Charlie Brown's little sister in Charles Schulz's comic strip "Peanuts." Her voice was provided by Erin Sullivan in the 1969 movie *A Boy Named Charlie Brown*, and by Hillary Momberger in the 1972 movie *Snoopy Come Home*. On "Peanuts" TV specials, Sally's voice was provided by Kathy Steinberg (1965–1968); Hillary Momberger (1969–1973); Lynn Mortensen (1974–1975); Gail Davis (1975–1976); and Cindi Reilly (1981).

**Sally Bowles**
Fictional Berlin cabaret singer of the 1920s, the subject of Christopher Isherwood's 1939 book *Berlin Stories*. She was played by Julie Harris in the 1955 movie *I Am a Camera* and by Liza Minnelli in the 1972 movie *Cabaret*. The character was loosely based on an acquaintance of Isherwood's named Jean Ross.

**Sally Rogers**

One of Rob Petrie's (Dick Van Dyke) co-writers on "The Alan Brady Show," played by Rose Marie on the TV series "The Dick Van Dyke Show." Sally was played by Sylvia Miles on the pilot show, called "Head of the Family."

**Sam**

Inger's family dog in the 1969 Jerry Lewis movie *Hook, Line, and Sinker*.

**Sam**

Drunk on the steps of Chicago's Plymouth Hotel in the 1980 movie *The Blues Brothers*.

**Sam**

Name that Eddie Haskell (Ken Osmond) sometimes called Wally Cleaver (Tony Dow) on the TV series "Leave It to Beaver."

**Sam**

Sergeant Frank Murphy's (Robert Stack) pet dog on the TV series *Strike Force*.

**Sam**

Statue of which the eyes light up. It was turned around to face the outside whenever the apartment was being occupied in the 1954 movie *Phffft!*

**Sam**

Ziggy's pet cat in "Ziggy" cartoons by Tom Wilson.

**Sam and Susie**

Two muskrats in the Captain and Tennille 1976 hit song "Muskrat Love."

**Samantha**

Colt Sievers's (Lee Majors) horse on the TV series "The Fall Guy."

**Sambo**

Characters played by Willie Best in the 1940 movie *I Take This Woman* and by Dale Jenkins in the 1968 movie *Will Penny*.

**Sam Marlowe**

Detective played by Humphrey Bogart lookalike Robert Sacchi in the 1980 movie *The Man with Bogart's Face* (retitled *Sam Marlowe, Private Eye*.)

**Samson**

Sally Rogers's pet goldfish in the TV series "The Dick Van Dyke Show."

**Samson and Delilah**

Betting routine at a bar, in the 1967 movie *Fitzwilly*, in which

Claude R. Fitzwilliam (Dick Van Dyke) bet fellow drinkers that Delilah did not cut Samson's hair. The relevant Bible passage (Judges 16:19) reveals that he is correct—Delilah had a man cut Samson's seven locks.

## Sam the Eagle
Mascot of the 1984 Olympics, held in Los Angeles.

## Samuelson, Ralph
Inventor of waterskiing, in 1922, at Lake Pepin, near Lake City, Minnesota. In 1925 he became the first person to make a ramp jump on water skis.

## Sandy Bar
Town setting of the 1955 Ronald Reagan movie *Tennessee's Partner*.

## Sandy Van Andy
TV news anchorman played by Bob Elliott in the 1965 movie *Cold Turkey*.

## San Fernando
California town setting for the 1959 movie *Plan 9 from Outer Space*.

## Sanford, John
Dred Scott's slave owner, whose name was part of the infamous Dred Scott case, Dred Scott vs. John Sanford (1857).

## "San Francisco"
Song composed in 1936 by Gus Kahn and Bronislau Kaper. The song can be heard in two Clark Gable movies, *San Francisco* (1936) and *Key to the City* (1950).

## San Francisco Sentinel
Newspaper for which Harry Jenkins (Ted Bessell) is a sportswriter on the TV series "Good Time Harry."

## San Jose Stallions
California pro baseball team for which Bubba Newman (John Ritter) played in the 1980 movie *The Comeback Kid*.

## Sanken, Barbara
Editorial researcher who, in May 1982, discovered that columnist Ann Landers was recycling her letters in her syndicated newspaper column. Landers admitted to using old letters occasionally.

## San Marino
Southern California city setting of the 1981 movie *Carbon Copy*.

## Santa Anna
(1795–1876) Mexican general and president of Mexico (1833–1836). He led the Mexican army against the Alamo mission held by

391

the Texans in 1836. He died in poverty in 1876. Santa Anna was portrayed by Manuel Sebastian in "The Siege of the Alamo," an episode of the "You Are There" TV program, and by C. Henry Gordon in the 1939 movie *Men of Conquest*.

## Santa Bello High
School setting of the 1958 movie *High School Confidential*.

## "Santa Claus Is Coming to Town"
Song that Arthur Bach (Dudley Moore) sang twice, first in his bathtub and later at his engagement party, in the 1981 movie *Arthur*. The Chipmunks sang the song over the closing credits of the 1983 movie *Deal of the Century*.

## Santa Claus School
First school to teach one how to act like Santa Claus. It opened in Albion, New York, on September 27, 1937.

## "Santa's Souped-Up Sleigh"
Song written and sung by Melvin Dummar (Paul LeMat) to Howard Hughes (Jason Robards, Jr.) in the 1980 movie *Melvin and Howard*.

## Santana
Name of Melvin Dummar's (Paul LeMat) brand new yacht, which he never got to use, in the 1980 movie *Melvin and Howard*.

## Sarah
Hooterville's telephone operator, played by Marie Earle, on the TV series "Green Acres." Sarah was the mother of Hank Kimble (Alvy Moore), the county agent.

## Sara Tucker
Proponent of Cool Whip topping at the Tucker Inn. Sara was played by Marge Redmond on TV commercials. Maude Eburne played a cook named Sara Tucker in the 1936 movie *Poppy*.

## Sardine can
Object used to smuggle gems into the United States in the 1949 movie *Love Happy*.

## Sarjeant, Marcus Simon
Seventeen-year-old youth from Folkstone, England, who was arrested after firing six blanks at Queen Elizabeth II as she rode horseback in London on June 13, 1981. Sarjeant was arrested under the 1842 Treason Act. The charge was "willfully discharging at the person of Her Majesty the Queen, a blank cartridge pistol, with intent to alarm her," Serjeant was wearing a Prince Charles and Lady Diana Spencer button.

**Sascha**
   Bartender at Rick's Cafe Americain, played by Leonid Kinskey, in the 1943 movie *Casablanca*.
**"Satin Doll"**
   Song that was being played by an orchestra at the Tea Dance at the Kansas City Hyatt Regency, when the third-floor walkway collapsed and crashed to the lobby floor, killing 113 people, at 7:01 P.M. on July 17, 1981. One of the banquet bartenders serving drinks in the lobby during the disaster was Rich Gale, pitcher for the Kansas City Royals. He was working there in the off-season. WHB radio newsman Chuck Hayes was one of those injured. "Satin Doll" was one of Duke Ellington's theme songs.
**"Satisfaction"**
   The Rolling Stones' 1965 hit song, "(I Can't Get No) Satisfaction," can be heard on the soundtracks of four nonmusical films: *Apocalypse Now* (1979), *Melvin and Howard* (1980), *High Risk* (1981), and *Starman* (1984).
**Satisfiers**
   Vocal group on Perry Como's radio show, who introduced the song "All I Want for Christmas Is My Two Front Teeth," in 1946.
**Saturday**
   Day of the week on which each episode of the radio/TV series "The Adventures of Ozzie and Harriet" took place. This was the reason why everyone was always home and why Ozzie never appeared to have a job. Saturday is the night of the week mentioned in Prince's 1983 hit song "Little Red Corvette."
**Saturday Nite Disco**
   Discotheque setting of the TV series "Makin' It."
**Saturday Night Fever**
   Movie (1977) starring John Travolta, which produced the best-selling soundtrack album of all time, with over 22 million copies sold. The movie was re-released with some scenes and language omitted in order to obtain a lower rating (PG). John Travolta's mother and sister both played bit roles. The movie produced four number-one hit records: "Stayin' Alive," by the Bee Gees; "Night Fever," by the Bee Gees; "If I Can't Have You," by Yvonne Elliman; and "How Deep Is Your Love," by the Bee Gees. Four previous number-one hits also appeared in the movie: "Disco Duck," by Rick Dees; "A Fifth of Beethoven," by Walter Murphy; and "You Should Be Dancing" and "Jive Talkin'," by the

Bee Gees.

**Saul**

First King of Israel, who was succeeded by David. He was killed by the Philistines at the battle of Mount Gilboa. Saul was portrayed by Jeff Corey on the TV series "Greatest Heroes of the Bible."

**Savarin Coffee**

Cans in which Chuck Lumley (Henry Winkler) kept his pimp money, in the 1982 movie *Night Shift*.

**"Save Your Kisses for Me"**

Hit record (1976) by the Brotherhood of Man, which was one of Princess Misha Al's favorite songs, as mentioned in the controversial 1980 film *Death of a Princess*.

**Saydis & Saydis Towing**

Tow truck at a Texaco service station from which Cheech (Richard Marin) and Chong (Thomas Chong) siphoned a garbage can full of gasoline in the 1980 movie *Cheech and Chong's Next Movie*.

**Scab Island**

Island nicknamed "The Rock," where Bluto took Swee' Pea after kidnapping him in the 1980 movie *Popeye*.

**Scaggs**

Andy Schmidt's (Henry Winkler) pet shaggy dog in the 1978 movie *The One and Only*.

**Scalplock**

Pilot movie (1966) for the 1966–1968 Dale Robertson TV series "The Iron Horse."

**Scarlet Circle, The, and The Amazing Mrs. Bainbridge**

Two movies seen by juror number four (E. G. Marshall) and his wife in the 1957 movie *Twelve Angry Men*.

**Scavenger Hunt**

Movie (1980) that involved the accumulation of the following items by five teams in San Diego. The prize was $200 million, left by game creator Milton Parker (Vincent Price).

| | | | |
|---|---|---|---|
| 1. | Toilet seat | 10. | Safe |
| 2. | Stuffed bear | 11. | Laughing gas |
| 3. | Beany | 12. | Globe |
| 4. | Box of bananas | 13. | Fox tail |
| 5. | Rolls-Royce radiator grille | 14. | Skeleton |
| 6. | Jack-in-the-box head | 15. | Bowling pin |
| 7. | Beehive | 16. | Bubblegum machine |
| 8. | False teeth | 17. | Policeman's uniform |
| 9. | Cash register | 18. | Cowbell |

| | |
|---|---|
| 19. Moose's head | 46. Horn |
| 20. Pogo stick | 47. Milk can |
| 21. Steeple | 48. Flag |
| 22. Baby carriage | 49. Microscope |
| 23. Drum | 50. Crystal ball |
| 24. Totem pole | 51. Cigar-store Indian |
| 25. Life preserver | 52. Punching bag |
| 26. Wedding dress | 53. Baseball bat |
| 27. Fat person | 54. Skis |
| 28. Piñata | 55. Stuffed bird |
| 29. Basketball hoop | 56. Canoe |
| 30. Inner tube | 57. Barbershop pole |
| 31. French horn | 58. Miner's cap |
| 32. Scooter | 59. Pylon |
| 33. Saddle | 60. Surfboard |
| 34. Bulletproof vest | 61. Hockey stick |
| 35. Parachute | 62. Gramophone |
| 36. Ostrich | 63. Merry-go-round horse |
| 37. Ship's lamp | 64. Old-fashioned bicycle |
| 38. Crutch | 65. Marlin |
| 39. Bomb | 66. Suit of armor |
| 40. Snowshoe | 67. Medicine ball |
| 41. Large bottle | 68. Football helmet |
| 42. Stilts | 69. Jackhammer |
| 43. Iron | 70. Parking meter |
| 44. Chess | Etc. |
| 45. Dress mannequin | |

## Scavullo, Francesco

Photographer who took the picture of eleven-month-old Brooke Shields as an Ivory Soap Baby.

## Scene 388

Scene from *Gone With the Wind* being filmed in the 1981 movie *Under the Rainbow*. The Munchkins and pet dogs ruin the scene.

## Scent of Mystery

Movie (1959) produced by Michael Todd, Jr., in which he used a gimmick called Smell-O-Vision that released fifty different scents throughout the movie theater during the film. The movie, in which Elizabeth Taylor made a cameo appearance, was later retitled *Holiday in Spain*.

## Schalk, Ray

(1892–1970) Chicago White Sox catcher who, in his seventeen-year career, caught more no-hitters (four—one of which was a perfect game) than any other catcher.

**Schantz, Barbara**

Springfield, Ohio, policewoman who posed for the May 1980 issue of *Playboy* magazine.

**Schary, Dore**

(1905–      ) Hollywood screenwriter and producer who headed MGM pictures for eight years. He wrote the play *Sunrise at Campobello* in 1956, and won an Academy Award for *Boys Town* (1938), as screenwriter. His autobiography is titled *Heyday*. Schary was portrayed by Stephen Keep in the 1980 TV mini-series "Moviola." He played himself on several occasions on the TV series "I Love Lucy."

**Schibe, Joseph**

Inventor of the first cork-centered baseball ever used in a World Series game (October 20, 1910).

**Schiffman, Frank**

White owner of Harlem's famous Apollo Theater during the 1950s. He was portrayed by Dick O'Neill as Sol Zuckerman in the 1978 movie *The Buddy Holly Story*.

**Schmidt, Mike**

(1949–      ) Philadelphia Phillies player who, in a 1974 game, hit the public address system speaker hanging from the Astrodome roof, 117 feet above the playing field (329 feet from home plate). He is credited as the only player ever to have hit an object hanging from the roof of the Astrodome during a regular game. "Mike Schmidt" is the answer given to the question "Best Philly?" in a Herman Joseph Beer TV commercial.

**Schmitt, Harrison**

Republican senator from New Mexico who, along with Ohio Senator John Glenn, was a former astronaut. Senator Schmitt died of cancer in 1983.

**Schneider, Eugene**

On July 1, 1966, he became the first Medicare patient. Schneider was treated at Polyclinic Hospital in New York City.

**Schneider, Jack**

Receiver of the first legal forward pass thrown in a football game. The pass was thrown by Bradbury Robinson of St. Louis University on September 5, 1906, in a game against Carroll College.

**Schomer, A. Thomas**

Sculptor of the statue of Rocky Balboa (Sylvester Stallone), dedicated by the city of Philadelphia, in the 1982 movie *Rocky III*.

**School Girls**

Book given to detective Phillip Marlowe (Robert Mitchum) in the 1978 movie *The Big Sleep*.

**Schriver, William "Pop"**

(1865–1932) First baseball player to catch a baseball thrown off the Washington Monument (April 26, 1894).

**Schroeder**

Pianist (he plays a toy piano) and Beethoven-lover who was introduced in Charles Schulz's comic strip "Peanuts" in 1951. His voice was provided by Andy Pforsich in the 1969 movie *A Boy Named Charlie Brown*, and by David Carey in the 1972 movie *Snoopy Come Home*. On "Peanuts" TV specials, Schroeder's voice was provided by Chris Doran (1965); Glenn Mendelson (1966–1967); Danny Hjelm (1971); Brian Kazanjian (1972); Greg Felton (1975–1976); Daniel Anderson (1977); and Christopher Donohue (1980–1981).

**Schroeder, Captain Gustav**

Captain of the passenger liner *St. Louis*, which departed Hamburg on May 27, 1939, bound for Havana, only to be refused permission to dock at this and other ports in other countries. The ship finally docked at Antwerp on June 17. Schroeder was portrayed by Max Von Sydow in the 1976 movie *Voyage of the Damned*.

**Schultz, Dave**

Holder of the NHL record of 2,706 penalty minutes (535 games). On July 8, 1982, he was elected commissioner of the Atlantic Coast Hockey League.

**Schweiker, Jim**

Photographer who was mistakenly awarded the Pulitzer Prize in 1978. Three days after the award was presented, it was taken back and correctly given to John Blair.

**Schwinn**

Brand of bicycle, ridden by Kermit, that was run over by a steamroller in the 1979 movie *The Muppet Movie*.

**Science Is Truth Found Out**

Motto of the Kleiman Institute, where unusual medical conditions are studied, in the 1981 movie *The Incredible Shrinking Woman*.

**Scobie, Reverend Jonathan**

American Baptist minister who, while living in Japan in 1869, invented the first rickshaw in order to move his invalid wife through the city of Yokohama.

**Scoble, Lisa and Teri**
Siamese twins who appear in the 1980 movie *The Elephant Man*.

**Scooby Doo**
Cartoon dog in Hanna-Barbera TV cartoon series; voice of Don Messick. He is seen on TV in the 1983 movie *Cujo*.

**Scott Banning**
Role played by Mike Farrell in the TV soap "Days of Our Lives," during the 1960s.

**Scott, Clifford**
Saxophone player on Bill Doggett's classic 1956 instrumental hit record "Honky Tonk."

**Scream**
Title of the story that Fred Felix Sherman (George Segal) read to Doris Wilgus (Barbra Streisand) in the 1970 movie *The Owl and the Pussycat*.

**Screen Actors Guild Annual Award**

| | |
|---|---|
| 1965 | Bob Hope |
| 1966 | Barbara Stanwyck |
| 1967 | William Gargan |
| 1968 | James Stewart |
| 1969 | Edward G. Robinson |
| 1970 | Gregory Peck |
| 1971 | Charlton Heston |
| 1972 | Frank Sinatra |
| 1973 | Martha Ray |
| 1974 | Walter Pidgeon |
| 1975 | Rosalind Russell |
| 1976 | Pearl Bailey |
| 1977 | James Cagney |
| 1978 | Edgar Bergen |
| 1979 | Katharine Hepburn |
| 1980 | Leon Ames |
| 1981 | No award (first considered was Ronald Reagan, but the Guild decided not to present the award) |
| 1982 | Danny Kaye |
| 1983 | Ralph Belamy |

**Scuttlebutt**
Martini-drinking duck featured in the 1961 Mickey Rooney/Buddy Hackett movie *Everything's Ducky*.

**Seafood**

Yacht piloted by Al (Rodney Dangerfield) in the 1980 movie *Caddyshack*.

**Sea Grass**

Thirty-foot fishing trawler on which the crew is mysteriously killed in the 1980 movie *The Fog*.

**Seagull**

Official state bird of Utah (since 1955).

**Sea Hag**

Ugly old woman who makes life miserable for Popeye and others. She debuted in newspaper comics on December 26, 1929. The voice of Marilyn Schreffler was used for Sea Hag in the TV cartoon series "The All-New Popeye Hour."

**Searcher**

Buck Rogers's (Gil Gerard) spaceship in the TV series "Buck Rogers in the 25th Century."

**Sears catalog**

Model Cheryl Tiegs has been on the cover of two Sears catalogs (1966 and 1967). In 1980 the Sears catalog put together a collection of sportswear with Cheryl Tiegs's name on it.

**Sea Shadows Inn**

Resort near Mendicino, California, where George Peters (Alan Alda) and Doris (Ellen Burstyn) met for a weekend romance once a year for twenty-six years, in the 1978 movie *Same Time Next Year*.

**Sea Shore Motel**

Santa Barbara motel where Fred Sanford (Redd Foxx) took his bride, Elizabeth, on their honeymoon in the TV series "Sanford."

**Seattle Rainers**

Pacific Coast League baseball team for which the Chicago Cubs Ron Santo was once a batboy.

**Seattle Stew**

Horse that provided the manure used in the 1978 movie *Harper Valley PTA*, according to the credits.

**Sea Witch**

Ship upon which Joe Rossi (Humphrey Bogart) was an officer in the 1943 movie *Action in the North Atlantic*.

**Sebring, Jimmy**

(1882–1909) Pittsburgh Pirates outfielder who hit the very first home run in a World Series game when, on October 1, 1903, he hit a home run in the first game of the Series, off pitcher Cy Young.

**Second Hand Lives**
Working title of Ayn Rand's novel *The Fountainhead*.

**Secretariat**
Winner of the 1973 Triple Crown, ridden by Ron Turcotte. Secretariat was the first horse to finish the Kentucky Derby in under two minutes (1:59.4). He was the son of the 1957 Preakness winner, Bold Ruler. Secretariat's photo was on the cover of *Time, Newsweek,* and *Sports Illustrated* in the same week.

**Secret Order of Beavers**
Fraternal lodge of which Dwayne Schneider (Pat Harrington) is a member on the TV series "One Day at a Time."

**Seddon, Rhea, and Robert Gibson**
First two U.S. astronauts to get married to each other (May 30, 1981).

**Sedgeman, Frank, and Ken McGregor**
Only men's doubles team ever to win the Grand Slam of tennis (1951).

**Seeker**
Space Academy's shuttle craft on the TV series "Space Academy."

**See You Next Wednesday**
Porno film (nonstop orgy) being shown at the Eros Cinema in Piccadilly Circus, in the 1981 movie *An American Werewolf in London*. The movie (actually fictitious) was previously advertised on a billboard in the 1980 movie *The Blues Brothers*. *See You Next Wednesday* was shown in "Feel-Around" at the Rialto Theater in the 1977 movie *Kentucky Fried Movie*. A poster for the film (appearing as a serious movie) can be seen on the wall of Jamie Lee Curtis's bedroom in the 1983 movie *Trading Places*. All of the films it was featured in were directed by John Landis. "See you next Wednesday" were the words written on a note in a movie at the Palace Theater, in John Landis's 1983 short subject *Thriller*, starring Michael Jackson.

**Seiko**
Watch worn by James Bond (Roger Moore) in the 1981 movie *For Your Eyes Only*.

**Selassie, Haile**
(1891–1975) Emperor of Ethiopia (1930–1974). He was driven out by the Italians in 1936, and lived in exile in England until he regained the throne in 1941. He was *Time* magazine's Man of the

Year for 1935. Selassie was portrayed by Leigh Whipper in the 1943 movie *Mission to Moscow*.

**Seminole Ritz Hotel**
Florida hotel where Sweet Sue and Her Society Syncopators performed in the 1959 movie *Some Like It Hot*. It was actually filmed at the Del Coronado hotel in San Diego.

**Semyonova, Yuliana**
Seven-foot-two-inch-tall member of the Soviet Union's women's basketball team, which won a gold medal in the 1976 Olympics.

**Senator Buckley Calls for Nixon to Resign**
Headline on the newspaper shown on the cover of Neil Young's album *On the Beach*.

**Senator William J. Tadlock**
United States senator played by Kirk Douglas in the 1967 movie *The Way West*.

**Senor Ka-Boom**
Archenemy of Mr. Fee-fi-fo (Chuckles the Clown) at the TV station WJM on the TV series "The Mary Tyler Moore Show." Senor Ka-Boom often hit Chuckles over the head with a giant cucumber.

**Sentinel, The**
Story by Arthur C. Clarke upon which the 1968 movie *2001: A Space Odyssey* is based.

**September 1**
Birthdate of two heavyweight boxing champions, James J. Corbett (1866) and Rocky Marciano (1923).

**September 1, 1961**
Date of the opening scenes of the 1982 movie *Grease 2*.

**September 9, 1981**
Last square-root date ($9 \times 9 = 81$) until January 1, 2001 ($1 \times 1 = 01$). The date prior to this was August 8, 1964 ($8 \times 8 = 64$).

**September 16**
Birthdate of Alice's (Linda Lavin) late husband, Don Hyatt, on the TV series "Alice."

**September 29, 1957**
Date of the last game played by both the New York Giants and the Brooklyn Dodgers.

**Sequoia**
English word that utilizes all five vowels.

**Serena Nobel, Doctor's Wife**
NBC TV soap, written by Nina Chapman Tracey (Judy Holliday),

in the 1954 movie *Phffft!*

**Sergeant Hulka**

Drill sergeant of Third Platoon, B Company, played by Warren Oates in the 1981 movie *Stripes*.

**Sergeant James "Fatso" Judson**

Crude U.S. Army NCO who instigated many fights with enlisted men. He was played by Ernest Borgnine in the 1953 movie *From Here to Eternity*, by Peter Boyle in the 1979 TV mini-series of the same title, and by Claude Jones in the 1980 spinoff TV series. In the 1953 movie, he was killed by Private Prewitt (Montgomery Clift).

**Sergeant Morgan Sylvester O'Rourke**

U.S. Calvary noncom who, with Corporal Randolph Agarn (Larry Storch), was always planning a new scheme. Played by Forrest Tucker in the 1965–1967 TV series "F Troop."

**Sergeant Paddy**

Mascot bulldog of Weinberg Military Academy in the 1980 movie *Up the Academy*.

**Sergeant Pryor**

Radio man at MASH headquarters in Seoul, Korea, who talked to Walter "Radar" O'Reilly (Gary Burghoff) at the 4077th on the TV series "M*A*S*H." Sergeant Pryor's nickname was Sparkie; his voice was that of Jon Arthur, and he was played in one episode by Dennis Fimple.

**Sergeant Frank Rock**

U.S. Army hero of *Sgt. Rock* comics. He debuted in *Showcase Comics* number 45 (August of 1963).

**Sergeant Zelmo Zale**

Supply sergeant at the 4077th MASH unit in the TV series "M*A*S*H," played by Johnny Haymer.

**Serpents and Choppers**

White and black rival motorcycle clubs featured in the 1970 movie *Black Angels*.

**SETH 16**

Texas license number of Maxwell Seth's (Mac Davis) Continental in the 1979 movie *North Dallas Forty*. As a quarterback for the North Dallas Bulls, his uniform number was 16.

**Seton, Mother Elizabeth Ann Bayley**

(1744–1821) First American saint. She was the founder of the U.S. branch of the Sisters of Charity. She was canonized on March 17, 1963. She was portrayed by Kate Mulgrew in the 1980 TV movie *A*

*Time for Miracles*.

**Seven Champions of Christendom**
> St. George of England
> St. Andrew of Scotland
> St. Patrick of Ireland
> St. David of Wales
> St. Denis of France
> St. James of Spain
> St. Anthony of Italy

**Seven Sisters**
> World's largest oil companies:
>> Exxon
>> Texaco
>> Mobil
>> Standard Oil of California
>> Gulf
>> British Petroleum
>> Royal Dutch Shell

**Seven Soldiers of Victory**
> Also called the Law's Legionnaires in 1940s comics. Members were Green Arrow, Speedy, the Star-Spangled Kid, Stripesy, the Crimson Avenger, the Vigilante, and the Shining Knight. Wins, the Crimson Avenger's sidekick, was an unofficial member.

**Seven Wise Men of Greece**
> Bias, Chilo, Cleobulus, Periander, Pittacus, Solon, and Thales.

**"Seventy-Six Trombones" and "Goodnight My Someone"**
> Two songs in the musical play by Meredith Willson, and in the 1962 movie *The Music Man*, which have the same melody, although they are sung at different tempos.

**Seward, William Henry**
> (1801–1872) American statesman, governor of New York (1839–1843), U.S. senator (1849–1861), and U.S. Secretary of State (1861–1869) under Presidents Abraham Lincoln and Andrew Johnson. Seward was portrayed by Charles W. Herzinger in the 1936 movie *The Plainsman*. The purchase of Alaska by the United States was called "Seward's Folly" or "Seward's Icebox" by those who didn't believe that he made the correct decision in purchasing the land from Russia.

**Seymour, Dan**
> Announcer of Orson Welles's classic 1938 radio broadcast of H.G. Well's novel *The War of the Worlds*.

**"Shadow of Your Smile"**

Song composed in 1965 by Johnny Mandel and Paul Francis Webster. It won the Academy Award for Best Song for the 1965 movie *The Sandpiper*. The song was sung by a woman in a nightclub in the 1980 movie *Hide in Plain Sight*.

**Shadow Pledge**

"I promise to bend all my efforts to give my moral and, when called upon, actual support to uphold law and order and down crooks." Members signed this pledge upon joining the Shadow Club, from the radio series "The Shadow."

**Shakespeare**

Actress Barbara Feldon's subject when she won the top prize on the TV quiz show "The $64,000 Question."

**Shamrock Meat Packers**

Meat-packing company where 190-pound Rocky Balboa (Sylvester Stallone) trained in the 1976 movie *Rocky*.

**Shamroy**

Rita Marlowe's (Jayne Mansfield) pet poodle in the 1957 movie *Will Success Spoil Rock Hunter?*

**Shanahan, Edward B.**

First FBI agent to be killed in the line of duty. He was shot by Martin James Durkin in 1929. At the time, there was no federal law against killing a federal officer.

**Shane, Mary**

First woman hired as a major-league baseball play-by-play TV announcer. She was signed by the Chicago White Sox on January 4, 1977.

**Sharkey, Jack**

(1902– ) Only man to have fought both Jack Dempsey (1927) and Joe Louis (1936—his last fight) in regular boxing matches. He was defeated by both. Born Joseph Zukauskas, he had adopted his ring name from two of his idols, Tom Sharkey and Jack Dempsey.

**Sharpe, David**

Efrem Zimbalist, Jr.'s stunt double on the TV series "The FBI." He previously doubled for Douglas Fairbanks, Jr., in five movies.

**Sharp, Zerna A.**

Author of the "Dick and Jane" primary reader series.

**Shaw, George Bernard**

(1856–1950) British playwright whose most famous works are *Caesar and Cleopatra* (1900), *Man and Superman* (1903), and *Pygmalion* (1912). He appeared in the 1914 film *Rosy Rapture*—

*The Pride of the Beauty and Chorus*. Shaw became the second person to refuse an Oscar, which he had won for the 1938 movie *Pygmalion* (Best Screenplay). (Dudley Nichols was the first person to refuse an Oscar, when he turned down his award for Best Screenplay for the 1935 movie *The Informer*.)

**Shaw, Sandra**
Actress who played the woman whom King Kong picked up mistakenly and then dropped off the Empire State Building, in the 1933 movie *King Kong* (in some copies this scene was edited out). Sandra Shaw (a.k.a. Veronica Balfe) later married actor Gary Cooper.

**Shaw, Thomas W.**
In 1923, dying at the age of ninety-one, he was the last survivor of the Light Brigade, which made the famous charge in 1854 against the Russians in the Crimean War. He was wounded in the charge, but luckily was nursed by Florence Nightingale.

**Shawkey, James Robert**
(1890– ) First New York Yankees pitcher to win a game in Yankee Stadium (opening day, April 18, 1923*). He won the game 4 to 1, pitching a three-hitter. The first batter he pitched to was Chick Foster of the Boston Red Sox, whom he struck out (his first pitch was a ball). Shawkey was the first to cross the plate, scoring the first run in the game. After retiring as an active player, Shawkey managed the Yankees during the 1930 season.

**Sheba**
Bengal tiger that frightened Ringo Starr in the 1965 movie *Help!*

**Sheen, Martin**
(1940– ) Hollywood actor born Ramon Estevez. He made his film debut in the 1967 movie *The Incident*. He portrayed Private Eddie Slovik in the 1974 TV movie *The Execution of Private Slovik*. While filming the 1979 movie *Apocalypse Now*, he had a heart attack. Martin Sheen was portrayed by James Hayden in the 1981 TV movie *The Patricia Neal Story*. Sheen is the only actor to have portrayed both Robert Kennedy and John F. Kennedy in television productions.

**Sheiba**
Sir Lancelot's (Robert Taylor) pet hawk in the 1954 movie *The Knights of the Round Table*.

---

*Babe Ruth hit a home run in that game—the first in Yankee Stadium.

**She knows all about love potions and lovely motions!**
Publicity line for the 1942 Fredric March/Veronica Lake movie *I Married a Witch*.

**Shell Oil**
Company to which Joe (Tony Curtis) pretended he was an heir in the 1959 movie *Some Like It Hot*.

**Shelton, Wesley**
Twenty-two-year-old Houston man who was stabbed to death at the Rolling Stones' concert at the Houston Astrodome on October 29, 1981.

**Shep**
Canine played by Buck the Wonder Dog in the 1954 movie *Fangs of the Wild*, starring Charles Chaplin, Jr.

**Shep**
Captain Rex Kramer's (Robert Stack) pet dog in the 1980 movie *Airplane!*

**Sheridan College**
Learning institute in Sheridan, where Professor Peter Boyd (Ronald Reagan) taught psychology in the 1951 movie *Bedtime for Bonzo*.

**Sheridan Falls**
Town setting where the Coopers lived on the radio series "My Favorite Husband."

**Sheriff Elroy S. Lobo**
Sheriff of Orlo County, who is always after B. J. McKay (Greg Evigan) on the TV series "B.J. and the Bear." He was played by Claude Akins on this series and on the spinoff, "The Misadventures of Sheriff Lobo."

**Sheriff Rosco P. Coltrane**
Dumb law enforcement officer of Hazzard County, played by James Best in the TV series "The Dukes of Hazzard."

**Sheriff Without a Gun**
Hollywood movie biography of Mayberry Sheriff Andy Taylor (Andy Griffith), who was portrayed in the film by Brian Bender (Gavin MacLeod) on an episode of the TV series "The Andy Griffith Show."

**Sherrill, Billy**
Nashville record producer who produced the early hits of singer Tammy Wynette. He was portrayed by James Hampton in the 1981 TV movie *Stand by Your Man*.

**Sherwood, Robert E.**
(1896–1955) Playwright, screenwriter, and winner of several Pulit-

zer Prizes. He won the Academy Award for the screenplay of the 1946 movie *The Best Years of Our Lives*. He was portrayed by Kenneth Moss in the 1963 movie *Act One*.

**Sherwood School**
Elementary school attended by Wednesday (Lisa Loring) and Pugsley Addams (Ken Weatherwax) on the TV series "The Addams Family."

**She's a Lady**
Eight-year-old Timothy "T.J." Joseph's (Ricky Schroder) racehorse, which fell during a race at Hialeah in the 1979 movie *The Champ*.

**"She's Funny That Way"**
Song that Nick Smith (Cecil Kellaway) sang and played on the guitar in the 1946 movie *The Postman Always Rings Twice*.

**She's got the biggest six-shooters in the West!**
Publicity line for the 1949 Betty Grable movie *The Beautiful Blonde from Bashful Bend*.

**Shield Pictures, Inc.**
Hollywood motion picture studio owned by Jonathan Shield (Kirk Douglas) in the 1953 movie *The Bad and the Beautiful*. The studio's motto was *Non Sans Droit*.

**Shields, Brooke**
(1965–    ) Child model and film actress. She made her movie debut in the 1977 movie *Alice Sweet Alice*.* Brooke Shields was featured on the cover of the *Harvard Lampoon* parody edition of *People* magazine, which was published in October of 1981. Miss Shields was pictured holding a big dead fish.

**Shields, James**
Only man to serve as a U.S. senator for three different states: Illinois, from 1849–1855, Minnesota, from 1858–1859, and Missouri, in 1879.

**Shinyo Maru**
Japanese ship which Lieutenant Commander Barney Doyle's (Glenn Ford) wife and daughter were aboard in the 1958 film *Torpedo Run*. As commander of the submarine *Greyfish*, Doyle sank the *Shinyo Maru*. The ship was an actual transport ship that was sunk off Mindanao on September 7, 1944, with the loss of 1,400 Filipino and American prisoners of war.

---

*Also called *Holy Terror* and *Communion*.

**Shoeless Joe Jackson**

Pseudonym used by musician Benny Goodman several times when he recorded as a sideman in Teddy Wilson's band for Victor Records. Obviously the name was taken from the great Chicago White Sox baseball player who was involved in the infamous 1919 Black Sox World Series scandal.

**Shoumatoff, Elizabeth**

Artist who painted the portrait of President Franklin D. Roosevelt, on February 14, 1884, just minutes before Roosevelt was stricken with a cerebral hemorrhage at Warm Springs, Georgia. The President's last words were: "Well, we've got fifteen minutes more to work."

**Shubbick, Chris**

Sarasota news reporter who shot and killed himself on live TV, after giving the evening news on July 15, 1974.

**Sicilian Project**

Code name for raising the ocean liner *Titanic* in order to locate the element byzantium, in the 1980 movie *Raise the Titanic!*

**Sideliners**

Cheerleaders for the Green Bay Packers football team.

**Sidney**

Gorilla who befriended and helped the shrinking Pat Kramer (Lily Tomlin), in the 1981 movie *The Incredible Shrinking Woman*. Sidney was played by Richard R. Baker.

**Silva, Flavius**

Roman general who fought against the Jews at Masada near the Dead Sea. He was portrayed by Peter O'Toole in the 1981 TV mini-series "Masada."

**Silver**

Lynx that is used in the TV and magazine commercials for Lincoln-Mercury's Lynx automobile. Silver's stand-in is another lynx, named Nicholas. Both animals were trained by S. Lloyd Beebe.

**Silver Dollar**

Saloon in the town of Northfork in the TV series "The Rifleman."

**Silver Palace Saloon**

Western town saloon setting of the huge fight scene in the 1965 movie *The Great Race*.

**Silver Sands**

Condominium in Fiddler Key, Florida, that is the setting of the 1980 TV mini-series "Condominium," based on the novel by John D. MacDonald.

**Silver Reef**
Location in Utah where Norman "Sonny" Steele (Robert Redford) let the $12 million thoroughbred horse Rising Star free in the 1979 movie *The Electric Horseman*. He earlier mentioned the bogus location of Rim Rock Canyon, ninety miles north of Silver Reef.

**Simmons, Al**
(1903–1956) Member of the Baseball Hall of Fame who, while playing for the Philadelphia A's on June 3, 1932, robbed Lou Gehrig of a fifth home run by catching a long fly ball. (No one has ever hit five home runs in one game.)

**Simmons, Curt**
(1929–     ) Philadelphia Phillies pitcher who, on August 1, 1950, became the first major-league player to be drafted into the Korean War.

**Simple Solution to Rubik's Cube, The**
Book that Chuck Lumley (Henry Winkler) was reading in bed in the 1982 movie *Night Shift*.

**Sincerely Yours**
Movie (1955) starring Liberace, with his brother George leading the orchestra. It was a remake of the 1932 movie *The Man Who Played God*. The screenplay for *Sincerely Yours* was written by Irving Wallace.

**Sinbad the Sailor**
Horse that Ronald Reagan rode on the TV series *Death Valley Days*. In 1982 the horse was struck by lightning and killed.

**Singing Troubador**
Nickname of singer Nick Lucas, who sang the song "Tiptoe Through the Tulips" at the wedding of Tiny Tim and Miss Vicki on Johnny Carson's "Tonight Show," on December 17, 1969.

**"Sing Your Own Song"**
TV theme song of Busch Beer, sung by Mark Lindsay, onetime lead singer of Paul Revere and the Raiders.

**Sir Bedivere**
Knight of the Round Table who threw King Arthur's sword, Excalibur, into the lake.

**Sir Dragonet**
Knight of the Round Table. He was portrayed by Reginald Beckwith in the 1963 movie *Sword of Lancelot*.

**Sir Galahad**
Knight of the Round Table who led the quest for the Holy Grail. He was portrayed by Richard Webb in the 1949 movie *A Connecticut*

*Yankee in King Arthur's Court,* and in the 1954 movie *Prince Valiant;* he was portrayed by Michael Palin in the 1974 movie *Monty Python and the Holy Grail.*

**Sir Gawain**

Nephew of King Arthur (according to some sources) and a Knight of the Round Table. He was portrayed in the following movies:

| | |
|---|---|
| *Prince Valiant* (1954) | Sterling Hayden |
| *Knights of the Round Table* (1954) | Robert Urquhart |
| *Sword of Lancelot* (1963) | George Baker |
| *Excalibur* (1981) | Liam Neeson |

**Sir Gent**

Men's magazine that printed detective Ron Harris's (Ron Glass) first written article, "John and Mary Ann." They changed the title to "Mary Ann and John and Harry and Frank," on the TV series "Barney Miller." Harris was paid $250 for the article.

**Sir Geoffrey**

Giraffe puppet on the 1951–1953 TV show "In the Park."

**Sir Kay**

Foster brother of King Arthur and a Knight of the Round Table, portrayed by Tom Conway in the 1954 movie *Prince Valiant.* Voiced by Norman Alden in the 1963 animated movie *The Sword in the Stone.*

**Sir Mordred**

Treacherous nephew/son of King Arthur and a Knight of the Round Table, who fatally wounded Arthur. He was portrayed by Stanley Baker in the 1954 movie *Knights of the Round Table* and by David Hemmings in the 1967 movie *Camelot.*

**Sir Percival**

Knight of the Round Table. He was portrayed by Gabriel Wolf in the 1954 movie *Knights of the Round Table* and by Paul Geoffrey in the 1981 movie *Excalibur.*

**Sister Angela**

Catholic nun, played by Deborah Kerr, in the 1957 movie *Heaven Knows, Mr. Allison.*

**Sister Beatrice**

Catholic nun, played by Martha Scott, in the 1974 movie *Airport 1975.*

**Sister Celestine**

Catholic nun, played by Binnie Barnes, in the 1966 movie *The Trouble with Angels,* and by Binnie again in the 1968 sequel *Where Angels Go, Trouble Follows.*

**Sister Janet Mead**
Nun who, in 1974, recorded a hit version of "The Lord's Prayer," which peaked at number four on the *Billboard* charts.

**Sister Jeanne**
Catholic nun, played by Vanessa Redgrave, in the 1971 movie *The Devils*.

**Sister Maria Angelica**
Father John Francis Patrick Mulcahy's (William Christopher) sister on the TV series "M*A*S*H." Mulcahy also had a sister named Kathy, who attended Holy Name Academy.

**Sister Mary Stigmata**
Catholic nun who headed the St. Helen of the Blessed Shroud Orphanage in Chicago. The Blues Brothers, Jake and Elwood, call her the Penguin. She was played by Kathleen Freeman in the 1980 movie *The Blues Brothers*.

**Sister Michelle**
Catholic nun, played by Mary Tyler Moore, in the 1969 movie *Change of Habit*.

**Sister Ruth**
Catholic nun, played by singer Helen Reddy, in her movie debut in the 1974 movie *Airport 1975*.

**"Situation of Gravity, A"**
Story by Samuel W. Taylor that appeared in the May 22, 1943, edition of *Liberty* magazine. It was the source of the movies *The Absent-Minded Professor* (1960) and *Son of Flubber* (1963).

**Six Feet Under**
Westport, Connecticut, firm that provided the hairstyles in the 1980 movie *Friday the 13th* (according to the closing credits).

**Six Fundamental Machines**
    Screw
    Lever
    Pulley
    Inclined plane
    Wedge
    Wheel

**Skagway**
Alaskan setting for the TV series "The Alaskans" and "Klondike."

**Skip**
Kramer family dog, who had to be sent away as Pat Kramer (Lily Tomlin) began shrinking in the 1981 movie *The Incredible Shrink-*

*ing Woman.*

**Skippy**

Mr. Matthews's (Cecil Kellaway) pet dog in the 1948 movie *A Portrait of Jennie*.

**Skunk Works**

Still in which the foul-smelling Kickapoo Joy Juice is made, in Al Capp's *Li'l Abner* comic strip.

**Sky Masterson**

New York gambler, played by Marlon Brando, in the 1955 movie *Guys and Dolls*. Gene Kelly wanted the role so badly that he felt he was as born to play it as Clark Gable was for Rhett Butler; however, MGM refused to loan him out.

**Slaughtered Lamb, The**

Pub in the small northern English town of East Proctor, whose customers lived in fear of a werewolf, in the 1981 movie *An American Werewolf in London*.

**Sleep 'n' Eat**

Demeaning name given to black actor Willie Best, when he first appeared in films.

**Sleeptite Pajamas**

Cedar Rapids, Iowa, clothing manufacturing factory setting for the 1957 movie *The Pajama Game*. The factory's softball team was called the Tigers.

**Slicker**

Seal featured in the 1938 movie *Spawn of the North*.

**Slimy Sam**

Production nickname given to the (mechanical) octopus that Popeye (Robin Williams) battled in the 1980 movie *Popeye*.

**Slipped Disco**

New York City nightclub featured in the 1966 movie *Cactus Flower*.

**Sliwa, Curtis**

Founder of the Guardian Angels of New York (originally from a group called the Magnificient 13), who voluntarily fight crime in the city's subways. Sliwa was portrayed loosely by Kevin Mahon (as Morgan "Case" Casey) in the 1981 TV movie *We're Fighting Back*.

**Smafield, Mrs. Ralph E.**

Housewife who, in 1948, won the first Pillsbury Bake-Off, with her water-rising twists.

**Smarty**
Original title of the 1927 musical play *Funny Face*.

**Smiley**
The Kent family canary, in the ABC TV special edition (1982) of the movie *Superman*.

**Smith, Al**
(1908–    ) White Sox outfielder who was accidentally doused by a cup of beer by a fan who was catching Dodger Charley Neal's 1959 World Series home run.

**Smith, Albert J.**
One-armed paperhanger about whom Robert L. Ripley wrote in his "Believe It or Not" column in 1927.

**Smith and Jones**
Aliases used by Butch Cassidy (Paul Newman) and the Sundance Kid (Robert Redford) while trying to "go straight" in Bolivia, in the 1969 movie *Butch Cassidy and the Sundance Kid*. This became the source for the title of the TV series "Alias Smith and Jones."

**Smith & Wesson**
Manufacturers of pistols and other weapons. Their first names were Horace and Daniel, respectively.

**Smith, Baldwin B.**
American lieutenant colonel who impersonated General Eisenhower during World War II to help conceal the general's actual whereabouts.

**Smith, Elmer**
(1892–    ) Cleveland Indians player who hit the first grand slam in World Series play (off Burleigh Grimes). The feat occurred on October 10, 1920, in the fifth game of the World Series between the Indians and the Brooklyn Dodgers. In that same game, William Wambsganss executed the only unassisted triple play in World Series play.

**Smith, George**
Taxi driver who, on September 10, 1897, became the first person to be convicted of drunk driving.

**Smith, Jimmy Lee**
Convicted murderer of Los Angeles police officer Ian Campbell. After spending nineteen years in prison, Smith was paroled in February 1982. He was portrayed by Franklyn Seales in the 1979 movie *The Onion Field* (based on the book by Joseph Wambaugh). Ian Campbell was portrayed by Ted Danson.

**Smith, Leonard B.**

American Navy flight ensign who, on May 26, 1941, spotted the German battleship *Bismarck*, which the British then sunk. Because Smith was flying with the British at the time, and the United States had yet to enter the war, he was not given official credit.

**Smith, Tommie, and John Carlo**

U.S. black athletes who gave the "black power" salute as the "Star-Spangled Banner" was being played after the presentation of their Olympic medals at the 1968 Olympics in Mexico City.

**"Smoke Gets in Your Eyes"**

Song written in 1933 by Otto Harbach and Jerome Kern, heard in three movies *Roberta* (1935), *Till the Clouds Roll By* (1946), and *Lovely to Look At* (1952). In 1958 the Platters had a number-one hit in both the United States and the United Kingdom with this song.

**Smokehouse**

Restaurant thanked on the liner notes of the Captain and Tennille's album, *Love Will Keep Us Together*.

**"Smoking kills. If you're killed, you've lost a very important part of your life . . ."**

Line said by Brooke Shields in her 1981 TV antismoking campaign commercial.

**"Smoke! Smoke! Smoke! (That Cigarette)"**

Hit recording, in 1947, by Tex Williams, which became Capitol Records' first million-seller.

**Smurfs**

Little figures and cuddly stuffed toys that first came on the U.S. market in 1980. The Smurfs are named Clumsy, Papa Smurf, Jokey, Brainy, Hefty, Lazy, Grouchy, Vanity, Greedy, Harmony, and Smurfette (female). They are manufactured in Korea by Wallace Berrie and Co., Inc., and were created by Peyo and Yvan Delponte. Gargamel created the female smurf (Smurfette) by mixing the following formula:

Blue clay (magical lump)
Dash of sugar and spice (but nothing nice)
Gram of crocodile tears
½ pack of lies
Chatter of magpies
Heart of stone

To which Papa Smurf added his own formula to create a new and improved Smurfette:

A touch of Venus

Moonbeams for light
    Essence of Smurfroot to Smurf her upright

Papa Smurf also changed her hair coloring from black to blond. On the TV cartoon show, Lucille Bliss provided the voice of Smurfette, and Paul Winchell provided Gargamel's voice. A picture of a group of Smurfs can be seen in a book in the 1966 movie *The Defector* (Montgomery Clift's final film). In 1983, Smurf-Berry Crunch breakfast cereal was introduced.

**Snickers**
Candy bar introduced by the Mars Candy Company in 1930.

**Snider, Duke**
(1926–    ) Brooklyn Dodger who, on September 22, 1957, hit the last home run at Ebbets Field.

**Sniffy**
Molly Middleton's (Shirley Temple) black Scotch terrier in the 1935 movie *Our Little Girl*.

**Snow, Hank**
(1914–    ) Country singer, born Clarence Eugene Snow, in Liverpool, Nova Scotia. He had a series of hit records from 1949 onward. It was Hank Snow who introduced Elvis Presley when Elvis first appeared on the Grand Ole Opry on September 25, 1954. Jimmie Snow, Hank's son, is a minister. Hank Snow was portrayed by Galen Thompson in the 1979 TV movie *Elvis*.

**Soar, Hank**
Versatile athlete who played halfback for the New York Giants football team from 1937 to 1946. He was a coach for the Providence Steamrollers basketball team in the BAA (Basketball Association of America) in 1947 and 1948, and an umpire in the American League from 1950 until 1971.

**S.O.B.**
Title of the 1981 Blake Edwards movie starring his wife, Julie Andrews. In the film, S.O.B. stands for Standard Operational Bullshit.

**Sobrek, Joe**
American sportsman who created the game of racquetball in the 1940s.

**Solar Challenger**
First solar-powered airplane to cross the English Channel. It was piloted for 5½ hours by Stephen Ptacek, on July 7, 1981.

**"So Little Time"**
Song sung by Andy Williams for the 1963 movie *55 Days at*

*Peking*.

**So long until tomorrow . . .**
Signoff of newscaster Lowell Thomas, from his first broadcast on KDKA in Pittsburgh in March 1925, until he resigned in May 1976.

**"Someone Who Cares"**
Theme song of the 1970 movie *Fools*, sung by Kenny Rogers and the First Edition.

**Something That Happened**
Original title considered by John Steinbeck for his 1937 movel *Of Mice and Men*.

**Son of Trigger**
Beau "Bandit" Darber's (Burt Reynolds) 1980 black turbo Trans Am in the 1980 movie *Smokey and the Bandit II*, Texas license BAN ONE.

**Song of Hiawatha**
Poem by Henry Wadsworth Longfellow (1855), that Bunny Watson (Katharine Hepburn) recited to a caller over the telephone, in the 1957 movie *Desk Set*.

**"Soon"**
Song composed in 1935 by Richard Rodgers and Lorenz Hart and introduced by Bing Crosby in the 1935 movie *Mississippi*. It was the first number-one song on radio's "Your Hit Parade" when the program debuted on April 20, 1935.

**Soon to Be a Major Motion Picture**
Title of Abbie Hoffman's autobiography.

**Sophisticatos**
Felix Unger's (Tony Randall) musical band on the TV series "The Odd Couple."

**Soul Food Cafe**
Restaurant in which Cledus (Jerry Reed) was beaten up by a gang of cyclists, after which he drove over their motorcycles with his truck in the 1977 movie *Smokey and the Bandit*.

**Soul Food Cafe**
Restaurant on Maxwell Street in Chicago, owned by Aretha Franklin in the 1980 movie *The Blues Brothers*.

**Sousa, John Philip**
(1854–1932) American bandmaster known as the March King. From 1880 to 1892 he was the bandmaster of the U.S. Marine Band. He composed such marches as "Semper Fidelis" (1888), "The Washington Post March" (1889), and "The Stars and Stripes

Forever'' (1897). He also composed several comic operas. John Philip Sousa conducted "The Star-Spangled Banner" at the official opening of Yankee Stadium on April 18, 1923. Liberace's father, Salvatore Liberace, was a French horn player with John Philip Sousa. Sousa was portrayed by Clifton Webb in the 1952 movie *Stars and Stripes Forever*.

**Southby**
Town near Southhampton where the byzantium (believed to have been on board the *Titanic* at the time of its sinking) was actually buried at the gravesite of Jake Hobart, whose tombstone indicated February 10, 1912, as the date of his death, in the 1980 movie *Raise the Titanic!* (based on the novel by Clive Cussler).

**Southern Comfort**
Singer Janis Joplin's favorite alcoholic beverage. The manufacturer was asked for permission to use the name Southern Comfort as the title of a 1981 movie starring Powers Booth and Keith Carradine.

**Southern Cross**
Clayton Farlow's ranch on the TV series "Dallas."

**Southern Military School**
Setting of the 1957 movie *The Strange One*.

**South Pacific soundtrack album**
First album to sell a million copies in Great Britain. This movie soundtrack was first released in 1958.

**Sovereign Airways**
Boeing 707 airliner that Inspector Harry Callahan (Clint Eastwood) sneaked onto in order to suppress a hijacking in the 1973 movie *Magnum Force*.

**SPCA**
Society for the Prevention of Cruelty to Animals. Organization founded in Great Britain in 1824 and in the United States in 1866.

**Space Invaders**
Pinball machine that Big Eddie (Richard Kiel) destroyed in front of his home on Prince Street in New York City in the 1981 movie *So Fine*.

**Spahn's Movie Ranch**
Home of Charles Manson and his "family" in the Santa Susanna Mountains, northwest of Los Angeles.

**Spahn, Warren**
(1921–      ) Member of the Baseball Hall of Fame and holder of the all-time record number of victories for a left-handed pitcher, with 363. He surrendered Willie Mays's first major-league home

run, on May 28, 1951. It was also Mays's first hit in the majors after going 0 for 12 at bat.

**Sparks**
Robot in the 1979 movie *The Shape of Things to Come*.

**Speak and Spell**
Toy computer that E.T. used as part of his machine to communicate with his people in his attempt to go home, in the 1982 movie *E.T. the Extra-Terrestrial*.

**Speaker, Tris**
(1888–1958) Member of the Baseball Hall of Fame. During the month of April, 1918, Tris Speaker, as a centerfielder for the Boston Red Sox, made two unassisted double plays.

**"Speak Softly Love"**
Vocal title of the "Love Theme from the Godfather," recorded by Al Martino on Capitol Records in 1972.

**Spence Andrews**
Role played by Daniel Travanti in the TV soap "General Hospital."

**Spencer, Daryl**
(1929–     ) First San Francisco Giant to hit a home run at Seals Stadium on opening day, April 15, 1958. The Giants defeated the Los Angeles Dodgers 8-0.

**Spencer, Percy L.**
American scientist who, in 1946, invented the microwave oven.

**Sphairistike**
Original name given to the game of tennis, when Major Walter Clopton Wingfield of Great Britain patented the game on February 23, 1874.

**Spike and Tyke**
Father-and-son bulldogs in MGM cartoons. Voices of Bill Thompson and Daws Butler. Debuted in "Dog Trouble" (April 18, 1942).

**Spilsbury, John**
English mapmaker who, in 1760, invented the jigsaw puzzle.

**Spirits of New England**
Cheerleaders for the New England Patriots football team.

**Spirit of the Bronx**
Vintage airplane flown by Wrong-Way Feldman (Hans Conried) on two episodes of the TV series "Gilligan's Island."

**Spitball**
Pitch that was officially banned from the major leagues in 1920, although seventeen pitchers who were using the pitch were allowed

to use it until they retired from baseball. The seventeen were:

| American League | National League |
|---|---|
| Y. W. "Doc" Ayers | Bill Doak |
| Ray Caldwell | Phil Douglas |
| Stan Coveleski | Dana Fillingrim |
| Urban Faber | Ray Fisher |
| H. B. "Dutch" Leonard | Marv Goodwin |
| Jack Quinn | Burleigh Grimes |
| Allan Russell | Clarence Mitchell |
| Urban Shocker | Dick Rudolph |
| Allen Sothoron | |

Grimes was the last to use the spitball with the New York Yankees in 1934.

**Splendour**

Sixty-foot, $250,000 yacht of Robert Wagner and his wife, Natalie Wood. Natalie drowned when she fell from the vessel's dinghy on November 29, 1981.

**Splet, Alan**

Recipient of a special award for sound editing for the film *The Black Stallion*, presented at the 1980 Academy Awards. Alan Splet was not present to receive the award, and became the butt of a series of jokes by MC Johnny Carson.

**Splinter and Knothead**

Woody Woodpecker's niece and nephew. They made their debut in the 1956 cartoon "Get Lost."

**Sports Illustrated**

Magazine whose debut issue was released on August 16, 1954. The three people on the cover were Eddie Mathews (batter), Wes Westram (catcher), and Augie Donatellie (umpire).

**Sports Life**

Magazine for which Sam Alston (John Schuck) was a writer on the TV series "Turnabout."

**Sportsman's Park**

Home of the old St. Louis Browns baseball team, before they moved to Baltimore in 1953; also the home of the St. Louis Cardinals until 1966.

**Spot**

Billy Pilgrim's (Michael Sacks) pet dog in the 1972 movie *Slaughterhouse Five* (based on the novel by Kurt Vonnegut, Jr.).

**SPRACAY**

Society for the Prevention of Rock and-roll and Corruption of

American Youth, an organization created to stomp out rock music in the 1956 movie *Shake, Rattle and Roll*.

**Spunky**
Arthur "Fonzie" Fonzarelli's (Henry Winkler) pet white terrier on the TV series "Happy Days."

**Spy Magazine**
Scandal magazine for which Mike Connor (James Stewart) and Liz Imbrie (Ruth Hussey) worked as reporters in the 1940 movie *The Philadelphia Story*.

**Square Deal Finance Company**
Firm that financed Wolf J. Flywheel's (Groucho Marx) automobile in the 1941 movie *The Big Store*.

**Square Deal Saloon**
Town bar run by Parker Tillman (Leonard Frey) in the town of Copper Creek in the TV series "Best of the West."

**Squeaker**
Buttons the Clown's (James Stewart) pet white dog in the 1952 movie *The Greatest Show on Earth*.

**Stacey Petrie**
Rob Petrie's (Dick Van Dyke) brother played by Jerry Van Dyke, real-life brother of Dick Van Dyke, on the TV series "The Dick Van Dyke Show."

**Stallion**
Midland, Texas, nightclub where the cowboys and their women drank and played in the 1981 movie *Hard Country*. The club served Lone Star beer.

**Standard**
Nevada gasoline station for which Melvin Dummar (Paul LeMat) worked in the 1980 movie *Melvin and Howard*.

**Stanley**
Chimpanzee in the 1964 movie *The Misadventures of Merlin Jones*, and the 1965 movie *The Monkey's Uncle*.

**Stanley**
Title of the 1925 British movie *Livingstone*, when it was released in the United States in 1933.

**Stanley and Geoffrey**
Alfred Hitchcock's two Sealyham terriers, which he led on a leash in a cameo outside a San Francisco pet store, in the 1963 movie *The Birds*.

**Starbrites**
Cheerleaders for the Miami Dolphins football team.

**Stardust**

New York City nightclub where Corky Withers (Anthony Hopkins) bombed as a magician, at their Eight O'Clock Amateur Hour, in the 1980 movie *Magic* (based on the novel by William Goldman).

**Starfish**

Deep-sea research vessel that imploded at a depth of over 12,000 feet, killing three crewmen, in the 1980 movie *Raise the Titanic!* (based on the novel by Clive Cussler).

**Star Rising**

Play starring Carlotta Marin, being presented in the 1954 movie *Black Widow*.

**Starr Twinkle**

Daughter of newspaper reporter Brenda Starr and her husband Basil St. John, in the comic strip "Brenda Starr."

**"Star-Spangled Banner, The"**

Title of a record that peaked at number 50 on the *Billboard* Hot 100 charts in 1968, sung by Jose Felicano on RCA records. Recorded at the fifth game of the World Series in Detroit, on October 7, 1968, it is the only hit record ever to be recorded at a baseball game and the only version of the National Anthem to make the charts.

**Starstreak**

Spaceship in the 1979 movie *The Shape of Things to Come*.

**"(Just Like) Starting Over"**

John Lennon's comeback single that went to the number-one slot on the charts one month after he was shot to death by Mark David Chapman in New York, on December 8, 1980.

**Star Wars movie series (to date)**

*Star Wars* (1977)

*The Empire Strikes Back* (1980)

*The Return of the Jedi* (1983—working title: *The Revenge of the Jedi*)

**State of Maine Pure Spruce Gum**

First brand of chewing gum. It was first marketed by John Curtis in 1848.

**Steady Star**

Horse that holds the mile record for a pacer. He set the record in 1971, at one minute and fifty-two seconds.

**Stebbins**

Janitor at the Springfield YMCA Training School who provided, for Dr. James Naismith, the first baskets for the newly invented game of basketball, in 1891. The baskets were two peach bushel

421

baskets.

**Steele, Alfred N.**
Member of the board of directors of the Pepsi-Cola Company and fourth husband of actress Joan Crawford. He was portrayed by Harry Goz in the 1981 movie *Mommie Dearest*.

**"Steeler and the Pittsburgh Kid, The"**
TV special feature (1981) in which "Mean" Joe Greene and Henry Thomas (Elliot of *E.T. the Extra-Terrestrial*) re-created and extended the famous Coca-Cola TV commercials.

**Stella's**
Coffee shop where attorney Ned Racine (William Hurt) often ate lunch, in the 1981 movie *Body Heat*.

**Stengel, Charles Dillon "Casey"**
(1890–1975) Major-league baseball manager who played center-field for the Dodgers in the first regular season game ever played at Ebbets Field, on April 9, 1913. (The very first game played at Ebbets Field was an exhibition game played between the Dodgers and the Yankees, on April 5, 1913, in which the Dodgers won 3 to 2.) In the fifth inning of that game, Casey Stengel hit the first home run in the park, an inside-the-park homer. Singer Nat "King" Cole named one of his twin girls Casey after the manager. Stengel was portrayed by William Duell in the 1981 PBS drama "Casey Stengel."

**Stepenfetchit**
Horse that finished third (out of twenty) in the fifty-eighth running of the Kentucky Derby, on May 7, 1932. It was this horse that lent its name to black actor Stepin Fetchit (Lincoln Theodore Monroe Andrew Perry).

**Stephens, Gene**
(1933–     ) Only man in the twentieth century to have made three hits in one inning in the major leagues. He accomplished the feat on June 18, 1953, with the Boston Red Sox.

**Stephens, S. L.**
Oklahoma state guard who came off the bench to tackle Iowa State quarterback Bucky Hardeman, in a game at Ames, Iowa, on November 24, 1973. The officials awarded Hardeman the touchdown.

**Stephens, Sozanne**
Seventeen-year-old cashier who was fired when she refused to serve customers in a store in Lake Ronkonkoma, Long Island,

during the ten-minute vigil for the late John Lennon, on December 14, 1980, between 2:00 and 2:10 P.M.

**Steve Garvey Junior High School**
School in Lindsay, California, that, on February 25, 1978, renamed itself after the Los Angeles Dodgers baseball player Steve Garvey, when the principal let the students choose the school's name (they had originally chosen Elvis Presley, but this was vetoed). Steve Garvey Junior High became the second school in the world to be named after a baseball player. Walter Johnson High School in Bethesda, Maryland, was the first. The school's library is named after Tom LaSorda, the Dodgers' manager. Roberto Clemente became the third ballplayer to have a school named for him.

**Steve Martin**
American reporter, played by Raymond Burr, in the 1956 Japanese movie *Godzilla, King of the Monsters* (U.S. edition only).

**Stevens, Tom**
First man to pedal a bicycle (a high-wheeler) around the world; beginning in 1884, he completed his trip in 1886.

**Stewart, Nels**
Player for the Montreal Maroons hockey team, who, in a game at Montreal on January 3, 1931, scored two goals in just four seconds.

**Stewart, Paul**
(1908–     ) Hollywood actor and TV director. He began his career on Orson Welles's "Mercury Theater" on radio in 1938. Along with other Mercury Theater players, he made his movie debut in the 1941 classic *Citizen Kane*. Paul Stewart was portrayed by Walter McGinn in the 1975 movie *The Night That Panicked America*.

**"Stewball"**
Record (1963) by Peter, Paul and Mary that is the only hit song about a racehorse (of the rock era since 1955).

**Stingley, Darryl**
New England Patriots wide receiver whom Jack Tatum of the Oakland Raiders paralyzed after hitting him during a pre-season game on August 12, 1978, breaking his neck in two places and damaging his spinal cord.

**Stockholm, Sweden**
Site of the equestrian events for the Fourteenth Olympic Games in 1956. The other events were all held in Melbourne, Australia

(Australia has rigid horse quarantine laws).

**Stokes, Carl B.**
Elected mayor of Cleveland in 1967, the first black to be elected mayor of a large American city.

**Stonefield**
Small-town setting of the 1938 Shirley Temple movie *Little Miss Broadway*. The town paper, the *Stonefield Democrat* was edited by Mike (Joel McCrae).

**Stone, Melville E.**
Publisher of the Chicago *Daily News* who, in 1875, introduced odd pricing of merchandise by subtracting a penny from the price (e.g., $1.99). He introduced the pricing through his advertisers.

**"Stop, Hey What's That Sound"**
Subtitle of Buffalo Springfield's 1967 hit record "For What It's Worth."

**Stop Magazine**
Scandal magazine for which Bob Weston (Tony Curtis) was a writer in the 1964 movie *Sex and the Single Girl*. *Stop*'s competitor was *Dirt Magazine*.

**Story of Civilization**
Eleven-volume series of history books written by Will Durant (1885–1981) over a period of fifty years; volumes 7–11 were written in collaboration with his wife, Ariel Durant.

1. *Our Oriental Heritage* (1935)
2. *The Life of Greece* (1939)
3. *Caesar and Christ* (1944)
4. *The Age of Faith* (1950)
5. *The Renaissance* (1953)
6. *The Reformation* (1957)
7. *The Age of Reason* (1961)
8. *The Age of Louis XIV* (1963)
9. *The Age of Voltaire* (1965)
10. *Rousseau and the Revolution* (1967) won a Pulitzer Prize
11. *The Age of Napoleon* (1975)

**Stowaway**
Shirley Temple movie (1936) that is shown over the opening and closing titles of the 1970 movie *Myra Breckenridge*. In the clips, Miss Temple sings "You Got to S-M-I-L-E."

**"Strange As It Seems"**
Radio series and series of books dealing with strange and unusual facts throughout the world, created by John Hix, from the late

1930s until the 1950s. It very closely resembled Robert L. Ripley's "Believe It or Not" series.

**Strange Cargo**

Clark Gable movie (1940) that was playing on Steve Nichols's (John Ritter) TV set in the 1980 movie *Hero at Large*.

**Stranger**

Willie Nelson's favorite horse. It was a gift from actor Robert Redford.

**Stratten, Dorothy**

Twenty-year-old girl who was *Playboy* magazine's Playmate of the Year for 1980. She was shot to death by her estranged husband, Paul Snider. Dorothy appeared in the 1980 movies *They All Laughed* and *Galaxina,* and was portrayed by Jamie Lee Curtis (the daughter of Tony Curtis and Janet Leigh) in the 1981 TV movie *Death of a Centerfold;* Paul Snider was portrayed by Bruce Weitz in the movie. Stratten was also portrayed by Mariel Hemingway in the 1983 movie *Star 80.*\*

**Strawberry**

Only fruit with its seeds on the outside.

**Strawberry Shortcake**

Cute doll that became popular in 1981. The character was first introduced via the American Greetings Company, which put her on greeting cards in 1980.

**Strawberry Shortcake's clan is made up of**

Huckleberry Pie, Blueberry Muffin, Apple Dumplin', Raspberry Tart, Lemon Meringue, Lime Chiffon, Little Chiffon, Apricot 'n' Hopsalot, Orange Blossom, Custard, and Pupcake (a dog).

**Stray Cats**

British group for which Jim MacLaine (David Essex) became the leader in the 1974 movie *Stardust*.

**"Streets of Laredo"**

Traditional cowboy song, from which the lyrics were borrowed for the 1956 TV play *Bang the Drum Slowly,* with Paul Newman and Albert Salmi, and the 1973 movie *Bang the Drum Slowly,* starring Robert DeNiro and Michael Moriarty. John Wayne sang the song in the 1973 movie *Cahill, United States Marshal*.

**Strife**

Magazine for which Jenny Ericson (Shirley MacLaine) is a photographer in the 1964 movie *John Goldfarb, Please Come Home*.

---

*STAR 80 was the license plate of Paul Snider's Mercedes.

**Strief, George, and Bill Joyce**
Only two major-league players to hit four triples in a single game. Strief, of Philadelphia, hit his on June 25, 1885, and Bill Joyce, of the New York Giants, hit his on May 18, 1897.

**"Strike It Rich"**
Game show hosted by Warren Hull which appeared on a TV set in the 1971 movie *The Last Picture Show*. In the movie, Hull asked a contestant to identify the tune "Shrimpboats Are A-Comin'."

**"String of Pearls, A"**
Dance song composed in 1942 by Jerry Gray and popularized by Glenn Miller. It was this tune to which Doc (Nick Nolte) and Suzy (Debra Winger) danced at the Bear Flag Restaurant in the 1982 movie *Cannery Row*.

**Strobridge, James**
Central Pacific construction boss who, with his railroad crew, on April 28, 1869, laid a record ten miles of new track over a twelve-hour period near Promontory, Utah. The record still stands.

**Stud**
Cologne worn by Consolidated Companies executive Franklin M. Hart, Jr. (Dabney Coleman), in the 1980 movie *9 to 5*.

**Stuhldreher, Harry**
(1901–1957) Quarterback member of Notre Dame's famed Four Horsemen. In his youth he often carried the helmet of Knute Rockne at Massillon so he could see the game for free. Stuhldreher was portrayed by Nick Lukats in the 1940 movie *Knute Rockne, All-American*.

**Stumble Steed**
Puppet horse on singer Willie Nelson's 1965 TV series.

**Stutz, Jodi**
Twenty-one-year-old secretary at Deere and Company, in Moline, Illinois, who was fired in 1980 for making a Xerox copy of her bottom.

**Sudol, Ed**
Major-league umpire who presided over the New York Mets' three longest games in their history: 1963 season (23 innings), 1968 season (24 innings), and 1974 season (25 innings).

**Sugar Bowl Soda Parlor**
Soda fountain where the teenagers hung out in Carl Ed's comic strip "Harold Teen."

**"Sugarbush"**
Top Ten hit record in Great Britain in 1952, sung in duet by Doris

Day and Frankie Laine.

**Sugar Daddy**
Candy manufactured by the Oxford Candy Company, founded by Robert Welch, Jr. (who was also the founder of the John Birch Society), in December of 1958.

**Suicide Capital of the World**
Uncomplimentary name sometimes conferred upon the city of San Francisco.

**Suicide King**
Name sometimes given to the king of hearts in a deck of cards.

**Suite 719**
Setting of the Neil Simon play *Plaza Suite*.

**Suite 1162**
Room at New York City Waldorf Astoria Hotel, where the Declaration of Independence of Panama was created and signed in 1903.

**Sullivan, Arthur**
(1842–1900) Half of the songwriting team of Gilbert and Sullivan. He was portrayed by Claude Allister in the 1940 movie *Lillian Russell*, and by Maurice Evans in the 1953 movie *Gilbert and Sullivan*.

**Sullivan, Mary**
New York City policewoman during the 1940s, who retold many of her experiences on the 1940s radio series "Police Woman," on which she portrayed herself (until replaced by Betty Garde).

**Sullivan, Roy**
Ranger at Shenandoah National Park, in Virginia, who has been hit by lightning eight times in his life. He appeared on the TV series "That's Incredible."

**Sullivan, Tom**
Multitalented blind young man who graduated from Harvard University, where he won a U.S. National title in wrestling. He also rowed in the British Henley Regatta, played golf (he came in third in the Inverary Pro-Am Tournament in Florida), as well as becoming a sky diver. In addition, Sullivan is a singer and musician. He has appeared on several TV series, such as *Mork and Mindy* and *Fame*. Tom Sullivan was portrayed by Marc Singer in the 1982 movie *If You Could See What I Hear*.

**Summer of '42**
Movie (1971) being watched by Wendy (Shelley Duvall) and Danny (Danny Lloyd) on TV at the Overlook Hotel in the 1980 movie *The Shining*.

**Sundblom, Haddon**
Artist who painted the jolly Santa Claus in Coca-Cola's Christmas advertisements. He used himself as the model.

**Sun Princess**
Luxury cruise liner commanded by Captain Thomas Allenford III (Ted Hamilton) in the 1976 TV pilot movie *The Love Boat I*.

**"Sunshine on My Shoulder"**
Theme song sung by John Denver for the 1975 TV series "Sunshine."

**Super Bowl VI**
Championship football game (1972) that Hunter S. Thompson (Bill Murray) is to write about in the 1980 movie *Where the Buffalo Roam*.

**Super Coupe**
Vehicle used by Super Chicken (TV cartoon show).

**Super Dome**
Fully enclosed playing field in New Orleans.

**Superior Properties, Inc.**
Investment firm that owns Ann's (Lynn Redgrave) apartment building in the TV series "House Calls."

**Super Star Sissy**
Dollhouse in which Mrs. Pat Kramer (Lily Tomlin) was forced to live within her real house in Tasty Meadows, in the 1981 movie *The Incredible Shrinking Woman*.

**Super Turf**
Surface used in the New England Patriots' Shaefer Stadium. They are the only home team to use super turf.

**Super X**
Brand of soap used at the Wash and Brush Up Company of Emerald City in the 1939 movie *The Wizard of Oz*.

**Supply**
U.S. Navy vessel, commanded by David Dixon Porter, that brought the first camels to America from Smyrna, Turkey, in 1856. Captain Porter was the foster brother of Captain David G. Farragut.

**Supreme Being**
The voice of the Supreme Being (played by Ralph Richardson) was that of Tony Jay in the 1981 movie *Time Bandits*.

**Supremium**
Rare mineral sought by villains (Martin Landau and Barbara Bain)

on the 1981 TV movie *The Harlem Globetrotters on Gilligan's Island*.

**Susan B. Anthony Hotel**

Women's hotel where Henry Desmond (Peter Scolari) and Kip Wilson (Tom Hanks) lived as women named Hildegarde and Buffy, on the TV series "Bosom Buddies."

**Susannah of the Mounties**

Movie (1939) in which Shirley Temple smoked a drug. She smoked an Indian peace pipe that made her "feel funny."

**Susie and Daisy**

Two girls mentioned in the lyrics of Little Richard's 1956 hit song "Tutti Frutti."

**Susy**

Name of Wallace Wooley's (Fredric March) pet cat in the 1942 movie *I Married a Witch*.

**Sutro, Adolph**

(1830–1893) Mining engineer who excavated a 20,000-foot-long tunnel into Mt. Davidson (1869–1878), in order to reach the rich Comstock Lode. Sutro served as mayor of San Francisco from 1894 to 1896. He was portrayed by Fred Kelsey in the 1942 movie *Gentleman Jim*.

**Sutter, John**

(1803–1880) Explorer and trader who founded a colony on the site of present-day Sacramento, California, building a fort there. It was John Sutter whom James Marshall first told of his gold discovery on his property at Sutter's Mill, on January 24, 1848. John Sutter was portrayed by Edward Arnold in the 1936 movie *Sutter's Gold*, by Edwin Maxwell in the 1940 movie *Kit Carson*, and by Royal Dano in the 1978 TV movie *Donner Pass: The Road to Survival*.

**Suzie**

Miniature poodle that Cary Grant gave to his bride Betsy Drake, whom he married on Christmas Day in 1949, in Phoenix. They were flown there by Howard Hughes.

**Swamp, the**

Tent at the 4077th MASH unit where the following surgeons have all lived, at one time or another, on the TV series "M*A*S*H":

Benjamin Franklin Pierce (Alan Alda)
John McIntyre (Wayne Rogers)
Spearchucker Jones (Timothy Brown)

Frank Burns (Larry Linville)

B. J. Hunnicut (Mike Farrell)

Charles Emerson Winchester (David Ogden Stiers)

**"Swanee"**

Recording by Al Jolson that is played to let Bill Grant (George Burns) know when it is 9:30 A.M. each day, in the 1979 movie *Just You and Me, Kid*.

**Swanee Inn**

Los Angeles nightclub where Nat "King" Cole first sang in public, in 1937, when he performed "Sweet Lorraine," as part of the group The King Cole Trio.

**Swash-buc-lers**

Cheerleaders for the Tampa Bay Buccaneers' football team.

**Sweeney, Joe**

Irishman who is credited with inventing the banjo. Music-lovers called his music Band Joe, because it sounded like a whole band.

**Sweeney, Peter**

Eight-year-old boy whose letter was read by President Ronald Reagan in his Address to Congress on April 28, 1981. The letter referred to Reagan's recovery from the assassination attempt. It said:

"I hope you get well quick. If you don't, you might have to make a speech in your pajamas. P.S., If you do have to make a speech in your pajamas, I warned you."

**"Sweet Georgia Brown"**

Song written by Ben Bernie, Maceo Pinkard, and Kenneth Casey in 1925, heard in the following movies:

*Broadway* (1942)

*The Harlem Globetrotters* (1951), whistled by Brother Bones

*The Helen Morgan Story* (1957)

*Some Like It Hot* (1959)

*To Be or Not to Be* (1983), sung in Polish by Mel Brooks and Anne Bancroft

Even the Beatles recorded the song while in Germany.

**Sweethaven Daily Poop**

Town newspaper in Popeye's hometown of Sweethaven in the 1980 movie *Popeye*. Selling for a penny an issue, its motto is "The print won't come off on your hands."

**Sweethaven Faerie Casino**

Gambling club in the 1980 movie *Popeye*.

**"Sweet Little Sixteen"**
Hit song (1958) by Chuck Berry that mentions the following cities in the lyrics: Boston, Pittsburgh, San Francisco, St. Louis, New Orleans, and Philadelphia.

**Sweet Thursday**
Novel by John Steinbeck that is the sequel to his earlier novel *Cannery Row*. Both novels were used as the basis for the 1982 movie *Cannery Row* (narrated by John Huston).

**Swinburne, Algernon Charles**
(1837–1909) British poet whose best work, *The Duke of Gandia*, was published in 1908. He was portrayed by Mike Lennox in the 1969 movie *The Best House in London*.

**"Swine Lake"**
Musical piece to which Miss Piggy and Rudolf Nureyev danced in the 1981 movie *The Great Muppet Caper*.

**Switched-On Bach**
Only million-selling record album by an artist who had a sex change, when Walter Carlos became Wendy Carlos in 1979.

**Switzer, Kathrine**
In 1967, wearing number 261, she became the first woman to run in the Boston Marathon. (During the race, officials attempted to stop her, since women at the time were banned from the race.)

**SY 2285**
Pasadena home phone number of Jack Amsterdam (Charles Durning), at 847 Wessex, in the 1981 movie *True Confessions*.

**Sylvanus Thayer Award**
The United States Military Academy's highest honor.

**Sylvester, Rick**
Stuntman who doubled for James Bond (Roger Moore) when he skied off the 3,000-foot Asgard Peak, on Canada's Baffin Island, in the 1977 movie *The Spy Who Loved Me*. He was paid $30,000 for the jump.

**Sylvester Sneedly**
Evil villain on the animated TV series "The Perils of Penelope Pitstop," voiced by Paul Lynde.

# T

**2N18869**
License number of Lois Lane's (Phyllis Coates) Nash Metropolitan automobile on the TV series "The Adventures of Superman."

**2X37796**
California automobile license number of Dr. Myles J. Binnell's (Kevin McCarthy) 1955 black-and-white Ford sedan in the 1956 movie *Invasion of the Body Snatchers*.

**2 inches**
Shortest touchdown pass in NFL history. It occurred in a game at Washington, D.C., on October 9, 1960, when Eddie LeBaron of Dallas threw to Dick Bielski.

**2.64 pounds**
Weight of the preserved brain of scientist Albert Einstein.

**2 to 1**
Final score of the last game played by the Brooklyn Dodgers, when, on September 29, 1957, they defeated the Philadelphia Phillies.

**3 Ages of archeology**
Stone Age
Bronze Age
Iron Age

**−3**
Blood pressure of Herman Munster (Fred Gwynne) on the TV series "The Munsters."

**3**
Number of ice cubes that Bob Hartley (Bob Newhart) prefers in his drinks, on the TV series "The Bob Newhart Show."

**3**

Number of rounds in an Olympic boxing match, each consisting of three minutes.

**3–3**

Tied score of a thirteen-inning night game played between the Los Angeles Dodgers and the Chicago Cubs, on September 20, 1961. It was the very last major-league baseball game played in the Los Angeles Coliseum.

**3 feet**

Maximum height that the U.S. Navy Vanguard missile reached off the launching pad on December 6, 1957, before blowing up, in an attempt to launch America's first satellite, which weighed only five pounds.

**3 M's**

The New York Yankees' Thurman Munson's first major-league home run came between two others, hit by fellow Yankees whose last names also began with *M* for three home runs in a row, hit on August 10, 1969. The other two runs were hit by Bobby Murcer and Gene Michael.

**10**

Major-league record number of consecutive strikeouts, pitched by Tom Seaver of the New York Mets, in a game on April 22, 1970, against the San Diego Padres.

**10**

Major-league record number of hits for two consecutive baseball games. It is held by Rennie Stennett, who got the hits on September 16 and 17, 1975.

**12**

Dallas Cowboys jersey number worn by Marie Thompson (Natalie Wood), when she played football in the 1980 movie *The Last Married Couple in America*.

**12**

Major-league record number of consecutive hits over several games. It is held by two players: the Boston Red Sox' "Pinky" Miller, Higgins, in 1938, and the Detroit Tigers' Walt Dropo, in 1952.

**12**

Major-league record for the most official appearances at the plate in a single game. Both John Milner and Felix Milan of the Mets set the record in a twenty-five-inning game on September 11, 1974.

**12**

Major-league record number of RBIs accumulated in one game. Jim Bottomley of the St. Louis Cardinals set the record in a game on September 16, 1924, when he had six hits for six times at bat, against the Brooklyn Dodgers, who lost 17–3. The American League record is held by Tony Lazzeri, with eleven RBIs.

**12**

Major-league record number of errors committed by one team during a game. Two teams share the record: the Detroit Tigers, on May 1, 1901, and the Chicago White Sox, on May 6, 1903.

**12**

Uniform number worn by Terry Bradshaw, Ken Stabler, Joe Namath, and Bob Griese, all of whom were quarterbacks who won Super Bowl games.

**12–0**

Pitching record of Yankee pitcher Tom Zachary. He set a major-league record in 1929 by winning the most games in one season without a defeat.

**12:05**

Time of the train mentioned in the lyrics of Sheena Easton's 1981 hit song, "Modern Girl."

**12:05**

Train that the singer is waiting for in the 1981 Juice Newton song "Queen of Hearts."

**13**

Major-league record of consecutive games won, set by the Atlanta Braves at the beginning of the 1982 baseball season. The Oakland A's had set the previous record the year before, with eleven straight wins.

**13th Precinct**

Manhattan South police precinct for which Lieutenant Theo Kojak (Telly Savalas) worked on the TV series "Kojak."

**13 to 3**

Final score of the July 4, 1980, softball game played in Plains, Georgia, in which President Jimmy Carter pitched for all nine innings. The President's team won in heat that hung around one hundred degrees. Carter was one for five at the plate, hitting a double, walking once, and getting to first base on an error. His brother, Billy, was the captain of the losing team.

**20**

Age at which Velvet Brown's (Elizabeth Taylor) mother (Anne

Revere) swam the English Channel in the 1944 movie *National Velvet*.

**20**

Major-league record number of players left on base during a nine-inning baseball game. The New York Yankees set the record on September 21, 1956, when they left twenty players stranded in a game against the Red Sox.

**20**

NBA record for consecutive games lost by a single team. The Philadelphia 76ers set the record in 1973.

**21**

Seconds in which Chicago Black Hawks player Bill Mosienko scored three goals against the New York Rangers, in an NHL game on March 23, 1952.

**22-5-17**

Combination to C. R. MacNamara's (James Cagney) office safe at the West Berlin Coca-Cola plant in the 1961 movie *One, Two, Three*.

**22nd Precinct**

New York City police precinct for which Frank Serpico (David Birney) was a police officer in the TV series "Serpico."

**22 Bleecker Street**

Greenwich Village home address of Dr. Stephen Strange (Peter Hooten) in the 1978 TV movie *Doctor Strange*.

**22 to 5**

Final score of the baseball game played between the New York Giants and the Philadelphia Phillies on June 1, 1923. The Giants scored in every inning, the first time this had ever occurred.

**23rd Precinct**

New York City police precinct for which Earl Eischied (Joe Don Baker) worked as chief of detectives in the TV series "Eischied."

**23**

Number of times that Washington Senators team pitcher, Walter Johnson, shut out the Philadelphia A's (out of 113 career shutouts thrown by Johnson, a record).

**24**

Football jersey number of Spearchucker Jones (Fred Williamson) during the football game between the 4077th and the 325th EVAC in the 1970 movie *M\*A\*S\*H*.

**24**

Record number of consecutive wins by a single pitcher. It was established by the New York Giants' Carl Hubbell, from July 17, 1936, to May 27, 1937.

**24**

Record number of tie games in the NHL, set by the Philadelphia Flyers during the 1969–1970 season.

**24 to 16**

Final score of the first American Football League Championship, played in January 1961, in which the Houston Oilers defeated Los Angeles in Houston.

**24-36**

Winning numbers on the roulette wheel that Melinda (Barbra Streisand) told Warren Pratt (Larry Blyden) to play in the 1970 movie *On a Clear Day You Can See Forever* (based on the Lerner and Lane musical play of the same title).

**25**

Correct answer that Bonzo the chimp wrote on a chalkboard at a carnival in response to the question from the audience, "If a banana and a half cost a cent and a half, how much would I get for a quarter?" in the 1952 movie *Bonzo Goes to College*.

**25**

Words per minute typed by Miss Piggy in the 1981 movie *The Great Muppet Caper*.

**27 to 24**

Final score of the longest professional football game ever played, when Garo Yepremian of the Miami Dolphins kicked the winning field goal to defeat the Kansas City Chiefs in the second period of sudden death in a game that lasted 82 minutes and 40 seconds, on December 25, 1971.

**28**

NHL record number of consecutive games won by one team. It was set by the Montreal Canadiens in the 1977–1978 hockey season.

**28**

Record number of successful free throws made in one game by a single player. It was set by the Philadelphia Warriors' Wilt Chamberlain, in a game against the New York Knicks on March 2, 1962, in which he attempted thirty-two free throws.

**28 days, 7 hours, 8 minutes, 22 seconds**

Length of Dagwood Bumstead's hunger strike, when his parents wouldn't allow him to marry Blondie, in the Chic Young comic strip "Blondie."

**29**

Number of crew members who perished in the wreck of the ship *Edmund Fitzgerald*, in the 1976 Gordon Lightfoot recording "The Wreck of the Edmund Fitzgerald."

**30 Briarcliff Lane**

Home address, in Wellesley, Boston, of Major Charles Emerson Winchester III (David Ogden Stiers) on the TV series "M*A*S*H." His phone number was LAwrence 3484.

**30**

Career number of stolen bases by Yogi Berra.

**32**

Number of the U.S. submarine that brought Ellen Arden (Doris Day) home in the 1963 movie *Move Over, Darling*.

**33 Gray Square**

Address of the flat in Mayfair owned by Caryl Hardwicke (Kim Novak) and rented to William Gridley (Jack Lemmon) in the 1962 movie *The Notorious Landlady*.

**33**

Number on the blue jersey worn by David Axelrod (Martin Hewitt) in the 1981 movie *Endless Love*.

**33**

NBA record number of the most consecutive games won by a team. It was set in 1971–1972 by the Los Angeles Lakers.

**33**

President Ronald Reagan's football uniform number at Eureka College.

**33 to 14**

Final score of a National Football League divisional playoff game in which the Chicago Bears defeated the Green Bay Packers at Wrigley Field on December 7, 1941.

**33⅔**

World Series record number of consecutive scoreless innings thrown set by the New York Yankees' Whitey Ford in the 1960, 1961, and 1962 World Series.

**35**

Major-league lifetime record number of times a player stole home, held by Ty Cobb.

**35 to 98**

Scoring range of the Rate-a-Record on Dick Clark's "American Bandstand" TV show.

**36**

Major-league record of triples hit in a single season. It was set in 1912 by the Pittsburgh Pirates' Owen Wilson.

**36**

NFL record number of touchdown passes thrown in a single season, set by George Blanda (1961), and matched by Y. A. Tittle (1963).

**36 B**

Size of Corporal Max Klinger's (Jamie Farr) high-rise bra in the TV series "M*A*S*H."

**37**

NFL record number of completed passes in one game. It was established by George Blanda, who was playing for the Houston Oilers, in a game against the Buffalo Bills on November 1, 1964.

**38**

Major-league record number of consecutive bases stolen, set by the Los Angeles Dodgers' Dave Lopes, from June 10 through August 24, 1974.

**38.6 seconds**

National collegiate record for the 440-yard relay. It was set on June 17, 1967, by four trackmen of the University of Southern California: Earl McCulloch, Fred Kuller, Lennox Miller, and O. J. Simpson.

**206**

Major-league record number of batters hit by a pitcher in a career. Walter Johnson holds the record.

**.211**

All-time lowest team batting average. It is held by the 1910 Chicago White Sox.

**212 Briarly**

Burlington, Vermont, address of Jade (Brooke Shields) in the 1981 movie *Endless Love*.

**213**

Number of the Trans Allied (Amtrak in reality) diesel engine that derailed and crashed in the 1979 TV movie *Disaster on the Coastliner*.

**216**

Number of stitches on an official baseball.

**217**

Major-league record for double plays by a team in a single season. It was set in 1949 by the Philadelphia Athletics.

**217 Southampton Street**
Chicago home address of the Random family on the 1979 TV series "Out of the Blue."

**220**
Number of space vehicles in the fleet led by the mother ship *Galactica*, on their trek to the planet Earth in the 1978 TV movie *Battlestar Galactica*.

**225**
Number of squares on a Scrabble board.

**228**
Number of the New York City courtroom setting of the 1957 movie *Twelve Angry Men*.

**228 Mulberry Street**
Address of Ernie's Tavern, the hangout of the law students, on the TV series "The Paper Chase."

**.237**
Major-league career batting average of "Marvelous" Marv Throneberry.

**240 Grover Avenue**
Yonkers, New York, home address of Harry Baker (Lee J. Cobb) and his family in the 1963 movie *Come Blow Your Horn*.

**247**
Home phone number of Thelma Lou in Mayberry, on the TV series "The Andy Griffith Show."

**.253**
Lowest lifetime batting average of any player, excluding pitchers, in the Baseball Hall of Fame. It is held by Chicago White Sox catcher Ray Schalk, who was elected in 1955.

**.254**
Ted Williams's batting average for the 1959 season. It was the only season of his major-league career in which he hit under .300.

**254**
Number of counties in the state of Texas.

**256 Hudson Street**
New York City address of the Hudson Street Home for Girls, established in 1891 and run by Miss Hannigan (Carol Burnett), in the 1982 movie *Annie*.

**257**
Major-league record number of hits in a single season. George Sisler, of the St. Louis Browns, set the record in 1920.

**258 GPP**

California license number of the yellow-and-white two-seater Thunderbird that Cheech (Cheech Marin) and Chong (Thomas Chong) blew up in the 1980 movie *Cheech and Chong's Next Movie*. The car belonged to their neighbor.

**258 Academy Street**

Houston, Texas, house address of Patricia Nash (Joanne Dru) in the 1952 movie *The Pride of St. Louis*.

**268 OHH**

California license number of Jeff Thompson's (George Segal) brown Jaguar automobile in the 1980 movie *The Last Married Couple in America*.

**268 pounds**

Extreme weight that five-foot-seven-inch diet fanatic Richard Simmons reached before he trimmed down to 137 pounds, after which he began promoting his diet programs on the TV series "The Richard Simmons Show."

**276**

Number of the U.S. submarine on which "Choir Boy" Jones (Gordon MacRae) was stationed in the 1953 movie *Three Sailors and a Girl*.

**277**

NFL record of career passes intercepted, held by quarterback George Blanda.

**282**

NFL record for consecutive games played, set by the Minnesota Vikings' defensive end Jim Marshall (1961–1979).

**294**

Number of consecutive passes thrown by Green Bay Packers' quarterback Bryan "Bart" Starr, without an interception (1964–1965 season). This is an NFL record.

**310 Orange Drive**

Home address of Dr. Alfred Bellows (Hayden Rorke), at Cocoa Beach, on the TV series "I Dream of Jeannie."

**312**

Major-league baseball's record career number of triples, held by Sam Crawford, who played from 1899 to 1917.

**315**

Correct answer that Bonzo the chimp wrote on a chalkboard in response to the question from the audience, "What was Joe DiMaggio's batting average in 1947?" at a carnival in the 1952 movie *Bonzo Goes to College*.

**320**
Record number of double plays that Hank Aaron has hit into, in his major-league career.

**320 Sycamore**
Home address in Bedford Falls of George and Mary Bailey (James Stewart and Donna Reed), in the 1946 Frank Capra movie *It's a Wonderful Life*.

**321 Harper Drive**
Home address of Hal Norton (Ronald Reagan) in the 1950 movie *Louisa*.

**325**
Number of novels featuring the crime fighter the Shadow, written between 1930 and 1949. The writers were Maxwell Grant (Walter B. Gibson), Theodore Tinsley, and Bruce Elliott. The 1938 novel *The Golden Vulture* was written by Lester Dent and Maxwell Grant. Between 1963 and 1967, ten more *Shadow* novels were written by Walter B. Gibson and Dennis Lynds, writing as Maxwell Grant.

**329 Elm Street**
Address of the haunted house in the 1982 movie *Saturday the 14th*. The only show that will appear on its TV is "The Twilight Zone." The gas stove in the kitchen is a Wedgewood.

**334XJB**
California license number of Violet Newstead's (Lily Tomlin) blue Buick in the 1980 movie *9 to 5*.

**335**
Issue number of *Rolling Stone* magazine (January 22, 1981) that was dedicated solely to one person, the late John Lennon.

**337**
Major-league record for the most hits made in a single day (July 16, 1950) throughout the majors. Fifteen games were played that day.

**.340**
Lifetime major-league batting average of Lou Gehrig.

**341 yards**
Longest drive in PGA records, hit by Jack Nicklaus in July of 1963.

**342**
Number of chests of tea thrown into Boston Harbor at Griffin's Wharf, at the Boston Tea Party, on December 16, 1773.

**342**
Total number of points scored in a single basketball game, played

on February 14, 1975, by the San Diego Conquistadores and the New York Nets, in which San Diego won 176 to 166.

**.360**

Batting average of country singer Otis Dewey "Slim" Whitman, in 1947, for the Plant City Berriers of the Orange Best League. His pitching record that season was 11–1.

**363**

Mayberry, North Carolina, phone number of Wally's Service Station on the TV series "The Andy Griffith Show."

**.367**

Lifetime batting average of the Detroit Tigers' Tyrus Raymond Cobb. It is the highest in major-league history. The average was given out as an answer over the telephone by the research department of the Federal Broadcasting Company in the 1957 movie *Desk Set*.

**367**

NBA record number of personal fouls in a single season, set in 1979 by Bill Robinzine of Kansas City.

**373**

Major-league career number of games won by both Grover Cleveland Alexander (1911–1930) and Christy Mathewson (1900–1916). Their losses were 208 and 188 respectively.

**375**

Number of members of the Mormon Tabernacle Choir.

**382**

National League record for the most strikeouts in a single season, set in 1965 by Sandy Koufax. Koufax also has the second highest number of strikeouts in a National League season, with 317 (1966).

**383**

American League record for the most strikeouts in a single season, set in 1973 by Nolan Ryan. Ryan also has the second highest number of strikeouts in a season, with 367 (1974).

**387 pounds**

Weight of Herman Munster (Fred Gwynne) on the TV series "The Munsters."

**2,000th hit**

Both Pete Rose (Reds) and Willie Davis (Dodgers) made their two-thousandth career hits on June 19, 1973. Rose hit a single against the Giants, and Davis hit a home run against the Braves.

**2,001**

Points scored by George Yardley of Detroit in the 1957–1958

season, becoming the first NBA player to score two thousand points in one season.

**2,002**

Points scored by George Blanda in his record-breaking football career (1949–1975).

**2,056**

Major-league record for walks in a career, held by Babe Ruth. Ted Williams is second, with 2,019.

**2,075**

Record number of mounts ridden by a jockey in a single year, set by Steve Cauthen in 1977. In that year he earned $6,157,750.

**2133**

Time setting of the 1974 movie *Planet Earth*.

**2,149**

NBA record number of rebounds made in a single season, set in 1961 by the Philadelphia Warrior's Wilt Chamberlain.

**2,218**

Major-league record number of games played by a shortstop. Luis Aparicio of the Chicago White Sox set the record (1930–1950, except for 1944).

**2238B**

Henleyville jail number of Norma Rae Wilson Williamson Webster (Sally Field) when she was arrested for disorderly conduct, in the 1979 movie *Norma Rae*.

**2,244**

Major-league record number of runs scored in a lifetime. The holder of the record is Ty Cobb (1905–1928).

**2283**

Date of the Romulan Ale given to Admiral James T. Kirk (William Shatner) by Dr. Leonard McCoy (DeForrest Kelley) in the 1982 movie *Star Trek II: The Wrath of Khan*.

**2,297**

Major-league record number of lifetime RBIs, held by Hank Aaron (1954–1976).

**2420 Metcalf**

Home address, in Metcalf, of Miriam Joyce Haines (Laura Elliott) in the 1951 Alfred Hitchcock movie *Strangers on a Train*.

**2,541**

Number of consecutive major-league games in which Bill McGowan appeared, which exceeded Lou Gehrig's 2,130 games. McGowan, an umpire, appeared from 1925 through 1954.

**2612 Houston Drive**

Dallas home address of Joanne (Savannah Smith), in the 1979 movie *North Dallas Forty*.

**2648 West Grand Avenue**

Address of Motown Records in Detroit, before it moved to Los Angeles.

**2721 Ocean Front Walk**

Venice, California, address of Molly Bell's (Lucie Arnaz) beachfront apartment, in the 1980 movie *The Jazz Singer*.

**2,856**

Consecutive episodes of the TV game show ''Jeopardy'' hosted by Art Fleming. He never missed a single show.

**3,000**

Career number of hits for major-league baseball player Roberto Clemente (1955–1972). Jon Matlack served up his final hit on September 20, 1972.

**3,000th**

Career hit by Paul Waner, which he accomplished at Braves Field on May 11, 1946, which was also the first night game ever played in Boston.

**3100 Willow Pond Road**

Bel-Air home address of Jonathan (Robert Wagner) and Jennifer (Stefanie Powers) Hart in the TV series ''Hart to Hart.''

**3152**

Prison number that Otis (Ned Beatty) wore while serving a prison term with Lex Luthor (Gene Hackman) in the 1981 movie *Superman II*. He resided in cell 383.

**3217 Valley Road**

Address of the New Deal used car lot in the 1981 movie *Used Cars*.

**3298**

Major-league record number of baseball games in which a single player appeared, held by Hank Aaron.

**.3429**

George Kell's batting average with the Detroit Tigers in 1949, which won him the American League batting title. He beat Ted Williams of Boston, who had an average of .3427.

**$3,500**

Bounty collected by bounty hunter Josh Randall (Steve McQueen) on the premiere episode (September 5, 1958) of the TV series

"Wanted: dead or Alive." The episode was titled "The Martin Poster."

**3,508**

Former major-league record number of career strikeouts, held by Walter Johnson (1907–1927) until surpassed by Steve Carlton, Nolan Ryan, and Gaylord Perry in 1983.

**3517 Grand Concourse**

Bronx address of Ida Morgenstern's (Nancy Walker) apartment (4G) on the TV series "Rhoda."

**3,600**

Exact number of National League hits made by Hank Aaron in his major-league career. He had 171 additional hits in the American League.

**3602 South Lowe**

Chicago address (Bridgeport area) where Mayor Richard Joseph Daley was born, on May 15, 1902.

**3,720 to 1**

Odds against safely navigating through an asteroid belt, as determined by R2D2 in the 1980 movie *The Empire Strikes Back*.

**3821**

Concord State Penitentiary prison number of Adam Worth (Michael Caine) in the 1976 movie *Harry and Walter Go to New York*.

**3,855**

NBA record number of personal lifetime fouls, set by Hal Greer (1959–1973).

**3959 Murraga Canyon**

Home address in Los Angeles of the *Tribune* managing editor, Charles Humes (Mason Adams), and his wife, Marion (Peggy McCay), in the TV series "Lou Grant."

**$20,500**

Poker pot won by Meredith's (Henry Fonda) wife, Mary (Joanne Woodward), in the 1966 movie *A Big Hand for the Little Lady*.

**20864**

Nevada license plate on the pursuing tanker truck in the 1971 movie *Duel*. There are also other plates on the truck.

**23471**

Sergeant Hans Schultz's (John Banner) German army service number in the TV series "Hogan's Heroes."

**23,924**

NBA record number of lifetime rebounds, set by Wilt Chamberlain (1960–1973).

**29450**

Prisoner number of Henry Brubaker (Robert Redford) when he first arrived incognito, as a prisoner, at Wakefield Prison in Arkansas, prior to declaring himself as the new warden in the 1980 movie *Brubaker*.

**31,419**

NBA record number of lifetime points scored, set by Wilt Chamberlain (1960–1973.)

**31874**

Engine number of the Scotland-bound train from which the German spy Henry Faber (Donald Sutherland) jumped in the 1981 movie *Eye of the Needle*.

**105353**

U.S. Army serial number of Lieutenant James Dunbar (Don Taylor) in the 1953 movie *Stalag 17*.

**218102**

Serial number of Sergeant Alvin York's (Gary Cooper) rifle in the 1941 movie *Sergeant York*.

**220–077**

License number of Alfred "Gloves" Donahue's (Humphrey Bogart) automobile in the 1942 movie *All Through the Night*.

**270,375**

Approximate number of times that the song "It's a Small World" is sung each year in Disneyland.

**272032**

Tail number of the B-17 in which Eddie Rickenbacker (Fred MacMurray) and the crew crash-landed in the Pacific Ocean in the 1945 movie *Captain Eddie*.

**274306**

Eddie's (Meatloaf) police identification number in the 1975 movie *The Rocky Horror Picture Show*.

**338171**

RAF service number of Aircraftman Shaw (pseudonym of adventurer/author Thomas Edward Lawrence).

**36–25–36**

Actress Ginger Grant's (Tina Louise) measurements on the TV series "Gilligan's Island."

**2350960**

Miss Piggy's London jail number in the 1981 movie *The Great Muppet Caper*.

**242–9970**

Private telephone number of Brenda Patimkin (Ali MacGraw) in the 1969 movie *Goodbye, Columbus*.

**2,500,000**

Approximate number of rivets in the Eiffel Tower.

**283-7451**

Philadelphia police hotline number given out over TV for information to aid in the capture of the Liberty Bell Murderer in the 1981 Brian DePalma movie *Blow Out*.

**362-4368**

Telephone number mentioned in the lyrics of the 1982 AC/DC song "Dirty Deeds Done Dirt Cheap."

**3,929,214**

Number of people counted in the first U.S. census, in 1790.

**32-816-775**

Sergeant Henry A. Kissinger's U.S. Army serial number during WWII.

**39150782**

Sergeant John Lawrence's (Ronald Reagan) U.S. Army serial number in the 1949 movie *John Loves Mary*.

**(202) 456-1414**

Telephone number of the White House.

**(207) 555-8000**

Phone number of the Institute for Advanced Concepts at Hanover, Maine, in the 1980 movie *Simon*.

**(212) 926-7058**

Phone number that Antoinette Lily (Sondra Locke) dialed collect to New York in the 1980 movie *Bronco Billy*. (It was busy.)

**$2,660,527.02**

Amount of the first robbery committed by Thomas Crown (Steve McQueen) in the 1968 movie *The Thomas Crown Affair*.

**(311) 555-1285**

Phone number of CIA boss Meyerson's (Ned Beatty) Georgia summer home, where Miles Kendig (Walter Matthau) hid out in the 1981 movie *Hopscotch*.

**T48X9**

Texas license plate number of Buck Bonham's (Willie Nelson)

touring bus in the 1980 movie *Honeysuckle Rose*.

**T5H270**

Florida license number of Megan Carter's (Sally Field) gray Mazda sports car in the 1981 movie *Absence of Malice*.

**Tab**

Diet soda bottled by Coca-Cola, first introduced in 1963.

**Tabei, Junko**

On May 16, 1975, she became the first woman to scale Mount Everest. Tabei led an all-female Japanese expedition up the mountain.

**Tabor, Charley**

Trumpet player on Bert Kaempfert's 1960 hit instrumental song "Wonderland by Night."

**TACKY**

California license number of actress Sally Struthers's Porsche 911.

**Taft Hotel**

Manhattan hotel where, on May 26, 1933, country singer Jimmie Rodgers, the Singing Brakeman, died of tuberculosis in his room.

**Take a Friend to Church**

Advertisement on a billboard on Highway 109, through which Sheriff Lyle Wallace (Ernest Borgnine) drove his police car in the 1978 movie *Convoy*.

**"Take Me Along"**

Song composed in 1959 by Bob Merrill and introduced by Walter Pidgeon and Jackie Gleason in the musical *Take Me Along*.

**"Take Me Back"**

Song sung by a streetcorner quartet in the 1976 movie *Rocky*. In actuality, they were a group called the Valentines, lead by Sylvester Stallone's brother, Frank Stallone.

**"Take Me for a Buggy Ride"**

Bessie Smith record being played on Liz Hamilton's (Jacqueline Bisset) record player in her New York apartment in the 1981 movie *Rich and Famous*.

**"Take Me Out to the Ball Game"**

Music inserted by the Marx Brothers in the orchestra's music score for the opera *Il Travatore* in the 1935 movie *A Night at the Opera*. The song was also sung by Doris Day in the 1952 Ronald Reagan movie *The Winning Team*.

**Take my wife—please . . .**

Tag line of comedian Henny Youngman.

**Takes the Ouch Out of Grouch**
Original slogan for 7-Up soft drink when it was introduced in 1929.

**Tale of the Tsar Saltan, His Son, the Famous and Mighty Prince Guidon Saltanovich, and the Beautiful Swan Princess**
Direct translation of the title of the Nicholas Rimsky-Korsakov opera that produced the "Flight of the Bumblebee."

**Tale of Two Cities, A**
Novel written in 1859 by Charles Dickens. Mr. Spock (Leonard Nimoy) gave an early edition of the book to Admiral James T. Kirk (William Shatner), who quoted from it several times in the 1982 movie *Star Trek II: The Wrath of Khan*.

**Tale of Two Kitties, A**
Merrie Melodies cartoon released on November 21, 1943, that caricatured comedians Bud Abbott and Lou Costello as two kittens.

**"Tallahassee"**
Song introduced in the 1947 movie *Variety Girl* by the duet of Alan Ladd and Dorothy Lamour.

**Tamarac**
Gas station that sold Fina gasoline, where Bo Hooper (Jerry Lewis) got a job for a short time in the 1981 movie *Hardly Working*.

**Tampa Bay Buccaneers**
NFL football team that set a record for consecutive losses by one team when, in 1976 and 1977, they lost twenty-six games in a row. They were also the first twenty-six games that the team ever played.

**T. and W. H. Clark Works**
British company for whose calendar Peter W. Sutcliffe posed, by sitting at the wheel of his Ford truck. Peter Sutcliffe was arrested on January 1, 1981, for being the Yorkshire Ripper, who is believed to have murdered thirteen women over the previous five years.

**Tangina**
Psychic who attempted to rid the Freeling house of the beast in the 1982 movie *Poltergeist*. Tangina was played by four-foot, three-inch, ninety-six-pound Zelda Rubinstein.

**Tanguay, Eva**
(1878–1948) Singer and dancer of the early 1900s. Her theme song was "I Don't Care." She was portrayed by Mitzi Gaynor in the 1953 movie *The I Don't Care Girl*.

**Tanis**
Ancient city in Egypt where the Ark of the Covenant was found, in

the 1981 movie *Raiders of the Lost Ark*.

**Tank in Attack**

Book written by German Field Marshal Erwin Rommel, and read by General George S. Patton (George C. Scott), in the 1970 movie *Patton*.

**Tarantula**

Movie (1955) about a gigantic spider, a scene of which is shown on the wall of a discotheque in the 1968 movie *Coogan's Bluff*. Clint Eastwood appeared in both films. He played the leader of a flight of jet fighters in *Tarantula*.

**Tarbaby**

Actual name of the horse that Ronald Reagan owned and rode in the films *Stallion Road* (1947) and *The Last Outpost* (1951).

**TARDIS**

Time and Relative Dimension in Space—Dr. Who's time-travel machine in the *Dr. Who* TV and movie series.

**Tarnower, Herman**

Doctor who was slain by his ex-lover, Jean Harris, while his book, *The Complete Scarsdale Medical Diet*, was at the top of the best-seller lists in 1980.

**"Tarpaper Stomp"**

Original title of the classic instrumental "In The Mood," written in 1939 by Andy Razaf and Joe Garland.

**Taxi Driver**

Movie (1976), starring Robert DeNiro and Jodie Foster, seen by John Hinckley, Jr., at the Ogden Theater on Colfax Avenue in Denver, on March 11, 1980. The attempted assassination of a political figure by DeNiro and the role of Foster as a twelve-year-old prostitute gave Hinckley a scenario for his attempted assassination of President Ronald Reagan.

**Taylor, Annie**

Forty-three-year-old woman who, on October 24, 1901, became the first person to go over Niagara Falls in a barrel and survive.

**Taylor, Colonel Edmund Haynes, Jr.**

Founder of Old Taylor Kentucky Straight Bourbon Whiskey, in 1887.

**Taylor, Ken**

Canada's Ambassador to Iran, who, on November 4, 1979, while the U.S. Embassy staff was being taken prisoner in Tehran, hid six Americans in the Canadian Embassy until they could safely escape three months later. Ken Taylor was portrayed by Gordon Pinsent in the 1981 TV movie *Escape from Iran: The Canadian Caper*.

**Taylor, Robert**
(1911–1969) Hollywood actor born Spangler Arlington Brugh. He made his debut in the 1934 movie *Handy Andy*. From 1939 until 1951, he was married to actress Barbara Stanwyck. He was billed as "The man with the perfect profile." Taylor was portrayed by Terrence McNally in the 1980 TV mini-series "Moviola."

**Taylor, Samuel**
Writer who was credited in the 1929 movie production of William Shakespeare's *A Midsummer Night's Dream—The Taming of the Shrew*, as providing additional dialogue. The credits read, "Script by William Shakespeare, additional dialogue by Samuel Taylor."

**Taylorville**
Illinois hometown of Sandy Stockton (Sandy Duncan) on the TV series "Funny Face."

**Taylor, Zachary**
(1784–1850) Twelfth President of the United States. He was the father-in-law of Confederate President Jefferson Davis. Taylor was portrayed by Harry Holden in the 1927 silent movie *The Yankee Clipper*, by Robert Barrat in the 1951 movie *Distant Drums*, and by Fay Roope in the 1953 movie *Seminole*.

**Tchaikovsky's Sixth Symphony (Pathétique), First Movement**
Theme song of the radio soap "The Road of Life."

**"Tea for Two"**
Song to which Bill Grant (George Burns) woke up and exercised in the 1979 movie *Just You and Me, Kid*.

**"Teen Angel"**
Title of a morbid 1960 hit record by Mark Dinning (MGM Records). Singer Frankie Avalon played the role of Teen Angel in the 1978 movie *Grease*. Alan Paul, who played the role of Teen Angel in the Broadway musical *Grease*, used the money he had saved to form his own rock group, which he called the Manhattan Transfer.

**Television network news capsules**
Telecast each evening for one minute:
"Newsbreak" (ABC)
"Newsbeat" (CBS)
"News Update" (NBC)

**Tell Me About Women**
News anchorman Harry Reasoner's only novel, which he wrote in 1946.

**TEmpleton 9-9871**

Home telephone number of Margo Channing (Bette Davis) in the 1950 movie *All About Eve*.

**Temptation**

Perfume worn by Laura Partridge (Judy Holliday) in the 1956 movie *The Solid Gold Cadillac*.

**Tenace, Gene**

Oakland A's catcher who, in his first two appearances in his first World Series game (1972), hit a home run.

**Tener, John Kinley**

(1863–1946) Irish-born governor of Pennsylvania (1909–1911). He had previously pitched in the major leagues (1885–1890).

**Tenby, HMS**

British destroyer from which James Bond (Sean Connery) was "buried at sea" in the 1967 movie *You Only Live Twice*.

**Tenderness**

Original title of D. H. Lawrence's novel *Lady Chatterley's Lover*.

**Tennessee**

State that Dinah Shore sang about in her 1949 hit song "Dear Hearts and Gentle People."

**Tennis, anyone?**

Popular catchline that originated in the 1923 broadway comedy play *Meet the Wife*. The words were first spoken by a then unknown actor named Humphrey Bogart. William Holden said "Tennis, anyone?" in the 1954 movie *Sabrina*.

**Tennis Cabinet**

Nickname of President Theodore Roosevelt's close friends and advisors.

**Tennyson, Alfred Lord**

(1809–1892) English poet whose most famous works were *The Charge of the Light Brigade* (1854) and *The Idylls of the King* (1859–1885). He is buried in Westminster Abbey. Tennyson was portrayed by Hugh Burden in the 1969 movie *The Best House in London*.

**Terasaki, Hidenari**

Japanese diplomat who was in the United States at the time of the Japanese attack on Pearl Harbor, on December 7, 1941. He was married to an American Caucasian named Gwen, whom he took back to Japan with him after the outbreak of the war. Hidenari and Gwen Terasaki were portrayed by James Shigeta and Carroll Baker in the 1961 movie *Bridge to the Sun*.

**Teresa Neele**
Name used by mystery writer Agatha Christie (Vanessa Redgrave), to check into the Old Swan Hotel in Harrowgate for eleven days in the 1979 movie *Agatha*.

**Terlingua**
Texas ghost town that is the site of the International Chili Society's annual cook-off.

**Terrace Restaurant**
Restaurant at the Quiet Little Motel where Steve Martin played a waiter for Kermit and Miss Piggy in the 1979 film *The Muppet Movie*.

**Terror of Tiny Town, The**
Columbia Pictures 1938 musical Western utilizing an all-midget cast. It starred Billy Curtis.

**"Terry's Theme"**
Alternate title of the song "Eternally," composed in 1953 by Geoffrey Parsons and Charles Chaplin. It is the theme song of the 1952 movie *Limelight*.

**Test-Tube Twins**
The world's first test-tube twins were born in Australia on June 6, 1981. Their names are Stephan (1:43 A.M.) and Amanda (1:44 A.M.).

**Texas, USS**
First battleship to become a state shrine. The vessel is moored in Houston, Texas.

**Thackeray Club**
Reserved London club established in 1864, where Jerry Travers (Fred Astaire) disturbed the members by making noise in the 1935 movie *Top Hat*.

**Thanks a million. Come back soon . . .**
Words on the doormat at Archie Bunker's Place on the TV series "Archie Bunker's Place."

**Thank Your Lucky Stars**
BBC television program on which the Rolling Stones made their TV debut on June 7, 1963.

**That's Amazing, America!**
Television series hosted by Bucky, Johnny, Skippy, Kenny, P.J., Barbie, and Bunny, on which Zonker Harris appeared as a suntan contestant, in the G. B. Trudeau comic strip "Doonesbury."

**"That's Entertainment"**
Song composed by Arthur Schwartz, with lyrics by Howard Dietz,

that can be heard on the soundtrack of the movies *The Band Wagon* (1953), *That's Entertainment!* (1974), *That's Entertainment! Part II* (1976), *King Kong* (1976), and *All the Marbles* (1981). It was also used as the theme song of the TV series "That's Hollywood."

**That's the trouble with directors. Always biting the hand that lays the golden egg . . .**

Saying credited to movie producer Samuel Goldwyn, known as a Goldwynism.

**That that is is that that is not is not is that it it is**

Words that Charly Gordon (Cliff Robertson) asked Alice Kinian (Claire Bloom) to punctuate in the 1968 movie *Charly*. Punctuated, it reads like this: "That that is, is. That that is not, is not. Is that it? It is!"

**That was the best ice cream soda I ever tasted . . .**

Last words of comedian Lou Costello, who died immediately after eating a strawberry ice cream soda in Doctor's Hospital in Beverly Hills on March 3, 1959.

**Thaw, Harry Kodall**

Jealous husband of Evelyn Nesbit, who was the lover of famed architect Stanford White. Thaw shot White to death at Madison Square Garden on June 25, 1906. He was portrayed by Farley Granger in the 1955 movie *The Girl in the Red Velvet Swing*, and by Robert Joy in the 1981 movie *Ragtime*.

**The Body**

Name of Captain Buzz Rickson's (Steve McQueen) B-17 in the 1962 movie *The War Lover*.

**The Bottle**

Story that Don Birnam (Ray Milland) attempted to write in the 1945 movie *The Lost Weekend*.

**The Cage**

Pub in the town of Valentine Bluff, where the miners hung out, drinking Moose Head beer, in the 1981 movie *My Bloody Valentine*.

**The End?**

How the 1958 movie *The Blob* and the 1980 movie *Flash Gordon* ended.

**The game ain't over until it's over . . .**

One of many famous statements made by Yogi Berra.

**The Great Man**

Original title of the 1941 screenplay for *Never Give a Sucker an Even Break*, written by W. C. Fields under the pseudonym of Otis

Criblecoblis.

**The lady with all the answers does not know the answer to this one . . .**

Statement by Ann Landers in her July 1, 1975, column when she admitted to her readers that she was getting a divorce.

**The Land Around Us**

Play produced by Phillip Cook, featuring singer Frank Elgin (Bing Crosby) in the 1954 movie *The Country Girl*.

**The Legion Is Our Homeland**

English translation of the Latin motto of the French Foreign Legion.

**The Living End**

Closing screen words for the 1956 movie *Rock Around the Clock*.

**Thelma Harper**

Eunice's mother (Vicki Lawrence), who passed away on a Special based on the TV series "The Carol Burnett Show." Her husband Carl (voice of Dick Clair), who was never seen, died in the bathroom. Thelma Harper starred in her own TV series, "Mama's Family" (1983–    ).

**The Marriage Market**

Saloon in the town of Sandy Bar, run by Elizabeth Farnum (Rhonda Fleming) in the 1955 Ronald Reagan movie *Tennessee's Partner*.

**The Mortgage the Merrier**

Title of the Bonners' home movie, in which they filmed the final payment on their mortgage for their country estate, Bonner Hill, in the 1949 movie *Adam's Rib*.

**The natives are restless tonight . . .**

Famous line, first said by Charles Laughton in the 1933 movie *The Island of Lost Souls*.

**Theodore McCoy**

Ex–baseball player whom Los Angeles Tribune reporter Billie Victoria Newman (Linda Kelsey) married on November 2, 1981, on the TV series "Lou Grant." McCoy was played by Cliff Potts.

**Theodore Roosevent High School**

Washington, D.C., school for which baseball Commissioner Bowie Kuhn played basketball. His coach was Red Auerbach.

**The Pits**

Huggy Bear's (Antonio Fargas) Los Angeles bar on the TV series "Starsky and Hutch."

**There are more chickens in America than there are people . . .**

True-or-false question that was used as the first question asked on the TV game show special "Ultra Quiz," telecast on November 10, 1981. The answer, which eliminated 121 people out of 732, was "true."

**"There's a New Girl in Town"**
Theme song of the TV series "Alice," sung by Linda Lavin.

**"There's No Business Like Show Business"**
Unofficial anthem of the theater. Ethel Merman sang the song in the 1954 movie *There's No Business Like Show Business*, and the 1980 movie *Airplane!* She can be heard singing it over the closing credits of the 1979 movie *All That Jazz*.

**There's No Business Like Show Business**
Movie (1954) directed by Walter Lang and starring Ethel Merman and Marilyn Monroe. It was the only movie appearance of singer Johnnie Ray, who played a priest.

**There's no need to fear, Underdog is here . . .**
Motto of the TV cartoon character Underdog (voiced by Wally Cox).

**There's something I've got to do in the rose garden . . .**
Line said by Ronald Reagan in the 1938 movie *Brother Rat*.

**"There Will Be Love"**
Theme song of the 1978–1979 TV series "Julie Farr, M.D." (originally titled "Having Babies"), sung by Marilyn McCoo.

**These are the times that try men's souls . . .**
Opening line of the 1959 Kingston Trio hit song "MTA." The line was coined by Thomas Paine in 1776, in his publication *Common Sense*.

**The Secrets of Life and Death**
Book written by Dr. Frankenstein, in the 1948 movie *Abbott and Costello Meet Frankenstein*.

**The Story of Salome**
Script that Norma Desmond (Gloria Swanson) had written and was waiting to film, in the 1950 movie *Sunset Boulevard*.

**The sum total of all emotion!**
Publicity line for the 1945 Gene Tierney/Cornel Wilde movie *Leave Her to Heaven*.

**The temperature hit ninety degrees the day she arrived . . .**
Opening line of Jacqueline Susann's 1966 best-seller, *Valley of the Dolls*.

**The Thing and Forbidden Planet**
Two classic science fiction movies being shown on TV in the 1978 movie *Halloween*.

**The White Rajah**
Errol Flynn movie (fictitious) that is being premiered at the Cathay Circle Theater in Los Angeles as Ronald Reagan comments as a radio announcer, in the 1938 James Cagney movie *Boy Meets Girl*. The title was borrowed from an actual screenplay that Errol Flynn once sold to Warner Bros. It was never filmed.

**The Who**
Featured rock 'n' roll group that was performing at Cincinnati's Riverfront Coliseum on the evening of December 3, 1979, when eleven teenagers were trampled to death.

**They Came from Denton High**
Original title of the 1975 cult film *The Rocky Horror Picture Show*.

**They Dare Not Love**
Movie (1941) starring George Brent and Martha Scott, which the babysitter (played by Kathleen Freeman) watched on the 7:30 movie in the 1969 movie *Hook, Line and Sinker*.

**They're young . . . they're in love . . . and they kill people . . .**
Publicity line for the 1967 Warren Beatty/Faye Dunaway movie *Bonnie and Clyde*.

**Thing with Two Heads, The**
Horror-movie (1972) monster that walked around with the heads of two men, played by Ray Milland and Rosie Grier.

**Think God**
Advertising slogan that young Tracy (LouAnne) thought up for God (George Burns) in the 1980 movie *Oh God, Book II*. The children wrote the slogan all over town.

**This world in which we live in . . .**
Redundant line in Paul and Linda McCartney's 1973 hit song, "Live and Let Die," from the James Bond movie of the same name.

**"This World Is Yours"**
Song sung by Jack Jones over the opening credits for the 1968 movie *Anzio*.

**Thomas**
Name of the horse that led the carriage that took Ma and Pa Kettle around Central Park in the 1950 movie *Ma and Pa Kettle Go to Town*.

**Thomas, Danny**
(1951–    ) Milwaukee Brewer designated hitter who refused to play baseball on Saturdays because of his religious beliefs. He played in only 32 major league games, all in 1976, and none on

Saturday.

**Thomas, Dylan**

(1914–1953) British poet, author of *Map of Love* (1939), *World War I Breathe* (1939), and *Portrait of the Artist as a Young Dog* (1940). In the 1979 movie *Norma Rae*, Norma Rae Webster (Sally Field) borrowed a book of poetry by Dylan Thomas from Rubin Washopsky (Ron Leibman).

**Thomas, Ira**

(1881–1958) Detroit Tiger who made the first pinch hit in a World Series game (1908). It was a single. He was hitting for shortstop Charley O'Leary.

**Thomas, Jerry**

Occidental Hotel bartender in San Francisco who, in 1860, invented the martini drink.

**Thomas, Richard and Alma**

Their triplet girls, born on August 25, 1981 are:

Barbara Ayla (6 pounds, 4 ounces)

Gwyneth Gonzales (4 pounds, 9 ounces)

Pilar Alma (5 pounds, 8 ounces)

**Tomkins, Patrick**

Fourth and rarely mentioned passenger in the taxicab accident in which singer Eddie Cochran was killed, and singer Gene Vincent and songwriter Sharon Sheely were injured, on April 17, 1960. The cab driver, George Martin, was unhurt.

**Thompson, Linda**

Former Miss Tennessee (1972), and third runner-up in the Miss U.S.A. Pageant, who was the live-in girlfriend of singer Elvis Presley from 1972 to 1976. She was a regular on TV's "Hee Haw." Thompson was portrayed by Stephanie Zimbalist in the 1981 TV movie *Elvis and the Beauty Queen*, and by Cheryl Needham in the 1981 movie *This Is Elvis*.

**Thornton, Dr. William**

Designer of the Capitol Building in Washington, D.C.

**Thornwell, James**

Victim of U.S. Army experiments in which the Army forced him to take LSD. His plight was told on a "60 Minutes" broadcast in January 1979, and later he was portrayed by Glynn Turman in the 1981 TV movie *Thornwell*.

**Thorson, Ralph "Papa"**

Six-foot, two-inch, 310-pound professional, modern-day bounty hunter. In more than thirty years he has arrested approximately

11,000 persons. Thorson was portrayed by Steve McQueen in the 1980 movie *The Hunter*.

**Thousand Thrills, and Hayley Mills!, A**
Publicity line for the 1962 Hayley Mills film *In Search of the Castaways*.

**Three B's of Basin Street**
Barrelhouse, boogie-woogie, and blues

**Three jacks and two nines**
Poker hand held by the robot Huey, to beat Lowell Freeman (Bruce Dern) in the 1972 movie *Silent Running*.

**"Three Little Fishes"**
Song composed in 1939 by Saxie Dowell. A 78-RPM recording by Kay Kyser can be heard in the 1976 movie *Alice, Sweet Alice* (a.k.a. *Holy Terror* and *Communion*).

**Three minutes, Rock . . .**
Three words said by Olympic champion Jim Thorpe, in a cameo appearance in the 1940 movie *Knute Rockne, All-American*.

**Three Musketeers**
Candy bar manufactured by MARS, which Joe Baxton (Richard Pryor) gave to a Doberman pinscher guard dog in the 1981 movie *Bustin' Loose*.

**Three Musketeers, The, and The Four Musketeers**
Alexander Salkind's two 1973 films, *The Three Musketeers* and *The Four Musketeers*, hold the distinction of being the first set of movies to be filmed simultaneously. *Superman* (1978) and *Superman II* (1981) were also largely filmed simulaneously.

**Three Rivers Stadium**
Pittsburgh home of the Pirates baseball team and the Steelers football team. The stadium is named for the three rivers that make a juncture near by: the Allegheny, the Monogahela, and the Ohio.

**Thrilla in Manila**
Name given to Muhammad Ali's third fight with Joe Frazier, held in Manila, the Philippines, on October 1, 1975.

**Throckmorton**
Sea serpent puppet on the 1951 TV show "Ozmoe."

**Throckmorton**
Name that Madie Lovington (Dyan Cannon) gave to a calf that she bottle-fed in the 1980 movie *Coast to Coast*.

**Thunderbird (T-Bird)**
Automobile mentioned in the lyrics of the Beach Boys' 1964 hit song "Fun Fun Fun."

**Thunderlips**
Professional wrestler weighing 325 pounds and standing six feet eight inches tall, whom Rocky Balboa (Sylvester Stallone) "fought" in a charity exhibition match in the 1982 movie *Rocky III*. Thunderlips was played by Hulk Hogan.

**THX 2238: 4EB**
Short story which was the basis for the 1969 movie *THX 1138*, which was the first film directed by George Lucas.

**Tickey, Bertha Reagan**
Softball pitcher for the Brakettes women's team, who won 735 games in her career (161 no-hitters).

**Ticlaw**
Small Florida town that went to great lengths to get a freeway off ramp in order to help their businesses, in the 1981 movie *Honky Tonk Freeway*.

**Tige**
Nickname of Mattie Appleyard's (James Stewart) glass right eye in the 1971 movie *Fool's Parade*.

**Tiger**
Ringo Starr's dog, which appeared in the 1967 TV film *Magical Mystery Tour*.

**Tiger Winds**
Yacht owned by gynecologist Mike Phillips (Arthur Hill) in the 1979 movie *The Champ*.

**Tijuana Heights**
New name for the city of San Diego after it was sold to Mexico in the 1979 movie *Americathon*.

**Tiki Restaurant**
Glendale, California, restaurant where Melvin Dummar (Paul LeMat) sang about his employer, Rockwood Dairy, to the tune of the Dave Dudley hit "Six Days on the Road," in the 1980 movie *Melvin and Howard*.

**"Till There Was You"**
Song composed in 1957 by Meredith Willson for *The Music Man*. It is the only song that the Beatles recorded that came from a Broadway musical.

**Timber Tom**
Host of the Canadian edition of the TV show "Howdy Doody Time," which debuted in 1954. Tom was played by Robert Goulet.

**Time Bandits**
Movie (1982) about a gang of six midget adventurers who traveled

through time tunnels in order to steal history's most precious objects. The bandits were Randall (David Rappaport), Strutter (Malcolm Dixon), Og (Mike Edmonds), Wally (Jack Purvis), Fidgit (Kenny Baker), and Vermin (Tiny Ross).

**Time for Love**
Radio series starring Marlene Dietrich as Dianne LaVolte.

**Time Warp**
Dance featured in the 1975 movie *The Rocky Horror Picture Show*.

**Timoshenko, Marshal Semyon**
Russian army commander. He was in charge of the Russian defense against the German invasion of Moscow in 1941. He served as the commander-in-chief of the southwestern front (1941–1942). Timoshenko was portrayed by Kurt Katch in the 1943 movie *Mission to Moscow*.

**Tinkerbelle**
Harry Hinkle (Jack Lemmon's) pet cat that ran away, as mentioned by him in the 1966 movie *The Fortune Cookie*.

**Tinkerbelle**
Felix Farmer's (Richard Mulligan) yacht, berthed at Marina Del Rey in the 1981 movie *S.O.B.*

**Tinkle Bells**
Original title of the song "Silver Bells," which debuted in the 1950 movie *The Lemon Drop Kid*.

**Tin Star, The**
Movie (1957) starring Henry Fonda and Anthony Perkins. A movie poster of *The Tin Star* can be seen on a wall in the original opening credit scenes of the TV series "Happy Days."

**Tippitoe**
Louisiana town mentioned in the lyrics of Jerry Reed's 1971 hit song "Amos Moses."

**Titan**
Cassadine family yacht on the TV series "General Hospital." Luke (Tony Geary) was given a deed to the yacht for saving Lake Charles.

**Titanic**
Dr. George Alonzo "Gonzo" Gates's (Gregory Harrison) 1968 motor home, parked across the street from San Francisco's Memorial Hospital on the TV series "Trapper John, M.D." The license plate number is 550MYL.

**Titanic**
Name of the yacht owned by Pete (Cliff Robertson) and Kit (Lana

Turner) Jordan in the 1965 movie *Love Has Many Faces*.

**Titano**

Super ape with Kryptonite powers featured in Superman comics.

**Titans**

Original name of the New York Jets AFL football team, before it was changed in 1962.

**TL-1469**

Tennessee license number of the 1952 white Cadillac convertible in which country singer Hank Williams died on January 1, 1953.

**TNA872**

California license number of Sandra Sue "Abby" Abbott Bradford's (Betty Buckley) MG sports car in the TV series "Eight Is Enough."

**Toby**

Luke Fuchs's (Jack Warden) pet Beagle in the 1980 movie *Used Cars*. Toby was played by Peanuts.

**"To bring the hope of a new future to mankind"**

Mission of the crew of Ark II on the TV series "Ark II."

**Todd's Livery Stable**

Location of the fight between Marshal Will Kane (Gary Cooper) and Harvey Pell (Lloyd Bridges) in the 1952 movie *High Noon*.

**"To Each His Own"**

Song written in 1946 by Jay Livingston and Ray Evans, but not used in the 1946 movie *To Each His Own*. It is the only song in *Billboard* history of which three different versions all reached number one. This occurred in the summer of 1946, with versions by Eddy Howard, Freddie Martin, and the Ink Spots. An orchestra played the song at a nightclub in the 1952 movie *Submarine Command*.

**To Have and Have Not**

Movie (1944) starring Humphrey Bogart, the screen debut of Lauren Bacall. It was the only movie based on a novel by a Nobel Prize-winning author (Ernest Hemingway) to have a second Nobel Prize-winning author (William Faulkner) as the author of its screenplay.

**Tol'able David**

Silent film (1921) shown at a theater in the 1959 movie *The Tingler*.

**Toledo Dolls**

Female tag-team champions whom the California Dolls beat in a championship wrestling bout at the MGM Grand Hotel in Reno, for

462

a prize of $10,000 in the 1981 movie *All the Marbles*. The MC for the bout was football great "Mean" Joe Green. The event was televised on KGIM TV (Channel 6).

**Toledo, Ohio**
Hometown of Corporal (later Sergeant) Maxwell Q. Klinger (Jamie Farr) on the TV series "M*A*S*H." Toledo is the city mentioned in the 1979 Kenny Rogers's hit song "Lucille."

**Tomato Plant**
Potted plant that the girl (Marilyn Monroe) knocked off the balcony, almost injuring Richard Sherman (Tom Ewell), in the 1955 movie *The Seven Year Itch*.

**Tombaugh, Clyde**
Astronomer at the Lowell Observatory in Flagstaff, Arizona, who, on February 18, 1930, discovered the planet Pluto. He had finally found proof of Percival Lowell's belief that the planet existed.

**Tommy**
Laura's boyfriend in Ray Peterson's 1960 hit record, "Tell Laura I Love Her."

**Tommy and Becky**
Young married couple mentioned in the lyrics of Kenny Rogers's number-one country song of 1980, "Coward of the County."

**Tommy's**
Hamburger stand where Marie Thompson (Natalie Wood) took her husband, Jeff (George Segal), to celebrate his birthday in the 1980 movie *The Last Married Couple in America*.

**Tomorrow's Sound Today**
Slogan of Phil Spector's Phillies Record label, popular in the 1960s.

**Tom Quartz and Slippers**
President Franklin D. Roosevelt's two pet cats.

**Tom Terrific**
Cartoon boy who owns a dog named Manfred. He debuted in the 1957 TV cartoon "Nasty Knight" on "The Captain Kangaroo Show."

**Tom Thumb**
Small hero of the sixteenth-century nursery tale "The History of Tom Thumb." He was played by Sumner Getchell in the 1934 movie *Babes in Toyland,* and by Russ Tamblyn in the 1958 movie *tom thumb*.

**"Tonight Show, The"**
On Johnny Carson's first show, on October 1, 1962, the guests

were Groucho Marx, Joan Crawford, Mel Brooks, Tony Bennett, and Rudy Vallee.

**Tony**
Danny "Doc" Torrence's (Danny Lloyd) imaginary friend in the 1980 movie *The Shining* (based on the novel by Stephen King).

**Tonya**
Novel written in 1960 by World War II U.S. Marine Ace, Major Gregory "Pappy" Boyington and published by Pocket Books.

**"Too Close to Paradise"**
Title song of the 1978 movie *Paradise Alley,* sung by Sylvester Stallone.

**"Too Little Time"**
Song sung by Nancy Wilson in the 1964 movie *The Killers*.

**Too Much Johnson**
Uncompleted 1938 movie directed by Orson Welles and produced by John Houseman. If it had been completed, it would have been Welles's first movie.

**Too Much Spring**
Play written by Richard Collier (Christopher Reeve) in the 1980 movie *Somewhere in Time*, in May 1972.

**To One Love . . .**
Inscription on Laura Petrie's (Mary Tyler Moore) wedding ring on the TV series "The Dick Van Dyke Show."

**Too Tall**
Nickname of six-foot, eight-inch defensive lineman Ed Jones, of the Dallas Cowboys.

**Toothless**
Mountain lion on the 1973–1975 cartoon TV series "Lassie's Rescue Rangers."

**Toots**
Author Eric Knight's collie, which was the inspiration for his 1938 novel *Lassie, Come Home*.

**Tootsie Frootsie**
Ice cream sold by Chico Marx in the 1937 movie *A Day at the Races,* and the ice cream cone eaten by Chico in the 1949 movie *Love Happy*.

**Tootsie Roll**
Candy that manufacturer Leo Hirschfield named after his daughter, Clara "Tootsie" Hirschfield, when he introduced it in 1896.

**"Too Young"**
Song that four-year-old Gladys Knight sang to win the $2,000

grand prize on "Ted Mack's Original Amateur Hour" in 1948.

**Top Hat**

Movie (1935) starring dancing partners Fred Astaire and Ginger Rogers. Scenes from the film were shown in the 1981 movie *Pennies from Heaven*.

**Tora! Tora! Tora!**

Movie (1970) about the Japanese surprise attack on Pearl Harbor, Sunday, December 7, 1941, recounting both the American and Japanese sides. Scenes from *Tora! Tora! Tora!* have been used in the films *The Final Countdown* (1979), *Enola Gay* (1980 TV movie), and *Pearl* (1980 TV mini-series).

**Torg**

Ridiculous-looking and cheaply made Martian robot, played by Josip Elic, seen in the ridiculous-looking and cheaply made 1964 movie *Santa Claus Conquers the Martians*.

**Toronto**

Canadian city that was the site in 1914 of the only home run that Babe Ruth ever hit in the minor leagues (playing with Baltimore).

**Torpedoes**

High school basketball team coached by Harry Casey (Joe Namath) on the TV series "The Waverly Wonders."

**Toy Boutique, The**

Toy store that is the front for the government agency known as UNIT on the TV series "A Man Called Sloane."

**Toymaker**

Role played by comedian Benny Hill in the 1968 movie *Chitty Chitty Bang Bang*.

**TR 1-3340**

Detroit telephone number of Motown Records. The number appeared on the early copies of the record label.

**Tracy**

Gorilla played by Bob Burns on the TV series "The Ghost Busters."

**"Tracy's Theme"**

Theme song of the 1940 movie *The Philadelphia Story*.

**Trade Winds Bar—1945**

Calendar inside Avenger Bomber number 33, found in the Sonoran Desert in Mexico in the 1977 movie *Close Encounters of the Third Kind*.

**Trail of '98, The**

Movie (1929) starring Dolores Del Rio, in which Lou Costello doubled for Miss Del Rio.

**Tramp**
David Maldon's (Van Johnson) pet dog in the 1950 movie *The Big Hangover*.

**Trans American Flight 209**
Aircraft in distress, piloted by Captain Oveur (Peter Graves) and copiloted by Roger Murdock (Kareem Abdul-Jabbar), in the 1980 movie *Airplane!*

**Trans Atlantic Flight 627**
DC-7 airliner that ditched successfully in the Atlantic Ocean on a flight from Lisbon to New York. All thirty-one (fifteen men, eight women, one boy, one infant, and six crew members) on board were picked up by Destroyer Escort 347 in the 1958 movie *Crash Landing*.

**Transcon Medi-Vac**
Ambulance (number 55) driven in the race to California by J. J. McClure (Burt Reynolds) and Victor (Dom DeLuise) in the 1981 movie *Cannonball Run*.

**Trans Global Flight 442**
Airliner (Boeing 747) that crashed into Santa Monica Bay, killing ninety-two people, featured on a 1981 episode of the TV series "Quincy, M.E."

**Travels Through Time**
Favorite book of Elise McKenna (Jane Seymour) in the 1980 movie *Somewhere in Time*.

**Travis Bickle**
Character played by Robert DeNiro in the 1976 movie *Taxi Driver*. It was this character that John Hinckley, Jr., was trying to emulate when he attempted to assassinate President Ronald Reagan.

**Traynor, Chuck**
Movie producer who has been married to porno queens Linda Lovelace (*Deep Throat*) and Marilyn Chambers (*Behind the Green Door*).

**"Trees"**
Poem by Joyce Kilmer that was referred to in two 1981 movies, *Superman II* and *Cannonball Run*.

**Treves, Dr. Frederick**
London hospital doctor who helped John Merrick, the Elephant Man. He was portrayed by Anthony Hopkins in the 1980 movie *The Elephant Man*.

**Trigger**
Beau "Bandit" Darber's (Burt Reynolds) 1978 black turbo Trans Am in the 1978 movie *Smokey and the Bandit*.

**"Triple B Ranch"**
New York City radio show on which "Buffalo" Bob Smith first introduced the marionette named Howdy Doody, in 1947.

**Triple Crown of Thoroughbreds (Britain)**
Derby
Two Thousand Guiners
St. Leger

**Triple Crown of Trotters**

| | |
|---|---|
| Hambletonian Stakes | DuQuoin, Illinois |
| Kentucky Futurity | Lexington, Kentucky |
| Yonkers Futurity | Yonkers, New York |

**Triple Rock**
Musical black Baptist church in Calumet City, where Jake (John Belushi) and Elwood (Dan Ackroyd) go in order to "see the light," in the 1980 movie *The Blues Brothers*.

**Tri-State League in the Lesser Antilles**
League of which Larson E. Whipsnade (W. C. Fields) stated that he was the Ping-Pong champion in the 1939 movie *You Can't Cheat an Honest Man*.

**Trixie Tinkle**
Ex-showgirl named Eliza Blob, whom Oliver "Daddy" Warbucks married in the "Little Orphan Annie" comic strip on February 29, 1932. Shortly afterwards, she mysteriously disappeared from the strip.

**Troubles**
Loyal Sheepdog belonging to the dead actor on the beach in the 1981 movie *S.O.B.*

**Troutt, Kathy**
Thirty-three-year-old diver who doubled for thirteen-year-old Brooke Shields in the underwater nude scene in the 1980 movie *The Blue Lagoon*.

**Truckadero**
Name of the cafe/bar frequented by Doug Quintain (Humphrey Bogart) in the 1937 movie *Stand-In*.

**Truck Shackley and the Critters**
Krofft puppets' hillbilly band, which appeared on the TV series "Barbara Mandrell and the Mandrell Sisters."

**Truman, Margaret**

(1924–     ) Daughter of President Harry S Truman; she has authored a number of books, including *Murder in the White House* (1981). Margaret Truman was portrayed by Nancy Morgan on the TV mini-series "Backstairs at the White House."

**Truman's Folly**

Name given by critics to the balcony that President Truman had built onto the White House.

**Trumpet Voluntary**

Musical piece by Jeremiah Clarke, performed at the bridal procession of the marriage of the Prince of Wales (Prince Charles) to Lady Diana Spencer, on July 29, 1981.

**Truro County**

Southern setting of the TV series "Flamingo Road."

**TSA**

Airline whose Boeing 747 crashed into a London skyscraper in the 1978 movie *The Medusa Touch*.

**Tubby's**

Los Angeles drive-in restaurant hangout of the Hollywood Knights automobile club on Wilshire Boulevard in the 1981 movie *Hollywood Nights*. Tubby's was "The Home of the Big One" for twenty-one years, until finally closed on November 1, 1965.

**Tuesday**

Day of the week on which the 1955 movie *Guys and Dolls* opens; the day on which the 1980 movie *9 to 5* opens; and the day on which the great shark was killed in the 1975 movie *Jaws*.

**Tuffy Leemans' Day**

Special Sunday set aside by the New York Giants football team to honor their running back, Tuffy Leemans. Unfortunately, on that day his team lost to the Brooklyn Dodgers, 21 to 7 (the date was December 7, 1941).

**Tupper, Earl W.**

Inventor who, in 1945, introduced Tupperware. He died in October 1983.

**Turkey**

Bird that Benjamin Franklin suggested as the national bird of the United States. However, the eagle won out.

**"Turkey for the President, A"**

Episode of "General Electric TV Theater" that starred Ronald Reagan and his wife, Nancy.

**Turner, Ted**
Owner of the Atlanta Braves baseball team. In 1977 he won the America's Cup and has been named Yachtsman of the Year four times. He founded Cable News Network (CNN), the world's first twenty-four-hour TV news network.

**Turning Point, The**
Movie (1977) directed by Herbert Ross, starring Anne Bancroft and Shirley MacLaine. It holds the record for being nominated for the most Oscars (eleven) without winning a single award.

**Tucson**
Arizona home town of Jo Jo, mentioned in the lyrics of The Beatles 1969 hit song, "Get Back."

**Tuttle's Muddle**
Silent film that movie producer H. H. Cobb (Brian Keith) spliced together from Leo Harrigan's (Ryan O'Neal) movie, *Romeo's Balloon*, and nine other films in the 1976 movie *Nickelodeon*.

**Twain, Mark**
(1835–1910) Pseudonym of author and humorist Samuel Langhorne Clemens, born in Florida, Missouri, and raised in Hannibal, Missouri. In his youth, he served as a riverboat pilot on the Mississippi (1857–1861). His most well-known works are *The Adventures of Tom Sawyer* (1876); *The Prince and the Pauper* (1882); *Life on the Mississippi* (1883); *The Adventures of Huckleberry Finn* (1885); and *A Connecticut Yankee in King Arthur's Court* (1889). He was the first author to produce a book on a typewriter. Mark Twain portrayed himself in the 1907 movie *A Curious Dream*, and was portrayed by Fredric March in the 1944 movie *The Adventures of Mark Twain;* by Christopher Connelly in the 1977 TV movie *The Incredible Rocky Mountain Race,* and by David Knell in the 1980 TV movie *Life on the Mississippi.* Hal Holbrook has portrayed him on both stage and television in his one-man show, *Mark Twain Tonight*.

**Tweety**
Yellow canary of the Freeling family, which died in the 1982 movie *Poltergeist*. He was buried in a King Edward Imperial cigar box containing:
Tweety
A small piece of red licorice (for when he is hungry)
A Polaroid photo of Carol, Anne, Robert, and E. Buzz (for when he's lonely)

A napkin (for when it's nighttime)

A red flower (for a better smell)

## Twilight

Original title of William Faulkner's 1929 novel *The Sound and the Fury*.

## Twilight Number 3

Perfume worn by actress Miss Peggy Courtney (Rhonda Fleming) in the 1957 movie *The Buster Keaton Story*.

## "Two Ladies in de Shade of de Banana Tree"

Song composed by Harold Arlen, with lyrics written by author Truman Capote. The song was introduced by Ada Moore and Enid Mosier in the 1954 movie *House of Flowers*.

## Ty Cobbs

Cheerleader's club on which a young girl is wearing a jacket in the closing credits of the TV series "Welcome Back Kotter."

## Tycoon

CB handle of (J.B.) Jethro Bodine (Ray Younge) in the 1981 TV movie *The Return of the Beverly Hillbillies*.

## Tyrell, Gary

Trombone player for the 140-member Stanford marching band who was knocked down by California defensive back Kevin Moen as he ran into the end zone for the game's winning touchdown with no time left on the clock (November 20, 1982).

## Tyrone

Bulldog nemesis of Waldo the Cat. Voiced by Allan Melvin on the 1975–1976 TV cartoon series "The Secret Lives of Waldo Kitty."

# U

### U-9
German submarine commanded by Captain Otto Weddigen that, on September 22, 1914, became the first sub to sink an enemy ship on the high seas. It sank the HMS *Aboukir* and, within minutes, the HMS *Hogue* and HMS *Cressy*.

### U-26
German submarine that transported the Ark of the Covenant to a secret German island in the 1981 movie *Raiders of the Lost Ark*. The same sub was previously used in the 1982 German movie *Das Boot*.

### U-53
German U-boat that surfaced off the coast of Scotland in an attempt to pick up the German spy Henry Faber (Donald Sutherland), in the 1981 movie *Eye of the Needle*. The serial number of the ship's clock was 19226.

### U-96
World War II German submarine featured in the 1982 movie *Das Boot*. Jurgen Prochnow played the captain (see U-26 above.)

### UNTCHBL
California license plate of actor Robert Stack's Mercedes 300SL.

### USES
United States Employment Service.

### US Festival
Rock festival thrown by Apple Computer co-founder Stephen Wozniak, on Labor Day weekend of 1982, at Glen Helen Regional Park near San Bernardino, California. The last song sung at the festival was "Go Your Own Way," by Fleetwood Mac.

**UTV**

TV network that broadcast the basketball game between the Harlem Globetrotters, coached by Dewey Stevens (Scatman Crothers), against the New Invisibles (Robots) for the deed to Gilligan's Island in the 1981 TV movie *The Harlem Globetrotters on Gilligan's Island*. The final score was 101 to 100, the Globetrotters' favor.

**Ufema, Joy**

Outspoken Pennsylvania nurse who dedicated herself to the helping of the terminally ill. She first appeared on an episode of "60 Minutes" in 1978 and was portrayed by Linda Lavin in the 1981 TV movie *A Matter of Life and Death*.

**Ugliest Man in Pictures**

Title conferred on character actor Rondo Hatton (1894–1946).

**Uncle Neddy**

Nom de plume under which Miles Fairley (George Sanders) wrote children's books in the 1947 movie *The Ghost and Mrs. Muir*.

**"Undercover Woman"**

Fictional TV series starring Joyce Whitman (Betty White) on the TV series "The Betty White Show."

**"Underneath the Mango Tree"**

Song sung by James Bond (Sean Connery) and Honeychile Rider (Ursula Andress) in the 1962 movie *Dr. No*. A few lines of Honeychile singing the song can again be heard in the 1969 movie *On Her Majesty's Secret Service*.

**Underwood**

Brand of typewriter that author Irving Wallace uses to type all of his books.

**Uniform Number 1**

Worn by Baseball Hall of Fame member Earl Combs.

**Uniform Number 2**

Worn by Baseball Hall of Fame members Charlie Gehringer and Billy Herman.

**Uniform Number 3**

Worn by Baseball Hall of Fame members Babe Ruth, Jimmie Foxx, Frankie Frisch, Bill Terry, Mickey Cochrane, Kiki Cuyler, Jim Bottomley, Heinie Manish and Earl Averill (the most of any one number, with nine wearers).

**Uniform Number 4**

Worn by Baseball Hall of Fame members Lou Gehrig, Goose Goslin, Chick Hafey, Hack Wilson, Mel Ott, Joe Cronin, Luke

Appling, and Ralph Kiner.

**Uniform Number 5**

Worn by Baseball Hall of Fame members Hank Greenberg, Lou Boudreau, and Joe DiMaggio.

**Uniform Number 6**

Worn by Baseball Hall of Fame member Stan Musial.

**Uniform Number 7**

Worn by Baseball Hall of Fame members Fred Lindstrom, Al Simmons, Joe Medwick, and Mickey Mantle.

**Uniform Number 8**

Worn by Baseball Hall of Fame members Bill Dickey and Yogi Berra.

**Uniform Number 9**

Worn by Baseball Hall of Fame members Gabby Hartnett and Ted Williams.

**Uniform Number 10**

Worn by Baseball Hall of Fame members Lefty Grove, Lloyd Waner, and Al Lopez.

**Union Motors**

Automobile manufacturing company that bought out Dodsworth Motors in the 1936 movie *Dodsworth*.

**Unique Employment Agency**

Los Angeles firm for which Lucille Carter (Lucille Ball) worked. The company's motto was "Unusual Jobs for Unusual People" on the TV series "Here's Lucy."

**University of Minnesota**

College attended by Mary Richards (Mary Tyler Moore), where she was a member of the Gamma Gamma Delta Sorority, on the TV series "The Mary Tyler Moore Show."

**University of Pittsburgh**

College that produced two consecutive winners in the Miss Cheerleader U.S.A. contest. The winners were Susan Murphy and Joyce Prokopovich.

**"Unknown Stuntman, The"**

Theme song of the TV series "Fall Guy," sung by the show's co-producer and star, Lee Majors. The actors and actresses mentioned in the song's lyrics are Farrah Fawcett, Sally Field, Bo Derek, Robert Redford, Cheryl Tiegs, Raquel Welch, and Clint Eastwood.

**"Up Your Income"**

Game show featured on an episode of "The Carol Burnett Show." The three categories were:

Sea Monsters of Lake Michigan

Gypsies Stolen at Birth

Disaster Movies Without Charlton Heston

Stella (Carol Burnett) was the contestant and the Sha Na Na Nunie Sisters (Pointer Sisters) were the panelists.

**"Up Your Street"**

KTLA TV show, hosted by Westbrook Van Voorhis, that visited the boardinghouse where Herbert H. Heebert (Jerry Lewis) worked in the 1961 movie *The Ladies' Man*.

**U.S. Camera**

Magazine in which the girl (Marilyn Monroe) posed in a scene called "Textures" (a combination of sand, driftwood, and her—in a pink polka-dotted bikini) in the 1954 movie *The Seven Year Itch*.

**U.S. Capitol**

C-54 aircraft that First Lady Bess Truman christened in 1945. Each time that she attempted to break the champagne bottle against its nose, the bottle refused to break. Several military men also attempted unsuccessfully to break the bottle, until finally it was broken with a hammer. The confusing and humorous scene has been shown in a movie newsreel.

# V

**VEGAS-1**

Nevada personalized license plate of all of singer Wayne Newton's automobiles. In order to get the same plate for all the cars, Newton had to obtain special permission from the Nevada governor.

**Valentine**

Camel that drank out of a bottle in the 1976 movie *Hawmps!*

**Valenzuela, Fernando**

Mexican-born Los Angeles Dodgers pitcher who was awarded the National League's Cy Young Award in 1981, becoming the first rookie ever to win both the Cy Young Award and the Rookie of the Year award.

**Valiant**

Name of the rubber dinghy from which actress Natalie Wood fell and drowned on the evening of November 29, 1981. The dinghy belonged to Natalie and her husband Robert Wagner's sixty-foot yacht, *Splendour*.

**Valiant Tobacco Company**

Large tobacco firm that offered the prize of $25 million to the town of Eagle Rock, Iowa, if its people could quit smoking for thirty days, in the 1971 movie *Cold Turkey*.

**Vallee, Rudy**

(1901–    ) Popular crooner, born Herbert Pryor Vallee, and nicknamed "The Vagabond Lover." "Heigh-ho, everybody" became his greeting. He was the first person to record "As Time Goes By." Vallee was loosely portrayed by Wilson Wood in the 1952 movie *Singin' in the Rain*.

**Valley Advocate**

Small San Fernando, California, newspaper for which Kate

Columbo (Kate Mulgrew) worked in the 1979 TV series "Kate Loves a Mystery" (a.k.a. "Mrs. Columbo").

**Valley Checker Cab**
San Diego taxicab number 25 (California license 1C11503) driven by Marvin Dummitz (Richard Mulligan) in the 1980 movie *Scavenger Hunt*.

**Valley of the Dolls**
Novel written by Jacqueline Susann, first published in 1966. The book holds the record for being the best-selling novel of all time, with twenty-two million copies sold through 1981. The book has inspired three movies: *Valley of the Dolls* (1967), *Beyond the Valley of the Dolls* (1970—inspiration only; no official connection), and *Valley of the Dolls 1981* (1981—TV). A paperback edition of Jacqueline Susann's novel was read in bed by Evelyn Stohler (Barbara Barrie) in the 1979 movie *Breaking Away*.

**Vanity Fair**
Magazine in which Apple Annie (Bette Davis) found the name of Lord Ferncliff, which she used when writing to her daughter, Louise (Ann-Margret) in the 1961 movie *Pocketful of Miracles*.

**Velazquez, Loretta Janeta**
Woman who fought for the Confederate Army during the Civil War, under the name of Harry T. Burford.

**Vecchio, Mary Ann**
Kent State student who was photographed kneeling over the body of a dead student after members of the Ohio National Guard opened fire on a protest demonstration on May 4, 1970. Because of the emotion shown in the photo, it became highly publicized.

**Vendors, The**
Movie (1970) produced, directed, written, and scored by Bobby Darin and starring Richard Bakalyan and Mariette Hartley, which has never been released.

**Venus DiMilo Arms**
Apartment house at 4960 Terrace Drive in Pastafasullo, Rome, where the Holiday family resided in the 1972–1973 TV cartoon series "The Roman Holidays."

**"Very Thought of You, The"**
Song composed in 1934 by Ray Noble. It was heard in the 1944 movie *The Very Thought of You* and was sung by Doris Day in the 1950 movie *Young Man with a Horn*, and by JoAnne Dru in the

1956 movie *Hell on Frisco Bay*.

**Vezina Trophy**

Award given annually by the NHL to the goaltender against which the fewest goals have been scored. The trophy was named for Georges Vezina, who died of tuberculosis a short time after collapsing during a game on November 28, 1925.

**Vice Presidents under President Franklin D. Roosevelt**

| John Nance Garner | 1933–1941 (two terms) |
| Henry Wallace | 1941–1945 |
| Harry S Truman | 1945 |

**Vicki Lester**

Stage name of actress Esther Blodgett, played by Janet Gaynor in the 1937 movie *A Star Is Born,* and by Judy Garland in the 1954 version.

**Victoria**

Secret Service code name of Mrs. Lyndon B. Johnson.

**Victoria Cross**

Britain's highest military honor.

**"Victors, The"**

University of Michigan's fight song.

**Victory has a hundred fathers, but defeat is an orphan . . .**

Saying coined by Count Galeazzo Ciano, the foreign minister of Benito Mussolini. President Kennedy used the quotation after the Bay of Pigs fiasco.

**Vidor, King**

(1894–1983) Hollywood movie producer and director of *The Champ* (1931) and *Northwest Passage* (1940). He directed a few scenes for *The Wizard of Oz* during the absence of Victor Fleming, and has been nominated for best director five times. Vidor, who made a cameo appearance in the 1934 movie *Our Daily Bread,* was portrayed by Joseph Hacker in the 1980 TV mini-series "Moviola."

**Viking**

Cuda Webber's (Clu Gulager) boat on the short-lived TV series "The MacKenzies of Paradise Cove."

**Vile Body**

Bluto's boat in the 1980 movie *Popeye.*

**Village People**

Rock group with such hits as "YMCA" and "In the Navy." The

original members were:

| Policeman/sailor | Victor Willis (lead—previously Ray Simpson) |
| Indian | Felipe Rose |
| Sailor/GI | Alex Briley |
| Cowboy | Randy Jones |
| Hardhat | David Hodo |
| Leatherman | Glen M. Hughes |

The group appeared in the 1980 movie *Can't Stop the Music*, in which Olympic decathlon champion Bruce Jenner made his movie debut.

**Village Virus, The**
Original title of Sinclair Lewis's 1921 novel *Main Street*.

**Violet**
Twelve-year-old prostitute played by Brooke Shields in the 1978 movie *Pretty Baby* (she made $27,500 for the film).

**Violet Rutherford**
Ten-year-old girl who gave Beaver Cleaver (Jerry Mathers) his first kiss from a girl; played by Veronica Cartwright on an episode of the TV series ''Leave It to Beaver.''

**Virginia Military Institute**
School setting of the 1938 Ronald Reagan movie *Brother Rat* and the 1940 sequel *Brother Rat and a Baby*. Both movies were filmed at the Valley Forge Military Academy (as was the 1981 movie *Taps*).

**Virgin Tramp, The**
News media name for the murder victim who was sawed in half in the 1981 movie *True Confessions* (based on the novel by John Gregory Dunne). She had a rose tattoo on her right thigh.

**Viscosity**
The condition of having relatively high resistance to flow. Term used in Castrol Astrol GTX Motor Oil commercials on TV.

**VISTA**
Volunteers in Service to America

**Vitameatavegamin**
Vitamin product that Lucy Ricardo (Lucille Ball) advertised on TV, only to become drunker and drunker as she spoke (the product contained 23 percent alcohol), on an episode of the TV series ''I Love Lucy.''

**Vogue Records**
Record label for which Frank Elgin (Bing Crosby) recorded in the

478

1954 movie *The Country Girl*.

**"Voice of Broadway"**

Dorothy Kilgallen's syndicated newspaper column.

**"Volga Boat Song"**

Song played as Mighty Joe Young and ten strongmen had a tug-of-war in the 1949 movie *Mighty Joe Young*.

**Volkswagen Bug**

One of the most popular automobile models ever built (1938–1978), with over 19 million cars produced.

**Vulcan**

Statue erected on Red Mountain in 1936, which today overlooks the city of Birmingham, Alabama.

**Vulture**

Spacecraft built by junkyard dealer Harry Broderick (Andy Griffith), and flown to the moon and back on the TV series "Salvage 1."

# W

## W2XBS

Experimental New York City TV station begun in 1930 by the National Broadcasting Company, that recorded several sports firsts.

| | |
|---|---|
| May 17, 1939 | Televised the first sporting event, when they showed the Princeton–Columbia baseball game at Baker Field in New York City. |
| February 25, 1940 | Televised the first American hockey game between the New York Dodgers and the Montreal Canadiens. |
| February 28, 1940 | Televised the first collegiate basketball game played between Pittsburgh and Fordham, and a second between New York University and Georgetown. |

On July 1, 1941, W2XBS became WNBT.

## WH11294

Military license plate number of the Mercedes German military truck hijacked by Indiana Jones (Harrison Ford) in the 1981 movie *Raiders of the Lost Ark*.

## WAACs

Women's Army Auxiliary Corps, authorized by Congress on May 15, 1942.

## WMDL

Television station in Midvale, Indiana, on which Clayton Poole (Jerry Lewis) appeared in the 1958 movie *Rock-a-Bye Baby*.

## WNYC

Radio station over which New York City Mayor Fiorello H.

LaGuardia read the Sunday comics to the children of the city each week during a 1937 newspaper strike.

**WOW**
Milwaukee 1950s radio station on the TV series "Happy Days." Also the call letters of a real radio station in Omaha, Nebraska.

**WTFB**
Middletown, Ohio, radio station, the first to broadcast in stereo.

**WXYZ**
Television station for which Sweet Polly Purebread worked on the TV cartoon series "Underdog." Also the real call letters for the ABC affiliate in Detroit.

**WZAZ**
Chicago disco radio station whose transmitter tower was knocked down by Trans American flight 209 (Boeing 707) in the 1980 movie *Airplane!*

**Wack**
Ziggy's pet duck in the "Ziggy" cartoons by Tom Wilson.

**Wacky**
Dummy that appeared on Bert Healy's (Peter Marshall) radio show in the 1982 movie *Annie*.

**Wade, Jennie**
Only civilian killed at the battle of Gettysburg, in July 1863. She was in her home at the time.

**Waikis, Eddy**
Answer to the question "Who played first base for the 1950 Philadelphia Phillies?" asked in the 1980 movie *Up the Academy*.

**Waggles**
Captain B. J. Hunnicut's (Mike Farrell) pet dog back home in the TV series "M*A*S*H."

**Wagon Wheel**
Nightclub where Henry Thomas (Steve McQueen) sang with his band, the Rockabillies,* in the 1965 movie *Baby the Rain Must Fall*.

**Wakefield Prison**
Arkansas prison farm built in 1903, of which Henry Brubaker (Robert Redford) became the new warden in the 1980 movie *Brubaker*.

**Walcott, Jersey Joe**
(1914–     ) Heavyweight boxing champ (1951–1952). The only

---

*One of the band's members was a young Glen Campbell, uncredited in the film.

man to lose three consecutive heavyweight championship bouts: twice to Joe Louis (1947 and 1948) and once to Ezzard Charles (1949). He has lost more heavyweight championship bouts than any other heavyweight champ, losing twice to Joe Louis, twice to Ezzard Charles, and twice to Rocky Marciano. In the 1956 movie *The Harder They Fall*, Walcott played a trainer. The Walcott-Marciano title fight was the only heavyweight title fight to be filmed in 3-D.

**Waldorf**
Bar where Wardell Franklin (Bill Cosby) and Steve Jackson (Sidney Poitier) got beaten up in the 1974 movie *Uptown Saturday Night*.

**Walker, Jimmy**
(1881–1946) Mayor of New York City, nicknamed Beau James. He was the host of the first scheduled TV program, telecast on July 21, 1931. Walker was once the president of Majestic Records, a popular label in the 1930s. He appeared as himself in the 1929 movie *Glorifying the American Girl*. Jimmy Walker was portrayed by Bob Hope in the 1957 movie *Beau James*.

**Walker, Nancy**
Comedienne who appeared in three TV series in one TV year (1976–1977): "Rhoda," "The Nancy Walker Show," and "Blansky's Beauties." She had previously appeared as Mildred the maid on the TV series "McMillan and Wife."

**Walker, Ricky**
Ten-year-old boy who won a thirty-five-foot steel replica of a spaceship as first prize in the "Space Patrol" Name the Planet contest, sponsored by Ralston-Purina in December 1953. His winning planet name was "Caesaria."

**Wallenberg, Raoul**
Swedish businessman who went to Budapest during the closing days of World War II, in order to save as many Jews as possible from the Auschwitz gas chambers. He is credited with having saved thirty thousand Jews. In 1945 he was arrested by the Russians, and his fate remains a mystery to this day.

**Walsh, Stella (Stanislawa Walasiewicz)**
Polish Olympic gold medal winner (1932) for track (she was the first woman to run 100 yards in less than 11 seconds, when she clocked 10.8 seconds). She has collected more than five thousand medals and awards. She was still setting track records at the age of forty-one. When Walsh died on December 4, 1980, at the age of

sixty-nine, killed by a robber, it was revealed that she was actually a male.

**Walter**

Old large rainbow trout sought for years by Norman Thayer (Henry Fonda) and finally caught by Billy Ray (Doug McKeon), only to be released, in the 1981 movie *On Golden Pond*.

**Walter Matuschanskayasky**

Actor who is credited with the role of the drunk in the 1974 movie *Earthquake*. It was Walter Matthau, using his real name.

**Wamba's Revenge**

Movie being filmed in the 1981 movie *Cheech and Chong's Next Movie*.

**War and Peace**

Novel written between 1865 and 1872 by Leo Tolstoy. The book became popular in both Great Britain and the United States during World War II, when the Germans began their invasion of Russia. The novel was filmed three times: in 1956 by the United States, in 1968 by the Soviet Union (in a version running over six hours), and as a PBS mini-series.

**War and Piece**

Porno movie to which Max Bialystock (Zero Mostel) took his accountant, Leo Bloom (Gene Wilder), in the 1968 movie *The Producers*.

**Ward, Arch**

Sports editor of the *Chicago Tribune* who originated the idea of the major-league All-Star Game in 1933.

**Warde, John**

Man who committed suicide by jumping from a New York City building on July 26, 1938. TV cameras were on the scene, making John Warde the first man to be televised while committing suicide.

**Ward, Jem**

British heavyweight boxing champion (1822–1831), who was born on September 26, 1800, Boxing Day.

**Warhop, Jack**

(1884–1960) New York Yankees pitcher who threw Babe Ruth the pitch that became Ruth's first major-league home run. It occurred at the Polo Grounds on May 6, 1915, when Ruth was a member of the Boston Red Sox.

**Warner, Jack L.**

(1892–1978) Hollywood executive, producer and co-founder of Warner Bros. Pictures. Warner was portrayed by Richard Dysart in the 1980 TV movie *Bogie*, and by Michael Lerner in the 1980 TV mini-series "Moviola."

**Warren, Annette**
Singer who dubbed in Ava Gardner's singing in the 1951 movie *Show Boat*. Gardner's voice, however, can be heard singing on the movie's soundtrack album.

**Warren, Earl**
(1891–1974) Chief Justice of the U.S. Supreme Court from 1953 until he retired in 1969. Earl Warren was the father-in-law of actor Richard Anderson. Warren was portrayed by John Houseman in the 1980 TV movie *Gideon's Trumpet*.

**Warren, Robert Penn**
Only person to win Pulitzer Prizes in both fiction (for *All the King's Men*, 1947) and poetry (for *Promises*, 1958).

**"Washboard Blues" and "Lazybones"**
Two Hoagy Carmichael songs that utilize the same melody.

**Washington**
Only state named for a President.

**Washington and Jefferson College**
Pennsylvania learning institute that became the first college to put numbers on its football players, introducing the practice in 1908.

**Wasson, Father William**
Catholic priest who founded a home for orphaned children in Mexico. He was portrayed by Jason Miller in the 1975 TV movie *A Home of Our Own*.

**"Watchdog Report"**
Melvin P. Thorpe's (Dom DeLuise) KPTV (Channel 4) crusading TV series in the 1982 movie *The Best Little Whorehouse in Texas*. Melvin's character was loosely based on that of Houston TV reporter Marvin Zindler.

**Watts, Isaac**
Father of English hymns.

**Wavy Gravy**
Leader of the Hog Farm Commune of New Mexico, who served as MC of the Woodstock Festival, on August 15, 1969. His real name is Hugh Romney.

**"Way Back Home"**
Recording by the Crusaders, which the SLA (Symbionese Liberation Army) claimed as their national anthem.

**Way We Were, The"**
Song written by Marvin Hamlish that can be heard in the movies
*The Way We Were* (1973), sung by Barbra Streisand, and *Starting
Over* (1979). A girl also sings the song at an audition at the High
School of the Performing Arts, in the 1980 movie *Fame*.

**We Are Family"**
Hit record (1979) by Sister Sledge, played on a Panasonic radio in
the Army barracks in the 1980 movie *Private Benjamin*. The
female recruits danced to the recording. The record had previously
become the theme song of the 1979 World Series-winning team,
the Pittsburgh Pirates.

**Weber, Manford**
Contestant on the TV game show "County Fair," hosted by Bert
Parks. On April 7, 1959, Weber was hospitalized after a stunt on
the show backfired, causing burns on his face and neck.

**We blew it!**
Last line said in the 1969 movie *Easy Rider*. It was spoken by
Captain America (Peter Fonda) before he died.

**Webster, Randy Allan**
Seventeen-year-old Louisiana boy who was shot to death by Houston police after a high-speed chase on February 8, 1977. His
parents eventually revealed a police coverup. Randy was portrayed
by Gary McCleery in the 1981 TV movie *The Killing Of Randy
Webster*. His parents, John and Billie, were portrayed by Hal
Holbrook and Dixie Carter.

**"We Could Have It All"**
Theme song of the 1980 movie *The Last Married Couple in America*, sung by Maureen McGovern.

**We could have made beautiful music together . . .**
Famous Hollywood line, first said by Gary Cooper to Madeleine
Carroll in the 1936 movie *The General Died at Dawn*.

**Weeghman Field**
Previous name of Cubs Park which in 1927 became Chicago's
Wrigley Field.

**Weemawee High**
High school setting of the TV series "Square Pegs."

**We have come to visit you in peace and good will . . .**
First words spoken by Klaatu (Michael Rennie) to the people of the
world in the 1951 movie *The Day the Earth Stood Still*.

**Weidmann, Eugene**
Last person in France to be guillotined in public (June 7, 1939).

**Weinberg, Mel**
Con man who, in conjunction with the FBI, set up the Abscam meetings in which several congressmen accepted bribes in 1982.

**Weinberg Military Academy**
Michigan setting of the 1980 movie *Up the Academy*, which was produced by *Mad* magazine. Butch Academy is the nearby girl's military school. It was filmed at the St. John's Military School in Kansas.

**Welcome**
Arizona town whose bank is robbed by Robert Marmaduke Hightower (John Wayne), Pete (Pedro Armendariz), and the Abilene Kid (Harry Carey, Jr.), in the 1948 movie *Three Godfathers*. Their destination was New Jerusalem, Arizona, with a baby that the trio found in a covered wagon.

**We'll always have Paris . . .**
Line said by Rick Blaine (Humphrey Bogart) in the 1943 movie *Casablanca*, and by Isaac Davis (Woody Allen) to his girlfriend, Tracy (Mariel Hemingway), in the 1979 movie *Manhattan*.

**We'll Get By**
Short-lived 1975 TV series created by Alan Alda.

**"Well, I'm gonna give ole' Red a break and do one of his songs..."**
Singer Hank Williams's last words before he died, on January 1, 1953. He had been talking to his chauffeur, Charles Carr, about singer Red Foley.

**"Well, King, this case is closed . . ."**
Ending to the weekly radio/TV series "Sergeant Preston of the Yukon."

**"Well, nobody's perfect . . ."**
Line said by Joe E. Brown when Jerry Daphne (Jack Lemmon) revealed to him that he was not a woman, but a man, in the closing scene of 1959 movie *Some Like It Hot*. This turned out to be one of the classic closing lines of all time.

**We love you, baby . . .**
Message addressed to singer Stevie Wonder in braille on the cover of Paul McCartney's *Red Rose Speedway* album.

**"We Love You, Call Collect"**
Song recorded by Art Linkletter in 1969, peaking at number 42 on

the *Billboard* charts. He recorded it shortly after the suicide of his daughter Diana, on October 4, 1969.

We met, we lived and dear we loved, then comes that fatal day, the love that felt so dear fades far away. Tonight love hath one done and lonesome, all that I could sing I you you (sic) still and always will, but that's the poison we have to pay.

Lyrics on a crumpled piece of paper found in the hand of the dead body of singer Hank Williams in the back seat of his Cadillac, on January 1, 1953.

**Wendy**
Rhoda's (Valerie Harper) favorite doll, as a girl, on the TV series "Rhoda."

**Wentworth Detention Centre**
Melbourne, Australia, women's prison setting of the TV series "Prisoner: Cell Block H."

**Werewolf 1**
Tactical call sign of Lieutenant Colonel Wilbur P. "Bull" Meechum's (Robert Duvall) F4C Marine fighter, that he stayed in to the end, so that it would not crash on the town of Beaufort, South Carolina, in the 1980 movie *The Great Santini* (based on the novel by Pat Convoy).

**WEst 3-0693**
Home phone number in Metropolis of reporter Clark Kent, on the TV series "The Adventures of Superman."

**Westcoast Airlines**
Airline company for which the Captain and Mandy fly in the comic strip "The Captain and Mandy."

**Westgate Hotel Apartments**
New York City building in which Michael Adropolis (Michael Douglas) lives in the 1979 movie *Running*.

**Westmore Brothers**
Hollywood's makeup artist family: Monty, Buddy, Ernest, Wally, and Percy.

**We was robbed!**
Famous line said by Max Schmeling's manager, Joe Jacobs, in a radio interview on June 21, 1932, the night that heavyweight Jack Sharkey defeated Schmeling in a fifteen-round decision.

**Whaleboat**
Secret Service code name for President Richard Nixon's press secretary, Ron Ziegler.

**Wharton, Edith**
   In 1921 she became the first woman to win the Pulitzer Prize for fiction, with her book *The Age of Innocence*.

**What a Man**
   British release title of the 1939 W. C. Fields movie *Never Give a Sucker an Even Break*.

**What are people who don't wear their seat belts called? Stupid . . .**
   Message on the billboard through which a police car traveled, in the 1974 movie *Dirty Mary, Crazy Larry*.

**"What'd I Say"**
   Song sung by Elvis Presley in the 1964 movie *Viva Las Vegas*, and by Ray Charles in the 1966 movie *Blues for Lovers*.

**Whatsit**
   Name of photographer Matthew Brady's wagon, which he used when traveling about to photograph the American Civil War. He took more than 3,500 photographs.

**What's Your Perversion?**
   TV quiz show hosted by Jack Barry in the 1972 Woody Allen movie *Everything You Always Wanted to Know About Sex (But Were Afraid to Ask)*. (This was Jack Barry's only movie appearance.)

**What to Do Before the Doctor Comes**
   Book read by Laura Petrie (Mary Tyler Moore) in bed just prior to Ritchie's birth on the TV series "The Dick Van Dyke Show."

**Wheaties**
   Cereal introduced in 1924 by General Mills. Two Olympic decathlon champions on the cover of the cereal boxes have been Bob Mathias and Bruce Jenner.

**Wheaton High School**
   Illinois high school to which Ned Racine (William Hurt) sent away for their 1968 yearbook, in order to see photographs of both Mary Ann Simpson, "The Vamp" (homecoming queen), and Matty Tyler Walker, "Smoochie," in the 1981 movie *Body Heat*. The school's team name was the Cougars.

**When you're slapped, you'll take it and like it . . .**
   Line said by Sam Spade (Humphrey Bogart) to Joel Cairo (Peter Lorre) in the 1941 movie *The Maltese Falcon*.

**Where's the Rest of Me?**
   Autobiography (1965) of Ronald Reagan, written with Richard G. Hubler. It was taken from a line said by Reagan in the 1949 movie

*King's Row*, just after he woke up in bed to find out that both of his legs had been amputated.

**WHIP US**
California license number of the 1955 Chevy convertible in which two beautiful girls were riding in the 1981 movie *Cheech & Chong's Nice Dreams*.

**White Cloud**
Steamboat that, while berthed in St. Louis, Missouri, on May 17, 1849, caught fire. The flames spread and destroyed twenty-three other steamboats and fifteen city blocks.

**White, Edward Douglass**
(1845–1921) Chief Justice of the Supreme Court (1910–1921), who had served in the Confederate Army between 1861 and 1863. He was portrayed by Joseph J. Greene in the 1944 movie *Wilson*.

**White Fang**
Kate Columbo's (Kate Mulgrew) pet basset hound on the TV series "Mrs. Columbo."

**White, Marian Rose**
Young girl who, because of a congenital defect in her vision, was committed by her mother to the Sonoma, California, State Home for the Feeble-Minded, in 1934. Marian was in fact sane, and after suffering many ordeals (including sterilization against her will), she was eventually released with the help of Bonnie MacNeil. White returned to the institution later to assist and teach the retarded children. She was portrayed by Nancy Cartwright in the 1981 TV movie *Marian Rose White*. Katharine Ross portrayed Bonnie MacNeil.

**White Orchid Cosmetics Company**
Firm for which Carol Evans (Hope Summers/Doris Rich) was employed on the radio soap "The Road of Life."

**White, Peregrine**
Child born on board the ship *Mayflower* in 1620.

**White Virgin of the Nile, The**
Movie being filmed by actress Carla Naples (Marilyn Maxwell) within the 1958 Jerry Lewis movie *Rock-a-Bye Baby*.

**Whitney High School**
School where Ralph Hinkley (William Katt) taught history on the TV series "The Greatest American Hero."

**Whitney, Richard**
President of the New York Stock Exchange the day of the great

stock market crash on November 29, 1929. He was later sent to Sing Sing Prison for grand larceny. Whitney was portrayed by Robert Vaughn in the 1980 TV movie *The Day the Bubble Broke*.

**Whitten, Reverend M. C.**

Minister who married singer Jerry Lee Lewis to his thirteen-year-old third cousin, Myra Gale Brown, on December 11, 1958. At the time of his marriage, Lewis had four more months to go until his divorce from his second wife, Jane, would be final. Jerry Lee had married his first wife, Dorothy, when he was just fifteen years old.

**Who Goes There?**

Novella by John W. Campbell, Jr., on which the 1951 movie *The Thing* was based.

**"Who, me? Oh no! I got a bellyache!"**

Donald Duck's first and only words in his 1934 film debut, *The Wise Little Hen*.

**Who, the**

British rock group. The four original members were Keith Moon, Roger Daltrey, Peter Townshend, and John Entwistle. Drummer Keith Moon died in 1978 and was replaced by Kenny Jones.

**Who will survive—and what will be left of them?**

Promotional line used in newspaper advertisements for the 1974 movie *The Texas Chainsaw Massacre*.

**Why can't a woman be more like a man?**

Line said by Rex Harrison in the 1964 movie *My Fair Lady*, and by Henry Fonda in the 1968 movie *Yours, Mine and Ours*.

**"Why, they couldn't hit an elephant at this dist—"**

Famous last words of Major General John Sedgwick, before he was killed at the Civil War battle of Spottsylvania on May 9, 1864.

**Wicked Lady**

Name of Mrs. Venable's (Katharine Hepburn) pet Venus's-flytrap plant in the 1959 movie *Suddenly, Last Summer*.

**Wicked, Wicked**

Movie (1973) that utilized the novelty gimmick of a split screen throughout the film, showing what both the heroine and a killer were doing at the same time.

**Wicked Witch of the West**

Surviving witch who attempted to get the red ruby slippers away from Dorothy Gale in *The Wizard of Oz*. She was played by twenty-year-old Margaret Hamilton in the 1939 movie *The Wizard of Oz*.

**Wilbur**

Teddy's (Richard Keith) small black-and-brown dog that survived, along with all of the passengers and crew, a ditching in the Atlantic in the 1958 movie *Crash Landing*.

**Wilbur Peabody**

Deaf mute played by Don Knotts on the TV soap "Search for Tomorrow." Wilbur's sister, Rose, was played by both Lee Grant and Nita Talbot.

**"Wild About Harry"**

Theme song of the TV series "Good Time Harry," sung by Norman Brooks.

**Wildfire**

Dog that starred in the 1955 movie *It's a Dog's Life*.

**Wild Jack Monroe**

Ex-Hollywood Western star (three hundred films) and owners of WJM Television in Minneapolis, played by Slim Pickens in the TV series "The Mary Tyler Moore Show." The station's letters are taken from his name.

**Wildwood, New Jersey**

Annual site of the National Marbles Tournament.

**Wiley, H. V.**

Lieutenant commander, executive officer, and one of the only three known survivors of the Navy Zeppelin USS *Akron II*, which crashed on April 4, 1933, off the New Jersey Coast, with seventy-two fatalities.

**Willard, Jess**

(1881–1968) Heavyweight boxing champ (1915–1919). He didn't fight in his first professional bout until he was twenty-nine years old, in 1911. Willard was portrayed by Clay Hodges in the 1983 TV movie *Dempsey*.

**Williams, Ike, and Beau Jack**

Two lightweight boxing champions; Williams (1945–1951) and Jack (1942–1944) fought each other in the very last fight of both men's careers. Williams defeated Jack in the ninth round of the fight, which took place on August 12, 1955.

**Williams, John**

(1932–      ) Composer who scored the following movies: *Daddy-O* (1959), *The Reivers* (1969), *The Poseidon Adventure* (1972), *The Cowboys* (1972), *The Towering Inferno* (1973), *Cinderella Liberty* (1973), *Earthquake* (1974), *The Paper Chase* (1974), *The Eiger Sanction* (1975), *Jaws* (1975), *Star Wars* (1977), *Close Encounters of the Third Kind* (1977), *E.T. the Extra-Terrestrial* (1982), and many others. John Williams is the son-in-law of actress Laurene

Tuttle. The 1974 movie *California Split* was dedicated to Barbara Ruick (1933–1973), the wife of John Williams, who had died on the movie set. Upon Arthur Fiedler's death in 1979, Williams became the conductor of the Boston Pops.

## Williams, Robin

His comic characters: Grandpa Funk (old man), Andrew (six-year-old child psychologist), Benign Neglect (blues singer), Nicky Lenin (Russian stand up comic), Reverend Ernest Avary, Walt Buzz Gay (film director), Mr. Sincerely (redneck used-car dealer).

## Williams, Sandy

First Miss Black America (Pennsylvania, 1968).

## "Willow Weep for Me"

Song written in 1932 by Ann Ronell and dedicated to composer George Gershwin.

## Will Scarlet

A member of Robin Hood's Merry Men of Sherwood Forest, played in movies by Patric Knowles, in *The Adventures of Robin Hood* (1938); John Abbott, in *The Bandits of Sherwood Forest* (1946); Douglas Mitchell, in *A Challenge for Robin Hood* (1968); and Denholm Elliott, in *Robin and Marian* (1976).

## Wilson, Charles

Secretary of Defense under President Eisenhower, who first said, "What's good for General Motors is good for the country and vice versa." Wilson had previously been president of General Motors (1941–1953).

## Wilson, Earl

Hollywood columnist and author. Earl Wilson played himself in the 1965 movie *Beach Blanket Bingo* and in the 1968 film *Where Were You When the Lights Went Out?* among other cameo appearances in movies.

## Wilson, Earl Lawrence

(1935–     ) Detroit pitcher who served up Mickey Mantle's 536th and final home run of his career, on September 20, 1968. He later changed his name to Robert Earl Wilson.

## Wilson, Horace

American teacher at Tokyo University who in 1873 introduced baseball to Japan.

## Winchester .45-60

Rifle used by Tom Horn (Steve McQueen) in the 1980 movie *Tom Horn*.

**Windowpane**
Object that hit Dorothy Gale (Judy Garland) in the back of the head, knocking her out, after which she dreamed of being in the land of Oz, in the 1939 movie *The Wizard of Oz*.

**Windsor Castle**
Name of the British C-47 aircraft seen in the 1981 movie *Eye of the Needle*.

**Windy**
Name of the sleeping horse (in bed) in the 1980 movie *Airplane!*

**Winfield, Kansas**
Hometown of Mary Ann Summers (Dawn Wells) on the TV series "Gilligan's Island."

**Wingfield, Major Walter Clopton**
Englishman who, in 1873, introduced the game of lawn tennis.

**Winner, The**
Horse that finished seventh (out of eight horses) in the twenty-second Kentucky Derby (May 6, 1896). The winning horse was Ben Brush. The question (better done orally) "Who was the winner of the twenty-second Kentucky Derby?" may be answered, "Ben Brush and a horse that finished seventh."

**Winstead**
Comedian "Doodles" Weaver's first name.

**Winston**
British beachmaster's bulldog in the 1962 movie *The Longest Day*.

**Wired for Sound**
Popular nightclub on the TV soap opera "The Guiding Light."

**Wisdom**
Secret service code name for Nixon's White House Adviser John D. Ehrlichman.

**Wisdom of Eve, The**
Story by Mary Orr, upon which the screenplay by Joseph L. Mankiewicz for the 1950 movie *All About Eve* was based.

**Wisdom of the Heart**
Play in which Elise McKenna (Jane Seymour) performed in 1912, in the 1980 movie *Somewhere in Time*. It was her last performance, even though she was quite young.

**Wise, Rick**
(1945–    ) Only major-league pitcher ever to have thrown a no-hitter and hit two home runs in the same game. He accomplished this feat with the Philadelphia Phillies on June 23, 1971, in a game

against the Cincinnati Reds (4–0.) Later in the season, he again hit two home runs in one game.

**Wissahickon Walk**
Location in Philadelphia where Jack Terry (John Travolta) tape-recorded the sound of a rifle shot just as Governor McRyan's automobile had a blowout and crashed in the 1981 Brian DePalma movie *Blow Out*.

**Witch of Wall Street**
Title conferred upon the millionairess Miss Hetty Green, who left $90 million when she died, yet lived like a pauper.

**Withington, Lothrop**
Harvard freshman who, in 1939, allegedly began the fad of goldfish-swallowing.

**Witt, Vicki**
Centerfold photo in the August 1978 edition of *Playboy* magazine that David Rosen (Lee Strasberg) was looking at in bed while his wife, Becky (Ruth Gordon), looked on, in the 1979 movie *Boardwalk*.

**Wolf**
Eddie Haskell's (Ken Osmond) German shepherd on the TV series "Leave It to Beaver."

**Wolfgang Sauerbraten**
Crazy disc jockey played by Ernie Kovacs on TV.

**Womack, Dooley**
(1939–   ) Last major-league pitcher to wear a single-digit number on his uniform. Womack (number 3) pitched for the Oakland A's for two games in 1970 (0–0).

**"Wonderful World"**
Hit (1960) song by Sam Cooke in which the following subjects are mentioned: history, biology, science, French, geometry, trigonometry, and algebra. The song was composed by Barbara Campbell (a pseudonym of Herb Alpert and Lou Adler), and can be heard in the 1983 Richard Gere film *Breathless*.

**"Wonderful World of Disney"**
Opening theme song composite of seven Disney movie themes: "Chim Chim Cheree," "Whistle While You Work," "It's a Small World," "Zip-A-Dee-Doo-Dah," "Ballad of Davy Crockett," "Bibbidi, Bobbidi, Boo," and "When You Wish Upon a Star."

**Wonder, Stevie**
Performer from whom a Moog synthesizer was borrowed in the novel *Close Encounters of the Third Kind*. (The fact, however, was

not mentioned in the 1977 movie.)

## "Won't You Play a Simple Melody?/Sam's Song"
Song recorded in 1950 and credited on the record label to "Gary Crosby and Friend." The friend, who was not named on the label, was his father, Bing Crosby.

## Woodcutter
Secret Service code name for Henry A. Kissinger.

## Woodley College
Women's college from which Eloise Winters (Susan Hayward) was expelled because Dean Whiting caught her and Walt Dreiser (Dana Andrews) kissing in the elevator in the 1949 movie *My Foolish Heart*.

## Wood, Natalie, and Robert Wagner movies
*All the Fine Young Cannibals* (1960), *The Affair* (1973—TV), and *Cat on a Hot Tin Roof* (1976—TV).

## Woodpecker Paradise
Name of country singer Slim Whitman's Florida country home (3830 Old Jennings Road).

## Woodstein
Collective name by which *Washington Post* reporters Bob Woodward and Carl Bernstein were known after they broke the Watergate story.

## World Cup Games (soccer)

|  | | | | |
|------|---------------|---|-----------------|-----------|
| 1930 | Uruguay | 4 | Argentina | 2 |
| 1934 | Italy | 2 | Czechoslovakia | 1 |
| 1938 | Italy | 4 | Hungary | 2 |
| 1950 | Uruguay | 2 | Brazil | 1 |
| 1954 | West Germany | 3 | Hungary | 2 |
| 1958 | Brazil | 5 | Sweden | 2 |
| 1962 | Brazil | 3 | Czechoslovakia | 1 |
| 1966 | England | 4 | West Germany | 2 |
| 1970 | Brazil | 4 | Italy | 1 |
| 1974 | West Germany | 2 | The Netherlands | 1 |
| 1978 | Argentina | 3 | The Netherlands | 1 (overtime) |
| 1982 | Italy | 3 | Germany | 1 |

## World for Two, A
Movie for which Vicki Lester (Judy Garland) was awarded an Academy Award for Best Actress, only to have her husband, Norman Maine (James Mason), accidentally slap her across the face at the presentations, in the 1954 movie *A Star Is Born*. The three actresses she defeated were Jane Brandon, for *Those Who*

*Seek;* Alice Tenny, for *The Great Chance;* and Shirley Bandor, for *Don't Cry My Love* (all the movies were, of course, fictitious).

**World Is Not Enough, The**
Motto of the Bond family in Ian Fleming's James Bond novels.

**World Wide Studios**
Hollywood motion picture studio headed by Roger Cross (Peter Lawford) in the 1974 TV movie *The Phantom of Hollywood*.

**Worms**
Objects that Jack Dunne (Henry Winkler) carried in a shoebox from New York City to Eureka, California, in the 1977 movie *Heroes*.

**Wozniak, Stephen**
Co-founder of the Apple Computer Company, who, on Labor Day weekend in 1982, paid $12.5 million to finance a three-day rock festival called the U.S. Festival, in San Bernadino County in California.

**Wrangell, Baron George**
Original "Man in the Hathaway Shirt," beginning in 1951. He wore an eyepatch over his right eye (although he actually had nothing wrong with his eyes).

**Wren, Sir Christopher**
(1632–1723) Designer and builder of St. Paul's Cathedral in London. He also built other churches in London.

**Wrestling World**
Magazine that featured an article on the California Dolls wrestling team (pages 87 and 88) in the 1981 movie *All the Marbles*.

**Wrong Way Bond**
Nickname that the UCLA football team gave to member (and future actor) Ward Bond, because during a USC-Stanford football game he sat on the bench facing the stands.

**Wuffles**
Mary Wilke's (Diane Keaton) pet dachshund in the 1979 movie *Manhattan*.

**Wurlitzer**
Brand of the jukebox at the Frosty Palace in the 1978 movie *Grease*.

**W. Wendell Weaver School**
Santa Barbara, California, school (1647 Lorraine Court) attended by the members of the baseball team called the Bad News Bears, on the TV series "The Bad News Bears." The principal of the school was Dr. Emily Rappant (Catherine Hicks).

**Wyatt Earp, Frontier Marshal**
Novel by Stuart N. Lake upon which the following films were

based: *Frontier Marshal* (1934), *Frontier Marshal* (1939), and *My Darling Clementine* (1946).

**Wykoff, Frank**

Only man to be a member of three different winning Olympic relay teams. He won a gold medal for the 1928, 1932, and 1936 Olympic Games, as a member of the U.S. 4-times-100-meter relay team.

**Wynken, Blynken and Nod**

Names of the three real goldfish that appeared on the set of the TV series "Ding Dong School."

**Wyoming**

State in which women were first given the right to vote in the United States. They achieved the right in 1869, while Wyoming was still a territory, twenty-one years before it became the forty-fourth state of the Union.

# X

**X**

Name of the puppet owl on ''The Mister Rogers' Neighborhood'' TV series. Voiced by Fred Rogers.

**X1W**

Registration number of Oliver ''Daddy'' Warbucks's (Albert Finney) orange autogyro in the 1982 movie *Annie*.

**X-9746**

Experiment number of the study of the Gill Man in the 1955 movie *Revenge of the Creature*.

**XF-11**

Plywood reconnaissance aircraft (originally designated DX-2) developed by Hughes Aircraft. On the aircraft's test in July 1946, the twin-engine plane (four-bladed propellers) crashed into several houses in Beverly Hills. Marine Sergeant William Lloyd Durkin pulled the test pilot, Howard Hughes, from the wreckage on Whittier Drive. Hughes gave Durkin a reward of $200 a month for life.

**XP**

Brand on the horses used by Pony Express riders (April 3, 1860, to October 24, 1861).

**XTRA**

Mexican radio station that introduced the all-news format in 1961.

**XT2941**

Call sign of the DC-3 aircraft on which Jeff Williams (Ronald Reagan) and Victoria Evans (Rhonda Fleming) were passengers when the aircraft lost its starboard engine in the 1951 movie *Hong Kong*.

**XZ-31**

Buck Rogers rocket pistol. When the toy gun first went on sale, on

November 17, 1934, two thousand people lined up outside of Macy's in New York City.

**Xavier**
Middle name of actor Francis X. Bushman.

**"Xavier Cugat Show, The"**
Variety TV show (1957) that is the only TV show ever to begin with the letter *X*.

# Y

**YESCA**

California license number of the truck made of marijuana fibers in the 1978 movie *Up in Smoke*.

**YMCA**

Young Men's Christian Association. "YMCA" was the title of a 1979 hit by the Village People. The very first game of basketball was played at the Springfield, Massachusetts, YMCA gym on January 20, 1892. It was organized by Dr. James Naismith.

**Ya Gotta Believe!**

Slogan of the 1973 New York Mets, who went from last place to win the National League Pennant. The expression was coined by pitcher Tug McGraw.

**Yamit**

Israeli city blown up and bulldozed into rubble when the Sinai Peninsula was returned to Egypt in April 1982. The town was destroyed by Israel after Egypt refused to pay a remittance for it.

**"Yankee Doodle"**

Official state song by Connecticut since 1978.

**Yellow Mountain**

Nebraska home of the horse named Wild Fire in the 1975 song "Wild Fire," recorded by Michael Murphey.

**Yellowstone**

First national park in the world, and largest in the United States.

**"Yes, I killed him and I'm glad, I tell you, glad, glad, glad!"**

Bette Davis's famous line in the 1941 movie *The Letter*.

**"Yes, We Have No Bananas"**

Record played by Linus Larabee (Humphrey Bogart) in a canoe in the 1954 movie *Sabrina*. In 1923, the Westman Publishing Company successfully sued the composer for taking part of the melody of the "Alleluia Chorus" from Handel's *Messiah* for the song.

**Yoda**
Wise little old creature (actually a Muppet) in the 1980 movie *The Empire Strikes Back,* and the 1983 movie *Return of the Jedi.* He was designed and operated by Frank Oz, who also provided his voice. His eyes were patterned after those of Albert Einstein. A small child wore a Yoda costume on Halloween night in the 1982 movie *E.T. the Extra-Terrestrial;* E.T. was attracted to the costume. Yoda died at the age of nine hundred in *Return of the Jedi.*

**Yorkshire Ripper**
Media name given to Peter Sutcliffe, self-confessed murderer of thirteen British women over a five-year period (1976–1981).

**"You and Me, Babe"**
Theme song of the short-lived TV series "Freebie and the Bean," sung by Bobby Hart.

**You and Your Vocabulary**
Paperback book that Doris Wilgus (Barbra Streisand) carried with her in the 1970 movie *The Owl and the Pussycat.*

**"You Are My Lucky Star"**
Song that Kathy Selden (Debbie Reynolds) sang to a billboard of Don Lockwood (Gene Kelly) in a scene cut from the final print of the 1952 movie *Singin' in the Rain.*

**"You'd Be So Nice to Come Home to"**
Recording by Sandy (Judi West) played by Harry Hinkle (Jack Lemmon) on his record player in the 1966 movie *The Fortune Cookie.*

**"You can fool all of the people some of the time, and some of the people all of the time, but you can't fool all the people all of the time . . ."**
Quotation by Abraham Lincoln that was written in the fortune cookie picked by Harry Hinkle (Jack Lemmon) in the 1966 movie *The Fortune Cookie.*

**"You can observe a lot just by watching . . ."**
One of many famous statements made by Yogi Berra.

**"You Can't Take That Away from Me"**
Recording made by heavyweight champion James J. Braddock and given to contender Joe Louis the day of their June 22, 1937, fight in which Joe did take the title away from him.

**You do things like this, no wonder your show is going off PBS . . .**
How host Johnny Carson replied to host Dick Cavett when Cavett

501

dropped his trousers in order to show his jogging shorts on "The Tonight Show" on May 13, 1982.

**You knew the job was dangerous when you took it . . .**

Motto of the TV cartoon character Super Chicken.

**"You Made Me Love You (I Didn't Want to Do It)"**

Song written in 1913 by Joe McCarthy and James V. Monaco, which appears in the following movies: *Wharf Angel* (1934); *The Broadway Melody of 1937* (1937), sung by Judy Garland; *Private Buckaroo* (1942); *Syncopation* (1942); *The Jolson Story* (1946); *Love Me or Leave Me* (1955); and *Somewhere in Time* (1980).* It was the song playing on the ship's radio as two Japanese Zero aircraft attacked and sank the yacht *Gatsby* in the 1980 movie *The Final Countdown*.

**" You must come up and see me some time . . ."**

Line said by W. C. Fields to Mae West in the 1940 movie *My Little Chickadee*.

**"You Must Have Been a Beautiful Baby"**

Song written in 1938 by Johnny Mercer and Harry Warren. Dick Powell introduced it in the 1938 movie *Hard to Get*. It also appeared in the films *Mildred Pierce* (1945) and *My Dream Is Yours* (1949). Lex Luthor (Gene Hackman) sang the song at a piano in the ABC TV special edition (1982) of the 1978 movie *Superman* (it was in one of the scenes added for the special showing).

**You never get any place worthwhile unless you stick your neck out . . .**

Motto of Turtledom, the popular Turtles organization, whose name stands for The United Resistance to Life's Everyday Setbacks.

**Young Americans, The**

Documentary film (1968) for which the producers, Robert Cohn and Alex Grosshoff, had to return an Oscar they had won, after it was discovered that the film had been shown within the previous year. This is one of only a few times that an Oscar had to be returned after it had been awarded. After the mixup, *Journey into Self* was awarded the Oscar.

**Young, Buddy**

First black player to score a touchdown in the Rose Bowl. Young scored the touchdown for Illinois in a game against UCLA on January 1, 1947. Illinois defeated UCLA 45 to 14.

---

*The scene in *Somewhere in Time* in which a woman sang the song was set on June 27, 1912. However, the song wasn't copyrighted until 1913.

**Young Lions, The**
Irwin Shaw's first novel that Joseph C. Gillis (William Holden) was reading in the 1950 movie *Sunset Boulevard*. *The Young Lions* was made into a movie in 1958, starring Marlon Brando, Montgomery Clift, and Dean Martin.

**Your Kaiser Dealer Presents Kaiser-Frazer "Adventures in Mystery," starring Betty Furness in "By-Line"**
Longest title of a TV series (1951).

**Young Men's Purity, Total Abstinence, and Snooker Pool Association**
Social club to which John Ford, John Wayne, Ward Bond, Gene Markey, Merian C. Cooper, Preston Foster, Frank Morgan, Johnny Weissmuller, Dudley Nichols, and others belonged in Hollywood in the 1930s. They met regularly at the Hollywood Athletic Club. Their slogan was "Jews but no dues." They later changed their name to Young Men's Purity, Total Abstinence, and Yachting Association, and then to Emerald Bay Yacht Club, with the slogan "The yacht club for people who don't like yacht clubs."

**Your Money or Your Life**
British game show seen on TV in the 1981 movie *Time Bandits*. One of the questions asked was "What famous film star begins with C?" (No answer was given.)

**"You've Got a Friend"**
Song written by James Taylor, of which Madie (Dyan Cannon) sings just two lines while sitting in the cab of a GMC truck, in the 1980 movie *Coast to Coast*.

**You Wanted to See It**
TV program for which Arthur "Fonzie" Fonzarelli (Henry Winkler) set a motorcycle jump record on the TV series "Happy Days."

**"Your Cheatin' Heart"**
Hank Williams song, sung by country singer Kitty Wells on the jukebox at Bob's Country Bunker, as Jake and Elwood enter in the 1980 movie *The Blues Brothers*.

**Yukk**
Mighty Man's pet dog, the world's ugliest, dog on the TV series "The Plastic Man Comedy Adventure Show."

**YUkon 2-8209**
San Francisco telephone number of detective Candy Matson (Natalie Masters) in the radio series "Candy Matson."

# Z

**00**

Jersey number of Oakland Raiders center Jim Otto, the last man to wear the number 00 in the NFL.

**044APD**

California license number of Kate Columbo's (Kate Mulgrew) automobile on the TV series "Mrs. Columbo" (a.k.a. "Kate Loves a Mystery").

**058ESL**

California license number of Joe Rossi's (Robert Walden) Mustang on the TV series "Lou Grant."

**061UOX**

California license number of the yellow Ford Mustang driven by Kelly Garrett (Jaclyn Smith) on the TV series "Charlie's Angels."

**06413357A**

Serial number of a giant $100 bill in the 1981 movie *Pennies from Heaven*.

**Zaharias, George**

Wrestler who married Olympic athlete Babe Didrickson. He was portrayed by Alex Karras in the 1975 TV movie *Babe*. Karras later married Susan Clark, who portrayed Miss Didrickson.

**Zak**

Dog that barks at the beginning of Rod Stewart's song "Sweet Little Rock 'n' Roller."

**Zambony**

Machine that cleans and resurfaces ice in an ice rink.

**Zangaron**

Fictional country in Africa that is invaded by mercenaries in the 1981 movie *The Dogs of War* (based on the novel by Fredrick Forsythe).

**Zanuck, Darryl F. (1902– )**

Hollywood movie producer who, after quitting Warner Bros., formed 20th Century Pictures in 1933 (the next year it became 20th Century-Fox). He produced his first film in 1929, with *Noah's Ark*. Some of his productions are *The Grapes of Wrath* (1940), *How Green Was My Valley* (1941), and *The Longest Day* (1962). He is the father of Richard Darryl Zanuck. Darryl Zanuck was portrayed by Peter Maloney in the 1980 TV mini-series "Moviola."

**Zatopek, Emil and Dana**
Czechoslovakian husband and wife who, while both competing in the 1952 Olympics at Helsinki, Finland, each won a gold medal on the same day. Emil won his for the five-thousand-meter race, while Dana won hers for the women's javelin throw.

**Zebra 1**
Call sign of Captain Buzz Rickson's (Steve McQueen) B-17, *The Body*, which he flew into the White Cliffs of Dover, in the 1962 movie *The War Lover*.

**Zeda**
Planet from which the robot 4-U-2 traveled to Earth in the 1979 children's TV series "Whitney and the Robot."

**Zenith International Studios**
Hollywood motion picture studio where Hubbell Gardner (Robert Redford) worked as a screenwriter in the 1973 movie *The Way We Were*.

**Zephyr Cigarettes**
"The Clean One"—account of which Eddie Anderson (Kirk Douglas) is in charge, in the 1968 movie *The Arrangement*.

**Zero Hour, The**
Radio series (1973) hosted by Rod Serling.

**Zesto Delicious Soup**
Product advertised on a billboard at Fourth and Oak, in which Beaver Cleaver (Jerry Mathers) got stuck inside a large cup, in an episode of the TV series "Leave It to Beaver." Part of this episode can be seen on a TV set in the 1982 movie *Fast Times at Ridgemont High*.

**Zeus**
Supreme God in Greek mythology, husband and brother of Hera. His home was on Mount Olympus, and among his children were Aphrodite, Artemis, Apollo, Athena, and Hermes. Portrayed in movies by Niall MacGinnis in *Jason and the Argonauts* (1963), Wilfrid Hyde-White (voice only) in *Xanadu* (1980), and Laurence Olivier in *Clash of the Titans* (1981).

**Ziggy**
Small cartoon character (three feet tall, two feet wide, and forty-two pounds) created by Tom Wilson. Ziggy also appears as a toy doll. His pets are Fuzz (dog), Sam (cat), and Wack (duck). He often plays Mantovani records for his plants.

**"Zing a Little Zong"**
Top 10 duet hit record in Great Britain, in 1952, for Bing Crosby

and Jane Wyman.

**Zip Girl**

Name given to actress Zelda Zanders (Rita Moreno) in the 1952 movie *Singin' in the Rain*.

**Zippy**

Chimpanzee sidekick of Captain Safari (Randy Kraft) on the TV series "Captain Safari of the Jungle Patrol."

**Zoo (Flying Zoo)**

Name of the Lockheed Electra aircraft (on loan from Evergreen International), used by the maintenance crew of Richard Nixon's Presidential campaign, in the 1980 movie *Where the Buffalo Roam*.

**Zoomar**

Novel written by comedian Ernie Kovacs in 1957.

**Zoot Zoot Black**

Name of the B-24 Liberator bomber in which Joseph P. Kennedy, Jr., was killed on August 12, 1944.

**Zorro and Florence Nightingale**

Costumes worn to a charity costume ball by Bob and Emily Hartley, on an episode of the TV series "The Bob Newhart Show."

**Zukor, Adolf**

(1873–1976) Hollywood movie producer and movie company president (Paramount Pictures). *The Public Is Never Wrong* was the title of his 1953 autobiography. Zukor, who died at the age of 103, portrayed himself in the 1929 movie *Glorifying the American Girl*.

**Zyl, Jane Rochelle Van**

First U.S. Naval Academy graduate to marry another U.S. Naval Academy graduate, when, on May 27, 1981, she married Francis Marion Knight II. They were married at the academy's chapel.

**Zyzzyva**

Rare yellow weevil found in Brazil, named by Dr. Tom Casey in 1922. It is the last entry in many dictionaries.

"That's all there is, there isn't any more."
— Ethel Barrymore

(For now, that is!)